Tolley's Taxation of Collective Investment

Tolley's
Taxation of Collective Investment

Edited by:

Stephen Newcombe
and a team of expert contributors

 LexisNexis™ UK

Members of the LexisNexis Group worldwide

United Kingdom	LexisNexis UK, a Division of Reed Elsevier (UK) Ltd, Halsbury House, 35 Chancery Lane, LONDON, WC2A 1EL, and 4 Hill Street, EDINBURGH EH2 3JZ
Argentina	LexisNexis Argentina, BUENOS AIRES
Australia	LexisNexis Butterworths, CHATSWOOD, New South Wales
Austria	LexisNexis Verlag ARD Orac GmbH & Co KG, VIENNA
Canada	LexisNexis Butterworths, MARKHAM, Ontario
Chile	LexisNexis Chile Ltda, SANTIAGO DE CHILE
Czech Republic	Nakladatelství Orac sro, PRAGUE
France	Editions du Juris-Classeur SA, PARIS
Germany	LexisNexis Deutschland GmbH, FRANKFURT and MUNSTER
Hong Kong	LexisNexis Butterworths, HONG KONG
Hungary	HVG-Orac, BUDAPEST
India	LexisNexis Butterworths, NEW DELHI
Ireland	LexisNexis, DUBLIN
Italy	Giuffrè Editore, MILAN
Malaysia	Malayan Law Journal Sdn Bhd, KUALA LUMPUR
New Zealand	LexisNexis Butterworths, WELLINGTON
Poland	Wydawnictwo Prawnicze LexisNexis, WARSAW
Singapore	LexisNexis Butterworths, SINGAPORE
South Africa	LexisNexis Butterworths, DURBAN
Switzerland	Stämpfli Verlag AG, BERNE
USA	LexisNexis, DAYTON, Ohio

© Reed Elsevier (UK) Ltd 2003

A CIP Catalogue record for this book is available from the British Library.

ISBN 0 4069 6530 7

Typeset by Columns Design Ltd, Reading, England
Printed and bound in Great Britain by Thomson Litho Ltd, East Kilbride, Scotland
Visit LexisNexis UK at www.lexisnexis.co.uk

Preface

When it was suggested to me that there seemed to be no publication that provided a wide-ranging guide to the taxation of Collective Investment I realised there was a need for a first stop publication that enables a reader to gain an understanding of a particular issue or for initial reference before embarking on more in depth research. I therefore produced the outline of a book for *Tolley's* that I would find useful as a guide in my everyday work.

The result is this two part book covering the taxation of collective investment vehicles in the first part and the taxation of the investors in the second part. In order to make the second part of greater value for those looking at the investor's tax position, sections on the taxation of life policy holders pension fund 'investors' and PEPs and ISAs have been included. This book should, therefore, be of assistance whether you are advising the product provider or the investor; however, often their interests are the same.

I am delighted that so many eminent experts in the field of the taxation of collective investment vehicles have contributed chapters to this volume. The list of authors includes leading experts in their field from City law firms, accountancy firms, trade bodies and the financial services industry. I have also particularly asked the authors to include potential pitfalls so that readers will be aware of many of the areas that can cause problems in practice.

One area that always surprises those who look at this area for the first time is the great variation in tax 'regimes' that apply to different collective investment vehicles and investment returns for investors, that can make radical differences to the investors' tax position. The underlying principle should be (and it is one that I understand the Inland Revenue support) that the taxation of the investor in a collective investment vehicle should be broadly similar to the taxation of the investor if he held directly the underlying investments of the fund. Identifying where this principle does not hold true is important when considering the alternative investment opportunities open to a particular investor.

An aspect of the UK tax system that fund providers and investors continue to find unsatisfactory is the tax regime for interests in offshore funds. Although reform has been promised, the regime outlined in the chapters from Martin Smith of *PwC* is likely to have greater longevity than we anticipated twelve months ago. Unfortunately, the tax position for investors (including retail investors) in offshore funds is still determined retrospectively, a wholly unacceptable position.

The variety of tax regimes for collective investment vehicles can cause confusion as to the tax treatment of a transaction in a particular fund and the effect that may have on the end investor. However, it is possible that we will witness many of these anomalies disappearing over the next few years with changes that may come about as a result of the new tax regimes required for

'CP185' funds and authorised property funds. The effect of possible reforms will be an important subject for subsequent editions of this book. Nevertheless, it would be unfortunate if changes to the existing regime for retail funds are so radical that investors no longer consider they understand how their investment returns will be taxed.

What this book attempts to provide is a guide to the taxation of collective investment vehicles and investors in those vehicles. It is not intended to be a technical manual but a starting point for those that are researching a particular area and provide comprehensive coverage of the wide range of investment funds and the taxation of investors in those funds. For many the content will be sufficient to provide an understanding of the taxation of funds and fund investors without further reference. As I have already mentioned the list of the contributors is impressive and draws on leading experts, therefore this book should also be a valuable companion to those that need to look in more technical detail at certain of the subject areas covered.

I have certainly learnt a lot from reading the author's contributions and will find this book an essential addition to those that I keep readily available at my desk. I hope that you do too.

Stephen Newcombe
October 2003

About the Authors

Patrica Allen graduated from Cambridge University and joined Ashursts in 1990. Patricia is a partner in Ashursts' tax department and advises on all forms of corporate and employee taxation. She has specialist experience of UK and overseas fund work, management buy outs and leverage buy outs and of advising on tax efficient methods of employee incentivisation.

David Cartwright is a partner in PricewaterhouseCoopers LLP. David advises venture capital and private equity firms on a range of tax issues and advises a majority of the Venture Capital Trusts established to date on compliance with the Venture Capital Trust legislation. David is also a member of the British Venture Capital Association's tax committee.

Simon Davies is a manager in the investment management and real estate consulting group at PricewaterhouseCoopers LLP and advises international fund managers and real estate funds on taxation issues affecting cross-border transactions. Simon also specialises in matters concerning the UK offshore fund legislation and has been involved in representations to the Inland Revenue on possible changes to the tax regime.

Eliza Dungworth is a tax partner in Deloitte's Insurance, Funds and Savings Tax Practice specialising in fund management and life assurance, heading the Funds tax practice in the UK. Her clients include fund managers as well as the funds themselves including Unit Trusts and OEICs, Venture Capital Trusts, Investment Trusts, Limited Liability Partnerships and Pension Funds. Eliza is a regular speaker at industry conferences and writes in the *International Tax Review* on fund-related topics such as investment structures and unfair tax competition.

Oliver Farnworth is a senior manager in the Deloitte Banking and Capital Markets tax group, based in London. He has experience of advising internationally-oriented collective investment schemes including authorised funds, investment trusts, unauthorised unit trusts and limited partnerships. He also advises a number of UK investment advisers and investment managers on international issues.

Nathan Hall qualified as a Chartered Accountant in 2000, having graduated in Classics. He then joined KPMG's Financial Sector tax practice. He has just completed a secondment to the Investment Management Association as tax adviser and secretary to the SORP working group. Nathan now forms part of KPMG's investment management and funds team.

Philip Hare is a senior tax manager in PricewaterhouseCoopers LLP's Entrepreneurial Companies and Private Clients division. Philip advises venture capital and private equity firms on tax issues and advises promoters and advisors of Venture Capital and Enterprise Investment Schemes.

Roger Leslie is a tax partner in the Investment Management Group of Ernst & Young LLP where he specialises in providing tax and other advice on all forms of funds, onshore and offshore. He frequently works with the Inland Revenue on industry issues including the creation of pension fund pooling vehicles and the initial taxation regulations for open ended investment companies. He is the author of the chapter on 'Collective Investment Schemes' in *Tolley's Tax Planning* and a regular speaker at conferences and seminars. Roger is a member of the Association of Investment Trust's Technical Committee advising in particular on taxation issues impacting investment trusts.

Chris Marshall is the Legal and Technical Services Manager for the Life Assurance Division of the Legal & General Group. He joined Legal & General in 1969 after obtaining an Honours Degree in Law at Liverpool University; he worked in various departments of the Legal & General's Life Group including claims, marketing and for a number of years as Compliance Officer. He deals with new product development, policy drafting, trusts, taxation and other legal matters. He has been a tutor of the Chartered Insurance Institute and is also the author of a number of their text books. He frequently lectures on insurance and tax planning. He is a member of the ABI Taxation (Life Policies) Panel.

Ian Sayers is the Technical Director of the Association of Investment Trust Companies (AITC). Ian is responsible for providing technical advice to the AITC's members and their managers on areas such as taxation, accounting, company law and regulation. He is also responsible for the AITC's public affairs activities and regularly lobbies the Government, the Treasury, the FSA, the DTI and the Inland Revenue on matters affecting the investment trust industry. He joined the AITC in 1998 from Ernst & Young, where he was a tax manager in the Investment Management Group specialising in investment trusts.

Peter Shipp, following time in printing and local government, joined a provincial stockbroking firm based in North Yorkshire in the mid-1980s. Following the announcement of Personal Equity Plans, Peter was responsible for setting up a PEP Administration centre for the firm and others in the same group, servicing the private clients of some 27 branches throughout the UK. Eight years later he joined the PEP Managers' Association (PEPMA) with responsibility for developing technical support and training for member firms. Peter is currently Technical Director of the successor organisation PIMA (the PEP & ISA Managers' Association).

Lucy Shirley is a senior manager with Deloitte in London. Between 2000 and 2002 Lucy was seconded as tax adviser to the Investment Management Association. While there she was heavily involved in the continuing discussions surrounding the introduction of the European Savings Directive, and made representations on subjects including reforms to the loan relationships regime. Since her return to Deloitte, Lucy has been working on advisory projects and is a member of the IMA tax committee.

Martin Smith is a partner in PricewaterhouseCoopers LLP's UK investment management consulting group, and advises international fund managers in the retail and institutional sectors alike on corporate and fund taxation issues and product development strategy. Before joining the firm in 1988, Martin worked with the Inland Revenue where, amongst other things, he led the implementation of the 1984 offshore fund legislation. He maintains a close interest in tax policy matters affecting the UK and offshore fund markets. As well as his association with the present publication, Martin is co-author of the UK Chapter of the IBFD's industry publication, *Taxation and Regulation of Investment Funds and their Investors.*

Camilla Spielman is a solicitor with Eversheds with considerable experience of the taxation of investment funds and products, both retail and institutional. She regularly advises on the conversion of authorised unit trust schemes, together with the mergers of authorised unit trusts and open-ended investment companies. She also advises on reconstructions of offshore funds and investment trusts. Her role includes advising fund management groups on product development. Following her involvement in the landmark 1998 unit trust stamp duty case, she has taken a particular interest in stamp taxes.

John Watson is a Partner in the City law firm Ashurst Morris Crisp. A Cambridge mathematics graduate and originally a barrister he is head of the firm's tax department and deals with all forms of taxation. His specialisations include enterprise zones, fund work, property finance and venture capital. He has served on the tax committee of the British Venture Capital Association and as honorary legal adviser to the Enterprise Zone Property Unit Trust Association. He led the discussions with the Inland Revenue that culminated in the introduction of Pension Fund Pooling Vehicles.

x

Contents

Contents

2 Unauthorised Unit Trusts

Roger Leslie

Ernst & Young

3 Stamp Duty and Stamp Duty Reserve Tax

Camilla Spielman

Eversheds

4 Offshore Funds

Martin Smith and Simon Davies

PricewaterhouseCoopers LLP

Contents

5 Onshore Limited Partnerships as Investment Funds

John Watson

Ashurst Morris Crisp

6 Offshore Limited Partnerships as Investment Funds

Patricia Allen

Ashurst Morris Crisp

7 Investment Trust Companies

Ian Sayers

AITC

Contents

8 Venture Capital Trusts

David Cartwright

PricewaterhouseCoopers LLP

9 Mergers and Reconstructions of Funds

Camilla Spielman

Eversheds

10 Pension Fund Pooling Vehicles

John Watson

Ashurst Morris Crisp

11 Foreign Taxes

Eliza Dungworth and Oliver Farnworth

Deloitte

Contents

PART II

TAXATION OF INVESTORS

Contents

15   Venture Capital Trusts

Philip Hare

PricewaterhouseCoopers LLP

16   Taxation of Holders of Life Policies

Chris Marshall

Legal & General

Abbreviations

ACD	=	authorised corporate director
ACT	=	advance corporation tax
AITC	=	Association of Investment Trust Companies
AUT	=	Authorised Unit Trust
AVC	=	additional voluntary contribution
BVCA	=	British Venture Capital Association
CCF	–	common collective fund
CETV	=	Cash Equivalent Transfer Value
CFC	=	Controlled Foreign Company
CGTA	=	Capital Gains Tax Act
CIS	=	Collective Investment Scheme
CP	=	Consultation Paper
DWP	=	Department for Work and Pensions
EC	=	European Commission
EEA	=	European Economic Area
EEC	=	European Economic Community
EEIG	=	European Economic Interest Grouping
EU		European Union
EUFT	=	eligible unrelieved foreign tax
FA	=	Finance Act
FCP	=	Fonds Communs de Placement
FID	=	foreign income dividend
FII	=	franked investment income
FIP	=	Foreign Indirect Participant
FOF	=	futures and options
FoF	=	fund of funds
FRS	=	Financial Reporting Standard
FSA	=	Financial Services Authority
FSAVC	=	free-standing additional voluntary contribution
FSMA	=	Financial Services and Markets Act
FURBS	=	Funded Unapproved Retirement Benefit Schemes
GAAP	=	generally accepted accounting principles
GFOF	=	geared futures and options
ICTA	=	Income and Corporation Taxes Act
IFRS	=	International Financial Reporting Standards
IHTA	=	Inheritance Tax Act
IME	=	Investment Manager Exemption
IMRO	=	Investment Management Regulatory Organisation
IPA	=	Individual Pension Account
IRS	=	Internal Revenue Service
ISA	=	Investment Savings Account
ISD	=	Investment Services Directive
IUMV	=	initial unrestricted market value
LLP	=	Limited Liability Partnership
MOU	=	Memorandum of Understanding

NAV	=	net asset value
NOR	=	not ordinarily resident
NQI	=	non-qualified intermediary
OECD	=	Organisation for Economic Cooperation and Development
OEIC	=	Open-ended Investment Company
OTC	=	over-the-counter market
para	=	paragraph
PCC	=	protected cell companies
PEP	=	Personal Equity Plan
PET	=	potentially exempt transfer
PFPS	=	Pension Fund Pooling Scheme
PFPV	=	pension fund pooling vehicle
PoA	=	Power of Attorney
PPS	=	priority profit share
QFI	=	Qualified Foreign Intermediary
QI	=	qualified intermediary
RDS	=	relevant discounted security
s	=	section
SA	=	Stamp Act
Sch	=	Schedule
SDRT	=	stamp duty reserve tax
SI	=	Statutory Instrument
SICAV	=	Société d'Investissement à Capital Variable
SIPP	=	Self Invested Personal Pension
SORP	=	Statement of Recommended Practice
SP	=	Inland Revenue Statement of Practice
TCGA	=	Taxation of Chargeable Gains Act
TESSA	=	Tax Exempt Special Savings Account
UBTI	=	unrelated business taxable income
UCITS	=	undertakings for collective investment in transferable securities
UKLA	=	United Kingdom Listing Authority
UURBS	=	Unfunded Unapproved Retirement Benefit Scheme
UUT	=	unauthorised unit trust
VAT	=	Value Added Tax
VATA	=	Value Added Tax Act
VCIC	=	variable capital investment company
VCOC	=	venture capital operating company
VCT	=	Venture Capital Trust

Table of Statutes

Paragraph numbers in bold type indicate where the legislation is set out in part or in full

Part I

Collective Investment Vehicles

Collective Investment Schemes

1   Authorised Unit Trusts and OEICs

Lucy Shirley

Deloitte

Introduction

1.1   This chapter is concerned with the taxation of authorised unit trusts (AUTs) and open-ended investment companies (OEICs). However, it begins by describing the regulation of these schemes, their history and some of the operational aspects of their day-to-day running. This is for two reasons.

1.2   Firstly, regulatory and legal matters are intrinsically caught up in the structure, establishment and operation of authorised unit trusts and OEICs and they bring with them a certain amount of jargon and technical terms. Unless these matters are put in context, a lot of the understanding of why these funds exist and why they are set up as they are is lost.

1.3   Secondly, the taxation of these schemes is, to a certain extent, predicated on the fact that they are authorised entities and are constitutionally different from other types of entity such as ordinary companies or trusts. Again, if their make up were not put in context, it would be harder to obtain a sense of why their tax treatment is as it is, and to compare this with other vehicles such as unauthorised unit trusts and investment trusts.

A. Regulation

1.4   Authorised funds are subject to extensive regulation originating both in the UK and in the European Union.

UK regulation

1.5   In the UK, regulation of deposit taking, insurance and investment business is performed by a single body, the Financial Services Authority (FSA). Around 10,000 different institutions fall within its supervision.

The legislation governing the authorisation and supervision of financial services firms is the *Financial Services and Markets Act 2000* (hereafter *FSMA 2000*).

1.6   The FSA's Investment Firms Division regulates firms including fund management operations, investment banks, stockbrokers and independent financial advisers, as well as professional firms such as lawyers and accountants carrying on mainstream investment business.

FSA Handbook

1.7   All the detailed rules regarding the activities overseen by the FSA are set out in its Handbook. With respect to collective investment schemes, the main part of the Handbook which is applicable is the Collective Investment Schemes (CIS) Sourcebook. The Sourcebook applies to OEICs, directors and depositaries of OEICs, managers and trustees of authorised unit trusts, and operators of recognised collective investment schemes, and its purpose is to set out rules for the day-to-day running of these products with the aim of protecting consumers. The degree of regulation applied is intended to ensure a high and uniform standard of protection for investors.

1.8   In addition to the CIS Sourcebook, other parts of the Handbook are also applicable to the investment management industry, such as the Authorisation and Supervision Manuals, the Conduct of Business Sourcebook and the Prudential Sourcebook. These books are more concerned with the general regulatory environment and stipulate conditions with which operators must comply in their general business activities as investment managers.

The number of rules surrounding the management and promotion of collective investment vehicles make them among the most tightly regulated products in the UK.

European regulation – the UCITS Directive

1.9   In 1985, the European Union agreed a Directive on the co-ordination of laws, regulations and administrative provisions relating to undertakings for collective investment in transferable securities. This Directive is known as the UCITS Directive and has been law in the UK since 1989.

The aim of the Directive was to facilitate the cross-border marketing of investment funds between European countries, and to achieve this a set of requirements for all UCITS funds' regulation and administration was agreed such that each state would regard them as equivalent to funds authorised by their own authorities. Accordingly, any fund which is certified by its competent authority as complying with the UCITS Directive may be freely marketed in another member state, subject to registration with the host state regulator.

1.10   In the UK, the only types of funds which are capable of being UCITS compliant are authorised funds and, until recently, only a subset of those. Authorised funds comprise two varieties of collective investment scheme, the authorised unit trust (AUT) and the open-ended investment company (OEIC).

Authorised Unit Trusts

1.11   An AUT is a scheme established in trust form where the property is held on trust for the beneficiaries by a trustee, and which the FSA has authorised to be sold to the public. Its objective is to provide an income and/or capital return on the investments it holds for the investors and spread investment risk by holding a range of different investments. The investors are issued with units which represent their entitlement to share in the profits, gains and losses of the trust.

Open-Ended Investment Companies

1.12   OEICs were introduced in 1997 as a corporate alternative to authorised unit trusts. While unit trusts were popular vehicles in the UK, their legal form was poorly understood abroad in countries which do not have the concept of trusts, and the industry argued that an authorised vehicle in corporate form was essential to allow it to compete for business on the Continent.

When they were first introduced, all OEICs were required to be set up to comply with the UCITS Directive's requirements. Since then, revised OEIC Regulations have been issued which allow non-compliant OEICs to be established. These second generation OEICs have been permitted since 1 December 2001.

1.13   An OEIC should, therefore, be thought of as a unit trust in corporate form. There are a number of legal and terminological differences between the two vehicles, but in many ways they can be regarded as equivalent.

Authorised unit trusts	OEICs
Units	Shares
Trust	Company
Manager	Authorised corporate director
Trustee	Depositary
Trustee legally owns investments	Company legally owns investments
Investors beneficially own investments	Company beneficially owns investments
Income or accumulation units	Income or accumulation shares, plus classes for different charging structures, currencies, investor types, etc.

Further explanation of the legal basis of AUTs and OEICs follows later in this chapter.

For the remainder of this chapter, the use of the terms 'unit trusts', 'units' and 'unitholders' should be read to indicate authorised unit trusts only, and to include rules relevant to OEICs, shares and shareholders unless the context demands otherwise.

Categories of scheme

1.14 Nine different forms of authorised scheme are permitted in UK Regulations, based on the different eligible asset classes, and the table below sets out the general investment restrictions to which each type is subject. However, the original UCITS Directive recognised only two of these types as having qualifying investments, namely securities schemes and warrants schemes. Accordingly, the first OEICs could only invest in securities or warrants in the manner prescribed by the UCITS Directive. Unit trusts which fell into other categories were not permitted to be UCITS funds, but could be sold in the UK.

Securities	A securities scheme may invest only in transferable securities such as bonds, shares, Government securities and units in other CISs.
Money market	A money market scheme may invest only in cash and near cash assets, including some debentures and bills of exchange, and units in other money market schemes.
Futures and options (FOF)	Futures and options schemes may invest in approved and over the counter derivatives.
Geared futures and options (GFOF)	Geared futures and options schemes are identical to FOFs except that they are permitted to take on greater exposure by putting up to 20% of scheme property into initial outlay on derivatives. Initial outlay is the amount which the fund is required to provide in order to obtain rights under a transaction in derivatives, excluding any payment or transfer on exercise of rights.
Property	Property schemes may invest in land or buildings (described as 'approved immovables' in the regulations), property-related assets and transferable securities.
Warrant	Warrant schemes are identical to securities schemes except that there is no limit on their ability to invest in warrants.
Feeder	A feeder fund is an AUT which is also a pension scheme, and which is invested in either a single UK authorised fund, recognised collective investment scheme or approved investment trust.
Fund of funds (FoF)	A scheme which may invest all its property in at least five other regulated collective investment schemes in any one category or type of scheme. No more than 20% of its property may be invested in any one of those schemes. The types of fund in which an FoF may invest are all except feeder funds and other FoFs. Recognised overseas schemes and subfunds thereof are eligible if they fall into one of the above categories.

Umbrella	A single scheme which has at least two subfunds between which unitholders are permitted to switch on demand. Each subfund must be invested in line with the regulations governing one of the preceding categories of scheme, but is not permitted to invest in units of any of its sister subfunds.

1.15 The investment strategies outlined above are only general; it is, of course, open to a scheme to restrict its investment strategy further in terms of specific classes of investment, the types of transactions it will enter into, etc. For example, a securities scheme may invest in any transferable securities, but its prospectus may limit it to invest only in equities of larger companies situated in North America, for example.

UCITS III

1.16 Even when the UCITS Directive was published, it was acknowledged that it excluded many funds on the basis of their investment policy or legal type and that a revised version of the Directive would be needed at a later stage to broaden the scope of what was permitted. It took until December 2001 for the revised version to be agreed and adopted, and later published in the Official Journal of the EU on 13 February 2002 (making this the date of entry into force).

1.17 Two Directives (*2001/108/EC* and *2001/107/EC*) have in fact been adopted. The first enlarges the scope of investment assets available to UCITS funds to include money market instruments, derivatives and units of other schemes, and the second makes changes relevant to the management companies. They are known as UCITS III collectively and the Product Directive and the Management Directive individually.

UCITS III again anticipates that further changes may be required in due course to fine tune its provisions and a general review clause has been inserted which obliges the European Commission to review the Directive within three years from its date of entry into force. Issues such as cross-border marketing, permitting institutional funds, real-estate funds, guaranteed funds etc to be certified, the use of derivatives and the way in which the management company passport works are all slated for review at that time. In addition, a report is due at the same time on the capital requirements introduced by the Management Directive which it is anticipated may need revision.

The Product Directive

1.18 Under the Product Directive, a wider range of investments is now permitted to be included within a UCITS scheme, such that the following are now UCITS compliant:

- Securities scheme

- Warrant scheme

- Money market scheme

- Futures and options scheme

- Fund of funds scheme

1.19   The Regulations now go further than they did previously in allowing a fund to invest in a mixture of asset types within a single fund (the so-called mixed fund structure). The change gives the scheme operator the ability to choose its own asset mix from these types of eligible investments, subject to limits on spread and other restrictions.

Non-UCITS categories, therefore, are GFOFs, property funds and feeder funds. Subfunds of umbrella funds have the investment powers applied to them separately in determining whether they qualify, although all subfunds of an umbrella OEIC will have to be qualifying if the OEIC itself is to be qualifying.

The following table sets out the categories of scheme which are now permitted for AUTs and OEICs.

	Type of scheme	AUTs	OEICs
	Umbrella	√	√
Permitted under UCITS I	Securities	√	√
	Warrant	√	√
Permitted under UCITS III	Money market	√	√
	Futures and Options Fund	√	√
	Fund of Funds	√	√
Non-UCITS	GFOF	√	√
	Property	√	√
	Feeder	√	x

The Management Directive

1.20   The Management Directive is intended to achieve three things.

- to introduce a 'Passport' regime similar to that under the Investment Services Directive (ISD) which allows UCITS management companies that are authorised in one member state to carry out cross-border investment services throughout the European Economic Area (EEA);

- to impose new financial resource requirements and conduct of business rules on the UCITS management company;

- to provide for a simplified prospectus to be used as a marketing document throughout the EEA.

1.21 At the time of writing, there is a lack of consensus across the EU as to whether the Directive does in fact provide the ability for a management company to be passported into different countries. The UK is among several countries that have concluded it is possible, but there is opposition to this viewpoint from several other countries including the Republic of Ireland. If passporting is eventually successful, it will mean that a local presence may no longer be required in each state in which a fund is marketed and could lead to significant cost savings for multinational groups.

UK approach to UCITS III

1.22 Under the timescales imposed by UCITS III, member states are required to transpose the law into their own legislation by 13 August 2003, and to apply it by 13 February 2004. In the UK, the FSA issued a consultation paper (CP 135) with HM Treasury at the end of April 2002 to implement the Product Directive. The provisions of CP 135 were transposed into law on 1 November 2002, substantially unchanged from the original consultation document.

At the time of writing, the changes introduced by the Management Directive have been passed by the FSA but will not formally be part of the FSA Handbook or fully effective until February 2004. The rules on the simplified prospectus are not likely to be implemented until March 2004 or to take effect until November 2004, owing to a lack of consensus within EU member states as to the exact interpretation of the simplified prospectus requirements.

1.23 Under transitional rules, UCITS authorised on or before 13 February 2002 may continue to be run under the old rules for up to five years from that date to give them time to adapt their investment policy to the new rules. The transitional rules also allow any UCITS scheme authorised between 14 February 2002 and 12 February 2004 to operate under the old investment policy requirements until 12 February 2004. There is also nothing to prevent non-UCITS schemes from converting into UCITS schemes whenever they wish.

The detailed rules on what each category is permitted to invest in are contained in the CIS Sourcebook, Chapter 5 for UCITS III-compliant funds and Chapter 5A for non-UCITS funds and UCITS funds operating under the transitional rules.

The UK regulatory environment

1.24 As mentioned earlier, the FSA Handbook sets out the detailed rules which prescribe the requirements for operators in the industry to follow, and their influence is far-reaching.

Approved persons

1.25   In order to ensure that the many requirements of the CIS Sourcebook are complied with by investment firms, the Regulations require that key functions are overseen by approved persons. These are generally individuals who have been judged to be fit and proper persons to perform controlled functions in the financial services industry.

The sorts of functions requiring an approved person's appointment include being a director, overseeing compliance or money laundering reporting, internal audit and dealing with customers in an advisory capacity.

Authorised persons

1.26   *FSMA 2000, s 19* stipulates that, in order to protect consumers, certain financial activities carried on in the UK must be regulated, and must only be carried out by authorised persons. The requirement to be authorised is taken extremely seriously – breaches are punishable by up to two years in prison and unlimited fines.

The activities in question include activities pivotal to the fund management industry, such as

- dealing in investments as principal or agent;

- arranging deals in investments;

- managing investments;

- safeguarding and administering investments;

- establishing, operating or winding up a collective investment scheme (whether regulated or unregulated);

- acting as trustee of an authorised unit trust scheme; and

- acting as the depositary or sole director of an open-ended investment company.

1.27   It therefore follows that any person wishing to operate as a fund manager, investment manager, custodian etc must obtain authorisation from the FSA. Such persons may be conducting more than one regulated activity – for example, a fund manager may both be operating a scheme, managing investments and dealing in investments either as agent or principal.

General prohibition on marketing to the public

1.28   Without authorisation, a person may not 'in the course of business, communicate an invitation or inducement to engage in investment activity' (*FSMA 2000, s 21*). That is, only authorised persons may market investment products to the general public in the UK.

1.29   *FSMA 2000, s 238* further provides that collective investment schemes may not be marketed to the general public in the UK, with three exceptions. These are UK AUTs, OEICs or recognised foreign schemes. It therefore follows that unauthorised unit trusts, while they must be established and managed by authorised persons according to the general rule in *s 19*, may not be marketed publicly. Recognition of foreign schemes is discussed below.

Authorisation may be obtained either by the person demonstrating he has UCITS certification (see below) or by obtaining permission from the FSA to carry on regulated activities.

Permission

1.30   Permission is granted upon application. The application must state the activities for which permission is sought, and any permission granted will be limited to those specified. If the person subsequently wishes to undertake an additional activity, a further permission will need to be obtained.

The application for permission must demonstrate compliance with a number of conditions, including adequacy of financial resources and suitability to carry on the activity.

1.31   Minimum financial requirements for firms carrying on investment services are set out by various European Directives and transposed into UK law by the FSA. The FSA will evaluate the applicant's resources in terms of quantity, quality and availability, examining in fact not only all of its financial resources, but also non-financial resources and means of managing those resources. This includes working capital, provisions against liabilities, holdings of cash and other liquid assets, human resources and effective means by which to manage risks using systems and controls.

The requirement for suitability means the applicant firm must be 'fit and proper' to be authorised, evaluated with reference to connections with other persons (such as the influence of other companies within a group), the range and nature of its proposed or current regulated activities and an assessment that its affairs are and will be conducted soundly and prudently. Evidence from overseas regulators may also be used in the evaluation process. It should be noted that it is the firm itself which is assessed for suitability. Any key personnel undertaking controlled functions will be assessed individually under the approved persons regime outlined earlier.

1.32   The person applying for authorisation may be either an individual, a body corporate, a branch of a body corporate, a partnership or an unincorporated association. In investment management, the authorised person will generally be a company (indeed, the manager and trustee of an AUT must be bodies corporate). Within that company, certain employees undertaking key roles will have to be approved persons as described above.

1.33 *Authorised Unit Trusts and OEICs*

An OEIC, being a body corporate, operates itself rather than being operated by another person. It is automatically an authorised person upon coming into existence, for it will already have gone through the process of being authorised as a product. In practice, the managers of OEICs are their Authorised Corporate Directors.

Regulation of non-UK funds marketed in UK

1.33 It was mentioned earlier that there is a general prohibition on collective investment schemes being marketed to the general public in the UK under *FSMA 2000, s 238*, and that that prohibition was not applied to a small number of types of vehicle including recognised foreign schemes.

1.34 As a general rule, schemes which are established outside the UK but which are subject to an equivalent level of supervision and regulation in their home country to that applicable to authorised UK funds, may obtain authorisation from the FSA to be sold to the general public.

This may be achieved in any of three ways.

1   Schemes constituted in other EEA States (UCITS)

   Funds which have been certified by their competent authority as UCITS-compliant in their home country and which give a two-month notice period and file certain information with the FSA. The recognition of these funds is permitted under *FSMA, s 264*.

2   Schemes authorised in certain designated countries or territories

   Funds which are not UCITS funds but which are authorised in a designated country or territory and the law and practice to which they are subject grants UK investors at least an equivalent level of protection to UK authorised funds and UCITS. Application for recognition must be made in writing and accompanied by certain documentation. These are recognised under *FSMA 2000, s 270*, and comprise all funds authorised in Guernsey, Jersey, the Isle of Man and Bermuda with the exception of feeder funds and Guernsey protected cell companies.

3   Individually recognised overseas schemes

   Schemes which are managed outside the UK and which may not be recognised under *s 264* or *s 270*, but which are subject to laws and regulations which grant UK investors adequate protection and ensure that the fund will be appropriately managed by appropriate persons. It is also required that there is an entitlement to redeem units at a price related to net asset value or a reasonably similar market price. Recognition of such schemes is permitted under *FSMA 2000, s 272*.

Offshore funds are discussed in greater detail in **CHAPTER 4**.

B. History and background

History of unit trusts

1.35   For much of the early history of collective investment schemes they were constituted as trust schemes. The reason for this was that trust law offers a great deal more flexibility for the investor to be granted exit rights than a company – corporate law places numerous restrictions and conditions on the ability of a company to repurchase its shares or increase or reduce its issued share capital, all features which are necessary if a scheme is to be open-ended and allow investors to invest and divest on demand.

Trusts, in comparison, can be established to grant the investor the right to redeem on demand and have complete flexibility on the number of investors who can be admitted.

1.36   The first unit trust was launched in 1868 but for many years the form of these funds was restrictive and made it difficult or impossible for the manager to vary the investments held. Known as fixed schemes, they provided for a set number of investment units to be purchased by a manager, which could be divided into sub-units for sale to investors. The number of sub-units allowed could be increased, but only if the trust deed provided for the creation of further investment units.

In 1879 it was ruled that unit trusts were unlawful associations, being unincorporated associations of more than 20 persons and considered to have been established in order to carry on a business in common with a view to profit. In response, all but one of those in existence quickly converted into limited companies. This action caused the creation of what we now know as investment trusts.

The case was later overruled when the Court of Appeal judged that, in fact, the investors shared no common relationship with one another, no business was being carried on and in any event it was not the unitholders who were carrying on any such business.

1.37   Municipal and General Securities launched the first unit trust which we would recognise today in 1931. Its remit was to invest in the shares of 24 companies whose composition did not change after that point, so it was still far more restrictive than modern schemes. However, it did grant investors the right to require the manager to repurchase their units at a price representing their share of the fund's underlying investments.

In 1934 the first unit trust to feature a flexible investment policy was established. By the end of the 1930s there were around 100 trusts in the UK, managing funds in the region of £80m. At the time of writing, Investment Management Association statistics show that 1,929 authorised funds are in existence, managed by 130 providers and comprising a total of £222bn. Of this, 927 funds and £96bn of assets remain in authorised unit trust form. The remainder are OEICs.

Reasons for investing in a collective investment scheme

1.38   Collective investment schemes offer a number of advantages over investing directly in the underlying assets:

- They achieve greater portfolio diversification than an average investor would be likely to do. Authorised schemes typically hold securities of around 40 different companies, thus spreading the risk of share price collapse and preventing any single company's results from being disproportionately important to overall performance. In addition, the stocks are chosen after a process of researching the companies' recent performance and future prospects, something which the average retail investor would not tend to have the time or expertise to do. Of course, the success of stock picking varies considerably from manager to manager but in general the investor is paying for professional management in the expectation that it will yield better results than he could have achieved alone.

- Some kinds of investments are out of the reach of many small investors to acquire on their own, such as gilts or property, and pooling resources with other people gives investors the buying power to gain exposure to such investments.

- As discussed earlier, the investment management industry is subject to a very high level of regulation and there are numerous safeguards in place to protect the consumer from excessive risks being taken with their money. This protection is not available to the same extent to an investor buying stocks and shares on its own account.

- Collective investment schemes are also subject to tax regimes which are in the main either favourable to the investor or at least put him on the same footing as he would have been had he invested directly, so that it is tax efficient to use these vehicles to manage his savings.

Factors influencing growth of authorised products

1.39   It was noted above that authorised funds have grown hugely over the decades, both in number and in terms of assets under management, and OEICs now account for around 56% of all the assets managed by authorised funds in the UK. OEICs have only really taken off to a significant extent in the last two years since the changes introduced by their new Regulations have relaxed the restrictions on their permitted investments such that they became attractive vehicles to operate.

There are a number of reasons for the growth experienced by the industry since the 1940s. Their tax treatment was made more advantageous in the early 1980s with the introduction of an exemption from tax on their capital gains, there has been a much improved public awareness of the benefits of equity investment and, most significantly of all, the launch of tax-exempt investments (Private Equity Plans from 1990 to 1999, and Individual Savings Accounts from then on) brought them to a far wider customer base than had ever been the case before.

C. Structure

Authorised Unit Trusts

Constitution – trust deed

1.40 A trust comes into existence when a person is the legal owner of property but is subject to an obligation to hold it for the benefit of other persons rather than for themselves. This person is the trustee of the trust.

Like any trust, an authorised unit trust is constituted by a trust deed. However, the parties to the deed not only include the trustee and the beneficiaries (unitholders), but also a manager. The powers and duties of the trustee and manager are set out in the regulations contained in the FSA's Collective Investment Schemes Sourcebook.

The trustee

1.41 The trustee performs a primarily caretaking role with respect to the investments, their management and the investors' rights to the property in the scheme.

Although any authorised body corporate may act as trustee to an AUT, in practice the role is invariably performed by a bank.

1.42 The trustee's first duty is to ensure that the scheme is managed by the manager in accordance with the general law, with the FSA regulations and with the trust deed. If there is any doubt that the fund is not being properly managed, the trustee must report any matters to the FSA.

Its specific responsibilities include:

- holding legal title to the fund property and ensuring its safe custody;
- ensuring that the scheme property is invested by the manager in accordance with the stated investment strategy of the fund;
- ensuring that the manager is pricing the units correctly;
- collecting income paid to the unit trust;
- making tax reclaims;
- keeping records to demonstrate its compliance with the regulations;
- maintaining the register of unitholders;
- paying distributions of income to the investors;
- creating and cancelling units upon instruction from the manager.

1.43 No part of the trustee's responsibilities may be delegated to the manager where they relate to custody of the property or oversight of the manager's activities. Custody may be delegated only if the appointed custodian is bound to obtain the trustee's permission for releasing documentation to a third party. Apart from these restrictions, other duties may be delegated to any person including the manager. The trustee will remain responsible for any acts or omissions of the manager in performing duties delegated by the trustee.

The manager

1.44   The manager's role may be described as the responsibility for the day-to-day running of the unit trust. The manager must be independent of the trustee and an authorised body corporate.

1.45   The manager's duties are of a fiduciary nature. The overriding duty is to manage the scheme in accordance with the trust deed, prospectus and FSA rules but the following activities are also involved:

- selecting and managing the fund's portfolio of investments;
- marketing the fund for sale to investors;
- making a market in the units, by pricing them in accordance with the rules and buying and selling units on demand from investors;
- instructing the trustee to create or cancel units as and when necessary to deal with investor demand;
- reporting to the trustee on matters such as compliance or otherwise with the rules, the amount of income to be distributed etc;
- maintaining records and accounts and appointing an auditor;
- preparing tax returns.

The manager may delegate any of these functions to any person. It will remain responsible for any acts or omissions of the delegate if they pertain to the management of the scheme property or if the delegate is the trustee or an associate of itself or the trustee.

Beneficial versus legal ownership

1.46   Under trust law, the trustee is the legal owner of the fund's investments, not the unitholders. They are, however, the beneficial owners of the investments.

OEICs

Legal basis

1.47   It was mentioned earlier that collective investment schemes originated in trust form because of the legal restrictions in what corporate structures are able to do. If OEICs were to be a feasible vehicle, they had to be set up with the capability to issue unlimited share capital and permit redemption of their shares as and when investors demanded it. These features prevent them from being governed by the *Companies Act* which does not grant such abilities to limited liability companies.

For ease and speed, OEICs were introduced in UK legislation using secondary legislation rather than an Act of Parliament, and as a consequence all amendments to their legal rights and duties are passed using statutory instruments.

1.48 The *European Communities Act 1972* enabled the Government to make the *Open-Ended Investment Companies (Investment Companies with Variable Capital) Regulations 1996 (SI 1996/2827)*, made on 11 November 1996 and in force from 6 January 1997. These Regulations made provision for the formation of a class of body corporate referred to in the Regulations as an investment company with variable capital, and for the authorisation of such companies and their subsequent supervision.

As mentioned earlier, the 1996 Regulations have now been revoked and the *Open-Ended Investment Companies Regulations 2001 (SI 2001/1228)* were introduced in their place. These Regulations establish the corporate code for OEICs and give the FSA power to make rules for their operation. It should be noted that the CIS Sourcebook refers to ICVCs, meaning investment companies with variable capital, rather than OEICs.

Constitution – articles

1.49 As an OEIC is an incorporated entity, it must prepare and file an instrument of incorporation which must make the following statements:

- where the head office of the company is situated;
- that the company is an open-ended investment company with variable share capital;
- that the shareholders are not liable for the debts of the company;
- that the scheme property is entrusted to a depositary for safekeeping (subject to any exceptions permitted by FSA rules); and
- that charges or expenses of the company may be taken out of the scheme property.

1.50 It must also provide:

- the name of the company;
- the object of the company (ie the type of property it will invest in, along with a statement that the object of the company is to invest in property of that kind with the aim of spreading investment risk and giving its shareholders the benefit of the results of the management of that property);

- any matter relating to the procedure for the appointment, retirement and removal of any director of the company for which provision is not made in these Regulations or FSA rules; and

- the currency in which the accounts of the company are to be prepared.

- the category, as specified in FSA rules, to which the company belongs if it is a Chapter 5A fund (non-UCITS or a UCITS operating under the transitional arrangements);

- the maximum and minimum sizes of the company's capital;

- in the case of an umbrella company, the investment objectives applicable to each part of the scheme property that is pooled separately;

- the classes of shares that the company may issue and their various rights.

These provisions may subsequently be changed if required, subject to the procedures laid down in the OEIC regulations and CIS sourcebook and, in some cases, shareholder approval.

Assuming that everything is in order, the FSA will authorise the company and at that point the OEIC will come into existence, as per Regulation 3 of the OEIC Regulations.

Depositary

1.51 The Regulations require that an OEIC must have a depositary. The depositary must be a firm (usually a bank) authorised under the FSMA, must be independent of the OEIC and of the persons appointed as directors of the OEIC.

The depositary's function is in many ways similar to that of the AUT's trustee. The investment property is held by the depositary in its own name. The depositary may appoint sub-custodians to take custody of the assets but it will remain ultimately responsible. The depositary also has responsibility for checking that the OEIC complies with the key regulatory requirements.

Authorised Corporate Director

1.52 Like any company, an OEIC is required to have a board, with a minimum of one director. One director must be a body corporate authorised under the FSMA, known as an authorised corporate director or ACD. If the OEIC has only one director, that director must be an ACD.

All of the directors must be approved as fit and proper persons, and the board must have appropriate expertise.

The ACD is broadly similar to the AUT's manager, in that its main duties involve dealing with the day-to-day operation of the company.

1.53   Where the OEIC has directors additional to the ACD, these have a general duty of oversight of the company's affairs, including checking that the ACD is fulfilling its duties in a competent manner. The duties of the additional directors also include non-compliance matters such as strategy and marketing policy, although these functions can be delegated to, for example, the ACD. In practice, additional directors are rare.

Beneficial versus legal ownership

1.54   The investments of the OEIC are owned by the depositary. However, unlike an AUT, an OEIC has legal personality and beneficial ownership of the investments lies with the OEIC itself, and shareholders have no rights to the underlying assets. Their rights to participate in or receive profits and income arising from the acquisition, holding, management or disposal of the scheme property are to be included in the OEIC's instrument of incorporation, in accordance with the OEIC Regulations.

Units and shares

1.55   The interests of investors in an AUT consist of units or fractions of units, each representing one undivided share in the AUT's scheme property.

Units may be issued in one of four forms:

- income units;
- accumulation units;
- limited issue income units;
- limited issue accumulation units.

1.56   An AUT will default to issuing income units unless one of the other kinds is provided for in its prospectus.

Holders of accumulation units do not receive distributions from the fund as income and instead their share of the income is credited to the capital value of their unit, increasing its redemption value.

Holders of income units receive the fund's distributions as income, which they may or may not have the option of using to purchase additional shares.

Limited issue funds are those which have a cap on the number or value of units which will be issued, or which place restrictions on the occasions when units will be issued. Units from these funds will either be income or accumulation units, as with any other AUT.

1.57   The interests of investors in an OEIC are represented by shares. The OEIC Regulations provide that rights attached to a share of any class may be expressed in two denominations, 'larger' and 'smaller'. The smaller denomination must be a set proportion of the larger denomination, and the larger denomination will be regarded as a standard share. In this way the value of an investor's holding can be allocated to a precise number of larger and smaller shares without the need for rounding up or down to a whole share.

OEICs are permitted to issue a wider range of shares than unit trusts. These are, as the Regulations currently stand:

- income shares;
- net accumulation shares;
- gross accumulation shares;
- currency class income shares;
- currency class net accumulation shares;
- currency class gross accumulation shares; and
- limited issue shares which will also be shares of another class.

Net and gross refer to the matter of whether a distribution can be accumulated with or without deducting any withholding tax at source. Generally, gross classes are reserved for non-resident investors and tax-exempt institutional investors.

Currency class shares are priced in a different currency from that used as the fund's base currency, and pay distributions in the designated currency of the class.

1.58 In addition, the OEIC may apply different charging structures to different share classes. This may be used to allow the OEIC to negotiate different rates of annual fee with different customers. For example, large institutional customers may pay lower rates than retail customers due to their economies of scale and bargaining power.

Although AUT units are only available in a relatively small number of classes at present, the FSA is, at the time of writing, consulting on whether to expand the range of unit classes to match those available to OEICs.

1.59 In most other respects, units and shares can be thought of as equivalent. Unitholders and shareholders both have the right to sell their shares back to the manager of the AUT or the OEIC on any dealing day when trading has not been suspended, and both units and shares may be in registered or bearer form.

Open-ended

1.60 Both AUTs and OEICs are open-ended types of scheme. Open-ended means that the number of units which the fund can issue can vary according to demand without an upper limit, and each share will be valued with reference to the fund's net asset value, unaffected by demand levels for the shares.

At the time of writing, the FSA was in the process of consulting on allowing limited redemption funds. These would be non-UCITS funds permitted to restrict the occasions on which redemptions by investors have to be accepted, up to a maximum of once every six months. The consultation paper proposes that this should only be allowed where the fund is invested in property or where the investment objective involves providing a set return over a specific period of time, such that the practicalities imposed by managing the investments require that investors have less than immediate access to their money.

D. Day-to-day operation

Investment restrictions

1.61 As mentioned earlier, the FSA permits authorised funds in a variety of classifications – securities, warrants, money market, futures and options, geared futures and options, property, umbrella, feeder and fund of funds structures are all permitted. There are detailed rules in the FSA Handbook covering the types of investment each scheme may make, along with limits on the amount of scheme property which can be invested in any one type of investment or in the instruments or securities of any one issuer.

Stocklending

1.62 The Regulations permit authorised funds to enter into stocklending transactions for the purposes of generating additional income with an acceptable degree of risk. Stock may only be lent to other authorised persons. Collateral at least equal in value to the stock being lent must be obtained, and in one of a prescribed number of forms, such as cash and Government securities. For the time that it is held, the collateral forms part of the scheme property.

Cash and borrowing

1.63 Strict limitations are placed on an authorised fund's ability to borrow and to hold cash (rather than investing it). Apart from when the fund is initially offered for sale, cash and near cash may be held by the fund only where it is necessary for facilitating the redemption of units, efficient management of the fund in accordance with its objectives, or purposes ancillary to the investment objectives of the fund. Money market schemes, FOFs and GFOFs are, however, permitted to hold cash and near cash in any amounts.

An OEIC or the trustee of an AUT, if instructed to do so by the manager, may borrow money for the fund's use with the borrowing repayable out of the scheme property. Money may only be borrowed from an eligible institution (broadly, approved credit institutions or other investment firms) or an approved bank.

The amount of borrowing must be no more than 10% of the fund's property at any time and must be on a temporary basis.

Pricing

1.64   The price of units in an authorised fund is unaffected by relative levels of supply and demand in the market, having instead a direct relationship with the value of the scheme property, the net asset value (NAV).

It is one of the roles of the ACD or unit trust manager that the fund must be valued on a regular basis and the price of units calculated and published, and there are a number of rules relating to the way in which pricing is performed.

Single pricing

1.65   All OEICs are subject to a requirement to calculate a single price for issuing shares to and repurchasing shares from investors. AUTs have the option of using a single price or a dual price for their units.

The price of a unit will essentially be calculated by dividing the scheme property attributable to a class of units by the number of units in issue at the time. Once that price is calculated, the manager has the option of adding or deducting a provision for SDRT and dilution levy which may be payable in the future on the fund's investments or the buying and selling of its own units.

Dual pricing

1.66   Under dual pricing, the manager of the AUT calculates two prices, one being the price at which units are sold to investors and one being the price at which they are repurchased. The starting point for the pricing is, as with single pricing, the net asset value of the fund divided by the number of units in issue, but the sale and redemption prices are then calculated so as to fall within parameters set by the Regulations.

The Regulations allow that the sale price of units may be increased by a preliminary charge, providing that the trust deed permits. The preliminary charge is the means by which the manager makes a profit margin on dealing in units, and is either a fixed amount per unit or a percentage of the issue price.

In addition to preliminary and redemption charges, the manager is entitled to apply an SDRT provision to incoming and outgoing investors if desired and if provided in the fund's prospectus.

Dilution levy

1.67   Under the rules for single pricing, the manager of the scheme has the option, but not the requirement, to impose a dilution levy on the price of units. A dilution levy may be required where investments have to be sold to finance a redemption of units and in so doing either significant transaction costs are incurred, or the fund suffers a loss through the margin between buying and selling price of the underlying investments, and is intended to compensate the fund (not the manager) for the loss. Typically, the levy is only applied when a large redemption occurs, for example as a consequence of an institutional investor selling a large block of units.

Creation/cancellation

1.68   When an investor redeems his units, the manager will repurchase them from him and hold them in what is known as the manager's box. The box represents the available supply of units which can be issued immediately to a new investor. Should demand rise or fall significantly, the manager may find that the manager's box contains too few or too many units to satisfy demand. If more are required, he will instruct the trustee to create more units, and if fewer are required, he will instruct the trustee to cancel them. Unless the fund is a limited issue fund, creations can be made without restriction.

Equalisation

1.69   At each distribution date set out in its prospectus, a fund will pay out all of its income available for distribution (or accumulate it, as applicable). At that point, if a new investor is introduced into the fund, his unit price will be calculated with reference only to the capital value of the fund and the income account will be empty.

If, however, he is introduced at any point between two distribution dates, he will be joining a fund which has begun to earn income on the investments owned by the existing unitholders. Because the fund manager will allocate all available income equally among all the units in issue at the distribution date, some process is required to ensure the new investor does not receive a share in the income which arose before he joined, but only that which arose afterwards. This process is equalisation, and it is also a way of ensuring that the value of existing unitholders' units is not detrimentally affected by the issue of new units.

1.70   To achieve this, when the new investor buys units, he pays a price that comprises both income earned since the last distribution date and the capital value of the fund. The income element is the equalisation. At the end of the distribution period, the manager takes all the equalisation received on creations and returns it to all new investors as part of the next distribution. The amount received will be an average per unit. Of the total distribution received, part will be the income earned since he was a unitholder and part will be equalisation, treated as a return of capital. The respective treatment of these items in the hands of the investor is considered in **CHAPTER 12**.

The process is best illustrated by way of an example.

EXAMPLE 1.70

> Suppose that Alison wishes to buy 5,000 units in a unit trust exactly six months into a twelve-month distribution period, and that income is earned at a steady rate of 10% pa by the fund. Also suppose that on day one of the distribution period, the fund had a capital value of £4,000 and had 10,000 units in issue, so the basic capital value of each unit was £0.40.
>
> By the time Alison approaches the fund manager, the unit trust's net asset value has grown to £4,200 (£4,000 capital, £200 income having been earned on the capital in six months). Each unit is worth £0.42 and therefore she must pay £0.42×5,000=£2,100 for her units so that all the 15,000 units now in issue are equally priced. The fund's total value is thus £6,300.
>
> On the fund's distribution date, it has £600 to distribute among 15,000 units, £500 of which is income and £100 of which is equalisation.
>
> The income is calculated as (£4,000×10%)+(£2,000×10%×6/12), as 10,000 of the units are entitled to twelve months of income, while Alison's 5,000 units are only entitled to six months.
>
> A distribution of 4p per unit is payable. All the pre-existing unitholders receive 4p of income for each unit held, whereas Alison receives 4p for each of her units, comprising 2p income and 2p equalisation.

Group I/Group II unitholders

1.71   In order to separate the unitholders to whom equalistion is payable from those to whom it is not, the fund manager will classify all unitholders as either Group I or Group II.

Group I unitholders are those who have been invested since the beginning of a distribution period, and are clearly entitled to receive all the income which is earned throughout the period.

Group II unitholders are those who, like Alison in the example above, join the fund part of the way through a distribution period. These investors receive some of their first distribution as income and some as equalisation.

1.72   If an existing investor buys more units at some point during a distribution period, his new holding will be classed as Group II and the original holding as Group I. He will, of course, only pay and receive equalisation on his new holding. The tax consequences of equalisation are explained in **CHAPTER 12**.

Distribution periods

1.73   Authorised funds are required by the CIS Sourcebook to allocate income to the units in issue at least annually, within four months of the accounting date of the fund. In addition they may, if provided for in their prospectus, make interim distributions. The period of time between distributions is known as a distribution period and may be as little as a day. Typically, funds will be run with six-monthly distribution periods although some bond funds or money market funds may make more frequent distributions.

Reports, accounts, meetings

1.74   The CIS Sourcebook requires that OEICs and AUTs must produce annual and half-yearly reports for unitholders, and the annual report must be audited.

The OEIC Regulations require that an OEIC must hold an annual general meeting each year in which the annual report and accounts are approved. However, if it holds its first meeting within 18 months of the date of the authorisation order, the OEIC need not hold a further AGM in the first two years following its incorporation. Not more than 15 months may elapse between AGMs.

SORPs

1.75   The accounts for AUTs and OEICs must be prepared in accordance with financial reporting standards currently in force and, additionally, in accordance with either the Statement of Recommended Practice (SORP) for OEICs or the SORP for AUTs as applicable.

The unit trust SORP was published by the Investment Management Regulatory Organisation (IMRO) in January 1997 and the OEIC SORP by the FSA in November 2000. Work is underway to produce a combined SORP for authorised funds, which will be published by the Investment Management Association, the trade body for the professional investment management industry in the UK. An exposure draft of the combined SORP was published in May 2003 and is, at the time of writing, intended to take effect for accounting periods beginning on or after 1 December 2003.

1.76   The SORPs cannot override any requirements of financial reporting standards in force but can add to them and clarify the approach which should be taken to ensure that the accounts of unit trusts and OEICs reflect a true and fair view of the entities' financial position. SORPs exist in other industries besides the management of authorised funds (for example, banking and investment trusts) but these SORPs are unique in having a mandatory adoption status. It is permitted to depart from the SORP's provisions in an aspect of the fund's accounts, but explanation must be given of the effect of any departure and the reason why it is appropriate to follow a different treatment.

As tax treatment of authorised funds moves closer to accounting treatment, the provisions of the SORP become increasingly important in determining their tax position. This is discussed further below in the section on taxation of loan relationships, foreign exchange and derivative contracts.

E. Taxation

Background

1.77 The overriding principle behind the taxation of authorised investment funds is that their investors should be in the same position, neither better nor worse off, through investing in a collective investment scheme than they would have been if they had held the underlying investments directly. This is largely achieved by the tax legislation, although there are certain exceptions, often due to the complexity that such a goal would otherwise bring with it. This book makes reference to this as appropriate.

History

1.78 The rules governing the taxation of authorised funds and the general scheme of corporation tax have been subject to a great deal of change in the last 10 to 15 years, for example with the introduction and abolition of foreign income dividends (FIDs), the abolition of *s 242* reclaims of dividend tax credits, the abolition of ACT and introduction of Shadow ACT rules, and changes to the types of distribution a fund could make. This chapter covers only the rules which currently affect authorised funds, or those which are subject to transitional change, and disregards those which have been repealed. Full details on the historic taxation of funds can be obtained from the Inland Revenue Manuals at COT3943 et seq.

General rules of corporation tax

1.79 As trusts, AUTs would be subject to income tax legislation were it not for a specific instruction in *ICTA 1988, s 468* that they should be regarded as companies for the purposes of the Tax Acts 'in respect of income arising to the trustees…and for the purposes of the provisions relating to relief for capital expenditure'. Consequently they are not necessarily subject to all the tax rules to which ordinary companies are subject, and may also be subject to a derogation from mainstream corporation tax rules regarding their income or expenditure. Where this is the case, this will be specifically noted (for example, under the *FA 1996* loan relationship legislation).

Similarly, *TCGA 1992, s 99* states that the provisions of that Act will apply to authorised unit trusts as though they were companies resident and ordinarily resident in the UK and as though the units were shares. This means that unitholdings are subject to the same rules on pooling, reorganisations, taper relief etc as orthodox company shares. The treatment of investors making disposals of units is covered in CHAPTER 12.

1.80 As companies, OEICs would be subject to corporation tax in any event, but their tax treatment is made equivalent to that of AUTs by modifications to the Tax Acts which ensure that they have effect for OEICs in a like manner as they do for AUTs. The *Open-Ended Investment Companies (Tax) Regulations 1997 (SI 1997/1154)* introduce amendments so that references to unit trusts are taken to include references to OEICs, and references to units in a unit trust are taken to include references to shares in an OEIC etc.

Accounting periods

1.81 As noted above, FSA regulations require that unit trusts draw up audited accounts as part of their annual report to investors. The accounting date chosen will be the unit trust's accounting date for tax purposes, and all the usual requirements for filing corporation tax self-assessment returns and paying tax apply as they would for a company.

Treatment of umbrella funds

1.82 For tax purposes, each subfund of an umbrella fund is regarded as a separate taxable entity, so they are taxed individually on their respective profits and must each complete separate tax returns. References in the Tax Acts to unit trusts are to be read as indicating subfunds of umbrellas separately.

Distribution periods

1.83 A distribution period is different from an accounting period. Funds must pay distributions at least annually, but the frequency of payments can be on a monthly, quarterly, six-monthly or annual basis. The length of time between payment of distributions is a distribution period. A number of the sections dealing with AUTs refer to distribution periods.

Specific legislation for authorised unit trusts and OEICs

1.84 *ICTA 1988, ss 468–468Q* (as modified by the OEIC Tax Regulations) set out the specific tax rules pertaining to the taxation of income and expenses of an AUT.

Rate of corporation tax

1.85   Under *s 468(1A)*, authorised funds are subject to corporation tax at the lower rate of income tax, which for 2003/04 is 20%, rather than the corporation tax rates. This is intended to ensure that investors are in the same position as if they received the underlying income direct, net of expenses.

Income

1.86   As entities subject to corporation tax, unit trusts pay tax on the excess of their taxable income over allowable expenses.

Non-taxable income

1.87   Like other companies, unit trusts are not taxable on UK dividend income (franked investment income, or FII), whether this is paid by a company or another unit trust. UK scrip dividends are also not taxable income.

All other forms of income are taxable as usual under the schedular system.

Taxable income and applicable Schedules

Schedule A

1.88   Profits made in connection with the holding of property will be taxed under Schedule A on an accruals basis on the same principles as they are for a Schedule D Case I trade.

Schedule D Case I

1.89   It is central to the tax treatment of a unit trust that it is regarded as holding investments and not trading in them. Were it to be regarded as trading, any capital gains arising on the investments would be taxable as income under Schedule D Case I, with no exemption, and yet the gains would be treated as capital for regulatory purposes. This would mean they could not be distributed to investors, so any tax paid could not be passed on via the distribution.

Trading activities would therefore lead authorised funds to have tax on their investments trapped in the fund, and as the investors would be taxed again on disposal of their units, double taxation of gains arising in the fund would be the consequence.

1.90   It is a possibility that a fund with high levels of investment turnover or that uses more sophisticated instruments such as derivatives to blur the line between capital and income might be accused of trading in investments. The

Inland Revenue is not believed generally to take the point, and indeed has stated in *Tax Bulletin 60* that there is a 'general and prevailing assumption' that a fund is set up for investment, not trading purposes.

Schedule D Case III

1.91   Items taxable and relievable under Schedule D Case III comprise non-trade loan relationship credits and debits, some profits and losses on derivative contracts and some foreign exchange gains and losses.

The treatment of these items changed under rules introduced in *FA 2002*. Accounting periods beginning before 1 October 2002 are subject to the old rules laid down in *Finance Acts 1993, 1994* and *1996*, while those beginning on or after 1 October 2002 are subject to the new rules, which appear in *FA 2002* and *FA 1996* as amended by *FA 2002*.

Accounting periods beginning before 1 October 2002

LOAN RELATIONSHIPS

1.92   *FA 1996, Sch 10 para 2* disapplied the loan relationships legislation for AUTs in respect of their creditor relationships (relationships where they stood in the position of creditor, ie as investors). AUTs were instead made subject to the income tax rules as applicable to unauthorised unit trusts, although on the basis of accounting period dates rather than years of assessment.

Application of the income tax rules meant that interest was taxable on a receipts rather than an accruals basis under Schedule D Case III, and that AUTs were excluded from the requirement to mark their bond holdings to market annually and tax the movement. The accrued income scheme applied to purchases and sales of bonds, and gains and losses on bond holdings were treated as capital, and thus fell within the AUT capital gains exemption. The only exception was for relevant discounted securities, for which the discount was taxed as Schedule D Case III income generally on disposal of the security.

1.93   AUTs were within the scope of the old loan relationship rules for their debtor relationships (relationships where they stood in the position of debtor, ie borrowers). Although AUTs are restricted by the Regulations in the amount of borrowing they are permitted to do, to the extent that they paid interest, it was relieved on the accruals basis.

ACCRUED INCOME SCHEME

1.94   The accrued income scheme seeks to prevent taxpayers from converting income into capital, which would be exempt for AUTs, by 'bond washing'. It ceased to apply to corporates from 1 April 1996 when the loan relationship rules of *FA 1996* took effect, but remains applicable in income tax legislation and to authorised funds for pre-2002 periods by virtue of their exclusion from the mainstream rules for creditor relationships.

Bond washing involves buying and selling securities timed such that interest coupons are not actually received and instead the accrued interest is reflected in the buying and selling price. Were there not legislation in place to prevent the sale or disposal from being treated as involving purely capital proceeds, taxpayers could obtain a tax advantage from the practice.

1.95 The AIS legislation works by stripping out any income which has accrued up to the date of sale of loan stock and similar securities and is, therefore, reflected in the sale price. Only the true capital value of the bond will be subject to capital gains treatment, and the accrued income is taxed or relieved as appropriate.

When a security is bought cum-interest, the purchaser is entitled to relief equivalent to the interest purchased, which by rights belongs to the previous owner. This relief is aggregated with other amounts calculated under AIS relating to the same kind of security. Any excess relief can then be set against the interest received on that security at the next interest payment date. This may not be in the same accounting period as that in which the purchase takes place.

When a security is bought ex-interest, the interest will be paid to another person but the purchaser will be treated as having received a sum equal to the gross amount of interest accruing from the date of purchase to the interest payment date. These sums are aggregated with other charges and reliefs under the scheme relating to the same kind of security. Any positive balance is chargeable to tax under Schedule D Case VI in the accounting period of the next payment date.

1.96 When a security is sold cum-interest, the vendor is treated as entitled to the interest accrued from the last payment date to the date of sale. Again, this is aggregated with other amounts and the balance, if positive, is chargeable under Schedule D Case VI.

When a security is sold ex-interest, the vendor is entitled to relief under AIS for an amount equal to the interest which has accrued from the date of sale to the next interest payment date. Again the aggregation rules apply and any excess relief is available for offset against the interest when it is received.

1.97 The unit trust and OEIC SORPs require funds to use 'clean accounting' in respect of their fixed interest securities, so that any accrued interest bought or sold will be separately identified in the accounts as income in the period in which the purchase or sale takes place. Therefore, the only difference between the accounting and tax treatment is one of timing. For tax purposes, amounts are taxed or relieved at the next payment date, which may be in the next accounting period. In practice, this shifts the tax charge from corporation tax to deferred tax.

RELEVANT DISCOUNTED SECURITIES

1.98 A relevant discounted security (RDS) is a security, whenever issued, where the amount payable on redemption is an amount which involves, or might involve, a deep gain.

The definition of an RDS refers to a security where the amount payable on redemption exceeds the issue price by more than the lower of 0.5% of the redemption amount for each year between the date of issue and date of redemption, or 15% of the redemption amount, where the life of the security is 30 years or greater. Where that period is not a complete number of years, each month shall be taken as one-twelfth of a year.

1.99 Certain securities are specifically excluded from being treated as relevant discounted securities, including gilt-edged securities which are not strips, excluded indexed securities and securities issued under the same prospectus as other securities which are not RDSs.

For example, where a security is issued for £90 with a redemption price of £100 and a life of ten years, the discount inherent in the pricing is £10 or 10% of the redemption amount. As the discount is greater than 10 years x 0.5%, or 5%, the security would be regarded as an RDS.

1.100 The legislation brings into charge the £10 discount on disposal of the security and any other income paid as an ordinary coupon is taxable on receipt. As the SORPs for AUTs and OEICs also require discounts on securities to be accounted for in this way, tax and accounting treatment should match and no adjustments to accounting profit should be required.

Upon transferring, redeeming or becoming entitled to redeem the security, the amount receivable is compared with the amount paid and any gain is taxed to Schedule D Case III in the period in which this event occurs. Where a loss arises, relief is available.

DERIVATIVE CONTRACTS

1.101 For accounting periods beginning before 1 October 2002, derivative contracts were termed financial instruments and their tax treatment was governed by *FA 1994*. Authorised funds were specifically excluded from the application of the financial instruments legislation by *FA 1994, s 154*, and were subject instead to income tax rules and *ICTA 1988, s 468AA*.

1.102 The question of whether a transaction has trading or non-trading purposes is settled on the particular facts and circumstances and guidance on the subject is provided by SP 03/02 (superseding SP 14/91). Profits, gains and losses arising out of authorised funds' holdings of financial instruments under the income tax rules were not taxable items. *ICTA 1988, s 128* and *TCGA 1992, s 143* serve to ensure that returns on non-trading activities are treated as capital gains or losses, and authorised funds are exempt from tax on capital gains. Where a transaction was entered into for trading purposes, *ICTA 1988, s 468AA* provided a specific exemption from tax on the profits, gains or losses of futures and options contracts.

Where the old rules apply, the exemptions described above mean that only other kinds of derivative contract, such as a contract for differences, entered into for trading purposes, could subject the unit trust to tax on the return. In practice, this was extremely rare.

FOREIGN EXCHANGE GAINS AND LOSSES

1.103   Authorised funds were also specifically excluded from the application of the foreign exchange legislation under *FA 1993, s 152*. This had a similar effect to that for financial instruments, in that treatment depended on whether the exchange movements arose on non-trading items (treated as capital and thus non-taxable and non-relievable) or on trading items (taxable under Schedule D Case I).

Accounting periods beginning on or after 1 October 2002

1.104   *FA 2002* introduced around 80 pages of new and revised legislation to cover the treatment of loan relationships, derivative contracts and foreign exchange gains and losses previously contained in *Finance Acts 1993, 1994* and *1996*.

The new legislation has consolidated and fundamentally overhauled these areas, and the way in which collective investment schemes are treated was revisited as part of the process.

1.105   In all cases, the changes made took effect from the first accounting period beginning on or after 1 October 2002, referred to as 'the first new accounting period' in the legislation.

Other terms used in the legislation are:

● 'the last old accounting period' (the last accounting period which began before 1 October 2002);

● 'the first new day' (the first day of the first new accounting period);

● 'the last old day' (the last day of the last old accounting period).

SORP-BASED APPROACH

1.106   The approach under *FA 2002* in general is to align tax treatment very closely with accounting treatment such that few amendments to accounting profits are needed in computing the tax liability. Given the unique structure and manner of operation of authorised funds, they have again been specially dealt with under the new legislation.

As it is mandatory for authorised funds to follow their Statements of Recommended Practice, the Inland Revenue has based the tax treatment of loan relationships, derivative contracts and foreign exchange gains and losses around the accounting treatment of these items laid down in the SORPs.

LOAN RELATIONSHIPS

1.107 The previous rule disapplying the loan relationships legislation from creditor relationships of authorised funds has been revoked, and they are now subject to tax on these items in the same way as a normal corporate on both debtor and creditor relationships, with one important exception.

The exception is that *FA 1996, Sch 10 paras 2A, 2B* (as amended by *FA 2002*) provide that profits, gains or losses on a creditor relationship are not taxable credits or debits if they are accounted for as capital under the SORP.

To be capital, they must be classified under either of the headings 'net gains/losses on investments during the period' or 'other gains/losses' in the fund's statement of total return for the period.

If they are classified under any other headings, they will be treated as income and either taxed or relieved as appropriate, as non-trade loan relationship debits or credits.

Maintaining the capital/income distinction is of crucial importance to authorised funds in order to ensure that investors are only taxed once on their capital gains.

DERIVATIVE CONTRACTS

1.108 In the same way as for loan relationships, the relevant SORP will be used to determine whether profits, gains and losses arising on derivative contracts are taxable or non-taxable.

The derivative contracts legislation in *FA 2002, Sch 26* covers the taxation of futures, options and contracts for differences involving most types of underlying subject matter, but notably excludes those whose subject matter is wholly equity.

Non-equity-based derivatives such as interest rate swaps are, therefore, taxable or exempt from tax on the basis of how they are accounted for. Equity-based derivative contracts, however, fall to be taxed as they would have been under the previous rules; that is, based on whether the transactions are entered into for trading or non-trading purposes. The difference now is that a trading contract will be taxable under Schedule D Case I rather than being exempted by *ICTA 1988, s 468AA* as this section was repealed by *FA 2002*.

FOREIGN EXCHANGE LEGISLATION

1.109 Any foreign exchange gains and losses will be dealt with under either loan relationships or derivative contracts legislation, as appropriate, so that the currency movements will be treated in the same way as the principal item.

OTHER POINTS

1.110 A consequential amendment arising out of *FA 2002* was made to *ICTA 1988, s 468L* (interest distributions), to expand the categories of qualifying investments for the purposes of the 60% test used to determine whether a fund is a bond fund for tax purposes (see below). That test now includes derivative contracts and contracts for differences whose underlying subject matter consists of the original classes of investment (money placed at interest, securities, shares in a building society, and shares/units in authorised bond funds).

Transitional rules

1.111 The transitional rules introduced to ensure that no items are taxed twice or relieved twice in the move from old to new rules are almost identical to the transitional rules introduced by *Finance Act 1996* for normal corporates.

For loan relationships, closing accruals in the last old accounting period will be added back to the accounts figure in the first new accounting period, in order to ensure that they are taxed.

Interest paid on bonds which currently fall within the accrued income scheme will be subject to transitional rules if paid after the start of the first new accounting period. The table below sets out the appropriate treatment for interest bought and sold, cum-div and ex-div.

	Cum-div	**Ex-div**
Bought	The fund is taxable on the entire interest receipt, but entitled to a non-trade loan relationship debit for interest accruing up to the date of purchase.	Although no interest is received, the fund is taxable on a non-trade loan relationship credit representing interest earned after the date of purchase.
Sold	Although no interest is received, the fund is taxable on a non-trade loan relationship credit representing interest earned before the date of sale.	The fund is taxable on the entire interest receipt, but entitled to a non-trade loan relationship debit for interest earned by the purchaser after the date of sale.

1.112   As the tax treatment of relevant discounted securities has changed to follow accounting treatment (any income being taxed on the accounts basis, any gain or loss being a tax 'nothing'), transitional rules are required to deal with holdings held prior to the new rules.

The rules are that the fund should mark the holdings to market on the last old day. If there is a gain or loss on a security, that amount will be brought into tax as a non-trading loan relationship credit or debit in the accounting period in which the earliest of the following dates falls:

- the first date on which the holder is entitled to require the security to be redeemed;
- the day on which the security is actually redeemed; or
- the day on which the security is disposed of.

Schedule D Case V

1.113   Overseas dividends are taxable under Schedule D Case V on an arising basis, in accordance with general principles. However, most unit trusts credit income to the accounts when shares go ex-div or bonds go ex-interest, rather than when the income is actually paid. By informal concession the Inland Revenue may allow a unit trust to be taxed on this ex-div basis rather than on the payment date.

Overseas interest is taxable as Schedule D Case III income under the loan relationships legislation (see below).

See CHAPTER 11 for discussion of foreign taxes.

Schedule D Case VI

1.114   Other income, such as underwriting commission and offshore income gains on disposal of interests in non-qualifying offshore funds, as well as charges and reliefs under the accrued income scheme as described earlier, are taxed under Schedule D Case VI.

Capital gains

1.115   *TCGA 1992, s 99* applies the Act to any unit trust scheme as if the scheme were a company and the units were shares, but specifically exempts them from corporation tax on their chargeable gains. *Section 99* also prescribes that AUTs are treated as if they were companies resident and ordinarily resident in the UK. The OEIC tax regulations extend the legislation to treat OEICs in the same manner.

Management expenses

1.116   *ICTA 1988, s 468(4)* stipulates that a unit trust is permitted relief for management expenses on the same basis as an investment company, irrespective of whether or not it is an investment company as defined by the legislation. It further provides that, whilst general principles apply in determining whether a given expense is revenue or capital in nature, and whether an expense falls to be relieved under this provision or other provisions such as the loan relationships legislation, sums periodically appropriated for manager's remuneration shall be treated as expenses of management.

Generally, expenses such as fees of the investment manager, registrar, trustee and auditor will be deductible for tax purposes. Costs incurred in connection with the buying and selling of investments are not.

Surplus management expenses will automatically be carried forward to future accounting periods, treated as management expenses of that period and be available for relief against taxable income. They cannot be carried back to earlier periods, nor are they available for group relief. Whilst the tax legislation treats the rights of the unitholder as shares in a company, the Inland Revenue takes the view that this is not 'ordinary share capital' and as a consequence, it is not possible for a unit trust to satisfy the 75% subsidiary test required to be able to claim or surrender group relief.

Capital allowances

1.117   While in practice authorised funds do not hold fixed assets on their own account and there are few authorised property funds in existence, should any capital allowances be capable of being claimed, *ICTA 1988, s 468(1)* (as amended where applicable by the OEIC Regulations at *SI 1997/1154*) makes clear that the allowances and balancing charges would accrue to the trustees of an AUT as if they were a company resident in the UK, and to the OEIC itself.

Distributions

1.118   The fund is required to treat the total amount shown in the distribution account as available for distribution as dividends or yearly interest (interest distributions). Amounts accumulated on behalf of unitholders are treated for tax purposes as a distribution. The distribution date will be the date specified in the terms of the trust or, if no such date is provided, the last day of the distribution period. Dividend distributions may be paid by either equity or bond funds, whereas interest distributions may only be paid by bond funds.

Within an umbrella it is possible to have a combination of equity and bond funds, so a combination of dividend and interest distributions may be paid. Within a single subfund, however, only one type of distribution is possible (that is, it is not possible to pay some unitholders a dividend and others interest).

Bond funds versus equity funds

1.119   Notwithstanding the various commercial fund classifications operated to distinguish between funds with different investment strategies, for tax purposes all authorised funds are divided into bond funds and equity funds. This distinction affects the treatment of a fund's distributions and is applied on a distribution period by distribution period basis.

A bond fund is one which has satisfied the qualifying investments test throughout a distribution period. The test is also known as the 60% test, because it is passed if the market value of a fund's holdings in qualifying investments exceeds 60% of its total investments.

Qualifying investments are those set out below.

- money placed at interest;

- securities;

- shares in a building society;

- qualifying entitlements to a share in the investments of another authorised bond fund;

- derivative contracts whose underlying subject matter consists wholly of one or more of the matters above (derivative contracts and contracts for differences only count as qualifying investments in accounting periods beginning on or after 1 October 2002);

- contracts for differences whose underlying subject matter consists wholly of interest rates, or creditworthiness, or both.

If any fund does not satisfy the qualifying investments test throughout a distribution period, it is an equity fund for tax purposes.

It should be noted that the 60% test must be passed at all times during a distribution period if the fund is to qualify as a bond fund. Consequently, if the test is breached even for a short period of time, the fund will not qualify and will be treated as an equity fund for that period.

1.120   Outside the tax world, a UK fund is usually only classified as a bond fund for marketing purposes if at least 80% of its investments are fixed interest securities. A fund would be classified as an equity fund if at least 80% of its investments were in equities. Consequently, it should be noted that some types of fund which invest in neither equities nor bonds per se, such as property or money market funds, may be given a label for tax purposes which does not reflect the actual nature of their investments.

A dividend distribution paid by a fund is treated in exactly the same way as one paid by an ordinary company in that it is paid out of post-tax profits and is not a deductible expense for tax purposes. The only difference in treatment is the corporate streaming rules, explained below.

1.121 An interest distribution is treated by *ICTA 1988, s 468L* as being annual interest in the hands of the investor, and is subject to the normal rules regarding deduction of tax at source. The fund must deduct tax at the lower rate when the recipient is a UK resident individual but tax need not be deducted if the recipient is an entity within the charge to corporation tax, a non-resident investor, an exempt investor (such as an approved pension fund, charity or local authority) or a PEP or ISA account holder. See below and CHAPTER 12 for further discussion of tax deducted at source.

Unlike a dividend, the interest distribution is treated as payable out of pre-tax profits and the net amount of the distribution shown in the accounts is deductible from profits chargeable to tax in the accounting period in which the last day of the distribution period falls (which is not necessarily the same as the distribution date). The legislation gives flexibility as to whether this is deductible before or after other deductions (such as management expenses) and any excess deduction may be carried forward and treated as deductible in the next accounting period. Although a bond fund has the option of paying a dividend, in practice it will always choose to pay interest because the matching of the income tax credits with the income received is more tax efficient for the investor.

Because the 60% test is conducted on a distribution period basis, it is possible for a fund to be a bond fund for part of its accounting period and an equity fund for the remainder, depending on how it is run. In this case, the interim and final distributions will be taken separately and will receive either dividend or interest treatment as appropriate.

See CHAPTER 12 for the tax consequences for investors of receiving distributions from authorised funds.

Corporate streaming

1.122 Where the recipient of a distribution from an authorised fund is subject to corporation tax on its income, a tax advantage could be obtained by investing in a balanced fund which pays dividend distributions. For example, if a fund has a 50/50 split of investments between equities and bonds, it will not qualify as a bond fund and will pay a dividend distribution, which is tax-exempt franked investment income for a corporate investor. However, if the investor had held the same investments directly, 50% of the income would have been received as interest, not dividends, and would have been taxed at the investor's appropriate rate.

Consequently, all corporate unitholders (other than the manager which receives dividends on its box units) are required to separate out the part of the dividend distribution derived from franked income and that part derived from unfranked income. These are known as the corporate streaming rules, and treat the two types of income in the appropriate manner. The unfranked element is deemed to have been paid under deduction of income tax at the lower rate which can be offset against the recipient's corporation tax liability or repaid.

1.123   This is really an issue for the investor in the fund rather than the fund itself, but the unit trust has to provide the necessary information to allow the investor to do the calculation.

Section 468Q sets out the calculation for corporate streaming, which is

$$U = \frac{A \times C}{D}$$

Where:

U = the unfranked part of the dividend distribution;

A = the amount of the dividend distribution, excluding equalisation;

C = gross income excluding franked investment income, as reduced by the trustees' net liability to corporation tax;

D = gross income as reduced by the trustees' net liability to corporation tax.

Gross income is defined as the gross amount entered in the distribution accounts for calculating the income available for distribution. This means that any franked investment income should be net of deemed tax credits.

The trustee's net liability to corporation tax is defined as the amount of the liability of the trustees to corporation tax, less double tax relief. Where an interim distribution is paid, the trustees will have to estimate what their net liability to corporation tax in the distribution period will be. The calculation done at the time of the final distribution will incorporate the total net liability for the period, less any net liabilities calculated at interim dates.

The net liability to tax can be thought of as the amount of tax the fund is obliged to pay in the UK, either in the current, past or future accounting periods. Consequently, the figures shown in the accounts for UK corporation tax, double tax relief, deferred tax charges or credits and prior year adjustments in relation to any of these should be included. Overseas taxes should be excluded.

If credit is taken for tax relief on expenses charged to capital, this should also be reflected in the corporation tax charge, provided that the expenses are allowable deductions for corporation tax purposes.

EXAMPLE 1.123

By way of an illustration, suppose that the ABC Fund has the following in its accounts, and is about to pay its first and final dividend distribution for the period of £1,350,000.

Income received on investments	£'000
Franked investment income	1,000
UK interest	800
Overseas dividends	500
Overseas interest	200
	2,500

Taxation	£'000
UK corporation tax	100
Overseas tax	150
Double tax relief	(100)
	150

For the purposes of the streaming calculation,

A will be £1,350,000

B will be ((£2,500,000 − £1,000,000) − £0) = £1,500,000

D will be (£2,500,000 − £0) = £2,500,000

U is calculated as £810,000, or 60% of the distribution.

The distribution of £1,350,000 is therefore streamed into £540,000 of franked investment income and £810,000 of unfranked investment income. A corporate unitholder owning 1% of the units in issue would receive £13,500 in total, of which £5,400 would be accounted for as FII and £8,100 would be grossed up and accounted for as interest received under deduction of tax.

1.124   To prevent the Inland Revenue being out of pocket as a consequence of the unitholder reclaiming more income tax than the fund has actually paid, the amount of income tax that a corporate unitholder is entitled to claim as a refund is restricted to their share of the net liability to corporation tax of the trustees (*ICTA 1988, s 468Q(5A)*). Their ability to offset against a corporation tax liability is not restricted in this way. In the example above, if the corporate investor had no tax liability of its own it would not be able to obtain a refund of the tax deemed to be deducted at source because the net liability to tax for the fund is nil. If it did have a tax liability of its own, however, it could offset £2,025 against it.

Corporate streaming of the dividend into franked and unfranked elements is not required where the manager is entitled to the distribution and receives it in the ordinary course of his business.

Deduction of tax at source

1.125   As mentioned earlier, the fund must deduct income tax at the lower rate when paying an interest distribution, in accordance with *ICTA 1988, s 349(2)*, unless the legislation specifically permits or requires the payment to be made gross.

ICTA 1988, ss 349A–D set out the occasions on which gross payment should be made.

Recipients which fall into the following categories, among others, should automatically be paid interest free of withholding tax:

- entities within the charge to UK corporation tax on the receipt (meaning UK-resident corporates and UK branches of overseas companies), which includes payments to other authorised unit trusts;

- tax-exempt recipients, including local authorities, charities and pension funds;

- managers of PEP or ISA plans, and their nominees;

- partnerships where each partner is either a tax-exempt recipient or is a UK company or branch as above (in other cases, tax should be deducted).

1.126   Payments to UK resident individuals must be made under deduction of tax, the only exception being where payment is made via a PEP or ISA plan as noted above.

Gross payment should, however, only be made if the payer has a 'reasonable belief' that the recipient falls into one of these categories. If tax is not withheld when it should have been, the payer is subject to interest and possible penalties on the underpayment of tax. How a reasonable belief may be established is not set out in legislation but in practice it may be safest to obtain a declaration from the investor confirming their legal or tax status.

1.127   In addition to the *ICTA 1988, ss 349A–D* exceptions to the general rule, *ss 468M–PB* also set out specific rules pertaining to the payment of gross interest by authorised funds.

Pre-16 October 2002, part or all of an interest distribution could be paid gross if the recipient was resident outside the UK and provided the fund with a valid not ordinarily resident (NOR) declaration.

The amount of the distribution available for gross payment depended on the proportion of income received by the fund relative to total income. Eligible income comprised all income except FII, Schedule A income and any income which has suffered overseas tax at a reduced rate under a double tax treaty. Where all income of the fund was eligible income, the entire distribution could be paid gross.

As of 16 October 2002, the concept of eligible income has fallen away and the full amount of an interest distribution may be paid gross in certain circumstances. Gross payment is still available if the unitholder has completed a declaration of non-residence, but the rules have been extended so that interest distributions may be made automatically without deduction of tax if the unitholder is a company investing on its own account or is the trustee of a unit trust scheme (nominee companies and corporate trustees of trusts are not so entitled).

1.128 Also entitled are unitholders who receive distributions via a company that is subject to the EC Money Laundering Directive (or equivalent non-EC provisions), or is associated with a company which is so subject, and the fund manager has reasonable grounds for believing that the unitholder is not a UK resident, and also non-resident beneficiaries of a trust, whether individuals or companies, on whose behalf a non-resident trustee legally holds their units. Where the whole of the income belongs beneficially to someone other than the trustees, a valid declaration of non-residence will need to be in place.

Tax vouchers

1.129 Upon paying a distribution, whether dividend or interest, a unit trust is required to provide the investor or his nominee with a voucher showing the amount of dividend or interest paid, the date of the payment and the amount of the tax credit arising on the payment.

The format of the voucher must be agreed in advance by the Inland Revenue Business Tax division. Apart from the above information demanded by *ICTA, s 234A*, it is also a requirement for the trustee's net liability to corporation tax to be disclosed on the tax voucher, in accordance with *s 468Q(5C)*. This information allows the recipient to determine the amount of income tax deemed to have been deducted at source for the purposes of any reclaims. Managers have the option, but not the requirement, to show a figure for net liability to corporation tax per unit to simplify calculations of the maximum allowable reclaim.

VAT

1.130 Authorised funds may specialise in a number of very diverse investments including property, derivatives contracts and securities. The VAT treatment of these investments, in particular property investments, is very complex. It would not be possible to set out the details of the VAT treatment of all of these investments in this section. Therefore, the comments below merely highlight the VAT matters that a fund must be aware of when accounting for VAT, rather than providing a comprehensive guide.

From a VAT perspective there are two main considerations arising in relation to authorised funds; will the fund be required to account for VAT on its activities (see **1.131** et seq below) and will the fund be able to reclaim any of the VAT it incurs in relation to its costs (see **1.136** et seq below).

Taxable and exempt activity

Schemes not investing in property

1.131 The sale of securities including shares, bonds and warrants is not normally liable to UK VAT. When such securities are sold to a UK or other EU counterparty, no entitlement to input tax credit will be available. However, when sold to a non-EU counterparty input tax credit will be available. Similar considerations apply to the issue of the units in a trust by the operator and the shares of an OEIC. Certain commodity transactions are liable to VAT. This is a complex area as a number of special regimes apply to commodities transactions and specialist advice should be sought.

Property schemes

1.132 The VAT treatment of property transactions is extremely complex and specialist advice should be sought before entering into such transactions. However, a number of general considerations apply, as outlined below.

Where an authorised fund owns either a leasehold or freehold interest in an investment property (rather than shares in a property owning company, see below) the income it receives will be either taxable or exempt for VAT purposes. The VAT liability of commercial rental income is, by default, exempt from VAT. However, any person owning an interest in a commercial property may apply to Customs and Excise to elect to charge VAT on its rental income. In addition, certain transactions (such as the sale of the freehold of a new commercial property) are always liable to VAT.

If the income received is exempt from VAT, then there is no requirement to account for output tax in relation to the property (however, see the comments below regarding the reverse charge). If the fund elects to charge UK VAT in relation to a particular property, then the fund will be obliged to charge VAT to its tenants, and to account for this to Customs and Excise.

The reverse charge

1.133 In practice, any fund which only invests in securities or only receives VAT exempt rental income will only have an output tax liability when it receives supplies of services from outside the UK that are subject to the reverse charge. For example, lawyer's services supplied from France to a UK fund may be subject to a VAT reverse charge (ie the fund, if registered or required to register for VAT, should self-assess the VAT in respect of the legal services). The receipt of such services may also trigger an obligation to register for VAT if the value of the services received exceeds the VAT registration threshold. At present the UK VAT registration threshold is £56,000.

Fund managers' fees

1.134 Fees charged for the management of the property of an authorised fund are exempt from VAT, in accordance with *EC 6th Directive, Art 13B(d)(6) (77/388/EEC)*. According to Customs and Excise, the 'management' of funds is made up of a variety of elements including:

- monitoring the performance of the scheme property;

- making investment decisions;

- dealing with the paperwork and bookkeeping;

- offering advice on the growth of the portfolio; and

- contracting with dealers to buy and sell assets on behalf of their client.

If these services are provided to an authorised unit trust, trust based scheme or an OEIC under a single management agreement they are exempt from VAT as 'management'. However, if only particular elements are provided, the VAT liability may vary, eg advice, advertising and data processing supplied individually will be standard rated.

1.135   In the past, UK VAT legislation specified that only the operator of a unit trust or authorised corporate director of an OEIC enjoyed VAT exemption for the management of the fund. However, from 1 August 2003, the legislation has been changed such that any company providing management services to a UK OEIC or UK authorised unit trust or trust-based scheme should apply the VAT exemption.

The UK VAT legislative definition of authorised unit trusts and OEICs for the purposes of the VAT exemption for management is contained within *FSMA 2000, ss 235, 236, 237*. Whilst it is arguable that certain overseas funds fall within these definitions, Customs published policy is that the supply of fund management services to funds belonging outside the UK is outside the scope of UK VAT with the right to recover associated input VAT.

The management of UK funds other than UK authorised unit trusts and OEICs (for example, of unauthorised unit trusts) is standard rated.

Input VAT

Property schemes

1.136   VAT incurred by the fund which is solely attributable to taxable property may be recovered in full. Conversely, VAT incurred by the fund which is solely attributable to VAT-exempt property may not be recovered unless the total input tax incurred by the fund falls beneath the de minimis threshold (see below). In practice, most funds agree a bespoke partial exemption method with Customs and Excise to calculate the recovery percentage for the remaining VAT which cannot be attributed to any specific supply. Such methods must be agreed in writing with the fund's local VAT office.

Other schemes

As the management of an authorised unit trust or an OEIC is exempt from VAT it is likely that it will incur only a very small, or relatively small, amount of VAT.

To recover any of the VAT it incurs the fund must register for VAT. Once registered, a fund would then usually agree a method to calculate the percentage of VAT recovery it is entitled to with Customs and Excise. This is referred to as a special partial exemption method. Agreements on the recovery of VAT should be confirmed in writing by the fund's local VAT office.

1.137   Generally, any method of attribution will be designed to determine how much of the fund's VAT is attributable to the sale of securities or warrants which carry the right to input tax recovery as a proportion of all of the supplies the fund makes. The only supplies made by a fund which carry the right to input tax recovery are likely to be those that, for VAT purposes, are deemed to be made outside of the EU. For VAT purposes, a supply is deemed to take place wherever the purchaser of the securities belongs. So only the sale of securities, warrants and (in the case of OEICs) its own shares to investors outside the EU carry the right to input tax recovery.

Easement

1.138   Customs recognise that it is not always possible to determine where the counterparty to a transaction belongs for VAT purposes. In cases where it is not possible to identify where the purchaser of securities belongs, Customs allow a series of alternative tests to be used when determining whether a sale of securities is treated as being to an EU or non-EU purchaser. If the place of the transaction is known, the sale is treated as being made to a person belonging in that place. Secondly, if the place of transaction is not known, it can be deemed to be where the security is listed. Thirdly, if a security is not listed or is listed on both an EU and non-EU exchange, then a sale can be deemed to be transacted where the final broker involved in the transaction belongs. This is a 'descending order' easement and once one of those tests above can be applied, that is the one which must be applied.

De minimis

1.139   If the total amount of VAT incurred by a fund which is attributable to exempt supplies is not more than:

(a)   £625 per month 'on average'; and

(b)   one-half of all input tax for the period concerned,

all such input tax may be treated as being attributable to taxable supplies and consequently may be recovered in full, subject to the normal rules.

2 Unauthorised Unit Trusts

Roger Leslie

Ernst & Young

Introduction

2.1 There are two main forms of UK-based collective investment schemes namely unit trusts and open-ended investment companies. This chapter looks at what in legislative terms is the basic form of a unit trust, namely an unauthorised unit trust. A detailed account of the taxation of authorised unit trusts and open-ended investment companies can be found in CHAPTER 1.

The taxation regime that applies to unauthorised unit trusts ('UUTs') is fundamentally based on the taxation of trusts in general and for that reason is arguably not best suited to a collective investment scheme priced for investors net of any tax liabilities.

2.2 As with any collective investment scheme, investors may be taxed at various levels, ie a tax charge on the scheme followed by tax on returns made by the investor with a possible credit for tax already paid by the scheme. In this respect UUTs can achieve a reasonable amount of tax efficiency for investors but do so in a manner which can seem unnecessarily complicated both in theory and in practice.

This chapter begins by looking in outline at some general matters concerning unit trusts and unitholders and then moves on to the tax regime that applies at present. Finally, some consideration is given to a possible future regime to simplify and modernise tax as it applies to UUTs and unitholders.

What is a unit trust?

2.3 A unit trust is an investment fund with an unspecified capital established by trust deed and which operates under general trust law. That requires the trust to account separately for trust income and trust capital. In trust terms the beneficiaries of a unit trust are the unitholders who share in both income and capital on the basis of the number of units held.

A unit trust is constituted by trust deed and governed by trust law. A trustee is appointed and is typically a large bank or insurance company. This trustee is responsible for safeguarding the trust's assets and generally looks after the interests of unitholders. A manager is also appointed to carry out the day-to-day management of the unit trust and will usually be responsible for investment decisions.

2.4   The Trust deed of a unit trust will include provisions concerning:

● investment objectives;

● managers' permitted periodic and preliminary charges;

● other charges;

● extent of investment and borrowing powers,

and in the case of a UUT will outline the mechanism by which costs and charges are recovered from unitholders.

2.5   A unit trust is 'open-ended', ie it has an unspecified capital. Its 'share capital' is units issued and the units in issue can typically increase or decrease each working day. In effect a unit trust is like a company that can both issue and repurchase shares on a daily basis. The capital value of a unit trust can therefore increase or decrease during an accounting period. If an ever increasing number of units is being issued there are more funds for investment and, assuming the value of investments remains constant in terms of share prices, the fund size will go up. If, on the other hand, unitholders are selling their units back to the manager and the manager cannot resell to new unitholders, the trustee will have to sell investments to provide cash to buy back units from the manager. In that way the fund size will almost certainly decrease.

The relationship between a unit trust, the trustee, the unit trust managers (where they run a stock of units) and the outside unitholders can best be illustrated by an example.

EXAMPLE 2.5

		Units held by	
	Total units	manager	unitholders
Units in issue brought forward	8,000	200	7,800
Creations	2,000	2,000	–
	10,000	2,200	7,800
Sales	–	(2,100)	2,100
	10,000	100	9,900
Repurchases	–	2,400	(2,400)
	10,000	2,500	7,500
Cancellations	2,250	(2,250)	–
Units in issue carried forward	7,750	250	7,500

At the beginning of the period there are 8,000 units in issue of which the manager holds 200. The managers anticipate a substantial demand for units and ask the trustee to create 2,000 units, thus increasing the number of units in issue and funds for investment within the UUT. The newly created units are acquired by the manager in the first instance and then 2,100 are sold to new investors, reducing the manager's holding to 100 units out of a total of 10,000 units.

Subsequently, several unitholders sell a total of 2,400 units back to the manager. The capital value of the UUT at that point is not reduced, although the allocation of the

10,000 units between manager and other unitholders is changed. If the manager is unable to sell his stock of units to new investors he will ask the trustee to cancel units and, in the example above, 2,250 units are cancelled, ie bought back from the manager.

2.6 As illustrated above, creations and cancellations affect the size of the unit trust as the units are brought into existence or liquidated by the trustee in accordance with the requests of the managers. Created units are sold to the managers, while cancelled units are sold by the managers back to the trustee for liquidation. Sales and repurchases do not affect the size of the unit trust because they merely reflect a change of ownership of the units in question. Outside unitholders are recorded in the unit register, while the managers are not. This is consistent with the fact that the managers deal in the units, whereas outside unitholders invest in them. Where the managers do not run a stock of units, all sales will be of newly created units and all repurchases will be instantly cancelled. There will, in this situation, be no re-sales of repurchased units.

2.7 Pricing of units is a complex issue and there are typically four different prices to consider.

1   Issue price. The price paid by managers when units are created.

2   Cancellation price. The price paid to managers when they sell units back to the trust.

3   Redemption price. The price paid by managers when they buy units from unitholders.

4   Sale price. The price at which managers will sell units to intending unitholders.

There are two different types of unit typically available to unitholders.

(i)   Income units, where income is paid out to unitholders in cash or is used to purchase additional units.

(ii) Accumulation units, where income is rolled up into existing units held, thereby increasing value per unit.

The value of units in a unit trust is fixed by the pricing mechanism. Investments are valued, often on a daily basis, to determine bid and offer prices of units. As units can be bought, sold, created or cancelled the number of buyers and sellers of units does not of itself determine movements in the value of units. The value of units held in a unit trust therefore closely approximates the value of the investments held and, in particular, is not at a discount in the same way that shares in some investment trusts are quoted at a discount to net asset value.

Unauthorised unit trusts

2.8 For UK taxation purposes the basic definition of 'unit trust scheme' is taken from *Financial Services and Markets Act 2000, s 237.* This definition finds its way into *ICTA 1988, s 469* which is the section mainly concerned with UUTs.

Any unit trust scheme which has not been authorised in terms of *FSMA 2000, s 243* is by default an unauthorised unit trust and as such will be subject to the taxation regime explained below. There are a few exceptions to this general rule specifically excluded by the *Income Tax (Definition of Unit Trust Scheme) Regulations 1988 (SI 1988/267)*.

In most cases the creation of a unit trust scheme is a deliberate act by a fund manager keen to manage funds for a fee. There is a trust deed and all parties are only too aware of the structure and tax regime that will apply. In practice it is sometimes possible that a fund sponsor or property manager brings investors together to co-invest and is not initially aware of the possible legal and tax consequences. If what is created is a collective investment scheme and the property is held on trust for the investors, this will be a unit trust scheme and the tax implications will follow. In practice this tends to happen most often with property co-investment and, unless all the investors are exempt from capital gains tax (see **2.20** below), what is created is a tax inefficient vehicle with capital gains tax charged inside the fund and in addition on investors selling units.

2.9 *SI 1988/267* includes a list of unit trust schemes which are not to be taxed in accordance with *ICTA 1988, s 469*, namely:

(a)   an enterprise zone property scheme;

(b)   a charitable unit trust scheme;

(c)   a limited partnership scheme;

(d)   a profit sharing scheme which has been approved in accordance with *ICTA 1988, Sch 9, Part I*;

(e)   an employee share ownership plan approved under *FA 2000, Sch 8*

In addition, the *Income Tax (Pension Funds Pooling Schemes) Regulations 1996 (SI 1996/1585)* provide that a unit trust scheme which is a pension funds pooling scheme will not be taxed in accordance with *ICTA 1988, s 469*.

Accounting for income and capital

2.10   A UUT is a trust and as such will account separately for income and capital. At its simplest a UUT makes investments for a return made up of income and (hopefully) capital appreciation. It incurs expenses which in accounting terms are deducted from the income property of the fund but which in tax terms are more typically deducted from any income distributions payable to investors. This is an important point explained in more detail below.

There is no Statement of Recommended Practice ('SORP') that sets out the format of accounts for a UUT. Typically, managers will adopt most if not all of the format set out for authorised unit trusts in accordance with the revised Statement of Recommended Practice for such trusts issued in January 1997. This SORP is currently being redrafted to incorporate recommended practice for both authorised unit trusts and open-ended investment companies. In due course managers will no doubt adopt this latest SORP as a basis for the preparation of accounts of a UUT.

2.11   As outlined in more detail below, for tax purposes investors are treated as receiving annual payments which, after deducting basic rate income tax, are equal in aggregate to the amount shown in the accounts of the UUT as income available for payment to unitholders. There is a practical issue here in that the format of accounts drawn up in accordance with the SORP does not easily lend itself to a conclusion as to what is the 'amount shown in the accounts of the UUT as income available for payment to unitholders'. There are at least two issues to consider in this respect.

2.12   Firstly, as is noted at **2.26** below, for most UUTs expenses are deducted from the income distribution and not in arriving at the income distribution. In other words, the measure of annual payments for unitholders is based on income before deduction of expenses. In practice accounts will typically deduct expenses from income in which case the accounts themselves will not 'show' the appropriate amount of income on which the annual payments are based. In practice accounts will separately include details of the distribution rate payable by the UUT and this information is typically in a format that appears on distribution vouchers as outlined at 2.40 below.

2.13   Secondly, as a UUT is open-ended it is necessary to consider the mechanism by which income is attributed to investors joining or leaving the UUT part way through a distribution period. This is achieved by equalisation, which for investors joining a UUT is explained in more detail at 2.38 below. The amount of equalisation paid out to such investors as part of their first distribution is not income and does not therefore come into the calculation of annual payments received by unitholders. A more difficult issue can arise where unitholders sell their units back to the manager for cancellation. When this happens, income is paid out on the units cancelled and reduces the amount of any distribution payable to unitholders on the normal pay date of the UUT. The measure of income, ie the amount of income available for payment to unitholders, is gross income less income tax. This is before the deduction of expenses. It is also before adding any income received on units created and before deducting any income paid out on units cancelled. This is generally accepted by the Inland Revenue although there may be some doubt as to the tax position of the manager and this is considered further at **2.47** below.

The accounting treatment of income etc will drive the tax position of investors. In practice the Inland Revenue rarely challenge the accounting treatment but they would do so where it was not obviously in accordance with UK generally acceptable accounting principles and the trust deed.

Overview of taxation of UUTs and investors

2.14   As already stated, a UUT is a trust and from that it follows that a UUT files a trust return for each fiscal year ending 5 April. In an ideal world a UUT's accounts should be drawn up to 5 April (or 31 March which the Inland Revenue will usually accept as being near enough!). In practice, UUT accounts are drawn up to other dates and that presents the first of several issues which unnecessarily complicate tax filing for UUTS.

If, for example, a UUT draws up accounts to 30 November each year then, when it files its trust income tax return for the year ended 5 April 2003, that return will have to include:

- income on an arising basis for the period 6 April 2002 to 30 November 2002 taken from and reconciled to the Accounts for the year ended 30 November 2002;

- income on an arising basis for the period 1 December 2002 to 5 April 2003 taken from and reconciled to the Accounts for the year ended 30 November 2003.

This apparently straightforward example throws up an obvious practical problem with the filing deadline which is 31 January 2004 for the income tax year ended 5 April 2003. It is unlikely the accounts to 30 November 2003 will be finalised and audited by 31 January 2004 and the obvious question arises as to how to prepare and submit the tax filing by that date. In practice a tax filing is often based on unaudited figures which will hopefully be easily reconcilable to the final audited accounts.

2.15   As well as having to give careful thought to the practicalities of tax filing, UUTs are almost always taxpaying for reasons explained below and pay their income tax in three instalments namely:

(i)   31 January in the year of assessment as a payment to account for the year;

(ii)   31 July after the year of assessment as another payment to account for that year;

(iii)   31 January after the year of assessment as a balancing payment for that year.

The first two of these three payments are typically based on one half of the previous year's final income tax liability subject to any claims to reduce in the usual way.

2.16   Another important issue which follows on from the basic taxation of trusts and income tax being an annual tax, is the possibility of a liability on the UUT in terms of *ICTA 1988, s 350*. There are relieving provisions dealt with at **2.41** below but at this stage it is important to understand how *s 350* applies.

A UUT is deemed to pay to its unitholders an amount equal to the aggregate shown in its accounts as income available for distribution and is deemed to pay that amount net of basic rate income tax. This is best illustrated by an example.

EXAMPLE 2.16

Assume that for the fiscal year 2002/03, a UUT has income brought into charge to income tax of £10,000. If in that fiscal year it pays out net distributions of £7,020 this is equivalent to gross distributions paid of £9,000, ie £7,020 grossed up at basic rate of income tax.

Looking then at the possible application of *s 350*, the UUT has:

income brought into charge to income tax	£10,000
gross income distributions paid out	£9,000

It follows that the gross income distributions paid out are paid wholly out of income brought into charge to income tax and there is no liability in terms of *s 350*.

If, however, changing the example, the UUT paid out net distributions of £8,580, ie gross distributions of £11,000, we than have:

income brought into charge to income tax	£10,000
gross income distributions paid out	£11,000

In this case £1,000 of the gross income distributions are not paid out of income brought into charge to income tax and there is a *s 350* tax liability at basic rate on £1,000.

The possibility of such a liability arises because *s 350* compares income brought into charge to income tax for a fiscal year with gross income distributions paid out in that fiscal year.

2.17 Typically a UUT will choose an accounting date for its accounts and a payment date for its income distribution. For example, a UUT may draw up accounts to 31 March each year and have a distribution pay date two months later, ie 31 May. In looking at a possible *s 350* liability for the year ended 5 April 2003 we have to compare income brought into charge to income tax for the year ended 5 April 2003 (Inland Revenue would typically accept 31 March 2003) with gross income distributions paid out 31 May 2002.

At the risk of stating the obvious, the income distribution paid 31 May 2002 is based on income in the UUT accounts to 31 March 2002 which may be more or less than the income in the UUT accounts to 31 March 2003. In any case the possibility of a *s 350* charge exists and it was for that reason that relieving provisions were introduced, initially as a concession and more recently in the legislation at *ICTA 1988, s 469(5A)* et seq. This is outlined in more detail at **2.44** below.

2.18 As with all collective investment schemes, the taxation of investors depends on the type of investor, ie individual, corporate, pension fund etc. In each case investors are deemed to receive an annual payment net of income tax at the basic rate. That income tax can be reclaimed by exempt investors and is available, where appropriate, to partly offset any investor level taxes at a higher rate.

Exempt UUTs and non-exempt UUTs

2.19 In practice the vast majority of UUTs are exempt UUTs based on the exemption in *TCGA 1992, s 100(2)*. If, throughout a year of assessment, all the issued units in a unit trust scheme are assets such that any gain accruing if they were disposed of by the unitholder would be wholly exempt from capital gains tax or corporation tax (otherwise than by reason of residence), gains accruing to the unit trust scheme in that year of assessment shall not be chargeable gains.

This is a fundamental aspect of launching an exempt UUT. In practice the draft trust deed of any proposed exempt UUT is sent to the Inland Revenue for approval in advance. That trust deed will make it very clear that all investors must be exempt from taxation of capital gains other than by reason of residence. Again, in practice each intending investor will provide the manager or trustee with a standard format self-certification of their exempt status including, where appropriate, an Inland Revenue reference number. In addition, each such investor also agrees to notify the manager or trustee immediately if this exempt status is lost. Finally, in most trust deeds each investor agrees to indemnify all unitholders of a UUT set up to be exempt should that investor lose its exempt status and hence cause the UUT to be non-exempt.

2.20 In relation to capital gains tax, in theory a UUT is either 100% exempt or 100% taxable. If only one investor is non-exempt the UUT will become 100% taxable on capital gains. Obviously the remaining investors will not readily accept a share of such a tax charge and hence each investor will typically give an indemnity to the trust.

EXAMPLE 2.20

> An example will highlight what is potentially a difficult issue. Assume an exempt UUT has 100 investors all owning exactly 1% of the trust which has total investment assets of £50m. In the year under review the UUT has realised capital gains of £12m. Also in relation to that year, one of the investors was non-exempt. That unitholder eventually disinvests from the UUT, ie encashes its £500,000 of units.
>
> The UUT, in theory, has a liability to capital gains tax on gains of £12m and would be taxed at 20%, ie at the capital gains tax rate applicable to trusts. This would give a total liability of £2.4m.
>
> The non-exempt investor was only invested in the amount of £500,000 but in terms of the indemnity might have to pay out £2.4m in respect of this capital gains tax. In practice this can be a difficult position to resolve.

Although the Inland Revenue are entitled to collect this full amount of capital gains tax from the UUT, in practice they can sometimes be persuaded to adopt a different approach which, at worst, ends up with a liability based on the non-exempt investor's share of the gains of the UUT There are two possibilities here. Either the investor was non-exempt at the point of investing into the UUT or was exempt but for some reason subsequently lost its exempt status. As regards the first of these two possibilities, if the trust had reasonable controls in place they are likely to receive a more sympathetic hearing than if there were no such controls. In any case, the trustee or manager will be asked to give a commitment that controls will be strengthened to ensure a similar situation does not arise in the future.

Where an exempt investor has subsequently lost status and not immediately advised the trustee, the Inland Revenue are likely to be sympathetic provided the trustee acts to remove the investor as soon as it becomes aware of the position.

2.21 In theory, all investors in an exempt UUT must be exempt from UK taxation of capital gains other than by reason of residence. The Inland Revenue accept that the manager of a UUT operating a box of units in the usual way will not cause the UUT to be non-exempt. There are then a relatively small number of potential investors in an exempt UUT, ie:

- UK approved pension funds

- UK charities

- Investment trusts

- Authorised unit trusts and OEICs

- Other exempt UUTs

2.22 There are obvious risks in having either investment trusts or other exempt UUTs as unitholders. In other words, if an investment company failed to achieve investment trust status for an accounting period it would no longer be exempt from tax on gains and that would make the underlying UUT non-exempt. For similar reasons there are risks where an exempt 'fund of funds' UUT is set up to invest in other exempt UUTs. Any loss of status at the fund of funds level would produce a domino effect and the loss of status for all the underlying exempt UUTs.

There are some UUTs that chose not to be exempt from tax on capital gains. Such UUTs are not a tax efficient vehicle for UK taxable investors. This is the case because the UUT will pay tax on gains and an investor selling units will also pay tax on gains with no credit for the fund's liability.

Taxation of income of a UUT

2.23 Any income arising to the trustees of a UUT is regarded for tax purposes as their income and not as income of the unitholders. In addition, the trustees and not the unitholders are regarded as the persons entitled to any capital allowances.

2.24 A UUT by definition is not authorised and hence not subject to any investment restrictions. Accordingly it can receive income from any number of sources. The inclusion of income in a tax filing will be based on general tax principles, eg overseas dividends are taxed on an arising basis as are UK dividends and bank interest. Rental income is taxed in accordance with the general rules of Schedule A which allow for certain costs to reduce rental receipts. So far as gilts and bonds are concerned, UUTs remain firmly within the accrued income scheme which seeks to tax interest income on a daily accruals basis. While arithmetically this is exactly what it does, the regime in place to achieve this is complicated. One aspect of the accrued income scheme is that where a UUT sells a bond with accrued interest in the price that accrued interest is deemed to arise to the UUT on the next interest payment date of the bond. That next interest payment date could well be in a different period of account and, more importantly, a different income tax year. This timing issue can give rise to *s 350* problems as described above in outline and more fully below.

In practice the taxation of underwriting commission received by a UUT is as follows:

- underwriting commission in relation to shares taken up by a UUT may be deducted from the cost of those shares and is not taxable;

- underwriting commission in relation to shares not taken up is taxable.

2.25 The relative income tax efficiency of a UUT is based on income items being accounted for and distributed as income. This efficiency is lost where any return properly accounted for as capital is for some reason nevertheless liable to income tax as outlined at **2.27** below.

The income of a UUT is the sum of all its various sources for a fiscal year and that total income is liable to income tax at the basic rate. In particular, although a considerable part of this income may be 'savings income' as referred to in *ICTA 1988, s 1A*, the rate of income tax is specifically stated in *ICTA 1988, s 469(2)* to be income tax at the basic rate.

Relief for expenses

2.26 In the vast majority of cases, ie for exempt UUTs, the trust deed will provide that expenses not deductible in arriving at an income source are to be paid out of the net income distribution payable to unitholders. Such expenses, ie the manager's fee and the trustee's fee, are not deductible for income tax purposes in the UUT and to ensure income tax efficiency each is deducted from the net income distribution of each unitholder.

EXAMPLE 2.26

This is best illustrated by a simple example where we assume each unitholder is exempt and hence can reclaim any income tax deducted at source by the exempt UUT.

If the UUT deducts the management fee etc to arrive at the income distribution we might have:

	£
Income	1,000
Expenses	200
	800
Income tax 1,000 @ 22%	220
Net distribution to unitholder	580
Income tax reclaim 22/78×580	164
Final position of unitholder	744

If, on the other hand, the UUT deducts the management fee etc from the income distribution we have:

	£
Income	1,000
Income tax 1,000 @ 22%	220
Income distribution	780
Expenses	200
Net distribution to unitholder	580
Income tax reclaim 22/78×780	220
Final position of unitholder	800

In this case, the final position of the unitholder is effectively £1,000 less the expenses of £200.

Charging income tax on capital profits

2.27   As already mentioned, the income tax efficiency of a UUT depends on income tax only applying to amounts accounted for and distributed as income. There are a number of returns which are properly accounted for in capital but nevertheless could be liable to income tax. These include:

(a) Trading profits

2.28   If a UUT deals in securities and accounts for any profits as income then it will be liable to income tax and will pass credit for this tax to investors with an income distribution. All of this maintains the tax efficiency.

If a UUT accepts that it is dealing in securities but accounts for any profits in capital, it will have an income tax liability in capital which cannot be passed through to investors. On the other hand if a UUT considers it is making investments but is challenged by the Inland Revenue that it is dealing in securities then any eventual income tax liability will be in capital.

It is important to note that a UUT can choose to deal in securities and provided it accounts for any returns in income it will maintain its income tax efficiency.

The more typical problem can arise where the UUT is challenged by the Inland Revenue running an argument in relation to dealing in securities.

UUTs frequently turn over the capital value of their investment portfolio several times a year and on an initial analysis this may appear to be trading in securities. There are, however, several factors to consider, not least of which is the open-ended nature of a UUT. If a number of investors sell their units to the manager and subsequently those units are cancelled, the UUT will have to encash investments to pay out the manager. It may then be the case that quite independently, within a month or so, a considerable amount is invested by a new investor, giving the UUT cash to purchase more investments.

The Inland Revenue has stated that the level of buying and selling activity is not, of itself, conclusive. In informal discussions they have also indicated that, at least in theory, each purchase and sale should be looked at in isolation. In other words, it is not all or nothing in terms of trading in securities. For the same UUT, some transactions may be trading and others for investment. This line of argument could lead to an extraordinarily difficult and time-consuming tax compliance exercise.

As a point of principle the argument against a UUT trading in securities runs along the following lines. A manager buys an investment as an investment. That is the intention at the date of acquisition and it is this intention which is crucial to any question of trading. Thereafter, the manager runs the investment portfolio of the UUT so as to provide investors with a performance which gives an above average return. To achieve this, he needs to react instantly to movements within the different markets or sectors in which the UUT is invested. If he fails to do so, the value of investments managed may go down as against those managed by other fund managers or held by other investors who reacted more quickly. External factors therefore cause a manager to change an investment decision and sell. That does not amount to trading in securities.

(b) Relevant discounted securities

2.29   Profits realised on the disposal of relevant discounted securities are liable to income tax at basic rate. Both the profits and this tax will be accounted for as capital items of the UUT.

(c) Offshore funds

2.30   Profits realised on the disposal of shares in an offshore fund are liable to income tax unless the offshore fund has distributor status throughout the period of ownership of the UUT. Such profits are correctly accounted for as capital but will nevertheless give rise to an income tax liability.

(d) Accrued Income Scheme ('AIS')

2.31   All returns from AIS securities are typically accounted for in income. There remains in *ICTA 1988, s 469(10)* a reference to an earlier accounting regime, where some returns, eg interest amounts included in disposal proceeds, were accounted for in capital. If, in fact, a UUT adopts such a regime it will have an income tax liability in capital.

Strictly speaking, the rate of income tax applying to returns described at (c) and (d) immediately above is the rate applicable to trusts, ie 34%, but this may not be the case in practice given the views of the Inland Revenue outlined immediately below.

Inland Revenue view of taxation of UUTs

2.32   In the view of the Inland Revenue the income tax computation of a UUT adds up all the various sources to arrive at total income. From that total income a UUT is entitled to deduct gross income distributions paid out in the fiscal year in question to arrive at net income liable to income tax.

The UUT then has a total liability being the sum of two amounts:

(i)   basic rate income tax withheld from the gross income distributions paid out in the fiscal year; plus

(ii) basic rate income tax on the net income liable to income tax, ie on the total income less gross income distributions paid out in the fiscal year.

At first glance, this looks like an unnecessarily complex way of charging total income to basic rate income tax but there have been, and are still, situations where it matters.

EXAMPLE 2.32

By way of an example, assume a UUT has total income of 10,000 and gross income distributions paid out of £8,000. In such an example, the income tax liability of the UUT is:

	£
(a) 22% withheld on £8,000, ie	1,760
Plus	
(b) 22% of (£10,000 less £8,000), ie	440
	2,200

which is, of course, 22% of £10,000.

2.33   Under *ICTA 1988, s 835(4)*, where a taxpayer is entitled to deduct an amount from total income, that deduction shall be treated as reducing income of different descriptions in the order which will result in the greatest reduction to the income tax liability.

2.34   *Unauthorised Unit Trusts*

As noted above some offshore income gains may be liable to income tax at 34% in accordance with *ICTA 1988, s 764*. Also, accrued income scheme amounts accounted for in capital may also be liable to income tax at this rate.

Bearing in mind *s 835(4)*, an example will illustrate the point:

EXAMPLE 2.33

	£
UK dividends	3,500
Overseas dividends	2,500
Offshore income gains (non–distributor)	4,000
	10,000
Less: Gross income distribution	8,000
Net income liable to income tax	2,000

In line with *s 835(4)* we can deduct the gross income distribution firstly from the offshore income gains with the result that the total income tax liability will be at 22%, ie £2,200.

2.34

EXAMPLE 2.34

If, on the other hand, we have a different example where offshore income gains were 8,500 then we have:

	£
UK dividends	1,000
Overseas dividends	500
Offshore income gains	8,500
	10,000
Less: Gross income distribution	8,000
Net income liable to income tax	2,000

The UUT would be liable to income tax as follows:

		£
(a) withheld from the gross income distribution 8,000 @ 22%		1,760
(b) chargeable on net income		
balance of offshore income gains	500 @ 34%	170
other income	1,500 @ 22%	330
		2,260

Double taxation relief

2.35 UUTs will invest overseas and receive overseas dividends net of overseas withholding tax. Any such overseas tax in excess of treaty rate will typically be reclaimed from the appropriate overseas tax authority.

A particularly difficult issue arises with overseas tax suffered at the treaty rate and the question as to how to get relief for such overseas tax. The legislation in point is *ICTA 1988, s 796(3)* which seeks to limit credit relief for overseas tax. This provides that the foreign tax to be allowed to a UUT against income tax for any year of assessment shall not exceed the total income tax payable by the UUT for the year of assessment, less any income tax which the UUT is entitled to charge against any other person. A UUT is entitled to charge basic rate income tax against unitholders by deducting it from gross income distributions.

2.36 For each year of assessment a UUT has to calculate its *s 350* position and its ability to take credit relief for overseas withholding tax. These two calculations are in fact based on the same amounts ie:

(a) gross income brought into charge to income tax for a year of assessment £A
(b) gross income distributions paid out in that year of assessment £B

The maximum amount of credit relief allowed to a UUT for a year of assessment is basic rate income tax, ie 22% of (£A less £B). In practice, if a UUT is growing in size year on year, £A will typically exceed £B and it may be possible to obtain some credit relief for overseas tax. If the UUT is falling in size or static then £A will be no more than £B and no credit relief is due for overseas tax. In such circumstances the UUT will 'expense' the overseas tax in line with *ICTA 1988, s 811*.

Taxation of investors

2.37 In accordance with *ICTA 1988, s 469(3)*, investors are treated as receiving annual payments made by the trustees under deduction of basic rate income tax. The date on which the annual payments are treated as made is the date or latest date provided by the terms of the scheme for any distribution in respect of the distribution period in question except that, if:

- the date so provided is more than 12 months after the end of the period; or
- no date is so provided,

the date on which the annual payments are treated as made shall be the last day of the distribution period.

Each investor will receive a distribution voucher from the UUT.

Equalisation of income

2.38   As already outlined at **2.5** above, a UUT is an open-ended vehicle and is priced to include the capital value of the fund plus income accrued to date in the distribution period.

When an investor invests part way through a distribution period, units will be purchased at a price inclusive of an amount paid to share in the income already accrued in that period. This 'payment for income' is the mechanism by which the existing income rights of unitholders are not diluted by the incoming investor.

The amount 'paid' by the incoming investor for income is accounted for in the income section of the Statement of Total Return of the UUT and is then returned to that investor as part of their first distribution.

The following example will help illustrate how this works in practice.

EXAMPLE 2.38

Assume a UUT has an annual distribution period ended on 31 March 2003 and its next following annual distribution period ends on 31 March 2004. Income accrues to the UUT on its investments from 1 April 2003 onwards and expenses will be incurred during the year to 31 March 2004.

Any investor who is invested at 31 March 2003 and 31 March 2004, ie throughout the distribution period, is termed a Group 1 investor. Any investor who invests during the distribution period and is an investor at 31 March 2004 (but not at 31 March 2003) is termed a Group 2 investor. The total distribution, in pence per unit, paid to Group 1 investors and to Group 2 investors is the same. For a Group 1 investor that total distribution is income. For a Group 2 investor part of that total distribution is an amount called equalisation and only the balance is income, for example:

	Net distribution	*Equalisation*	*Total*
Group 1 investor	18	–	18
Group 2 investor	15	3	18

For example, in the accounts of a UUT and on the reverse of the distribution voucher received by each unitholder will be a statement along the following lines.

'Equalisation applies only to units purchased during the distribution period (Group 2 units). It is the average amount of income included in the purchase price of all Group 2 units and is refunded to unitholders of these units as a return of capital. Being capital, it is not liable to income tax, but must be deducted from the costs of units for capital gains tax purposes.'

2.39   What this means is that when an investor buys units during the period and hence becomes a Group 2 unitholder, part of the price paid is for the income already accrued in the UUT since its last distribution date. Such a 'payment for income' flows through the income section of the Statement of Total Return and is distributed after the year end.

Continuing the example above, the Group 2 unitholder that receives a net distribution of 15 plus equalisation of 3 may have invested in units during the period at a price of 200. The capital gains cost of those units is 200 less 3, ie 197.

Distribution vouchers

2.40   Each investor will be entitled to a distribution voucher which will certify how much income tax has been deducted.

In most cases the expenses of a UUT are deducted from the net income distribution to arrive at the distribution paid or accumulated on behalf of unitholders.

Using amounts by way of illustration, the information on a voucher will include:

Gross income before tax	100
Less: Income tax at basic rate	22
	78
Less: Share of expenses	10
	68
Add: Equalisation (if Group 2)	2
Distribution paid or accumulated	70

In most cases investors will be exempt and will want to reclaim income tax of 22 based on this voucher.

Uncredited surpluses

2.41   As already outlined, a UUT is treated as making annual payments out of income and passes a credit for basic rate income tax to unitholders with each income distribution. The theory here is that the UUT pays income tax and separately unitholders reclaim that income tax. It seems a pointlessly complicated exercise which may well be consigned to history on a change to the taxation regime as outlined below.

Pending such a change it is perfectly possible for a UUT to pay out gross income distributions in a fiscal year that exceed the income brought into charge to income tax for that year. This gives the UUT a *s 350* liability at basic rate on the difference.

2.42   In the mid-1980s it was recognised that, with a few exceptions, a UUT would only have a *s 350* liability because of the interaction of the annual nature of income tax and timing differences. In other words, over the life of a UUT, ie from launch to termination, the gross income brought into charge to income tax would equal gross distributions paid out to investors.

Consider the following example:

EXAMPLE 2.42

	1999/00	2000/01	2001/02	2002/03
Gross income charged to income tax	10,000	12,000	8,000	2,000
Gross income distributions	Nil	10,000	12,000	10,000

Over the life of the UUT, ie 1999/2000 until 2002/03 the gross income charged to income tax is £32,000 as are the total gross income distributions.

However, looking at each income tax year in isolation the UUT would have a *s 350* liability in 2001/02 of £4,000 x 22% and in 2002/03 of £8,000 x 22%.

It then follows that the UUT would, over the four years, be charged to income tax on a total of £42,000 whereas the unitholders would only be entitled to reclaim income tax on a total of £32,000. In practice it is not quite so simple and a UUT will typically account for its *s 350* position on what might be described as a 'death of funds' basis to ensure equity among different generations of unitholders.

2.43   With all of this in mind a concession was introduced in 1987 followed by legislation which is now at *ICTA 1988, s 469(5A)* et seq.

At its simplest this allows a UUT to carry forward any uncredited surplus from a fiscal year. For this purpose an uncredited surplus is the amount by which the gross income charged to income tax exceeds gross income distributions paid. Extending the example we then have:

EXAMPLE 2.43

	1999/00	2000/01	2001/02	2002/03
Gross income charged to income tax	10,000	12,000	8,000	2,000
Gross income distributions	Nil	10,000	12,000	10,000
Section 350 deficit	Nil	Nil	4,000	8,000
Uncredited surplus	10,000	2,000	Nil	Nil
Uncredited surplus brought forward	Nil	10,000	12,000	8,000
Uncredited surplus carried forward	10,000	12,000	8,000	Nil

In this relatively simple example the UUT will not incur any *s 350* liability.

2.44   While all of this seems relatively straightforward, in practice the issue of *s 350* liabilities and uncredited surpluses is not always dealt with as part of an income tax filing. This is frequently down to a lack of understanding on behalf of the UUTs which in turn may go unchallenged by the Inland Revenue for a number of years.

An obvious difficulty can then arise if a new tax adviser or a new Inspector of Taxes asks the question. There is in fact another issue that can bring the matter to a head and that is when a UUT is wound up or converted into another type of fund, eg into an authorised unit trust or open-ended investment company. In each of these cases the UUT will in fact be wound up and the trustee will ask the Inland Revenue to confirm that there are no outstanding tax liabilities. It is at this stage that there is a serious risk, especially if a local Inspector of Taxes takes advice from his head office colleagues, that the question of *s 350* liabilities might be raised.

2.45   As outlined above, the theory of a UUT is that over its existence, ie from launch to wind-up, it should not have a *s 350* liability. The purpose of the relieving provisions in *TA 1988,s 469(5A)* et seq is to smooth out the potential for a *s 350* liability that would otherwise only arise because of the annual nature of income tax. The serious difficulty that can arise in practice is quite simply trying to recreate the history of uncredited surpluses bearing in mind the number of years that may be involved. Over the life of a UUT, an eventual *s 350* liability will arise if the UUT has received some non-taxable income which is accounted for as income and distributed as such.

In the majority of cases, over the life of a UUT, there will be no eventual *s 350* liability. While it is reasonably easy to explain the theory of this to the Inland Revenue, they are more likely to ask for calculations, the information for which may or may not be to hand.

2.46   There may be a particular problem for a UUT substantially invested in gilts and bonds and this arises because of the interaction of the accrued income scheme, the accounting date of the UUT and *s 350*. For some UUTs, the income distribution is paid very shortly after the year end. If, for instance, a UUT has a 28 February 2003 year end and a 31 March 2003 pay date for its distribution, it is possible that some of the income for the year ended 28 February 2003 (all of which is distributed 31 March 2003), may not be taxed until after 5 April 2003, ie may not be taxed until the following fiscal year. This is actually the reverse of the norm where income is taxed before it is distributed and *s 350* allows for the carry forward of uncredited surpluses etc as already described. Ideally here we need to carry back an uncredited surplus but the Inland Revenue have not, to date, been willing to accept such a suggestion. There is a practical solution here which is to accelerate the taxability of income into the fiscal year in which it is distributed and by doing this the *s 350* liability will not arise. Generally speaking the Inland Revenue are unlikely to challenge this approach.

The UUT manager

2.47   As already noted at **2.21** above, the fact that a UUT manager may own units in a UUT from time to time will not of itself prejudice the exempt status of an exempt UUT.

There is, however, another issue which arises for the UUT and the manager and that concerns the maintenance of the tax efficiency of the exempt UUT in the context of income paid out on units cancelled. The theory behind the tax efficiency for the UUT and its exempt investors comes from the fact that the UUT pays income tax and the investors reclaim this income tax. The ability to reclaim this income tax attaches to the income distributions paid to investors including those rolled up into the value of accumulation units.

2.48   As is noted at **2.11** above, the measure of annual payments for investors is based on the amount shown in the accounts as income available for distribution to investors. When an investor sells units to the manager who in turn cancels the units with the trustee, part of the price received by the manager is accounted for by the UUT as income paid out on units cancelled. Again, as outlined at **2.13** above, the measure of income for investors is gross income less income tax of the UUT and, in effect, this includes any income paid out on units cancelled.

What this means is that for the purposes of calculating any *s 350* liabilities or uncredited surpluses, any amounts of income paid out on units cancelled are income distributions from which income tax at basic rate has been withheld. Conversely, this should mean that when a manager cancels units with the trustee, that part of the price received which relates to income paid out on units cancelled is income received net of income tax and the corporation tax computation of the manager should include such income on that basis.

There is some sense in which all of this seems reasonable. Namely, if the income paid out on units cancelled is an income distribution that could give rise to a *s 350* liability, it should conversely follow that the manager is treated as being in receipt of income that has suffered basic rate income tax.

2.49   In practice the position of the manager is not obviously supported by *TA 1988, s 469*. It is questionable whether income paid out on units cancelled is part of the amount shown in the accounts of the UUT as income available for distribution to unitholders. The Inland Revenue sometimes argue that income paid out on units cancelled is not an income distribution. If that is the case then such income should not be treated as a distribution when calculating *s 350* liabilities.

Referring back to the difficulties of recreating calculations of uncredited surpluses over a number of years, it is very important to establish the position on income paid out on units cancelled.

UUTs and gross pricing

2.50   The taxation regime for an exempt UUT and its investors is unnecessarily complicated. The exempt UUT pays income tax and investors reclaim income tax.

Given that all the investors are exempt there is an opportunity for the manager to 'gross price' the fund. This does not simplify the various tax filings but it does in some senses seem a more obvious pricing basis.

In order to set up the UUT to be gross priced, each intending investor will have to mandate the managers to reclaim UK income tax on their behalf and pay it into the UUT.

This would work most easily with accumulation units. In effect the UUT has a basic rate income tax charge against income in the usual way but, in addition, it carries a debtor for this basic rate income tax being the reclaims to be made in due course. In that way the fund is gross priced.

UUTs and a possible future regime

2.51   The current regime is clearly far too complicated bearing in mind that for exempt UUTs the end result is no net tax receipts for the Treasury, ie tax is collected from the UUT and repaid to the unitholders.

In achieving this we have the following complications:

- tax filing to 5 April irrespective of UUT year end;

- need for detailed records of uncredited surplus;

- continuing complexity of the accrued income scheme.

On the other hand, the tax legislation for authorised funds allows for interest distributions to be paid gross to a range of investors including approved pension funds.

2.52   It seems a reasonably straightforward proposition to bring exempt UUTs within the corporation tax regime. There would be a special category of exempt authorised unit trusts or OEICs that could only be invested in by exempt investors, ie exactly as at present. That special category of exempt fund would not be liable to corporation tax and would pay gross distributions to investors.

The Inland Revenue are currently reviewing the taxation of UK onshore funds following the issue of CP 185 which outlines a new regime for UK regulated funds. CP 185 refers to the introduction of non-retail funds and to the need for the Treasury and the Inland Revenue to give some thought to a tax regime for such funds. This would seem to be an opportune moment to introduce a simplified tax regime for exempt UUTs.

3 Stamp Duty and Stamp Duty Reserve Tax

Camilla Spielman

Eversheds

Introduction

3.1 This chapter covers stamp duty and stamp duty reserve tax ('SDRT') on UK unit trust schemes and OEICs (Northern Ireland has a distinct legislative regime for stamp duty but not for SDRT).

Definition of unit trust scheme and OEIC for Stamp Duty and SDRT

Unit trust schemes

Definition

3.2 For the purposes of stamp duty and SDRT, 'unit trust scheme' has the same meaning as in *FSMA 2000, s 237* (*FA 1999, Sch 19 para 14*).

Accordingly, both authorised and unauthorised unit trust schemes are treated in the same way for both stamp duty and SDRT. Definitions of various related expressions are found in *FA 1999, Sch 19 para 14(3)*.

Exclusions

3.3 A number of types of unit trust scheme are carved out of the stamp duty and SDRT regimes for unit trust schemes by being excluded from the definition for stamp duty and SDRT purposes. These are:

- common investment schemes and common deposit schemes under the Charities Acts (see *FA 1999, Sch 19 para 15(a) and (b)*);

- unit trust schemes under the terms of which units may only be held by charities (see *FA 1999, Sch 19 para 15(c)*);

- common investment arrangements by the trustees of exempt approved schemes under *ICTA 1988, s 592* established solely for the purposes of those schemes (see *FA1999, Sch 19 para 16*);

- limited partnerships registered under the *Limited Partnerships Act 1907* (see the *Stamp Duty and Stamp Duty Reserve Tax (Definition of Unit Trust Scheme) Regulations 1988 (SI 1988/268)*;

- profit sharing schemes approved under *FA 1978, Sch 9 (FA 1999, Sch 19 para 14)*;

- court common investment funds made under *Administration of Justice Act 1982, s 42 (Stamp Duty and Stamp Duty Reserve Tax (Definition of Unit Trust Scheme) Regulations 1992 (SI 1992/3287))*;

- pension funds pooling schemes (*Stamp Duty and Stamp Duty Reserve Tax (Pension Funds Pooling Schemes) Regulations 1996 (SI 1996/1585)*); and

- unit trust schemes under the terms of which units may be held only within Individual Pension Accounts (*Stamp Duty and Stamp Duty Reserve Tax (Definition of Unit Trust Scheme and Open-ended Investment Company) Regulations 2001 (SI 2001/964)*).

The Treasury has power to exclude further types of unit trust scheme under *FA 1999, Sch 19 para 17*.

Umbrella unit trust schemes

3.4 For stamp duty and SDRT purposes, each of the parts of an umbrella scheme is regarded as a separate unit trust scheme, while the actual umbrella scheme is looked through (*FA 1999, Sch 19 para 18*). An umbrella scheme is defined for this purpose as a unit trust scheme that provides for separate pooling in subfunds both of the unitholders' contributions and of the profits or income out of which payments are to be made to them. In addition, the unitholders must be entitled to exchange units in one subfund for units in another.

OEICs

3.5 The Treasury was given the power in *FA 1995, s 152* to make regulations applying the stamp duty and SDRT enactments relating to unit trusts to OEICs. The stated intention was that the enactments should apply to OEICs in a manner corresponding to the manner in which they have effect for unit trusts, subject to appropriate modifications.

Definition

3.6 For stamp duty and SDRT purposes, an OEIC is defined by reference to the amendments to *ICTA1988, s 468* made by *Regulation 2* of the *Open-ended Investment Companies (Tax) Regulations 1997 (SI 1997/1154*, made under *FA 1995, s 152*), which insert *subsections (10)–(18)* into *section 468 (Stamp Duty and Stamp Duty Reserve Tax (Open-ended Investment Companies) Regulations 1997 (SI 1997/1156) as amended*). As a result, 'open-ended investment company' means a company incorporated in the UK that falls within *FSMA 2000, s 236*. The sub-sections inserted into *section 468* also define various related expressions.

Umbrella unit trust schemes

3.7   Each subfund of an umbrella company is treated as a separate OEIC for stamp duty and SDRT purposes, and references to shareholders are to shareholders in the appropriate subfund (*FA 1999, Sch 19 para 18*). Each subfund is treated as a separate OEIC for the purposes of the *Schedule 19* SDRT regime, however, under *ICTA 1988, s 468(11)*.

Exclusion

3.8   Following the introduction of Individual Pension Accounts in *FA 2001*, where OEIC shares may be held only within an Individual Pension Account, the OEIC is excluded from the definition and is therefore outside the *Schedule 19* SDRT regime for collective investment schemes. Further the shares do not constitute chargeable securities for the purposes of SDRT in *FA 1986* (*FA 1986, s 99(5C)* inserted by the *Stamp Duty and Stamp Duty Reserve Tax (Open-ended Investment Companies) Regulations 1997 (SI 1997/1156)* as amended).

Creation and seeding of unit trust schemes and OEICS

Creation of unit trust schemes and OEICs

3.9   Unit trust instrument duty on the trust deed of a unit trust was abolished in 1988. The trust deed is, however, liable to fixed stamp duty of £5 as a declaration of trust under *FA 1999, Sch 13 para 17*. There is no equivalent liability on OEICs.

Seeding unit trust schemes

3.10   The transfer by a single investor to a new unit trust scheme in exchange for the initial issue of units does not result in a change of beneficial ownership of the investments transferred. Any stock transfer form or other transfer document therefore attracts a fixed £5 stamp under *FA 1999, Sch 13 para16*, unless the property being transferred is outside the stamp duty net. SDRT under *FA 1986, s 87* (the principal charge) does not arise, as there is no consideration.

In some cases a number of prospective unitholders have portfolios that mirror each others; for instance, after an investment company has been unitised (see **CHAPTER 9**). It is understood that Inland Revenue (Stamp Taxes) accepts that these may be transferred together into a new unit trust scheme in exchange for the issue of units to each of the initial unitholders without triggering a liability to stamp duty or SDRT. The reason is that described in the previous paragraph.

All subsequent transfers of property into a unit trust scheme that are not in exchange for the initial issue of units are sales for stamp duty purposes. They carry ad valorem stamp duty at 0.5% in the case of shares and securities within the charge to stamp duty (rounded up to the nearest £5). This results from units being included in the definition of stock (*FA 1999, Sch 19 para 19* (applied by reference under *SI 1997/1156* for OEICs). Stock is dutiable consideration so the transfer of dutiable shares or securities in exchange for the issue of stock is treated as a sale for stamp duty purposes where there is a transfer document, under the principle in *J & P Coates Limited v IRC* [1897] 1 QB 423. This charge arises notwithstanding the abolition of stamp duty on the transfer of units under *FA 1999, Sch 19 para 1*, because the units here are the consideration for the transfer of other property.

Seeding OEICs

3.11 Even an initial transfer of assets to an OEIC in exchange for the first shares to be issued triggers a liability to stamp duty and SDRT, if applicable, on the assets concerned. This results from OEICs being bodies corporate so that they are the beneficial owners of their assets. There is therefore always a change of beneficial ownership on the transfer of assets to them and the principle in *J & P Coates* applies.

Issue of units/shares

Unit trust schemes

3.12 The issue of registered units to the manager or investors does not trigger a liability to stamp duty or SDRT.

In contrast, the issue of bearer units (*FA 1999, Sch 15* and *Sch 19 para 19*) in the UK or in relation to a unit trust scheme established in the UK gives rise to a charge to stamp duty at 1.5%, as does the first transfer on sale in the UK of a bearer unit not chargeable on issue. The issue of units to a depository or clearance system generally attracts the higher rate SDRT charge of 1.5% on the consideration or value.

OEIC

3.13 There is no charge to stamp duty or SDRT on the issue of shares in registered form to the manager or investors.

The position regarding bearer shares and shares issued to depository and clearance systems is as described above for units.

Acquisition of investments by unit trust schemes/OEICS

3.14   Stamp duty or SDRT has to be paid by a unit trust scheme or OEIC in the normal way on purchases of investments in the market that are not exempt. The funds will also have to pay any relevant foreign transfer taxes.

Where an investor subscribes to a unit trust scheme or OEIC in specie then stamp duty or SDRT will be payable on all assets subject to stamp duty or SDRT under the principle in *J & P Coates* described in **3.10** above. This is because units in a unit trust scheme are deemed to be stock (*FA 1999, Sch 19 para 19* (applied by reference under *SI 1997/1156* for OEICs)). Exceptionally, Inland Revenue (Stamp Taxes) accepts that if a prospective unitholder in a unit trust scheme has a portfolio that exactly mirrors the scheme property, then the subscription of the assets does not trigger stamp duty or SDRT on the grounds that there is no change of beneficial ownership.

Dealings in units in unit trust schemes and in shares in OEICS

3.15   *FA 1999, Sch 19* abolished the *FA 1946* stamp duty regime for UK unit trusts in favour of an SDRT regime with effect from 6 February 2000. The old stamp duty regime had been extended to OEICs by the *Stamp Duty and Stamp Duty Reserve Tax (Open-ended Investment Companies) Regulations 1997 (SI 1997/1156)* and corresponding changes were made for OEICs so that the *Schedule 19* regime applies to them by reference from 6 February 2000 (*Stamp Duty and Stamp Duty Reserve Tax (Open-ended Investment Companies) (Amendment No 2) Regulations 1999 (SI 1999/3261)*).

Outline

3.16   The substantive legislation is set out in *FA 1999, s 122* and *Sch 19*. The Inland Revenue Stamp Taxes Manual describes how the SDRT regime applies, as well as giving practical information on compliance issues. It is based on the initial guidance issued by Inland Revenue (Stamp Taxes) on 1 September 1999.

- Stamp duty on documents relating to units in unit trust schemes and shares in OEICs was abolished from 6 February 2000 with two exceptions. These are:

  (a) where the units/shares form the consideration for the sale of other property; and

  (b) where the units/shares are in bearer form.

- A special SDRT regime for collective investment schemes in *Schedule 19* applies to transfers of the legal title to units/shares to or via the unit trust manager or ACD (a 0.5% charge arises on surrenders, which is proportionately reduced both where surrenders exceed issues and any of the underlying investments in the fund are exempt, subject to various exceptions); and

- The principal charge to SDRT at 0.5% under *FA 1986, s 87* applies to the assignment of an equitable interest (as opposed to the legal title) in units/shares transferred direct from one investor to another without going through the manager or ACD, subject to various exemptions.

SDRT charge

3.17   SDRT at 0.5% arises where an investor surrenders units in a unit trust scheme or shares in an OEIC, subject to various exclusions and exemptions (*FA 1999, Sch 19 para 2*). A surrender is defined as taking place in one of two circumstances. These are, first, where a person authorises or requires the trustees or managers under a unit trust scheme or the ACD of an OEIC to treat him as no longer interested in a unit/share and, secondly, where a unit/share is transferred to the managers or ACD respectively. A charge arises wherever the surrender takes place or the parties are or are resident. It is limited to cases where the units/shares are chargeable securities (see **3.23** below).

The charge is on the market value of the units/shares. This is defined as the higher of the price they would fetch in a sale on the open market and their cancellation or redemption price (*FA 1999, Sch 19 para 3*). In practice, the Inland Revenue normally accepts the price paid.

A surrender is generally regarded by the Inland Revenue as occurring at the valuation point for the transaction. This will allow the normal dealing record to be used as the basis for the charge (Inland Revenue Stamp Taxes Manual 15.15).

Reduction fractions

3.18   The charge is on the value of surrenders in a week. It is reduced proportionately by two reduction fractions that operate on a two-week rolling basis. The relevant weeks are the week the surrenders take place and the following week. The reduction fractions apply separately to each subfund of an umbrella scheme (*FA 1999, Sch 19 para 18*).

Reduction of tax where surrenders exceed issues – FA 1999, Sch 19 para 4

3.19   The amount of tax chargeable is proportionately reduced if the number of units/shares that are surrendered to the managers/ACD in the relevant two-week period exceeds the number of units/shares issued by the manager/ACD in that period. This is achieved by applying the fraction I/S to the amount of SDRT otherwise chargeable, where 'I' is the number of units/shares issued in the two week period and 'S' the number of surrenders in that period.

legislation is drafted in terms of classes of units/shares. The Inland Revenue Stamp Taxes Manual makes clear, however, at paragraphs 15.18–24 that the calculations should in practice be done where there is more than one class in issue by first restating the classes into a base class, and then doing the calculations for the entire fund or subfund, as appropriate. The regulation provides for the consolidation or sub-division of units. This would cover switches between classes of units/shares, which are not regarded as either surrenders or issues.

3.20   Only surrenders for cash may be brought into the number of issues or surrenders under the reduction fraction. In specie transfers are therefore excluded, as are exempt transfers, for instance, gifts between investors (see **3.33** below).

Where there are cancelled or altered deals, the manager/ACD may either consistently include them as amendments in the charging period and relevant two-week period in which they occur or else consistently do a full recomputation (Inland Revenue Stamp Taxes Manual paragraph 15.26).

Reduction of tax where exempt investments are held – **FA 1999, Sch 19 para 5**

3.21   The charge on the value of surrenders in a week is further reduced if the fund holds any exempt investments. The reduction is made by applying the fraction $N/(N+E)$ to the amount of SDRT otherwise chargeable. 'N' and 'E' are the average market values of the non-exempt and exempt investments over the relevant two-week period.

The Inland Revenue Stamp Taxes Manual states at 15.3.1 that cash or other funds held for day-to-day management are not classed as investments. It also provides guidance on acceptable methods for averaging at paragraph 15.3.3.

3.22   Exempt investments for this purpose are:

- investments which are not 'chargeable securities' for SDRT purposes or subject to ad valorem stamp duty on transfer;

- units in an authorised unit trust or shares in an OEIC under the terms of which scheme property can be invested only in exempt investments producing Schedule D Case III income (certain gilt or bond funds); or

- derivatives which relate wholly to exempt investments.

All other investments are non-exempt investments for the purposes of the reduction fraction.

The Inland Revenue Stamp Taxes Manual helpfully states at 15.38 that investments which would not generally attract ad valorem stamp duty, such as shares in a foreign company without a UK share register, should be treated as exempt.

3.23 Stamp Duty and Stamp Duty Reserve Tax

The main categories of non-exempt investments are UK equities, equity-linked bonds and UK land. The main categories of exempt investments are foreign equities and bonds and UK bonds that are not equity-linked.

Exempt unit trusts and OEICs

3.23 The SDRT charge on surrenders applies only where the units/shares are chargeable securities. Units and shares in authorised funds restricted to exempt investments, and in foreign funds, are not chargeable securities, so the funds themselves fall outside the *Schedule 19* SDRT regime. Likewise, collective investment schemes that fall outside the definition of unit trust schemes or OEICs (see **3.3** and **3.8** above) and open-ended investment companies incorporated outside the UK are all outside the *Schedule 19* SDRT regime.

Authorised funds restricted to exempt investments – FA 1986, s 99(5A)(b)

3.24 To qualify, the terms of the scheme must restrict its investments to those that are not chargeable to ad valorem stamp duty on transfer and are not chargeable securities for SDRT purposes. In addition, the scheme property may not be invested so as to give rise to income chargeable otherwise than under Schedule D Case III. The restrictions may be in the trust deed, instrument of incorporation or prospectus. It is usual to put them into the prospectus since this can be changed more easily than a trust deed or instrument. It is also usual for them to be set out in full, although the Inland Revenue will accept the proviso being expressed by reference to *FA 1986, s 99(5B)(b)(i)* and *(ii)* (inserted by *FA 1999, Sch 19 para 12(3)*).

Foreign unit trust schemes – FA 1986, s 99(5A)(a)

3.25 Unit trust schemes where their trustees are resident outside the UK and the units are not registered in a register kept in the UK by or on behalf of the trustees fall outside the *Schedule 19* regime.

In specie redemptions

3.26 Investors are entitled to request an in specie redemption of units/shares if their holdings exceed the threshold allowance laid down in the prospectus, typically 5%. This gives rise to potential transfer tax liabilities at two levels: on the transfer of the underlying assets to the investor and on the redemption of the units/shares.

Transfer of portfolio investments

3.27 The transfer of investments from the trustee/OEIC to the investor is exempt from SDRT whether or not the investor receives a proportionate share of each asset (*FA 1986, s 90(1B)*, inserted by *FA 1999, Sch 19 para 11*). Similarly, where there is a stock transfer form or other instrument, this will attract fixed stamp duty of £5. There may be foreign transfer taxes in certain jurisdictions.

Surrender of units/shares in pro rata in specie redemptions

3.28   No SDRT arises under *Schedule 19* on a pro rata in specie redemption (*FA 1999, Sch 19 para 7*) and the redemption is excluded from the number of surrenders for the I/S reduction fraction. To qualify, the investor must receive an exact share of each holding in the fund or a share in each holding that is as nearly as practicable proportionate. The Inland Revenue judges this by reference to trading constraints, allowing percentages to be adjusted to a whole number of shares or, where applicable, deliverable lots (Inland Revenue Stamp Taxes Manual 15.47).

Surrender of units/shares in non-pro rata in specie redemptions

3.29   Surrenders of units/shares in non-pro rata in specie redemptions are within the *Schedule 19* charge on surrenders triggering a 0.5% liability. They are excluded from the I/S reduction fraction figures, however, as this reduction fraction does not apply where the redemption is not solely for money. The charge may be reduced by the exempt investments reduction faction where relevant to the fund.

Funds of funds

3.30   The *Schedule 19* regime operates harshly in the case of funds of funds. This results from the definition of exempt assets for the N/(N+E) reduction fraction. The only holdings in a collective investment scheme that are exempt assets for a fund of funds are those authorised funds that not only in practice invest solely in gilts and bonds but whose terms also provide that they cannot invest more widely (see **3.24**). As a result an authorised unit trust scheme or OEIC investing only in non-UK equities is not an exempt investment for the purpose of the N/(N+E) reduction fraction, even though the fund itself will pay no SDRT under *Schedule 19* because all its investments are non-UK. Accordingly, if a fund of funds invests in international equity funds it does not benefit from a reduction under the N/(N+E) reduction fraction.

Third party transfers

3.31   There are two types of third party transfer.

Third party transfers on the register

3.32   Where the manager, trustee or ACD handles the transfer and alters the register showing the ownership of the units/shares, the Inland Revenue regards the transfers as being both surrenders and issues for *Schedule 19* purposes (Inland Revenue Stamp Taxes Manual 15.50). The Revenue considers that these surrenders and issues occur on the day that the register is changed to reflect the transfer. The value of the units/shares surrendered for *Schedule 19* purposes is their market value on that date (not the value of any consideration passing between the investors).

In some cases, the manager/ACD may require the parties to the transfer to pay an SDRT provision against the *Schedule 19* liability that would otherwise fall on the fund (Collective Investment Schemes Sourcebook 4.6.3R). As the liability depends on the market value of the holding being transferred, the Inland Revenue will accept the redemption price at the time the holder sends the transfer instructions to the manager, trustee or ACD so long as they are acted on promptly.

Although agreements to transfer units/shares that result in a change to the register appear to be chargeable to SDRT at 0.5% under *FA 1986, s 87* (the principal charge) as well as under *Schedule 19* because the exemption in *section 90(1)* of that Act does not apply, Inland Revenue practice is not to look for this charge (Stamp Office letter of 25 June 1999 to AUTIF). There is therefore in practice no double charge.

Exemptions

3.33   There are a number of exemptions from the *Schedule 19* charge for transfers on the register of units/shares (*FA 1999, Sch 19 para 6*). In these cases, both the surrender and issue are excluded from the I/S reduction fraction.

The exemptions cover:

- gifts and transfers to a nominee without consideration in money or money's worth;

- transfers to charities and certain heritage bodies;

- where stamp duty group relief would apply under *FA 1930, s 42* if there were a transfer document; and

- transfers which would be exempt from fixed rate stamp duty under the *Stamp Duty (Exempt Instruments) Regulations 1987 (SI 1987/516)*.

The exemptions do not require an instrument or to be adjudicated but the manager/ACD will need to be satisfied that the relevant conditions have been met, and in turn be able to satisfy the Inland Revenue, if required. The Revenue will normally accept a stock transfer form bearing an appropriate certificate as sufficient evidence.

Third party transfers off the register

3.34   Where there is a third party transfer that does not go through the manager/ACD there will be no charge to SDRT under *Schedule 19*. Rather there is a 0.5% charge to SDRT under *FA 1986, s 87* (the principal charge) in the normal way if the units/shares are chargeable securities (see **3.24** above). The buyer will be liable to pay the tax, subject to various reliefs. These include those that would be available from stamp duty for intra-group transfers and transfers that would fall within the *Stamp Duty (Exempt Instruments) Regulations 1987*, by virtue of *FA 1986, s 90(1A)*.

Particular types of third party transfer

Transfers of units/shares to a life company as premium for the issue of a policy

3.35   Before the special SDRT regime for collective investment schemes was introduced by *FA 1999, Sch 19*, it was standard practice to use a stock transfer form or letter of direction to effect the transfer. The instrument was liable to fixed duty (50p or £5) only as the issue of the policy was not dutiable consideration (provided that the parties avoided the transfer being in satisfaction of a debt). The stamp duty cancelled the SDRT that arose on the basis that the issue of the policy constituted 'money's worth' for the purposes of *FA 1986, s 87*. (It is arguable that the issue of a policy (a non-assignable contractual right to an unascertained sum) is not money's worth for *FA 1986, s 87* purposes, but Inland Revenue (Stamp Taxes) takes the view that it is.)

Since stamp duty on the transfer of units/shares was abolished by *paragraph 1* of *Schedule 19*, it has not been possible to stamp an instrument transferring them to a life company as premium for the issue of a policy. Consequently, where there is such a transfer of units/shares and no change of legal title on the register, SDRT arises under *FA 1986, s 87*. In other cases, where the register is changed, the units/shares will be surrendered and re-issued for the purposes of the *Schedule 19* SDRT regime and the SDRT suffered may be borne by the fund concerned or by one of the parties, depending on the fund's policy.

Transfers of units/shares on the merger of pension schemes

3.36   The Inland Revenue for some time took the view that the transfer of units/shares from a discontinuing pension scheme to a continuing scheme is money's worth because of the continuing scheme taking over the obligations of the discontinuing one. This triggered SDRT under *FA 1986, s 87* where there was no change of legal owner or under *Schedule 19* where there was such a change. As explained in the previous section, after stamp duty on the transfers of units/shares was abolished by *FA 1999, Sch 19*, there was no way of using an instrument stamped with fixed duty to cancel the SDRT.

It is understood that the Inland Revenue now accepts that the assumption of liabilities by the continuing pension scheme in a pension scheme merger is not money's worth for the purposes of SDRT. Accordingly, no SDRT will arise on the transfer of units/shares under either *FA 1986, s 87* in the case of the transfer not effected in the register or under *Schedule 19* for transfers requiring the registration.

Property funds

3.37   There are no special rules for unit trusts, whether authorised or unauthorised, investing in property. Rather they are subject to the *FA 1999, Sch 19* regime in the normal way.

From 1 December 2003, units/shares in unit trust schemes and OEICs (*FA 2003, ss 101* and *102* respectively) are effectively excluded from stamp duty land tax, although the funds themselves will be liable to it on the purchase of property investments.

Change of trustee/depositary

3.38   A deed of retirement and appointment of new trustee may be certified as exempt under Category A of the *Stamp Duty (Exempt Instruments) Regulations 1987*.

Changes of depositary of an OEIC require either a deed of novation or a new agreement, neither of which is stampable.

Winding up of unit trust schemes and OEICs

3.39   If a unit trust scheme or OEIC is wound up and its assets distributed in specie to its investors, this will not trigger SDRT under *Schedule 19*. (Even if this should constitute surrenders by the investors under *paragraph 2* of *Schedule 19*, they would not be chargeable by virtue of *paragraph 7*.) No SDRT would normally arise if the fund contained chargeable securities (broadly, UK equities and equity-linked bonds) but any instruments of transfer would attract fixed £5 stamp duty.

Conversions and mergers

3.40   The SDRT and stamp duty implications of conversions of authorised unit trust schemes and mergers are set out in CHAPTER 9.

Individual pension accounts

3.41 With effect from 6 April 2001, exemption from the *Schedule 19* SDRT charge was introduced for transactions in units/shares held in Individual Pension Accounts ('IPAs') (*FA 2001, ss 93, 94*). There are three ways in which units/shares may qualify for the exemption:

1   The terms of a unit trust scheme or OEIC may require that all units are held within an *IPA (Stamp Duty and Stamp Duty Reserve Tax (Definition of Unit Trust Scheme and Open-ended Investment Company) Regulations 2001 (SI 2001/964))*. All surrenders of units/shares in such a fund would be exempt from SDRT, and no SDRT return need be made.

2   Where an OEIC has an IPA-only share class, then surrenders of shares in the IPA class will not trigger SDRT under *Schedule 19*, and surrenders and issues of IPA class shares should be excluded from the *Schedule 19* computation (*FA 2001, s 94*).

3   Where a unit trust is operated with a mixture of IPA and non-IPA unitholders, then surrenders and issues of IPA units may be excluded from the *Schedule 19* charge and computation only if the person making it provides to the Revenue a certificate (*FA 1999, Sch 19 paras 4(6), 6A* (inserted by *FA 2001, s 93*)). This must confirm that, during the period of the return, the manager or trustee making it could, firstly, identify which of the units were held within an IPA, and secondly that no SDRT had been paid, directly or indirectly, by them.

Compliance

3.42 The *Unit Trust Records Regulations 1946* have been repealed and not replaced.

Accountability

3.43 The trustee or the OEIC is the person ultimately liable for SDRT arising under *Schedule 19* (*FA 1999, Sch 19 para 2*). The accountable person, that is the person responsible for paying the tax in the first instance, is the manager or ACD (*Stamp Duty Reserve Tax Regulations 1986 SI 1986/1711* (as amended)).

Liability

3.44 The *Stamp Duty Reserve Tax Regulations 1986* have been amended by the *Stamp Duty Reserve Tax Amendment (No 2) Regulations 1999 (SI 1999/3264)* to incorporate provisions for the administration and enforcement of the *Schedule 19* SDRT regime. The regime is administered by SDRT Operations Unit, Worthing.

A monthly return, covering surrenders occurring in the weeks for which the relevant two-week periods end during that month, is required not later than the 14th of the following month (the 'accountable date'). Any SDRT due should also be paid not later than the accountable date. Strictly, the return is a notice under *Regulation 4B* of the *Stamp Duty Reserve Tax Regulations 1986* and the Regulation lays down what information must be provided. The Inland Revenue Stamp Taxes Manual sets out an illustrative model return form at 15.74.

3.45   If SDRT due under *Schedule 19* is not paid by the accountable date, interest will be payable on it, in the same way as with other SDRT. Late returns are also subject to a fixed penalty of £100 unless there is a reasonable excuse. If a return is submitted more than a year after the accountable date there is a tax-geared penalty.

If a return is incorrect as a result of negligence, there is also a tax-geared penalty, which may be up to the amount of the tax not accurately returned by the accountable date. The Revenue may mitigate these penalties in the normal way, which is dependent on the circumstances of the disclosure and co-operation shown.

Audit

3.46   The SDRT Operations Unit, Worthing, has a rolling audit programme, aiming to visit managers every three years.

4 Offshore Funds

Martin Smith and Simon Davies

PricewaterhouseCoopers LLP

What is an offshore fund?

4.1   The phrase 'offshore fund' refers in its general sense to any non-UK vehicle for collective investment. The term is used to describe a wide range of fund products for both retail and institutional investors: including non-UK resident investment companies; unit trust schemes with non-UK resident trustees; contractual arrangements such as a Luxembourg Fonds Commun de Placement ('FCP'); and overseas partnerships. The common feature of all these vehicles is that they provide arrangements which enable investors to pool their funds available for investment and to share in the financial benefits arising from the common management of their pooled investments.

Offshore funds are frequently perceived to have a tax advantage over their 'onshore' counterparts in that they are almost invariably established in jurisdictions that levy little or no tax either on the fund or on the fund's distributions to international investors. This absence of tax at the fund's local level, together with the degree of privacy enjoyed by many offshore funds, could be an absolute benefit to any investor intent upon evading his tax responsibilities, or simply wanting a discreet means of investment. Even assuming full tax disclosure of the investment return, however, an offshore fund that 'rolls up' its income can, under current UK tax law, provide an element of tax deferral that would not be possible within a UK-based fund. However, the technical analysis is complicated both by the impact of UK anti-foreign fund tax rules and by the fact that offshore funds generally suffer greater levels of worldwide withholding tax on their underlying income (and sometimes on their capital gains) as a result of their tax-favoured status in their country of domicile.

In many cases, however, the popularity of certain offshore funds for UK and, indeed, other cross-border investors can simply be attributed to their comparative lack of regulation, enabling the use of investment strategies that would not currently be permitted within an onshore, highly regulated fund environment.

It is important to recognise that although the phrase 'offshore fund' can encompass a wide range of non-UK investment vehicles, this is not to be confused with the definition of an 'offshore fund' in the UK tax legislation. This definition, which is restricted to offshore funds with particular structural characteristics, can impact on the tax treatment of holdings by UK investors in such vehicles (see CHAPTER 13).

Typical investment structures

4.2 Offshore funds can be distinguished in various ways, for example according to:

- their legal form (company, unit trust, contractual arrangement, partnership etc);

- their structure (single strategy fund, 'umbrella' fund, fund of funds, feeder fund etc);

- whether they are 'open-ended' or 'closed-ended';

- their investment strategy (equities, bonds, cash and money market instruments, balanced investment, derivatives, 'hedge' fund, private equity, property etc);

- whether they are primarily marketed to retail or to institutional investors; and

- the extent to which they can be freely marketed in the UK.

Certain of the above characteristics are discussed further below.

Legal form

Companies

4.3 Most offshore funds are formed as limited liability **companies** with share capital. A corporate fund will have a board of directors in whose hands ultimate executive control of the fund will rest. Depending upon the local regulatory framework within which the fund operates, day-to-day responsibility for the fund's operations may be delegated in their entirety to a separate, local fund management company. This management company may in turn sub-contract certain of its responsibilities, eg investment management, transfer agency or fund accounting. Certain corporate funds may however be self-administered by their board of directors, in which case it would be usual for the directors to delegate their various day-to-day responsibilities to separate service providers. Whatever the arrangements for the day-to-day management of the corporate offshore fund's affairs, the safekeeping of the fund's assets will invariably be entrusted to an independent custodian or depository company to ensure investor protection.

Unit trusts

4.4 Funds constituted as unit trusts are commonly established in jurisdictions founded on Anglo-Saxon common law, and will therefore mostly be found in the Channel Islands, the Republic of Ireland, the Isle of Man and other offshore centres that are, or originated as, British dependencies (including a number of the Caribbean states). Unit trust funds do not exist as such on the continent of Europe, where the Anglo-Saxon concept of a trust is not recognised in civil law.

A unit trust is a legal arrangement under which a trustee and a manager agree to hold and invest assets on behalf of participating investors, whose beneficial interests in the trust's assets are evidenced by the issue to them of units. As in the case of a corporate offshore fund, the actual safekeeping of the unit trust's assets is entrusted to an independent custodian (usually, although not necessarily, a company in the same group as the trustee). The unit trust manager may, as in the case of the manager of a corporate fund, delegate to others certain of the day-to-day fund operations, including the management of the unit trust's investments.

Although an offshore unit trust will function from day-to-day in much the same way as a corporate offshore fund, there are important legal, and thus tax differences in the respective entitlements of corporate shareholders and trust unitholders to income, gains and assets of the fund.

Contractual arrangements

4.5   Whereas unit trust funds as such do not exist on the continent of Europe, somewhat equivalent contractual arrangements for the co-ownership and co-management of investments exist in Belgium, France and Luxembourg in the form of Fonds Communs de Placement ('FCPs'). See **4.15** below for further details.

Investment partnerships

4.6   Offshore limited investment partnerships are commonly established as vehicles for international private equity and hedge fund investment. Their usage and characteristics are more fully described at **4.27** et seq ('Specialist funds).

Fund structures

4.7   A **single strategy fund** is a stand-alone fund, of whatever legal form, that invests in a particular asset class or sector.

Many offshore funds – generally established as companies – are constituted as **'umbrella' funds**. Umbrella funds issue different classes of shares, each of which is solely entitled to the income and gains from a segregated pool of assets (a 'subfund'). An umbrella fund may comprise any number of separate subfunds, each with a distinct investment strategy. Umbrella funds can enjoy economies of scale and administrative efficiencies that would not be available if each subfund were established as a separate, stand-alone investment fund. They are commonly, although by no means exclusively, used as investment vehicles for the retail market.

A **'fund of funds'** is an offshore fund that invests in a range of other offshore funds. Whereas a single strategy fund is designed to spread risk by investing in a range of underlying companies, the higher investment risks and greater volatility associated with many hedge funds in particular have led to the increasing popularity of funds of hedge funds. These might appeal to more conservative institutional and high net worth investors looking for the potential for enhanced investment returns but with a balanced approach to risk. The fund of funds structure is also used for more traditional investment in the securities markets as a convenient means of overall asset allocation and re-allocation.

A **'feeder fund'** is an offshore fund that invests exclusively in a single, underlying fund. A feeder fund structure (which may involve a number of separate funds feeding into the same underlying fund) is generally used as a means of offering different types of investor the opportunity to invest in the same underlying investments, but via a fund vehicle whose tax or other legal characteristics are most suited to the relevant class of investor. A typical example can be found in the hedge fund market, where it is not uncommon for investment in an underlying 'master' partnership vehicle to be routed via either another investment partnership (into which US taxable institutions may prefer to invest) or alternatively an investment company (into which US tax-exempt institutions and other non-US investors may prefer to invest).

'Open-ended' versus 'closed-ended'

4.8   At its simplest, the distinction between an 'open-ended' and 'closed-ended' fund is illustrated on the one hand by an unquoted investment company with a variable ('open') amount of issued share capital, which issues and redeems shares on a continuous basis (either directly to investors or via the fund's manager); and on the other hand by a quoted investment company with a fixed ('closed') amount of issued share capital, whose shares can only be realised by sale on the secondary market. In the UK, open-ended investment companies ('OEICs') and authorised unit trusts are examples of open-ended funds. By contrast, a UK investment trust company whose shares are traded on the London stock exchange is an example of a closed-ended fund.

An open-ended investment fund offers its investors the opportunity, on a daily basis in the case of most retail and some institutional funds, and on a less frequent basis in the case of certain institutional or specialist funds, to redeem their shares at a value equivalent to their relevant proportion of the value of the fund's underlying assets. By contrast, the value at any time of shares in a closed-ended investment fund is entirely dependent upon external supply and demand. Most closed-ended funds designed for retail investors will provide investors with the means to invest in and disinvest from the fund through dealings on a stock exchange. However, in these cases the share price will be driven by market forces, and shares will generally trade at a discount to (or occasionally at a premium over) the proportionate underlying net asset value of the fund.

A number of offshore, closed-ended funds sold to only institutional or professional investors are established for a fixed term of years (usually anywhere between five and ten years), and offer their investors no ready means of realising their investment until the fund is liquidated. There may, however, be a staged return of capital. Such fund structures tend to be associated with long-term investment in illiquid assets such as private equity or property, where institutional investors are prepared to accept a greater level of risk and inflexibility for the opportunity of an enhanced investment return.

Marketing of offshore funds to UK investors

4.9   The *Financial Services and Markets Act 2000* ('*FSMA 2000*') and associated regulations provide a comprehensive regulatory framework for the marketing of non-UK funds to UK investors. A detailed commentary on this regulatory framework is outside the scope of this publication, but in broad terms the UK regulations aim to restrict the promotion of non-UK collective investment vehicles to UK retail investors to those funds that are subject to prudential supervision in their home territory that is broadly equivalent to that which would apply to a UK authorised investment fund.

Offshore funds that are either unregulated, or subject to a materially lower degree of regulation than that of a UK authorised fund, may not be promoted to UK retail investors. However, there are channels through which such funds may be sold to certain high net worth, professional and institutional investors who are better equipped to assess and manage the risks inherent in an unregulated investment.

In principle, there are three categories of non-UK fund that, subject to registration with the UK Financial Services Authority ('FSA'), can be freely marketed to the general public in the UK.

4.10   The first category comprises investment funds established within the European Economic Area ('EEA') and which adhere to investment parameters laid down by the EU UCITS Directive ('Undertakings for Collective Investment in Transferable Securities'). The original UCITS Directive (see Table below) was introduced in 1985, but a new Directive (sometimes referred to as the 'UCITS III Product Directive') has recently been enacted (see Table below) and is in the process of being implemented by EU and certain EEA member states.

Original UCITS Directive	Directive 85/611/EEC of 20 December 1985 on the coordination of laws, regulations and administrative provisions relating to undertakings for collective investment in transferable securities (UCITS)
UCITS III Product Directive	Directive 2001/108/EC of the European Parliament and of the Council of 21 January 2002 amending Council Directive 85/611/EEC on the coordination of laws, regulations and administrative provisions relating to undertakings for collective investment in transferable securities (UCITS), with regard to investments of UCITS

The Product Directive has widened the investment powers of 'UCITS' schemes, which under the original UCITS directive were limited to transferable securities (predominantly bonds or shares). Funds established under or converted to the UCITS III Product Directive are permitted to invest in a wider range of assets such as deposits, certain types of money market instruments, derivatives (for a wider purpose than permitted previously) and units or shares of other collective investment schemes (to a wider extent than permitted under the original UCITS directive). A fuller discussion is included at the end of this chapter (see **4.113** et seq). In order to maintain an appropriate risk profile for UCITS schemes, the old as well as the new UCITS Directive prescribes requirements relating to spread of investments and risk. Investment funds that comply with the standards of the UCITS Directive may be freely sold to investors in other member states under a single European 'passport'.

4.11   The second category comprises locally authorised investment funds established in certain non-EEA countries ('designated territories') where agreement has been reached with the FSA that the relevant class of fund is suitable for promotion to UK investors. Such designated territories include Jersey, Guernsey, the Isle of Man and Bermuda.

4.12   Finally, it is in principle open to the promoter of any non–UK fund falling outside the above two categories to approach the FSA for individual registration to market that particular fund to UK retail investors. This facility is, however, used relatively infrequently, given the high registration fee and the strict registration requirements with which the FSMA requires these schemes to comply.

Vehicles available in different offshore jurisdictions

4.13   Outlined below are those vehicles which are more commonly used for cross-border investment in selected jurisdictions.

Luxembourg

4.14 Luxembourg is the largest European market place for investment funds that are sold cross-border. Luxembourg UCITS (or non–UCITS) funds may be organised under either a contractual or corporate structure.

FCPs

4.15 The contractual structure is the 'Fonds Commun de Placement' ('FCP') which is defined as 'any undivided collection of assets made up of and managed according to the principle of risk spreading, on behalf of joint owners who are liable only to the extent of their contribution and whose rights are represented by units'. A management company, in accordance with the management regulations set up together with the custodian bank, manages the FCP. Investors in an FCP participate in the underlying fund property via 'units' and generally have no voting rights.

In relation to UK investors, the Inland Revenue have confirmed (*Tax Bulletin 50*) that they will treat an FCP as a transparent vehicle as regards its income. As a result, UK investors will in theory be taxed on their share of the underlying income (and arguably, on their share of the capital gains) of the FCP as these arise within the FCP, irrespective of whether the income/gains are distributed in cash, and possibly without the benefit of obtaining a tax deduction for the FCP's management expenses. This would pose a serious cash flow disadvantage for UK taxpaying investors (and a permanent tax disadvantage if no deduction were available for management expenses). On the plus side, there is potential for UK resident investors to reclaim foreign tax credits on underlying sources of income received by the FCP, by reference to the UK's double tax treaty network, as there would be in the case of a direct investment by the UK investor in the relevant underlying security.

In practice, the authors suspect that the taxation of UK investors in an FCP will often proceed by default as though the fund were corporate in nature, with net income recognised for tax purposes only on a cash distribution by the FCP; and capital gains (subject to any application of the offshore fund rules) recognised only on redemption of the investor's units in the FCP. It is also suspected that few operators of FCPs provide the detailed breakdown of underlying income, capital gains and expenses that would be required for a technically accurate UK tax filing. In any event, evidence would suggest that investment in FCPs by UK investors is relatively uncommon.

SICAVs

4.16 An alternative (and, for UK investors, more common) corporate fund structure exists as a separate legal entity, generally in the form of a 'Société Anonyme' (SA or public limited company), which may be organised with a fixed or variable capital structure. The more commonly promoted structure is the latter – 'Société d'Investissement à Capital Variable' ('SICAV') – where the amount of capital varies and is at all times equal to the net asset value of the company.

The SICAV is a corporate entity and as such is opaque (ie not transparent) for UK tax purposes. Therefore UK investors are only taxed on income to the extent that cash distributions are made by the fund, and they are taxed on underlying capital gains only upon the disposal of their shares in the fund. A SICAV is a flexible investment vehicle and is often formed as an umbrella structure with a number of subfunds, each pursuing a distinct investment policy. As noted earlier, this has an advantage over single fund structures in that it enables the fund manager to pool resources and to obtain cost savings through economies of scale.

The Luxembourg SICAV is probably the best known 'offshore' investment vehicle marketed in the UK by virtue of its UCITS 'passport' (see **4.10** above), and is particularly prominent in the retail sector. The vehicle itself is similar to a UK OEIC, and UK investors tend to understand the tax implications of investing in such a vehicle much better than those of investing in a vehicle such as an FCP.

Ireland

4.17   Over recent years the Irish Government has made a concerted effort to promote the attraction of Irish investment funds as a means of cross-border investment by UK and other international investors. Although many Irish funds avail, like Luxembourg funds, of the UCITS passport for retail investors, Ireland has established a particular reputation as a centre for institutional fund investment. The following are the main entities available for cross-border investment.

VCICs

4.18   A variable capital investment company ('VCIC') is a designated investment company with variable share capital incorporated as a public limited company that operates as a fund. The share capital of a VCIC does not have a nominal value and is equal to the value of the net assets of the fund. A VCIC is similar to a Luxembourg SICAV in that it is treated as opaque by the Inland Revenue, and it too can be formed as an umbrella fund with more than one subfund.

Unit trusts

4.19   As with the United Kingdom, Ireland also offers investment funds constituted as unit trusts. Structurally, these vehicles are essentially the same as their UK counterparts. One thing to note is that these vehicles are generally regarded as quasi-transparent for income purposes. In other words a unitholder is deemed to be beneficially entitled to their share of the income (but not, for

UK tax purposes, of the capital gains) of the unit trust, irrespective of whether it is distributed or not. In practice, however, offshore unit trusts can sometimes give rise to similar problems to those associated with investing in a Luxembourg FCP, in that the correct information required by UK investors for their tax returns may not always be provided. See further discussion of offshore unit trusts in CHAPTER 13.

CCFs

4.20   The common collective fund ('CCF') is a new institutional investment vehicle that is currently being launched in Ireland. It is a contractual arrangement, based upon the concept of a Luxembourg FCP. Investors participate in the underlying assets of the fund via units in the CCF. The particular intention is that the CCF will facilitate tax-efficient cross-border pension pooling due to the fact that it has been designed to be tax transparent with respect to both its income and its capital gains. Thus, for instance, a UK pension fund that invests in US shares via an Irish CCF should be deemed, for the purposes of the UK/USA double tax treaty, to have invested directly in those shares and to be entitled to a zero rate of US withholding tax on share dividends.

Channel Islands

4.21   As with other major offshore jurisdictions, Jersey and Guernsey provide a domicile for both open- and closed-ended investment funds. The main vehicles offered are as follows:

●   Unit trusts

●   Open-ended investment companies

●   Limited partnerships

In the open-ended sector the majority of investment funds are established as companies or as unit trusts. In the closed-ended sector the majority of investment vehicles are companies, but a significant percentage of funds have been established as limited partnerships, especially for private equity investment.

In addition, legislation has been enacted in Guernsey (but not in Jersey) to allow for the formation of protected cell companies ('PCCs') and the conversion of existing companies into PCCs. The significance of the legislation is that it permits a PCC to have separate and distinct 'cells' or 'subfunds'. Unlike some other umbrella fund structures, the assets and liabilities of each subfund are legally segregated from those of other subfunds, and those assets are not available to creditors of the other subfunds in a corporate insolvency. In other words, PCCs do not suffer from 'contagion'.

4.22   *Offshore Funds*

Cayman Islands

4.22   The laws of the Cayman Islands provide a high degree of flexibility for establishing offshore funds. The three vehicles commonly used are:

- the exempted company;
- the exempted limited partnership; and
- the exempted unit trust.

Exempted companies

4.23   The most common vehicle used is the exempted company with limited liability. An exempted company is incorporated under the *Companies Law (Revised)* through the registration of its Memorandum and Articles of Association with the Registrar of Companies, a declaration signed by a subscriber to the effect that the proposed exempted company will be operated mainly outside the Cayman Islands, and payment of the prescribed fee. The exempted company may operate as either an open-ended or closed-ended corporate fund.

Exempted limited partnerships

4.24   Almost all partnerships are incorporated under the *Exempted Limited Partnership Law (Revised)*, rather than the *Partnership Law (Revised)*, due to several desirable advantages, particularly in relation to the return of capital. Exempted limited partnerships are generally used for private equity funds with a limited number of investors. The limited partner(s) and general partner(s) can be domiciled in any part of the world provided at least one general partner is either:

(i) an individual resident in the Cayman Islands;

(ii) a company incorporated in the Cayman Islands, or registered as a foreign company under the *Companies Law (Revised)*; or

(iii) a partnership registered pursuant to the *Exempted Limited Partnership Law (Revised)*.

Exempted unit trusts

4.25   A fund can be created under common law and subject to the *Trusts Law (Revised)* whereby a trust deed is declared by a trustee or agreed with a manager. Such a fund is invariably referred to as a unit trust. Unit trusts are often used for investors in jurisdictions where participation in a unit trust is more acceptable or attractive than shares in a company.

Other jurisdictions

4.26   There are two other offshore jurisdictions, namely Bermuda and the British Virgin Islands, which are of traditional interest for UK investors. These jurisdictions offer vehicles that are broadly similar to those available in the UK. The laws of Bermuda offer vehicles structured as investment companies, unit trusts and investment partnerships, while under the laws of the British Virgin Islands, vehicles structured as trusts, open-ended companies and limited partnerships are permitted.

Specialist funds

Private equity funds

4.27   The British Venture Capital Association (BVCA) describes private equity as:

> 'a mechanism of financing companies that represents an alternative to raising funds on public equity or debt markets. Especially where the perceived level of risk and uncertainty with the investment is too great for the debt providers and the public markets.'

Private equity generally backs companies seen as too high a risk for the public market or offering too distant a return. The providers of private equity are generally independent private equity funds, which raise funds from institutional investors such as banks, insurance companies and pension funds. There are also captive funds, which receive their funds from parent organisations, usually financial institutions. These structures have been used in the past to encourage high performance within banks by passing a share of the return to those who make the investment decisions. High net worth individuals may also seek to invest in such funds for the higher returns they typically bring.

Typical structure

4.28   These funds are typically set up using a limited partnership structure, often via a UK limited partnership but equally via limited partnerships established in offshore jurisdictions such as the Cayman Islands, the Channel Islands or certain states of the USA, such as through a Delaware limited partnership.

Where an offshore jurisdiction is involved the vehicles used can, however, range from tax efficient corporate entities in jurisdictions such as Luxembourg through to limited partnerships. The choice of vehicle will be influenced by issues such as the need for access to double tax treaties, local taxation at the entity level of income and gains or specific exemptions (for example, EU Directives such as the Parent-Subsidiary Directive), and investor appetite for investing in offshore jurisdictions.

4.29   *Offshore Funds*

In choosing an offshore jurisdiction issues such as the legal character of the entity and level of legal liability need to be considered as well as the tax characteristics of the vehicle. The choice of offshore vehicle has to be tax effective for potential investors, the target investments and the sponsoring private equity firm and its key individuals.

4.29   In a typical limited partnership structure the limited partners will invest a certain amount of capital and/or loans into the partnership and the general partner will manage the fund and its investments on a day-to-day basis. In return for this the general partner receives a priority profit share ('PPS'), which must come out of the income or gains of the partnership before any limited partner receives their share. In addition to the PPS the general partner and/or some related vehicle or party will usually receive a performance related share of the return if a predetermined level of return is achieved, known as 'carry'.

From a UK perspective the Inland Revenue tend to view offshore limited partnerships as being tax transparent; however, advice should always be taken in this regard.

Where the partnership is transparent for UK tax purposes, the investors themselves (being the limited partners) are taxed on their allocation of income and gains as these arise. The partnership itself is not subject to tax. This can be attractive to certain types of investor as it avoids double taxation.

As with other forms of transparent entity, accounting for the investment returns to investors for the purposes of tax returns can be very complex and time consuming.

Hedge funds

4.30   'Hedge' funds are offshore funds that are generally established as open-ended vehicles and typically attract institutional and high net worth investors. Hedge funds are differentiated from traditional investment funds by virtue of their alternative investment strategies. The hedge fund manager will often take both long and short positions in securities, which can vary from something as simple as shares and debt securities (both listed and unlisted) to currencies, commodities and derivatives.

Hedge funds seek to capitalise on market inefficiencies and aim to achieve high absolute performance regardless of market movements.

Some strategies used by hedge fund managers

SHORT SELLING

4.31   This usually involves the immediate sale of borrowed securities which are considered overvalued, in the expectation that the subsequent purchase of similar securities to repay the stock 'loan' will result in a profit.

HEDGING

4.32 This involves defensive strategies to mitigate risk at a fraction of the cost of the risk itself. Different types of risk can be hedged (eg market risk, currency risk, company risk, credit risk) and each can be hedged in different ways. A manager seeking 'absolute' (ie non-market-correlated) investment returns will employ techniques to discount the relative effect of general movements in a particular market, thus isolating the pure return on a targeted share or security.

ARBITRAGE

4.33 This exploits temporary market inefficiencies or discrepancies in the pricing of securities.

LEVERAGING

4.34 This involves borrowing money to increase the size of the portfolio or increase the margin in a particular investment.

Typical structure

4.35 The fund will generally take the form of either an open-ended company or a limited partnership, and is typically located offshore to take advantage of low levels of regulation and in order that the returns generated are taxed at a favourable rate or not at all.

The fund is frequently advised by a 'primary' investment manager located in an offshore jurisdiction (which, in the case of a limited partnership fund, will also constitute, or will otherwise report to, an offshore general partner company), which in turn has a sub-advisory agreement with an onshore investment adviser in the UK. These management companies are usually under common ownership. Together, they will manage the fund's portfolio on a daily basis, following the investment strategy laid down by the fund's board of directors (in the case of a corporate fund) or by the general partner (in the case of a partnership fund). The relevant investment strategy will also be detailed in the fund's prospectus or information memorandum. The investment manager(s) receive a management fee based on the value of assets under management and usually also a performance fee based on the increase in value of the fund over a period, subject as appropriate to hurdle rates and high-water marks. The UK Inland Revenue are currently pursuing a robust investigation of these structures, and their attendant transfer pricing methodologies, as there is concern that a disproportionate amount of the investment manager's fee is, in some cases, retained offshore.

Property funds

4.36 Property funds are another specialist category of funds and are often distinguished by their unique tax implications and investor requirements. As the investments of a property fund consist of large investments in property it is difficult to offer a vehicle that is marketable to a wide range of investors. This is due to the fact that most investors will want to invest in an open-ended fund whereby they have the ability to redeem their shares and get their cash out at any time. This is not a problem for a fund that invests in shares or debt, as the fund manager will simply sell a portion of the underlying assets as and when required to fund redemptions. However with a property asset with a value worth several million pounds this is not so easy. Therefore, in general, property funds are more actively marketed to large institutional investors, such as pension funds and life companies, which are willing to take the risk of keeping their money in the fund until the end of its life.

Typical structure

4.37 Property funds can take many structural forms, including both onshore and offshore fund vehicles, depending on both the target investors and target investments. For UK tax-exempt institutional investors there will be distinct preferences for the type of fund structures that invest in UK property as opposed to those structures that are used to invest in non-UK property.

The main aim of such investors is to avoid any tax costs that would arise as a result of investing in property via a fund as opposed to investing directly into the property, where there would be no direct tax costs for a tax-exempt investor. An offshore fund might therefore seem to be the ideal solution for such investors. However, where UK property is held by an offshore corporate entity, any rental income (and potential trading gains) generated by the property would be subject to income tax in the UK (or possibly corporation tax on trading gains). As a result, where a fund intends to attract UK institutional investors and subsequently invest in UK property, it is often structured as a tax-exempt onshore vehicle (ie an exempt unauthorised unit trust scheme) or more commonly as a fully transparent vehicle, located either onshore or offshore. These days many property funds are structured as either limited partnerships (UK and offshore) or offshore unit trusts which are managed and controlled outside the UK and where the trustees are resident outside the UK.

Taxation of funds

Basis of taxation

4.38 In deciding where to invest their money, investors will be primarily concerned with the return that their investments will generate for them. One variable that can affect the return on an investment are the associated tax costs. These tax costs can take many guises, the most visible being a direct tax on the income or gains of the fund, an indirect tax on the assets of the fund, or a withholding tax on dividend and interest payments out of the fund. UK investors will ultimately be subject to tax on their periodic and final investment returns and would therefore seek to avoid additional levels of taxation at the fund level, particularly where offsetting credits against UK taxation are unavailable.

As a result, offshore fund vehicles are generally based in nil or low tax jurisdictions where, in the case of investment funds sold to international investors, direct taxes or withholding taxes at the fund level are minimal or non-existent.

Direct taxation/corporate tax

4.39   None of the well known, commercially available offshore funds, eg Luxembourg SICAVs, Dublin VCICs and exempt Channel Island funds, are subject to any form of corporate income tax on their net income or gains, and as such have at least a cosmetic advantage over their UK-based counterparts.

Local asset taxes

4.40   With the notable exception of Luxembourg, the vast majority of offshore jurisdictions do not apply any other form of taxation to the fund. Luxembourg investment funds are subject to a subscription tax ('taxe d'abonnement') at a default rate of 0.05% per annum on the total net asset value of the fund, as evaluated at the end of each quarter. This rate is reduced to 0.01% per annum for funds invested solely in money market instruments and bank deposits and also for institutional investment funds. The tax does not apply to a fund of funds to the extent that the assets of the underlying funds have themselves been subject to subscription tax. The principal reason for the reduction over the years in the level of the subscription tax on Luxembourg funds (and in particular that on institutional funds) is the fact that equivalent investment funds in Dublin (Luxembourg's main competitor in the pan-European market place) do not suffer an equivalent asset tax.

Withholding taxes

4.41   Like direct taxes, withholding taxes applicable on the payment of dividends and other distributions from an offshore investment fund would be a disincentive to prospective international investors (although UK taxpaying investors could expect an equivalent credit against their domestic tax liability on the income). Offshore jurisdictions have for the most part recognised this fact, and have not sought to withhold tax on distributions to international fund investors.

Howevr, the arrival of the EU Savings Directive (see CHAPTER 13) will complicate this situation. Luxembourg (along with Austria and Belgium) has opted to subject cross-border interest payments to individual beneficial owners in other EU member states to a progressive rate of withholding tax rather than exchange information with counterpart EU tax authorities. The definition of interest payments is wide ranging but is intended to apply to both income distributions and share redemptions from investment funds whose assets include debt instruments (subject to certain de minimis rules).

Moreover, a number of the truly 'offshore' centres for cross-border investment funds, being current or former dependencies of EU member states such as the UK, have had their hands forced over the application of equivalent withholding tax or exchange of information regimes for interest-based distributions to EU individual investors. Time will tell whether the implementation of the Savings Directive (and any future extension to other, EU cross-border payments such as equity dividends) will create greater tax competition amongst the traditional offshore fund centres, or cause new ones to emerge.

Tax transparent funds

4.42   The term 'transparent' is used to describe a fund whose income and, in some cases, capital gains are deemed for tax purposes to arise directly in the hands of its investors, ie the fund is 'look-through'. It will depend on the view of the tax authorities in each country of investor residence as to whether they regard the fund vehicle in question as transparent for their domestic purposes, and tax domestic investors on their shares of underlying income (and gains) accruing in the fund, irrespective of the cash distributions from the fund. Tax transparency can result from the legal characteristics of the fund itself, or from an overlay of tax rules in those countries in which investors reside. A discussion of the UK tax position is contained in CHAPTER 13.

Treaty access for fund structures

4.43   Although often overlooked by investors, there is another level at which tax costs can adversely impact on their eventual return, namely withholding or other taxes levied on local source income or gains by those countries in which an offshore fund invests. From the standpoint of a UK investor, it is here that a superficial comparison of the tax attraction of an offshore fund over a domestic fund can often break down, depending upon the investment profile of the fund.

In contrast to their offshore counterparts, UK OEICs and authorised unit trusts do, as a rule, benefit fully from the extensive tax treaty network developed by the United Kingdom. Offshore funds are, however, often established in jurisdictions that have no double taxation agreements; or, where a treaty network does exist (for example in Luxembourg and Ireland), locally-based investment funds can avail of those treaties to only a limited extent by reason of their tax-advantaged status.

Luxembourg

4.44   Withholding taxes levied at source on income received by a Luxembourg fund are normally not refundable. In addition, while Luxembourg funds formed as investment companies may benefit from certain (but not all) double tax treaties, FCPs will generally not benefit unless the unitholders themselves are able to claim reduced rates under double tax treaties between their own state of residence and the underlying country of investment.

The Luxembourg tax administration has formalised its position in various notes regarding the application of tax treaties to Luxembourg investment funds.

Fonds communs de placement (FCPs)

4.45 FCPs cannot generally benefit from tax treaties concluded by Luxembourg, since they are not taxable entities. An exception is the Ireland–Luxembourg treaty, which FCPs are able to access.

Even though, in theory, a FCP investor resident in a territory which has a double tax treaty with the underlying country of investment might be able to secure relevant tax benefits as regards their share of the FCP's income from that country, there is no guarantee that the tax administration of that country will accept this position. For example, France refuses to allow treaty benefits in the case where French source income is paid to a Luxembourg FCP, irrespective of where its unitholders are resident.

SICAVs/SICAFs

4.46 The Luxembourg tax administration considers Luxembourg SICAVs and SICAFs to be Luxembourg resident, but recognises that tax treaties concluded by Luxembourg do not necessarily enable them to apply for treaty benefits. At the time of writing, the countries with which the tax treaties signed by Luxembourg clearly apply to Luxembourg SICAVs and SICAFs are the following:

- Austria
- China
- Finland
- Germany
- Indonesia
- Ireland
- Malta
- Morocco
- Poland
- Portugal
- Romania
- Singapore

- Slovakia

- South Korea (though there is some debate here)

- Spain (but limited)

- Thailand

- Tunisia

- Uzbekistan

- Vietnam

This list may appear long, but, with the notable exception of Germany, it excludes most of the industrialised countries in which investment might be expected to be made, such as the USA, UK and Japan.

For all other countries with which Luxembourg has signed a tax treaty, either there is a clear non-application of the treaty to Luxembourg SICAVs and SICAFs, or there is uncertainty as to the application of the treaty.

Ireland

4.47   Ireland has favourable double taxation treaties with around 40 countries. The question of access to these tax treaties is complex, and opinions differ as to how the provisions and benefits accorded to Irish entities should be interpreted in relation to tax-exempt funds. The possibility of treaty access cannot be ruled out but equally cannot be relied upon.

The only treaty on which a legal ruling has been obtained in relation to its applicability to Irish funds is the Ireland–South Korea treaty. In many treaties, limitations apply to curtail the benefits available to funds – for example the Ireland–US treaty has a limitation of benefits clause (see **4.49** below).

Many Irish funds are in practice able to recover withholding tax suffered in excess of the treaty rate from overseas jurisdictions. However, it is less than clear that the funds would be strictly entitled to these benefits if the question were tested in court.

Other offshore centres

4.48   Jurisdictions such as the Cayman Islands, Bermuda and the British Virgin Islands have no double tax treaties in force. Jersey and Guernsey have bilateral treaties with each other and with the United Kingdom, though the latter is limited in scope and of little relevance in the context of investment funds.

Treaty shopping and limitation on benefits

4.49 Based on the comments above, it is easy to understand how tax treaty access can have a significant impact on the relative performance of an offshore fund. The investment fund industry recognises this, and attempts are sometimes made to structure an investment via an entity based in a jurisdiction that has the benefit of a preferential treaty rate with the country (or countries) where the underlying investments are held. Such a strategy is often referred to as 'treaty shopping'.

Tax authorities are understandably concerned about treaty shopping, and look to combat it. Some authorities have insisted that the entity claiming the benefit of the tax treaty with their country must be able to demonstrate sufficient business substance and that it is not just a so-called 'letter box', established simply to obtain treaty benefits. If sufficient substance cannot be demonstrated, the tax authorities will deny those benefits.

Other tax authorities have gone one step further and introduced specific anti-'treaty shopping' provisions within their double taxation treaties with other countries, generally referred to as limitation on benefits clauses. These work by allowing the benefits of a tax treaty only to those entities resident in another jurisdiction which also have a certain portion of their investors resident in the same jurisdiction.

Nevertheless, a number of relatively well known structures have in the past been used by investment funds in order to reduce withholding taxes on their underlying investments.

Under a typical such structure, investment in a particular country would be made by the investment fund via a subsidiary company based in a third country which has a tax treaty with the underlying country of investment. Obviously for this to work effectively, there needs to be no or very little tax chargeable on the profits of the subsidiary, and no or very little withholding tax on the repatriation of dividends and other proceeds from the subsidiary to the fund itself. This last requirement can only be met if the country where the subsidiary is located does not require tax to be withheld on distributions, or if the withholding tax rate is reduced under the double tax treaty between the country where the fund is resident and that where the subsidiary is resident. This is not an easy task, bearing in mind the limitation on treaty access for offshore funds in general. However, Luxembourg SICAVs have historically been able to benefit from certain such structures, using Cypriot subsidiaries to invest in Russian securities and Mauritius subsidiaries to invest in Indian securities.

The forthcoming implementation of the UCITS III Directive will curtail the use of many such structures; although at the same time the new Directive may permit more limited use of such techniques by allowing so-called 'funds of funds' in the future. UCITS III is discussed in more detail at **4.113** et seq. The increasing use of equity-linked derivatives within offshore fund portfolios can also provide opportunities to bypass the withholding tax issues frequently associated with direct investment in equities.

UK tax issues for offshore funds

Residency of fund – general

4.50   The principle of tax residency is a long-standing one, and one might question why it should be an issue for offshore investment funds more than for any other non-UK entity. The simple answer is that an offshore fund will invariably be situated in a nil or low tax jurisdiction, which in some cases may offer little more than a basic administrative structure for the fund's operations; whereas the fund can only access the world stage for investment opportunities through the value-added activities of investment professionals who will usually (although not always) be located in the major onshore financial centres. Thus, in the case of offshore funds promoted by UK investment houses, the UK Inland Revenue will be particularly keen to establish that the affairs of the fund itself (as distinct from those of its UK investors and its management professionals) are properly controlled offshore, and as such fall outside the UK tax net.

The ability of an offshore fund to demonstrate that it is not tax resident in the UK is therefore essential. That said, the authors do believe that the UK Treasury and the Inland Revenue recognise the importance of the UK, and London in particular, as an international financial centre, and would not, as a matter of policy, seek to undermine the benefits of the associated revenue flows by an overly heavy-handed approach to the tax residency of non-UK investment funds, particularly where investors in the fund are internationally-based. Other checks and balances exist, either as regards the domestic taxation of the individual or institutional UK investor in an offshore fund, or as regards the UK taxation of an appropriate level of commercial profit in the hands of the fund's UK manager. Consequently, challenges to the tax residency of offshore funds have been comparatively rare over the years. Nevertheless, the UK promoter of any offshore fund would be ill-advised to ignore the risk.

Residency of fund – corporate

4.51   Under UK taxation principles governing the residency of companies, a corporate investment fund established outside the UK would nevertheless be deemed to be resident in the UK for tax purposes if its 'central management and control' were exercised within the UK. While 'central management and control' has no statutory definition, and is a question of fact in each particular case, the courts have held it to be the highest form of control and direction of a company's affairs, as distinct from the management of the company's day-to-day operations.

What constitutes 'central management and control'?

4.52   In general, decisions that reflect the central management and control of a company are those that would ordinarily be taken by the directors alone, rather than delegated to operational management. The extent of these decisions will depend upon the nature of the company and the complexity of its affairs, but core matters would include:

- Appointment of officers of the company, and approval of major service contracts;

- Employee relations;

- Changes in capital structure, and strategic shareholder relations;

- Approval of financial statements;

- Dividend policy;

- Corporate strategy;

- Major financing and capital expenditure; and

- Strategic investment decisions.

Most of the above would feature in the context of a corporate offshore fund as they would with any company. Even though, as an investment 'product', an offshore fund's framework and operations will be set out in its prospectus, the fund's directors must still consider and approve the company's offering to its investors, as well as any subsequent changes to this.

In the case of an investment company, the determination of investment strategy and any changes thereto is a vital ingredient of central management and control. Thus, in circumstances where day-to-day responsibility for the management of the fund's portfolio is delegated to a UK-based manager, the greatest care must be taken to ensure that the investment manager's decisions are always taken within the overall investment parameters set out within the fund's prospectus, approved by the fund's board of directors and subject to the board's regular review and ratification.

How and where is 'central management and control' exercised?

4.53 As indicated above, the highest executive level of a company's management and decision-making would be in the hands of its directors and would be expected to be exercised by them at board meetings. Accordingly the location of central management and control will often be determined by the place at which the board meetings are conducted. It is, however, important to recognise that this will not always be the case, particularly if it emerges that the board meetings are not in fact the forum in which major decisions are actually being made.

This point is highlighted in the Inland Revenue's Statement of Practice SP 1/90 which states that:

> 'Generally however, where doubts arise about a particular company's residence status, the Revenue adopt the following approach –
>
> - They first try to ascertain whether the directors of the company in fact exercise central management and control;
>
> - If so, they seek to determine where the directors exercise this central management and control (which is not necessarily where they meet);

- In cases where the directors apparently do not exercise central management and control of the company, the Inland Revenue look to establish where and by whom it is exercised.'

4.54   Typical guidelines recommended in order to maintain central management and control offshore include the following:

- The board should comprise a majority of non–UK resident directors with sufficient business experience and seniority to take responsibility for corporate governance, and any UK directors should not constitute a decision-making quorum. Ideally, the chairman should not be UK resident, but if he or she is then they should act in a non-executive capacity.

- The location of all board meetings should be offshore, and should whenever possible be held in person. Board meetings should be held sufficiently frequently to amply demonstrate that these meetings are the true forum through which control of the fund is exercised.

- Full minutes should be kept of each board meeting, and should demonstrate the active discussion and determination of relevant issues (including a considered appraisal of investment performance). The directors must not merely 'rubber-stamp' decisions already made elsewhere

Residency of fund – non-corporate

4.55   Many non-corporate fund structures are established as offshore trusts whose income would be subject to UK income tax, and whose gains would be subject to UK capital gains tax, should the trust be deemed to be tax resident in the UK. The residence rules for income tax and capital gains tax differ from those for corporation tax.

For income tax purposes the residence of a trust is dependent on the residence status of its trustee(s). Where any of the trustees is a corporate entity, then it is necessary to revert to the corporate rules (ie the central management and control test) in order to determine that trustee's tax residency.

The capital gains tax determination of residency is slightly more complex, and hinges on whether the trust can be considered a unit trust scheme under the *Financial Services and Markets Act 2000*. Should it fall outside this definition, and not be considered either a 'bare' trust or otherwise transparent in nature, the tests to determine residence would then become those laid down in the *Taxation of Chargeable Gains Act 1992, s 69*. This section states that for a trust to be non-UK resident, both of the following conditions must apply:

(a) The majority of the trustees are not resident or not ordinarily resident in the UK.

(b) The general administration of the trust is carried on outside the UK.

Arguably, the 'general administration' test has a wider scope than the corporate test of a company's central management and control. However, it is believed that the delegation to a UK person of responsibility for carrying on the day-to-day management of the investment portfolio of the trust should not in itself put the trust at risk of being deemed UK resident. Conversely, the delegation of core, trust administration functions to a UK person may create such a risk. Should all the investors in the trust be non-UK resident, it may be possible to apply the 'professional trustee' exemption contained within the above-mentioned section such that the trust is not deemed UK resident.

4.56 It is a moot point for capital gains tax purposes whether, for a unit trust scheme, one should apply the corporate rules (as under *Taxation of Chargeable Gains Act 1992, s 99* these vehicles are deemed to be companies), or the method described above for trusts generally. The authors favour the former approach, which would in effect treat the unit trust as though it were a company, and consider the joint activities of the trustee and the unit trust manager in the context of the exercise of the fund's 'central management and control'. Both entities should, of course, be incorporated outside the UK.

4.57 Entities such as Luxembourg FCPs and offshore investment partnerships, which are constituted neither as companies, trusts or unit trust schemes are usually considered transparent for UK tax purposes. In such cases each investor's share of the underlying income and gains of the fund will be directly taxable in the hands of the investor, and the treatment applied will depend on whether the return is UK-sourced and whether the investor is UK resident.

Specific issues

4.58 In specific instances where the authors have seen the Inland Revenue question the tax residence of corporate offshore funds, key concerns have included the following:

- Whether the entire operation of the fund was in fact carried out through the UK investment manager;

- Whether the UK investment manager was managing the fund's liabilities as well as its assets;

- Whether matters were routinely referred to the fund's directors 'for approval', rather than couched as advice/recommendations for active debate by them;

- Whether there was evidence that UK resident fund directors did not regularly attend board meetings (suggesting that decisions may have already been taken elsewhere);

- Whether marketing documentation focused entirely on the UK investment manager and did not include sufficient consideration of the offshore fund's board of directors;

- Whether the fund's directors were actively involved in establishing and approving contracts with service providers.

4.59 A particular problem relates to 'founder' or 'management' shares issued by a corporate offshore fund, should they have attached to them extra rights concerning the appointment and dismissal of the investment manager. Founder shares have been used in a number of offshore fund structures (particularly in the hedge fund arena) as a tool to allow the fund's manager to have exclusive rights to determine whether the fund should be wound up. However, over time these rights have sometimes developed to cover matters relating to the appointment and dismissal of the investment manager, and even the power to amend the memorandum and articles of the fund. If such shares do contain the exclusive right to appoint the investment manager (or to protect the manager from dismissal) or to make fundamental decisions as regards the continuation or constitution of the fund, then the Inland Revenue could well consider this a key power that overrides the general powers of the offshore board of directors. If these shares are held by UK persons then this creates a significant risk that the central management and control of the fund could be brought onshore for taxation purposes. As founder shares have created risks not only in relation to fund residency but also for the Investment Manager Exemption (discussed at **4.77** et seq below), it is generally recommended that the capital of affected funds be reorganised so as either not to include shares with such rights attached, or to alter the way in which such rights are framed.

An additional risk is that such rights could ultimately mean that if the owner of the founder shares is the UK investment manager, this could result in the consolidation of the fund in the UK manager's accounts, as a subsidiary, due to the investment manager having deemed control of the fund.

UK taxation of the fund's income and gains

4.60 The great majority of offshore investment funds are just that: namely, funds that invest in underlying assets (eg shares, securities, money market instruments or property) for a periodic income yield and the prospect of longer-term capital gain on their disposal. In these cases, provided the offshore fund is non-UK tax resident, the fund's capital gains are not subject to UK taxation, even if the underlying investments are UK-based ones. As regards the fund's income, this is only subject to UK taxation if it is UK-sourced, for example UK dividends, UK interest or rental income from UK property. Except in the case of UK rental income, however, the UK income tax liability of the fund will generally be limited to any UK tax that is withheld at source on payment of the income. UK dividends are not subject to withholding tax, and nowadays very few categories of UK-source portfolio interest are subject to withholding tax – the main exception being annual interest paid by a UK company to a non-UK person, for example on domestic corporate bonds.

In the case of a fully tax transparent offshore fund such as a Luxembourg FCP or an offshore investment partnership, it is the investors in the fund, rather than the fund itself, who would according to the above rules be exempt from, or liable to, UK taxation on their respective shares of underlying income and capital gains, depending upon their individual tax residency status and the source of the income.

In the case of an offshore unit trust, the *Taxation of Chargeable Gains Act 1992, s 99* will usually deem the unit trust to be a company for capital gains tax purposes. Thus the capital gains of the fund (from whatever source) will not be subject to UK taxation provided the unit trust is not tax resident in the UK (see previous discussion on tax residency at **4.50** et seq). UK-source income of the unit trust will in principle be subject to UK taxation, irrespective of the tax residency of unitholders, but subject to the limitations on liability mentioned above for non-resident unitholders.

Trading, UK agency and UK permanent establishment issues

4.61   The position becomes considerably more complex if the offshore fund's 'investment' activities fall to be characterised as a 'trade' under general UK tax principles. Under long-standing UK tax rules, a non-UK person (which would include an offshore corporate fund and also a non-UK resident investor in a tax transparent offshore fund) is, in principle, subject to UK taxation on the profits of a trade carried out in the UK, unless exemption from UK taxation is afforded by a relevant double taxation treaty. Under previous legislation that was overhauled in *Finance Act 2003* for companies subject to corporation tax in respect of accounting periods commencing on or after 1 January 2003, a non-UK resident corporate fund (or, in the appropriate cases, a non-UK corporate investor in a tax transparent fund) was subject to UK corporation tax on profits attributable to a trade carried on through a UK branch or agency (*ICTA 1988, s 11*), and remains subject to UK basic rate income tax on profits attributable to a trade carried on in the UK other than through such a UK branch or agency (*ICTA 1988, ss 6(2)* and *18*). Investors in a tax transparent fund who are non-UK resident individuals are subject to UK taxation at their relevant marginal rates of income tax on their share of the profits of a trade carried on by the fund within the UK, whether or not the trade is conducted through a UK branch or agency (*ICTA 1988, s 18*).

A UK resident individual investor in a tax transparent offshore fund that carries on a trade would, under normal UK tax principles, be subject to tax on their share of the fund's profits.

What is trading?

4.62   There is no statutory definition of 'trading', and reliance is placed on case law and Inland Revenue interpretation.

In 1955 the Royal Commission listed various 'badges of trade', and these have been considered and developed by the courts in numerous cases over the years. Unfortunately, these cases have generally involved commercial operations outside the financial sector. Some guidance in the area of investment management is, however, provided by the Inland Revenue in Statement of Practice SP 1/01, which confirms amongst other things that the active management of a portfolio of shares, bonds and money market instruments will not usually be considered to constitute a trade. The most important badges of trade to consider when determining whether the management of a portfolio of securities constitutes a trading, as opposed to an investment activity, are motive, frequency of transactions and length of holding period.

4.63   High turnover in securities can never be more than an indication that trading might be taking place. However, the level of an offshore fund's turnover is generally visible in the fund's financial statements, and therefore is often the starting point for further enquiries. There are different views as to how to measure turnover, but a generally accepted formula is:

$$\frac{1/2 \; (\textit{value of purchase} \, + \, \textit{value of sales}) \times 100}{\textit{average net asset value}}$$

Turnover in excess of 100% might, in the Inland Revenue's view, warrant more detailed enquiry into the number of securities transactions entered into during a particular period, and the duration of portfolio holdings. However, high turnover can on occasion simply be associated with high levels of fund share issues or redemptions; and the need to acquire underlying securities as a fund expands, or to sell them as it contracts, is in no way indicative of trading.

4.64   Ultimately, the key factor in determining whether a fund invests or trades in securities is likely to be that of motive. Investment generally denotes an intention to buy and hold securities for medium to longer term capital growth, usually with the prospect of income yield in the interim holding period. The purchase of a security with a simple view to securing a profit on its disposal in the short term is more characteristic of trading. This is why the selling of securities 'short', where the disposal actually precedes the subsequent purchase at a lower price, has, in the Revenue's eyes, traditionally been seen as a trading transaction. Similarly, transactions undertaken over a short period of time with a view to arbitraging temporary market anomalies for profit have little of the flavour of an investment.

Strategies of this type are typically associated with hedge funds, and these funds are more often than not branded as 'traders'. They rarely apply for UK distributor status (for fear of being forced to distribute their portfolio profits on an annual basis – see **4.95** et seq), and are particularly sensitive to possible UK tax exposure through the activities of a UK adviser or manager (see **4.68** et seq). However, it is too easy to brand all hedge funds alike, and many of them (for example, 'market neutral' funds that seek absolute returns on securities by hedging out general movements in the surrounding markets) are merely pursuing a more rarefied form of long-term investment return. The short-selling strategies that go hand-in-hand with the 'long' holding of securities in such funds may be viewed in this wider investment context, rather than as individual trading transactions in their own right.

4.65   As a rule, offshore funds that pursue, even on an active basis, more traditional, long-only investment strategies are, as SP 1/01 confirms, less likely to be considered to be trading. However, any strategy under which securities are acquired, and automatically sold when a predetermined point occurs (eg when the securities reach a particular price), without any intervening judgement by the investment manager, could be open to challenge on trading grounds – and some have been challenged in practice.

Whereas it will be crucial in borderline cases to understand the investment manager's motive on a transaction-by-transaction basis, the description of investment strategy within the fund's prospectus and marketing material, and manager reports accompanying its accounts, may contain relevant evidence of overall intentions.

4.66   Finally, the use of financial derivatives is another area where trading considerations will often come to the fore. The Inland Revenue's Statement of Practice SP 3/02 discusses the taxation treatment of financial futures and options. Broadly speaking, where the use of the financial future or option is ancillary to an underlying position in securities, the treatment of the profit or loss on the derivative instrument will follow that of the underlying position. Thus, the use of stock index futures to hedge against a fall in value of portfolio securities held as an investment would be viewed as a capital transaction, provided the hedging transaction could be shown to be economically appropriate. Equally, the use of a forward currency contract or future to hedge against the fall in value of the currency in which a portfolio of investment securities is denominated, as against the reference currency of the fund itself, would be viewed as capital.

Where a position in financial futures or options is taken on a 'stand-alone' basis, or does not have sufficient economic linkage to an underlying asset or position (eg entering into a cross-currency future that has no connection with either the currency in which portfolio securities are denominated, or the currency of the fund or of the fund's share capital), the derivative transaction would be analysed in its own right in order to determine whether it was by way of investment or trading.

4.67   By way of postscript, the Inland Revenue have recently issued *Tax Bulletin 66*, in which they suggest that financial swaps generally cannot be considered as 'financial futures' for the purposes of Statement of Practice SP 3/02 or other UK tax rules. The detail is not covered here, but the Revenue's position on this runs counter to many years of tax and industry practice, and could generate difficulties for offshore funds that seek UK distributor status. Other difficulties that *Tax Bulletin 66* was initially seen to create for offshore funds that may be carrying on a securities trade in the UK have now been partially resolved (see **4.84**).

Implication of trading – UK investment management

4.68   The above issues are of practical significance if, as is frequently the case, the portfolio of a 'trading' offshore fund is managed by a UK company, either directly or under delegated authority from a lead offshore fund manager. The activities of the UK investment manager will, in most cases, cause the offshore fund (or the corporate investors in a tax transparent fund) to trade through a UK agency, and thus, in principle, expose the attributable trading profits (eg gains made on the purchase and sale of securities) to UK corporation tax. In the case of non-UK individual investors in a tax transparent fund, the UK investment manager's activities would, for all practical purposes, also render their attributable trading profits liable to UK income tax.

Moreover, under the UK self-assessment tax regimes, the UK investment manager in such a position would have a statutory obligation to account to the Inland Revenue for any UK tax on the relevant trading profits of the fund (or of its non-UK resident investors).

4.69   In the same way that the making of investment decisions by a UK manager could create a UK agency tax liability for a trading offshore fund, the execution of securities transactions by a UK resident broker could similarly cause the profits of such a fund to fall within the UK tax net. In both cases, however, there is an important tax exemption available for UK investment managers and brokers acting on an arm's length basis for non-UK resident clients, including offshore funds. This is described more fully at **4.77** et seq below.

Finance Act 2003

4.70   The *Finance Act 2003* changes referred to above are only of relevance to non-UK resident corporate trading entities (including non-UK resident corporate investors in tax transparent funds). Whereas such companies were previously only subject to UK corporation tax if the trade was carried on through a UK branch or agency, the future corporation tax position will turn on whether or not the trade is carried on through a UK 'permanent establishment'. Additionally, the trading profits attributable to a UK permanent establishment are subject to more detailed statutory definition than was previously the case, and this is likely to result in a greater level of UK corporation tax in the relevant cases. The changes have been designed to create a closer correlation between the level of UK trading presence required of a non-UK company before its profits become subject to corporation tax, and that which, under the OECD model tax treaty, determines whether the UK can retain taxing rights over the profits of a company resident in another treaty country.

4.71   The new UK definition of a permanent establishment is broadly that of a 'fixed place of business' in the UK through which the business of the company is wholly or partly carried on; or an agent in the UK who acts on behalf of the company and has, and habitually exercises, authority to do business on behalf of the company (*FA 2003, s 148(1)*).

Investment advice versus investment management

4.72   The activities of an offshore fund's UK investment adviser or manager can range from the simple provision of general investment research, to the full discretionary management of the fund's investment portfolio. Whereas the latter services have, in the past, undoubtedly constituted a UK agency of the fund (and would, subject to the Investment Manager Exemption described at **4.77** et seq below, also constitute a UK permanent establishment of the fund under the *FA 2003* rules), it has generally been argued that where a UK adviser does no more than provide investment research and recommendations, and actual investment decisions are made by a lead fund or investment manager offshore, the UK adviser has not constituted a taxable UK agency of the fund. This argument would appear robust enough if there is a genuine division of responsibilities as regards the investment portfolio decisions. Where, however, the facts suggest that the division is more one of form than substance (for example, an absence of credible investment professionals based in the offshore jurisdiction), it might have been more difficult to argue that the UK investment adviser did not, in reality, act in the capacity of the fund's UK branch or agent. The mere use of the term 'echo system' (whereby investment recommendations are provided and usually agreed by return) has significant connotations here.

4.73   The *FA 2003* changes could impact on the above analysis in situations where the UK adviser is unable to claim exemption from permanent establishment status under the independent agent rules. This is because the UK definition of permanent establishment could extend to UK activities on behalf of the offshore fund that fall short of the actual conclusion of contracts. The new provisions state that no permanent establishment will exist if the activities performed in the UK are only of a preparatory or auxiliary character in relation to the business of the non-UK company on a whole. Whereas it might be possible to argue that the provision of general investment research is merely 'preparatory' to the selection, purchase and sale of individual investments, that argument would be much more difficult to sustain if the UK adviser's activities extended to specific investment recommendations.

UK permanent establishment – measure of taxable profits

4.74   In relevant situations, new *section 11AA* of *ICTA 1988* lays down the method to be used in order to ascertain the trading profits of a UK permanent establishment for corporation tax purposes, and this is very similar to the OECD model. Note that in circumstances where a non-resident company is subject to income tax rather than corporation tax on its UK trading income (ie where UK activities are insufficient to create a permanent establishment), and also where a non-resident individual is deemed to trade in the UK (eg as a participator in a tax transparent offshore fund), there remain no statutory rules to determine the measure of the profits attributable to the UK trade.

The new rules effectively serve to bring more taxable profits into the UK corporation tax net, although the main effect on offshore funds would be in line with the magnitude of the financing deductions they attempt to claim, and the level of debt existing in any UK permanent establishment. The provisions have no effect on passive, non-trade income such as rent and interest.

4.75   Three specific provisions take effect:

1   The profits of the permanent establishment shall be those calculated as if it were a distinguishable (functionally separate) entity engaged in similar activities, dealing at arm's length with its offshore 'owner'. The conditions for similar activities and operating conditions will require that the deemed entity's functions, assets and risks are identified and pricing is set accordingly – which adds further weight to transfer pricing requirements as discussed within the section on the Investment Manager Exemption at **4.81** et seq below.

2   Deductible expenses are those incurred for the deemed entity's purposes anywhere in the world, including general administration expenses.

3   The UK permanent establishment will be deemed to have the same capital/equity as if it were operated as a subsidiary – ie the same credit rating as the actual entity worldwide, and no more loan capital than its equity can support.

4.76   Problems that can be envisaged generally in relation to these provisions include:

–   Whether the permanent establishment's profits can exceed the worldwide profits of the offshore fund. This appears not to have been addressed in the current provisions.

–   Should the profits allocated to the UK permanent establishment be calculated on the basis of the offshore fund's commercial profits, or its UK profits as adjusted for UK tax principles?

Thankfully, the existence of the UK investment manager and broker exemptions should make it a rare occurrence for an offshore fund to be required to calculate the measure of its UK trading profits under the new corporation tax rules.

Investment Manager Exemption ('IME')

4.77   The full exercise by the UK of its taxing rights as regards offshore funds that were deemed to be trading in the UK through the activities of a UK investment manager would severely damage the UK investment management industry, as funds would opt in favour of expertise from a jurisdiction without such rules. Therefore there are important 'safe harbour' provisions contained within both *FA 1995, s 127* and the new rules on permanent establishment (*FA 2003, Sch 26*), which protect the trading profits of an offshore fund (or other non-UK person) from becoming subject to UK tax, should the UK manager meet six specific criteria. These criteria are designed to exempt what the Inland Revenue view as bona fide independent investment management services that are being provided from the UK to an offshore entity on a fully arm's length basis.

It should be noted that the following tests are applied on a period-by-period basis. Therefore for each individual accounting period of the offshore fund, the

UK manager must meet these criteria or face being liable to tax on the profits of the fund for that period.

Test (a) – whether the UK manager is carrying on the business of providing investment management services

4.78   This test is generally uncontentious, and is not prejudiced if the UK manager conducts a wider business, only part of which is that of investment management.

Test (b) – whether the services provided to the particular offshore fund are in the ordinary course of that business

4.79   This test might be expected to be satisfied where the contractual arrangements are standard, and at arm's length. However, services might not be provided in the ordinary course of the business should the UK manager fail to secure an adequate fee for its services (see also **4.83** below), or should the terms of the agreement with the offshore fund not be comparable to the usual terms of an investment management agreement.

Test (c) – whether the UK manager provides services to the offshore fund in an 'independent capacity'

4.80   The legislation states that the manager shall not be regarded as acting in an independent capacity unless, having regard to its legal, financial and commercial characteristics, the relationship between the manager and the offshore fund is one between persons carrying on independent businesses dealing with each other at arm's length. The Inland Revenue have, within Statement of Practice SP 1/01, identified specific circumstances where it will generally deem this test to be satisfied:

(i) Where the provision of services to the offshore fund and any parties connected with the offshore fund does not comprise a 'substantial' part of the UK manager's investment management business. The Statement indicates that no more than 70% of the UK manager's business should be derived from the fund and the fund's connected parties (if any), usually by reference to fee income, although another measure (such as assets under management) might be permissible in a particular case.

One such case might be where the arrangements with the offshore fund include the payment of performance fees (or a priority profit share in the case of a partnership fund) which could swamp fixed fee rates from other client contracts during periods of high fund performance.

The Statement confirms that where investment management services are provided to a transparent fund such as a partnership, the deemed connection of partners for tax purposes will not apply in determining the level of the UK manager's business with any one partner.

(ii) Where, in the case of a start-up investment management business, the criterion at (i) above is satisfied within 18 months of commencement.

(iii) Where neither (i) nor (ii) above have been met for reasons outside the control of the UK manager, but it can be demonstrated that all reasonable steps have been taken by the manager to attempt to satisfy the criteria.

(iv) Where the services are provided to a collective fund which is quoted on a recognised stock exchange, or is otherwise freely marketed.

It has sometimes been assumed that the mere listing of a fund on a recognised stock exchange (for example in Ireland) would be sufficient to meet this test. However, the Revenue have indicated that 'freely marketed' means that there should usually be at least monthly liquidity and that the price of the fund's shares should be calculated and published on that basis. In the case of a listed fund, active trading of the fund's shares should thus be demonstrated.

(v) Where the services are provided to a 'widely held' collective fund. A 'widely held' fund is defined as one in which no majority interest is held by five or fewer persons or persons connected with them, or in which no interest of more than 20% is held by a single person or persons connected with him.

Satisfaction of the independent capacity test can often be problematic for hedge funds, as these tend to be heavily seeded at the outset (sometimes by the manager), due to the entrepreneurial character of this type of fund, and in order to inspire confidence in the manager's operations and provide an established track record to attract third party investors.

'Connected persons' for the purposes of this test are taken to be those defined in *ICTA 1988, s 839* and the definition of 'control' is in *ICTA 1988, s 416*. The latter definition includes direct and indirect control of the fund by reason of share capital, voting rights, rights to income or entitlement to assets on a winding up. Parallel seeding of a number of hedge funds by either the manager or a particular institutional investor could cause the funds to become connected, and the management income from all the funds to be aggregated for the purposes of the '70%' test.

Test (d) – whether the UK manager and/or persons connected with the manager are beneficially entitled to more than 20% of the profits of the fund

4.81   The UK manager and/or persons connected with the manager must not have a beneficial entitlement to more than 20% of the fund's taxable trading income arising from transactions carried out through the manager. For the purposes of this test, contractual fees paid to the UK manager for his professional services (be they normal management fees or performance-based fees) are not generally taken into account. However, care should be taken in the case of partnership funds where the performance-related return to the UK manager (or to an entity affiliated with the manager) is received by way of an allocation of partnership profit.

Where the 20% test is failed, **but all other IME tests are satisfied**, only that part of the income of the offshore fund to which the UK manager and persons connected with the manager are entitled will fall into the UK tax net.

The connected party rules for the purposes of this test follow the same definitions as those for test (c) (**4.80** above). Care should be taken in the case of hedge funds in particular, that the rights attached to any founder or management shares do not give the UK manager (or an entity affiliated with the manager) control of the offshore fund. Otherwise, the 20% test will be failed, and the entire profits of the fund will fall to be taxed on the UK manager. (See detailed discussion of founder shares in the context of tax residency issues at **4.59** above.)

4.82   It is important to note that the 20% test is one of **intention**, and can be deemed to be met throughout a reference period not exceeding five years, provided the UK manager's average entitlement (including that of any persons connected with the manager) to the fund's taxable income over the reference period arising from investment transactions carried out by the manager, meets the 20% test. This obtains even if, for one or more individual account periods within a longer reference period, the threshold has been exceeded.

The 20% test is also treated as satisfied if the manager intended to meet the condition but failed to do so for reasons outside his control, as long as he can be proven to have taken reasonable steps in order to attempt to meet the condition. Therefore the investment manager should make every effort to satisfy the 20% test within a chosen reference period, but need not do this at all costs if there are valid commercial reasons why satisfying the test has not been possible.

Heavy seeding of an offshore hedge fund by its manager can thus result in problems with the 20% test as well as the independent capacity test (see above), unless there is a robust business plan for the manager's interest in the fund to be diluted over time.

There are, however, provisions which assist the UK manager's satisfaction of the 20% test in circumstances where this would otherwise be prejudiced through the existence of partnership arrangements.

Test (e) – whether the UK manager's remuneration for his services is at a rate which is not less than would be customary for the relevant class of business

4.83   There are three situations in particular in which this test might be prejudiced:

(i) where the offshore fund itself is connected with the UK manager or the wider management group, and might therefore be paying less than an arm's-length rate of remuneration to its management. In such a case, however, the 20% test above would, by definition, generally also be failed.

(ii) where the UK manager's remuneration from an unconnected offshore fund with which it contracts directly might be adversely influenced by separate remuneration paid for other management or administration services to offshore companies connected with the UK manager. The offshore fund itself would only be concerned with the aggregate remuneration it pays for all management services.

(iii) where an unconnected offshore fund contracts at arm's length for umbrella management services with an offshore affiliate of the UK manager, but the transfer pricing of sub-advisory services provided by the UK manager to its offshore affiliate is at less than arm's length.

Thus, in both (ii) and (iii) above, the internal policies of the management group may prejudice the offshore fund's position as regards the IME. In such cases it will be necessary to establish and document that the remuneration received by the UK manager for its direct or indirect services to the fund is at least equivalent to the customary market rate that it would receive in a fully arm's-length situation. Documentation for these purposes requires a functional analysis assessing the risks, assets and functions of the UK business as regards the relationship with the offshore fund concerned, together with an appropriate benchmarking study that compares the remuneration received with that which would be received by third parties for similar services. Moreover, because the UK manager is subject to tax self-assessment obligations, it is incumbent upon the manager to determine that its remuneration meets the required level before it can adopt a UK filing position to the effect that all the IME conditions have been satisfied. It is not sufficient to await an Inland Revenue audit.

Test (f) – whether the UK manager falls to be treated as the UK representative or permanent establishment of the offshore fund in relation to other, non-exempted income of the fund

4.84   An offshore fund's exemption from UK tax on its trading profits under the IME relies on all profits being generated through 'investment transactions' as defined in *FA 1995, s 127(12)* or *FA 2003, Sch 26 para 3(3)*, as appropriate. These transactions are restricted to:

(i) transactions in shares, stock, futures contracts, options contracts or other securities of any description (but excluding futures or options contracts relating to land);

(ii) transactions consisting in the buying or selling of any foreign currency or in the placing of money at interest; and

(iii) such other transactions as the UK Treasury may designate in regulations. (Until very recently, there have been none.)

Were a UK investment manager to engage in even a single non-qualifying 'investment transaction', the offshore fund's entire immunity from UK taxation would be lost.

Whereas the above list of qualifying transactions has, in the past, been considered sufficiently wide to cover the vast majority of financial transactions entered into by a typical UK investment manager on behalf of an offshore fund, there do remain exceptions. For example, the purchase and realisation of second-hand endowment life policies would be a non-qualifying transaction. More troublesome were statements made in the Inland Revenue's *Tax Bulletin 66* to the effect that it would no longer regard a 'swap' of any description as a 'financial future'. While it seems clear that the Revenue's latest guidance was designed to address the UK taxation of such derivatives generally in the hands of non-corporates, the specific implications for the satisfaction of the IME were potentially serious. The UK Treasury has since issued Regulations (*SIs 2003/2172* and *2003/2173*), taking effect from 12 September 2003, which deem certain, cash-settled financial swaps, contracts for differences and similar instruments (other than those that relate to land, or that comprise contracts of insurance) to be 'investment transactions' for the purposes of the IME. However, the designated transactions would not appear to cover swaps that involve the physical delivery of assets other than currency (eg certain credit derivative swaps), and at present do not therefore provide a full solution to the problem.

4.85   If a UK manager provides services to the offshore fund beyond those of investment management, it will again be necessary to consider the implications, if any, for the satisfaction of test (f). Broking services are covered briefly below (see **4.86**). Other services that a UK manager might commonly provide would be those of marketing or selling agent for the offshore fund's shares. It is the authors' view that although, depending upon the facts, such activities could, in themselves, conceivably cause the UK manager to become a UK representative or permanent establishment of the fund, the 'income' of the fund potentially subject to UK taxation would, in the ordinary course, be that directly generated through the manager's investment management operations on behalf of the fund. Thus, it is not considered likely that test (f) would be failed in these circumstances. Nevertheless, a word of caution is merited. To the extent that this is viewed as a potential risk area, it might be helpful to arrange for the relevant non-investment management services to be provided by a different company within the management stable. This would pave the way for the satisfaction of the IME; although it would not deal conclusively with the possibility that the UK company providing the additional services might itself constitute a taxable establishment of the fund. The position would therefore need to be considered on a case-by-case basis.

UK broker exemption

4.86   A similar provision to the Investment Manager Exemption exists for trading income of an offshore fund attributable to transactions carried out through a UK broker. A broker will invariably be involved in the execution of a trade in a security; and, in the case of hedge funds, a prime broker will provide greater levels of service to the fund.

The tests to be satisfied for the UK broker exemption are similarly designed to ensure that relief from UK taxation in the broker's hands is only available in situations where the broker engages at arm's length with the offshore fund, although significantly the 'independent capacity' test (**4.80** above) and the '20% test' (**4.81** above) are not replicated within the UK broker exemption. The four remaining tests within the IME must, however, be satisfied in the case of a broker, except that for brokers (as distinct from investment managers) there is no statutory limitation on the category of transactions that may be undertaken.

UK property investment

4.87   An offshore fund structured as a corporate entity is liable to UK income tax under Schedule A on rental income from UK properties. Credit for the UK tax paid by the corporate fund cannot, in the ordinary course, be given against the tax liability of UK investors in the fund on distributions of net income to them (or, where relevant, on the disposal of their investment in the fund).

Offshore fund structures that are constituted as tax transparent partnerships or bare trusts (eg offshore enterprise zone unit trusts) should not be caught by this regime. In these cases investors in the fund should be taxed on their share of the fund's rental income and expenditure, based on their own personal tax circumstances.

Other offshore unit trusts are viewed by the Inland Revenue as quasi-tax transparent (see discussion in **CHAPTER 13**). The strict technical position is open to interpretation, but in practice most such unit trusts account for the entirety of the UK Schedule A liability on an annual basis, and the investors receive an individual income tax credit on the periodic distribution or accumulation of the fund's income.

It is probably not possible to obtain an exemption from the charge on rental income under any of the existing UK double tax treaties, even assuming that the offshore fund could access one of them.

4.88   Most offshore funds will seek to restrict the UK income tax liability arising on the rental income by financing the property by way of a loan so that it can deduct interest payments from the rental income in computing the Schedule A charge. The income tax rules as to what interest is allowable, and not the corporation tax rules, need to be met.

As with any other property-related expense, to qualify as a deduction, the interest payment must be wholly and exclusively incurred for the purposes of the Schedule A business. It will then be deductible on an accruals basis. It is therefore common to see non-resident investment funds accruing all of the interest on loans to finance UK property, claiming a deduction in their tax returns and then simply repaying the loans and accrued interest on the ultimate disposal of the property. Withholding tax on UK-source interest paid to non-residents will normally dictate that the borrowing should be from a bank in the UK unless the borrowing fund can otherwise ensure the loan is non-UK source. There is no reason in principle why the borrowing should not be from another non-UK entity associated with the investment fund. This overcomes the problem of security – a factor in determining whether the interest is UK-source or not. However the Inland Revenue are likely to enquire into such an arrangement if they believe the level of interest being charged is in excess of what they believe would be charged in arm's-length circumstances. An arm's-length price is defined as a bargain arrived at between two parties acting independently.

4.89   Non-resident landlord investment funds liable to income tax are required to self assess their profits in accordance with arm's-length principles under *ICTA 1988, Sch 28AA*. The Inland Revenue have published guidance on the application of arm's-length principles for non-resident landlords in *Tax Bulletin 46*. In the *Bulletin*, the Revenue comment that in their experience third party lenders are primarily concerned with the value of the property they are being asked to lend against and that offers of advances appear typically to be in the range of 65–80% of value if there is a satisfactory projected income stream.

Property trading

4.90   The tax treatment of an offshore fund on the sale of UK property depends on whether the property transaction was by way of investment or trade. To the extent that the fund trades in UK property, it is chargeable to UK tax on its UK trading profits. The extent of UK liability on UK trading profits will depend upon the nature of the offshore fund (corporate or transparent) and whether or not trading is undertaken through a UK permanent establishment (see earlier discussion at **4.74** et seq). On the other hand, if an offshore fund disposes of a UK property that was held as an investment, there is usually no UK tax liability on the capital gains in the offshore fund, but substantial UK investors (more than 10% holding) may be liable to tax on their apportioned capital gains if the offshore fund is closely held (see **CHAPTER 13**).

In general terms a property is bought as an investment if it is acquired in order to generate rental income, while a property is bought as trading stock if it is acquired in order to generate a profit from reselling it. As discussed earlier (see **4.62** above), there is considerable case law as to what constitutes an investment/trading transaction. In addition the Inland Revenue and the courts have established a number of basic tests which evidence whether a transaction is likely to be investment or trading. The following factors will be relevant in any case:

(a)   The motive for the property acquisition.

(b)   The method of financing the property.

(c)   The period of property ownership.

(d)   Whether the property is income producing.

(e)   The reason for the property disposal.

As the difference between an investment and trading transaction can ultimately determine whether there will be any tax due in the UK, the distinction is critical.

Value Added Tax (VAT)

VAT issues from the perspective of the UK investment manager of an offshore fund

4.91   The key VAT issue affecting the UK management of an offshore fund is whether VAT incurred on costs and general expenditure (input tax) can be recovered. Fund management services to an offshore fund will be classed either as financial intermediary services (exempt services) or as investment advisory/asset management services (potentially taxable services). If a transaction-based investment management fee is levied, this is likely to point towards exempt services; whereas a periodic charge usually points towards the latter category of taxable services.

Both of the above categories of services are contained within *VATA 1994, Sch 5*, and therefore are outside the scope of UK VAT when supplied to a customer outside the UK. However, intermediary services are classed as financial services, and therefore do not give rise to input tax deduction unless the offshore fund is outside the EU. UK managers of offshore funds therefore tend to find themselves in the position of being outside the scope of charging UK VAT on their services, but in the most part with input tax recovery (unless they are providing financial services to EU funds). Thus, UK VAT does not become a real cost to the manager, and the UK industry can remain competitive as a location for providers of investment management services to offshore funds. It should also be noted that for EU funds, the payment for these services could give rise to a local VAT charge, if they are not viewed as exempt services under local VAT law. However, the scope for exemption tends to be widely drawn in EU states such as Ireland and Luxembourg.

4.92   In addition to the services described above, elements of fund management, such as specific portfolio management or administration, may be outsourced. These outsourced services can be subject to VAT, but this is recoverable by UK investment managers in relation to most offshore funds. In certain cases, administration services and the associated VAT may be charged direct to an offshore manager of a fund. If the offshore manager can prove that it is in business, it should be able to recover this VAT using the procedures provided for in the *8th* and *13th EU VAT Directives*.

4.93   A key issue for UK managers of offshore funds, given the above rules for input tax, arises when they enter into bespoke contracts for one investor (eg a pension fund). If a large proportion of the assets managed relate to a single client, an element of double charging of fees may result at the combined levels of the primary client contract and the offshore fund. To overcome this issue, fee rebates are usually made to the investor. However, the VAT treatment of these rebates can be complex and should be carefully structured to ensure that the investor incurs the least amount of VAT.

VAT issues from the offshore fund's perspective

4.94   Where the fund is established in a non–EU country, there are usually no UK VAT issues and fees charged by any UK manager will, as discussed above, also be outside the scope of UK VAT. Where the fund is established in another EU state, it will be subject to the relevant national value added tax regime, the conditions and complexity of which will depend on the particular jurisdiction. For example, the value added tax treatment of funds in Ireland and Luxembourg differs from that in the UK. There is, however, an exception to this, in that for an EU fund whose activities are deemed under UK legislation not to be by way of their business, UK VAT would then become chargeable.

UK offshore fund legislation

Introduction

4.95   The main offshore fund legislation can be found in *ICTA 1988* within *sections 757–764* and *Schedules 27* and *28*. The legislation was introduced in *Finance Act 1984* in response to what the Inland Revenue perceived to be the widespread avoidance of UK tax liabilities through the use of offshore, money market investment vehicles to roll up interest income, thus converting this from higher taxable income into lower taxable capital gain. The differential was considerably greater in the early 1980s when high inflation allowances could frequently eliminate taxable gains altogether. The legislation broadly attempts to differentiate between those offshore funds that distribute the great majority of their income ('distributing funds') and those that roll up their income ('non-qualifying funds').

It is important to note that not all non-UK investment vehicles described as offshore funds in a commercial sense fall within the statutory definition of an 'offshore fund' for the purposes of the UK legislation. A full discussion of this definition is contained in CHAPTER 13.

Distributing versus non-qualifying offshore funds

4.96   *ICTA 1988, s 760(1)* states that an offshore fund is a non-qualifying fund except during an account period of the fund in respect of which the fund is certified by the Board of the Inland Revenue as a distributing fund (commonly referred to as having 'distributor status').

An 'account period' of an offshore fund for these purposes is generally the same as the fund's financial accounting period, but cannot exceed twelve months.

Certification is given retrospectively.

In order for a fund to be certified as a distributing fund in respect of any account period the fund must comply with the following conditions:

1   The fund must pursue a 'full distribution policy', within the meaning of *Schedule 27, Part I*; and

2   The fund must comply with certain investment restrictions.

If the offshore fund were not to comply with either part of these requirements in any account period, it would fail to be certified as a 'distributing' fund for the period concerned. The detailed rules governing 1 and 2 above are complex, but can be summarised as follows:

1 *Full distribution policy*

4.97   *ICTA 1988, Sch 27* outlines the requirements that must be met for an account period for an offshore fund to be deemed to have pursued a full distribution policy.

Broadly, an offshore fund is treated as pursuing a full distribution policy if a distribution is made for an account period and the amount of the distribution which is paid:

 (i)   represents at least 85% of the income of the fund for that period; and

 (ii) is not less than 85% of the fund's 'UK equivalent profits' for that period.

In addition the distribution must be made within six months of the end of the account period, and must be in such a form that, if it were received by a UK resident person and were not part of a trade (and thus subject to tax under Schedule D Case I or II), it would be taxable under Schedule D Case IV or V. It should be noted however that the Inland Revenue do have statutory discretion in allowing distributions to be made later than six months from the end of the account period. In the authors' experience, the Inland Revenue have rarely failed to exercise this discretion where a late distribution, or further distribution is required to meet the distribution standard. However, offshore funds would be ill advised to rely upon the automatic exercise of discretion.

4.98   Special care should be taken when a fund (or possibly even a subfund within an umbrella fund) is to be put into liquidation. In these circumstances, any distributions due and payable once the liquidator has been appointed will generally be deemed to be a capital payment to investors, and as such would not constitute a qualifying distribution. Best practice on these occasions is for an accurate estimate to be made of income that will accrue up to the date the liquidator is appointed, and for the appropriate income distribution to be made prior to the relevant date.

4.99   For the purposes of the first leg of the distribution test, a fund's 'income' is generally the net investment income after expenses disclosed in the fund's accounts.

A fund's 'UK equivalent profits' are those profits, excluding chargeable gains and after relevant deductions, on which corporation tax would be charged if the fund were a UK resident company for the relevant account period. The purpose of this double test is to ensure that 85% of the accounts income is distributed, while at the same time preventing any untoward circumvention of this distribution requirement through the manipulation of accounting policies. It is far from clear that this test of notional UK income is really required going forward, now that offshore funds are increasingly required to draw up their accounts in line with internationally recognised accounting standards. The current test can give rise to real problems in that items of income and expenditure that are recognised in the accounts for one account period may be recognised in the UK equivalent profits calculation for another period. As a result situations can arise where a fund has to distribute an amount of income twice in different periods, thus somewhat unfairly increasing the amount of income that must be distributed over the fund's life. It is sincerely hoped that the outcome of the Inland Revenue's current consultation on the reform of the offshore fund legislation (see **4.111** below) will, amongst other things, eliminate this injustice and its associated compliance burden.

Exceptions to the basic distribution rule

4.100 There are two broad exceptions to the above distribution rule:

(i) Where the gross income of the fund does not exceed 1% of the average value of the fund's assets during the relevant period, no distribution is required. No statutory formula is laid down for this test, although the Inland Revenue have stated that they will accept calculations based upon the average opening and closing asset value on both an annual or monthly basis as long as consistency is shown. In practice it is suggested that any reasonable calculation of average asset value that demonstrates the satisfaction of this de minimis test should be acceptable.

The statutory de minimis rule was introduced in order to avoid previous case-by-case negotiations where it was argued that the administrative cost of making a small distribution would exceed the amount of the distribution. Consequently the Inland Revenue would be unlikely to entertain such discussions now.

(ii) To the extent that a fund is, for any account period, subject to a restriction, imposed by the law of any non-UK territory, on the amount of distribution it may make, and that restriction operates by reason of an excess of losses over profits as understood for the purposes of that law, the fund's distribution standard is reduced accordingly.

It is important to note that the restriction in question must stem from the (eg corporate) law of a particular country. It is insufficient, for example, that a fund's own bye-laws provide for some limit on the amounts the fund may distribute.

Calculation of UK equivalent profits

4.101 The examples listed below are not exhaustive, but do account for the common adjusting factors that go into a UK equivalent profits calculation:

(a) Any expenditure which might be considered to be of a capital nature or incurred other than in the management of the fund's investments (eg amortisation of formation costs, depreciation, legal and professional costs of a capital nature) must be excluded.

(b) Exchange gains and losses included in the income of the fund, but which relate to the fund's capital investments, must be excluded.

(c) Any dividends or other income, excluding pure stock dividends, which are not included in gross income (eg dividends taken to capital, such as those subject to a dividend reinvestment plan (DRIP)) must be included.

(d) Stock dividends or enhanced scrip dividends received by way of a bonus issue must be excluded.

(e) Profits on treasury bills and certificates of deposit must be included.

(f) Strictly, UK taxation of both interest income and foreign dividends is on an arising (ie received) basis, rather than the accruals and ex-dividend basis generally adopted in a fund's accounts. An analysis would thus be required of income included in the accounts, including details of opening and closing accruals. This information may not in practice be required if in prior years it has been agreed with the UK Inland Revenue that the UK equivalent profit calculation may be submitted on an 'accruals' basis, and the effect of adjustment would be relatively minor.

(g) In the case of interest income purchased and sold on bonds, UK tax rules (the 'Accrued Income Scheme') would ultimately bring in the same measure of 'earned' income as would be recognised by a fund that 'clean accounted' for such interest. However, timing differences will frequently occur as regards the account periods of the fund in which the related income or income deduction is recognised for (i) accounting, and (ii) UK equivalent profit purposes. Whereas the Inland Revenue have, in the past, often accepted the absence of technical adjustments under the Accrued Income Scheme, current guidance is that such adjustments may, in the future, be required if material amounts are involved. This is more likely to be the case for bond funds or subfunds than for equity or balanced funds.

(h) Gains realised on 'relevant discounted securities' (defined as securities issued at a discount to maturity in excess of 15% or, where the life of the security is less than 30 years, in excess of half the life of the security expressed as a percentage) must be included.

(i) Gains realised on the disposal of holdings in non-qualifying offshore funds must be included, together with any 'equalisation' gains on the disposal of holdings in distributing offshore funds that operate equalisation. The gains arising on such disposals are treated as income for the purposes of the UK equivalent profit calculation, and not as capital gains.

(j) Any profits derived from transactions deemed to be in the nature of trade will fall to be included in the calculation of the fund's UK equivalent profits. A discussion of the criteria used in determining whether a transaction of purchase and sale is a trading, as opposed to an investment transaction, is contained in **4.62** et seq above.

(k) Profits from commodity dealings are subject to special treatment, in that one half of any such income (net of associated expenditure calculated on a just and reasonable basis) is left out of account for the purpose of calculating both the fund's accounts income and its UK equivalent profits. Any net loss from commodity dealings remains unadjusted in each case. (Commodities do not include currency, debts, or assets of a financial nature but include tangible assets which are dealt with on a commodity exchange, including respective futures and options trading eg coffee, sugar etc.)

2 Investment restrictions

4.102 As indicated earlier, certification does not depend solely on adequate distributions of income. The investment restrictions contained in the legislation mean that additional consideration has to be given to the structure and content of the fund's portfolio.

In summary, there are three fundamental rules on investment restrictions:

(a) At no time in the account period must more than 5% by value of the assets of the fund consist of interests in other, non-qualifying offshore funds. Investments in other offshore funds that are, or could be certified as distributing funds for their corresponding account periods, are ignored for the purposes of both this, and the other investment limits; but the fund must then impute to itself the appropriate share of the investments of the underlying fund, and its UK equivalent profits must be increased by its proportionate share of any amount by which the underlying fund's distributions fall short of that fund's own UK equivalent profits.

(b) At no time in the account period must more than 10% by value of the assets of the fund consist of interests in a single company (relaxed to 20% for investments in non-financial trading companies). Importantly, this limit is fixed on the most recent occasion on which an investment in the relevant company was acquired, or increased, for consideration in money or money's worth. Thus, any subsequent movement in the market value of the investment as a proportion of the value of the fund's overall assets is ignored.

(c) At no time in the account period must the assets of the fund include more than 10% of any class of the issued share capital in any company (relaxed to 50% for investments in non-financial trading companies).

Care must be taken in determining whether the extended investment limit applies to an investment in a non-financial trading company, as the Inland Revenue have indicated that they will look to the activities of the company in which the investment is directly made. Thus an investment in the holding company of an otherwise non-financial trading group would not be viewed as qualifying for the relaxation.

4.103 There are specific relaxations of the investment limits for an offshore fund's investment in a wholly-owned subsidiary company, and in a company associated with the management of the fund or dealings in its shares.

There is also a specific relaxation for investments that would breach rule (c) above, but do not, together with any investment in non-qualifying offshore funds, amount to more than 5% by value of the fund's assets.

Finally, the Inland Revenue have statutory discretion to disregard a breach of any of the investment limits if they are satisfied that the failure occurred inadvertently and was remedied without unreasonable delay.

Certification procedure

4.104   To obtain certification as a distributing fund for an account period, an offshore fund must make a formal application to the Inland Revenue within six months of the end of that period, or at such time as may be allowed at the Revenue's discretion.

The application should be accompanied by the final audited accounts of the fund covering the relevant period, which should consist of a balance sheet, income and expenditure account and investors' report, together with certain other information, including a calculation of the fund's UK equivalent profits and details of actual or planned distributions.

The Revenue have recently published a pro forma application, whose use is recommended.

Specific issues

Equalisation

4.105   Income 'equalisation' is a method adopted by virtually all UK authorised funds, and also many offshore open-ended funds, for arranging that, on the occasion of each income distribution, the same total amount per share/unit is distributed to each investor in the fund, irrespective of the fact that they may have acquired shares/units in the fund since the previous distribution date, whilst also ensuring that an investor only receives his share of that income which has been earned by the fund during his period of ownership of fund shares/units.

Under equalisation arrangements, that part of the overall purchase price paid by an incoming investor which comprises fund income earned since the date of the previous distribution is credited to the fund's income account and returned to the relevant investor in capital form at the next distribution date, together with the income earned since the investor entered the fund.

4.106   It is a feature of funds that operate equalisation (and most probably of those that do not) that the redemption price paid to an outgoing investor includes an amount reflecting the accrued income of the fund since the previous distribution date. In the absence of a statutory tax rule on this particular point, it is possible that the payment of such accrued income by the fund might constitute a capital payment. Certainly the Inland Revenue appear to have taken this view when developing the offshore fund rules, as a specific provision is incorporated that deems such a payment of accrued income on a share etc redemption to be income taxable on a UK investor, and equally deems a qualifying income distribution to have been made by the fund. The problem is that this provision only applies if the fund in question operates equalisation arrangements. Thus, an offshore fund that does not operate equalisation, but makes a payment of accrued income on the occasion of a share etc redemption, may find itself in difficulties as regards satisfying the distribution test for a period during which it has suffered disproportionately high redemptions, since it will have utilised a significant part of its otherwise distributable income through earlier payments that could well be deemed to be capital payments.

Dividend reinvestment schemes

4.107   Dividend reinvestment schemes are a common feature of offshore funds that wish to satisfy the conditions for UK distributor status, while offering their investors a ready means of retaining their income within the fund. This is achieved by making an income distribution, but immediately reinvesting the distribution in additional fund shares. A variation on this theme would be to reinvest the distribution in such a way as to add to the value of existing shares in the fund.

Inland Revenue guidance states: 'a Fund that operates a reinvestment mechanism must meet the criteria that it has *"paid"* a distribution that is capable of being construed as income for UK tax purposes'.

The Revenue have taken the view that, provided the distribution passes out of the fund's control, and into the hands of a third party, who can clearly be seen to receive the distribution and to reinvest it in further shares/units (or to increase the capital value of the existing shares/units) on behalf of the relevant shareholder, this would satisfy their definition of 'paid'.

Care should therefore be taken, when establishing arrangements for 'automatic' dividend reinvestment, that the arrangements achieve the desired effect. A good litmus test is whether, in the exceptional case that a particular investor might want his 'agent' to actually pay over his distribution in cash, it would be possible to do so.

Umbrella funds

4.108   *ICTA 1988, s 760(3)(d)* creates an additional requirement for certification based on the actual structure of the fund. If, at any time in the relevant account period, there is more than one class of material interest in the offshore fund, then each class must receive full distribution benefits before the whole fund can be certified. For this purpose, each class of interest, together with attributable assets and income, should be treated as though it were a separate offshore fund, and must demonstrate that a full distribution policy has been followed.

Consequently, each subfund of an umbrella fund must have satisfied its notional distribution test before the umbrella as a whole can be certified as a distributing fund. Equally, an offshore fund (or subfund) that issues different classes of share capital that share in a common pool of assets, but are distinct in terms of currency, management charges etc, must be able to demonstrate that a notional segregation of the fund's assets and income amongst the various share classes would result in each class receiving full distribution benefits. For this reason, corporate offshore funds that issue both distribution and accumulation shares are, under the current rules, unable to obtain distributor status (other than by default, in the event that the fund has no income to distribute), as qualifying income distributions will not be made on the accumulation shares. (See, however, **4.110** below.)

4.109   This requirement to distribute 85% of the income of each subfund in order for the umbrella fund as a whole to obtain distributor status has been one of the main criticisms of the offshore funds regime. It prevents fund promoters from operating a single fund structure that can offer 'distributing' subfunds or share classes to certain investors (ie UK investors) and 'accumulating' subfunds or share classes to other investors.

It should be noted that whereas the distribution test is applied to each and every subfund, the investment limits are considered by reference to the assets of the whole umbrella, rather than by reference to the assets of each subfund individually.

Transparent funds

4.110   As will be seen in **CHAPTER 13**, the offshore fund rules can only apply to a UK investor on the disposal (or deemed disposal) of a relevant interest in an offshore fund that would also constitute the disposal of an asset for UK capital gains tax purposes.

Offshore funds that are viewed as transparent for UK capital gains tax purposes (for example, most offshore limited partnerships) will, in principle therefore, have no reason to apply for UK distributor status, as UK investors are treated as owning fractional shares of the fund's underlying assets (and, as such, entitled to their share of income and gains therefrom as these arise within the fund), rather than a capital gains asset comprised of an interest in the fund itself. Technically, the same analysis would apply in the case of a contractual fund such as a Luxembourg FCP, although given our earlier remarks about how UK investors are sometimes taxed in practice (ie as though they held interests in a corporate fund), it would not be surprising to find that certain such investment funds do apply for distributor status.

A qualification to the above is where the actual or potential distributor status of a tax-transparent offshore partnership or FCP becomes a factor in determining the ability of another offshore fund that invests in the partnership or FCP to obtain distributor status itself, by virtue of the restriction in the amount that may be invested in other non-qualifying offshore funds. This is despite the fact that the transparent nature of the underlying fund would prevent any income roll-up at the lower tier.

Despite the legal entitlements of their unitholders, UK investors in most offshore unit trusts are treated for UK capital gains tax purposes as though they held shares in an offshore company (*TCGA 1992, s 99*). Thus, offshore funds must, as a rule, seek and obtain UK distributor status if they wish to preserve the relevant UK tax benefits for their UK investors. However, as will be seen from the discussion in CHAPTER 13, UK unitholders in an offshore unit trust will, in practice, generally be taxed as though they were fully entitled to (and taxable on) their shares of the fund's income at the time of each periodic distribution or accumulation of that income. Consequently, *ICTA 1988, Sch 27 para 3* will apply so as not to require a cash distribution in order for the fund to satisfy the distribution test. However, the unit trust must still adhere to the various investment limits if it is to be certified as a distributing fund.

The Future

Consultation process on the offshore funds regime

4.111 On 22 April 2002, the Inland Revenue issued a consultation document confirming the Government's commitment to review and, if appropriate, make changes to the current offshore funds regime to reflect market developments since the original rules were introduced in 1984.

The Government confirmed that the initial aim of the legislation still remained relevant today, ie to prevent investors using offshore funds to reduce, or even eliminate the tax they would otherwise pay on their savings income. At the same time, however, they recognised that there have been significant changes since 1984 in the commercial and regulatory environment in which many funds operate which mean that the existing rules may no longer be appropriate. They also recognised the importance of having a UK tax regime that should be easy to understand and comply with, and which should allow the fund management industry to promote funds internationally without unnecessary duplication of fund ranges and undue compliance burdens.

The present legislation has, in the view of many, imposed levels of compliance which are inconsistent with the free movement of financial services within the European Union, and constitute unfair discrimination. Although there was nothing in the consultation document which overtly acknowledged this complaint, it was significant that the document made reference to the fact that any legislative change should be fully compliant with EC law.

4.112 The Inland Revenue identified four distinct routes for the future of the offshore funds legislation:

- No change to the existing legislation; or

- Abolition of the existing legislation without replacement; or

- Reform of the existing regime to counter the most significant problems encountered to date; or

- Replacement of the existing regime with a brand new regime.

A large number of interested parties took the opportunity to respond to the Inland Revenue's request for responses on each of these suggestions.

The Inland Revenue published these responses on 27 November 2002 and it was clear from their paper that views expressed had been many and diverse. There were strong recommendations to simply dispense with the legislation, while other commentators wanted the existing regime to be modified only (eg to allow subfunds of umbrella funds to be certified in their own right). Others wanted the regime to be replaced by an information provision regime (highly topical in light of the Savings Directive).

What does seem unlikely is that the Inland Revenue will simply abolish the regime without replacement, as the Government believes that offshore funds would then be at an advantage to their UK counterparts. In addition it would seem unlikely for the offshore regime to remain as it is in light of recent successful European Court of Justice cases against the free movement of capital throughout the EU, and the clear impediments to commercial business that are contained in the present rules.

Perhaps unsurprisingly, the Revenue's paper indicated that further consultation was needed, and looked forward to the introduction of changes in *Finance Act 2004*. At the time of writing (autumn 2003), it has become apparent that the Revenue's review of the taxation of offshore funds is now being influenced by a wider review of the taxation of savings and investment (including the taxation of onshore funds), and other developments such as corporate tax reform. Any legislative change on offshore funds in 2004 is therefore likely to be limited to some 'quick fixes', pending the announcement of a permanent (and integrated) future approach.

UCITS III

Introduction

4.113   Two new EU directives (together commonly known as 'UCITS III') came into force with their publication in the Official Journal of the European Communities on 13 February 2002, with a view to widening:

(i) the scope of investment products available to co-ordinated UCITS (the 'Product Directive' – Directive *2001/108/EC* of the European Parliament and of the Council of 21 January 2002 amending Council Directive *85/611/EEC* on the co-ordination of laws, regulations and administrative provisions relating to undertakings for collective investment in transferable securities, with regard to investments of UCITS); and

(ii) the scope of activities which may be carried out by management companies of co-ordinated UCITS (the 'Management Company Directive' – Directive *2001/107/EC* of the European Parliament and of the Council of 21 January 2002 amending Council Directive *85/611/EEC* on the co-ordination of laws, regulations and administrative provisions relating to undertakings for collective investment in transferable securities, with a view to regulating management companies and simplified prospectuses).

Both directives modify the earlier Directive *85/611/EEC* ('UCITS I' – Directive *85/611/EEC* of 20 December 1985 on the co-ordination of laws, regulations and administrative provisions relating to undertakings for collective investment in transferable securities), and member states were required to implement them in their national laws before 13 August 2003, and to start effectively applying them by 13 February 2004. A UCITS established prior to 13 February 2002 will have to comply with the national legislation from 13 February 2007. However, a UCITS authorised after 13 February 2002 must comply with the provisions by 13 February 2004. The Management Company Directive's transitional provisions allow management companies of UCITS authorised before 13 February 2004 to continue under the existing rules until 13 February 2007. After that time, compliance with the Directive becomes mandatory. The transitional provisions of both Directives are, however, subject to implementation by member states in their national law, and member states may adopt more stringent requirements.

The Product Directive

4.114   The Product Directive substantially extends the instruments in which a UCITS fund can invest. In addition to investments in shares and bonds, UCITS will now be permitted to invest in money market instruments, cash instruments, bank deposits and other investment funds. Furthermore, the rules on the use of financial derivatives traded on regulated or over-the-counter ('OTC') markets are eased, as are the investment restrictions applying to funds that replicate indexes. This means that money market funds, cash funds, funds of funds and index funds will now benefit, under certain conditions, from the 'European passport'.

Money market instruments

4.115   Money market instruments are defined as 'instruments normally dealt in on the money markets which are liquid, and have a value which can be accurately determined at any time'.

Deposits

4.116   Deposits will be allowed with credit institutions from member states and certain credit institutions from non-EU countries. A co-ordinated UCITS may not invest more than 20% of its net assets in deposits made with the same body.

Units of investment funds

4.117   For investments in units of investment funds, the Product Directive states that a UCITS may acquire the units of other UCITS and collective investment undertakings provided that no more than 10% of its net assets are invested in units of a single co-ordinated UCITS or other collective investment undertaking. Member states may raise this limit to a maximum of 20%. The Product Directive states that target funds are not eligible if they in turn invest more than 10% of their net assets in other undertakings for collective investment.

Investments made in non-UCITS funds may not exceed, in aggregate, 30% of the net assets of the coordinated UCITS. However, non-UCITS are eligible investments only to the extent that they are subject to prudential supervision and a level of shareholder protection similar to that of a UCITS, thereby ruling out the possibility of UCITS funds being able to invest in hedge funds.

Derivatives

4.118   The Product Directive introduces rules for the use of derivatives. In order to assess a UCITS's exposure to derivatives, a UCITS management company or investment company must adopt a risk management process to monitor and measure the risk of the UCITS's derivatives positions and their contribution to the overall risk profile of the UCITS.

Index tracker funds

4.119   The Product Directive also introduces more flexible risk spreading rules for UCITS whose investment objective is to replicate the composition of certain stock or debt securities indices. Previously, UCITS index tracker funds encountered difficulties in circumstances where the UCITS was restricted from investing more than 10% in any one issuer and where the weighting of a particular stock in an index rose above 10%. The Product Directive now permits UCITS to raise this limit to 20% in any one issuer (and 35% in certain circumstances) where, according to the fund's rules, the objective is to replicate the composition of the index and provided the index is appropriately recognised and published.

Group concept

4.120   Apart from imposing various spread requirements for the instruments mentioned above, the Product Directive also introduces the concept of a group limit in that companies which are included in the same group (defined as those companies required to be consolidated under the relevant directive or International Accounting Standards) are regarded as a single body for the purpose of calculating most investment limits prescribed by the Product Directive.

Non-EU subsidiary companies

4.121   A significant provision in the Product Directive is that a UCITS cannot set up a subsidiary in a non-EU member state as an investment vehicle, and therefore UCITS funds can no longer establish subsidiary vehicles in jurisdictions such as Mauritius and Cyprus to minimise withholding taxes (see earlier discussion as regards double tax treaty access at **4.49** et seq). UCITS funds authorised before 13 February 2002 will have until 13 February 2007 to dispose of their investments in these vehicles.

While UCITS funds are no longer able to use non-EU subsidiary companies, the ability to invest in other investment funds means that it may still be possible to structure a UCITS fund to give it better access to tax treaties.

The Management Company Directive

4.122   The Management Company Directive introduces a more regulated environment for the management companies of UCITS, and establishes equivalent market access rules, operating conditions and capital adequacy requirements. The Management Company Directive also introduces a passport for UCITS management companies, along the lines of the passport provided to investment firms by the Investment Services Directive (Council Directive *93/22/EEC* of 10 May 1993 on investment services in the securities field). With this passport, a UCITS management company can offer certain services (as permitted by the Management Company Directive, and for which it has been authorised in its home state) in other member states through the establishment of a branch or the provision of cross-border services. Thus for example, in principle, it will be possible for corporate UCITS such as UK OEICs to be managed by a Dublin-based management company. This passport will not extend to the cross-border management of a non-corporate UCITS. The Management Company Directive also authorises management companies to carry out other activities, such as managing private portfolios or pension fund assets.

The Directive also introduces a harmonised simplified prospectus that must be produced in addition to the full prospectus and can be used in any country where the fund is sold, simply by translating it into the local language. Prospectuses will be more marketing-orientated and less legalistic, giving a clear and easily understandable description of the fund, including its overall risk profile and investor profile. Member states will no longer be able to demand additional information or documentation.

Conclusion

4.123   In conclusion, although member states are left to interpret many of the provisions on a local basis, the new Directives should benefit investors by extending their choice of UCITS investment products and are a further step towards a single European investment funds market.

5   Onshore Limited Partnerships as Investment Funds

John Watson

Ashurst Morris Crisp

The BVCA Memorandum

5.1   Since 1987 the number of registered English limited partnerships has increased sevenfold. This extraordinary upsurge in use reflects the acceptance of the limited partnership as an investment vehicle following the publication by the British Venture Capital Association in 1987 of a 'Statement approved by the Inland Revenue and the Department of Trade and Industry on the use of limited partnerships as venture capital investment funds' ('the BVCA Memorandum'). The memorandum is available on the website of the British Venture Capital Association and can also be found, shorn of its final annexes, at paragraph 3258 of the Inland Revenue's Company Tax Manual.

The BVCA Memorandum was the culmination of a joint initiative between the venture capital industry and the authorities to promote an effective onshore fund vehicle; it sets out the treatment of limited partnerships and their members from a tax and regulatory point of view. It has been relied on by the promoters of private equity funds since 1987 and, although it states in terms that it sets out an agreement with the Inland Revenue as to the tax treatments of partnerships used 'as vehicles for raising funds wholly or partly for equity investment in unquoted companies', the insights it gives into official thinking have enabled the promoters of partnerships formed as funds to hold other types of asset to predict their tax treatment as well.

5.2   The issues which inhibited the use of limited partnerships as investment funds prior to 1987 arose whether the partnerships invested in private equity, debt or land and the views expressed in the BVCA Memorandum shed light on the treatment of limited partnership funds investing in all these areas. Nonetheless, it is always important to keep in mind whether a particular fund is within the intended scope of the memorandum, in which case a departure from the memorandum by the authorities might be the foundation of an action for judicial review, or whether the memorandum is simply being used as an indication of official views. Where a partnership's investments are other than unquoted equity – for example it invests in quoted companies, in mezzanine debt or in land – comfort drawn from the memorandum clearly falls into the latter category. Less obviously, perhaps, a partnership only truly falls within the scope of the memorandum if it is used to raise funds for investment and its structure is broadly analogous to that set out in Annexe A to the memorandum.

5.3   Paragraph 2.1 of Annex A makes it clear that the Revenue may not follow the BVCA Memorandum where there is a 'material deviation' from the structure set out at paragraph 2.2, but without saying what a material deviation is. In fact, no modern venture capital fund is ever constructed entirely as set out in para 2.2 so there will always be some element of deviation. The question is when that deviation becomes material.

At paragraph 5 of Annex A it was stated that for the period of twelve months from the publication of the memorandum the Inland Revenue would do its best to comment on variations from the guidelines. Although this period has long expired, the fact that the Inland Revenue offered this facility at all indicates that deviations were always expected; the fact that there have been so few disputes over the years indicates that those deviations have to be wide before they become material. It seems therefore that a deviation in form will only result in the guidelines being disapplied where it goes to the nature of the fund in question.

5.4   It should be noted those parts of the guidelines which deal with taxation under the *Income Tax (Earnings and Pensions) Act 2003* (ie paragraph 2 of the main text of the memorandum and paragraph 3 of Annex A) have been overtaken by the enactment of the new regime for 'employment-related securities' introduced by *Finance Act 2003*. Comments on the way in which the new regime applies to carried interest in private equity funds will be found below. It is not as yet clear to what extent similar principles will be applied to limited partnership funds generally.

The demands which shaped the fund structure

5.5   Before discussing how limited partnerships are used as investment funds it may be helpful to look at some of the commercial considerations which drive the use of the partnership structure and how these factors have influenced its development. Although limited partnerships can be used to hold most types of asset, their main use is to hold assets which are relatively illiquid – such as shares in private companies or land. Since the development of the limited partnership fund structure has been led by the private equity industry, it may be helpful to analyse the advantages of limited partnerships by reference to the requirements of those who wish to invest in that asset class.

5.6   By their very nature, investments in private equity are unquoted and in the case of any investment in an unquoted company both the achievement of a return and the recovery of the capital invested depend upon an exit being achieved; exits normally takes the form of a sale or listing and the requirement for such a transaction introduces an element of risk additional to that present in, say, a quoted portfolio. This additional risk, and indeed the general risk intrinsic to investment in immature assets, can be controlled in two ways:

- by spreading investment over a wide portfolio. Obviously this underlines the requirement for a fund; and

● by managing the development of each investment and its progress towards exit. The equity risk endemic in private equity investment needs to be balanced by an involvement in management. This may mean control; alternatively, it may mean board representation backed by rights to make or veto particular decisions. In either case the rights need to be exercised by individuals with experience in this type of investment. Not every institution has the relevant experience. By participating in a fund the institution effectively delegates this function to the fund manager.

5.7 Quite apart from creating a demand for funds, the nature of private equity dictates the form which the fund structure must take. Each investment is bespoke and has to be sourced, negotiated and agreed in a process which will take weeks or months. Of necessity then, a private equity portfolio is assembled over a period – and most funds now provide a window, known as the 'investment period', of three to five years for this to occur. It would suit nobody for investors' funds to be drawn down before the monies are needed. Investors would not wish to provide money which will sit on deposit until the right opportunity arises: managers would not want to hold funds which are not invested in private equity. To do so would dilute their returns and thus inhibit their ability to raise further funds in future. It follows that a successful fund structure should enable investors to make a commitment initially and for that commitment to be drawn down as and when investment opportunities arise.

5.8 Looking at the other end of the process, successful private equity investments are generally realised when a favourable sale or floatation can be achieved. A direct investor will reap his rewards at that point and will then decide whether to reinvest in private equity or to use the monies realised elsewhere. Generally speaking, private equity funds are designed to mirror this. On realisation of an investment, the proceeds (whether in cash or in quoted shares) are returned to the investors who will make their own decisions on whether to invest in a successor fund. It is unusual for the manager to have power to reinvest, save in special cases such as where an investment is syndicated or realised within a short period of its acquisition.

Of course there are exceptions. A number of UK houses operate highly successful investment trusts where monies realised are reinvested in private equity. Such entities have the advantage that their shares are readily realisable and may be held by retail investors; still the preferred institutional model is an open-ended one and it is this model on which the limited partnership funds discussed in this chapter are based.

5.9 Much of what is said above in relation to private equity can be said in relation to other classes of illiquid asset. For example, investments in property take a long time to make and cannot be realised until a purchaser has been found. Investments in mezzanine debt are also bespoke and their realisation is likely to depend upon the attitude of the management and equity holders of the investee companies.

This chapter deals with limited partnership funds managed from the UK. Limited partnerships managed from outside the UK are dealt with separately at CHAPTER **6**.

Why partnerships?

5.10   It is often said that the main attraction of the limited partnership as a vehicle is that it delivers tax transparency and, before turning to the detail of the structure, it is worth reflecting on this statement.

In appraising a fund structure, a good starting point is to ask the general question whether institutions investing through the fund will suffer more tax than would have been borne if those institutions had invested direct. Unless the answer to that question is 'no' or 'not materially' (and where a fund is being invested wholly for capital growth, 'not materially' might mean 'only in respect of income') the structure will probably not be a viable one.

In fact the answer to the question depends on the tax profile of the investors. Take, for example, a UK pension fund. By virtue of its exempt approved status such an investor will not pay UK tax on investment income or capital gains. To a pension fund, any fund structure which involves tax being levied on gains realised on the portfolio will be unacceptable because it will give a materially worse tax treatment than direct investment. It follows that a pension fund will only invest in a fund structured as a UK company if it is clear that the capital gains of that company will escape tax – for instance because it only invests in substantial shareholdings on the disposal of which relief under the *TCGA 1992, Sch 7AC* should be available. On the other hand a corporate investor, which would pay tax on income and gains derived from a real property portfolio at 30%, may be content for a property fund vehicle to pay corporation tax provided that no further tax arises on distribution.

5.11   It is in the nature of fund-raising that the tax profile of investors will differ; indeed it will often not be possible to predict the spread of investors until much of the marketing has been completed. To an extent, then, a successful fund structure has to be efficient in the general sense that it will be able to accommodate investors of all likely types.

It is the words 'all likely types' which set the test against which the limited partnership must be measured. At first sight the results are mixed. Limited partnerships work for UK institutions investing in UK assets because the UK regards them as tax transparent, but that treatment is by no means universal. In France and Italy, for example, the tax authorities regard them as opaque. The Netherlands will only regard them as transparent if special provisions are made to align them with the local closed CV. Nonetheless they are the chosen vehicle of the US private equity industry and, as a result of this, international investors are familiar with them and have set themselves up in such a manner that they are able to participate as partners. In the end those promoters who structure their funds as limited partnerships will encounter few surprises when those funds are offered to investors and that is a very considerable commercial advantage.

5.12   The prominence of limited partnerships as private equity funds has also meant that standard solutions have emerged to deal with those difficulties which their use can cause at the level of the investment. For example the fact that the French authorities regard a limited partnership as a taxable entity which has no treaty protection is generally dealt with by the interposition of a Luxembourg holding company above an investment in a French company. *FA 2002* introduced special amendments to those provisions of the loan relationships regime which defer the tax deduction for certain accrued interest and discounts on the borrowings of close companies until it is actually paid. These amendments, now found at *FA 1996, Sch 9 paras 2(1B)* and *18(1)(c)*, provide exemptions for debt owned by 'a limited partnership which is collective investment scheme within the meaning of *section 235* of *Financial Services and Markets Act 2000*'. Accordingly, UK close companies may obtain a deduction for accruing discount or rolled-up interest on debt owed to limited partnerships which hold their equity in circumstances where such a deduction would not be available if the equity and securities were held directly by investors.

5.13   Following the introduction of the substantial shareholding exemption, also by *FA 2002*, one might consider a UK investment company as an alternative structure for certain types of private equity fund. However, lack of experience of the substantial shareholding exemption and the consciousness that moving away from the limited partnership is going 'off piste' has so far inhibited the development of this route. The international private equity community has become comfortable with the limited partnership and it will take a lot to move them away from it.

The requirements for a business

5.14   Before the limited partnership could be adopted as a vehicle for UK investment funds, a number of preliminary issues had to be dealt with. The first of these was whether investment could amount to a business for the purposes of *Partnership Act 1890, s 1(1)*. *Section 1(1)* defines partnership as being 'the relation which subsists between persons carrying on a business in common with a view of profit'. It follows that where there is no business there cannot be a partnership. Such a conclusion would result in the purported partnership being a company within *ICTA 1988, s 832*, with corporation tax charged on its profits. (For an example of this treatment, see *Blackpool Morton Rotary Club v Martin* 62 TC 686.)

The term 'business' is defined by *Partnership Act 1890, s 45* as *including* 'every trade, occupation or profession'. Clearly the natural meaning of the term goes further than this but, since *section 2(1)* of the Act specifies that 'joint tenancy, tenancy in common, joint property, common property or part-ownership does not of itself create a partnership as to anything so held or owned whether the tenants or owners do or do not share any profits made by the use thereby', it seems that an entirely passive holding of assets is not enough.

5.15   The latter principle is illustrated by the case of *Smith v Anderson (1880)* 15 Chancery 247 which examined the word 'business' in the context of its use in the *Companies Act 1862*. There is no reason to think that it is differently used in the *Partnership Act*. The case related to the establishment of a trust to make pooled investments in a high-risk portfolio of shares with the intention of spreading risk. The activities of the trust were insufficient to constitute a business. However, it should be noted that the trust intended to make changes to its investment portfolio only infrequently and that there were specific restrictions on the ability of the trustee to buy and sell portfolio companies.

Although there are probably some 'activities' which could never constitute a business, such as the holding of a particular investment, there is Canadian authority in the case of *A E Lepage Limited v Kamex Developments Limited* (1979) 2 SCR 155 for a distinction between those who intend to carry on a venture together and those who simply hold assets jointly through trustees. This suggests that in some cases the holding of investments would be a business if carried on in partnerships, although there would be no business if the investments were simply held by trustees. In the case of most funds investing in illiquid assets the institutions act together in a planned scheme of laying out money by way of investment and subsequent realisation. Certainly that seems to carry the hallmarks of business.

5.16   In the case of private equity, the BVCA Memorandum specifically addresses whether the business of investing in unquoted companies is sufficient to found a partnership business. Without giving any reasoning, paragraph 1.1 states:

> 'A limited partnership established for the purpose of raising funds for investment into companies will be regarded as carrying on a business and will represent a partnership within the definition in section 1 of the Partnership Act 1890 for the purposes of United Kingdom taxation.'

Two points should be noted here. First, whilst this statement was endorsed by both the Inland Revenue and the Department of Trade, it is only their view and has no legislative effect. Accordingly it is still open to third parties to argue that, in law, a fund does not carry on a business – although, bearing in mind the large number of funds established as partnerships over the last 15 years, a court might be reluctant to come to this conclusion.

Second, the statement refers specifically to 'investment into companies' and this, in view of the introduction to the BVCA Memorandum, may be taken as referable only to investment in unquoted equity. So it gives no comfort in respect of limited partnerships formed to hold other asset classes such as investment in land or buildings. Here a view has to be taken on the law but, as indicated above, it would be surprising if a properly organised partnership investment programme did not involve a business.

Finally it should be observed that the statement does not deal with the possibility that a partnership is formed for the sole purpose of holding the carried interest in another partnership. Indeed, in the author's view, a single passive holding of this nature would probably not amount to a business at all.

Avoiding treatment as a unit trust

5.17   The second preliminary issue is whether or not a limited partnership formed to hold an investment portfolio could amount to a unit trust under what is now *FSMA 2000, s 237*. Were that the case, tax transparency would not be available at all because in the case of an unauthorised unit trust (that is, a unit trust other than authorised unit trust – the latter would not be relevant in this context):

(a)   the unit trust is treated for the purposes of capital gains tax as if it were a company and the rights of the unitholders were shares in that company (*TCGA 1992, s 99*). The gains of the trust are charged, however, to capital gains tax rather than to corporation tax. It follows that, subject to the exception mentioned below, an unauthorised unit trust which is resident in the UK will pay capital gains tax whenever a gain is realised on its assets. That would be a highly undesirable impost for an investment fund; and

(b)   where the trustees of the unit trust are resident in the UK, *ICTA 1988, s 469* requires them to pay income tax on their income at the basic rate. That may be less serious than the capital gains tax charge both because illiquid portfolios often aim to generate capital gains rather than income and because the mechanisms of the income tax regime will generally allow investors to obtain credit in respect of that tax.

5.18   The effect of the capital gains tax treatment is to make it impracticable to use a UK unauthorised unit trust as a fund vehicle unless it benefits from the exemption from the capital gains tax charge provided by *TCGA 1992, s 100(2)*. That exemption only applies where all units are held by unitholders who are themselves exempt from tax on their capital gains (other than by reason of non-residence); accordingly, it would not typically fit the requirement of a private equity fund which, even in the relatively unusual circumstance that all the investors are UK institutions with the relevant exemption, would normally give direct participation to a taxable general partner and to individuals involved in management.

5.19   It is clearly essential that a limited partnership used as a fund should not be categorised as a unit trust and concerns on this score led to regulations being laid in 1988 to exclude 'a limited partnership scheme' from the definition of 'unit trust scheme' for the purposes of capital gains tax (*CGT (Definition of Unit Trust Scheme) Regulations 1988 (SI 1988/266)*), income tax (*IT (Definition of Unit Trust Scheme) Regulations 1988 (SI 1988/267)*), and stamp duty and stamp duty reserve tax (*Stamp Duty and Stamp Duty Reserve Tax (Definitions of Unit Trust Scheme) Regulations 1988 (SI 1988/268)*); in each set of regulations 'limited partnership scheme' is defined as 'a unit trust scheme ... when the scheme property is held on trust for the general partners and the limited partners in a limited partnership'. At first sight this is curious because partnership assets are not generally held on trust unless they comprise land, when *Partnership Act 1890, s 20(2)* imposes a statutory trust. The key to the drafting lies in *FSMA 2000, s 237* which defines a unit trust as 'a collective investment scheme under which the property is held on trust for the participants'.

It will be seen that this provision dovetails with the definition used in the regulations so that there is no room for a limited partnership to fall down the middle and lose its tax transparency. If a partnership does not involve the assets being held on trust, it will not be a unit trust. If it does involve assets being held on trust, the exemptions conferred by the regulations will apply.

5.20   It is important to note that in each set of regulations the expression 'limited partnership' is restricted to a limited partnership registered under the *Limited Partnerships Act 1907*. Where there is no registration (for example if the partnership is established overseas), whether a partnership is treated as a unit trust for tax purposes depends solely on whether the definition in *FSMA 2000, s 237* is satisfied. In the case of limited partnerships which hold shares, there would normally only be a trust if the partnership holds them through a nominee company. Clearly this fact on its own cannot make such a partnership a unit trust because otherwise unit trust status would vary as assets were transferred to or from the nominee. In the author's view a collective investment scheme only becomes a unit trust if the trust delineates the rights of the partners themselves. On that basis one would not expect a partnership to become a unit trust simply because it held interests in land.

Trading for tax purposes

5.21   Generally speaking, the partners in a UK investment partnership will expect profits to be taxed in the UK as investment income and capital gains rather than under Case 1 of Schedule D.

The question of how the profits are to be taxed is, of course, one which falls to be determined at the level of the partners rather than at the level of the partnership because, as has been mentioned, partnerships are transparent for UK tax purposes. That is to say that the profits are attributed to the partners and taxed in their hands. Before we turn to the question of when an investor's share of profits from an investment partnership are likely to be taxed as the profits of a trade, it may be helpful to show the importance of that question by explaining the effect which the characterisation of partnership profits as trading income would have on partners.

5.22   A UK partner, will in the absence of a specific exemption, pay tax on its share of gains realised by the fund on the disposal of investments either as capital or as income. The headline rates of tax on capital and income being the same, it might be thought that whether such gains are trading profit or capital gains was academic. In fact that is not the case at all. Although the headline rates may be similar, the tax base is different for the two regimes. For example:

(a)   capital gains will be reduced by indexation allowance (in the case of companies) or taper relief (in the case of individuals and settlements). Neither relief is available in a tax computation relating to trading profits;

(b)   where a UK resident company receives a dividend from UK shares held as an investment, that dividend will be exempt from tax by virtue of *ICTA*

1988, s 208. Where the recipient is a dealer in securities, the dividend will be brought into account in computing his trading profit by virtue of *ICTA 1988, s 95*;

(c)   individuals have separate allowances for income and capital gains;

(d)   the rules for relieving trading losses and capital losses are different.

5.23   Where a UK partner benefits from a specific exemption, the difference between the two treatments is likely to be even more pronounced. Certain categories of UK investor are exempt from tax on capital gains; however, those which commonly arise in practice benefit from no matching exemption for trading profits. In particular:

(a)   an exempt approved pension scheme is exempt from capital gains tax under *TCGA 1992, s 271(5)*, but the matching income tax exemption conferred by *ICTA 1988, s 592* only covers 'income derived from investments or deposits' held for the purposes of the scheme. That would not cover trading profits;

(b)   *TCGA 1992, s 100* confers exemption from corporation tax on capital gains on an authorised unit trust or an investment trust. There is no corresponding exemption from corporation tax on trading profits; and

(c)   although the capital gains of charities benefit from the exemption under *TCGA 1992, s 256*, the exemption for trading profits conferred by *ICTA 1988, s 505(1)* is very limited and would not cover profits made by dealing in securities.

Any of these investors is likely to regard the characterisation of the profits which it derives from a partnership as trading profits as disastrous.

5.24   For a non-resident member of a UK partnership, the issue is also important. If no trade is carried on it should not pay UK tax on its share of partnership profit, save insofar as it may bear UK withholding tax on UK interest. If, however, that partner is carrying on a trade and the investments made by the partnership are connected with that trade, the position is entirely different. In the case of a UK partnership, a non-resident partner which carries on a trade will be carrying it on through a UK branch or agency – or in the case of a corporate partner, a UK permanent establishment. On this basis its share of the partnership profits could be assessable to UK tax in one of two ways:

(a)   if the partnership or the partnership investments are current assets of the trade, profits will be assessable under Case 1 of Schedule D; and

(b)   if the investment in the partnership is a capital asset used for the purposes of the trade or the branch or permanent establishment, gains realised by the partnership will be subject to UK tax on chargeable gains.

Either way, the fact that a non-UK resident partner is trading is likely to result in gains on the partnership portfolio being taxed in the UK.

5.25   The tax regimes for both corporate and non-corporate investors allow tax due from a non-resident to be collected from that non-resident's UK representative, a term which could include the general partner either as agent or representing the partnership itself. That means that tax due on the non-resident's share of profits could be collected from the general partner and that the general partner must withhold monies to meet that tax from distributions. Since whether a partner's share of profits derives from a trade depends in part on the activities of that partner, it is a question which the general partner or manager of the fund itself will not be able to answer. Accordingly, it is usual to protect the partnership from any liability to tax in respect of profits of non-resident partners in two ways:

(a) by including in the partnership deed indemnities under which each partner is liable to indemnify the others for tax suffered on its behalf; and

(b) by including in the application form a warranty from each partner that it is not acquiring its interest in connection with an activity which amounts to trading for UK tax purposes. That ensures that the general partner is put on notice of any need to deduct and should also make it possible to avoid the need for deduction arising in practice. If it appears that a potential investor is carrying on a trade (for example if that investor is a dealer in securities, a bank or a general insurance company) it should be possible to arrange for that investor to participate in the partnership through a non-trading entity.

In the case of private equity funds a possible alternative approach to requiring trading investors to invest through a non-trading entity is to place reliance on the exemption for investment managers now found at *FA 2003, Sch 26* for corporate non-resident investors and *FA 1995, s 127* for non-corporates. The hedge fund industry has long used the exemption to avoid a UK tax charge where a non-resident uses a UK manager. Why should private equity funds not do the same?

5.26   On funds constructed on the standard model it is often difficult to see why the manager would not satisfy the terms of the exemption but there are features of private equity funds which fit ill with its terms. For example:

(a) the general partner itself is the agent of the investors but would appear to be neither independent in fact nor an investment manager; and

(b) the complex arrangements surrounding private equity funds may result in the manager failing one or more of the statutory tests.

Rather than get into this difficult area it is generally preferable simply to ensure that dealing entities do not make a direct investment. It should be noted that in any event the investment manager's exemption does not apply to property funds.

5.27   Additionally, trading status will adversely affect the position of a non-resident partner under any double tax treaty between its home jurisdiction and the UK. Typically, such treaties limit withholding tax on interest and permit a proportion of the tax credit attaching to UK dividends to be repaid. Since the drop in the level of the tax credit attaching to a dividend to one-ninth in April 1999, the latter reclaim has generally disappeared. Nonetheless if a partnership receives interest from a UK source, tax will be withheld from that interest at 20%. In these circumstances a treaty between the UK and the jurisdiction of the investor could enable a non-resident partner to reclaim all or part of the withholding tax provided that the interest is not connected with a UK permanent establishment of the investor. The UK Revenue have confirmed in writing that they would not regard the general partner of a private equity fund set up in accordance with the BVCA Memorandum as being a permanent establishment of a non-resident investor under an OECD-style double tax treaty, unless that non-resident investor is trading in respect of its participation in the fund.

Whether a private equity fund carries on a trade

5.28   For the above reasons it is important to establish whether an investor in an investment limited partnership carries on a trade. To determine whether this is the case two separate enquiries have to be made:

(a)   whether the business of the partnership is such that it can be regarded as trading; and

(b)   if this is not the case, whether the activities of the partner itself are such that it is holding its investment in the fund as trading stock, or at the least, as the capital asset of a trade.

5.29   First we will consider the activities of the partnership itself and again we will begin with unquoted shares. Generally speaking the holding of investments is not regarded as a trading activity, even where those investments are actively managed. That is particularly the case where the investments are held by an individual. In considering the positions of a private equity limited partnership, it is necessary to consider whether there is some specific feature of its activity which removes it from the investment category. The main features which might be regarded as pointing to trading are generally as follows:

(a)   the fact that the investments typically yield little or no income and are held with a view to a profit being realised on their disposal; and

(b)   the fact that the manager or investment adviser to the fund will typically work in the development of the target company.

5.30   The first of these factors is not as significant as it was. As long ago as 1986, Sir Nicholas Browne-Wilkinson said in *Marson v Morton* 1986 STC 463 at 472:

> 'It is true that in the Reinhold case the Court of Session did rely on the fact that there would be income in rents as a relevant factor, and in my judgement it plainly is a relevant factor. But in my judgment in 1986 it is not any longer self-evident that unless land is producing income it cannot

be an investment. The legal principle of course cannot change with the passage of time: but life does. Since the arrival of inflation and high rates of tax on income new approaches to investment have emerged putting the emphasis in investment on the making of capital profit at the expense of income yield. For example, the purchase of short-dated stocks giving a capital yield on redemption but no income has become commonplace. Similarly, split level investment trusts have been invented which produce capital profits on one type of share and income on another. Again, institutions now purchase works of art by way of investment. In my judgement those are plainly not trading deals; yet no income is produced from them. I can see no reason why land should be any different and the mere fact that land is not income-producing should not be decisive or even virtually decisive on the question whether it was bought as an investment.'

Many large institutions now also have private equity portfolios.

5.31   As to the second factor, it should be borne in mind that the work on the development of the target will generally be carried out by the manager's appointees to the company's board. This is a far cry from the work done by owners in those cases where activity has been taken to indicate a trade (eg *IRC v Livingstone* 11 TC 538, where a vessel was acquired and converted to steam prior to sale). Against this background it seems most unlikely that a court would regard the business of investing in private equity as a trade and it appears that the Inland Revenue share that view.

5.32   The BVCA Memorandum states at paragraph 1.4 that, save in the exceptional circumstances where a venture capital limited partnership is carrying on a business of lending money and the holding of shares is ancillary to that business, a limited partnership which 'purchases shares and securities with the intention of holding them as investments' will not be assessed on profits realised on those shares and securities under Case I of Schedule D. On a literal level, the fact that this confirmation only applies where the underlying shares or securities are acquired 'with the intention of holding them as investments' reduces its value. If one cannot decide whether a fund is trading, one is hardly likely to be able to decide whether it acquired its holdings by way of investment. Still, the passage does seem to indicate that 'normal' private equity investment will not be regarded as trading; so concerns on this score should only arise where the fund is doing something unusual such as taking arbitrage positions, acquiring shares when a short-term exit had already been prepared, acquiring shares for immediate on-sale etc. Typically then, the assumptions made in an opinion letter to the effect that the fund activity should not itself result in partners carrying on a trade might include:

(a) that the partnership will invest on terms common for investors in the venture capital industry;

(b) that investments will be made without any arrangements for a specific exit being in place;

(c) that the general expectation on making investments is that they will normally be held for somewhere in the region of [insert relevant figure] years and above; and

(d) that shares and securities which are to be realised in the short term, for example pursuant to underwriting arrangements or where it is proposed to syndicate, and which may be realised at a price greater than that paid for them, will be held in a specially formed company belonging to the partnerships and/or other co-investors. In fact, as is explained later (see **4.58**) this point is usually finessed by taking the carrying cost and any profit to the manager of the fund as a fee.

5.33   The test of whether the way in which the fund portfolio is managed indicates that a trade is being carried on will vary according to the asset class. One would expect most portfolios of securities to be judged by the above rules and these rules have been used to justify non-trading status in the case of funds holding mezzanine debt. Where the underlying assets comprise land, however, the position becomes more complex because of the variety of different situations which can arise. This is particularly the case where the land is to be developed, because the narrow line between development for letting but with an eye to the capital profit which may arise on the ultimate sale (normally investment) and developing to sell after boosting the value by pre-letting (probably trading) is hard to discern. It all depends on the facts.

5.34   Generally speaking the business of an investment fund will be carried on in a manner which ensures that it does not itself result in the partners carrying on a trade. If that is done, the only way in which the investors could hold their interests as current assets of a trade would be if they had dealing status themselves. It is of course possible that an interest in a fund will be held by a dealer as part of his trading stock. It is much more likely, however, that it will be held by either a bank or a general insurance company. Both banks and general insurance companies carry on trades for UK tax purposes and it follows that if such an entity participates in a fund, it will generally hold its interest in that fund as part of its trading stock. If it does this, all its gains on the fund will be taken to trading account. Life assurance companies also technically carry on a trade although in some cases they are taxed as investors. Generally the Revenue offer overseas life companies concessionary treatment in that provided certain conditions are satisfied their investment in a BVCA partnership is not treated as giving rise to a permanent establishment for the purposes of any double tax treaty constructed on the OECD model. This may enable them to invest in such a partnership without UK tax.

Tax transparency

5.35   The main feature of limited partnerships which is used to justify their role as a fund vehicle is that of tax transparency, and it is important to bear in mind here that transparency can arise in two quite different ways. First the nature of the entity itself may require that for tax purposes the income of each participant is simply a proportion of (or if there is only one participant, the whole of) the income of the entity. A good example of this can be found in the field of trusts, where for income tax purposes the holder of a life interest is regarded as entitled to the income which arises to the trustees. This type of transparency arises from the general nature of income tax and can be contrasted with the second type of transparency which is specifically laid down by statute.

5.36   In the case of partnerships, authority for the first type of transparency can be found in two cases dealing with double tax treaties. In *Padmore v IRC* 1989 STC 495 one issue was whether the profits derived by a UK individual from a Jersey partnership which carried on a trade on the Island were excluded from UK tax by paragraph 3(2) of the UK/Jersey treaty which exempted 'the industrial or commercial profits of a Jersey enterprise'. In deciding that they were Fox LJ held (at page 501) that:

'The source of the income of an individual partner is the same as the source of income for all the partners, namely the trading operations of the partnership. If a partner is entitled, as a partner, to a share of the income of the partnership and that income is itself exempted from United Kingdom tax, it seems to me that his share is similarly exempted in the absence of a direction to the contrary. That is because what he is entitled to (and what he would be taxed on if he were taxed) is a share of the profits of the enterprise and the Arrangement says that the profits of the enterprise are not subject to United Kingdom tax.'

In the later case of *Memec v IRC* 1998 STC 754 it was accepted by all parties that this principle applied to English and Scottish partnerships. (See the judgment of the Peter Gibson LJ at 763(g).)

5.37   Although, the first type of transparency is important for double tax claims, in relation to domestic taxation it is overridden by statutory regimes which confer transparency on a more specific basis. In the case of income this is achieved through *ICTA 1988, s 111(1)* which, reading in those adjustments which *section 111(10)* dictates for investment partnerships, provides that:

'where a business is carried on by persons in partnership, the partnership shall not, unless the contrary intention appears, be treated for the purposes of the Tax Act as an entity which is separate and distinct from those persons.'

In other words, it is the partners not the partnership who are treated as receiving the income. In the case of capital gains, transparency is achieved through *TCGA 1992, s 59* which, having stated that taxes are to be assessed and charged on the partners separately, goes on to say: 'Any partnership dealings shall be treated as dealings by the partners and not by the firm as such...'

5.38   It should be noted that both of these provisions apply where business is carried on 'in partnership' and that the term 'partnership' is not itself statutorily defined. There is no reason to think then that the expression is confined to partnerships written under UK law and on that basis the Inland Revenue treat Delaware and certain other limited partnerships which are differently constituted from the UK models in the same way. This treatment does not, however, extend to structures which fall entirely outside the idea of partnership as understood in the UK even if the word 'partnership' is used to describe them locally. The question of when an overseas partnership is regarded as transparent is discussed at **CHAPTER 6**.

5.39 It should also be noted that although these provisions govern the taxation of UK parties, they have no effect on how the structure will be viewed by other jurisdictions either when seeking to assess the position of any of their own residents who invest or when determining whether withholding tax should be levied on payments of interest or dividend to a partnership in relation to investments in their jurisdictions.

The principles of allocation

5.40 The fact that a limited partnership is transparent and that its income and gains are allocated amongst the partners demands rules for how the allocation is to be performed. The theory underlying the rules for the allocation of income is different from the theory which underlies the rules for the allocation of capital gains and, although the two sets of rules often produce similar results in practice, they must be analysed separately.

5.41 Taking income first, the legislation governing allocation differs according to whether the partner in question is within the charge to corporation tax or pays income tax. Broadly, corporation tax is paid by UK companies, and also by overseas companies which carry on a trade through a UK permanent establishment. Income tax is paid by all other entities including, in particular, individuals and trusts.

The allocation of income to partners subject to income tax is governed by *ICTA 1988, s 111*. That allocation to each partner is carried through in two stages. First, the income of the partnership is computed as it would be if the partnership itself were an individual. Where the allocation to a UK resident partner is in point this computation is carried out as if the hypothetical individual was also a UK resident. If the partner is non-resident the hypothetical individual is also non-resident. Second, that partner is attributed a share of that income 'according to the profits of the partners during the period'.

5.42 The rules for partners who pay corporation tax are set out in *ICTA 1988, s 114* and work in a broadly similar matter but, not surprisingly, the profits to be allocated are computed as if the partnership was a company which paid corporation tax. There are three statutory glosses on this:

(a) no account is taken of distributions. This rule was presumably introduced to exclude advance corporation tax and the effect of its set-off against mainstream tax. With the abolition of advance corporation tax much of its significance is lost;

(b) capital allowances are computed and allocated separately; and

(c) if on a change of partners there remain corporate partners but none of them was previously a partner, the business is regarded as being transferred to another company.

The general approach of carrying out the initial computation on the basis that the partnership pays tax on the same basis as the partner in question, makes clear sense. In each case it ensures that the income finally allocated is calculated on the basis appropriate to that partner. In some cases, however, a direction to compute the profits of the partnership as if it were a company is not enough, because the treatment of some profits varies from one type of company to another. Take loan relationships as an example. The authorised accruals basis of accounting by reference to which investment trusts are taxed on their loan relationships will exclude capital movements; in the case of investment companies which are not investment trusts such movements are taken into account. The notional computation under *section 114* needs to reflect these different treatments depending on the identity of the partner to whom the allocation will be made. Thus the gain apportioned to an investment trust in relation to a partnership's loan relationships needs to be differently computed from that apportioned to a simple investment company.

5.43   Before *FA 2002*, the use of different types of notional computation for different types of corporate partner was stipulated by *FA 1994, s 172*. That provision, however, applied for the financial instruments legislation only. The absence of similar provisions in the legislation governing the charge to corporation tax in respect of exchange differences and loan relationships was made good by the Inland Revenue practice set out in SP 4/98.

FA 2002 amalgamated the corporation tax provisions governing loan relationships and foreign exchange differences and as part of the general reform dealt specifically with this issue. *FA 1996, Sch 9 para 19*, as inserted by that Act for accounting periods beginning after 30 September 2002, now requires that in relation to loan relationships a separate notional calculation is carried out for each partner on the basis which would prevail if the relevant debt were owed by or to him rather than by or to the partnership. The partner is then attributed a proportion of the result, appropriate to his share of profits.

The effect of this is that the amount allocated to each company partner is computed on the basis appropriate to that partner. An investment trust, for example, will receive an allocation of profits calculated on investment trust principles.

5.44   *Paragraph 19* also stipulates that an authorised accruals basis should be used in the notional computation unless the particular partner uses an authorised mark-to-market basis in relation to his interest in the partnership. In the latter case – unless an authorised accruals basis is stipulated by some other provision – a mark-to-market basis will be used in the notional computation of profits to be apportioned.

The identification of the notional computation with the particular corporate partner which is to be taxed, has other effects. The computation of profits is carried out by reference to the latter's accounting period. Whether debt is to be regarded as made with a party with which there is a connection (with a resultant prohibition of mark-to-market and a restriction of bad debt relief) is determined by the relationship between that counterparty and the corporate partner itself. To supplement the provisions of *FA 1986, s 87* in this context, *paragraph 19(7)* provides that where the creditor or debtor of the partnership is itself a company partner and the latter (with other company partners under the same control) controls the partnership, then in computing the allocation of profits to any company partner the loan shall be regarded as made by or to a person with whom there is a connection for the purposes of *section 87(3)*.

5.45   Although *paragraph 19* directs one to look at the company partner rather than the partnership in a number of respects, it has to be borne in mind that in the end the relationships being taxed are real ones and that it is the actions of the partnership and not of the particular partners which will determine their shape. Accordingly it is provided that although the notional computation is carried out as if the corporate partner was itself party to the loan relationships, it must be assumed that 'anything done by or in relation to the firm in connection with the money debt shall be treated as done by or in relation to the company partner'. Moreover, exchange gains and losses will only be excluded from profits under *section 84A* on the grounds that they are carried to reserves where that accounting treatment is followed by the partnership itself.

5.46   Finally it should be noted that, exceptionally, gains on discounted securities are computed on corporate principles and allocated to all partners – presumably to avoid mismatches between the income tax and corporation tax treatments.

For analogous provisions dealing with derivative contracts the reader is referred to *FA 2002, Sch 26 paras 49* and *50*.

Before leaving the principles of allocation of income for corporation tax purposes, mention should be made of *ICTA 1988, s 115*, which deals with the position where a company partner is not resident in the UK. In the case of a non-resident company, the corporation tax charge is restricted to profits attributed to any UK permanent establishment through which it carried on a trade. It will come as no surprise to the reader that where such a company is a partner, the notional computation operates by reference to a non-resident company.

5.47   Finally it should be noted that one consequence of tax transparency is that where a partnership makes losses, each partner will be treated as incurring a proportion of them. In the case of limited partners, *ICTA 1988, ss 117* and *118* limit the ways in which trading losses and deductions for interest and charges can be used. Since these provisions only apply where the partnership carries on a trade, however, they are not considered in detail here.

Allocations of capital gains

5.48   The capital gains tax legislation relating to partnerships is contained in *TCGA 1992, s 59* which is pleasingly brief. After stating that each partner will be taxed separately, it simply stipulates that, and only that: 'any partnership dealings shall be treated as dealings by the partners and not by the firm as such'.

The flesh is placed on these somewhat spare bones by Statement of Practice D12. Paragraphs 1 and 2 of the Statement stipulate that, for the purposes of tax on chargeable gains, each partner will be regarded as owning a fractional share of each of the partnership assets so that when an asset is disposed of one looks at the position of each partner separately. That is to say that as consideration one brings in that partner's share of the disposal proceeds: as a deduction one brings in his share of the acquisition cost and any enhancement expenditure. A number of consequences, also set out in the Statement of Practice, flow from this. Two are particularly interesting.

5.49   The first relates to distributions in specie. In the case of private equity funds such distributions often occur where investments are floated by way of exit. The fund will not wish to retain quoted shares so these will typically be distributed to the partners to hold or sell as they decide. Where a distribution in specie is paid pro rata to the partners' entitlement to the asset in question there is no disposal. Instead they continue to own their shares of the (now separated) asset, retaining their proportion of the original base cost. This treatment, which is confirmed by paragraph 3 of the Statement of Practice, takes no account of the argument that the partner in question is exchanging an undivided share in the entire asset for a divided part of it and is thus affecting some sort of 'swap'. This treatment, which may at first appear generous, is probably no more than the law following the Court of Appeal decision in *Booth v Ellard* 1980 STC 555.

5.50   Also important are the comments on changes in partnership sharing ratios. Where there is a change in ratios and a capital asset stands in the partnership accounts at book value, any transfer of an interest in that asset will be on a no gain/no loss basis. That is because the partner giving up a share in the asset has made no profit on it, a point easily illustrated by example:

EXAMPLE 5.50

Suppose there are two partners who share in profits equally and the asset cost the partnership £200. Then if that was the only asset and the partners had put the money in as cash, the partnership accounts would stand as follows:

Asset Account	Partner A Account	Partner B
£	£	£
200	100	100

Partner C now comes in to replace partner A and no money moves outside the books. The accounts will be:

Asset	Ex-Partner A	Partner B	Partner C
£	£	£	£
200	100	100	–

Although future appreciation will now be shared between Partner B and Partner C, Partner A still has a balance of £100 which he will receive back in due course. He has thus made no profit.

A change in sharing ratios would, however, give rise to a profit, in three circumstances:

(a) where a payment is made outside the accounts to the partner whose share decreases (in our case Partner A). Here he is clearly getting extra consideration so one would expect to see a gain;

(b) if the asset has been revalued in the accounts. Were that the case partner A would expect to get more than £100 when his capital was repaid, so again he has made a commercial profit;

(c) where the partner giving up his share and the partner receiving an additional share are connected persons or not at arm's length, so that *TCGA 1992, s 17* applies to substitute market value. Under *section 286(4)* transfers between partners are not regarded as being between connected persons per se if pursuant to bona fide commercial arrangements. Connection is therefore restricted to matters extraneous to the partnership itself.

As will be seen, the treatment of revaluations has lead to very great confusions in the case of private equity funds.

Profit sharing and contingencies

5.51 Although the rules laid down for the allocation of partnership income and chargeable gains work well in many circumstances, they suffer from a lack of flexibility when the question of who benefits from profit depends on future contingencies. Suppose that a profit (in the shape of either income or a capital gain) arises in a particular year but the question of who will benefit from it will not be decided until a later year. Then how should one carry out the allocation under *ICTA 1988, ss 111* or *114*? Alternatively, which partners should be regarded as disposing of a part of the asset for the purposes of *TCGA 1992, s 59* and Statement of Practice D12?

This is not just a theoretical question. In many limited partnerships (and almost always in private equity funds) the manager or its executives will be entitled to a share of the overall profits of the fund, known as a 'carried interest' provided that the investors recover the money they invest together with a hurdle, which for the purpose of illustration let us take at 8%. If at the end of the day the investors receive a compound return of 8% per annum on their contributions, the holders of carried interest will participate in every profit made by the fund (whether before or after the hurdle is achieved). If the hurdle is never achieved they will not benefit from any profit at all.

5.52 Bearing in mind that the tax legislation makes no provision for subsequent reallocation of income or gains, there are two obvious ways of dealing with this for fiscal purposes:

(a) to allocate each profit (whether income or gain) between investors and carried interest holders in the ratio 80:20. If the hurdle is never achieved this will leave the carried interest holders with a tax charge but no cash from which to pay the tax; or

(b) to allocate nothing to carried interest holders until the hurdle is achieved and then to make a tax free reallocation of the gains in their favour (this reallocation is often described as a 'base cost shift' because its effect is to ensure that carried interest holders receive 20% of all consideration from future realisations although they did not contribute to base cost).

This issue was debated extensively between the BVCA and the Inland Revenue in the discussions which culminated in the BVCA Memorandum. In the end the decision was made to follow the accounts, meaning that in practice all income and gains up to the achievement of the hurdle (insofar as they exceed the general partner's fixed share) are allocated to the investors. When the hurdle is achieved, a transfer is made from the accounts of the investors to the accounts of the holders of carried interest, reflecting the latter's share in prior gains. In the simplest case that transfer should line those accounts up with future profit share to support the future pattern of distributions. A very simplistic illustration can be found at Annex C to the BVCA Memorandum. This Annex is not reproduced in the Company Tax Manual but can be obtained from the BVCA.

5.53   This transfer of reserves representing existing profits from the investors to the holders of carried interest has no tax consequences. Since it follows from this that overall the investors are allocated for tax purposes a higher proportion of income and gains than they actually receive with a corresponding tax advantage for the holders of carried interest, the BVCA Memorandum contemplates that an offsetting commercial adjustment may be made. Paragraph 3.2 provides that such an adjustment (and in practice such adjustments are rare) will not be regarded as consideration for the change in partnership shares.

5.54   The transfer of reserves is of course accompanied by a change of profit share, because from then on the carried interest holders will be entitled to 20% of all profits. The BVCA Memorandum proceeds on the basis that this profit share is of the same quality as those referred to in Statement of Practice D12 so that if there has been a revaluation in the accounts there must be a capital gain. That seems to be wrong. Where a change in profit share arises from a contemporaneous bargain, the fact that partnership assets have been revalued alters that bargain – for example it increases or reduces the amount which the reducing partner will subsequently be able to draw from the partnership accounts. Where, however, the change in profit share is pre-set, as in the case of the carried interest, a revaluation makes no difference to the commercial position of the parties at all. If, due to a revaluation, greater profits are attributed to the investor prior to the achievement of the hurdle then a greater amount will have to be reapportioned to carried interest holders. That is all. Still, in the light of the BVCA Memorandum a cautious manager will avoid revaluing assets in the partnership accounts in order to avoid contention. There is of course no reason why one should not keep the assets at book value in the accounts and provide a separate statement showing current valuations.

Limited partnerships and Value Added Tax

5.55 Although *VATA 1994, s 45* provides a regime under which a partnership may be registered in the firms name and be treated as an entity distinct from its members for VAT purposes, the treatment of limited partnerships is different. Here, following the tribunal case of *Saunders v C & E Commissioners* 1980 VATTR 53, the partnership is treated as if the business was carried on by the general partner alone so that the supplies and inputs of the partnership are entered on the general partner's VAT return. As a result of this:

(a) general partner and partnership form a single VAT 'entity' and the nature of the partnership's supplies will effect the ability of the general partner to recover input VAT both on the expenses incurred by the partnership and its own private expenses; and

(b) where the general partner is a member of a VAT group, that group will be regarded as making all the supplies which are actually made by the partnership. As will be seen the ability to include the general partner in a VAT group is fundamental to the way in which the VAT affairs of BVCA-style partnership funds are planned.

BVCA model partnerships

5.56 Having set out the general principles on which limited partnerships and their members are taxed, we will now consider some of the issues which arise in relation to private equity funds set up in accordance with the BVCA Memorandum.

The model proposed by the Memorandum has three different categories of partner:

(a) The general partner, responsible for the management of the partnership but not entitled to profit beyond a fixed amount. As will be seen, actual management is normally carried out by a manager ('the manager') which owns the general partner.

(b) The holders of carried interest will often include the manager or executives of the manager (described in the BVCA Memorandum as 'founders'). They will be entitled to a carried interest, typically 20% of the overall gains made by the partnership, but only if investor limited partners receive an amount equal to their original investment plus a return thereon at the hurdle rate.

(c) The investor limited partners ('investors') who put up the money.

Each type of partner needs to be considered separately in the light of the principles set out above.

The general partner

5.57 The general partner has unlimited exposure to partnership liabilities and takes responsibility for the operation of the partnership. In return for that it will commonly be entitled to a share in partnership profits up to a fixed level each year. This fixed share will vary over the life of the partnership. For example, during the investment period it will normally be a fixed percentage (say 2%) of the total commitment by the investors. Once the partnership has ceased to invest (and the partnership deed will put a limit on the investment period) the fixed share will commonly reduce both as a percentage and by reference to the extent to which commitments have been drawn down and investments realised. Sometimes, of course, in particular at the early stages of a partnership, there are insufficient profits to satisfy the fixed share. Where that is the case, advances will normally be made to the general partner to be discharged from additional allocations of future profits. If the profits never materialise the outstanding loans will normally be written off.

It is relatively unusual for the general partner to manage the partnership itself. Normally it will delegate management to the manager, which will be a company in its own group, and the manager will then enter into an agreement with the partnership itself on the basis that it is being remunerated by the general partner. This can be achieved in a way which makes it unnecessary for the general partner (but not, of course, the manager) to seek FSMA authorisation by the manager being appointed to carry on all activities of operating the partnership and managing its assets to the exclusion of the general partner. Prior to that appointment, the manager will also have been responsible for making arrangements to establish the partnership. In this way, the FSMA-regulated activities of establishing and operating a collective investment scheme (ie the partnership) and managing investments will only ever be carried on by the authorised manager and not by the general partner.

5.58 A typical management group will thus commonly comprise a management company, which employs the executives, and a series of subsidiaries, each of which is the general partner of a separate partnership and delegates the management back to that company.

Under this structure the general partner's profits are simply those profits of the fund which are allocated in discharge of its share. It follows that those profits comprise investment income and capital gain and that the general partner will not normally be regarded as carrying on a trade. This treatment is confirmed at Paragraph 4 of the BVCA Memorandum which goes on to say that, as an investment company, the general partner should be able to obtain a deduction for expenses of management under *ICTA 1988, s 75*. On that basis the fee paid to the manager should be deductible so that the general partner should simply act as a conduit and not pay tax. The manager will be a trading company. It should be noted that monitoring fees, arrangement fees, underwriting fees and syndication fees which are paid by the companies in which the fund invests or by those institutions to which fund investments are syndicated, are usually paid to the manager. This is preferable to their receipt by the fund, where they would represent income taxed under Case I or Case VI of Schedule D. That would be unattractive for investors such as UK pension funds who are exempt from tax on investment income but not receipts of this type. Including such sums in the trading profit of the manager avoids these problems but raises a commercial issue. How can investors obtain their share of the benefits? This is done by reducing the general partners fixed share by all or part of the fees so that investors receive their benefit indirectly.

5.59 As has already been seen, no distinction is made for VAT purposes between the general partner and the partnership. If, then, the general partner and the manager are included within the same VAT group through an election under *VATA 1994, s 43*, there will be a single VAT unit comprising manager, general partner and fund as shown below.

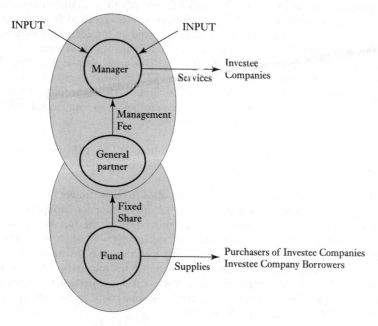

Typically supplies will be made at two levels:

(a)   the manager will make supplies of services in return for the arrangement, monitoring and other fees received from companies in which the fund invests. In the case of a fund which invests within the EU, many of the supplies will be exempt; and

(b)   at the fund level money will be lent at interest and shares and securities will be sold. Again if the recipient of the services is in the EU, the supplies will be exempt.

5.60 The high level of exempt supplies means that the VAT group will be partially exempt and will only recover a proportion of the input tax on supplies received. It is here that VAT consolidation of manager, general partner and fund operates to minimise the VAT loss. Both the fixed profit share paid to the general partner and the fee paid by the general partner to the manager are within the consolidation so that they would not themselves be subject to VAT. It follows that the group's VAT input tax will be limited to VAT on the expenses incurred by the manager. If most of the manager's expenses comprise the payment of salary and staff benefits, neither of which bear VAT in the first place, the total input tax could be quite small. On this basis any loss of input tax due to partial exemption may not be material.

Matters become more complex when the manager sources deals through teams based overseas. Conventionally such teams are employed by overseas companies within the manager's group which provide advice and information to the manager, the board of the manager making the final decision. Unfortunately, as the recipient of such services, the manager will incur VAT, generally through the reverse charge mechanism which levies UK VAT on advisory services received from abroad. If this VAT was only recaptured in part the cost could be considerable. One answer to this is to set up the overseas advisory teams as branches of the manager rather than as separate companies. That assists the VAT position because those branches are branches of a company within the overall VAT consolidation and there is no VAT on 'charges' within a single entity. The input VAT loss is thus confined to external non-employee expenses. This may reduce VAT loss to an acceptable level albeit at the cost of a complicated branch structure.

The other approach is to site the fund outside the EU but this topic properly belongs in **Chapter 6** which deals with non-resident funds.

5.61   One further point should be mentioned here: under *VATA 1994, s 43B(5)* the Commissioners may refuse an application for grouping if that appears to them to be necessary for the protection of the revenue. Customs practice in relation to this is set out in Business Brief 15/99 where they indicate that they will not normally refuse grouping where any tax saving results from the elimination of a VATable supply between group members. The business brief would seem to cover the structures discussed above, particularly when it is borne in mind that the same VAT position would result if the manager and general partner were in fact one company.

Carried interest holders

5.62   In theory it would be possible to introduce the holders of carried interest directly into the limited partnership comprising the fund. Formerly, this would have caused difficulties under the 20-partner limit but that limit no longer applies to partnerships of this type following the *Regulatory Reform (Removal of 20 Member Limit in Partnerships etc) Order 2002 (SI 2002/3203)*. Nonetheless, the manager will not normally want the investors to see all details of how the carried interest is held and the practice is for holders of the carried interest to come in indirectly. There are two ways in which this can be achieved. The first is to bring in a company from the manager's group as the holder of the carried interest and then arrange for that company to assign slices of the carried interest to the executives of the manager under *Partnership Act 1890, s 31*. Such an assignment entitles the assignee to a share of the profits of the partnership but does not make him a partner. From a tax point of view, however, his position should be the same as if he had become a partner in the partnership itself.

One advantage of this system is that the carried interest holders do not become partners and so are not 'associates' for the purposes of *ICTA 1988, s 417*. This can be useful, for example, in preventing companies which they control from becoming close. On the other hand the system involves complex documentation since the interests created by assignment are distinct and further carried interest can only be issued by assigning part of the carry originally allotted.

5.63 A partnership with a carried interest set up on this basis may be illustrated as follows.

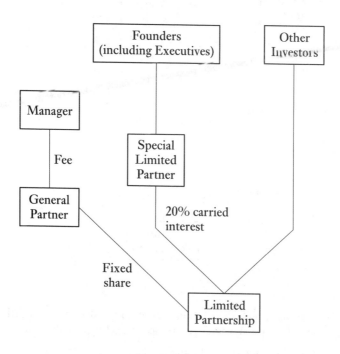

5.64 The alternative approach is to use as the general partner a partnership formed under Scottish Law which takes both the general partner's share and the carried interest in the fund partnership. Note that if an English law partnership was used it would become part of the same overall partnership as the fund itself. A Scottish partnership, which has legal personality, will retain its separate identity. That leaves the general partner of the Scottish partnership, normally a Scottish company, with responsibility for both the Scottish and the fund partnerships. In practice both roles are delegated to the manager.

The Scottish partnership itself will have two categories of partner. The first is its own general partner to which it will pay the fixed share received from the fund partnership. That general partner will normally use the money to pay fees to the manager. The limited partners will be the carried interest holders, between whom carried interest will be split according to their partnership share. This gives the following structure.

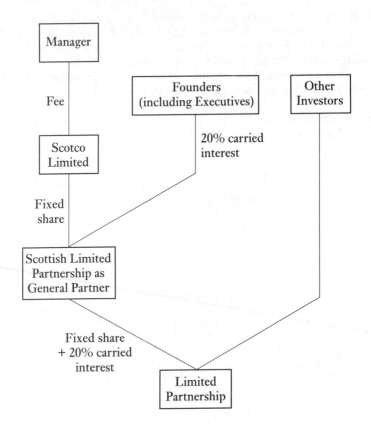

5.65   Both systems have their advantages although the latter is a little more common. On either system there are two tax issues for the holders of carry:

(a) How are income and gains allocated to them?

(b) How will carried interest be taxed under the *Income Tax (Earnings and Pensions) Act 2003*?

These issues are discussed below.

Carried interest and the allocation of income and gains

5.66   As explained above, the level of income and gains attributed to carried interest holders for tax purposes is likely to be less than that from which they may benefit economically because of the attribution of initial gains to investors and the subsequent reallocation of reserves.

This, however, is not the only reallocation of profits which may occur. A simple 20% whole-fund carried interest with a hurdle might work on the basis that cash not required to satisfy the general partner's share is distributed in the following order of priority:

(a) to investors until they have been repaid monies drawn down;

(b) to investors to the extent required to ensure that they receive the hurdle return on that money;

(c) to the holders of carried interest until the amount distributed to them is equal to 20% of the aggregate amount distributed under subparagraph (b) above and this subparagraph (c); and

(d) 80:20 between investors and holders of carried interest thereafter.

5.67 If in its early stages the fund makes sufficient distributions to trigger the carry but the return on later investments is flat or negative, it may be that at the end of the fund either:

(a) carried interest holders will have received more than 20% of the overall gain; or

(b) carried interest will have been taken although, looking at the fund as a whole, the investors will not have achieved the hurdle return on monies drawn down.

To protect investors against these outcomes, claw-back arrangements are commonly put in place under which carried interest has to be repaid until the position had been rectified. Sometimes the carried interest goes into escrow in support of those claw-back obligations; sometimes it does not. Either way, however, operation of the claw-back involves a payment to investors out of income, or out of the proceeds from disposals the gains on which have already been taxed; as we have already seen such payments will not realign the historic tax liability. To remove the risk that carried interest holders end up paying more in tax than they are left with after the claw-back, the claw-back should operate on a net of tax basis and any escrow in support should allow for releases to meet tax liabilities.

Carried interest as an employment-related security

5.68 Although the entitlement of executives of the manager to invest in carried interest clearly bears a relationship to their employment, paragraph 2 of the BVCA Memorandum provided that as long as they received arm's-length remuneration for the services they performed, they would not be considered to acquire either their partnership interest or their interest in underlying investments made by the partnership 'by reasons of rights conferred upon them or opportunities offered to them as directors or employees of any body corporate for the purposes of section 79 of the Finance Act 1972'. This protected carried interest and any interest from the underlying shares from the growth in value charge imposed by *section 79* and the confirmation was subsequently refreshed to cover the growth in value charge imposed by the conditional share legislation. It did not, however, refer specifically to the taxable emolument which might arise if, when carry was acquired, its realisable value exceeded the amount paid for it. Nevertheless, an argument that carry was a reward for services would have been entirely inconsistent with the stance taken on *section 79* and the point has not generally arisen in practice.

5.69 The introduction of a new regime for 'employment-related securities' by *FA 2003* altered the basis of taxation in this area. Although it is quite possible that the draftsman did not originally have carried interest in mind, the statutory definitions seem to be wide enough to catch it. That is certainly the Inland Revenue's view and they have made it clear that they do not regard the comfort given by the BVCA Memorandum as applying to the new regime.

5.70 The new *section 420* of the *Income Tax (Earnings and Pensions) Act 2003* specifies that the term 'securities' includes 'units in a collective investment scheme'. Here the expression 'collective investment scheme' is widely defined and would certainly cover an investment in a limited partnership operating as a fund. It is more questionable whether carried interest can constitute 'units' but the better view, probably, is that it could. On this basis, since the new regime defines the relationship with employment very widely, carried interest acquired by executives of a management company will now be 'employment-related securities'.

In most cases an interest in carry will also be a restricted security because it will not be freely transferable and the executive (or the family trust of the executive which acquires the carry) will have to surrender all or part of it at cost if the executive leaves employment.

5.71 Under the new legislation (the relevant part of which applies generally to interests in carry acquired on or after 16 April 2003) there is a choice:

(a) either an election may be made by the manager as employer and the employee under *ICTA 1988, s 431*. In this case the carried interest acquired by the executive will be excluded from the new regime relating to employment-related securities but any initial emolument charged on its receipt will be calculated by reference to the value which it would have had if it was unrestricted (the 'initial unrestricted market value' or 'IUMV'). In determining the IUMV no account is taken of restrictions on transfer or any obligation to surrender the carry on leaving employment; or

(b) the carried interest may be left within the provisions. If that is done payroll tax and national insurance contributions will arise on the proportion of the IUMV which is neither paid for nor taxed up front at a later stage. Since the whole purpose of carry is that if the fund is successful it should grow quickly, deferring the tax charge until later is an unattractive strategy.

5.72 From a tax planning point of view, the obviously strategy is to exhaust the charge at the time when the carry is conferred either by arranging for the executive to pay the full IUMV (in which case the charge is exhausted whether an election is made or not) or by making an election so that the difference between the IUMV and the amount paid initially is subject to an immediate tax charge. Either way any tax is computed whilst the carry is still of little value. However, although that may minimise the overall amount charged, any uncertainty as to what the IUMV might be would still give rise to a problem. After all, if no election is made, how would one know that there would not be subsequent charges because the amount paid by the executive fell short of the IUMV? If an election was made the tax and national insurance on that shortfall would need to be paid up front. If the amounts were considerable there could be unfunded liabilities.

In order to deal with these very real concerns the Inland Revenue agreed guidelines with the BVCA setting out how the new provisions would apply to carried interest. The memorandum of understanding setting out those guidelines can be found at Issue 30 of *Simon's Tax Intelligence 2003*.

5.73   Before examining the comfort given by the guidelines, it is important to appreciate their nature. First, they do not in any sense replace the legislation itself. A taxpayer who wishes to do so is entitled to argue valuation issues on their merits, and indeed where the guidelines do not apply this is the only approach available. The guidelines then simply create a safe harbour in which the Inland Revenue is able to give specified comfort. Second, the scope of the guidance is limited to funds which carry on 'a genuine VC fund business'. To define the scope of this the guidelines draw on the definition of a 'Venture Capital Investment Partnership' at *TCGA 1992, Sch 7AD para 2* which sets the parameters of such a partnership by reference to three conditions which must be, and have always been, met. These are:

(a)   that the sole or main purpose of the partnership is to invest in unquoted shares or securities. That condition can only be met where it is supported by the partnership agreement or prospectus;

(b)   the partnership does not carry on a trade. This question is analysed above and since this chapter deals only with investment partnership nothing further will be said about it here; and

(c)   90% of the book value of the partnership's investments must be attributable to investments which are either shares or securities which were unquoted when they were acquired or shares which were acquired as quoted shares but which it was then reasonable to believe would cease to be quoted within the next twelve months. That might be the case where the shares were in a company which was the target of a public-to-private transaction. It should be noted that in relation to this condition, no account is taken of cash unless it was acquired with the purpose of realising a gain on its disposal or of quoted shares or securities which have been acquired in exchange for unquoted holdings. The 90% is established by reference to the accounts at the end of each accounting period of the partnership.

It follows from all this that a fund formed to hold investments in small quoted companies or in other funds would not be protected by the guidelines. It remains to be seen where the Revenue would in fact apply a similar treatment in analogous cases. For the moment, however, such funds will have to rely on their valuers.

5.74 The guidelines also state that the Revenue will not be bound where a significant purpose of the arrangements is to avoid tax or national insurance, where arrangements have changed post-closing (save as specifically envisaged by the guidelines) or where there are material deviations from the fund structures described. It is important, therefore, that those relying on the memorandum of understanding should carefully compare the structure of their fund against the structures described at paragraphs 7 and 8 of the guidelines. That being said, those paragraphs were designed to describe the fund structures in common use so that in most cases any deviation will be minimal.

5.75 When the above conditions are satisfied the Revenue will regard the IUMV of the carried interest acquired by executives of the manager as being the amounts actually paid for it, provided that:

(a) the executives are paid full market salaries and bonuses for their work;

(b) the carried interest does not relate to the work performance of particular executives but to the performance of the fund;

(c) the carried interest is acquired before the fund makes its first investment;

(d) negotiations between investors and those managing the fund are at arms' length. If the negotiations are not actually carried out at arm's length, it is sufficient to show that the terms are comparable with those agreed between unconnected third parties;

(e) the fund follows certain specific structures set out in the guidelines. The commonest of these is the standard BVCA structure with a small amount of capital being put up by carried interest holders and investors, of which the proportion subscribed by the carried interest holders is not less than their maximum fraction of the profits (commonly 20%). The remainder of the investors' commitment is then advanced by way of loan. Other forms of fund are also discussed but the requirement that the carried interest holders pay their proportion of the equity capital is fundamental;

(f) the carried interest holder pays the same rate for his capital as the investors pay for theirs (ignoring for this purpose the investors' loans); and

(g) the only restrictions applied to the carried interest are leaver, vesting restrictions and general transfer restrictions.

In the normal case, then, the executives will have to pay very little for their carried interest provided they obtain it before the fund makes its first investment. The guidelines extend this treatment to the case where the fund had started making investments before carry is allotted but it can be shown that the aggregate value of the funds investments has not increased above their aggregate acquisition costs.

5.76 In addition to giving comfort on values, the guidelines also confirm that where a fund falls within their scope the change in profit sharing ratios which occurs when the hurdle is achieved does not represent an 'increase' in the carry which would be regarded as the acquisition of a new security within *section 421D(5)*, and also that, provided that the partnership follows one of the structures set out in the guidelines, the partners will not be regarded as having separate interests in the underlying securities held by the fund for the purposes of the employment-related securities regime. It is arguable that in relation to these points the guidelines merely reflect the law.

5.77 Finally, the guidelines state specifically that if, when a leaver surrenders his or her interest, it is allocated (whether automatically or not) to other carried interest holders, the latter will be regarded as receiving a new employment-related security. Assuming this is correct (and in the author's view the position is not entirely clear, at least where the reallocation simply reflects the leaver's withdrawal from a partnership) care must be taken to avoid arrangements under which reallocation is automatic; such arrangements could involve an unfunded liability for tax and national insurance, if implemented when values are high. A safer course might be to entrust the entire question of reallocation to the manager – perhaps on the basis that any carry which is not reallocated will be used to pay bonuses.

The investors

5.78 The most important category of partner is of course the investor and, since in the end the investor has the choice of walking away and investing elsewhere, there is little point in a fund structure which does not meet his needs. These needs fall into two categories. Some affect all investors and derive from the fund structure; others relate to investors in particular categories. Beginning with the general requirements, an investor will commit to provide funds for investment over a period and will then expect to be repaid as the investments are realised. If the funds were initially provided as partnership capital that would give rise to a difficulty. The *Limited Partnerships Act 1907, s 4(3)* provides that a limited partner should not, during the continuance of the partnership, draw out or receive back any part of his contribution and to the extent he does so shall be liable for partnership debts up to that amount. To prevent distributions gradually stripping the partners of their limited liability it is important that the proceeds of investments should not be distributed by way of repayment of capital.

5.79 One answer to this is for partners to contribute a very small amount of equity to the partnership and to advance the rest of the contribution by way of interest-free loan. This deals with the point on the *Limited Partnerships Act 1907* but also has certain disadvantages. In the hands of a corporate partner the loan would be a loan relationship within *FA 1996*. This could introduce an element of complexity into the tax affairs of the partner. In addition any distribution in specie in discharge of the loan would bear stamp duty by reference to the value discharged under *Stamp Act 1891, s 57*. An alternative approach, and one in general use, is to advance the remainder of the investor's capital by way of unregistered loan capital which, although it can be left out of account in the registered capital of the partnership, is, technically speaking, only recoverable in an action for account. Such capital is not really debt and its discharge does not form consideration for any shares distributed. Nor does it give rise to stamp duty when a portfolio of shares is contributed by a new partner.

5.80 Turning to specific categories of investor, since the BVCA limited partnership structure is fiscally transparent in the UK, it is generally suitable for investment by UK taxpayers. A UK corporate will receive its share of any dividend paid by UK companies in which the partnership invests as franked investment income and accordingly will not pay tax upon it. A UK pension fund will be able to utilise its tax exemptions as if it had made direct investment in the underlying securities.

5.81 One vehicle which is less suited by the partnership, however, is a quoted UK investment trust. An investment trust is entitled to exemption from UK tax on chargeable gains provided that it satisfies the conditions set out in *ICTA 1988, s 842*. One of those conditions (*section 842(1)(b)*) is that the investment trust has no holding in a company (other than another investment trust or a company which would qualify as such were it quoted) which represents more than 15% by value of the investment trust's investments. Taken on its own, that condition would leave the investment trust at risk of disqualification if an investment rose dramatically in value. The point is secured, however, by *section 842(2)* which provides that the condition is satisfied in respect of each investment provided that it was satisfied when that investment was acquired or when an addition was last made to it. If an investment trust invests in a limited partnership it becomes hard to be certain that that condition will always be satisfied. The limited partnership structure, with its fluctuations of allocation between carried interest and investors' interests, can result in acquisitions by the investors occurring without their taking any action. That means that if the partnership's interest in a particular company represents a substantial part by value of the investment trust portfolio, the investment trust may lose status inadvertently because the holding in that company may exceed 15% by value of the investment trust assets at a time when the trust is regarded as acquiring a further interest in that company. Where an investment trust is being used as a feeder through which retail investors can participate in the partnership, so that the partnership represents all – or at least a large part of – the investment trust's holdings, it is necessary to construct the partnership specially, to ensure that the investment trust is not at risk of disqualification through changes in profit share.

5.82 It should also be noted that *TCGA 1992, Sch 7AD* sets a special regime for an insurance company whose long-term insurance fund invests as a limited partner in a venture capital investment partnership (as to the definition of this, see **5.73** above). Broadly, the affect of the provisions is to regard the investment in the partnership (excluding such part of the partner's assets as comprised in qualifying corporate bonds) as being a single asset for the purposes of tax on capital gains. Accordingly, distributions of capital are regarded as part disposals of a single asset. There are specific provisions to prevent this regime being used to avoid tax by retention of proceeds for more than twelve months.

5.83 Those promoting an investment partnership will frequently find that investors of particular jurisdictions have particular requirements. The most common source of overseas investment is the US and in relation to US investors there are a number of requirements which need to be borne in mind. Two issues in particular arise frequently:

(a) If an investor is subject to the *US Employee Retirement Income Security Act of 1974* ('ERISA'), the assets of the fund in which he invests will also become 'plan assets' subject to ERISA and the manager will become an ERISA fiduciary of those assets, with attending liability, unless either the 25% exemption applies (ie the interest in the relevant partnership owned by all 'benefit plan investors' is 'not significant' as defined in the applicable regulations – a test which can be hard to meet because benefit plan investors are widely defined, including for example non–US retirement plans) or another exemption is available. Where the 25% does not apply, the usual course is to ensure that the fund qualifies as a 'venture capital operating company' ('VCOC') concurrently with the partnership's first investment. To do this, it must meet two criteria at the outset and annually thereafter. The first is that 50% of the fund's assets valued at cost must be invested in operating companies (ie not investment companies) with respect to which the fund has obtained management rights. The second is that the fund must exercise those rights as to at least one of its portfolio companies. To avoid the risk that a fund may not achieve a VCOC status, the contributions of ERISA investors are often postponed until the fund's first investment is made or, if called, are applied only to certain expenses of formation and management. VCOC qualification requires annual maintenance and has special rules applicable to a fund's run-off activities. While sometimes the manager of a BVCA fund splits all the ERISA investors into a separate partnership in relation to which these requirements can be respected, there are countervailing considerations as regards secondary transfers of fund interests.

(b) US tax exempt investors such as pension funds, endowments, private foundations and other charitable organisations will generally require the fund to be run in a manner that avoids their realising 'unrelated business taxable income' ('UBTI'). Such income would fall outside their tax exemption and there is a considerable overlap between this income and the income which would give a UK pension fund an analogous problem. The receipt of fees and income derived from business operations, for example, is a common problem. The system of diverting fees to the manager mentioned above and giving credit against the general partner's share suits both the US and the UK. One area where UBTI imposes its own constraints, however, is that of partnership borrowings which, if incurred, are generally limited to short-term borrowings if UBTI is to be avoided; even then there could be a problem if the financed investments were realised or produced income before or within twelve months after the borrowings are repaid.

Where investment is invited from the US, specific advice will need to be taken on these issues as it will also on US securities law.

Partnerships as property funds

5.84 Although limited partnerships used as mezzanine funds and funds of funds are broadly designed on the BVCA model, limited partnerships used as real property investment funds tend to be very different.

First, the general partner will normally only take a minimal profit share to establish its status as a partner. Instead of management being rewarded by a fixed profit share, managers and other providers of professional services will normally be remunerated by way of fee. From a tax point of view, a management fee will normally be deductible from rents in computing the amounts charged to partners under Schedule A. Where the properties in which the fund invests are elected for VAT purposes, any VAT on the fees should be recoverable.

5.85   In general, then, a fee structure is an efficient way of remunerating companies who contribute expertise and services to the partnership business. In the case of property investment funds, that remuneration will include any form of incentive profit share or 'kicker' because there is no general practice of allowing individuals involved in management to take a direct carried interest in the vehicle itself. Generally speaking, then, property funds are more straightforward in form than private equity funds with fees being used to pay for services and the profit sharing of the fund itself being set on relatively straightforward lines.

That being said, however, the tax principles which govern the two types of funds are the same and the provisions of *ICTA 1988, s 111* and *TCGA 1992, s 59* apply to both. It follows that the profits and losses are attributed to the partners as mentioned above and that partners will be able to use their own tax reliefs to mitigate the tax on their share of the partnership profits.

5.86   The capital gains tax transparency of the partnership conferred by *section 59* can make a partnership vehicle unsuitable where there are partners within the charge to tax on capital gains and the partnership business plan contemplates the admission of further partners at a later stage. For example:

EXAMPLE 5.86

Suppose that:

(a)   the partnership has a general partner with a trivial share and two limited partners A and B, each of whom subscribed £100,000;

(b)   the £200,000 of partnership funds are spent on an investment property which then doubles in value. At that point the assets of the partnership are revalued so that the capital accounts of each of A and B stand at £200,000;

(c)   in order to recapitalise the partnership a further investor, C, takes a one-third share for which he subscribes capital of £200,000.

In these circumstances, each of A and B has given up one third of its property asset (base cost £33,333) in return for consideration worth £66,666. Accordingly, it realises a capital gain at a time when there is no money to pay the tax. That does not matter where A and B are exempt funds but if they are taxable entities it would be an unattractive conclusion. It is for this reason that property funds are often structured as overseas unit trusts so that each investor is regarded as owning his units for the purposes of tax on chargeable gains and the introduction of a further investor does not result in those already in place paying tax.

5.87   Partnerships are also frequently used for dealing projects carried out by UK corporates, but that use is beyond the scope of this chapter.

5.88   Finally, on the topic of property investment partnerships it should be noted that:

(a) where partners are not resident in the UK, income chargeable under Schedule A will be subject to the provisions for the assessment and charging of income tax to overseas investors in UK related property set out in *ICTA 1988, s 42A*; and

(b) although the replacement of stamp duty on UK real property transactions by stamp duty land tax, effected by *FA 2003*, does not affect contributions of land to, and distributions of land by, partnerships or the transfer of partnership interests where the partnership owns land, an extension of the stamp duty land tax regime covering these areas is expected to be introduced by *FA 2004*.

LLPs as fund vehicles

5.89   The *Limited Liability Partnership Act 2000* introduced a new vehicle to English law. A limited liability partnership ('LLP') is regarded as a 'body corporate' for the purposes of company law and yet for UK direct tax purposes it is regarded as having the transparency of a partnership.

This treatment as a partnership is achieved in two ways. First, the Taxes Acts specify that the activities and property of an LLP are to be regarded for tax purposes as the activities and property of a partnership (*ICTA 1988, s 118ZA(1)* for taxation of income, *TCGA 1992, s 59A(1)* for capital gains tax). Second, references to 'a partnership' in the Taxes Acts are to be taken as including references to 'a limited liability partnership' (*s 118ZA(2)* and *s 59A(2)*). The upshot of this is that for most direct tax purposes the partnership is to be treated as transparent and the income and gains are to be allocated to the partners under the rules for limited partnerships as discussed above.

5.90   There are, however, some exceptions. The above treatment of limited liability partnerships only survives provided that the LLP is carrying on a trade or business with a view to profit, during a temporary cessation of this state of affairs or during a winding-up following a cessation of business where the winding-up has no connection with tax avoidance and is not unreasonably prolonged. Where, however, these conditions are breached, where a liquidator is appointed or where a winding-up order being made by a court or an equivalent event under foreign law, the LLP will cease to be regarded as transparent and from then on will be taxed as a company. One effect of this is that transparency for the purposes of tax on capital gains is replaced by a regime where the company itself is regarded as owning its assets and the members are regarded as owning interests in the LLP. That transition does not itself result in a chargeable gain (save in so far as gains have previously been rolled over into or deferred by reference to the assets of the LLP) but, on subsequent disposals of the underlying assets or of interests in the LLP itself, gains would be computed as if the LLP had never had transparent status.

5.91   The restrictions on set-off of trading losses which apply to limited partnerships by virtue of *ICTA 1988, ss 117* and *118* are applied in the case of LLPs with various adjustments. In the case of investment LLPs, however, they should have no application.

5.92   Although an LLP is transparent for direct tax it is treated as an entity separate from its partners for both VAT and stamp duty. In relation to the first it is capable of forming part of a VAT group, but where the LLP is a fund vehicle it would not normally be possible to group it with the manager along the lines suggested for the general partner of a limited partnership.

Where it is desired to use an LLP as a vehicle for a private equity fund, it would probably be possible to get through the VAT point by allowing the LLP to employ the individual managers direct. Even where this is achieved, however, the corporate nature of the vehicle makes it less satisfactory for International funds because of the risk that overseas jurisdictions will regard corporate identity as a block to transparency under their own legal systems. For that reason the LLP is unlikely to supplant the limited partnership as the private equity fund vehicle of choice.

5.93   As a vehicle for property funds, the LLP is deliberately put at a disadvantage by specific statutory provisions. *Section 842B* defines a 'property investment LLP' as an LLP whose business consists wholly or mainly in investment in land and the principal part of whose income is derived therefrom. Tax-exempt investors participating in a property investment LLP are, generally speaking, specifically prohibited from using their exemptions in relation to income and gain allocated to them. That clearly puts the property investment LLP at a massive disadvantage in comparison with the analogous limited partnership structure.

6 Offshore Limited Partnerships as Investment Funds

Patricia Allen

Ashurst Morris Crisp

Introduction

6.1 Since the publication of the British Venture Capital Association Memorandum in 1987 it has been possible to structure private equity funds as UK Limited Partnerships. As explained in CHAPTER 5 the business of those funds can be carried on in the UK and, generally speaking, the fund (as opposed to its participants) will not bear UK direct tax. Despite this, funds based on the expertise of UK resident individuals are often based in offshore centres such as the Channel Islands. That involves an increase in the costs of running the fund and also considerable inconvenience. Those who run the funds in this way would only do so if they had identified advantages. In this chapter those advantages and the structures necessary to obtain them will be explored.

6.2 The main reason for placing a private equity fund offshore is normally to reduce VAT costs. In the case of a UK fund investing in companies within the EU, a preponderance of exempt supplies for VAT is likely to mean that only a part of the Value Added Tax on services received by the manager will be recoverable. By moving the fund outside the EU this VAT loss can be avoided.

A second possible reason for setting up the fund offshore is to simplify the admission of investors. A UK Limited Partnership will be the UK branch or permanent establishment of overseas investors so that if those investors are themselves carrying on a trade they will be liable for tax in respect of their share of the fund's profit and the general partner or manager of the fund will be liable to collect that tax. That is normally dealt with by requiring any overseas traders to invest in the fund through special purpose investment vehicles but the efficacy of this depends upon an ability to identify exactly who the investors are. Although warranties are normally sought as part of the application process, these are only as good as the knowledge of those giving them and with complex investors (eg overseas fund-of-funds) mistakes may easily occur. Using an offshore structure without a UK agent would typically allow the fund and its participants to step away from this problem.

Equally, there are certain advantages in using an overseas limited partnership where investors include non-UK domiciled individuals. Individual partners who are resident in the UK but are not domiciled in the UK (or, in the case of Commonwealth or Republic of Ireland citizens, are not ordinarily resident in the UK) will be taxed on their share of the UK income of an offshore fund under Schedule D Case I or II, but will be taxed on their share of any overseas profit only on the remittance basis (Schedule D Case V) (*section 112(1A)*).

The nature of the investments to be acquired by the fund may also point towards an overseas structure. For example, the sale of an interest in a UK limited partnership which invests in real property is subject to stamp duty at 4%, although in practice one might leave a transfer of a UK partnership interest unstamped. A sale of an interest in a foreign partnership should not attract stamp duty at all.

6.3   Against this, where the expertise which supports the fund is in the UK, the offshore route has serious disadvantages. The first of these is that if the fund is to be run from overseas, it will be necessary to demonstrate that certain decisions are made outside the UK. In the case of a hedge fund, overseas management is sometimes demonstrated by using an overseas board which devolves its decision-making through a UK investment manager. That is justified on the basis that it is the appointment of the manager which is the crucial decision and that the fund board, by making that appointment and then reviewing the progress of the manager, is able to keep the residence of the fund overseas. The position on a private equity fund is a little different. Here we are not talking about a commercial broker which can be instructed to carry out a series of market transactions under a discretionary management agreement. In the case of a private equity fund, each transaction is major in itself and it is important to ensure that sufficient decision making on each transaction occurs overseas if the overseas nature of the fund is to be secured.

6.4   The procedures required to protect the fund's offshore status will depend upon which of these advantages is being sought. For example the structures required to avoid loss of VAT input tax would not always protect the position of overseas traders. In setting up an overseas structure, therefore, it is necessary to be clear precisely what advantages are required and when considering the analysis which underlies the various advantages consideration will be given to the steps necessary to obtain them.

Before turning to look at the above issues in detail, it may be helpful to consider a number of other issues which should be borne in mind in choosing between an onshore and an offshore structure.

Tax transparency

6.5   The first point to make is that offshore structures are not required in order to prevent tax arising at the fund level (ignoring here the collection of tax due from overseas investors). Provided that an offshore fund is accepted as being a partnership (see further **CHAPTER 5**) it should be tax transparent for precisely the same reasons as a UK fund. In respect of income, tax transparency should be conferred by *Taxes Act, s 111* which provides a mechanism through which income can be attributed to the partners. For the purposes of capital gains the fund is regarded as transparent pursuant to *TCGA 1992, s 59* which regards the assets of the fund as being held by the partners themselves.

Investors should ensure that any overseas partnership in which they are investing will be regarded as tax transparent. The English Limited Partnership is a well-known vehicle and, having no corporate identity, is regarded by the UK authorities as transparent for double tax treaty purposes. A number of other jurisdictions follow this lead. Whether an overseas partnership will obtain a similar treatment depends upon its structure.

6.6 In *Memec plc v Commissioners of Inland Revenue* 71 TC 77, the court considered whether a German silent partnership ('stille Gesellschaft') was equivalent to an English or Scottish partnership. The court proposed two tests:

(a) whether the partnership was transparent. The court acknowledged that Scottish partnerships are not as transparent as English ones, so presumably a lesser degree of transparency would also be expected of an overseas partnership. However, the silent partnership failed this test because the silent partner lacked 'any proprietary right, legal or equitable...in the shares of the [partnership's] subsidiaries or in the dividends accruing on those shares'.

(b) whether business is carried on by the partners in common with a view to profit, and with joint liability amongst the partners for the debts and obligations of the business. The silent partnership failed this test because one partner was effectively sole owner of the business, with no joint liability between the partners as against third parties for the debts and obligations of the business.

These tests should be borne in mind when looking at any overseas structure to determine its tax treatment.

BVCA Memorandum

6.7 Technically speaking, overseas structures fall outside the comfort regarding UK tax treatment given by the BVCA Memorandum. In many cases, of course, the Inland Revenue, by indicating their approval of that memorandum, were really indicating that they agreed with the views expressed as a technical matter. In such cases, the position should be the same whether the partnership is written under UK law or a similar foreign law. Where the memorandum includes an element of concession, however, the position is more difficult. It seems likely that limited partnerships written under the law of an EU member state could require the same concessions to be provided to them by virtue of Article 43 of the Treaty of Rome. See *Commission v United Kingdom* C-246/89 [1991] ECR I-4585 which held that discrimination against a company that is rooted in nationality is impermissible. Although this case concerned a company a similar principle is likely to apply in the case of a partnership. See also *Imperial Chemicals Industries plc v Colmer (Inspector of Taxes)* C-264/96 [1988] STC 874 where it was held that Article 43 (then Article 52) precluded national legislation which made a form of tax relief subject to a residence requirement. Where, however, a partnership is placed outside the EU, the Treaty of Rome will not apply and the Revenue will not be bound by their comments in relation to the UK structure. It follows that use of an overseas structure gives less comfort on those areas where the law is known to be uncertain.

FSA authorisation

6.8 There are five principal activities that are usually carried on in relation to a limited partnership any of which, if carried on in the UK, may constitute a regulated activity for the purposes of the *Financial Services and Markets Act 2000* ('FSMA'). These principal activities are: 'establishing, operating and winding up a collective investment scheme'; 'managing investments'; 'safeguarding and administering investments'; 'advising on investments'; and 'arranging deals in investments' (*FSMA 2000 (Regulated Activities) Order 2001, articles 25, 37, 40, 51* and *53*).

6.9 In relation to an offshore limited partnership, the first three of these activities would often be carried on entirely outside the UK and, therefore, would not require authorisation from the UK Financial Services Authority for the purposes of the FSMA. The latter two activities might, however, still be carried on in the UK if there is a UK-based investment adviser. In order to avoid a requirement to be authorised in the UK, a UK-based investment adviser would need to restrict its activities to providing advice to an offshore manager/general partner that is in the same group as the investment adviser, taking advantage of a group exclusion to the otherwise regulated activity of 'advising on investments'; although it may be able to provide certain other services for the manager/general partner of the fund within strict limits or on a one-off basis. In practice, however, a typical UK-based private equity investment adviser often finds the scope of what it can do in the UK without carrying on a regulated activity is too restrictive in the medium and long term of a fund. This is because the advisory team often adds its significant value by being fully involved in the activity of 'arranging deals in investments' (eg structuring MBOs, syndication, exits etc) as well as, possibly, corporate finance activities (investment advice and arranging deals) for investee companies and third parties.

In each case, the individual structure of a fund will need to be considered to determine what authorisation may be required or the parameters to avoid contravening the FSMA, which can otherwise result in serious sanctions.

Investor preference

6.10 The technical equivalence for direct tax purposes between onshore and offshore funds is generally matched by investors' indifference as to which structure is used. Both are commonplace and although one will occasionally hear it said that investors prefer a structure which is run exclusively from a tax haven, the authors have seen little evidence that this is really the case. On the contrary the current EU drive against tax havens has meant that many large reputable organisations are happier dealing with a vehicle run from an EU member state.

Different houses take different views on whether to base their funds in the UK or elsewhere. Generally, speaking, however, it seems undesirable to involve a manager in the complexity and uncertainty of an offshore structure unless there is a very good reason to do so. The best approach seems to be, therefore, to put a value on the matters referred to above (together with any commercial advantage there may be) and to see whether these compel an overseas solution.

VAT

6.11   It has been explained in CHAPTER 5 that in the case of a UK limited partnership it is usual to arrange for the general partner to receive a fixed profit share of an amount sufficient to reward it for managing the partnership. The general partner will not actually manage the partnership but instead will delegate this role to a manager within the same VAT group. Although the manager acts as manager of the partnership, it is paid by the general partner which in effect passes on all the profit share it has received.

Under such a structure, the VAT outputs will be largely those of the fund and if those relate to European securities almost all the corresponding VAT input tax (including that on the manager's costs) will be lost. In calculating the disallowance of input tax it is important to bear in mind that:

- neither salaries nor pensions bear VAT;

- some costs of premises etc will bear VAT; and

- if there are advisory companies in other jurisdictions which invoice the manager, the manager will suffer VAT on those fees under the reverse charge mechanism.

The branch solution

6.12   In a normal case there is little serious VAT wastage unless advisory companies are set up in other jurisdictions and fees are paid to those advisory companies from the manager in the UK. The manager will suffer a reverse charge in the UK, which in the case of a fund investing in Europe will give rise to an irrecoverable VAT cost. One potential way of dealing with this problem is to replace the overseas advisory subsidiaries with overseas advisory branches, as mentioned in CHAPTER 5. There should be no VAT between the overseas branch and the 'remainder' of the manager so the appropriate part of the monies received by the manager (no VAT because of the group election between the general partner and the UK manager) can be passed out to the local jurisdiction without VAT. It is clearly important to check whether the local tax regime permits arrangements of this sort and whether the fund could in some way be regarded as becoming resident in the local jurisdiction. Using this technique a typical structure might be as follows:

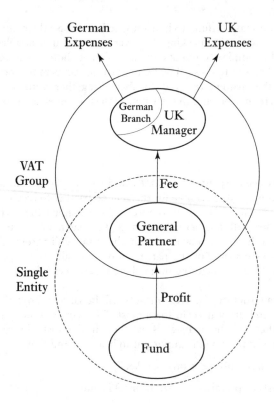

6.13   The above branch solution may work in certain jurisdictions (eg Germany) but, for both direct and indirect tax reasons, it is unlikely that this structure could be used throughout Europe. As a result, setting up in the UK is likely to give rise to a real VAT cost if several European advisers are to be employed. If there are to be advisory companies throughout Europe then to avoid a large irrecoverable VAT cost in the UK under the reverse charge mechanism it is generally advisable to set the fund vehicle up outside the EU.

Going offshore for VAT

6.14

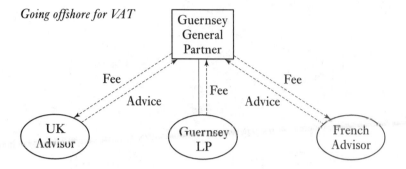

Going offshore for VAT

The above diagram shows the typical structure of a partnership established outside the EU to mitigate an irrecoverable VAT cost.

6.15   If the fund is established in, say, Guernsey, VAT will not be chargeable by the UK adviser on the supply of advisory services to the general partner in the Channel Islands. For VAT purposes the advisory services will be treated as a supply of consultancy bureaux services within *VATA 1994, s 5 para 3* which are treated as made for VAT purposes where they are received (*VATA 1994, s 7(11)* and *VAT (Place of Supply of Services) Order (SI 1992/3121), art 16*). Moreover, the UK adviser will be able to recover all its input VAT by virtue of the fact that it is making supplies outside the UK which would be taxable supplies if they were made in the UK (*VATA 1994, s 26(2)(b)*).

The VAT analysis is of course dependent on the fact that the services of the UK adviser are treated as supplied outside the EU.

Hybrid structure

6.16   Historically, to protect this analysis when establishing an offshore limited partnership, the view has been taken that the team in the UK must only give advice – the actual decision-making and signing authority should rest with the board of the general partner in the Channel Islands or with a person with delegated authority from that board in the Channel Islands. However, recently there has been a movement towards a form of hybrid structure under which the general partner is established in the Channel Islands but there is a manager in the UK with authority to manage the fund on behalf of the general partner.

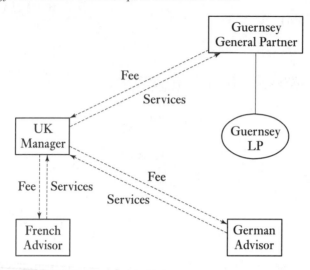

How robust are these hybrid structures from a VAT perspective? Can one successfully argue that the UK manager should be regarded as supplying services outside the UK pursuant to Article 9(2)(e) of the Sixth Directive?

6.17   Article 9(2)(e) of the Sixth Directive states that services such as those provided by the manager shall be deemed to be supplied in the place where the customer has 'established his business or has a fixed establishment to which the service is supplied'. There are, therefore, two tests which the fund must pass for the supply to be deemed to take place offshore:

(a)   the fund does not have its 'business' in the UK; and

(b)   the fund does not have has a fixed establishment in the UK to which the service is supplied.

The crucial test set out in Article 9 of the Sixth Directive must be considered in the light of a string of cases in which Customs have successfully been challenging VAT avoidance schemes.

Ensuring that the fund does not have its business in the UK

6.18   What a company's 'place of business' is for the purposes of Article 9 of the Sixth Directive was considered by the VAT Tribunal in *British United Provident Association Limited v the Commissioners of Customs & Excise* (VAT Decision No 17286). The tribunal held (at paragraph 92) that the 'place of business' was 'not the registered office [of the business, but the] establishment of the business, in the economic sense'. The tribunal pointed out that, in other language versions of the Sixth Directive, the term 'seat of...economic activity' is used instead of place of business. In determining where the company had its 'place of business', the tribunal considered matters such as the company's centre of control and place of business, as well as the location of its staff and of its board meetings.

A limited partnership established overseas must therefore ensure that it does not delegate so much power to the UK manager that the place of central management and control of the fund is in fact the UK because all decisions are made there. For example, if an offshore general partner delegated full power to make and realise investments to a UK manager, and that delegation was only revocable in the event of default by the manager, or of a partnership resolution to that effect, it could well be argued that the general partner had an almost entirely administrative role, and that the real 'place of business' of the fund was in the UK.

It is advisable therefore for the board of the general partner to be involved in top-level decision making (eg reviewing the investments and approving them in principle). Authority to complete negotiations and execute documents may be delegated to a UK manager, but this delegation should be kept under review: it should be revocable, and preferably should be renewed periodically.

Ensuring that the services are not supplied to a fixed establishment in the UK

6.19   Although the UK manager is unlikely to be established as a branch of the general partner, it will be acting as an agent for the fund. It was confirmed in *Customs & Excise Commissioners v Chinese Channel (Hong Kong) Limited* [1998] STC 352 that an agent will be a fixed establishment from which a service is supplied if:

(a)   it has the permanent human and technical resources to make the relevant supplies;

(b)   the agent does not act independently from the principal in 'function and substance [as well as] legal form'; and

(c)   the service is supplied by the agent.

The *Chinese Channel* case (as with most case law in this area) concerned a company making supplies, not receiving them; however, it is considered that the test for receipt of services must be similar, since it would be illogical for supplies received by a company to be treated differently from supplies made by that same company. However, the above test must be modified so as to refer to the receipt rather than the making of supplies.

In the case of a UK manager of a private equity fund, there is unlikely to be any doubt that the manager will have the resources to receive the supplies. It therefore needs to be considered whether or not the manager is independent from the fund, and whether or not the services are in fact supplied to the manager rather than the fund.

Is the manager independent of the fund?

6.20   In most cases, the manager will be in same group as the general partner, but not in the same group as the economic owners of the fund. As is explained in CHAPTER 5, following *Saunders v CCE* 1980 VATTR 53, the fund will be regarded as being in the same VAT group as the general partner.

The European Court in *Customs & Excise Commissioners v DFDS A/S* [1997] STC 400 (Case C–260/95) held that an agent which was a UK subsidiary of DFDS was 'not independent' of DFDS where it had so little autonomy from its principal under an agency agreement that it had 'no effective independence from the [principal] in the conduct of its business'; it acted merely 'as an auxiliary organ' of the principal. This should not be the case for a UK fund manager, which will expect to have wide discretion on investments, to make its own profits, and to take fees from investee companies as well as from the fund.

6.21   However, the law on the independence of agents is currently in a turbulent state, and it would be unwise to take much comfort from *DFDS*. The VAT tribunal in *RAL (Channel Islands) Limited and others* (VAT Decision No 17914) considered a case where, unlike in *DFDS*, an agent had some discretion in its operations under the contract with its principal. However, the tribunal held that the agent was a 'mere auxiliary' to its principal, because:

(a)   the agent was a member of the same group as the principal;

(b)   the agent was established for the purpose of allowing the principal to make supplies using resources provided by the agent;

(c)   there were contracts in place between the principal and the agent permitting the principal to make supplies using the resources provided by the agent; and

(d)   services were in fact made as a result of those contracts.

The circumstances of an offshore fund with a UK manager are clearly very different to the situation in *RAL*, which was a decision reached in the context of an avoidance scheme in which the parties worked according to a pre-arranged plan; however the wording of the decision is very broad.

6.22   It may, therefore, be difficult to demonstrate the independence of the manager following *RAL*. Ideally, the manager should not be in the same VAT group as the fund. This might be achieved by introducing a second, external general partner to the fund (for example, a further administrative general partner owned by an offshore trust corporation), which would break the linkage between the partnership and the general partner under the test in *Saunders*. This would make it much harder to suggest that the partnership and the manager were linked.

Are the services supplied to the manager?

6.23   If it is decided that the UK manager may be a 'fixed establishment' of the fund, it becomes necessary to consider whether the services could be said to be supplied to that establishment.

The presumption of the courts is that the supply will be attributed to the principal place of business (in this case the Channel Islands) unless it would be 'irrational' to do so. The European Court in *Gunther Berkholz v Finanzampt Hamburg-Mitte-Altstadt* (Case 168–84) (a case in which the issue was the jurisdiction from which supplies were made (rather than where they were received)) stated that 'the place where the supplier has established his business is a primary point of reference'; supplies should only be regarded as being made from somewhere else if it would 'not lead to a rational result for tax purposes or [would create] a conflict with another member state' to attribute them to the principal place of business.

In practice, it is considered that irrationality will only occur where the policy and scheme for VAT would otherwise be undermined.

6.24 The question, therefore, is whether it would be irrational to attribute the supplies of the UK manager to the fund's offshore place of business. This question may depend on the nature of the investors in the fund. If they are themselves offshore, it is difficult to see what distortion of competition or damage to the VAT system arises by treating the supplies as received by the fund's place of business in the Channel Islands, since this merely gives the benefit of offshore treatment to a fund consisting of largely offshore investors. This situation is very different from that in *RAL*, where the court emphasised the fact that the services were inevitably provided in the UK to UK consumers. However, the position of an offshore fund might be more precarious if the majority of investors were EU based.

6.25 In the present developing state of the VAT authorities it is clearly important that the heart of the fund's operation is kept offshore as this will:

• ensure that the fund's place of business is offshore; and

• enable the UK manager to rely on the fact that attributing supplies to that UK place of business would be irrational.

Further, there is some credibility in the argument that for the structure to work the Commissioners could well expect to see a fund which purported to be offshore going through a certain amount of inconvenience.

6.26 One needs, therefore, to ensure that sufficient decision making authority sits offshore. Assuming one has a Guernsey LP the board of the Guernsey GP should meet regularly to consider each proposal recommended by the UK manager, consider the performance of the fund and delegate authority to the UK manager to complete negotiations and execute documents in the UK. This authority should be revocable and needs to be reviewed approximately every three months.

The meetings of the board of the GP should be held outside the UK.

The members of the board of the GP should be of adequate weight to make investment decisions and, although they will no doubt be conscious that the

181

limited partners have invested with a view to exploiting the investment manager's expertise, will exercise their own judgement and reach their own decisions. The production of agendas, minutes, accounts etc and other secretarial functions should take place outside the UK.

The domestic legislation

6.27   The domestic legislation in *Value Added Tax Act 1994, s 9(5)(a)* is drafted more widely than the Sixth Directive. It states that 'a person carrying on a business through a branch or agency in any country shall be treated as having a business establishment there'. However, it is considered that this section must be read in the light of the Sixth Directive and of case law, and so it adds little to the analysis above.

Permanent establishment/branch or agency in UK

6.28   When setting up an overseas fund, it is important to consider whether the structure will give rise to a branch or agency and/or permanent establishment of the partners in the UK. This is important if either the fund itself or any of the overseas partners is trading. If the fund itself is trading (which in the case of a private equity or mezzanine fund is unlikely), an agency and/or permanent establishment in the UK would result in all the overseas partners being charged to UK tax on their profits. Where the fund itself is not trading, an agency and/or permanent establishment in the UK would result in those overseas partners who do trade being subject to UK tax.

The regimes differ slightly depending on whether the partners are individuals or companies. Where a foreign non-corporate entity carries on a trade, tax on its trading profit will be assessed on any UK branch or agency through which that trade is carried on.

6.29   Where a foreign corporate entity carries on a trade, tax on its trading profit will be assessed on any UK permanent establishment through which that trade is carried on. The term 'permanent establishment' is defined in *Finance Act 2003, s 148*. Under that section a company has a permanent establishment in a territory if, and only if:

● it has a fixed place of business there through which the business of the company is wholly or partly carried on; or

● an agent acting on behalf of the company has and habitually exercises their authority to do business on behalf of the company.

An 'agent' is a person who has the authority or capacity to act on behalf of a principal, and create legal relations between the principal and third parties. The existence of an agency relationship is a question of fact, and agency may arise even where an agreement states that it will not (*Customs and Excise Commissioners v Pools Finance (1937) Ltd* [1952] 1 All ER 775, CA).

6.30   The safest way to avoid the structure of the partnership creating an agency or a permanent establishment in the UK is to ensure that the partnership is managed from overseas and that the role of any UK team is restricted to the sourcing and recommendation of deals; the UK team should have no authority to commit either the manager or the fund. However, as mentioned above, the trend in structuring overseas partnerships is away from this model. To give UK executives the flexibility to negotiate and/or to sign documentation in the UK there has been a movement towards overseas partnerships being established with a UK manager as opposed to only a UK adviser. The existence of such a UK manager with delegated authority both to negotiate deals on behalf of the partnership and authority to sign documentation in the UK may well mean that the overseas fund/partners will have an agency/permanent establishment in the UK.

6.31   As mentioned above the tax regimes for both corporate and non-corporate investors allow tax due from a non-resident to be collected from that non-resident's UK representative, a term which could include, in the case of a corporate investor, the UK manager and in the case of a non-corporate investor, any UK resident partner. This means that tax due on the non-resident's share of profits can be collected from the UK manager/individual partner. Monies must be withheld to meet that tax from distributions. To avoid the obvious complexities of putting in place such a mechanism it is usual in the case of a UK partnership to protect the partnership from any liability to tax in respect of the profits of non-resident partners by including indemnities in the partnership and a warranty from each partner that it is not acquiring its interest in connection with an activity which amounts to trading for UK tax purposes. If such a warranty cannot be given then the overseas partner should invest in the fund via a special purpose vehicle. If the model of overseas partnership which is being used includes a UK manager as opposed to a UK adviser then these protections will also need to be included in the terms of the overseas partnership documentation.

An alternative approach would be to place reliance on the exemption for investment managers found in *FA 2003, Sch 26* for corporate non-resident investors and *FA 1995, s 127* for non-corporates. However, in practice, it is unlikely that the tests for the investment manager exemption to apply will be satisfied in the context of a limited partnership arrangement.

Mezzanine funds

6.32   Funds which invest in European mezzanine investments – a combination of debt and warrants – are traditionally set up offshore. The normal model is as follows:

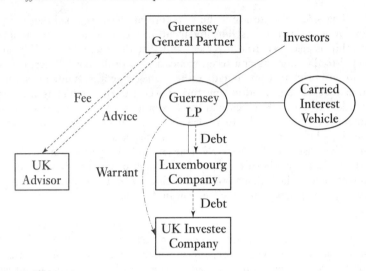

When establishing a mezzanine fund offshore, in addition to the normal VAT and direct tax issues referred to above, the issue of withholding tax also needs to be addressed.

Withholding tax

6.33   If the offshore partnership were to invest directly in debt instruments then it is unlikely that withholding tax on interest in the investee company jurisdiction could be avoided and partners will be thrown back on either making claims for repayment of such tax under a double tax treaty or suffering a real cost if resident in a non-double tax treaty jurisdiction. In theory, it may be possible to claim treaty relief either in the name of the limited partnership itself, or of the limited partners. However, in practice, only the partners will be able to make such a claim.

6.34   Under certain double tax treaties the partnership itself is regarded as a 'person' which can prima facie receive the benefit of tax relief under the treaty. The Court of Appeal in *Padmore v Inland Revenue Commissioners* [1989] STC 493 considered the UK–Jersey treaty, in which a 'person' is defined as 'any body of persons, corporate or not corporate'. The Court held that this definition includes a partnership for the purposes of treaty relief even though, under both UK and Jersey tax legislation, partnerships are treated as transparent. Other double tax treaties contain provisions which may be interpreted in a similar way. However, in practice this interpretation of the word 'person' is unlikely to help in a claim for tax treaty relief. First, the UK–Jersey double tax treaty (and certain others) do not give relief for withholding tax on interest payments, and secondly, treaties which do grant relief on interest will require the person claiming relief to be a taxpayer in its home jurisdiction; it is very unlikely that a limited partnership will pay tax in its home jurisdictions. The limited partnership will not therefore be able to claim treaty relief on its own account.

6.35   Technically, there is an argument that even the limited partners should not be entitled to claim double tax treaty relief (even if they are themselves resident in a country with a suitable tax treaty). As with most treaties, a partner resident in, for example, France will only get relief under the UK–France tax treaty if it is the 'beneficial owner of the interest' (France–UK Income Tax Treaty, Art 11(1)). However, the Privy Council in *Hadlee and another v Commissioner of Inland Revenue* [1993] STC 294, referring to *Lindley on Partnerships* (15th edition, 1984, p 516), made the point that a partner only has a beneficial *interest* in the partnership assets, which is in the nature of a future interest taking effect in possession on (and not before) the determination of the partnership. It is considered that technically such a beneficial interest in assets does not equate to being the beneficial *owner* of those assets.

In practice, however, the Revenue do not take this technical point and will look through the partnership and grant treaty relief (where available) to the limited partners. The Revenue have confirmed in correspondence that they will give such relief to investors from various countries (including France, the USA and Italy) who are partners in UK Limited Partnerships. It is understood that the Revenue take a similar approach in relation to investors in overseas partnerships in respect of UK income.

6.36   A more serious problem in practice may be that, as a result of the profit sharing arrangements under the partnership agreement, it may be very difficult to identify which partners are entitled to the relevant income in respect of which double tax treaty relief is sought until the end of each accounting year. This will mean that, even if it turns out that the partners are entitled to treaty relief, withholding tax will initially be charged and it will be up to the partners to reclaim it at the end of the year. It may be possible to draft the partnership deed in such a way that partnership shares are fixed in advance for each accounting year – in that case, the investee companies will know the identities of those entitled to the income at the time of payment of the interest, and so payments may be made without withholding tax. Such a structure will obviously add a layer of complexity to the documentation.

6.37   Practically, therefore, most mezzanine funds will invest in jurisdictions with local withholding tax on interest via a company which is resident in a jurisdiction which has a good tax treaty network and which does not itself levy withholding tax on interest. Historically, Luxembourg has been used for this purpose.

It is critical when putting in place such a structure that the Luxembourg company is clearly tax resident in Luxembourg to enable it to obtain the benefit of the treaty and to avoid it having a permanent establishment in the UK.

In the case of a mezzanine fund which has set up a company in, for example, Luxembourg through which it makes investments then it is obviously critical that the activities carried out in the UK are not of such substance that the Luxembourg company could be said to be managed and controlled from the UK and thus tax resident in the UK. Therefore, it is prudent to restrict the activities in the UK to an advisory function as opposed to the hybrid UK manager structure.

Carried interest in an overseas partnership

6.38   In CHAPTER 5 there is a detailed explanation of the new income tax provisions in *Finance Act 2003* and an analysis of the Memorandum of Understanding ('MOU') which has been agreed between the Inland Revenue and the BVCA setting out how the new provisions in the *Finance Act* apply to carried interest. The following points, which are of specific application to a carried interest obtained in an overseas partnership, are worth noting.

6.39   The MOU gives executives and their employers comfort that they will not crystallise an up-front income tax/national insurance charge when they acquire a carried interest provided that the fund they are investing in follows the model set out in the MOU. The MOU notes that in a typical UK fund structure with a fund of, say, £100 million, investors will actually subscribe £10,000 for capital and will make loan commitments of £99,990,000. The carried interest holders would then subscribe for capital of £2,500, which would then represent 20% of the total capital contributions of £12,500 (£10,000 from the outside investors and £2,500 from the carried interest holders). In a typical overseas structure, investors do not contribute capital and loans but put all their money in by way of capital. The MOU addresses this point and in paragraph 8.1 there is an acknowledgement that the economics of such an overseas fund are identical to that of a UK fund provided that under the overseas model there is some form of 'GP participation', which ranks first for the priority profit share (the 'management fee'), and an 'LP participation', which ranks next for return of capital and the preferred return/hurdle, then a 'carry participation', which ranks last for 20% of overall profits once the prior ranking profit share has been satisfied. Provided this form of overseas structure is used then the MOU provides that the 'price paid for the "carry participation" in such a partnership is commensurate with what is paid under the loan structure'. As a result, those acquiring a carry in an overseas partnership should be comfortable that the Revenue will regard the initial investment market value ('IUMV') of the carried interest acquired by executives as being the amount actually paid for it and so no income tax/national security liability will arise. In practice this means that one should assume that the capital contributed by investors is 0.01% of the fund (see paragraph 7.1 of the MOU), and on that basis the capital attributed to the entire carried interest would be 0.0025% and UK executives acquiring carry should pay the appropriate proportion of that. The Revenue have been asked to confirm this approach is correct.

6.40   The MOU also acknowledges that in overseas partnerships the terms of the carried interest arrangement are less likely to follow the whole of fund model. In particular, carried interest might be payable in relation to each investment by applying the agreed preferred return to each realisation – however, investors will almost invariably require that no carried interest holder is able to receive (or retain) any monies unless, looking at the fund as a whole, the investors have received the same result as on a whole of fund calculation. Again, this gives comfort that if a deal-by-deal carry is being put in place in an overseas fund then it is still possible to fall within the safe harbour of the MOU.

7 Investment Trust Companies

Ian Sayers

AITC

Introduction

7.1 Investment trust companies are the closed-ended form of collective investment scheme available in the UK. As at 30 June 2003, there were some 370 investment trusts in existence, managing assets of approximately £51bn

It should be noted that, although the term 'collective investment scheme' has been used in the context of investment trusts, this is also a defined term for UK regulatory purposes. Investment trusts, being closed-ended funds whose shareholders have no right to the redemption of their shares, do not fall within the regulatory definition of 'collective investment scheme'. This is important for tax purposes where the tax legislation employs the regulatory definition of 'collective investment scheme' to determine a particular tax treatment, as such legislation will not apply to investment trusts.

Closed-ended

7.2 Developments in the UK funds market mean that the terms 'open-ended' and 'closed-ended' are far less absolute than has been the case in the past. Traditionally, the concept of a closed-ended fund was a fund which raised money for investment on launch and issued a fixed number of shares which, by and large, would remain fixed during the life of the fund. Trading in the shares by investors would by done via the stock market.

By contrast, trading in the units or shares of open-ended funds would be facilitated by the operator of the fund, with the fund issuing new units or shares or redeeming them according to demand. The fund would therefore expand and contract in size depending on whether there were more buyers or sellers of the units or shares.

7.3 Investment trusts' status as closed-ended funds has therefore made them particularly suitable for less liquid investments such as unquoted investments, as the fund manager does not have to be concerned about having to realise investments to raise money to meet redemptions. Venture Capital Trusts (see CHAPTER 8), which invest almost exclusively in unquoted investments, are very similar in structure to investment trusts and some aspects of the tax regime were based on the investment trust model. However, there are many investment trusts which invest in listed securities in much the same way as open-ended funds and compete directly with open-ended funds. Like authorised unit trusts and open-ended investment companies, the shares of investment trusts are owned by both institutional and retail investors.

The dividing line between open and closed-ended funds, in terms of the fixed capital structure, is likely to narrow considerably over coming years due to a number of developments:

- The abolition of advance corporation tax, and changes to UK company law, have made it far easier for investment trusts to buy back their shares than in the past. In addition, future changes to company law will enable investment trusts to buy-back and hold their shares temporarily 'in treasury', so that they can then be sold back to the market at a later date.

- The UK Financial Services Authority has recently proposed changes to the rules which apply to open-ended funds to permit certain types of limited issue and limited redemption funds (see Consultation Paper 185 *The CIS sourcebook – A new approach* issued by the FSA in May 2003).

7.4   For the future, the key distinction between open and closed-ended funds in the UK is likely to be that shareholders in closed-ended funds, unlike open-ended funds, will have no *right* to the redemption of their shares, with this remaining at the discretion of the board of the company. It is also likely that the price at which shares are sold and bought back will be driven by the prevailing stock market price, whereas in open-ended funds it will be driven by the value of the underlying assets.

The structure of investment trusts

7.5   Although they are referred to as trusts, this is very much by way of historical accident, as investment trusts are not trusts in any legal sense, but limited liability companies incorporated under UK company law and listed on the London Stock Exchange.

In fact, there is no requirement for an investment trust to be incorporated in the UK and it is possible for a non-UK incorporated company to become an investment trust providing it is UK tax resident (see **7.18**). Recent years have also seen the development of offshore closed-ended funds which are structured in much the same way as investment trusts, and like investment trusts are listed on the London Stock Exchange, but which are not technically investment trusts due to the fact that they are not UK tax resident. Invariably, such funds will be located in tax jurisdictions which provide closed-ended funds with tax benefits at least equivalent to UK investment trusts. For the remainder of this chapter, it should be assumed, unless otherwise stated, that references to investment trusts refer to companies which are both incorporated and UK tax resident.

Split capital investment trusts

7.6   One major regulatory difference between closed-ended funds and open-ended funds in the UK is the ability for closed-ended funds to issue different classes of shares with different entitlements to the income and capital profits generated by the investment portfolio. Such investment trusts will often be launched with limited lives (normally 7–10 years).

Although the structure of each split capital investment trust varies, a split capital trust is normally constructed with a share capital structure compromising two or more of the following broad types of share:

- zero dividend preference shares – shares which offer a predetermined capital return on liquidation;

- income shares – shares which offer a high level of income during the life of the trust, payable out of the income generated by the trust's investments, and, in some cases, a predetermined return of capital (eg a return of the initial invested capital) on liquidation;

- capital shares – shares which receive the balance of any sum remaining on liquidation after the payments due to other classes of shareholder.

7.7 In the years leading up to 2000, launches of new investment trusts were dominated by launches of split capital investment trusts. However, the bear market from 2000 onwards, coupled with the extensive use of gearing and cross-investment by a proportion of these funds, meant that a number of these split capital investment trusts suffered dramatic losses and led to investigations by the regulatory authorities. It is likely that these developments, and the reputational damage that has been done as a result to this type of structure, will limit the prospects of split capital investment trust launches in the future.

The general scheme of taxation

7.8 Investment trusts are companies and, therefore, subject to specific provisions to the contrary, all corporate tax legislation applies to them. The main areas of UK tax legislation that have particular relevance to investment trusts are:

- *ICTA 1988, s 842*, which sets out the conditions which a company must meet to be approved as an investment trust;

- *TCGA 1992, s 100*, which provides an investment trust with an exemption from tax on its chargeable gains;

- *FA 1996, Sch 10 para 1A*, which provides for a different tax treatment of an investment trust's investments in loan relationships; and

- *FA 2002, Sch 26 paras 38–39*, which provides a similar treatment in respect of certain derivative contracts.

An exemption from tax on its chargeable gains is a feature common to nearly all collective investment schemes and it is essential to prevent the double taxation of investors. A consideration of the conditions that must be met in order for a company to be approved as an investment trust therefore forms a significant part of this chapter. However, the mechanism by which a company obtains approval as an investment trust is very different from that of open-ended funds.

Obtaining approval as an investment trust

7.9   In order to be approved as an investment trust, a company must meet seven conditions. The major difference between investment trusts and open-ended funds in terms of obtaining their exemption from tax on chargeable gains is that, for investment trusts, these conditions must be met for each tax accounting period. This, for the most part, will be the same as the period for which the annual accounts are drawn up but if, for example, the annual accounts are drawn up for a period exceeding twelve months, then the company will have two tax accounting periods and the conditions must be met for each period. Failure to meet these conditions for any one tax accounting period will mean that the company will not be approved as an investment trust for that period and therefore will not benefit from the exemption from tax on chargeable gains (though the company can regain its approval in subsequent periods).

This can be compared to the position with authorised unit trusts and open-ended investment companies, which obtain their exemption from tax on chargeable gains by virtue of being authorised by the UK FSA, which naturally requires the fund and fund operator to meet many conditions. However, should the fund or fund operator breach any of these conditions, this may open the fund operator up to sanction by the regulatory authorities, but will not change the tax position of the fund itself, which will continue to benefit from its exemption from tax on chargeable gains. It is therefore crucial for an investment trust to continue to obtain approval in order to maintain its competitive position vis-a-vis open-ended funds.

Granting of approval by the Inland Revenue

7.10   *ICTA, s 842(1)* states that ' ... the Board shall not approve any company unless it is shown to their satisfaction ... ' that the relevant conditions are met. It does not state that approval *will* be given if all the tests are met.

The Inland Revenue's Capital Gains Manual (CG1408) states:

> 'Where the officer (of the Board) is satisfied that all the conditions ... are fulfilled the company may be approved as an investment trust. If the company is merely holding shares in a number of subsidiary companies so that it is no more than a holding company, or if there is any other doubt about the admissibility of the claim, the case should be referred to Financial Institutions Division (Investment Trusts).'

The phrasing of the legislation and the terms of the Inland Revenue's guidance to its own Inspectors suggest that the Inland Revenue may have some residual discretion to withhold approval even if the relevant conditions are met.

Although it has never been formally confirmed by the Inland Revenue, it is widely accepted amongst tax professionals that the Inland Revenue could not exert their discretion in this way and that, if the company meets the relevant conditions, the Inland Revenue is under an obligation to grant approval.

Interaction with corporate tax self-assessment

7.11   The failure to obtain approval as an investment trust could be potentially disastrous for a company. The board of directors of investment trusts are therefore naturally very keen to be able to confirm that they have obtained approval for any given period as early as possible. Indeed, the UK Listing Rules (Chapter 21 paragraph 21.22(a)) require the accounts of an investment trust to include:

> 'a statement confirming that the Inland Revenue has approved the company as an investment trust for the purpose of section 842 of the Income and Corporation Taxes Act, specifying the last accounting period for which approval is given'

Ideally, boards of investment trusts wish to confirm in their annual accounts that approval has been given for the previous year. However, the basic position under corporate tax self-assessment is that the Inland Revenue can initiate an enquiry into the tax computations of a company at any time up to two years after the accounting period concerned. This raised the concern within the investment trust industry that a company applying for approval would have to wait at least two years before it could be sure that approval had been obtained and potentially much longer if an enquiry was not raised until just before the end of the two year period.

7.12   After discussions with the industry's trade body, the Association of Investment Trust Companies (AITC), an agreement was reached so that, if requested by the company concerned, the consideration and granting of approval will be handled by the Inland Revenue outside the self-assessment process and deadlines. Guidance to local Inspectors indicates that they should, where possible, grant approval within three months of an application. It remains an option for a company to obtain approval via the normal self-assessment process and timescales but, for the reasons given above, this is rarely, if ever, the case.

The exemption from tax on chargeable gains

7.13   Although it is commonly said that investment trusts are exempt from tax on chargeable gains, *TCGA 1992, s 100(1)* states that 'Gains accruing to ... an investment trust ... shall not be chargeable gains.'.

In other words, the legislation deems the gains not to be chargeable gains, in which case there are simply no profits of a capital nature which can be taxed.

7.14   This can be relevant for those areas of tax legislation which talk in terms of 'chargeable assets' (eg *FA 1996, s 93*). If a chargeable asset is defined for the purposes of the relevant legislation (as it is for *section 93*) as one on which any gain accruing would be a chargeable gain, then it follows that most assets of an investment trust will not be chargeable assets, even though the assets concerned are of a type which would normally be considered to be chargeable (eg shares). It also follows that, if a company fails to obtain approval, then these assets will revert to being chargeable assets.

The exemption from tax on chargeable gains also applies when a company which acquired chargeable assets when it was not an investment trust later becomes an investment trust and disposes of those assets. Care has to be taken if assets are acquired where under the nil gain/nil loss provisions applying to companies in the same capital gains group and the acquiring company then becomes an investment trust at a later date, as there is an exception to this rule when the assets have been transferred to the company as part of a reconstruction and transfer of business (see **7.80**).

ICTA 1988, s 842

7.15   The most significant piece of tax legislation relating specifically to investment trusts is *ICTA 1988, s 842*, which deals with the conditions that a company must meet in order to obtain approval as an investment trust and therefore obtain its exemption from tax on chargeable gains. In order to be approved as an investment trust, a company must meet seven conditions for the tax accounting period concerned.

In brief these are that:

(a)   The company is not a close company ('the close company test').

(b)   The company is resident in the UK ('the UK residence test').

(c)   The company's income consists wholly or mainly of eligible investment income ('the income test').

(d)   No holding in a company represents, on acquisition, more than 15% by value of the investing company's investments ('the investment test').

(e)   The company's ordinary share capital is listed on the London Stock Exchange ('the share capital test').

(f)   The distribution as dividend of surpluses arising from the realisation of investments is prohibited by the company's Memorandum or Articles of Association ('the distribution of surpluses test').

(g)   The company does not retain more than 15% of its eligible investment income ('the retention test').

It is important to appreciate that tests a, b, d, e and f must be complied with throughout the accounting period concerned and that to breach any of them, even for one day, would strictly mean that approval cannot be given. The nature of tests c and g mean that they can only be applied after the end of the accounting period concerned.

The close company test

7.16 The generous tax benefits that are made available to investment trusts are, in part, a public policy measure by the Government to encourage individuals, particularly those on lower incomes, to save for their long-term futures. There would be a concern if the investment trust structure was exploited by wealthy individuals to avoid tax. The close company test, in conjunction with the share capital test, helps to ensure that an investment trust is a widely owned company and not one under the control of a few private individuals. The test of close company status is no different for an investment trust than it is for any other company.

In brief, for a company to be a close company it must be under the control of five or fewer 'participators' (ie shareholders, although the definition is actually much broader), or any number of participators who are directors (*ICTA 1988, s 414(1)*). In considering whether this is the case, shares held by companies which are themselves not close are ignored, which ensures that many of the major institutional investors would not be considered to be participators, and the same applies to investment trusts which invest in other investment trusts. Although the definition of control (*ICTA 1988, s 416*) is broad, for most companies applying for investment trust status the close company rules are not a concern.

7.17 In addition, even in the unlikely case that a company applying for approval as an investment trust were a close company under first principles, its quoted company status might mean that it would not be treated as a close company due to a specific exemption for quoted companies (*ICTA 1988, s 415*). For this exemption to apply, very broadly at least 35% of the voting shares must be owned by the general public and must have been traded on the London Stock Exchange over the last twelve months. The exemption does not apply when substantial shareholders (ie greater than 5%) own collectively more than 85% of the company's voting shares.

The UK residence test

7.18 Again, the question of a company's tax residence is no different for an investment trust than it is for any other company. However, a company will be treated as UK resident for tax purposes if:

- it is UK incorporated (*FA 1988, s 66*); or

- it is 'centrally managed and controlled' in the UK.

The question of what constitutes central management and control is beyond the scope of this document but a company wishing to become UK tax resident is likely to ensure, amongst other things, that it holds all its board meetings in the UK (see Inland Revenue Statement of Practice 1/90).

As a result, it is possible for an overseas incorporated company to obtain approval as an investment trust by moving its central management and control to the UK and thereby becoming UK resident for tax purposes. However, this is fairly rare and this chapter has confined itself to the tax issues arising in respect of companies that are incorporated in the UK.

The income test

7.19 *ICTA 1988, s 842(1)(a)* requires that 'the company's income consists wholly or mainly of eligible investment income'.

Income

7.20 The Inland Revenue's view is that 'income' is a tax measure of income, computed on normal taxation principles (including franked investment income) and before the deduction of management expenses, charges, corporation tax and before the granting of any tax reliefs, including double tax relief. In other words, the measure of income for these purposes is a tax measure (not, for example, an accounts measure, except of course where the accounts measure and the tax measure are the same) and generally before expenses are deducted

Where expenses are concerned, it is important to recognise that the measure of income is the amount of income which is assessable under a particular Schedule or Case. So, if tax law permits expenses to be deducted *in arriving at* the amount of income assessable under any particular Schedule or Case (eg some Schedule A income) then it is considered that the amount of income for the purposes of the income test is the 'net' amount. By contrast, expenses which are deductible from a company's total income in arriving at its profits chargeable to corporation tax (eg management expenses deductible under *ICTA 1988, s 75*) are ignored in measuring income for the purposes of the income test.

Wholly or mainly

7.21 'Wholly or mainly' is interpreted by the Inland Revenue as being at least 70%. This is reduced, by concession, to at least 50% in a new investment trust's first tax accounting period. This concession only applies to a company's first tax accounting period (not the first period it applies for approval as an investment trust), as it is aimed at the difficulties faced by newly formed investment trusts where delays may occur between the raising of capital and its investment. In such circumstances, an investment trust often puts the subscription monies on deposit pending investment, which may generate income which is not eligible investment income.

As the 70% level is not particularly onerous for most investment trusts to meet, the Inland Revenue's interpretation has never been seriously challenged by the investment trust industry. However, there is certainly an argument that the term 'mainly' implies that anything in excess of 50% should meet the condition. Indeed, the Inland Revenue have indicated that a company can still obtain approval if eligible investment income is close to 70% and the circumstances which gave rise to the test being breached are unusual and unlikely to continue. In addition, the Revenue have also stated that they will consider cases where failure has arisen due to transactions in futures and options (see **7.35**).

Eligible investment income

7.22 *ICTA 1988, s 842(1AA)* defines eligible investment income as either:

- income from shares and securities; or
- eligible rental income.

Income from shares

UK dividends

7.23 The basic principle that income is a tax measure occasionally raises the question as to how UK dividends are treated for the purposes of the income test, as UK dividends are exempt from tax when received by a UK corporate.

However, the Inland Revenue's position is that the tax measure, where UK dividends are concerned, is the measure of franked investment income (ie the amount of the dividend plus any associated tax credit). This also provides a good example of the basic position that the measure of income is a tax measure rather than an accounts measure. Following changes to the way in which UK dividends were taxed in the 1990s, the accounting treatment for UK dividends changed, so that UK dividends were no longer grossed up by reference to the tax credit that comes with it (ie dividend income of £9, with a £1 tax credit, began to be shown as £9 in the accounts, not £10 as previously). However, the Inland Revenue have confirmed that the measure of income for the purposes of the income test remains the amount of franked investment income (ie £10).

Scrip (stock) dividends

7.24 A scrip dividend is a distribution of shares by a company to a shareholder which the shareholder has elected to receive instead of cash in respect of whole or part of any dividend payable or proposed by the company. An enhanced scrip dividend means a scrip dividend incorporating a bonus element such that the market value of the shares exceeds the cash amount of the dividend the shareholder has elected to forego.

The Inland Revenue's basic position, however, is that a scrip dividend is not a distribution by a company at all but simply an issue of new shares by the company and therefore more akin to a bonus issue. The Revenue therefore takes the view that such dividends do not constitute income in the hands of a recipient company. The position is different for UK resident individuals in receipt of UK scrip dividends because there is specific legislation (*ICTA 1988, s 249*) which deems such dividends to be income. In the absence of specific legislation for companies, such dividends are not taxable income in the hands of an investment trust and therefore cannot constitute income from shares and securities.

7.25   Whilst the view that a scrip dividend is not income from shares and securities is reasonably secure as regards UK scrip dividends, the tax position is less clear as regards overseas scrip dividends.

The question of whether a receipt from an overseas company has the quality of income has been established by case law to be a question of local (ie overseas) law. There are certain overseas jurisdictions where, even though the distribution may be called a scrip dividend, local law treats it, for example, akin to a dividend followed by a reinvestment of the proceeds in new shares. In these cases, scrip dividends may be considered to be taxable as income of the investment trust and, in such cases, should therefore also constitute income from shares and securities.

As most investment trusts are non-taxpaying, having deductible expenses in excess of taxable income, it is not always the case that treating overseas scrip dividends as non-taxable income is beneficial to the trust, particularly those trusts which have difficulty meeting the 70% limit for the income test.

Manufactured dividends

7.26   The Inland Revenue, by concession, are prepared to treat a manufactured dividend (ie a payment in lieu of interest and dividends payable on lent securities during the period of the loan) as income from shares and securities to the same extent as the original income would have been so treated.

Fees received from stocklending activities and interest on the late payment of manufactured dividends are regarded as income not from shares and securities.

Authorised unit trusts/Open-ended investment companies

7.27   The Inland Revenue have accepted for a number of years that, for the purposes of the income test, units in a UK authorised unit trust can be treated as shares in a company (Statement of Practice 7/94, now superseded by SP3/97). This means that all distributions, including interest distributions, of an authorised unit trust will be treated as income from shares and securities.

UK open-ended investment companies have a share capital and therefore investment trusts invested in open-ended investment companies might not need to rely upon the above concession as regards the income test, as a dividend from an open-ended investment company would appear to be income from shares and securities under first principles. Notwithstanding this, the Inland Revenue have confirmed that UK open-ended investment companies will be treated in the same way as authorised unit trusts for the purposes of the income test (Statement of Practice 3/97).

Security

7.28   There is no precise definition of the term 'security'. However, the Inland Revenue have agreed with the AITC that the definition in *TCGA 1992, s 132* will apply (although there is no statutory reason why it should). This states that:

> '"security" includes any loan stock or similar security whether of the Government of the United Kingdom or of any other government, or of any public or local authority in the United Kingdom, or elsewhere or of any company, and whether secured or unsecured.'

7.29   The question as to what constitutes a 'similar security' has been addressed in a number of cases, principally those concerned with the determination of what constitutes a 'debt on a security'. Some of the factors which indicate that a debt instrument is more likely to be considered a security are:

- it is issued for a specified amount, with a defined term and with stated terms of repayment;

- it has the characteristics of a marketable security and is capable of being sold or assigned;

- its capital value fluctuates in accordance with changes in interest rates;

- it is traded on an active and readily available market.

A security need not be a secured debt.

Notwithstanding the above general principles, case law has indicated that there are no hard and fast rules as to what constitutes a security and that the term has no precise meaning. The Inland Revenue, however, have indicated that they believe 'that the term security implies a degree of permanence in the investment in question'.

Loan relationships

7.30   When the loan relationship legislation was introduced in *FA 1996*, the capital v revenue distinction disappeared where companies were concerned. This was problematical for investment trusts and other collective funds, where the exemption from taxation on chargeable gains is an essential part of their tax efficiency, in order to prevent the potential double taxation of investors. For some years, investment trusts operated under secondary legislation for loan relationships that was introduced under enabling powers provided in *FA 1996*. These regulations were never entirely satisfactory and *FA 2002* took the opportunity to enshrine the taxation of loan relationships in primary legislation in a clearer and more practical manner.

It is important when considering the taxation of loan relationships of investment trusts to distinguish between creditor relationships (eg investments that investment trusts hold in loan relationships) and debtor relationships (eg borrowings that an investment trust have taken out, perhaps for gearing purposes).

7.31   Where debtor relationships are concerned, investment trusts are taxed in an almost identical manner to other companies. Therefore, an investment trust is generally able to claim a deduction for the debits arising irrespective of how they are accounted for. By the same token, any credits arising are taxable. Although it is rare for a debtor relationship to give rise to an overall credit, this might arise, for example, if a trust arranged to wind up a long-term debenture with a coupon well below prevailing interest rates. In such circumstances, the debenture holders might be prepared to allow the debenture to be redeemed at a price below par, giving rise to an accounting profit which would be taxable under *FA 1996*.

Where creditor relationships are concerned, the taxability or otherwise of any profit or gain arising depends upon the accounting treatment (*FA 1996, Sch 10 para 1*). If the profit or gain is accounted for in the revenue account of the investment trust in accordance with the AITC's Statement of Recommended Practice (SORP) that profit or gain is taxable. If the profit or gain is accounted for in capital reserves, then the profit or gain is not brought into account (and any losses are denied relief).

Section 842 considerations

7.32   *FA 2002, Sch 25* also introduced a clarification as to how 'income' should be measured where loan relationships are concerned.

The basic principle of *FA 1996* is that debits and credits arising on the entirety of a company's loan relationships are aggregated and then, if an overall credit arises, this is taxed and, if an overall debit arises, this can be relieved. This could have caused problems in measuring 'income' for the purposes of the income and retention tests. Firstly, many investment trusts take out substantial borrowings for gearing purposes and there was a concern that the debits arising could reduce a particular trust's 'income', making it harder to meet the 70% level required for the income test. More importantly, any reduction in the level of a trust's income from shares and securities could potentially require the trust to pay higher dividends to meet the retention condition, thereby reducing its dividend flexibility. Also, this 'net' figure taxable under Schedule D Case III would be an amalgam of debits and credits, some arising on loan relationships which are securities, others not, making it difficult to establish what proportion, if any, represented income from shares and securities.

Though there was some doubt over whether this was the correct analysis of the relevant legislation, the insertion of a new *section 1AB* into *ICTA 1988, s 842* makes it clear that, in computing the measure of income for the purposes of income and retention tests, debtor relationships are ignored.

Trading

7.33   It has been confirmed by the Inland Revenue that all trading profits are not to be considered income from shares and securities, even if those profits arise from trading in shares and securities.

In reality, given the circumstances in which investment trusts are launched, the representations they make in their prospectuses and their investment objectives, it is unlikely that investment trusts would be considered to be trading in shares and securities outright (ie a shares and securities dealer). Therefore the question of trading is only likely to arise in respect of either individual unusual transactions or in respect of certain types of transactions. Transactions in derivatives have traditionally been the most frequent cause of concern from a trading perspective.

7.34   The question of whether a transaction is in the nature of the trade is no different for investment trusts than other companies and a detailed discussion of what constitutes trading is considered beyond the scope of this chapter. However, where derivatives are concerned, transactions which are speculative tend, by their nature, to give rise to profits and losses which are volatile in nature. Therefore, whilst trading profits can amount to up to 30% of a trust's income for a particular tax accounting period, a trust is likely to be extremely reluctant to want to generate trading profits on derivative contracts for fear that a particularly 'successful' period of trading would prevent it obtaining investment trust status, causing it be subject to tax not only on its trading profits, but also on its chargeable gains.

Transactions in derivatives

7.35   In determining the correct tax treatment of derivatives transactions, a dividing line can be drawn between two major groups of derivatives where tax legislation is concerned:

• futures and options falling within the scope of *TCGA 1992, s 143* (and not falling within *FA 2002, Sch 26*); and

• derivatives falling within *FA 2002, Sch 26*.

Depending on the nature of the derivative, both a (non-trading) income and capital gains tax treatment can arise. However, although the tax legislation applicable to, and resulting tax treatment of, the two groups of derivatives is very different, both sets of legislation share one feature in common, namely that the legislation is constructed in such a way that ensures that, if any gains are trading in nature, this takes precedence over an income and/or capital gains tax treatment and are assessed under Schedule D Case I.

Futures and options (other than those falling within FA 2002, Sch 26)

7.36   As a general rule, gains arising on transactions in futures and options are treated as capital in nature (*TCGA 1992, s 143(1)* and *ICTA 1988, s 128*). The main exception to this rule is if the activities from which the gains arise amount, in themselves, to a trade for tax purposes. As a result, an approved investment trust (being exempt from tax on chargeable gains) will only be taxed on the profits arising from transactions in futures and options if the transactions amount to a trade.

Statement of Practice 14/91 sets out the Inland Revenue's position with regard to whether a transaction in futures and options is trading in nature or not. Most of this relates to companies generally. However, paragraphs 17 and 18 of the statement do relate specifically to investment trusts. Paragraph 17 says:

> 'In the Revenue's view, any profit on a financial futures or options transaction which falls to be treated as of a revenue nature would constitute income not derived from shares or securities.'

7.37   The reference to profits of a 'revenue' nature can be slightly confusing, as the primary performance statement of an investment trust's accounts (its Statement of Total Return) is divided into three columns ('Revenue', 'Capital' and 'Total') and it is possible for profits arising on futures and options contracts to be accounted for as 'revenue' items for accounting purposes but not for this to amount to a trade for tax purposes. It has been confirmed by the Inland Revenue that the reference to profits of a revenue nature is only intended to apply to profits of a trading nature.

The Statement continues by saying:

> 'The Inland Revenue will be prepared to review any case where an investment trust infringes the test in Section 842(1)(a) in consequence only of a profit on a financial futures or options transaction being treated as of a revenue nature for tax purposes, and the infringement of the test is an isolated occurrence and the trust income derived from shares and securities for the accounting period does not fall far below 70 per cent. But the Revenue can give no categoric and universal assurance that, in such circumstances, a trust will never lose its approved status.'

Clearly, the adverse consequences of particular transactions being classified as trading (as opposed to exempt chargeable gains) could be out of proportion to the scale of the 'offence'. There has therefore been a history of the AITC attempting to get a change to the law so that trading profits, whilst remaining taxable, would not count in determining whether the income test had been met. Whilst these attempts have been resisted, the Inland Revenue did provide further guidance as to situations which investment trusts typically face and their view as to whether such situations might give rise to enquiries of a trading nature. This guidance is available in the Inland Revenue's Manuals, beginning at CG41445.

7.38 What this guidance suggests is that, if an investment trust uses derivatives with the intention of protecting the value of the investment portfolio, or to reduce risk, then these transactions are unlikely to amount to trading. Transactions which meet the 'Hedge Criteria' under the terms of the SORP are likely to fall within these terms. If, on the other hand, the decision to acquire derivatives is one taken in isolation, without reference to the other activities of the investment trust, then these are more likely to be speculative in nature and their purchase and sale may give rise to trading profits.

So, for example, if an investment trust were to purchase a put option to protect against the fall in value of one its equities currently in its portfolio that it felt might be overvalued, this would not amount to trading in the derivative, even if the put option were subsequently sold but the equity not. However, if an investment trust were to purchase and sell Yen futures, when it held no Japanese investments at all, it is more likely that this would amount to trading, as the purchase of the future is unconnected to the other activities of the investment trust and can only be considered to be speculative in nature.

Finance Act 2002, Sch 26

7.39 In broad terms, there are two elements in determining whether a derivative contract is covered by *FA 2002, Sch 26*:

- the nature of the derivative instrument;

- where futures and options are concerned, its underlying subject matter.

In terms of the nature of the derivative instrument, *FA 2002, Sch 26* only applies to 'relevant contracts' which are defined as options (including warrants), futures and contracts for difference.

7.40 In terms of the underlying subject matter where futures and options are concerned, there are a number of forms of 'excluded property' which, if they are the underlying subject matter of the future or option, mean that the future or option is not a relevant contract for the purposes of *Schedule 26*. These include land, rights under a unit trust scheme and, perhaps most importantly of all where investment trusts are concerned, shares in a company. As a result, currency futures being purchased by an investment trust to hedge foreign exchange risk on its overseas investments would be expected to fall within the scope of *Schedule 26*, whereas a put option over the shares of a company being purchased by the investment trust to protect itself against a fall in value of these shares would not. Interest rate swaps, on the other hand, fall within the scope of *Schedule 26*, which raises some particular issues for investment trusts.

FA 2002 continues a trend of relating the taxability of an item to how it is accounted for. If a gain or loss on a derivative contract which falls with the scope of *FA 2002, Sch 26* is taken to the capital reserve of an investment trust in accordance with the SORP, that gain or loss is not brought into account for tax purposes (*FA 2002, Sch 26 para 38*). If it is taken to the revenue account, then it will be taxed or relieved accordingly.

7.41 The SORP does not address the question of accounting for derivative contracts directly in any particular section. However, the basic principle for determining whether a particular return should be accounted for in capital or revenue is encapsulated in the recommendation in respect of hedging. Given the concerns referred to over the possibility of derivative transactions being classified as trading, it is likely that most derivative contracts purchased by investment trusts will be intended to be used for hedging purposes.

Paragraph 78 of the SORP reads:

> 'Where a transaction meets the Hedge Criteria then, both as regards the timing of recognition and the location – capital reserves or the revenue account – of recognition, the gain or loss on the hedging instrument or hedge position should be treated consistently with the gain or loss on the position being hedged.'

As a result, a profit or loss on a currency future being used to hedge foreign exchange differences arising on the capital value of an investment trust's overseas portfolio would be accounted for in capital reserves, as any exchange differences arising would similarly be accounted for entirely in capital reserves. Profits on the currency future would therefore not be taxable and losses not relievable.

7.42 Profits and losses on an interest rate swap, on the other hand, would be taken to capital and revenue in the same proportion as the interest being swapped. So, if an investment trust had a policy of charging 50% of its interest expense to revenue, and 50% to capital, and had entered into an interest rate swap to swap its variable rate loan to fixed, it would allocate half of any payments under the interest rate swap to revenue (and therefore treat this as either taxable or deductible) and 50% to capital (and therefore not bring these into account for corporation tax purposes).

Trading subsidiaries

7.43 Investment trusts wishing to carry out transactions in futures, options or warrants which are clearly speculative or trading in nature, indeed any activities which may amount to trading, can do so by means of a trading subsidiary. Any profits made by the subsidiary can be paid to the investment trust as a dividend, which effectively means that trading profits will be converted into income from shares and securities. The dividend payments can also be 'timed' to fall into an investment trust's accounting period when the investment trust is close to the 70% income limit.

However, the use of trading subsidiary can be a double-edged sword and great care has to be taken that the investment test is not breached, in particular where the financing of the subsidiary's activities is involved. A danger arises by virtue of the anti-avoidance provisions relating to companies in the same group (see 7.58). A number of investment trusts have experienced problems of this nature in the past, so this is not a route that should be undertaken without proper internal controls in place.

Underwriting commission

7.44   Paragraph 46(d) of the AITC SORP states that underwriting commission should be recognised in the accounts of an investment trusts as follows:

> 'Underwriting commission should generally be recognised as income, and taken to the income account when the issue underwritten closes. Where, however, the ITC is required to take up all of the shares underwritten, the commission received in respect of the underwriting commitment should be regarded as an offset against the cost of the shares taken up. Where the ITC is required to take up a proportion of the shares underwritten, the same proportion of the commission received should be treated as a deduction from the cost of shares taken up, with the balance taken to income.'

The Inland Revenue's position with regard to whether a charge arises under Schedule D Case VI is that any liability under Case VI is computed by reference to the commission on the shares of which the underwriter has been relieved by public subscription. The commission on shares which the underwriter has to take up is regarded as an adjustment to the cost to it of those shares. As a result, an investment trust complying with the SORP should only be assessable under Schedule D Case VI on the amount of underwriting commission reflected in the revenue account. Any other amounts would be considered to be items which would be taken into account in calculating chargeable gains and, therefore, given an investment trust's exemption from tax on chargeable gains, effectively disregarded for tax purposes.

Any amount taxable under Schedule D Case VI would constitute income not from shares and securities.

Offshore income gains

7.45   The Inland Revenue have confirmed that any disposal of a share or security in an offshore fund which gives rise to an offshore income gain (under

ICTA 1988, s 761) will be treated as income derived from shares and securities. However, this will only be the case if the holding in the offshore fund is in the form of shares or securities. Given the huge variety of structures that are sometimes collectively grouped as 'funds', it is critical, if the ability to meet the income test is likely to be materially affected by whether offshore income gains are income from shares and securities, that each holding in an offshore fund is considered on a case-by-case basis to establish the correct tax position.

Income from/not from shares and securities

7.46   The table below summarises what qualifies as income from shares and securities and what is income not from shares and securities:

Income from shares and securities	Not income from shares and securities
Dividends (excluding scrip dividends)	Bank deposit interest
Gilt interest	Short-term local authority loan interest
UK Treasury Bill income	Trading profits
Loan stock, debenture interest	Underwriting commission
Distributions by AUTs/OEICs	Stocklending fees
Some overseas 'scrip' dividends	UK scrip dividends

Foreign Treasury Bills vary according to the terms under which they are issued (for example, US Treasury Bills have been accepted to be securities in the past, but Australian Treasury Bills have not).

7.47   The Inland Revenue's Capital Gains Manual (CG41418) states that, if a claim is made by an investment trust that a short-term loan to a local authority is a security, the Inspector should obtain a copy of the prospectus of the issue of the loan and then refer the matter to Financial Institutions Division (Investment Trusts).

Eligible rental income

7.48   The inclusion of eligible rental income within the definition of eligible investment income (introduced by *FA 1996*) was required in order to allow approval of Housing Investment Trusts, an initiative aimed at stimulating the UK retail rental market. However, at the time of writing, no Housing Investment Trust has been successfully launched, and it is perhaps increasingly unlikely that one will be launched in the foreseeable future unless changes are made to the law. This is because the financial limits that were imposed on the value of properties that may be acquired which would generate eligible rental income (see below) are beginning to look very outdated in light of the property boom that has happened in the UK since the introduction of the legislation.

Although it is anticipated that a Housing Investment Trust's eligible investment income will be almost exclusively eligible rental income and that other investment trusts' eligible investment income will be exclusively income from shares and securities, there is nothing in the legislation to prevent an investment trust having a mixture of both. However, it is extremely unlikely that a retail orientated equity investment trust would wish to generate any eligible rental income, as the existence of any eligible rental income would mean that the shares of the investment trust could not be held in an Individual Savings Account (*SI 1998/1870, reg 7(7)*).

7.49   Eligible rental income is defined as rents or other receipts deriving from the letting of eligible properties (*ICTA 1988, s 508A(2)*). Where an investment trust has eligible rental income, the rate of corporation tax chargeable on this income (less allowable expenses) is set at the small companies' rate (currently 19%). Eligible properties are residential properties in which the investment trust first acquires its interest after 31 March 1996 and subsequently lets on assured tenancies providing:

- the investment trust's interest is either a freehold interest or an interest under a long lease at low rent;

- each property is unlet or let on an assured shorthold tenancy when acquired;

- each property did not cost the investment trust more than £125,000 in Greater London and £85,000 elsewhere; and

- the investment trust has not made any arrangement for letting the property when it acquires its interest.

Example of income test

EXAMPLE 7.49

An investment trust has the following income for tax purposes for an accounting period:

	£'000
Franked investment income	200
UK bank interest	85
Foreign bank interest	50
Underwriting commission	30
US debenture interest	60
Foreign dividends receivable	150
Total income	575

Income from shares and securities is therefore:

	£'000
Franked investment income	200
US debenture interest	60
Foreign dividends receivable	150
Total income from shares and securities	410

Income from shares and securities is 71.3% of total income and therefore the investment trust has passed the income test.

The investment test

Introduction

7.50 The investment test is perhaps the most complicated of the investment trust tests due to the existence of various anti-avoidance rules relating to groups (see **7.58**). Whilst investment trusts do occasionally fail to obtain approval for other reasons (eg the income test), the investment test holds the most traps for the unwary and anecdotal reports to the AITC suggest that, where investment trust approval has been refused, the investment test is the most frequent test that is at issue. One reason for this is that, unlike the income test, where it may be possible to identify a problem before the end of the accounting period and take corrective action, the investment test, once breached, even if only for one day, should strictly mean that approval will not be given for the accounting period concerned.

ICTA 1988, s 842(1)(b) requires that:

> 'no holding in a company, other than an investment trust or a company which would qualify as an investment trust but for (the share capital test), represents more than 15 per cent by value of the investing company's investments;'

7.51 It is important to note that the restriction only applies to holdings in a *company*. Therefore an investment trust can hold an unlimited amount of gilts etc. Though there have occasionally been concerns raised that the Government, for example, could technically amount to a body corporate, and therefore could be a company for the purposes of the holding condition (such that gilts would be a holding in this company), the AITC has written assurances from the Board of the Inland Revenue that they do not interpret the legislation in this way. As the above also makes clear, there is also no restriction on the amount an investment trust can hold in another investment trust, which can be important in fund of funds type structures and in takeover situations.

The above requirement could appear to require an investment trust to constantly monitor the value of all its 'holdings' in companies through the accounting period, compare these values to the value of all its 'investments' and see whether this is greater than 15%. Certainly, if the 15% limit has not been breached *at any time* in the accounting period on this basis, the company can be sure that the investment test has been met. In practice, a number of short cuts can be taken and, even if the 15% limit has been exceeded, the investment trust may still be able to meet the investment test due to the existence of various qualifications to the general rule.

7.52 The most important exception (*ICTA 1988, s 842(2)*) is that the 15% limit does not apply:

to a holding in a company which, when it was acquired, represented not more than 15 per cent by value of the (investment trust's) investments; so long as no addition is made to the holding.'

In other words, if a company acquires a holding in a company that represents 10% of its investments, it does not have to be concerned if the value of this investment increases substantially in relation to the rest of the portfolio, taking it above 15% on current valuations, providing it does not then acquire any additional holdings in the company.

In practice, therefore, an investment trust could simply perform the holding test immediately before any acquisition of an investment. However, generally management groups will perform more regular valuations of the portfolio, if only to identify holdings which may be approaching the 15% limit to ensure that these are identified as holdings with which greater care needs to be taken. Indeed, many investment trusts have few, if any, holdings in companies which would represent in excess of 5% of their investments.

Holding

7.53   *ICTA 1988, s 842(3)(a)* defines a 'holding' as 'the shares or securities (whether of one class or more than one class) held in any one company;'.

As a result, it is necessary to aggregate the value of all the shares and securities held in a company to arrive at the value of the holding in the company.

Value

7.54   The Inland Revenue consider that the value of a holding is its open market value (ie the price that a willing buyer would pay a willing seller). Subject to rare exceptions, in the case of quoted investments stock market values can be taken. Where unquoted investments are concerned, the Inland Revenue will normally accept the directors' valuations, although the Inland Revenue understandably reserve the right to challenge these.

Investments

7.55   Historically, the term investment has been stated to mean all assets capable of producing income through ownership. This would mean that interest-bearing bank deposits constitute an investment but interest-free intercompany loans do not. For similar reasons, property owned for the purposes of generating rental income would be considered to be an investment, whereas property occupied by a self-managed investment trust for the purposes of its investment business is not. However, this reference is fairly old and it is perhaps unlikely that the definition should be drawn so narrowly by reference to income producing potential but should perhaps be considered by reference to the motive in acquiring the asset concerned. In practice, the question is rarely material.

Additions

7.56   For the reasons discussed above, the investment test is only normally an issue whenever an addition is made to a holding. It is therefore extremely important to establish when an addition is made for the purposes of the investment test.

ICTA 1988, s 842(3)(b) states that an addition is made to a holding:

> 'whenever the investing company acquires shares or securities of that one company, otherwise than being allotted shares or securities without becoming liable to give any consideration, and if an addition is made to a holding that holding is acquired when the addition or latest addition is made to the holding;'

The fact that a holding is deemed to have been acquired when the latest addition is made to it means that it is necessary to revalue the entire holding whenever an addition is made to ensure that the 15% limit has not been breached. For example, if an investment trust acquires loan stock in a company in which it already owns shares, it would be necessary to revalue the shares at the date of the acquisition of the loan stock and add it to the value of the loan stock to arrive at the value of the holding in the company. This would then have to be compared to the total value of the investment trust's investments at that point (which in turn means that the investment trust's whole portfolio of investments would have to be revalued at the same time).

7.57   There are two exceptions to the normal rule for when an addition is made. The first, as stated in the above quote, is when the shares or securities are allocated for no consideration, which is primarily aimed at situations like bonus issues.

The second exception (*ICTA 1988, s 842(3)(c)*) is:

> 'where in connection with a scheme of reconstruction, a company issues shares or securities to persons holding shares or securities in a second company in respect of and in proportion to (or as nearly as may be in proportion to) their holdings in the second company, without those persons becoming liable to give any consideration, a holding of the shares or securities in the second company and a corresponding holding of the shares and securities so issued shall be regarded as the same holding.'

The definition of scheme of reconstruction is that given in the new *TCGA 1992, s 136* which was amended by *FA 2002* as a result of potential problems that were identified with the existing legislation as a result of the decision in the *Fallon v Fellows* case.

Groups

7.58   Where the investment test is concerned (and it is important to remember that it is only for the purposes of the investment test) there are a couple of rules which extend the meaning of a holding in a company. The first (*ICTA 1988, s 842(1A)(a)*) is that:

> 'holdings in companies which are members of a group (whether or not including the (investment trust) ... shall be treated as holdings in a single company;'

It is fairly clear that one of the intentions of this rule is to prevent investment trusts splitting their total investment in a group of companies among individual companies in the group (rather than simply investing in the holding company) to avoid breaching the 15% limit.

7.59   The definition of a 'group' for these purposes is a company and all its 51% subsidiaries (as defined by *ICTA 1988, s 838*). As a result, it is necessary to aggregate the value of all the shares and securities that make up an investment trust's total investment in such a group before performing The investment test.

The second rule (*ICTA 1988, s 842 (1A)(b)*) relates to where an investment trust is itself a member of a group. It states:

> 'where the (investment trust) is a member of a group, money owed to it by another member of the group shall be treated as a security of the latter held by the (investment trust) and accordingly as, or part of, the holding of the (investment trust) in the company owing the money;'

If an investment trust had a 100% subsidiary which was currently above the 15% limit (but was not when the subsidiary was acquired) and wished to inject further capital into the subsidiary, it could not do so by subscribing for new shares in the subsidiary without breaching the test. This rule prevents the investment trust achieving the same result by making an intercompany loan in a form that does not constitute a security in its usual sense (eg an interest-free loan) and therefore would not be treated as an addition to the holding in the subsidiary.

7.60   This rule occasionally causes some confusion and some commentators have assumed that, as a result of the above, interest on an intercompany loan to an investment trust's subsidiary would constitute income from shares and securities for the purposes of the income test by virtue of it being deemed a security by this section. However, the opening words of section *ICTA 1988, s 842(1A)* make it clear that such a loan would only be a security for the purposes of the investment test and this has been confirmed by the Inland Revenue.

It does mean, however, that whenever an amount becomes 'owed' to an investment trust by a subsidiary, this constitutes an addition to the holding in the subsidiary (and, of course, any other 51% subsidiaries in the same group). The wording of the legislation is interesting here, in that it does not refer to money 'lent' but simply 'owed'. This therefore brings into the scope of the rule far more than just intercompany loans. It could, for example, apply to any intercompany balance left outstanding in the subsidiary's books. Exactly how strictly the Revenue would apply this rule is not known.

Exceptions

7.61 The normal 15% by value test is subject to two main exceptions. The first, as stated above, is where the holding is in another investment trust, in which case no limit applies. This exception also applies where the investee company would have been able to obtain approval but for the share capital test.

Authorised Unit Trusts (AUTs)/Open-Ended Investment Companies (OEICs)

7.62 An AUT is not, of course, a company and therefore the exception referred to above should strictly not be available for investments in such entities. However, the Inland Revenue consider (see Statement of Practice 3/97) that, providing it meets one condition, an AUT can be regarded as a company which would qualify as an investment trust but for the share capital test. As a result, there is no restriction on the size of an investment in that AUT. The same considerations apply to investments in OEICs as for AUTs.

The condition is that, for the period of time in the investing company's accounting period during which it held units in the AUT/OEIC concerned, the AUT's/OEIC's income was derived wholly or mainly from eligible investment income. In addition, the Inland Revenue also state that this condition will always be satisfied where the AUT/OEIC concerned is a securities fund/company for the purposes of the Securities and Investments Board's Regulations for AUTs/OEICs (or a sub-fund of an umbrella scheme/company which would be a securities fund/company if it were itself the subject of an authorisation order). The reference to the Securities and Investments Board is outdated and should now read Financial Services Authority.

Capitalisation of debts

7.63 In some cases, an increase in the paid up share capital of a company can be achieved without an injection of actual funds. This can be done by the capitalisation of existing advances to that company. The Inland Revenue have confirmed that they do not generally consider that the capitalisation of a debt in subscribing for shares would represent an addition to a holding. An investment trust would therefore not have to perform the investment test at this time to ensure the 15% limit had not been breached.

Stocklending

7.64   The Inland Revenue have confirmed that the transfer and retransfer of shares or securities under an approved stocklending arrangement will not be treated as a disposal and addition for the purposes of the investment test.

Scrip (stock) dividends

7.65   The Inland Revenue do not believe that the receipt of a scrip (stock) dividend gives rise to an addition for the purposes of the investment test due to the fact that this would represent an allotment of shares without the investment trust being liable to give any consideration.

Example of the investment test

EXAMPLE 7.65

Company A obtained approval as an investment trust in Year 1 and has an investment of shares in Company B. It acquires some loan stock in Company C, which is a 100% subsidiary of Company B, in Year 3 which it believes has caused it to breach the investment test. It therefore sells half of its shares in Company B as soon as possible to bring it below the 15% level.

The following table shows the values of the shares and loan stock at various times during the first five years. In each case the position shown is the worst position during the year as regards passing the investment test (ie the time where the value of the investments in companies B and C, when taken together, is the greatest percentage of the value of Company A's total portfolio of investments):

	Company B	Company C	Total Investments
	£'000	£'000	£'000
Year 1	1,400	–	10,000
Year 2	1,800	–	11,000
Year 3			
(value on acquisition of loan stock)	2,000	1,000	16,000
(value post sale of B shares)	1,000	1,000	15,000
Year 4	1,100	1,000	16,000
Year 5	1,500	1,000	16,500

The situation with regard to the investment test is as follows:

Year 1

Company A met the investment test as its holding in Company B only amounted to a maximum of 14% of the value of Company A's investments at any time in Year 1.

213

Year 2

The holding in Company B did, at some time in Year 2, exceed 15% of the value of Company A's investments, due to an increase in the relative value of the shares in Company B. However, as the holding in Company B did not breach the 15% limit when it was acquired in Year 1 and no addition to the holding in Company B has been made since it exceeded the 15% limit, Company A would meet the investment test in Year 2.

Year 3

When Company A acquires the loan stock it clearly makes an addition to its holding in Company C. However, as the company is also in the same 51% group as Company B the investments in Company B and Company C are treated as holdings in a single company. They must therefore be added together before the 15% test is performed.

In addition, as a holding is deemed to be acquired at the date of the latest addition, the total value of the holding in Companies B and C must be taken as the value of the shares held in Company B plus the loan stock, at the value they stood at the time the loan stock was acquired. This gives a total value of the holding in Companies B and C of £3m, which is greater than 15% of the value of Company A's total investments of £16m.

Company A has therefore failed the investment test in Year 3.

Year 4

At no time in the year did Company A's total holding in Companies B and C exceed 15% of the value of Company A's investments and therefore the company has met the investment test.

Year 5

Company A's total holding in Companies B and C has exceeded 15% of the value of Company A's investments at some time during the year. It might appear to be common sense that this breach has only occurred because of an increase in the relative value of the shares in Company B and that, as no addition has been made to the holding in Companies B and C, Company A can rely on the exception to the basic rule as it did in Year 2. Whilst it is true to say that investment trust approval will be given, this is not the complete story.

In order to rely on the exception as discussed above, the value of Company A's holding in Companies B and C must not have exceeded 15% of the value of Company A's investments at the time it was acquired. This, however, is taken to be the time of the latest addition, namely when the loan stock was acquired, and the Inland Revenue considers the value of a holding to be the value of all the shares and securities that made up that holding at that time (ie not adjusted for any subsequent disposals). At that time, the value of the holding in Companies B and C (£3m) was in excess of 15% of the value of Company A's investments (£16m) and therefore Company A cannot strictly rely on the exception. The fact that Company A subsequently disposed of half of its shares in Company B is strictly irrelevant.

One solution to the problem would, of course, have been for Company A to immediately reacquire, say, £200,000 of the £1m of shares in Company B it sold in

Year 3. This repurchase would constitute an addition and therefore one would revalue the entire holding in Companies B and C at this point, which would then be deemed to be the time at which the total holding in Companies B and C was acquired. At this stage the holding in Companies B and C (£2.2m) was below 15% of the value of Company A's investments (£15.2m). As a result, in Year 5, Company A could rely on the exception as in Year 2.

7.66   However, the Inland Revenue does not pursue this type of breach of the investment test. The Inland Revenue's Capital Gains Manual (CG41422) states:

> 'If a company has a holding which … at the date of acquisition exceeded (15 per cent) it may dispose of part to bring the reduced holding within the 15 per cent limit. So long as no addition is made to the holding, approval should not be withdrawn for any subsequent accounting period solely because the reduced holding has appreciated in value so that it exceeds 15 per cent of the company's investments.'

The share capital test

7.67   *ICTA 1988, s 842(1)(c)* requires that:

> 'the shares making up the company's ordinary share capital (or, if there are such shares of more than one class, those of each class) are listed in the Official List of the Stock Exchange;'

Ordinary share capital

7.68   *ICTA 1988, s 832(1)* defines ordinary share capital as:

> 'all the issued share capital (by whatever name called) of the company, other than capital the holders of which have a right to a dividend at a fixed rate but have no other right to share in the profits of the company;'

As a result, it would be possible for an investment trust to have certain classes of fixed-rate preference shares which are not listed.

Listed

7.69   Prior to *FA 1996*, the share capital test referred to shares having to be 'quoted on' the Stock Exchange rather being 'listed in the Official List'. The requirement to be 'quoted' did cause some investment trust problems at the beginning and end of the company's life. As a result, there were two concessions relating to the quotation test and it is assumed that the Inland Revenue are prepared to continue the same concessions if the same problems arise in respect of maintaining a listing.

7.70   The first concession is that, for an investment trust's first accounting period, providing the company's shares are quoted within one month of the beginning of the accounting period (or if the company is a private company which has converted into a public company, within one month of the commencement of the company's first accounting period following conversion), the Inland Revenue will treat the investment trust as if its shares have been quoted for the whole period.

This concession was introduced to deal with the delay between the company receiving the subscription monies and the day the shares actually became quoted. When the company put this money on deposit, it would acquire a source of income and therefore an accounting period would begin. However, at the beginning of this accounting period it would not be quoted and therefore, strictly, could not meet the share capital test for its first accounting period.

7.71   The second concession relates to an investment trust in liquidation. A quoted company going into liquidation normally loses its quotation when the liquidator is appointed. In practice, the Revenue are prepared to continue the exemption from tax on chargeable gains during liquidation, providing the assets are disposed of while the ordinary share capital is still listed and the other tests are met.

The Inland Revenue's Capital Gains Manual (CG41424) also states that where an investment trust is placed into liquidation and it appears that the above condition will not be fulfilled, the case should be referred to Financial Institutions Division (Investment Trusts).

The distribution of surpluses test

7.72   *ICTA 1988, s 842(1)(d)* requires that:

> 'the distribution as dividend of surpluses arising from the realisation of investments is prohibited by the company's memorandum or articles of association;'

The Inland Revenue have confirmed that their practice as regards this test is only to examine the Memorandum and Articles to ensure that the necessary prohibition exists. The question of whether there has been any actual breach of this prohibition in the accounting period is a matter of company law, not taxation law, and is therefore irrelevant for the purposes of the test.

Whilst this may seem a generous position for the Inland Revenue to take, the consequences of a company paying a dividend out of such profits, in contravention of the company's articles (and almost certainly in contravention of company law, which imposes a similar condition on investment companies), is that the dividend would be illegal and the directors could be held personally liable to account for the money to the company. It is therefore extremely unlikely that any board of an investment trust would knowingly sanction such a course of action.

The retention test

7.73   *ICTA 1988, s 842(1)(e)* requires that 'the company does not retain in respect of any accounting period more than 15 per cent of its eligible investment income.'.

Income versus retained income

7.74   The Inland Revenue's position with regard to the application of the retention test is that it is necessary to compare an investment trust's 'income' from shares and securities (strictly eligible investment income) with 'retained income'. If the amount retained is greater than 15% of the income from shares and securities the investment trust will have failed the test, subject to a few exceptions.

'Income', for the purposes of the retention test, has the same meaning as for the income test. Certain exceptions were granted in the past where the measure of income could be taken as that included in the accounts for the period (eg when investment trusts moved from accounting for dividends on a cash basis to an ex-div basis). However, it would be unwise for an investment trust to rely on using an accounts based measure without prior agreement from the Inland Revenue and the safer position is to assume that this is a tax based measure of income.

'Retained income', however, has been stated by the Revenue as 'the amount shown as retained in the accounts, being the increase over the accounting period in the amount of the unappropriated profits before any transfers to or from reserves but after allowing for proper provision for liabilities.' It is, therefore, primarily an accounts based measure.

7.75   The Revenue have stated, however, that, for an accounts based measure of retention to apply, the accounts would have to have been prepared under normal accounting principles which have been consistently applied (subject to legitimate changes, such as when required in order to comply with the SORP). The Inland Revenue's Capital Gains Manual (CG41427) confirms that the accounts measure of retained income will apply when the accounts of an investment trust comply with the SORP for accounting periods commencing on or after 1 January 1996.

For cases where the investment trust fails to comply with the SORP, the Inland Revenue's Capital Gains Manual (CG41429) states:

> 'Where the accounts of the company are not prepared in accordance with the ... SORP ... then adjustments may be needed to the accounts figure to arrive at the amount of retained income. In such cases the measure of retained income will be (based upon) the gross statutory income computed on normal taxation principles,'

Although the title of the SORP refers to it being 'recommended' practice, its force, in reality, is far stronger than this and departures from the SORP are extremely rare. In practice, therefore, the measure of retained income can usually be safely taken to be the amount shown as retained (or transferred to reserves) after the payment of dividends in the revenue column of the Statement of Total Return.

Relaxation of the test

7.76 The strict retention test is subject to two statutory concessions. The first (*ICTA 1988, s 842(2C)*) is that the retention test will be treated as being met if the amount that the company would be required to distribute in order to meet the test is less than £10,000 or, if the accounting period is less than twelve months, a proportionately reduced amount.

The second (*ICTA 1988, s 842(2A)*) is where the company is required to retain income by virtue of a restriction imposed by law and the amount that is retained is greater than 15% of the company's income from shares and securities. Perhaps surprisingly, the phrase 'eligible investment income' was not substituted by *FA 1996* for income from shares and securities for the purposes of this relaxation. However, it is unlikely to be a problem as income from shares and securities should logically never be more than eligible investment income.

The second relaxation does not apply (*ICTA 1988, s 842(2B)*) where the amount of income actually retained exceeds the amount required to be retained by virtue of a restriction imposed by law and the amount of the excess, plus any distributions made during the period, is greater than £10,000, or a proportionately reduced amount.

7.77 The term 'imposed by law' is taken to mean specific legislative restrictions and does not extend to other forms of restriction (eg restrictions imposed by the company's articles, even though to breach these would be to breach company law). Recent examples of such restrictions imposed by law were brought about by problems relating to certain split capital investment trusts with bank debt in place. One of the additional conditions imposed on 'investment companies' (in return for greater flexibility over dividend payments), in broad terms, is that dividends may not be paid if their assets are less than one and a half times their liabilities. Due to the collapse in value of their investments, some of these trusts found they were unable to pay dividends due to this restriction. However, this did not affect their ability to obtain investment trust status though, not surprisingly, it was extremely unlikely that such trusts would have any significant chargeable gains, and almost certainly had overall capital losses.

Prior year adjustments

7.78 One area of concern that occasionally arises is where an investment trust is required to restate prior year figures as a result of a change in accounting policy and the restated figures would appear to indicate that the retention test was not complied with in the earlier period.

Although the Inland Revenue have not stated that they will never seek to reopen their enquiries into the retention test merely as a result of a prior year adjustment, they have indicated that where such an adjustment is made as a result of a genuine change in accounting policy (eg to comply with the SORP) the status of the prior period will not normally be challenged.

Example of retention test

EXAMPLE 7.78

An investment trusts accounts (which have complied with the SORP) show the following revenue account:

	£'000
UK dividends	180
Overseas dividends	100
UK bank interest	20
Underwriting commission	30
Total income	330
Expenses	(100)
	230
Taxation	(60)
Income available for distribution	170
Dividends	(135)
Retained	35

Overseas dividends include scrip dividends of £50k which are not considered to be taxable. Other than the grossing up of UK dividend income, there are no other adjustments required to the accounts figures in arriving at the amounts considered to be 'income' for the purposes of the retention test.

Income from shares and securities is £250k (UK dividend income of £180k, grossed up to £200k, plus overseas dividend income of £50k). The maximum amount that can be retained is therefore £250k x 15% = £37,500.

The company has complied with the SORP and therefore the measure of retained income is that shown as retained in the accounts (ie £35,000). As this is less than the maximum amount that can be retained, the company has met the retention test.

Acquisitions, mergers and reconstructions

General principles

7.79 *ICTA 1988, s 171(2)(c)* ensures that disposals by or to an investment trust or to or from a company in the same capital gains group cannot be made under the nil gain/nil loss provisions of *TCGA 1992, s 171*. As a result, any such transactions would be deemed to take place at market value, following the usual rules for transactions between connected persons.

This is not, however, the same as saying that an investment trust cannot be a member, or even the principal company, of a capital gains group and that therefore, if an investment trust has two subsidiaries, transfers of assets between the two would take place at nil gain/nil loss.

Transfer of business

7.80   *TCGA 1992, s 139(4)* prevents the nil gain/nil loss rules relating to a transfer of whole or part of a company's business as part of a scheme of reconstruction applying to transfers *to* an ITC.

Under *TCGA 1992, s 101(1)*, the *section 842* exemption from tax on chargeable gains may not apply when a company transfers (as part of a reconstruction to which *TCGA 1992, s 139* applies) its business (in whole or in part) to a company which is not, at that time, an approved investment trust. If, at any time after the transfer, the recipient company becomes an approved investment trust and still owns any of the assets transferred at the beginning of the accounting period for which it is first approved, the company will be assessed to tax on the chargeable gain (or allowable loss) which would have arisen if the remaining assets had been sold at their market value at the time of the transfer (*TCGA 1992, s 101(2)*).

7.81   With the introduction of self-assessment, the chargeable gain or allowable loss will be assessed on the company for the accounting period immediately before the one in which the company becomes an investment trust (*TCGA 1992, s 101(1A)*). The calculation of the gain or loss will still be based on the market values at the date of the transfer of business.

The above rules make it difficult for the assets of an investment company (which is not an investment trust) to be acquired by an investment trust without a tax charge arising in the investment company or investment trust. The investment company can, however, meet the conditions for approval as an investment trust, dispose of its assets and still benefit from the exemption from tax on chargeable gains.

Stamp duty

7.82   The stamp duty position of investment trusts (for which read Stamp Duty Reserve Tax where applicable) is almost identical to that of other listed companies. Therefore, on the issue of new shares (eg on launch) no stamp duty is charged, but purchases in the secondary market will normally carry a 0.5% ad valorem charge.

If an investment trust buys-back shares (an increasingly common feature of the sector), it will also incur 0.5% stamp duty. New legislation (see **7.85**) will enable investment trusts to buy-back shares into treasury and then sell them at a later date. For stamp duty purposes, a sale of treasury shares is treated in the same way as an issue of new shares, and therefore does not attract stamp duty.

VAT

7.83 Currently the management of an AUT and OEIC is exempt from VAT (see *VATA 1994, Sch 9 Gp 5 Items 9, 10*). This is an implementation of *EC 6th VAT Directive, Art 13B(d)(6)* that exempts the 'management of special investment funds as defined by Member States'. To date, the Government has not been prepared to extend UK legislation to cover investment trusts, with the result that the management fees levied by their fund managers are subject to VAT at 17.5%.

The ability to reclaim this input VAT, by and large, relates to the geographical regions in which the investment trust is invested. So, investment trusts largely invested outside the UK and EU will be able to reclaim the majority of this VAT (as its 'supplies', being sales of shares and securities, will generally be zero-rated) whereas investment trusts invested predominantly in the UK and EU will not be able to reclaim the majority, if any, of this VAT (as its supplies will be exempt).

7.84 The AITC considers that this VAT distinction between investment trusts and AUTs/OEIC is unfair and anti-competitive and may also not be legal under the terms of EU law. It is also surprising that VAT legislation constructed under EU law should penalise an investment fund for investing in the EU. It has therefore been lobbying the Government for investment trusts to be provided with an equivalent exemption to AUTs/OEICs and a consultation exercise was conducted by the UK authorities in January 2003. A decision is expected in October 2003 and the AITC has indicated that, if it is unsuccessful in its lobbying, it is prepared to bring a test case to challenge the UK's interpretation of EU law.

Treasury shares

7.85 Currently, when an investment trust buys-back its shares, it must cancel them (ie they cease to exist). The company's share capital, and funds under management, are therefore 'permanently' reduced. The treasury shares legislation, when it comes into force on 1 December 2003, will permit an investment trust, having carried out a share buy-back, to hold up to 10% of its share capital (or 10% of a particular class of shares) 'in treasury'.

When shares are held in treasury, they effectively go into a state of limbo. Although they still exist (the registered shareholder being the company itself) and are shown as issued share capital on the company's balance sheet, they do not carry any voting rights, dividends on them are suspended and they have no entitlements on a winding-up. Once bought back into treasury, the company can hold them indefinitely and then choose, at a later date, either to cancel them, or sell them at a price generally no less than 10% below the mid-market price at the time the sale takes place.

7.86 As a general rule, changes to law and regulation (including tax) will treat shares in treasury as if they had been bought back and cancelled. So, for example, where rules impose obligations on parties (including the company itself) by reference to whether certain percentage limits of the company's share capital have been exceeded, these percentages will in future be calculated ignoring any shares held in treasury.

The basic framework of the tax legislation applicable to treasury shares is that, if a company buys-back shares, holds them in treasury and then sells them at a later date, it will be treated for tax purposes as if it had bought back the shares, cancelled them and then made an issue of new shares. As a result, no taxable profit (or relievable loss) arises on the sale of treasury shares. In addition, no stamp duty is paid by a shareholder acquiring treasury shares.

Section 842 considerations

7.87   The holding of shares in treasury, and sale of shares from treasury, would appear only to have implications for one of the seven conditions, namely that no holding in a company must represent, on acquisition, more than 15% of the investment trust's investments. This raises two questions:

- does a holding of treasury shares constitute a holding in a company subject to the 15% limit (though it is difficult to conceive of many situations where a holding of treasury shares, being limited to 10% of a company's share capital, could exceed the 15% limit); and

- are treasury shares investments for the purposes of measuring whether any holding in a company exceeds the 15% limit (ie part of the denominator)?

7.88   The tax legislation provides that, where a company acquires treasury shares, the shares are not to be treated as the acquisition of an asset and that shares so acquired are to be treated for tax purposes as if they had been cancelled. The Inland Revenue have indicated that, as a result, treasury shares should not be considered a holding in a company subject to the 15% limit and also should not be considered as investments for the purposes of measuring whether this limit has been exceeded.

This is administratively the most convenient position and means that, by and large, the use of treasury shares should have no impact on a company's status as an investment trust.

8 Venture Capital Trusts

David Cartwright

PricewaterhouseCoopers LLP

History

8.1 Venture Capital Trusts (VCTs) are quoted companies, similar to investment trusts, that principally invest the funds available to them by subscribing for new shares and securities in unquoted trading companies, including companies listed on the Alternative Investment Market.

During the 1980s the Government tried to assist the funding of smaller unquoted trading companies by providing individuals with tax incentives to invest in such companies which had traditionally found it difficult to raise equity capital. This comprised the Business Start-up Scheme in 1981 and 1982 and then the Business Expansion Scheme from 1983.

8.2 The Business Expansion Scheme was terminated in 1993 and was replaced in 1994 with the Enterprise Investment Scheme which was similar to the Business Expansion Scheme but which also sought to attract business angels to invest in early-stage companies.

At the same time, in 1994 the Government commenced discussions with the venture capital industry with a view to setting up a new scheme which would establish new investment vehicles that would invest up to £1m at a time in unquoted trading companies.

8.3 What evolved was the VCT, a new investment vehicle which:

- would invest in unquoted trading companies;

- was financed by individual investors who were provided with an attractive package of tax incentives (see below);

- was professionally managed by experienced venture capital fund managers (see below); and

- was to be quoted on the London Stock Exchange.

VCTs were established by new tax legislation introduced in 1995 (effective from 6 April 1995), and the first VCTs were launched and established in the second half of 1995.

Tax breaks for investors

8.4   To attract individuals to invest in VCTs the Government needed to put together a very attractive package of tax incentives.

An individual who is over 18 years old and UK resident can enjoy the following tax reliefs in respect of an investment of up to £100,000 in new ordinary shares of a VCT for each tax year (to 5 April):

- an initial income tax relief of 20% of the amount subscribed for;

- the deferral of tax payable (up to 40%) on chargeable gains which have occurred on disposals of any assets which have taken place in a period beginning twelve months before the subscription and ending twelve months after the subscription.

8.5   In addition, the following tax reliefs are available to individuals who subscribe for or purchase new ordinary shares of a VCT:

- no income tax payable on dividends received;

- no tax is payable on gains realised on the disposal of shares in a VCT.

The tax free dividend is particularly attractive as it applies to both distributions of income and capital (and unlike investment trusts VCTs are able to distribute capital).

Professionally managed funds

8.6   Investors were also attracted to invest in VCTs as the investment managers had to prove a track record in investing in these types of unquoted investments.

Size of the sector

8.7   At 5 April 2003 over £1,500m had been raised by 73 VCTs, which were managed by 30 managers.

Year to 5 April	Estimated funds raised from investors (£ million)
1996	160
1997	170
1998	189
1999	164
2000	271
2001	433
2002	125
2003	50
	1,562

The above profile reflects

- circa £150m to £200m raised in each of the first four years as investors and their advisers understood VCTs and became regular investors;

- above average funds raised in the fifth and sixth years as VCTs began to establish investment performance largely characterised by capital distributions and investors were increasingly attracted by the ability to defer capital gains tax liabilities;

- a significant reduction in funds raised in the seventh and eighth years as VCTs' share prices and net asset values fell below the issue price reflecting the position in the equity markets.

Taxation of VCTs

8.8   VCTs are only taxed on their investment income less expenses, principally the management charges that are charged to revenue and capital. VCTs are not taxed on the gains made on their investments in shares and securities.

Obtaining and maintaining VCT approval

Conditions for full approval

8.9   To be approved as a VCT a company must not be a close company and must satisfy the Inland Revenue that in relation to its most recent complete accounting period:

- its income in that accounting period was derived wholly or mainly from shares and securities (in practice over 70%);

- at least 70% by value of its investments were in qualifying holdings of shares or securities throughout that accounting period;

- at least 30% by value of its qualifying holdings were in holdings of eligible shares throughout that accounting period;

- no holding in any company represented more than 15% by value of the VCT's investments at any time during that accounting period;

- its ordinary share capital was quoted on the London Stock Exchange throughout that accounting period; and

- it did not retain more than 15% of its income derived in that accounting period from shares and securities.

8.10   The company must also satisfy the Inland Revenue that these conditions will be met in relation to the accounting period which is current when the application for approval is made.

A company satisfying these conditions will receive an approval notice specifying:

- the date on which the approval is given; and

- the date from which approval shall have effect

Conditions for provisional approval

8.11   A company which does not meet the conditions for full approval may be given provisional approval where it satisfies the Inland Revenue that, in relation to the accounting period which is current when the application is made, or the next accounting period, and in the following accounting periods:

- its income in them will be derived wholly or mainly from shares or securities;

- no holding in any company will represent more than 15% by value of its investments at any time during them;

- it ordinary share capital will be quoted on the London Stock Exchange throughout them; and

- it will not retain more than 15% of its income derived in them from shares and securities.

In relation to an accounting period of the company beginning no more than three years after approval is given or, if earlier, when approval takes effect, and in following accounting periods:

- at least 70% by value of its investments will be in qualifying holdings of shares and securities throughout them; and

- at least 30% by value of its qualifying holdings will be in holdings of eligible shares throughout them.

A company meeting the conditions for provisional approval will be sent an approval notice specifying:

- the date on which the approval is given; and

- the date from which approval shall have effect.

8.12   If the approval is to take effect from a date later than that on which approval is given, the three-year period mentioned in the second bullet point runs from that later date.

Notices giving provisional approval may show additional conditions to be met by the company which are designed to ensure that it meets the conditions outlined above. Provisional approval is normally sought where a VCT issues a prospectus to raise new funds from investors.

Where further share issues take place

8.13 There is a relaxation in relation to the 70% and 30% investment tests where a VCT has issued further ordinary shares.

The relaxation applies where there is an issue of ordinary shares after an earlier issue of ordinary shares, which took place whilst a company was approved as a VCT. In these circumstances, the 70% and 30% investment tests do not apply to the funds raised by the further issue in accounting periods up to and including any accounting period ending before three years after the further issue is made (the 'disregard period'). For accounting periods after this, the tests apply to all VCTs' investments, whether funded by earlier issues or by the further issue of ordinary shares.

Applications for approval

8.14 Applications for approval must be made in writing to the Inland Revenue. There is no formal application form.

Applications for full approval should contain:

- details of the VCT's stock exchange listing;

- a copy of the VCT's latest audited accounts;

- a copy of the VCT's up-to-date Memorandum and Articles of Association and details of any proposed changes;

- a report giving details to demonstrate that the conditions at *ICTA 1988, s 842AA(2)* (ie those detailed at **8.9** above) have been met in relation to its last complete accounting period;

- the address of the VCT's registered office, and details of its tax office and tax reference number.

Applications for provisional approval should contain:

- details of the VCT's stock exchange listing (or its plans for a stock exchange listing);

- a copy of the VCT's latest audited accounts (or where it is a new company a current statement of affairs or balance sheet);

- a copy of the VCT's up-to-date Memorandum and Articles of Association and details of any proposed changes;

- a copy of the draft prospectus;

- a business plan describing how the VCT can meet the conditions at *ICTA 1988, s 842AA(2)* (although the draft prospectus will usually be sufficient for this purpose);

- the address of the VCT's registered office and its tax office and tax reference number (if known).

8.15 The application for full or provisional approval must contain a declaration that to the best of the VCT's knowledge and belief:

(a) where the application is for full approval,

- the conditions for approval were met in relation to the last complete accounting period of the VCT;

- the conditions will be met in relation to the current accounting period; and

- the particulars given are true and correct.

(b) where the application is for provisional approval,

- the conditions for full approval will be met within the prescribed time periods; and

- the particulars given are true and correct.

Provisional approvals will evolve into full approvals when the conditions for full approval are satisfied. No further application or approval notice is necessary.

Valuation of investments

8.16 VCTs, in preparing their published accounts, will have to comply with accounting conventions and British Venture Capital Association guidelines in valuing their investments.

However, in evaluating compliance with the VCT requirements for the 70%, 30% and 15% investment tests (see **8.9** above) the Inland Revenue provide different rules.

8.17 Where a VCT makes an additional investment in a share or security of an investee company the whole of the remaining investment is valued at the latest subscription price, regardless of the amount of the additional investment and whether there has been a part disposal of the investment.

Also, where an investee company is placed into administration, receivership or liquidation (after March 2000) the VCT's investment in that company is maintained at cost (or its VCT value, if different) until the investment is sold or the investee company is struck off the Register of Companies (or its equivalent).

Potential problem areas with VCT compliance and inadvertent breaches

Potential problem areas with VCT compliance

8.18 The most likely problem areas relate to compliance with the investment tests.

The 15% investment test

8.19   In relation to the 15% investment test the problem can arise where a VCT wishes to make a further investment of the same class and description in an investee company and the VCT valuation rules apply (see **8.17** above).

EXAMPLE 8.19

A VCT has

- 10 qualifying holdings at a cost of £7.5m;

- total investments of £10m (£7.5m in qualifying holdings and £2.5m of non-qualifying holdings);

- one particular investment of 100,000 ordinary shares in Company X (in the above figures) where the subscription price was £1 per share.

The VCT proposes to take up its rights under a rights issue to be made by Company X and subscribe for a further 1,000 ordinary shares at £20 per share.

If that investment proceeded the position on the 15% investment test would be:

	£
Valuation of holding in Company X (101,000 times £20) equals	2,020,000
Valuation of VCT's total investments	
• existing investments	7,500,000
• new investment in Company X	20,000
• uplift in VCT valuation of existing investment in Company X (100,000 times £20 minus £1)	1,900,000
	9,420,000

£2,020,000 divided by £9,420,000 equals 21.4%, ie 15 per investment test not complied with.

The 70% investment test

8.20   For a VCT that has achieved the 70% investment test within the three-year relevant period that test must continue to be met by the VCT after the end of the three-year relevant period.

Because the VCT's investments in qualifying holdings will be in minority, uninfluential, holdings, particularly where those investments are in AIM companies it is possible that there could be cash offers for some of those investee companies such that the VCT's investments in qualifying holdings fell below the requisite 70% of total investments. In such situations, where there is a period of time before the VCT can distribute a capital profit arising from those disposals or the VCT does not have sufficient resources to make a capital distribution and therefore requires a period of time to make additional qualifying investments to meet and exceed the 70% investment level, the Inland Revenue can regard the breach as an inadvertent breach and apply their 'care and maintenance provisions' (see **8.22** below).

8.21   For a VCT that is approaching the end of its relevant investment period, there may be difficulty in attaining and exceeding the 70% investment requirement by the end of the period. This may arise because:

• due diligence, in relation to a proposed qualifying investment, is prolonged and delaying the completion of the investment;

• investee companies decline to complete an investment or following due diligence the VCT declines to complete an investment.

In such a situation the VCT may wish to place a requisite amount of funds on non-interest bearing account.

Because the amount on non-interest bearing accounts are not regarded as investments the VCT can meet the 70% investment test.

EXAMPLE 8.21

• investment in qualifying investments   £6,600,000 *
• total investments   £9,100,000 *
* excludes £900,000 placed on non-interest bearing account pending investment of those funds in qualifying investments
£6,600,000 divided by £9,100,000 equals   72%
If the earmarked funds had been left in an interest bearing account the position would have been:
£6,600,000 divided by £10,000,000 equals   66%
After the further qualifying investments of £900,000 have been made the position is:
• investment in qualifying investments   £7,500,000
• total investments   £10,000,000
• £7,500,000 divided by £10,000,000 equals   75%

Inadvertent breaches

8.22   Where inadvertent breach takes place (see Example **8.21** above) the Inland Revenue are empowered to provide a period of time for the VCT to rectify the situation.

In the case mentioned above the Inland Revenue will want the VCT to have comfortably exceeded the 70% level of qualifying holdings and for the events (taking the level of qualifying holdings below 70% of total investments) to be outside the control of the VCT.

The VCT will need to advise the Inland Revenue of the breach promptly and provide full details of how the breach arose and how it is to be rectified.

The period of time to rectify the position (to regain at least 70% of its total investments in qualifying holdings) will be negotiated between the VCT and the Inland Revenue and for example will take into account the VCT's investment record (rate).

Returns to be made to the Inland Revenue

8.23   The Inland Revenue (see also **8.24** below) monitor compliance with the legislative requirements by way of a review of the Company's annual report and accounts and a 'Regulation 22' return that is normally submitted with the Company's corporation tax return.

The Regulation 22 return should disclose:

- the value of each investment held at the beginning of the period;

- the dates and valuations of any new investments made in the period together with revaluations if appropriate for investments arising from a further issue of shares;

- details of disposals or part disposals;

- whether the investment is or is not a qualifying holding;

- for each qualifying holding the name and address of the company invested in.

The Regulation 22 must be signed by the secretary or a director of the VCT who must certify that the conditions for approval have been met and that the return is, to the best of the VCT's knowledge and belief, true and correct.

Inland Revenue structure and organisation for VCTs

8.24   The Inland Revenue is organised for VCTs as follows:

- Tax Districts

- Technical Division

- Policy Division

There are three specific tax districts (Small Company Enterprise Centres) in Cardiff, Dundee and Maidstone that deal with applications for provisional clearances of the VCT status of investee companies and the proposed investment by VCTs by the investee companies' advisers (with the applications being sent initially to the Small Company Enterprise Centre TIDO, Ty Glas, Llanishen, Cardiff, CF14 5ZG).

In addition, the tax districts at Cardiff and Dundee deal with the VCTs' annual report and accounts, the corporation tax and the Regulation 22 returns, monitoring compliance with the VCT legislative requirements (see also **8.23** above).

8.25   The Inland Revenue has an adviser within its Technical Division responsible for VCTs; that adviser provides guidance on the interpretation of the legislation (*ICTA 1988, s 842AA, Sch 28B*) and practice as it affects VCTs, and gives provisional approvals (see **8.11** above).

The Inland Revenue also has a policy adviser focused on VCTs; that adviser formulates policy on new developments. For example, the policy adviser has been responsible for developing legislative provisions to enable the merger of VCTs and the winding up of VCTs without loss of tax reliefs.

Likely future developments

8.26 The Government are currently considering the ways in which smaller unquoted companies are financed.

VCTs are being reviewed as part of that consultation process and it is envisaged that there may be changes, in 2004, to the way VCTs are structured.

9 Mergers and Reconstructions of Funds

Camilla Spielman

Eversheds

Reasons for mergers and reconstructions

9.1 Various commercial reasons may cause a fund manager to propose the merger or reconstruction of a fund. Regulatory change is also a key driver for fund managers in this area. Structural reasons in closed-ended funds may also lead their boards to propose some form of reorganisation.

UK open-ended funds

9.2 A fund manager may decide that a fund is no longer commercially viable, perhaps because of investment conditions, for instance the end of the technology boom in 2002/03. In these circumstances the fund manager may propose to merge the fund affected into a stronger fund in its range. The converse can also arise. For example, it was relatively common to launch Japan and Pacific Basin funds in the 1980s and early 1990s, and as the economies of the two diverged, fund managers sought to reconstruct the funds into their component parts.

When a fund manager buys another fund manager, or in some cases its fund management business, there is likely to be duplication between fund ranges. To deal with this the acquiring fund manager often seeks to merge duplicated funds. If one of the managers has already converted its AUTs to OEICs then the proposals will almost invariably include the conversion of the acquired AUTs to OEICs.

From the introduction of OEICs in 1997, many fund managers have converted entire ranges of AUTs into OEICs, typically in umbrella form with a number of subfunds. A key driver was frequently the OEIC's ability to issue classes of share with different charging structures and other features. With the proposal to introduce flexible unit classes in AUTs in CP 185, however, investment houses that have not yet converted their range of AUTs to OEICs may not now do so.

Offshore open-ended funds

9.3 The reasons for merging or reconstructing offshore open-ended funds mirror many of those for onshore ones, that is, to reflect changing investment conditions and the rationalisation of funds after one fund manager acquires another's fund business. Offshore fund managers may also wish to 'redomicile' their funds into another jurisdiction, for example, to rationalise their administration and management centres.

Investment trusts

9.4   There are two basic reasons for reconstructing or merging an investment trust. First, where a fixed life investment trust is approaching a continuation vote and the board doubts whether the investment trust will be allowed to continue. In these circumstances, the board might wish to give shareholders the option of remaining invested in a vehicle with similar investment objectives or of disposing of their shareholdings for cash. Merging or reconstructing the investment trust into another investment trust or an open-ended fund, while offering cash as an alternative, satisfies both requirements.

Secondly, where an investment trust is trading at a discount, the board may be under pressure from shareholders, possibly including arbitrageurs, to narrow the discount. There are various routes which may be used to try to achieve this; restructuring the investment trust using a merger or reconstruction is one of them.

In this chapter, a merger refers to one vehicle (or more) amalgamating with another of the same type, for example, an AUT with another AUT. A conversion is where one (or more) AUTs converts into an OEIC, or more usually, an OEIC subfund. The word 'reconstruction' is used to cover other types of scheme in which the original vehicle is split in some way. References to OEICs include references to subfunds of umbrella OEICs, unless they are referred to separately.

UK open-ended funds

Background and basic outline of schemes of merger and reconstruction

Collective Investment Schemes Regulations

9.5   It is standard practice for managers to put forward a scheme that qualifies as a scheme of arrangement within the CIS Sourcebook, more commonly known as mergers or reconstructions (FSA Handbook Collective Investment Schemes Sourcebook (CIS Sourcebook), section 11.5 'Schemes of Arrangement').

Section 11.5, headed 'Schemes of Arrangement', lays down requirements at 11.5.2. The material point for these purposes is that investors in the original fund must vote in favour of the proposals. A resolution to implement a scheme of arrangement which has been duly carried will be binding even on those that did not vote. This compulsion is important both for the fund manager proposing the scheme and for capital gains tax purposes. In some cases the holders of the successor fund or funds must vote to accept the proposals.

The CIS Sourcebook does not prescribe the form that a scheme of arrangement must take.

Circular to investors

9.6 Typically the fund manager of the original fund will send a circular to its holders. The circular normally contains a letter from the fund manager to the holders outlining the proposals and the benefits they offer, the formal scheme, details of the original and successor fund or funds and formal documentation for the necessary meeting or meetings.

Schemes of arrangement tend to take a similar form, although the details necessarily vary according to the transaction proposed.

The scheme is normally expressed to be subject to unit/shareholder approval. The transfer of investments from the original fund to the successor fund or funds takes place at a time and date laid down in the scheme, and is frequently referred to as the 'effective date'. The key elements are that:

(a) dealings in the units/shares of the original fund will cease at a time shortly before the transfer of investments from the original fund to the successor fund;

(b) usually, the current accounting period of the original fund will end at a particular time, normally immediately before the transfer takes place (note, this may not be the case for all mergers and reconstructions);

(c) any actual and estimated income available for allocation in the original fund will be allocated in respect of the accounting period ending immediately before the relevant transfer;

(d) the valuation of the original fund and (if relevant) the successor fund or funds will be calculated at a time immediately before the relevant transfer;

(e) the assets of the original fund, less an amount retained to meet its actual and contingent liabilities, will be transferred to the successor fund or funds, as appropriate, on the effective date;

(f) holders in the original fund will receive new units/shares in the successor fund or funds of a value equal or as nearly as possible equal to the value of their original holding; and

(g) once the transfers have been effected and all liabilities discharged, the appropriate steps will be taken to terminate the original fund.

9.7 The simplest form of scheme of arrangement can be represented as shown below.

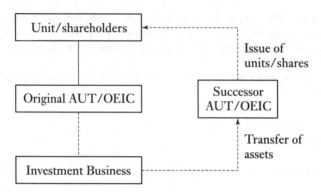

Mergers

9.8 The tax consequences of a merger of an AUT with another AUT, an OEIC with another OEIC, or more likely an OEIC subfund with another OEIC subfund (whether in the same or in a different umbrella fund) are similar. This section therefore covers all three types of merger together, unless otherwise indicated. The same principles apply when more than one authorised fund merges into a single successor fund.

Distribution of income to investors

9.9 The scheme of arrangement put to holders of the original fund will usually provide for the distribution (or where it is accumulated, allocation) of any actual and estimated income for the accounting period ending immediately before the effective date when the assets are transferred to the successor fund.

The income available for distribution allocated to income units/shares will be transferred to the distribution account of the original fund. Typically it will be distributed after the effective date of the merger, that is, in the post-merger accounting period. The procedure for these payments is the same as in a continuing fund.

In contrast, however, available income allocated to accumulation units/shares is normally transferred to the capital account of the original fund and allocated to the accumulation units/shares and reflected in their value. This income is then taken into account when calculating the number of new units/shares to be issued in the successor fund under the scheme.

The investors will be taxable on income distributed or allocated in the normal way according to the type of distribution and their personal circumstances.

Capital gains of investors

9.10 Investors in merging funds will generally wish to avoid having the exchange of their investment in the original fund for that in the successor fund trigger a chargeable disposal for capital gains tax purposes. As explained more fully in CHAPTER 1 above, both AUTs and OEICs are deemed to be companies for the purposes of *TCGA 1992*. Consequently the relieving provisions governing mergers of companies in *TCGA 1992, s 136* can apply to mergers of funds. Where *section 136* relief applies, the new units or shares issued in the successor fund will take on the acquisition cost and date of the original holding which they have replaced.

9.11   For the statutory roll-over relief in *section 136* to apply, the merger must constitute a 'scheme of reconstruction' as defined in *TCGA 1992, Sch 5AA*. For a merger of funds to qualify, the merger scheme must involve the issue of units/shares in the successor fund to the holders of units/shares in the original fund (the first condition). The second condition in *Schedule 5AA* is that all investors receive the same proportion of the new units/shares in the successor fund as they held in the original fund. Where there is more than one class of unit/share, the holders of each class must receive the same proportion of the new units/shares. Thirdly, the business or substantially the whole of the business of the original fund must be carried on by the successor fund after the merger. For this purpose the Inland Revenue accept that an investment business is passing from the original fund to the successor fund so long as the obligation to manage the assets passes with them (Inland Revenue Manual CG52709). They also disregard any cash or assets that are retained to meet liabilities and liquidation costs of the original fund (Inland Revenue Manual CG52726). None of these conditions should present problems for mergers that qualify as schemes of arrangement within the CIS Sourcebook.

Schedule 5AA has had effect for mergers effective on or after 17 April 2002. Before that date it was necessary to look to the case law definition of a 'reconstruction or amalgamation', augmented by the Inland Revenue Statement of Practice 5/85.

9.12   Where the technical conditions of *section 136* relief are met, then relief under the section will apply. There is an exception, however, for holders (including connected persons) holding more than 5% of, or of any class of the units/shares, in the original fund (*TCGA 1992, s 137*). For these holders to be entitled to *section 136* relief, the merger must be effected for bona fide commercial reasons. Further, it must not form part of a scheme or arrangements of which the main purpose, or one of the main purposes, is the avoidance of liability to capital gains tax or corporation tax on chargeable gains.

The Inland Revenue currently take the bona fide commercial requirement to mean that the scheme must provide a benefit for the holders in the original fund. Examples of such a benefit might include a more favourable charging structure in the successor fund, lower fixed costs per unit in the successor fund but only if the holders will benefit (as opposed to the fund manager), or better investment prospects in the successor fund. Before the introduction of *Schedule 5AA*, the Inland Revenue applied less rigorous standards to this test.

9.13   It is standard practice for fund managers proposing a scheme intended to provide roll-over relief under *section 136* to apply for clearance under *section 138* that the scheme is being effected for bona fide commercial reasons and not to avoid tax on capital gains. This is a precautionary measure to protect substantial investors in the original fund as the fund manager will not normally know, when it proposes the scheme, whether any investors will breach the 5% limit when the merger takes place. The clearance from the Inland Revenue does not confirm, however, that the proposed scheme will qualify as a scheme of reconstruction as required for *section 136* roll-over relief, but only that they are satisfied that *section 137(1)* should not have effect to prevent *section 136* roll-over relief applying.

Note that before the enactment of *Schedule 5AA*, the position was different. Recognising that the case law test of a reconstruction or amalgamation led to uncertainty, Revenue practice was for the Capital Gains Clearance Section to indicate if, in their view, arrangements submitted to them did not constitute a scheme of reconstruction or amalgamation.

9.14   Details of how the *section 136* clearance application should be made are available on the Inland Revenue website. The information provided in support of the application must fully and accurately disclose all the relevant facts; it is usual to enclose a copy of the circular to investors (this will normally be a late draft). Where clearance under *ICTA 1988, s 707* is also being sought (this is explained in **9.15**), the two applications should be contained in a single letter to the Business Tax Clearance Team. The Inland Revenue have a thirty-day period in which to grant the clearance applied for or to ask for further particulars of the transaction.

9.15   It is also usual to apply for an *ICTA 1988, s 707* clearance. The anti-avoidance provisions in *sections 703–709* apply where, briefly, a tax advantage is obtained as a result of a transaction in securities which falls within one of the five sets of circumstances set out in section 704. In such a case the Inland Revenue may serve a notice on the investor to counteract the tax advantage. It is difficult to see how this could apply to a merger where the income for the distribution period ending immediately before the effective date is distributed in the normal way and capital only is transferred to the successor fund. As stated above, however, an application for this clearance now requires only an additional paragraph in the *TCGA 1992, s 138* application letter.

An exception to the general principles described above applies to corporate investors in bond funds. They are subject to a mark-to-market basis for taxation under *FA 1996, Sch 10* and do not benefit from any form of roll-over relief. Their overall tax position should not normally, however, be effected by the disposal and acquisition.

Stamp taxes

Cancellation of units or shares in the original fund

9.16   Technically the original fund will be liable to stamp duty reserve tax (SDRT) under *FA 1999, Sch 19 para 2* on the cancellation of its units/shares to the extent that their value is attributable to UK equities and equity linked convertibles transferred to the successor fund. The exemption from SDRT for pro rata in specie redemptions in *paragraph 7* applies only where the investors receive their share of the underlying investments. In a merger the investments are passed directly to the successor fund and not the investors.

The practice of Inland Revenue (Stamp Taxes) is not, however, to treat the cancellation of units/shares in the original fund as triggering a charge under *Schedule 19* where a scheme in the normal form is employed.

Transfer of the original fund's investments

9.17   The position of AUTs is different to that of OEICs, so this section deals with them separately. It should be noted, however, that there might be foreign transfer taxes levied on transfers of portfolio investments in a limited number of jurisdictions. Where the fund concerned invests in land and other property, it will be necessary to consider the special provisions that apply to it, including stamp duty land tax after 30 November 2003.

AUTs

9.18   The basic position is that a transfer of trust property from the trustee of the original unit trust to the trustee of a successor unit trust may be dutiable as a conveyance on sale: this is certainly the Inland Revenue's view. The Inland Revenue previously regarded SDRT as applying to the transfer of chargeable securities, broadly UK equities and equity linked convertibles, on the merger of unit trust schemes. Their position on this has shifted following the decision in *Save & Prosper Securities Limited v IRC* [2000] STC (SCD) 408, described further below.

There was, however, an exemption from stamp duty and SDRT on the merger of AUTs, which lasted from 19 March 1997 to 30 June 1999 (see, for stamp duty: *FA 1997, s 95*; for SDRT: *FA 1997, ss 100* and *101*). This accompanied the introduction of OEICs and the generous exemptions for conversions.

9.19   In the case of foreign investments, the foreign transfer forms may technically, depending on the nature of the security, be chargeable to UK stamp duty because the consideration units are issued by a UK unit trust. So long as the foreign transfer forms are executed and remain outside the UK at all times then the time for stamping will not start to run and so no stamp duty will be payable. (Once registered, the foreign transfer forms would not normally serve any further purpose.) It is not, in any event, normal practice for a foreign registrar to be concerned with UK stamp duty. The only possible disadvantage in not stamping foreign transfer forms would arise if they were required in the UK. This would normally only be as evidence in legal proceedings, in which case the duty would need to be paid together with interest, but the late stamping penalty could be avoided so long as they were stamped within thirty days of being brought into the UK.

9.20 The issue of whether SDRT is payable on chargeable securities on the merger of AUTs receded following the Special Commissioner's case, *Save & Prosper Securities Limited v IRC* [2000] STC (SCD) 408. The two AUTs involved shared a common trustee and manager. The Special Commissioner, Dr A N Brice, held that there was no agreement for SDRT purposes in the merger process. Rather, the scheme took effect by operation of law under the provisions of the *Financial Services Act 1986* and the *Financial Services (Regulated Schemes) Regulations 1991* (now the *Financial Services and Markets Act 2000* and the CIS Sourcebook) with the essential ingredient being the passing of the unitholder resolution to implement the scheme of amalgamation. There was also no transfer from the unitholders in the merging fund to the continuing fund; both sets of unitholders gave up their beneficial interests in their respective funds and received new equitable interests in the enlarged scheme. The Inland Revenue withdrew an appeal and, on 26 February 2001, acknowledged in a draft Customer Newsletter that no SDRT was payable in cases along the same lines as the *Save & Prosper* case.

Many mergers of AUTs take place within a fund manager's range where there is a common trustee, so they fall squarely within the facts of *Save & Prosper*.

9.21 The position on mergers of AUTs with separate trustees is not clear. The logical position following the *Save & Prosper* decision is that SDRT would not be payable, but there has been no public indication that the Inland Revenue take this position. To avoid this uncertainty, a fund manager could align the trustees of the two AUTs before the merger. It should, however, consider the potential impact of *FA 1965, s 90* before doing so if it is the trustee of the original fund that is to change, and any of the investments in the AUT will require stock transfer forms, or a letter of direction will be required. *Section 90* states that any instrument whereby property is conveyed or transferred to any person in contemplation of a sale of that property shall be treated for the purposes of the *Stamp Act 1891* as a conveyance or transfer on sale of that property for a consideration equal to the value of that property. This anti-avoidance provision catches transfers to a nominee in contemplation of sale and charges stamp duty on them as if the transfer were a sale, for a consideration equal to the value of the property transferred. Inland Revenue (Stamp Taxes) contend that this provision applies to mergers of unit trusts where the trustee of the merging fund is changed to facilitate the merger. Unwritten Revenue practice is to regard a transfer to a nominee, including a change of trustee of a merging fund, in the year leading up to the 'sale' in question as being caught by the provision, unless the transfer took place for a bona fide commercial reason. An example of such a reason is where the retiring trustee of the merging fund is unwilling to carry through the merger process (which is not unreasonable as their remuneration arrangements will not normally compensate them for the additional work required in a merger), in which case it will need to be replaced before the merger can proceed. Although *section 90* is rarely invoked in practice, the fund manager of a fund where a trustee retires and is replaced to facilitate a merger should ensure where appropriate that proper evidence exists that the retirement and new appointment took place for bona fide commercial reasons.

9.22   Where a trustee of a successor fund retires and is replaced before a merger and this results in a common trustee, the converse does not apply and the anti-avoidance provision, *FA 1965, s 90*, does not bite. Similarly the section has no application to a mere change of fund manager.

OEICs

9.23   Turning to the merger of OEICs, the position is that stamp duty is payable on any stock transfer forms as described above for AUTs. Inland Revenue (Stamp Taxes) considered that SDRT was payable on an agreement to transfer chargeable securities on a merger. The *Save & Prosper* case and 2001 Inland Revenue draft Customer Newsletter did not address mergers of OEICs. The position of Inland Revenue (Stamp Taxes) on the merger of OEICs has changed. In correspondence with the IMA and others in January 2000, it was accepted that mergers of OEICs with a common depositary would not trigger SDRT. Technically this would appear to be correct following Dr Brice's decision in the *Save & Prosper* case that a fund merger took place by operation of law under the relevant regulations, which apply equally to AUTs and OEICs.

Inland Revenue (Stamp Taxes) reconsidered the SDRT position on the merger of OEIC subfunds with a common depositary at the end of 2002 on the basis of a second element to Dr Brice's decision in the *Save & Prosper* case. This was that the unitholders in both unit trusts surrendered their beneficial interests and received new beneficial interests in the enlarged continuing unit trust so that there was no transfer from the unitholders of the merging fund to the unitholders of the continuing fund. This can strictly apply only to AUTs because it is through their trust-based constitution that unitholders have a beneficial interest in the underlying assets in the trust fund. In contrast, shareholders in OEICs have an interest only in the shares of the OEIC, while the corporate OEIC is the beneficial owner of its assets. This second point was used by Dr Brice to bolster her first argument and so does not appear essential to the decision. At present Inland Revenue (Stamp Taxes) take a pragmatic approach and do not look for SDRT on the merger of OEIC subfunds with a common depositary, whether they are subfunds of one or more umbrella OEICs.

9.24   There is an additional argument against SDRT arising on the merger of subfunds within a single OEIC. In this case there will be no change in the beneficial ownership of the scheme assets. The *Stamp Duty and Stamp Duty Reserve Tax (Open-ended Investment Companies) Regulations 1997 (SI 1997/1156)* provide, by way of complex modifications to the definitions in *ICTA 1988, s 468*, that each subfund of an OEIC is treated as a separate OEIC for stamp duty and SDRT purposes, except where the context otherwise requires. It is not clear that the deeming provisions in this legislation go far enough as drafted to trigger a charge.

9.25   The position on mergers of OEICs with separate depositaries is not clear. The logical position following the *Save & Prosper* decision is that SDRT would not be payable but there has been no public indication that the Inland Revenue take this position. The points made in the context of AUTs will apply equally here.

Fund's tax position

Gains

9.26   Gains realised in the original fund in the course of a merger will not be subject to tax because of the exemption in *TCGA 1992, s 100*. This exemption applies directly to AUTs, but it is extended to OEICs under the *Open-ended Investment Companies (Tax) Regulations 1997 (SI 1997/1154)*.

Income

9.27   An AUT's pre-merger accounting period will normally end immediately before the time of the merger. This will also end its corporation tax accounting period. Despite the merger, all the tax balances of the original fund will carry forward into the post-merger accounting period in the normal way. So there will not therefore normally be any liability to corporation tax arising after the merger takes place. Where an OEIC subfund is merging, it is not possible to foreshorten (or lengthen) its accounting period without affecting the entire umbrella OEIC, so it is normal in this case to end an interim accounting period. Some fund managers are doing the same for AUT mergers.

Equalisation

9.28   If the successor fund operates equalisation and the effective date of the merger is not also an accounting date for the successor fund, then the trustee/depositary is likely to insist that the new units/shares issued in the course of the merger are Group II units. When the holders receive their first income distribution or allocation in the successor fund, part of it will consist of equalisation. This is effectively an allowance for the income element purchased when the capital from the original fund was used to acquire units/shares in the successor fund. Equalisation is a return of capital and so not taxable in investors' hands. The equalisation amount will, however, need to be deducted from the acquisition cost of the holdings in the successor fund. In other words, the original acquisition cost of the holdings in the original fund, which has been rolled over to become the base cost of the holdings in the successor fund, will need to be reduced to reflect the equalisation payment. Investors who dispose of their holdings in the successor fund before the distribution will not be affected by the equalisation adjustment.

Conversions

9.29   The basic form of conversion is where a single AUT is converted into a new subfund of a new or pre-existing umbrella OEIC (conversions into single

OEICs are rare) by way of a scheme of arrangement under the CIS Sourcebook. A conversion can, however, take place where an AUT converts into an existing subfund of an umbrella OEIC or existing OEIC (described as an amalgamation in the OEICs' tax legislation). Two or more AUTs can also convert into a new, or existing, OEIC subfund or OEIC. The basic principles remain the same whatever the variant, so they are not considered separately, other than for SDRT and stamp duty where the difference is important.

Conversions for tax purposes are simply a form of scheme of reconstruction and accordingly their basic tax treatment follows that of mergers. The Government in 1997, however, wanted to encourage the fund industry to convert AUTs into OEICs and so the 1997 OEICs' tax legislation contained a number of statutory concessions that applied where AUTs were converted. These concessions remain in place. An unusual feature of OEIC conversions is that they take place, or are deemed to take place, at midnight in order to allow for continuity of tax treatment between the AUT and the OEIC, as explained at **9.39** below (*Open-ended Investment Companies (Tax) Regulations 1996 (SI 1997/1154), regulations 25–27*). The other concessions relate to SDRT and stamp duty.

Distribution of income to investors

9.30   As with a merger, the first step in a conversion is to deal with the income accruing in the pre-conversion accounting period of the AUT. A scheme of arrangement implementing the conversion will provide for the current accounting period of the AUT to cease immediately before the effective date, that is, the time at which the conversion is deemed to take place. Any actual and estimated income available for distribution or allocation will be paid into the distribution account or retained as capital in the AUT, as appropriate. The income distribution will need to be made in the post-conversion accounting period of the AUT. Where there are accumulation units in issue, and the scheme provides for the pre-conversion income to be accumulated, this will be transferred to the OEIC and increase the value of the shareholding in the OEIC issued to the former holders of accumulation units.

Capital gains of investors

9.31   There are no special rules for capital gains tax on the conversion of AUTs. The provisions set out for mergers therefore apply. Both AUTs and OEICs are deemed to be companies for the purposes of the *Taxation of Chargeable Gains Act 1992 (TCGA 1992, s 99* in the case of unit trusts and *section 99* as applied by the *Open-ended Investment Companies (Tax) Regulations 1996 (SI 1997/1154)* in the case of OEICs), so relief under *section 136* will be available. Consequently, so long as the necessary conditions are satisfied, the new shares issued to investors will be treated for capital gains tax purposes as having been acquired at the time and for the consideration applicable to their original holdings in the AUT.

9.32   The technical conditions for roll-over relief to apply are set out in *TCGA 1992, s 136* supplemented by *Schedule 5AA*. This sets out the conditions for there to be a 'scheme of reconstruction'.

A conversion will satisfy the first condition of *Schedule 5AA* because it will involve the issue of shares in the OEIC to the unitholders. Secondly, all the unitholders, or if there is more than one class, all the unitholders in that class, must receive the same proportion of the new shares as they previously held. Finally, the business or substantially the whole of the business of the AUT must be carried on by the OEIC after the conversion. The Inland Revenue accept that this is the case where the only assets left in the AUT are to meet liabilities and liquidation costs, and a portfolio of investments is transferred together with the obligation to manage it.

9.33   As explained above for mergers, even where the technical conditions of *section 136* relief have been satisfied, where an investor (together with connected persons) holds more than 5% of the AUT, or of any class of units in the AUT, the conversion must be entered into for bona fide commercial reasons and not to avoid capital gains tax for that investor to qualify for roll-over tax treatment (*TCGA 1992, s 137*). It is standard practice to apply for clearance under *section 138* in every case.

As with mergers, it is also standard practice to apply under *ICTA 1988, s 707* to obtain clearance from the Inland Revenue that they will not issue a notice cancelling a tax advantage. Likewise, it is not obvious that any of the prescribed circumstances set out in *section 704* that can give rise to tax advantages to be cancelled can apply.

Stamp taxes

Cancellation of units in the original fund

9.34   The position on the cancellation of units in the course of a conversion is the same as set out for the merger of funds. In short, it is necessary to rely on the Inland Revenue's confirmation that they will not normally look for SDRT under *FA 1999, Sch 19* on the surrender of the units in the AUT. Technically the cancellation does, however, fall within the ambit of *paragraph 2* to that Schedule.

Under the *FA 1946* stamp duty regime for unit trust schemes any stamp duty payable in connection with the units would have been refundable, so no stamp duty would actually have been suffered. Consequently there was no exemption for conversions in the 1997 legislation. This might account for the absence of any specific provision in *Schedule 19*.

Transfer of the original fund's investments

9.35   Where an AUT is converted into an OEIC and the statutory conditions set out in *regulation 7* of the *Stamp Duty and Stamp Duty Reserve Tax (Open-*

ended Investment Companies) Regulations 1997 (SI 1997/1156) are satisfied then stamp duty is not chargeable on instruments transferring property from the trustee to the depositary. The conditions are, broadly, that all the available property of the AUT is transferred into a new OEIC. The investors' units must be exchanged for the appropriate proportion of newly issued shares in the OEIC. The OEIC may take over the liabilities of the AUT (which is sometimes done to enable the AUT to be terminated shortly after the conversion). These conditions will be satisfied in any normal conversion scheme.

9.36 In practice, stamp duty will rarely be a major concern for two reasons. First, few AUTs will still hold UK securities outside CREST. Secondly, the trustee of a converting AUT is often also the depositary of the OEIC. As explained for mergers above, being the trustee of a fund that is converting into an OEIC results in additional work (and potential liabilities) normally without any right to additional remuneration. Fund trustees that are not being retained after the conversion therefore tend to retire and be replaced beforehand. The exemption may be helpful, however, even where there is a common trustee/depositary, because it will allow documents to be created recording the unitholder resolution and, in particular, directing the custodian to hold the trust assets for the OEIC without any risk of stamp duty being payable on them.

It should be noted that any claim for exemption from stamp duty under *regulation 7* must be adjudicated.

9.37 An equivalent exemption from the principal charge to SDRT under *FA 1986, s 87* on the transfer of chargeable securities from the trustee of a converting AUT to an OEIC depositary is contained in *regulation 8*. There is no need to claim this exemption; rather the parties should simply retain sufficient evidence to prove that the conditions have been satisfied.

There are equivalent provisions for stamp duty and SDRT relief in *regulations 9* and *10* respectively that apply where an AUT is converted into an existing OEIC, that is, an OEIC that already owns assets (described as an amalgamation in the legislation). The conditions for these reliefs to apply are the same as those for straightforward conversions with the exception that the OEIC must already contain assets. These exemptions were originally due to end on 30 June 1999 but in the event were extended by the *Stamp Duty and Stamp Duty Reserve Tax (Open-ended Investment Companies) (Amendment) Regulations 1999 (SI 1999/1467)*, and have now been made permanent (Treasury Press Release of 16 October 2002 (105/02)).

CREST transaction stamp status flag 6 was introduced from 19 October 1998 to cater for the various exemptions for conversions where securities are moved within CREST.

There may be foreign transfer taxes, though these arise only in a limited number of jurisdictions.

Fund's tax position

Gains

9.38   As with mergers, the exemption from tax on capital gains within an AUT under *TCGA 1992, s 100* will cover the transfer of investments to the OEIC and any necessary sales to cover expenses.

Income

CONTINUITY OF TAX TREATMENT

9.39   The *Open-ended Investment Companies (Tax) Regulations 1997 (SI 1997/1154), reg 25* provides for continuity of tax treatment between the AUT and the OEIC where the conditions set out in the regulations are met. These may be summarised as the transfer to an OEIC of all the available scheme property of an AUT, in exchange for the issue of new shares in the OEIC to the unitholders in proportion to their original unitholdings, which are then cancelled. The OEIC may assume or discharge the liabilities of the AUT but otherwise the consideration must be limited to the issue of new shares in the OEIC. This will invariably be the case in a scheme of arrangement under the CIS Sourcebook. Where the conditions described above apply to a conversion, *regulation 25(2)* provides for the pre-transfer accounting period to end immediately before the transfer date. All of the available scheme property is then treated for corporation tax purposes as having been transferred to the OEIC immediately after the end of that accounting period. The intention behind this provision was that the AUT's corporation tax accounting period would run up to and including the day before the conversion took place. The various tax balances of the converting AUT specified in the Regulations would be treated as tax balances of the OEIC, with effect from the transfer date, so that they would be available to the OEIC in its accounting period ending on or after the transfer date.

9.40   Whilst the Inland Revenue have indicated that they are not prescriptive about the exact time that the AUT's accounting period ends on the day before the conversion takes place, it is recommended that the period should end at a time as near to midnight as possible, ideally 11.59 pm. The effective date of the scheme of arrangement converting the AUT into an OEIC would then take place, or be deemed to take place, as soon as possible after midnight, for instance at 12.01 am. The reason for having as small a gap as possible between the ending of the accounting period of the AUT and the scheme taking effect is to avoid income arising in the intervening period.

9.41   The tax reliefs passing on the conversion (surplus advance corporation tax (ACT), surplus franked investment income (FII), surplus foreign income dividends (FIDs) and excess management expenses) were of considerable importance under the corporation tax regime in force in 1997. This was also the case with the provisions in *regulation 26* dealing with dual running. The provisions are no longer normally of importance, other than for excess management expenses. They are discussed at **9.46** below.

9.42 Where a conversion takes place at the end of an accounting period that begins on or after 1 October 2002, the AUT will come within the modified loan relationships regime (described in CHAPTER 1). This should not give rise to difficulties on the conversion.

For conversions that took place at the end of an accounting period that began on or before 30 September 2002, there will be a charge to corporation tax on deemed sums arising on the transfer of gilts and bonds (that is, chargeable securities as defined for accrued income scheme purposes) under the accrued income scheme (described in CHAPTER 1) (*ICTA 1988, ss 710–728*). The corollary of this is that the OEIC would obtain purchased interest relief in relation to the acquisition of the chargeable securities. On a strict interpretation of the legislation, any 'deemed sums' arising on the transfer of the gilts and bonds are taxable in the post-conversion accounting period of the AUT. Any tax reliefs that were available to the AUT before the conversion have been automatically transferred to the OEIC, potentially giving rise to a corporation tax liability in the AUT. The Inland Revenue have agreed that where this would create a corporation tax liability in an AUT's post-conversion accounting period, it may be possible to reduce or eliminate this by allowing these sums to be taxed in the OEIC's accounting period that includes the conversion (see, letter dated 7 September 2000 from Inland Revenue Financial Institutions Division to the Association of Unit Trusts and Investment Funds (now the Investment Management Association)). This is in accordance with *regulation 25(9)*.

SURPLUS ACT

9.43 Under *regulation 25*, any surplus ACT of the AUT at the conversion date will be transferred to the OEIC and be treated as brought forward under *ICTA 1988, s 239(4)* into the accounting period of the OEIC that includes the conversion.

It is possible in a conversion into an existing OEIC for it to carry back the transferred ACT, although this is unlikely to take place in practice.

Few, if any, AUTs or OEICs recover surplus ACT because of the way in which the shadow ACT regime operates and the regulatory requirement for them to distribute all their income in each distribution period. It is theoretically possible, however. The Revenue currently consider that for conversions on or before 5 April 1999, any surplus ACT is carried forward from the AUT to the OEIC, and is available for the OEIC to recover under the shadow ACT regime. For subsequent conversions, the Revenue take the opposite view, considering that the interaction of the OEICs' tax regulations and the legislation abolishing

ACT results in any surplus ACT of the AUT remaining with it, and probably being carried forward into its post-conversion accounting period.

SURPLUS FII

9.44 Any surplus FII arising on a conversion on or before 5 April 1999 is transferred to the OEIC to be treated by it as an amount received on the conversion date for the purposes of *ICTA 1988, Sch 13* (quarterly accounting on forms CT61). For later conversions, the position probably mirrors that for surplus ACT.

UK dividend income receivable, but not yet received by an AUT at the conversion date, is not strictly covered by the regulations. The Revenue have agreed, however, that it may be treated as falling within *regulation 25(9)(b)* and be transferred to the OEIC.

SURPLUS FIDs

9.45 For conversions on or before 5 April 1999, the position is as for surplus FII. Since then, surplus FIDs have been valueless.

EXCESS MANAGEMENT EXPENSES

9.46 Any excess management expenses of the AUT at the conversion date are treated for the purposes of *ICTA 1988, s 75(3)* as transferred into the accounting period of the OEIC in which the conversion takes place. They are not available to the AUT in its post-conversion accounting period.

DUAL RUNNING

9.47 'Dual running' is the phrase used to describe the situation in a conversion where a corporation tax accounting period of the AUT ceases immediately before the conversion date, and another, the post-conversion accounting period, begins on the following day. The payment out of any final income distribution and the payment of various liabilities will take place in this post-conversion accounting period, including, before its abolition, the payment of ACT. The AUT's post-conversion accounting period will be brought to an end by the trustee asking the FSA to withdraw the AUT's certificate of authorisation, at which point the AUT will cease to exist. The corporation tax accounting period of the OEIC will have begun on or before the date of the conversion. It is necessary to deal with this dual running period.

Most of the difficulties of dual running probably fell away with the abolition of ACT for distributions payable on or after 6 April 1999. For a discussion of the issues surrounding dual running for conversions that took place before the abolition of ACT, see the chapter 'Open-Ended Investment Companies' in *Tolley's Tax Planning*, 1999/2000 edition.

Equalisation

9.48   If the OEIC operates equalisation, where a conversion takes place into a new OEIC, the new shares issued will be Group I shares. This will also be so if a conversion is into an existing OEIC the distribution period of which has been brought to an end on the effective date of the conversion. In a case where a conversion takes place into an existing OEIC part way through the distribution period, the OEIC will normally issue Group II shares. In this case, former unitholders who remain in the OEIC until after its next distribution date will receive an element of equalisation with their income distribution or allocation. This amount should be deducted from the base cost carried across from their unitholding into the OEIC shares.

Other forms of reconstruction

9.49   Schemes of reconstruction can take other forms while still qualifying as schemes of arrangement within the CIS Sourcebook so that all the investors are bound by an extraordinary general resolution. An authorised fund can be split into two (or more, in theory) parts and each one merged into another authorised fund. The successor funds can be new or existing funds in each case. The precise tax consequences will depend on the facts, although the basic position will be common to all schemes where a fund is split.

Distribution of income to investors

9.50   The first step will be to distribute the net income, actual and accrued, to the holders of the original fund. The position will be identical to that described in **9.9** above.

Capital gains of investors

9.51   It is essential for any proposed scheme to qualify as a scheme of reconstruction under *TCGA 1992, Sch 5AA* in order for the investors in the original fund to be able to claim roll-over relief under *section 136* of the Act.

Where an existing fund is split with all investors receiving the same proportionate interest in two (or more) successor funds, this will meet the first three conditions set out in *TCGA 1992, Sch 5AA* and qualify as a scheme of reconstruction. The conditions are discussed at **9.10** et seq above.

9.52   A reconstruction of a fund, which takes place along the lines of the existing classes, will also fall squarely within the conditions in *Schedule 5AA*. An example of this unusual type of reconstruction is where the retail share class switches into a particular subfund of a retail OEIC, with institutional class holders similarly exchanging their holdings for shares in a particular subfund of an institutional OEIC. Such reconstructions may become more common when institutional funds are permitted.

9.53 *Mergers and Reconstructions of Funds*

It is standard practice to apply for clearance under *TCGA 1992, s 138* and also *ICTA 1988, s 707*. These are covered in detail at **9.13** et seq above.

Where, under a scheme of reconstruction, a holder receives new holdings in more than one successor fund, then it is necessary for the original acquisition cost to be apportioned between the new holdings. This is done under *TCGA 1992, s 130* (with necessary adaptations) on the basis of published prices on the first day following the effective date of the scheme.

Stamp taxes

Cancellation of units or shares in the original fund

9.53 There should be no charge under *FA 1999, Sch 19* so long as the scheme of reconstruction is carried out using standard form documentation in light of the statement made by Inland Revenue (Stamp Taxes), discussed at **9.16** above.

Transfer of the original fund's investments

9.54 Any transfer documents will attract ad valorem stamp duty in the normal way, as explained at **9.17** et seq above.

The position on SDRT on chargeable securities is uncertain. Before the *Save & Prosper* decision, Inland Revenue (Stamp Taxes) looked for SDRT where a fund containing chargeable securities was split in any way. The result in practice was that funds with chargeable securities were rarely split. Inland Revenue (Stamp Taxes) are reviewing the position, which should lead to greater clarity in this area.

There may be foreign transfer taxes.

Fund's tax position

9.55 There are no special rules for funds that are reconstructed into more than one fund; the position is therefore as described at **9.26** and **9.27** above for mergers.

Equalisation

9.56 As described at **9.28** above for mergers, equalisation will be paid to former holders of the original fund with their first income distribution or allocation in the successor funds only if the reconstruction takes place part way through a distribution period of a successor fund. In this case, any equalisation received should be deducted from the acquisition cost attributed to the holding in the successor fund. The equalisation is treated as a non-taxable return of capital.

Offshore open-ended funds

9.57 This section covers the merger and reconstruction of offshore open-ended funds from a UK perspective. The re-domiciling of funds is achieved by way of a merger and so is not discussed separately.

Background and basic outline of schemes of merger and reconstruction

9.58 It is obviously essential for any proposed merger or reconstruction scheme to comply with the relevant local regulations. In jurisdictions within the EU these should comply with the relevant Directives and so their regulatory regime should be similar to that in the UK. This is not, however, always the case. For instance, Ireland has only recently allowed UCITS funds to be merged into UCITS funds outside Ireland.

Offshore funds rules

9.59 As explained in CHAPTER 13, open-ended offshore funds marketed to the UK are either distributing funds certified annually by the Inland Revenue or non-distributor status funds which normally roll up their income within the fund (*ICTA 1988, ss 757–764* and *Sch 27* and *28*). It will be important for UK investors in a distributing fund that undergoes a merger with another distributing fund or a UK fund that neither the original fund nor, if relevant, the successor fund ceases to qualify as a result of actions taken during the merger, and the same applies for reconstructions.

Circular to investors

9.60 The manager of the original fund will normally send a circular to investors, which will be very similar to one for a UK scheme of arrangement. The circular will generally contain a formal scheme. This again will normally mirror UK arrangements although it may be slightly different to reflect local requirements and comply with the offshore funds legislation.

Mergers and reconstructions

Distribution of income to investors

9.61 The treatment of income arising in the accounting period of the original fund before a merger or reconstruction will normally depend on whether it and the successor fund or funds are distributing funds.

Distributing funds

9.62   It is essential where the funds concerned are distributing funds that all income of the original fund is distributed to the investors in the form of income (if there is not full distribution of income for the accounting period within *ICTA 1988, Sch 27*, the exchange of investments will constitute a taxable disposal under *section 757(6)* of the Act). This is normally achieved by there being an income distribution in the original fund of the actual and estimated income of the accounting period ending immediately before the effective date of the scheme and which takes place either before the effective date or shortly after it. If, for administrative reasons, the distribution date has to be earlier than the accounting period, a sensible precaution is to provide in the scheme for a second distribution to be made, if required to meet the offshore funds legislation distribution requirements. The investors in the original fund will be taxable on the income distributions in the normal way depending on their circumstances.

9.63   Where a holder disposes of a material interest in an offshore fund that has been certified as a distributing fund throughout the investor's period of ownership and the fund is operating equalisation arrangements, then the equalisation element in the disposal proceeds is charged to tax as income (*ICTA 1988, s 758*). This is the case whether or not gains are rolled over under *TCGA 1992, s 136* (described below).

Non-distributor status funds

9.64   Where income arising in a fund is normally rolled up, any income held in the income account immediately before a scheme of merger or reconstruction is also likely to be rolled up. If so, it will be reflected in the value of the new holdings in the successor fund or funds issued under the scheme.

Capital gains of investors

9.65   Investors in offshore funds subject to a merger or reconstruction will generally wish to avoid it triggering a chargeable disposal for UK tax purposes. The rules for exchanges of holdings in *TCGA 1992, s 136* apply to offshore funds in the same way as they do for onshore funds. This is the case for offshore unit trusts too, as the deeming provisions for unit trusts in *section 99* apply equally to non-UK unit trusts. This allows them and their unitholders to benefit from the capital gains tax roll-over relief in *section 136*. Accordingly the points made in the sections on mergers and reconstructions of onshore open-ended funds regarding *section 136* and *Schedule 5AA* (schemes of reconstruction) apply equally to offshore funds. Generally, a merger or reconstruction of an offshore fund will qualify as a scheme of reconstruction. Accordingly, *section 136* will apply so that the new holding or holdings will take on the acquisition cost and date of the original (apportioned as necessary) for capital gains tax purposes and the scheme will not trigger a chargeable gain or allowable loss.

It should be noted, however, that where the original fund operates equalisation, a charge to income tax on the equalisation element will arise under *ICTA 1988, s 758.* The amount of this equalisation gain should be deducted from the rolled-over acquisition cost of the original holding for capital gains tax purposes.

9.66   The basic roll-over relief provisions of *TCGA 1992, s 136* and *Sch 5AA* are overlaid, however, by the offshore funds legislation at *ICTA 1988, s 757(6)*. This applies to investors whose holding in the original fund contains a latent gain, if any of the funds concerned is not a distributing fund. *Section 757(6)* provides for offshore income gains to be rolled over under *TCGA 1992, s 136* where both the original fund and the successor fund or funds are not distributing funds under the offshore funds legislation. It specifically provides for a disposal of the original holding to be recognised for tax purposes, however, if it is a material interest in a fund which is not a distributing fund and the successor fund or funds are distributing funds. The disposal is for a consideration equal to the market value of the holding at the time of the exchange.

9.67   The position may be summarised:

Original Fund	Successor fund or funds	Roll-over of gains under *ICTA 1988, s 757(6)*	Roll-over of gains and losses under the CGT rules
Distributing status	Distributing status	N/A	Yes
Non-distributing status	Non-distributing status	Yes	Yes
Distributing status	Non-distributing status	N/A	Yes
Non-distributing status	Distributing status	No	Yes

9.68   It is standard practice to apply for clearance under *TCGA 1992, s 138* in relation to offshore fund mergers and reconstructions in the same way as for UK open-ended schemes. The application should give details of the fund's status under the offshore funds legislation. It is good practice to set out the implications of roll-over relief applying if there are any unusual circumstances, for instance some investors may be rolling over losses.

As with onshore funds, it is also normal to apply for clearance under *ICTA 1988, s 707* at the same time.

Stamp taxes

Cancellation of units or shares in the original fund

9.69   There will normally be no liability to local taxes on the cancellation of the holdings in the original fund.

Transfer of the original fund's investments

9.70   If any UK equities are transferred using stock transfer forms these will be dutiable ad valorem at 0.5%. The basic position for SDRT is that it will arise on chargeable securities, broadly UK equities and equity linked convertibles. Following the *Save & Prosper* decision, this may not be the case, however, where there is (a) a common trustee/depositary and (b) the scheme takes place in a regulatory environment similar to the UK's, and (c) it is possible to argue that it takes place by operation of law without an agreement to transfer chargeable securities. It may also be possible to run this argument where there is no common trustee/depositary. The position of Inland Revenue (Stamp Taxes) on this is likely to be revealed shortly.

There may be local transfer taxes on the transfer of investments in certain jurisdictions.

Fund's tax position

9.71   There will normally be no local tax on profits payable by the fund.

Equalisation

9.72   As with UK open-ended funds, there may be income equalisation in the successor fund or funds, although it is less common offshore. The issue is explained in detail for onshore open-ended funds at **9.28** above under the heading 'Mergers'.

Investment trusts

9.73   There are a number of ways of restructuring investment trusts, as with other *Companies Act* companies. In addition to mergers and reconstructions, it is possible for an investment trust to use a court-approved reduction of capital under *Companies Act 1985, s 425*, or, if it has enough distributable reserves, simply to buy back the required quantity of shares. These are both outside the scope of this chapter.

Background and basic outline of schemes of merger and reconstruction

UKLA listing rules

9.74   As investment trusts are public companies whose shares are listed on the London Stock Exchange, they must comply with the relevant provisions of the Listing Rules of the UK Listing Authority as well as with the requirements of the Companies Act 1985 (*ICTA 1988, s 842(1)(c)*). Under the Listing Rules, admission to the Official List, for which the FSA acting as the UK Listing

Authority is responsible, and admission by the London Stock Exchange to trading, together constitute official listing on a stock exchange.

The circular to shareholders

9.75   Typically, circulars to shareholders of investment trusts are longer and more formal documents than circulars in open-ended funds, but they cover similar ground. A circular normally contains a letter from the chairman outlining the proposals and their benefits, a formal offer or scheme, details of the investment trust and the successor vehicle or vehicles and notices of the various company meetings required. Investment trusts often have more than one class of share in issue. Depending on the precise scheme, there may need to be separate class meetings, as well as one or more company meetings.

There will almost invariably be a cash option in a scheme to restructure or take over an investment trust.

Reconstructions

9.76   Schemes of reconstruction for investment trusts are frequently referred to as unitisation schemes, reflecting the fact that in the past the successor fund was normally an authorised unit trust scheme. The successor vehicle may be a UK or offshore OEIC or another investment trust, however.

The liquidation of the investment trust is an essential part of a scheme of reconstruction. This is because distributions made by a company in respect of share capital in a winding up are not qualifying distributions under *ICTA 1988, s 209*. Accordingly, they do not attract income tax treatment either for the company or the shareholders.

Schemes of reconstruction involve the solvent liquidation of the investment trust under *Insolvency Act 1986, s 110*. This enables the liquidator to transfer the company's assets to one or more successor vehicles in exchange for their issuing shares or units to the investment trust's shareholders. The liquidator will also pay cash to shareholders looking for an exit. The potential liquidator will be involved at an early stage.

Unlike in open-ended funds, shareholders in investment trusts have a right to dissent under *Insolvency Act 1986, s 111* in the period of seven days after the extraordinary general meeting approving the scheme of reconstruction takes place. As a result it is necessary to leave time for this process before the second extraordinary general meeting takes place to put the investment trust into liquidation and appoint the liquidator. The notices of both meetings will be contained in the same circular to shareholders.

9.77   Investors will generally expect the scheme of reconstruction of an investment trust to offer a cash alternative for those investors who wish to realise their investment. Until a few years ago, it was standard practice to offer units in a cash unit trust. Shareholders taking the cash exit would take this option and realise their units on receipt. More recently, most schemes provided for investors simply to be paid cash in the liquidation. After the decision in *Fallon and another v Fellows* [2001] STC 1409 it looked briefly as if the industry would need to revert to using cash unit trusts to provide a cash exit. Fortunately, the 2002 amendments to *TCGA 1992, s 136* specifically permit shareholders to be paid cash by the liquidator (*TCGA 1988, Sch 5AA para 4(4)*), provided that those shareholders form a separate class.

Distribution of income to investors

9.78 It is essential for the target investment trust to retain approved investment trust status until its assets have been disposed of. To this end it is necessary for the directors to announce the final (interim) dividend payable to ordinary shareholders, of an amount sufficient for it to meet the 15% floor in *ICTA 1988, s 842(1)(e)*. The dividend will reflect the board's best estimate of the accrued and anticipated income in order to meet the 15% floor required for the target investment trust to qualify as an approved investment trust for the accounting period. It may include accumulated undistributed revenue reserves, although there is no need for it to do so.

Capital gains of investors

9.79 Investors who elect to exchange their shares for an investment in the successor vehicle will expect the reconstruction not to constitute a disposal by them of their holdings for capital gains tax. Rather they will expect the original acquisition cost (apportioned if necessary) and the acquisition date to apply to their new holding or holdings, so that the transaction takes place on a no gain/no loss basis. To achieve this the scheme must qualify for relief under *TCGA 1992, s 136*.

Section 136 applies where there is an arrangement between the company (company A) and the shareholders in it, or where there are different classes of them, the persons holding any class, which is entered into for the purposes of, or in connection with, a scheme of reconstruction as defined in *Schedule 5AA*. Under the arrangement, another company (company B) must issue shares to those persons in respect of and in proportion to their relevant holdings in company A, and these are retained, cancelled or extinguished.

9.80 To qualify as a scheme of reconstruction under *Schedule 5AA*, the scheme must meet three conditions, conditions 1, 2 and 3. Condition 4 (an alternative to 3) will not be relevant. The first condition in the context of a scheme of reconstruction is that it involves the issue of ordinary share capital of one or more companies to holders of the ordinary share capital of the target company, or where it had more than one class of ordinary share capital, to holders of those classes. Secondly, the proportionate entitlement of each investor to acquire new shares must be identical to that of the other investors in the target company, or appropriate share class, as applicable. Lastly, the effect of the restructuring must be to pass the business or substantially the whole of the business from the target company to the successor company or companies. The holding and management of any assets, retained by the target company in order to make a capital distribution in respect of shares, is disregarded when considering whether substantially the whole business has gone across. In an investment trust reconstruction, the successor vehicle or vehicles can be investment trusts, authorised unit trusts, or OEICs (by which is normally meant OEIC subfunds) or offshore funds. (AUTs are deemed to be companies by *TCGA 1992, s 99*. This deeming is extended to OEICs by the *Open-ended Investment Companies (Tax) Regulations 1997 (SI 1997/1154)*.)

9.81 In addition to any existing share classes of the target investment trust, there will need to be separate classes to reflect any elections made under the scheme of reconstruction. Where, for example, a target investment trust has ordinary shares and is being restructured into a new investment trust with a single class of shares but the shareholders will be offered a cash alternative, the original investment trust would need to have its ordinary shares reclassified into two classes. One of the new classes would be for those shareholders that have elected to go across to the new vehicle, and the other would be for those seeking a cash exit. Each new class must be listed, as explained at **9.86** below under the heading 'Investment trust's tax position'. At the same time as the shares are reclassified, the board will need to divide the assets of the investment trust into separate pools reflecting the elections. This will allow them to be managed in accordance with their respective investment objective.

9.82 Substantially the whole of the target investment trust's business must pass to the successor vehicle. For the purpose of this test, the holding and management of any assets retained by the target company to fund capital distributions is disregarded (*TCGA 1992, Sch 5AA para 4(4)*). The Inland Revenue Manual states their acceptance that the transfer of a portfolio is a business for this purpose so long as the obligation to manage the investments passes with them (CG52709).

A practical issue which sometimes arises is the desire of the investment managers to dispose of a substantial proportion of the portfolio and to transfer cash (or rather near cash for the reasons stated below) to the successor vehicle. A certain level of cash and highly liquid assets is normally held within an investment portfolio. If the investment manager wants to exceed a normal level, the Revenue would look for compelling commercial reasons for doing so before accepting that an investment business is being transferred. Where this is proposed, it would be a sensible precaution to discuss the reasons with the Inland Revenue before proceeding.

9.83 To retain approved investment trust status, the company's income must comply with *ICTA 1988, s 842(1)(a)* even in the final pre-liquidation accounting period. This section requires that 'the company's income consists wholly or mainly of eligible investment income'. Eligible investment income is now defined as including 'income derived from shares or securities' together with 'eligible rental income'. Shares for this purpose include units in authorised unit trust schemes and shares in OEICs. 'Securities' is not defined in *section 842*, but it is understood that the Revenue generally apply the definition in *TCGA 1992, s 132*. The Inland Revenue Capital Gains Manual (CG41418) states that they regard 'securities' as including Treasury bills and US Treasury notes but not certain types of corporate debt such as certificates of deposit and short-term commercial paper, nor sterling loans to local authorities. The Inland Revenue consider the phrase 'income from shares or securities' in *section 842(1)(a)* to mean gross statutory income, which includes tax credits on franked investment income, but is calculated before management expenses, income and corporation tax, and interest are deducted. The Revenue have also stated that scrip dividends by UK companies do not constitute gross statutory income. Further, the amounts to be brought into account in respect of the investment trust's loan relationships must be calculated without reference to any debtor relationships of the company (*ICTA 1988, s 842(1AB)*).

9.84 The Inland Revenue normally accept that income is derived 'wholly or mainly' from eligible investment income if at least 70% does so (Inland Revenue Capital Gains Manual CG41414). To avoid breaching this limit, where the investment manager realises portfolio investments in the run-up to the reconstruction, the proceeds should be re-invested in assets accepted by the Revenue as being securities. Typically gilts or Treasury bills are used.

Stamp taxes

9.85 There will normally be a charge to SDRT on chargeable securities transferred by the liquidator to the successor vehicle or stamp duty, in either case at 0.5% (unless the assets are non-UK investments or UK investments exempt from stamp taxes). If the successor vehicle is a new unit trust (but not an OEIC), then it should be possible to carry out the transfer by a distribution in the liquidation without a sale, and so without stamp taxes arising.

In the unlikely event that an investment trust is being restructured into two new investment trusts and there is an absolute identity of shareholdings between all three, then it would be possible to avoid stamp duty by ensuring the transaction fulfils the conditions for relief under *FA 1986, s 75*.

Foreign transfer taxes can arise, though only certain jurisdictions impose them.

Investment trust's tax position

9.86 The investors in the original investment trust will expect it to be able to transfer assets to a successor vehicle, or dispose of them, free of tax, despite the restructuring. To achieve this, the investment trust must retain its approved investment trust status until its last asset has been realised. This in turn depends on all its ordinary shares being listed in the Official List of the Stock Exchange until that point (*ICTA 1988, s 842(1)(c)*). The target investment trust will not satisfy the requirements of *ICTA 1988, s 842* throughout the accounting period after it has been put into liquidation because putting the company into liquidation will begin a new accounting period, and it will not be listed throughout the period. Technically the target investment trust will therefore lose approved investment trust status when it is put into liquidation. Its assets, however, will not be transferred until after the liquidation begins. In practice the Inspector of Taxes will normally agree that approved investment trust status will continue until all the assets have been disposed of, so long as the shares continue to be listed and the various other requirements of *ICTA 1988, s 842* continue to be satisfied while it still holds assets.

Mergers

9.87   A merger of investment trusts normally takes place by way of one investment trust offering its shares in exchange for the shares of another investment trust. The conduct of the offer will be regulated by the Panel on Takeovers and Mergers under the City Code on Takeovers and Mergers. The offeror may be a newly launched investment trust where the intention is to offer a continuation vehicle for a fixed life investment trust but there is some reason why a reconstruction under *Insolvency Act 1986, s 110* as described at **9.76** above is not appropriate. Alternatively, the offeror can be an existing investment trust, in which case the offer may either be recommended by the board of the target investment trust or be a hostile takeover bid.

Where the successor investment trust will be a substantial holder of the original investment trust for a material time, the UK Listing Authority may require them to enter into an agreement regulating the relationship between them by way of demonstrating that the target investment trust can carry on business independently and that the transactions between the two investment trusts will be at arm's length and on a normal commercial basis.

9.88   Where a share exchange offer is used to reconstruct an investment trust, the offer may enable investors in the target investment trust either to accept it and receive shares in the successor investment trust, or else to receive cash. There are two ways of providing the cash. First, the shareholders wanting cash may continue to hold their shares until the winding-up; this would be particularly suitable for a fixed life investment trust nearing the end of its life. Alternatively, the offeror could provide a cash alternative under its offer or arrange for institutional shareholders to purchase for cash the consideration shares issued to shareholders in the target investment trust.

9.89   Where the cash is to be provided in the winding-up of the target investment trust, the interests of the shareholders who have accepted a share exchange offer and want the company's assets to remain invested will diverge from those wanting a cash exit. Accordingly, to enable the board to meet these conflicting requirements, the shareholders of the original investment trust will normally be asked to approve a capital reorganisation to be implemented upon the offer becoming unconditional. This would create two classes of ordinary share capital out of each class that previously existed. Those shares in respect of which the offer is accepted would be redesignated as, say, 'A' shares and would be owned by the successor investment trust, and those of shareholders not accepting the offer would be redesignated as, say, 'B' shares and remain with the original shareholders.

The assets of the original investment trust will also need to be divided into two pools which will be accounted for and managed separately. Effectively the board will split the company's assets in proportion to the acceptances into an 'A' pool to go to the 'A' shareholder (the offeror investment trust) and a 'B' pool, which will be realised to pay out the 'B' shareholders. The board will then be able to manage the two pools of assets in line with their investment objectives and take the liquidation costs and any other expenses of the target company from the two pools rateably.

There may be more than one class of ordinary shares, but the principles will remain the same.

Distribution of income to investors

9.90   As explained under the heading 'Reconstructions' at **9.78** above, to qualify as an approved investment trust the company may only retain in respect of an accounting period an amount which is not greater than 15% of its eligible investment income (*ICTA 1988, s 842(1)(e)*). It will be essential for the original investment trust to retain its approved investment trust status for capital gains tax purposes, as described below at **9.94**. For this reason it will be necessary for the original investment trust to distribute its eligible investment income for its final pre-liquidation accounting period as a dividend before the liquidation. It is normal for the board to declare a final interim dividend which will be payable to the holders on the register at the latest practical date before the winding-up.

Capital gains of investors

9.91   Shareholders in the target investment trust who accept the offer and exchange their shareholding for a holding in the offeror investment trust will not expect this to be a disposal for capital gains tax. Rather they will expect that any gain or loss arising in respect of the ordinary shares in the target investment trust will be rolled over into the new shares in the offeror investment trust received as consideration under the offer. In other words, they will expect the new shares to be treated for capital gains tax purposes as being the same asset as their previous shareholding and as having been acquired at the same time and for the same cost as it was. Roll-over relief under *TCGA 1992, s 135* will normally be available as the circumstances set out in *Case 2* will be satisfied. The relevant conditions in these circumstances are that a company (company B) issues shares to a person in exchange for shares in another company (company A) as the result of a general offer made to members of company A or any class of them. It must be made in the first instance on a condition such that if it were satisfied company B would have control of company A.

9.92   For relief to be available to those holding more than 5% of any class of shares, the scheme must be effected for bona fide commercial reasons and not form part of a scheme or arrangements of which the main purpose, or one of the main purposes, is avoidance of liability to capital gains tax or corporation tax on chargeable gains (*TCGA 1992, s 137*). As with open-ended funds, it is standard practice to apply for clearance under *TCGA 1992, s 138*, regardless of the size of the shareholdings.

Any shareholders that receive cash in the winding-up of the target investment trust will be treated as disposing of their original shareholding. If there is more than one payment by the liquidator then the shareholder will need to treat the payments as part disposals for capital gains tax purposes.

Clearance under *ICTA 1988, s 707* is also normally applied for at the same time as the capital gains tax clearance application is submitted. As with open-ended funds, it is, however, difficult to see how a tax advantage (as defined) could arise as all or substantially all of the income arising in the target investment trust will have been distributed and only capital transferred to the successor vehicle.

Stamp taxes

9.93   Where the shares of the original investment trust are held in CREST, the offeror investment trust will be liable to SDRT in relation to the shares it acquires in the target investment trust. In any case where the shares are not held in CREST, stamp duty at 0.5% would be payable on the stock transfer forms.

When the target investment trust is wound up and the liquidator transfers its assets to the successor investment trust there should be no SDRT (the appropriate flag should be alleged within CREST to avoid it being deducted automatically). Exemption from stamp duty may be claimed under Category I of the *Stamp Duty (Exempt Instruments) Regulations 1987 (SI 1987/516)*. If the target investment trust held foreign securities, then foreign transfer taxes may arise, but only in certain jurisdictions.

Investment trust's tax position

9.94   It is important to ensure that the assets of the target investment trust pass to the successor investment trust without a tax charge on any gains triggered in the process. This is dependent on the target investment trust retaining its approved investment trust status at all material times, which in turn depends on its ordinary share capital, or each class if there is more than one, being listed in the Official List of the London Stock Exchange (*ICTA 1988, s 842(1)(c)*). This gives rise to two potential areas of difficulty.

9.95   First, following the capital reorganisation into 'A' and 'B' shares, both classes must be listed and dealings permitted on the London Stock Exchange from the date on which the offer becomes unconditional to the date on which the target investment trust is wound up.

Secondly, putting the company into liquidation will begin a new accounting period, and the new investment trust will not be listed throughout. Strictly the target investment trust will therefore lose approved investment trust status when it is put into liquidation but its assets will not be transferred until after the liquidation begins. In practice the Inspector of Taxes will normally agree that approved investment trust status may continue, so long as the shares continue to be listed and the various other requirements of *ICTA 1988, s 842* are satisfied until it has disposed of its assets.

10 Pension Fund Pooling Vehicles

John Watson

Ashurst Morris Crisp

Overview

10.1   On 11 July 1996 the *Capital Gains Tax (Pension Funds Pooling Schemes) Regulations 1996 (SI1996/1583)*, the *Income Tax (Pension Funds Pooling Schemes) Regulations 1996 (SI 1996/1585)* and the *Stamp Duty and Stamp Duty Reserve Tax (Pension Funds Pooling Schemes) Regulations 1996 (SI 1996/1584)* came into force. As their names indicate they together laid the fiscal framework for the pension funds pooling scheme (better known as the 'pension fund pooling vehicle' or 'PFPV'), a new vehicle sponsored by a steering group of the Institutional Fund Managers Association with the assistance of the UK tax authorities.

The demand for a vehicle to pool international pension funds came from two different places. First, multinationals, aware that the investment performance of the pension funds set up by their subsidiaries around the world would ultimately affect their own bottom line, saw pooling as a way to ensure that the assets of their schemes were effectively invested. If all the funds could be contributed to a common pool the appointment of investment managers could be centralised. This would not just save costs and give the investment managers the advantage of greater weight; it would also enable management to be carried out under the eye of the multinational itself and would reduce the likelihood of inconsistent strategies. If there is a single pool there is less likelihood that one pension fund will decide to buy a particular range of assets at the same time as another pension fund decides to sell them.

10.2   The second source of demand was, of course, the fund managers. They already had a UK vehicle in the shape of the exempt unauthorised unit trust, through which UK tax exempt funds could be pooled. However, foreign participants may not be admitted to exempt unit trusts so that overseas pension funds are excluded.

The pension funds pooling vehicle is designed to accommodate both groups and, of course, to provide the pension schemes themselves with an attractive vehicle for common investment. Pension funds which commit their assets to a pooling vehicle will need to be satisfied that they are not adding to the fiscal cost of their investments. If they did so then, unless that fiscal cost was less than the administrative savings which the pooling achieved, they would be failing in their duty to their pensioners. It follows that a successful vehicle for the pooling of international pension funds needs to have the following attributes:

- it must not itself bear tax. Obviously any tax charge on the vehicle (whether direct tax or VAT) is likely to make it inefficient;

- it must preserve double tax treaty benefits. That means that the jurisdictions in which it invests must accept that the profits from assets in those jurisdictions belong to the participants and apply their network of double tax treaties accordingly. Under the new US/UK double tax treaty there is no withholding on dividends paid from a US company to a UK pension fund. A UK pension fund investing in a PFPV would be disappointed if its share of the US dividends paid to the PFPV bore US withholding tax which could not be reclaimed. Investment by a PFPV in a particular jurisdiction is, therefore, dependent on the authorities in that jurisdiction regarding the PFPV as transparent; and

- the PFPV will need to be acceptable in the jurisdictions from which investments are made. For a start it must be an acceptable investment for a pension fund under the regulatory regime. In addition, if there is any local tax and credit is required for withholding tax on the underlying investments, this will only be available if transparency is respected.

10.3 In looking for a vehicle those promoting the PFPV concentrated on transparency and eschewed the alternative courses of:

(a) using a tax exempt company to avoid domestic tax. Exempt vehicles do not generally attract treaty protection; or

(b) seeking an opaque vehicle in a jurisdiction which boasted an excellent network of treaties with a view to using those treaties to restrict the taxes withheld from income at source. Although there might be cases where the treaties applicable to the vehicle jurisdiction give a lower rate of withholding than transparency, this solution would be unstable because there would also be cases where transparency gave the better result. It would be a brave pension fund trustee who took a bet that the former would outweigh the latter. In any case it is difficult to find a vehicle with comprehensive treaty protection which does not itself pay tax.

10.4 Two types of UK vehicle were considered as possibilities. The first of these was the limited partnership. Although there is authority (see *Padmore v IRC* 1989 STC 495 and *Memec v IRC* 1998 STC 754) that a partnership should be viewed as transparent by the UK for double tax relief purposes, the international position is more difficult. Countries generally decide whether to give benefits under a double tax treaty by asking who owns the income as it arises as a matter of partnership law. The answer is not entirely clear.

The second possibility was to use a trust structure under which each participant in the PFPV participates in a trust and the trust uses these contributions to buy international assets. This was the approach chosen and it may be helpful to look at how treaty claims would need to operate in this context.

Supposing that pension funds from jurisdictions A, B C and D invest equally in a PFPV and the portfolio includes securities in country A, income on which would (but for treaty claims) bear withholding tax:

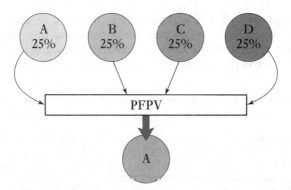

10.5   Tax neutrality will only be achieved if the authorities in country A regard the PFPV as transparent for domestic purposes (so that the tax treatment of the income derived from country A investments which corresponds to the fraction of the PFPV owned by pension funds in country A is the same as if those pension funds had directly invested) and if country A permits reduction/repayment of its withholding tax on those parts of the income attributed to pension funds in countries B–D respectively by reference to its treaties with those jurisdictions.

Although in a fiscal sense the PFPV may be an innovation, the structure itself is not. Arrangements under which assets are acquired by a trustee which holds them on trust for a number of beneficiaries in common are a well known feature of English commercial law. The assets are registered in the name of the trustee and each beneficiary is entitled to its undivided share of those assets. Such structures are known as unit trusts and **CHAPTER 1** of this book discusses them in detail. Readers will note, however, that the tax provisions which govern UK unauthorised unit trusts belie the simplicity of their structure. In particular:

(c)   the trustees are charged to tax on the income even though it does not really belong to them (*ICTA 1988, ss 468, 469*);

(d)   unitholders are charged to tax on capital gains by reference to the gain on their units and not by reference to their proportion of the gains on the underlying assets; and

(e)   units are chargeable securities for the purposes of stamp duty and SDRT.

10.6   All this artificial tax complexity has been superimposed on unit trusts to make their tax treatment more manageable. Were the income tax not treated as that of the trustees it would be necessary to allocate it between a fluctuating body of unitholders. If a unit trust was not treated as a company for capital gains tax purposes the issue of additional units would involve realisations by existing unitholders.

These rules are entirely appropriate where the participants in the unit trust include UK taxpayers, but they are unnecessary where the only UK holders of units will be tax exempt. In addition, they are inconsistent with the tax treatment required by a PFPV. Before a unit trust can be used as a PFPV, therefore, it is necessary to disapply these rules and the purpose of the Regulations is to do just that when the conditions which define a PFPV are satisfied. That leaves the unit trusts with their natural UK tax treatment under which:

- the income of the trust belongs to the unitholders as it arises and it is the unitholders and not the trustee which are taxable in respect of it;

- any capital gains of the trust are regarded as gains of the participants by virtue of *TCGA, s 60*. In fact restrictions on the entities which can invest in a PFPV ensure that its capital gains will not bear UK tax; and

- for stamp duty purposes the units are treated like interests under a partnership.

Since the key to the success of PFPVs is the international recognition of transparency, the efficiency of the structure for an investor in a particular jurisdiction depends on the views of the authorities there. Accordingly an approach was made by Ernst & Young to the authorities of a number of jurisdictions and the results they have obtained are posted on their website.

The Regulations

10.7 The definition of 'Pension Funds Pooling Scheme' for all three sets of Regulations is contained in the *Income Tax (Pension Funds Pooling Schemes) Regulations 1996 (SI 1996/1585)* ('the Regulations') and the other two sets of regulations cross-refer to these. The definition contains a number of conditions to be satisfied before a unit trust can qualify as a PFPV and it is not proposed to deal with them in full. The reader is referred here to the text of the Regulations themselves from which it will be seen that the conditions fall into a number of categories. It should be noted that if a PFPV ceases to satisfy the conditions at any time in a tax year it will lose its status for the entire year.

The first category of regulations deal with the types of entity which may invest in a PFPV. These are found at *sub-paragraphs (a)* and *(b)* of *Regulation 4(3)* of the Regulations. Before turning to the identity of the potential investors, it should be noted that the trustees of a PFPV must not admit any investor until investment by that investor into that particular PFPV has been approved by the UK Revenue. That approval, which is obtained by the trustee or manager of the PFPV, will be referred to as 'investment approval' to stress that it is quite separate from any approval the participant may require from the UK Revenue, or any other taxing authority, to confirm its tax status for its own domestic purposes.

10.8 There are two types of possible UK investor. The first is the exempt approved scheme, which is the traditional form for a UK company pension scheme. Such a scheme has itself to be approved by the Inland Revenue to confirm its tax status, a status which carries exemptions both from income tax on investment income and from capital gains tax. Frequently, that approval can take some time to obtain and to enable the scheme to invest in a PFPV during that period, the Regulations permit the scheme to be admitted while it is 'before the Board [of the Inland Revenue] in order for them to decide whether the scheme qualifies as an exempt approved scheme…'. In these circumstances, of course, investment approval can only be given provisionally and the Regulations duly cater for admission of the scheme on that basis. If, of course, the scheme does not in the event achieve approval, it will have to be expelled from the PFPV.

A similar regime applies for statutory superannuation schemes as defined in *ICTA 1988, s 615(6)*. These are schemes to provide superannuation benefits in respect of persons employed in trades or undertakings outside the UK and they enjoy exemptions from income tax on income derived from investments under *ICTA 1988, s 614(5)* and from capital gains tax under *TCGA 1992, s 271*. Again there is provision for provisional investment approval pending approval of the scheme's status.

10.9 Looking from the perspective of 2003, this seems a short list. From its earlier position of almost universal acceptance, the exempt approved scheme has suffered a considerable decline and modern pensions are provided through a number of different schemes including, for example, the personal pension. It seems odd that these other schemes cannot invest in a PFPV. Early in 2003, the Government produced a consultative paper suggesting that tax relief on pension schemes should be rationalised so that an individual would have a single lifetime total of tax privileged funds. If these proposals move forward it is hoped the opportunity will be taken to include all of these tax privileged funds within the ranks of potential investors.

An overseas pension fund may be accepted as an investor in a PFPV if it is 'for the time being accepted by the Board as equivalent to a retirement benefits scheme approved by the Board for the purposes of Chapter 1 of Part XIV of the Taxes Act' (*Regulation 2(1)*) – ie to an exempt approved scheme. That Chapter provides for two types of approval, mandatory approval under *ICTA 1988, s 590*, available only where the scheme meets a very narrow set of conditions and the much more usual discretionary approval which is given under *ICTA 1988, s 591* in accordance with published Revenue practice. To test whether an overseas scheme is eligible to invest in a PFPV, one needs to compare the benefits etc with those conferred by the schemes which are commonly approved under these heads.

10.10 Those operating the PFPV must, of course, obtain investment approval for an overseas scheme before the scheme can be admitted and, in order to allow the Inland Revenue to judge whether the benefits are equivalent to those under approved schemes, considerable detail has to be given as to the amounts and circumstances of the payments which can be made by the scheme to its pensioners. A review of all this information can take considerable time so, to prevent an unnecessary delay arising in straightforward cases, only limited information (and no analysis of available benefits) is required where the Board of Inland Revenue have announced that they are satisfied as to the eligibility of that particular class of scheme. So far they have expressed satisfaction in respect of specified schemes in Australia, Belgium, France, Germany, Guernsey, Ireland, the Isle of Man, Jersey, the Netherlands and New Zealand together with ERISA schemes in the USA.

It will be appreciated, of course, that the mere fact that the Inland Revenue have stated that they are happy to accept short particulars on a particular type of scheme does not mean that the scheme is entitled to invest in a PFPV under its own laws or indeed that the jurisdiction in which the scheme is situated will regard the PFPV as tax transparent.

10.11 On occasion, investment approval will be withdrawn after the investor has been admitted as a member of the PFPV. This could happen either because the original approval was provisional and the condition has not been satisfied or because it becomes apparent that a particular participant in the PFPV does not satisfy or no longer satisfies the requisite conditions. On receipt of notification by a participant that it is not or may not be eligible to participate (a participant who becomes aware that this is the case must notify the trustee of the PFPV in writing within seven days) or on the trustee becoming aware of non-eligibility (or in the case of an overseas scheme likely non-eligibility) the trustees must give notice to the Board within 14 days. Once investment approval has been revoked by the Board the trustee must ensure that the units of the participant are, within 28 days, either sold to an eligible participant or cancelled. Otherwise, the scheme will be treated as having ceased to have been a PFPV from the date on which the Board revoked the approval of the participant.

In the case of an illiquid fund, it will often be impossible to realise assets within this time scale so that the expelled unitholder will not receive money until later. In these circumstances, the unitholder's rights to be paid would still diminish on a drop in the market so that, in a sense, it is sharing the losses of the PFPV. It is understood that the Inland Revenue will regard units as cancelled even though the amount to be paid in respect of that cancellation could be reduced if the assets of the PFPV declined before payment or even though interest is payable on the outstanding amount.

The second class of conditions go to the structure of the PFPV itself. Under *sub-paragraph (c)* of *Regulation 4(3)* the participants have to be jointly absolutely entitled against the trustee within the meaning of *TCGA 1992, s 60*. This seems to add little since, were it not the case, the PFPV would pay tax on its capital gains whether the Regulations applied or not. Similarly, *sub-paragraph (g)* requires all participants to have the same rights or interest. Again, one would expect that to be so in any event for commercial reasons.

The third type of condition goes to the types of assets which may be held by the scheme and on which the contributions of the participants may be spent. These categories are very broad and, quite apart from shares, securities etc include land and buildings and the provision of machinery or plant which is integral to them. This gives rise to a tax complication in that overseas participants would be entitled to capital allowances on the plant and changes in participants in the PFPV could greatly complicate those allowances. To reduce the complexity, the Regulations provide that where a PFPV expends monies in a way which might give rise to capital allowances, the terms of the PFPV must impose a number of conditions designed to ensure that:

- the only circumstance in which the number of units can vary is a 'cancellation event' where the rights and interests of a participant are wholly redeemed, purchased or cancelled; and

- save in the case of a cancellation event, the rights of unitholders and their successors will always remain the same.

The actual regulations on this are quite complex and should be considered carefully by any PFPV making an investment of this sort.

10.12 The final set of conditions is administrative. PFPV status is only available where the trustees of the PFPV elect for the Regulations to apply and take responsibility for agreeing with the Inland Revenue the method of calculating the amount of any income arising from the scheme property and the allocation and amounts of income, capital allowances etc. The trustees are also required to provide a certificate to each participant within three months after the end of each accounting period showing the necessary information relating to that participant's entitlement for that period and, within three months after the end of each tax year; they must also provide annual returns to the Board of the information required under *Regulation 11*.

Collection of tax from PFPV

10.13 Although fiscal transparency means that the PFPV does not suffer UK tax in its own right, in certain circumstances the trustee or the manager can be obliged to collect tax due from a participant. Obligations to collect tax and account for it to the Inland Revenue could arise in a number of ways.

Where an overseas participant in a PFPV is regarded as carrying on a trade it is likely that the trustee, or where the investment manager's exemption does not apply, the manager will be a UK tax representative within *FA 1995, s 126* (or will in the case of a corporate participant be a permanent establishment). In these circumstances the overseas participant would be taxable in the UK on its trading profit and the trustee or the manager of the PFPV could be liable to account for that tax. From a practical point of view an overseas participant in a PFPV could carry on a trade for either of two reasons. First, the overseas pension fund could itself be carrying on a trade. This would be highly unusual bearing in mind the types of funds which can invest in a PFPV but nonetheless a warranty should be taken at the time when each participant subscribes. The second possibility is that the activities of the PFPV amount to trading in themselves. In the case of a UK exempt approved scheme, the tax exemption provided under *ICTA 1988, s 592(2)* for income desired from investments is extended by *ICTA 1988, s 659A* to cover income derived from transactions relating to futures and options. There is, however, no similar exemption for superannuation funds or overseas pension schemes. It follows that a PFPV in which the latter participate must eschew transactions in derivatives where those transactions would amount to trading under normal tax principles. The Inland Revenue's views on when this would be the case are set out in Statement of Practice SP 3/02.

10.14 It should also be noted in this context that, where an overseas participant in a PFPV is regarded as receiving trading receipts in respect of its investment, the PFPV is likely to be a UK permanent establishment for the purposes of any double tax treaty. It follows that the trading profit will not be protected from tax by treaty relief.

Another circumstance in which the PFPV may be obliged to collect tax on behalf of overseas participants is where the PFPV invests in UK land. There the collection regime as set out in Section 42A Taxes Act 1988 can, in certain circumstances, require agents to deduct tax from rental income owned by overseas entities.

Claims mechanisms

10.15 Since the pension fund pooling vehicle is designed to enable participants to obtain treaty benefits, the manner in which reclaims of withholding tax are handled is of some importance. Where an overseas pension fund invests in the debt of a UK company, the UK Revenue will, on appropriate claims being filed, issue a direction to the company to the effect that tax only need be withheld on interest at the treaty rate. Ideally, if an overseas pension fund was a participant in a PFPV which invested in UK corporate debt, the lower treaty rate of withholding should be similarly applied to its share of any interest. In practice, however, such a system would be hard to engineer because it depends upon the company paying the interest knowing who the participants in the pension fund pooling vehicle are at the relevant time. Accordingly, the UK would withhold tax on interest paid by a UK company at the full rate on the basis that the excess over the treaty rate would be reclaimed by each participant.

Although this is clearly a disadvantage of the PFPV against direct investment, the fact that the UK does not deduct withholding tax and dividends from UK companies means that it is often of little commercial importance. Where dividends and interest are paid to a PFPV by an overseas company the question whether tax should be withheld and, if so, how it can be reclaimed depends on the local tax regime.

10.16 As part of the documentation surrounding a PFPV, participants may authorise the manager to make any UK tax reclaim on their behalf. Where they do so, the claim in respect of UK participants has to be made to the participants own Tax Inspector; claims in respect of overseas participants can be made centrally.

The ability to have tax collected by the manager is particularly useful because it means that the tax recovery may be assigned back to the PFPV in return for further units. Alternatively, a PFPV may be designed so that tax reclaims are simply paid back into the fund with no issue of further units. This system only works, however, where all participants obtain repayment of tax at the same rate.

Value added tax

10.17 To be viable as an investment vehicle the pension fund pooling vehicle must also be neutral from a VAT viewpoint. At first sight one would not expect this to be the case because supplies, and in particular supplies of management services, are made to the trustees and, unless the business of the PFPV is wholly outside the EU, at best part of any VAT on such supplies will be recoverable as input tax. It should be noted here that the VAT exemption for fund management services provided by *VATA 1994, Sch 9 Gp 5* is restricted to services provided to an authorised unit trust, a trust based scheme or an open-ended company. A PFPV will not normally be any of these and therefore VAT will need to be charged on management services supplied to it.

Where management services are provided by a UK manager to an overseas investor, the VAT treatment will depend upon the status of that investor. Broadly, where the recipient of the services is in the EU the services will be standard rated. If, however, the recipient is outside the EU there will be no VAT charge on the services but the manager will be able to recover input tax on the services it itself obtains insofar as these are attributable to the supply. Non-EU institutions, therefore, do not expect to bear VAT on their management expenses and it is unlikely that they would invest in a PFPV if the structure imposed this.

10.18 The solution to this quandary hinges on the form of the PFPV documentation. Instead of providing that the manager provides the services to the trustee of the PFPV, it is possible to construct the documentation so that the manager's services are provided to each investor separately, the service in each case being one of managing investments through a PFPV structure. Where that is achieved each investor will pay the management charge appropriate to him and VAT will be added or omitted accordingly. It follows that each investor suffers the same amount of VAT as if it had invested direct.

Stamp duty and stamp duty reserve tax

10.19 The regulations relating to stamp duty and stamp duty reserve tax provide that a PFPV is not to be regarded as a unit scheme for the purposes of the stamp duty legislation. That has a number of effects:

(a) the regime for unit trusts at *FA 1999, Sch 19* does not apply;

(b) units in a PFPV are not regarded as stock for stamp duty purposes so that they are not consideration as mentioned at *Stamp Act 1891, s 55*; and

(c) the units are not chargeable securities as defined in *FA 1986, s 99* for the purposes of stamp duty reserve tax.

10.20 On this basis, the regime for PFPVs which only holds assets other than land is as follows.

Although investors who subscribe cash for new units in a PFPV certainly acquire an interest in the underlying investments, that acquisition is not pursuant to a transaction of sale. It follows that there should be no stamp duty and no SDRT. Where, however, a new investor subscribes securities in specie to an PFPV, the fact that the units obtained by the investor are not regarded as chargeable consideration for stamp duty purposes (see (b) above) means that the document affecting the transfer need only be stamped £5. Stamping the document with this amount will eliminate the stamp duty reserve tax charge which arises on the agreement to carry out the transfer.

In the case of distributions, the same logic works in reverse. Distributions of cash do not carry stamp duty or stamp duty reserve tax, either under the general rules or under Schedule 19 FA 1999. Where, however, a withdrawing investor takes investments in specie, a £5 stamp will suffice both to render the transfer fully stamped and to eliminate the SDRT charge.

10.21 As units in a PFPV are not chargeable securities their transfer is not affected by SDRT but the stamp duty on the transfer itself would bear the full rate at up to 4%. It is important to get the transfer stamped because otherwise the new holder cannot be entered on any register of unitholders without a breach of *Stamp Act 1891, s 17*. In fact, the high rate of duty on transfers of units does not greatly matter because the fact that PFPVs are not regarded as unit trusts for the purposes of *FA 1999, Sch 19* means that instead of A selling his units to B, A can simply withdraw money and at the same time B can subscribe the same amount.

Where the PFPV holds real property the position is more difficult and an interest in a PFPV is probably regarded as an interest in the underlying land for stamp duty purposes. By analogy with the Stamp Office's treatment of partnerships, however, it may be argued that a contribution of land in specie to a PFPV should not generally be regarded as a transaction of sale. The position, however, is not entirely clear and in any case will need to be reconsidered following the introduction of Stamp Duty Land Tax.

Conclusion

10.22 The pension fund pooling vehicle has been slow to develop. In part this is because of the amount of work which has to be done in relation to each jurisdiction in which a PFPV is to invest. Confirmation is required that the jurisdiction will treat the PFPV as transparent and, in addition, systems have to be constructed for the limitation of withholding tax or alternatively its reclaim. In addition to this, the attractiveness of the vehicle in the UK has been limited by the restricted class of UK pension funds which can invest. It is no longer the case that the UK pensions industry is dominated by exempt approved schemes.

Two changes point to an increased use of the vehicle. The first is that the Government is currently carrying out a consultation exercise on the reform of pensions. It is likely that limits etc will be applied by reference to an individual's 'tax privileged funds' and that the latter funds will therefore be defined. It is hoped that the opportunity will be taken to ensure that all these funds can invest in PFPVs.

The second important factor is a trend in double tax treaties to exempt from withholding tax, dividends which are paid to pension funds (see for example article 10 paragraph 3(b) of the current US/UK treaty which prohibits withholding tax on a dividend paid to a pension fund in the other contracting state). This sets a premium on a vehicle which works on a transparent basis and gives it an advantage over insurance based products.

11 Foreign Taxes

Eliza Dungworth and Oliver Farnworth

Deloitte

Introduction

11.1 The pursuit of cross-border investment opportunities exposes UK investment funds to the risk that they will be taxed both in the UK and in the foreign jurisdictions that they have invested in. The potential impact of this on investment returns, particularly in periods of economic downturn, means that assessment and management of this risk is likely to be a key issue in managing foreign investments for a UK investment fund. Typically this will require consideration of three issues:

(i) The exposure to foreign tax liabilities on the investment

(ii) The impact of foreign taxation on the investor's UK tax position

(iii) The availability of treaty benefits

Clearly (i) will depend upon the domestic tax legislation of the relevant foreign jurisdiction, hence it is not possible to make more than general comment in the present work. The focus of this chapter will therefore be consideration of (ii) and (iii), together with coverage of particular foreign tax issues of practical interest to investment funds, namely:

- the US Qualified Intermediary regulations;

- the impact of the new UK/US double taxation treaty;

- the French *avoir fiscal*;

- the withholding tax exemption on Japanese government bonds;

- foreign scrip dividends.

UK relief for foreign taxes

11.2 There are no special provisions governing relief for foreign taxes for collective investment schemes. Instead they must rely on the basic rules and principles described briefly below and covered fully in *Tolley's Double Taxation Relief.*

The UK legislative framework

11.3 The UK provisions covering double taxation relief in respect of income tax and corporation tax are set out in *ICTA 1988, Part XVIII.*

Chapter I (sections 788–791) sets out the principal reliefs, namely:

- relief by agreement with other territories (*ss 788* and *789*); and

- unilateral relief (*s 790*).

Under both headings, credit is available for foreign taxes suffered directly on income and gains in the hands of a UK resident. This encompasses both withholding taxes on dividends, interest and other income and other taxes assessed directly on the UK resident, for example foreign tax on branch profits or capital gains.

Credit relief may also be available for the foreign tax suffered on profits from which a dividend is paid, which is known as underlying tax. This may be permitted under the terms of a double taxation agreement or may be obtained under the unilateral relief provisions.

11.4 *Chapter II (sections 792–806)* covers the rules governing credit relief, and is itself subdivided under four headings:

- General (*ss 792–798*). These sections define some of the main terms and set out the key computational principles.

- Tax underlying dividends (*ss 799–803A*). These sections set out the rules for underlying tax relief.

- Miscellaneous rules (*ss 804–806*). These sections include special rules for insurance companies, the ability to elect against credit relief and the time limits for claims.

- Foreign dividends: onshore pooling and utilisation of eligible unrelieved foreign tax (*ss 806A–806M*). These sections set out the rules for the onshore pooling regime introduced by *FA 2000*, together with the rules for unrelieved foreign tax arising in a foreign branch or agency of a UK resident company and will be of limited application to collective investment schemes.

Chapter III (sections 807–816) comprises miscellaneous provisions. Of these, the most relevant one for collective investment schemes is *section 811*, governing expense relief.

Definitions

11.5 *ICTA 1988, s 792* includes definitions of certain key terms used in the rules concerning credit relief.

- 'Arrangements' means any arrangements having effect by virtue of *section 788*, ie double taxation agreements concluded with territories outside the UK.

- 'Foreign tax' means tax charged by a territory with which the UK has a double taxation agreement, for which credit relief is available under the agreement.

- 'The United Kingdom taxes' means income tax and corporation tax. Capital gains tax is also included by virtue of *TCGA 1992, s 277*.

- 'Underlying tax' means, in relation to any dividend, tax which is not chargeable in respect of that dividend directly or by deduction. The computation of underlying tax is dealt with in *section 799*, which uses the phrase 'so much of the foreign tax borne on the relevant profits by the body corporate paying the dividend'. The meaning is therefore tax on the profits out of which a dividend is paid.

- 'Unilateral relief' means relief under *section 790*. This provides for credit relief where there is no agreement with the particular territory or where the tax in question is not covered by the terms of the agreement

- 'Subsidiary' has a special definition in this context. One company is a subsidiary of another if the other company controls, directly or indirectly, not less than 50% of the voting power in the first company. This is unusual in that a holding of just 50% held by one company in the voting power of another is sufficient to make it a subsidiary, yet exactly 50% would not give voting control.

Creditable foreign taxes

11.6   The taxes for which credit relief is available under the terms of a double taxation agreement will be specified in the relevant agreement. For treaties following the OECD model, and most UK treaties, the taxes covered are dealt with in Article 2 of the treaty, which will list specific taxes of both contracting states. However, this should be read in conjunction with the 'elimination of double taxation' article later in the treaty as that may narrow the scope of taxes covered for the purposes of credit relief. Normally the 'taxes covered' article will also include a provision to the effect that the treaty will apply to identical or substantially similar taxes imposed by either contracting state after the treaty comes into force. The principle underlying the specified taxes will be that they are taxes on income or gains, whether paid by companies or individuals.

For collective investment schemes the taxes of most relevance are likely to be withholding taxes on dividends or interest, available tax credits and taxes on capital gains.

11.7   The same principle is evident in the equivalent unilateral relief provision, *ICTA 1988, s 790(12)*, which applies in the absence of a double taxation treaty.

Section 790(12) also deals with the question of taxes paid under the laws of provinces, states, other parts of countries, municipalities or other local bodies, which are levied on income in a number of jurisdictions, notably the US. These are also capable of being treated as corresponding to UK income tax or corporation tax.

11.8   The Inland Revenue Booklet 146, published in March 1995, contained a list of admissible (creditable) and inadmissible (non-creditable) taxes for a large number of countries. However, it should be noted that the booklet was not revised subsequent to its original publication and has now been officially withdrawn by the Inland Revenue. The only up-to-date list is now included in the Inland Revenue Double Taxation Relief Manual, which can be accessed on the Inland Revenue website, www.inlandrevenue.gov.uk.

The residence requirement

11.9   In general, credit relief shall not be allowed under any arrangements, or unilaterally, against UK tax for any chargeable period unless the person whose income and gains are chargeable to UK tax is resident in the UK for that period.

Exceptions to this include:

(a)   tax paid under the law of the Isle of Man or any of the Channel Islands, if the person in question is, for the chargeable period in question, resident either in the UK or in the Isle of Man or any of the Channel Islands, as the case may be;

(b)   tax paid under the law of any territory and computed by reference to income from an office or employment the duties of which are performed wholly or mainly in that territory, against income tax chargeable under Schedule E and computed by reference to that income; and

(c)   tax paid under the law of any territory outside the UK in respect of the income or chargeable gains of a branch or agency in the UK of a person who is not resident in the UK, where the following conditions are fulfilled, namely:

- that the territory under whose law the tax was paid is not one in which the person is liable to tax by reason of domicile, residence or place of management; and

- that the amount of relief claimed does not exceed (or is by the claim expressly limited to) that which would have been available if the branch or agency had been a person resident in the UK and the income or gains in question had been income or gains of that person.

Residence of collective investment schemes

11.10   For the purposes of UK double taxation relief provisions, the residence of the various types of collective investment scheme is determined as follows:

- Investment trusts and OEICs, being companies, will be treated as UK resident if they are incorporated in the UK (*FA 1988, s 66*) or if their 'central management and control' is exercised in the UK. The latter test is a matter of case law, the application of which is discussed in Inland Revenue Statement of Practice 1/90.

- The trustees of an authorised unit trust are deemed to be a company resident in the UK by virtue of *ICTA 1988, s 468(1)(a)*.

- An unauthorised unit trust will be treated as resident in the UK if the trustees are resident in the UK.

- An approved pension scheme established in the UK is regarded by the Inland Revenue as resident in the UK.

Source of income – general rules

11.11   In order for credit relief to be granted in the UK for foreign tax, it is necessary for the income on which relief is being claimed to have its source within the country where the foreign tax is payable *(ICTA 1988, s 790(4))*. This is determined by specific provisions in the relevant double taxation treaty or under UK rules which in general source the income or gains in the territory of the underlying asset.

The UK income requirement

11.12   *ICTA 1988, s 790(4)* specifies that unilateral credit relief will be allowed for foreign tax paid on an income or gain against UK income tax or corporation tax 'computed by reference to that income or gain'. To obtain relief it is therefore generally necessary to ensure that foreign taxes arising are matched by a UK liability on the same income or gains.

Most UK double taxation agreements replicate this rule, as does the OECD model treaty in Article 23B on the credit method. Note that Article 23A of the model treaty deals with the exemption method, which is the alternative method for eliminating double taxation.

Calculation of credit relief

11.13   Double taxation relief is available for foreign tax against UK tax arising on the same income or gain. Credit is available for the foreign tax borne on the income or gain, limited to the UK tax liability on the same income or gain, ie relief is available for the lower of the foreign and UK taxes.

The foreign tax borne for these purposes is the amount withheld at source from the income or paid directly by the taxpayer. Strictly the sterling value of the foreign tax should be derived using the exchange rate ruling on the date when the tax became payable. In practice it is common to use the exchange rate on the date the tax was paid or the date when the income was received after deduction of withholding tax. Provided a consistent approach is taken by the taxpayer, the Inland Revenue are unlikely to challenge this, unless the amount of tax involved is significant.

11.14   With regard to corporation tax the key provisions are that:

- The amount of credit for foreign tax to be allowed under any arrangements in respect of any income or gain should not exceed the corporation tax attributable to the relevant income or gain.

- The corporation tax attributable to the relevant income or gain is determined by calculating the corporation tax liability of the company on its whole profit, before credit relief, to derive an average rate of corporation tax applicable to the company's taxable income and gains. Authorised unit trusts and OEICs are always subject to a rate of corporation tax equal to the lower rate of income tax, hence always have the same limitation on credit regardless of their profits for the period.

EXAMPLE 11.14A

Nelson Investment Trust Plc is a UK resident investment trust with no associated companies. Its income comprises UK interest and overseas dividends on which withholding tax has been suffered. During the year ended 31 March 2004 it has profits chargeable to corporation tax of £500,000. It is accordingly entitled to marginal relief in accordance with *ICTA 1988, s 13(2)*.

	£
Profits chargeable to corporation tax	500,000
UK corporation tax at 30%	150,000
Marginal relief: $(1,500,000-500,000)\times\dfrac{500,000}{500,000}\times\dfrac{11}{400}=$	(27,500)
Corporation tax due before double tax relief	122,500

The company's average rate of corporation tax for the period is therefore 24.5% and credit relief for the withholding tax suffered on its Case V income will be restricted to that rate.

- Charges on income, management expenses or other amounts that can be deducted from or set against profits of more than one description may be allocated by the company as it sees fit (*s 797(3)*). In some cases this may have the result that the relevant income or gain is extinguished, hence no UK income or gain exists against which credit relief can be taken.

EXAMPLE 11.14B

The Crown European Fund is a UK authorised unit trust investing in a mixture of UK and European equities and bonds. During the year ended 31 December 2003 it has UK, Italian and German dividend income, and UK and Netherlands interest income. It has management expenses to set off against part of its income.

	UK Case III	Netherlands Case III	Italy Case V	Germany Case V
Foreign tax rate		10%	15%	15%
	£	£	£	£
Income per source	250,000	400,000	300,000	175,000
Management expenses	(250,000)	(200,000)	(75,000)	–
Income chargeable to corporation tax	Nil	200,000	225,000	175,000
UK corporation tax at 20%	–	40,000	45,000	35,000
Double taxation relief (limited to UK tax)	–	(40,000)	(45,000)	(26,250)
UK corporation tax payable	Nil	Nil	Nil	8,750

By allocating the management expenses first against the UK source income, then the income suffering the lower rate of foreign tax, the credit relief on the Case V income is maximised.

● If the credit limit is exceeded, then the excess may represent eligible unrelieved foreign tax relievable under the onshore pooling regime introduced by *FA 2000* if it arises on foreign dividend income (see 11.21 below). Any excess arising on foreign branch income taxable under Schedule D Case I (uncommon for a collective investment scheme) may be eligible for carry forward or carry back against the UK tax liability on foreign income from the same foreign branch under *ICTA 1988, s 806L*. Any excess credits arising in respect of other types of income are not relievable under the onshore pooling regime, hence the only alternative for using them is expense relief.

11.15 The general rules applicable for income tax purposes under *ICTA 1988, s 796* are as follows:

● The credit allowed for foreign tax under any arrangements is limited to the difference between:

– The income tax liability for the year on the person's total income, taking account of all reductions available under the Income Tax Acts, but excluding credit for foreign tax, and

– The income tax liability for the year, computed as above, but excluding the income in respect of which credit relief is claimed.

● The above calculation must be performed separately for each source of foreign income, each time excluding from the calculation foreign source income for which the maximum credit has already been computed.

● The total credit for foreign tax to be allowed shall not exceed the total income tax payable for the year of assessment, less any income tax which the person is entitled to charge against any other person, for example by retention from annual payments. The effect of this provision on unauthorised unit trusts is discussed below.

Expense relief

11.16   Under *ICTA 1988, s 811*, foreign source income will be treated as reduced by foreign tax paid on it where credit relief is not available for the foreign tax. This is commonly known as 'expense relief'.

Expense relief is commonly used by authorised unit trusts, OEICs and investment trusts because they often have excess management expenses, and hence no UK tax liability against which credit relief can be claimed. The relief is normally claimed in the tax computation by showing the relevant foreign tax as a deduction from each gross item of foreign income. It is not possible to claim both expense relief and credit relief for a particular item of income. However, it is possible to claim credit relief on one source of income and expense relief on another.

It should be noted in particular that expense relief is available for taxes that are classified as inadmissible for credit relief by the Inland Revenue.

An obligation is imposed on taxpayers by *section 811(5)* to notify the Inland Revenue where the expense relief previously claimed becomes excessive as a result of a reduction in the amount of foreign tax payable. This must be done within one year of the adjustment rendering the relief excessive to avoid liability to a penalty equal to the tax effect of the excess relief claimed.

Tax sparing relief

11.17   Many countries, particularly in the developing world, have tax incentives to stimulate their economies and encourage foreign investors. Examples include exempting profits from new ventures from taxation for a specified number of years and withholding tax benefits on approved investments. In order to prevent the effect of the foreign tax incentives being cancelled out by a corresponding increase in UK tax, *ICTA 1988, s 788(5)* permits relief by agreement for these incentives (unilateral relief is not available in such circumstances). As a result, a small number of the UK's double taxation agreements provide for credit to be given in the UK for foreign tax that would have been payable on income or gains but for the existence of particular reliefs specified in the relevant treaty. This is known as 'tax sparing relief'.

Loan relationships

11.18   Entitlement to credit relief for foreign tax depends upon identifying UK taxation attributable to the particular income or gain that has been subject to foreign taxation. However, the general rule in *FA 1996, s 82(4)* is that non-trading loan relationship debits and credits should be aggregated before being brought into account for tax purposes. Without further amendment, this rule would limit the ability to obtain credit for foreign tax suffered on, for example, overseas interest income, as it would be shown net of non-trade loan relationship debits for tax purposes. Special provisions are therefore included in *ICTA 1988, ss 797A, 797 (3A)* and *797(3B)* to ensure for double taxation relief purposes that overseas interest is dealt with gross and non-trade loan relationship deficits can be allocated with the same flexibility as charges on income and management expenses.

11.19   Where a company has overseas non-trading interest in respect of which a foreign tax credit is available, *section 797A* provides that:

● The company's non-trade loan relationship credits should be calculated for tax purposes without deduction of any non-trade loan relationship debits.

● The company's non-trade loan relationship debits should be adjusted to reflect any claims to carry back, group relieve or carry forward deficits of the period. The adjusted amount of debits can then be set off against profits of any description for the accounting period, including non-trade loan relationship credits. However, this allocation must reflect any claim to offset deficits against profits of the current period under *FA 1996, s 83(2)(a)*.

EXAMPLE 11.19

The Swan Trust Plc is a UK resident investment trust. It has income and expenses as follows:

UK interest income	1,000
Non-UK interest income	750 (with a foreign tax credit of 150)
Schedule A income	500
Loan relationship debits	(2,000)
Management expenses	(500)

It has a trading subsidiary with a profit of 200. Claims will be made as follows:

	Loan relationship debits	UK interest	Non-UK interest	Schedule A
	(2,000)	1,000	750	500
Management expenses				(500)
Group relief	200			
Section 797(3)	1,250	(1,000)	(250)	
Section 83(3A)	550			
Profit	Nil	Nil	500	Nil
UK corporation tax at 30%			150	
Double tax relief			(150)	
Tax liability			Nil	

Where a company has no overseas non-trading interest on which foreign tax is creditable, any non-trade loan relationship deficit subject to a claim under *section 83(2)(a)* should be allocated under *section 797* in accordance with that claim.

Dividends and relief from underlying tax

11.20   The payment of dividends from the post-tax profits of a foreign company and their subsequent taxation in the hands of a UK investor results in double taxation of those profits. In certain circumstances the UK therefore permits credit relief for the foreign tax suffered on the underlying profits from which dividends have been paid, that is, the 'underlying tax'.

Normally the UK's double taxation agreements provide that relief for underlying tax is available in respect of dividends paid by a foreign company to a UK resident company which controls directly or indirectly at least 10% of the voting power in the foreign company.

Where relief is not available by agreement, unilateral relief is available for underlying tax on a similar basis to that afforded by most UK treaties.

Given the requirement regarding voting power, it is relatively unusual for collective investment schemes, which are by their nature portfolio investors, to be eligible for underlying tax relief. The complex rules governing the availability and calculation of this relief are therefore not considered in further detail here and reference should be made to *Tolley's Double Taxation Relief*.

Eligible unrelieved foreign tax – provisions applicable to collective investment schemes

11.21   *Finance Act 2000* made significant changes to the rules governing credit relief for the purposes of corporation tax, with the introduction of the so-called 'mixer cap' and the onshore pooling regime. The complexities of the new regime are well known, and readers are referred to *Tolley's Double Taxation Relief* for a comprehensive explanation of the rules. In particular, as discussed above, the rules governing relief for underlying tax are not covered here. The provisions that may be relevant to collective investment schemes can be summarised as follows:

- Unrelieved foreign tax arising on certain foreign dividends is known as 'eligible unrelieved foreign tax' ('EUFT'), which can be used against the residual UK tax liability on 'qualifying foreign dividends'.

- The dividends that give rise to EUFT are defined in *ICTA 1988 s 806A(2)*. They comprise any dividends chargeable under Schedule D Case V, subject to a list of exclusions, notably dividends treated as reduced by expense relief under *section 811*.

- Foreign withholding taxes will give rise to EUFT where the UK tax payable on the foreign dividend is less than the creditable foreign tax. This is known as 'Case A' EUFT (*section 806A(4)*).

- Case A EUFT cannot exceed the amount of foreign tax that would have been creditable had the UK corporation tax rate been 45% (*section 806B(2)*).

- The Revenue have confirmed that Case A EUFT will arise not only where foreign withholding taxes exceed the UK corporation tax rate of 30%, but also where the UK tax charge is low because of the availability of losses or the application of the small companies rate.

- EUFT is available for relief against the UK tax liability on 'qualifying foreign dividends'. These comprise all dividends chargeable under Schedule D Case V, with the exception of (*section 806C(1)*):

  - acceptable distribution policy dividends paid by a controlled foreign company direct to a UK company;

  - dividends representing an acceptable distribution policy dividend paid by a controlled foreign company lower in the dividend chain;

  - dividends giving rise to an amount of EUFT;

  - dividends that are excluded from giving rise to EUFT by the exclusions in *section 806A(2)*.

- Qualifying foreign dividends are sub-divided into related and unrelated dividends. Related qualifying foreign dividends are those received from companies in which an interest of 10% or more is held in the voting power. All others are classified as unrelated (*section 806C(2)*).

- For the purposes of calculating the relief available, the related qualifying foreign dividends are aggregated and treated as one source called the 'single related dividend'. The unrelated qualifying foreign dividends are aggregated to form the 'single unrelated dividend' (*section 806C(3), (4)*).

- EUFT arising on the qualifying dividends, other than underlying tax, is aggregated and credit relief may be taken for the tax wholly or partly as required against either the single related dividend or the single unrelated dividend of the accounting period (*section 806(4)(d)*).

- The EUFT can also be carried back and credited on a LIFO basis against the UK tax liability on the single related or unrelated dividends of accounting periods beginning not more than three years before the accounting period in which the EUFT arose (*section 806E(2)*).

- The EUFT can also be carried forward indefinitely to be utilised against the UK tax liability on the single related or unrelated dividends of future accounting periods (*section 806D(5)(b)*).

Inland Revenue guidance on double taxation relief

11.22   The Inland Revenue's own guidance on double taxation relief is included in the Double Taxation Relief Manual, accessible on the Inland Revenue website, www.inlandrevenue.gov.uk.

Application to investment funds

11.23   As collective investment schemes enjoy various exemptions from UK taxation, they are less exposed to the risk of double taxation than other taxpayers. The practical issues for each type of vehicle are considered below.

Authorised unit trusts, OEICs and investment trusts

11.24   As these vehicles enjoy exemption from UK taxation on chargeable gains, they are not subject to double taxation on those. Care should be taken to ensure that foreign taxation on capital gains is in accordance with the provisions of the applicable double taxation treaty.

With regard to foreign income, these vehicles are subject to UK corporation tax, and are hence at risk of double taxation depending upon the foreign tax position. For funds with excess management expenses for an accounting period, credit relief will not be available, and claiming expense relief will be the only option. Funds that are consistently in this position should ensure that full advantage is taken of available treaty benefits and where possible look to other ways of reducing foreign tax suffered to yield a real improvement in their post-tax return. For funds that have a UK tax liability, credit relief can be maximised by allocating management expenses in the most advantageous manner, as permitted by *ICTA 1988, s 797(3)*. This involves allocating the management expenses against UK income first, then against foreign income with the lowest foreign tax rates, so that ultimately the UK tax liability arises on the foreign income that has suffered the highest rate of tax, hence maximising the potential credit relief obtained.

11.25   Following discussions with the AITC and IMA (then AUTIF), the Inland Revenue agreed a recommended manner for members of those organisations to present claims to double taxation relief in their computations. The recommendation is to show separately for each source country the amounts of interest and dividend income and the foreign tax suffered on each, and to provide details of items which distort the normal rate of tax shown on a particular income source. This is designed to facilitate the Inland Revenue's examination of claims. In consideration for this approach being adopted, it will not be necessary to submit itemised schedules and supporting vouchers, provided that these will be supplied on request.

Unauthorised unit trusts

11.26   Unauthorised unit trusts are normally exempt from UK taxation on chargeable gains by virtue of *TCGA 1992, s 100(2)*. This affords exemption to the unit trust provided all the unitholders in the trust are themselves exempt from capital gains tax or corporation tax on capital gains, other than by reason of residence. As a result, an unauthorised unit trust will not normally suffer double taxation on capital gains, although again a fund may look to minimise any foreign taxes suffered on capital gains.

11.27   With regard to foreign taxes on income, an unauthorised unit trust is prevented from obtaining full credit relief by *ICTA 1988, s 796(3)*. This limits the total credit for foreign tax to the total income tax payable for the year of assessment, less any income tax which the trustees are entitled to charge against any other person, for example by retention from annual payments. The unitholders of an unauthorised unit trust are deemed to receive an annual payment equal to the income of the trust available for distribution in the accounts, grossed up for the basic rate of income tax. The credit permitted under *section 796(3)* will therefore usually be nil, if no adjustment is made to the amount available for payment by the trust. Therefore the foreign taxes suffered should be treated as a deduction from the income available for distribution, hence reducing the deemed annual payment to the unitholders. The taxable income of the trustees will however remain the same, and as a result the foreign tax credit permitted under *section 796(3)* will be increased.

EXAMPLE 11.27

An unauthorised unit trust has income of £1,000 in 2002/2003, subject to withholding tax of £100. There are no expenses charged in the fund.

The gross income of the fund available for distribution will be £900, less tax deducted on the annual payment of £198.

The taxable income of the fund is £1,000, giving rise to a total UK tax liability of £220 before credit relief.

Under *section 796(3)*, credit for foreign tax of £22 will be available to the trustees, being the total UK tax liability of £220 less the £198 deducted from the annual payment. In effect, the trustees thereby receive expense relief for the foreign tax suffered.

Pension fund pooling schemes

11.28   Regulations concerning pension fund pooling schemes ('PFPSs') are set out in the *Income Tax (Pensions Funds Pooling Schemes) Regulations 1996 (SI 1996/1585)*. In form, PFPSs are unit trusts. However, they are explicitly excluded from the Income Tax definition of unit trust by the Regulations. As a result, it is the participants and not the trustees who are entitled to the income arising to the fund in proportion to their interest in the fund, and the participants are regarded as liable to any tax charge arising. The schemes are therefore treated as transparent for tax purposes.

As the participants in a PFPS are not liable in their own right to taxation in the UK, being exempt approved retirement benefit schemes, superannuation funds or overseas equivalents, any foreign taxes suffered on their income cannot be relieved against a UK tax liability. The objective for PFPSs should therefore be to eliminate foreign taxation of their income through making appropriate claims for relief from taxation under applicable double taxation treaties (see **11.46** below regarding treaty access).

Treaty access

11.29   Post-tax income and capital returns may vary significantly between treaty-protected and non treaty-protected investors. Successfully accessing the benefits available under double taxation agreements is therefore clearly of great importance to collective investment schemes making cross-border investments. Whether this is possible in a given case will depend upon consideration of all the provisions of the particular treaty, but the following areas will provide the framework:

- Personal scope of the treaty

- The definition of resident for treaty purposes

- Taxes covered

These are considered below for collective investment schemes in the context of the UK treaty network.

UK tax treaties

11.30   There are more than 1,300 double taxation agreements worldwide. The UK, with comprehensive double taxation agreements covering more than 100 jurisdictions, has the largest network of treaties in the world. This network of agreements is subject to an annual review process by the Government to ensure that it remains in line with current international practice and continues to meet the needs of UK businesses and individuals. The programme announced in Inland Revenue Press Release 62/03 for the year to 31 March 2004 comprises a mixture of work on existing treaties and negotiations for the creation of new agreements. Work is to be completed on new treaties with Australia, Chile, Croatia, France and Slovenia and new protocols to existing treaties with Belgium, Italy and New Zealand, whilst negotiations are to be progressed with Bahrain, Botswana, Georgia, Germany, Namibia and Saudi Arabia. Work is also to commence on new or updated treaties with Hong Kong, Iran, Luxembourg, Poland, Serbia and Montenegro, and Thailand. An update regarding progress was issued by the Inland Revenue in its August 2003 *Tax Bulletin, Issue 66*.

Persons covered

11.31   Most UK treaties now contain a 'personal scope' article, typically stating that the agreement applies to persons who are residents of one or both of the contracting states. This is in line with the OECD model.

The term 'person' is normally defined in the 'general definitions' article of UK treaties based upon the OECD model as including 'an individual, company or any other body of persons'. 'Company' is normally defined as 'any body corporate or any entity that is treated as a body corporate for tax purposes'.

The term 'resident of a contracting state' is also usually defined in UK treaties in accordance with the OECD model treaty, which uses the following definition:

'For the purposes of this Convention, the term "resident of a Contracting State" means any person who, under the laws of that State, is liable to tax therein by reason of his domicile, residence, place of management or any other criterion of a similar nature, and also includes that State and any political subdivision or local authority thereof. This term, however, does not include any person who is liable to tax in that State in respect only of income from sources in that State or capital situated therein.'

Authorised unit trusts

11.32 *ICTA 1988, s 468(1)* provides that, as regards income arising to the trustees and for the purposes of the provisions relating to relief for capital expenditure, the Tax Acts shall have effect as if:

- the trustees were a company resident in the UK; and

- the rights of the unitholders were shares in a company.

As discussed above, treaties following the OECD model as regards the persons covered will define the term 'company' as any body corporate or any entity that is treated as a body corporate for tax purposes. The effect of *section 468(1)* is to treat authorised unit trusts as companies for tax purposes, hence they should be within the scope of the persons covered where the wording of the treaty follows that model. As they are also liable to tax in the UK by reason of residence, they will be treated as UK resident for the purposes of such treaties. This analysis in fact holds good for most UK treaties, which use the definition of 'company' above. There are however a few older treaties, such as that with Greece, where the definition of company is simply 'any body corporate' which does not encompass a unit trust. However, these treaties usually include 'any body of persons' within the definition of 'person' and a unit trust is regarded as falling within this definition.

11.33 As an authorised unit trust is treated as a company, and hence not transparent for tax purposes, and is subject to UK tax on its income, it will usually be entitled to full treaty benefits in respect of income arising in treaty countries. The precise wording of the relevant treaty article and any limitation of benefits provisions should, however, always be consulted (see **11.77** below regarding the difficulties posed by the new UK/US treaty).

11.34 The position regarding capital gains treaty benefits is less certain, as an authorised unit trust is exempt from UK taxation on such gains. For treaties with a capital gains article following the OECD model, the exemption should not prevent a unit trust benefiting under the treaty, as the application of the capital gains article depends only on the investor being liable to tax in the UK. However, in some cases a requirement that the investor be subject to tax on gains or a particular type of gain will also be included in the capital gains article.

In such cases an authorised unit trust, being exempt from taxation on capital gains, would potentially not be entitled to the relevant benefit.

Open-ended investment companies

11.35 An OEIC, being a company, will be within the definition of 'person' on which the definition of 'resident' is based for the purposes of all current UK treaties. An OEIC resident in the UK, being liable to tax in the UK by reason of residence will be treated as UK resident for the purposes of all current UK treaties.

Like an authorised unit trust, an OEIC should usually be entitled to full treaty benefits in respect of income arising in treaty countries, but may have a restricted entitlement to benefits under capital gains articles in treaties because of its exemption from UK taxation on capital gains.

Investment trusts

11.36 A UK resident investment trust is legally a limited company. It will therefore be within the definition of 'person' on which the definition of 'resident' is based for the purposes of all current UK treaties. As investment trusts are also liable to tax in the UK by reason of residence, they should be UK residents for the purposes of all current UK treaties.

Investment trusts should usually be entitled to full treaty benefits in respect of income arising in treaty countries. As for the authorised funds, their entitlement to benefits under capital gains articles may in some cases be affected by their exemption from UK taxation on capital gains.

Unauthorised unit trusts

11.37 Unlike authorised unit trusts, unauthorised unit trusts are not treated as companies for UK tax purposes and it is the trustees of the scheme who are liable to taxation. As a result, their ability to access double taxation treaties using the OECD model treaty definition of 'person' depends upon being within the scope of the phrase 'any other body of persons'. Provided this wording is present in a UK treaty, it will be accepted that the trustees should be regarded as a 'person' for the purposes of the treaty residence article. As the trustees are regarded as liable to taxation in the UK on the income of the scheme, the scheme will therefore be treated as UK resident for treaty purposes.

In theory the trust structure poses a further question in that the benefits of the dividend and interest articles of UK treaties normally apply only to the beneficial owners of the income, which will be the unitholders in the case of an unauthorised unit trust. However, in practice, analysis of the beneficial ownership of the vehicle is not normally required to substantiate a claim to treaty benefits. Unauthorised unit trusts therefore generally obtain the same withholding tax benefits as authorised unit trusts.

Partnerships

11.38   The tax treatment of partnerships under domestic law varies markedly between different countries. Some jurisdictions, for example the UK and the US, treat partnerships as transparent for tax purposes and tax the individual partners directly on their share of the partnership profits. Others, for example France, treat partnerships as entities taxable in their own right, or even treat them as companies. As a result, the OECD model treaty has to date not included special provisions for partnerships, on the assumption that countries negotiating agreements should make appropriate provisions between themselves based upon the legal and tax treatment of partnerships in their particular jurisdictions.

The OECD did however publish a report, 'The Application of the OECD Model Tax Convention to Partnerships' (adopted by the OECD Committee on Fiscal Affairs on 20 January 1999), content from which was incorporated in the revised commentary on the OECD model treaty published in April 2000. This commentary now indicates that partnerships may be treated as 'persons' for treaty purposes. Depending upon how they are treated for tax purposes, they may fall within the definition of 'company' under the OECD model. Alternatively, if they are not deemed to be companies, they can be regarded as falling within the heading 'any other body of persons'. However, although a partnership may be characterised as a 'person' for treaty purposes, that alone would not make it a resident under the OECD model treaty, as it is also necessary for the person to be 'liable to tax' in its jurisdiction of residence. A partnership treated as fiscally transparent cannot satisfy this requirement, as the liability to tax falls upon the individual partners.

11.39   In the UK, the Inland Revenue historically took the view that treaties did not apply to partnerships unless they were specifically mentioned, which was not generally the case. This position was consistent with the usual treatment of partnerships in UK domestic tax law, as set out in *ICTA 1988, s 111(1)*:

> 'Where a trade or profession is carried on by persons in partnership, the partnership shall not, unless the contrary intention appears, be treated for the purposes of the Tax Acts as an entity which is distinct from those persons.'

The UK position therefore remains that unless there are specific provisions determining whether partnerships have access to a treaty, it will be the treaty rights of the individual partners that will determine the benefits available.

That being said, it has become more common for the UK's treaties to make specific provision for partnerships. The agreements with Italy, Iceland and India are examples of those specifically excluding partnerships from the definition of 'person' (subject in the case of India to a specific exception for a particular type of Indian partnership treated as a taxable unit). By contrast, the new agreement with the US specifically includes partnerships within the definition of 'person'. However, a UK partnership, being fiscally transparent, would not qualify as a resident under the terms of that treaty.

Venture capital limited partnerships

11.40   The factors discussed above with regard to partnerships generally apply equally to a venture capital limited partnership established under the *Limited Partnership Act 1907* to raise funds for investment as venture capital. As indicated above, it will normally be the treaty status of the individual partners that will determine whether treaty benefits can be obtained. It is not unusual for the partners in such a partnership to include non-residents, and it will be necessary to scrutinise the terms of the double taxation agreements with their particular jurisdictions to determine their position as regards income received by the partnership.

Where the non-residents are banks or other financial traders, a potential issue to be considered is whether the activities of the limited partnership can be regarded as trading in the UK through a permanent establishment. If so, the availability of treaty benefits may be restricted by the treaty on the basis that the income in question is effectively connected with a UK permanent establishment.

European Economic Interest Groupings

11.41   European Economic Interest Groupings ('EEIGs') are a form of fiscally transparent business association designed to facilitate cross-border co-operation between businesses within the EU. They were created on 25 July 1985 by EC Regulation 2137/85, which entered into force on 1 July 1989. In the UK regulations for the registration of EEIGs were issued under the *European Economic Interest Grouping Regulations 1989 (SI 1989 No 638)*. These treat an EEIG registered in the UK as a body corporate with legal capacity to act in its own name. As such, an EEIG registered in the UK is regarded as resident in the UK by virtue of *FA 1988, s 66*.

11.42   The UK tax treatment is covered in *ICTA 1988, s 510A*, which is designed to implement the principle in Article 40 of the EC Regulations that profits and losses resulting from the activities of an EEIG shall be taxable only in the hands of its members. In summary, therefore, *section 510A* treats the EEIG as an agent of its members for the purposes of assessing them to taxation on income and gains, and any trade or profession carried on by an EEIG is treated as being carried on by a partnership. Hence the EEIG itself has no liability to taxation.

The position of an EEIG and its members under double taxation agreements is therefore similar to that of partnerships, notwithstanding the fact that it may be treated legally as a body corporate, as in the UK. If the residence article of the relevant treaty follows the OECD model treaty, then an EEIG will not be treated as a resident of any state for treaty purposes, as the EEIG is not liable to taxation. Depending upon their own status, the members of an EEIG may be able to claim treaty benefits in their own right. This may be complicated in some cases as the members of an EEIG can include partnerships, in which case it would usually be necessary to consider the treaty position of the individual partners.

Charities

11.43   Charities will usually take the form of a body corporate, and hence fall within the definition of 'person' used in treaties following the OECD model. Failing that they are likely to be treated as falling within the scope of 'any other body of persons'. The question that then arises is whether they can be treated as persons 'liable to tax' given the exemptions from taxation that they enjoy. The UK takes the view that they should be treated as residents in accordance with this test, on the basis that the exemptions are conditional on satisfying specific requirements set out in *ICTA 1988, s 505*. Broadly the requirement is that profits and gains should be applied to charitable purposes only. In the case of trading profits, the trade concerned should either be part of the actual carrying out of the primary purpose of the charity or the work in connection with the trade should be mainly carried out by the beneficiaries of the charity.

Some states may not consider that such entities are 'liable to tax' on this basis, hence will not regard them as residents for treaty purposes unless they are expressly covered by the treaty in question.

11.44   Under some agreements, a resident of the UK will only be entitled to exemption or relief from foreign tax on certain types of income if they are 'subject to tax' on that income in the UK. The Inland Revenue take the view that a person should not be regarded as subject to tax in the UK if the income in question is exempted from UK tax by an extra-statutory concession or statutory exemption. Accordingly the Revenue do not regard charities as subject to tax on their income. This will restrict their entitlement to benefits under certain treaties. For example, not being 'subject to tax', a charity is precluded from recovering the French *avoir fiscal*.

Pension schemes

11.45   For treaties following the OECD model, Inland Revenue approved retirement benefit schemes will generally be regarded as falling within 'any body of persons' in the definitions article. Such schemes are regarded by the Inland Revenue as 'liable to tax', but not 'subject to tax'. Under most UK treaties they should therefore be treated as residents of the UK for treaty purposes, but may have restricted access to benefits where being 'subject to tax' is a condition.

Readers should note that this is an area where theory and practice do not always equate. Where significant sums are involved it may be appropriate to get tax rulings from the relevant tax authorities.

Pension fund pooling schemes

11.46   As discussed above, PFPSs are treated as transparent for tax purposes. Accordingly, access to treaty benefits will be determined as if the participants in the scheme held the investments directly. In principle a PFPS should be in a similar position to pension schemes, as discussed above. However, the inclusion amongst the participators of overseas schemes equivalent to UK approved schemes will increase the complexity of treaty claims in practice as it will be necessary to have recourse to the treaties of jurisdictions other than the UK to determine the scheme's entitlement to benefits. In such situations the comments made above about practice and theory are particularly relevant.

Offshore funds

11.47   Offshore funds may need to access the interest articles of UK treaties. However, their ability to benefit under double taxation agreements with the UK will in the first instance depend upon the terms of the particular treaty and the classification of the entity under the law of the foreign jurisdiction.

If the entity itself does not have rights under the treaty because, for example, it is treated as transparent by the foreign jurisdiction, the persons behind the entity could still be permitted to benefit by claims in their own name, depending upon their treaty status.

Overseas tax reclaims (commentary)

11.48   Collective investment schemes may need to pursue overseas tax reclaims for two reasons:

- to maximise the post-tax return on investments, in particular where credit relief is unavailable because they are exempt bodies or have losses ensuring that there is no UK tax liability to credit the foreign tax against; and

- to comply with the obligation to minimise foreign taxes imposed for the purposes of credit relief by *ICTA 1988, s 795A*.

Minimisation of foreign tax

11.49   The obligation to minimise foreign taxes was made explicit by *FA 2000*, which inserted the new *section 795A*, though it should be noted that the Revenue have always regarded the obligation as implicit. Under this section the onus is placed upon taxpayers to take all reasonable steps under the law of the foreign territory and any applicable double taxation arrangements to minimise the amount of foreign tax payable. 'Reasonable steps' include:

(a) claiming, or otherwise securing the benefit of, reliefs, deductions, reductions or allowances; and

(b) making elections for tax purposes.

Credit relief will not be granted for foreign tax in excess of the minimum foreign tax computed on this basis.

Whether 'reasonable steps' have been taken will be assessed by considering what the person might reasonably have been expected to have done if UK double taxation relief had not been available.

11.50   The Inland Revenue has published some guidance on interpretation of these provisions, including the following points:

●   Taxpayers are expected to claim the normal reliefs and allowances available to all entities under the standard tax regime for the territory concerned.

●   Examples of situations or conduct where the limit may apply include:

–   acceptance of an estimated tax assessment in the other territory which is likely to prove excessive;

–   not claiming an allowance or relief (eg capital allowances or losses) which is generally known to be available);

–   where the other territory's domestic law or the relevant double taxation agreement provides for alternative bases of taxation, not choosing the basis which would produce the lowest tax bill.

●   In deciding what steps to take, it is reasonable for a taxpayer to have regard on the one hand to the amount of time, effort and expense involved in discussing his case with the foreign tax authorities, and on the other to the amount of the expected tax reduction.

11.51   An Inspector will refer to International Division any case where:

●   the taxpayer makes a claim to relief from foreign tax to the foreign tax authority but the claim is refused for procedural reasons, for example failure to observe time limits, or the foreign tax authority does not respond to or act upon the claim, or

●   the foreign country imposes tax on income that does not arise in that country.

Management of foreign taxes

11.52   Collective investment schemes may have exposures to foreign taxes in numerous jurisdictions. Good housekeeping and process management will therefore be important to achieving the dual goals of minimising foreign taxes and collecting recoverable amounts on a timely basis. Ideally the foreign tax implications of foreign investments should be examined in advance of making the investments. This would entail consideration of and knowledge gathering concerning the following issues:

- The extent of foreign taxes applicable to the expected investment returns, whether in the form of interest, dividends or capital gains.

- The application of the relevant double taxation agreement for the investing body.

- The availability of relief at source in the event that relief is available under the treaty.

- The procedures for obtaining relief at source.

- The procedures for reclaiming excess foreign tax from the foreign tax authority.

- Time limits for recovery of foreign taxes.

Clearly obtaining relief from foreign taxes at source is greatly to be preferred over reclaiming the excess over treaty rates from foreign tax authorities. Relief at source not only optimises cash flow, but also may lead to greater recovery in absolute terms, as the time, effort and expense of dealing with certain jurisdictions, coupled with tardy repayment prospects, notably in Italy and Spain, may ultimately lead UK investors not to pursue repayment claims. This may then result in uncertainty regarding claims for credit relief in respect of excess foreign tax suffered.

If it is necessary to rely on reclaiming foreign taxes from the foreign tax authorities, time limits should be observed with care to avoid losing entitlement to recovery. As noted above, the policy of the Inland Revenue is to refer claims for credit relief in such circumstances to International Division, in which case credit relief may be denied for the excess foreign tax.

Treaty forms

11.53   In many cases, foreign tax authorities require claims for relief at source or repayment of tax in excess of treaty rates to be submitted on specific forms. These will normally require certification by the Inspector responsible for the claimant's tax affairs, and it is the claimant or their agent who should make the request. Depending upon the terms of the treaty, the form may merely require confirmation that the claimant is resident for tax purposes in the UK or it may require confirmation that the claimant is subject to tax in respect of particular income. It should be noted that the Inland Revenue will not provide certification to a mere nominee. Claims must be submitted in the name of the beneficial owner.

The Inland Revenue's Financial Intermediaries and Claims Office (FICO) does hold stocks of the forms required for some of the more common claims. These can otherwise be obtained from the relevant foreign tax authority.

Obtaining certification of residence from the Inland Revenue

11.54   In some cases there is no standard form available to make a particular treaty claim. In such cases it should be possible to forward an appropriate pro forma certificate to the claimant's Inspector for certification and to provide this to the foreign tax authority. On request, the Inspector may be able to provide such a certificate in bilingual form.

The US Qualified Intermediary Regulations – status of investment funds

Background

11.55   The US withholding tax and reporting regulations, which came into effect on 1 January 2001, introduced stringent documentation and reporting requirements for all intermediaries that make payments of US-source interest, dividends, royalties and other specified types of income. The rationale for the changes was to:

- eliminate the possibility of tax evasion by US citizens who have accounts held overseas; and

- to prevent non-US residents from claiming a reduced rate of withholding tax under a tax treaty for which they are not eligible.

Intermediaries may enter into an agreement with the IRS to become a qualified intermediary ('QI'), whereby treaty benefits can be obtained at source whilst maintaining client and market confidentiality. Intermediaries who have not entered into a QI agreement are by default classified as non-qualified intermediaries ('NQIs'). An NQI is required to disclose fully a beneficial owner's identity and details of US-source income received to the upstream withholding agent and ultimately to the IRS.

Although there are many advantages to entering into a QI agreement, a QI is generally required to have an audit of its compliance for both the second and fifth year – for most QIs this will be 2002 and 2005. It is possible to have the audit carried out by the IRS, although only a handful of QIs have taken up this option: most have engaged one of the larger accountancy practices.

Application to collective investment schemes

11.56   The significance of the regulations for collective investment schemes lies in the potential impact it has on:

- the documentation to be provided by the schemes to payers of their US-source income; and

- the potential inconvenience caused by submission of incorrect or insufficient documentation, and hence the risk that relief will not be obtained for US withholding tax at source.

Assuming the scheme is the beneficial owner entitled to treaty benefits, and it receives a payment from a QI, it will need to pass a completed Form W8-Ben to the QI asserting the scheme's entitlement to claim benefits under the treaty. The QI must hold complete and accurate documentation if a claim under the treaty is to be made. If the documentation supplied is incomplete, incorrect or unreliable, the QI should withhold tax at the standard rate of 30% until the correct information is supplied.

If the collective investment scheme is itself an intermediary, for example possibly a limited partnership, then documentation relating to investors must be obtained and passed to the QI. The investors are likely to be treated as indirect customers of the QI and their details passed on as described above. In these circumstances the collective investment scheme may consider the benefits of becoming a QI itself or whether to avail itself of the new non-withholding foreign partnership or trust status.

The French 'avoir fiscal'

Overview

11.57   The *avoir fiscal* is an imputed tax credit attached to certain French source dividends, which UK investors may be entitled to recover under the terms of the UK–France double taxation treaty. Non-residents have no entitlement to recover the *avoir fiscal* except as provided for in French treaties.

The draft French Finance Bill for 2004, which is expected to be voted on in December 2003, proposes the abolition of the *avoir fiscal*, with effect for distributions paid to corporate shareholders on or after 1 January 2004 and for distributions paid to individual shareholders on or after 1 January 2005. At present, no alternative arrangements have been proposed to replace the tax credit for companies. Therefore, UK investors in French equities who currently benefit under the UK-France double taxation treaty are likely to be disadvantaged. However, pending finalisation of the amending provisions, the future position will remain uncertain. The commentary below therefore describes the position according to currently enacted legislation.

11.58   The following conditions must be met for a dividend to qualify for the *avoir fiscal*:

- the company paying the dividend must have its head office in France and must be subject to corporate income tax;

- the dividend must be a dividend that is regularly and periodically distributed, either in cash or kind;

- the dividend must be declared by resolution of the annual shareholders' meeting (interim dividends distributed prior to the approval of the accounts of the current year also qualify).

11.59   The following types of distribution do not qualify for the *avoir fiscal*:

- exceptional distributions of reserves resolved in shareholders' meetings other than the annual general meeting called to approve the accounts. These constitute a partial capital allocation and not a dividend distribution;

- amounts allocated to shareholders in return for a capital reduction;

- amounts or capital allocated to shareholders when a company repurchases its own shares and reduces its capital;

- distributions by investment companies, which are normally exempt from tax. There is however a mechanism whereby they can transfer the benefit of the *avoir fiscal* on dividends they receive to their own shareholders, thus putting them in the same position as if they had invested directly in the investment company's portfolio. This applies, for example, to FCPs;

- bonus share distributions;

- distributions, profit shares or fees to directors;

- hidden profit distributions;

- both interim and final distributions of surpluses on liquidations;

- distributions by French branches of foreign companies.

Entitlement to the 'avoir fiscal' under the UK–France double taxation treaty

11.60   Article 9 of the UK's agreement with France makes provision for residents of the UK receiving dividends from a French resident company to recover from the French Treasury amounts equal to the *avoir fiscal* that a French resident would recover on those dividends. The benefit of this provision is, however, limited to UK residents who are:

- individuals;

- companies; or

- pension funds approved for tax purposes.

11.61   Article 3 of the treaty defines a resident of a contracting state as 'any person who, under the laws of that State, is liable to tax therein by reason of his domicile, residence, place of management or any other criterion of a similar nature'. The *avoir fiscal* provision in Article 9 is more restrictive as it also includes the requirement for individuals and companies that they should be 'subject to United Kingdom tax'. Pension funds approved for tax purposes are not subject to this requirement, which, as discussed above, they would not meet.

11.62   The size of the UK investor's holding is also relevant to determining entitlement to the *avoir fiscal*. Companies or pension funds, which control the company paying the dividend, are not entitled to the *avoir fiscal*. For this purpose 'control' is defined by paragraph 11 of Article 9:

'For the purposes of this Article, a company shall be deemed to control another company when either alone or together with one or more associated companies it controls directly or indirectly at least 10 per cent of the voting power in that other company, and two companies shall be deemed to be associated if one is controlled directly or indirectly by the other, or both are controlled directly or indirectly by a third company.'

As it is probably unusual in practice for an investment fund to hold as much as a 10% interest in an investment, this restriction may not be significant in this context.

There is also a prohibition on recovery by companies or pension funds if they are entitled to take into account French tax payable on the profits out of which the dividends are paid for the purposes of computing their entitlement to credit relief. This should in any case not be possible given the UK's minimum 10% ownership requirement to obtain relief for underlying tax.

11.63 Article 2 of the UK–France double taxation treaty provides that a 'company' means any body corporate or any entity which is treated as a body corporate for tax purposes. Therefore the following collective investment schemes should be eligible to benefit from the *avoir fiscal* under the treaty:

- authorised unit trusts;
- investment trusts and venture capital trusts;
- open-ended investment companies;
- pension fund pooling vehicles.

'Avoir fiscal' rates

11.64 UK resident individuals are entitled to recover an *avoir fiscal* credit equal to 50% of the dividend received.

UK companies with a holding of 5% or more of the French company's capital are also entitled to the full 50% credit.

Approved pension funds and UK companies with an interest below 5% in the French company's capital were entitled to a reduced credit equal to 15% of the dividend until 15 January 2003. *Avoir fiscal* after that date is at a rate of 10%, ie *avoir fiscal* attached to dividends paid in 2002.

Withholding tax

11.65 Article 9 of the UK–France double taxation treaty specifically provides that payments from the French Treasury to UK residents under these provisions are deemed to be dividends for the purposes of the treaty. As a result they are subject to withholding tax of 15%.

Recovery of the 'avoir fiscal'

11.66   The *avoir fiscal* is not paid to the UK shareholder at the same time as the dividend to which it relates. Instead, in order to claim the *avoir fiscal*, the UK shareholder must file Form RF 4 GB, certified by the Inland Revenue and proving entitlement under the treaty, with the paying entity. This should be done before the end of the year in which the distribution is made to ensure timely receipt of the *avoir fiscal*. Following receipt of the required documentation, the paying company will make a second payment comprising the *avoir fiscal* credit, less withholding tax. This payment will not be made before 15 January of the year following distribution of the dividend itself. It is the responsibility of the paying company itself to collect the *avoir fiscal* credit from the French Treasury by means of a subsequent set-off against withholding taxes due from that company to the Treasury.

EXAMPLE 11.66

> A UK investment trust with a 6% holding in a French company receives a gross dividend of 100 in April 2003. The UK investment trust is entitled to the *avoir fiscal* under the provisions of Article 9 of the UK–France double taxation treaty. Withholding tax of 15% is applicable to the dividend, hence the amount paid in April 2003 to the UK investment trust is 85. Following submission of documentary proof of entitlement by the investment trust, a further payment of 42.5 is made by the French company (ie *avoir fiscal* of 50 less 15% withholding tax). This will be made after 15 January 2004. The total received by the UK investment trust would be 127.5.

Tax and accounting treatment in the hands of a UK investor

11.67   *Avoir fiscal* received by a UK investor is taxable on a receipts basis under Schedule D Case V.

Since the introduction of FRS 16 'Current taxation', the accounting treatment of *avoir fiscal* receipts in the hands of investors preparing UK GAAP financial statements has been the cause of some confusion. Historically, *avoir fiscal* was treated as additional dividend income, in line with the UK tax treatment. However, under FRS 16, the appropriate treatment is to report *avoir fiscal* receipts as a credit in the tax line, which has had the effect of reducing levels of gross income reported.

Equalisation tax ('precompte')

11.68   The *precompte* is an equalisation tax designed to ensure that the *avoir fiscal* applies only to income in a French company that has borne the normal corporate income tax rate. It applies where distributed income has not been subject to corporate income tax at the normal rate or where the distributed income was derived more than five years before the distribution date. If, as expected, the *avoir fiscal* is abolished, then it is likely that the *precompte* will also be abolished. At present, however, where applicable it is charged at a rate of 50%

of the dividends distributed by the French company to the extent that they represent profits that have not borne the normal corporate income tax. Under Article 9(8) of the UK–France treaty, UK resident investors who are not entitled to recover the *avoir fiscal* under the terms of the treaty are entitled to a refund of the *precompte*, subject to deduction of withholding tax. Repayments of *precompte* are deemed to be dividends for treaty and UK tax purposes.

Impact of new UK/US treaty on UK investment funds

11.69 The new double taxation agreement with the US was signed on 24 July 2001, with an amending protocol being signed on 19 July 2002. The treaty entered into force on 31 March 2003, having been given effect in the UK by *Double Taxation Relief (Taxes on Income) (The United States of America) Order 2002 (SI 2002/2848)*.

Significant changes have been made to articles concerning dividends, gains, pensions, mutual agreement and the exchange of information, and there are a number of articles and provisions that are completely new, including:

- the article dealing with pension schemes;

- the limitation on benefits article;

- the conduit arrangement provisions found in the dividend, interest, royalty and other income articles;

- the provision restricting relief where the tax treatment of income is different in each country in the relief from double taxation article;

- the Exchange of Notes.

The more notable provisions affecting collective investment schemes are considered below.

Persons covered

11.70 Article 3 includes the following definitions:

(a) the term 'person' includes an individual, an estate, a trust, a partnership, a company, and any other body of persons;

(b) the term 'company' means any body corporate or any entity that is treated as a body corporate for tax purposes;

The inclusion of trusts and partnerships in the definition makes the treaty clearer and more specific than the OECD model. However, although partnerships are included in the definition of person above, Article 1(8) makes it clear that income derived through a fiscally transparent entity under the laws of either contracting state will be treated as the income of a resident only to the extent that it is treated for tax purposes as the income of a resident under the tax laws of either country. If so, treaty benefits may be available to the resident rather than to the fiscally transparent entity. UK partnerships themselves are therefore not entitled to benefits under the treaty.

The specific reference to trusts means that both authorised unit trusts and unauthorised unit trusts may in principle be treated as residents under the treaty, subject to the limitation of benefits provisions discussed below.

11.71   Article 4, the residence article, specifically includes as 'residents of a Contracting State':

- a pension scheme;

- a plan, scheme, fund, trust, company or other arrangement established in a contracting state that is operated exclusively to administer or provide employee benefits and that, by reason of its nature as such, is generally exempt from income taxation in that state;

- an organisation that is established exclusively for religious, charitable, scientific, artistic, cultural, or educational purposes and that is a resident of a contracting state according to its laws, notwithstanding that all or part of its income or gains may be exempt from tax under the domestic law of that state; and

- a qualified governmental entity that is, is part of, or is established in, that state.

11.72   'Pension scheme' is defined in Article 3(1)(o) as:

'any plan, scheme, fund, trust or other arrangement established in a contracting state, which is:

  (i) generally exempt from income taxation in that State; and

  (ii) operated principally to administer or provide pension or retirement benefits or to earn income for the benefit of one or more such arrangements.'

The Exchange of Notes make clear that from a UK perspective this covers employment-related arrangements (other than a social security scheme) approved as retirement benefit schemes for the purposes of *ICTA 1988, Part XIV Chapter I* and personal pension schemes approved under *Part XIV Chapter IV*.

Limitation of benefits (Article 23)

11.73   This treaty is the first UK agreement to include limitation of benefits provisions, though these are a common feature of recent US treaties, including those with the Netherlands, Ireland and Luxembourg. The provisions are designed to ensure that UK and US residents benefit from the treaty, whilst ensuring that residents of third countries who establish legal entities in either jurisdiction for the principal purpose of accessing treaty benefits, rather than for legitimate commercial and economic reasons, do not benefit.

Article 23 achieves its objective by providing that only residents of the UK and US who are 'qualified persons' under paragraph 2 will be entitled to all the benefits of the treaty. If a resident is not a 'qualified person', they may still be entitled to benefits in respect of specific items of income, profits or gains:

- through satisfying the 'derivative benefits test' in paragraph 3; or

- through satisfying the 'active conduct of a trade or business' test in paragraph 4; or

- at the discretion of the competent authority of the other jurisdiction under paragraph 6.

11.74 The rules for determining whether residents are 'qualified persons' are extremely complex. However, broadly speaking a 'qualified person' is a UK or US resident who is either:

- an individual;

- a qualified governmental entity as defined in Article 3, essentially the contracting states, political sub-divisions, local authorities and entities wholly owned by such bodies that do not carry on a business;

- a publicly traded company (listed in the UK or US);

- a company more than 50% owned by five or fewer publicly traded companies (listed in the UK or US);

- a publicly traded trust (listed in the UK or US);

- a trust more than 50% owned by publicly traded companies or publicly traded trusts (listed in the UK or US);

- a pension scheme where more than 50% of the beneficiaries, members or participants are individuals who are UK or US resident;

- a tax exempt employee benefit scheme where more than 50% of the beneficiaries, members or participants are individuals who are UK or US resident;

- a religious, charitable, scientific, artistic, cultural or educational organisation;

- a 'person' other than an individual that is for more than 50% of the chargeable period owned by certain 'qualified persons', and less than 50% of whose gross income is paid or accrued directly or indirectly in a tax deductible form to persons other than UK or US residents (the 'base erosion' test);

- a trust, or trustee of a trust in their capacity as such, if the trust is more than 50% owned by certain 'qualified persons' or by 'equivalent beneficiaries' (defined in paragraph 7), provided it satisfies the 'base erosion' test.

11.75   The combined effect of the definition of residents and the limitation of benefits provisions on UK collective investment schemes is as follows.

11.76   UK investment trusts qualify as residents and will be treated as 'qualified persons' under Article 23(2)(c)(i) as their ordinary share capital is listed on the London Stock Exchange. They are therefore entitled to full treaty benefits.

11.77   Authorised unit trusts are within the definition of UK resident under the treaty. However, they may face difficulties in attempting to satisfy the 'qualified person' tests, being reliant upon Article 23(2)(g). This essentially requires 50% or more of the fund's investors to be 'qualified persons' or 'equivalent beneficiaries' and specifies that less than half of their gross income can be paid or accrued as tax deductible payments to non-residents. Satisfying the tests would be inherently difficult because of the need to ascertain the status of all unitholders, which may not in any event be clear. The representative body for authorised UK funds, the Investment Management Association, has made representations to the IRS concerning authorised funds' access to treaty benefits and pension funds' ability to receive income gross if investing via an unauthorised unit trust. However, the view the IRS will take remains to be seen and at present authorised unit trusts should be considering how they can qualify. Note that a competent authority application could also be pursued by such funds on the basis that obtaining benefits under the treaty is not their principal purpose. However, despite the assurances of the IRS that such applications will be dealt with 'as expeditiously as possible', past experience suggests that this could be a lengthy process, especially given the fact that the US competent authority would be obliged under the treaty to consult with the UK competent authority before reaching a final decision.

11.78   OEICs are in a similar position to authorised unit trusts, being UK resident for the purposes of the treaty, but not easily satisfying one of the tests to be 'qualified persons'. The test they can potentially meet is that in Article 23(2)(f) which requires them to satisfy both an ownership test and the 'base erosion' test referred to above. However, the ownership test may be difficult to meet in practice, hence they are also lobbying the IRS to obtain automatic access.

11.79   Unauthorised unit trusts are also treated as residents of the UK under the new treaty. They will, however, face the same hurdles as authorised unit trusts as regards whether or not they are 'qualified persons'.

11.80   Approved pension schemes where more than 50% of the beneficiaries, members or participants are UK or US resident individuals will be both UK resident and treated as 'qualified persons' under Article 23(2)(e), hence will be entitled to full treaty benefits.

Dividends (Article 10)

11.81   The standard rate of withholding tax on dividends under US domestic law is 30%.

The treaty rate of withholding tax is generally 15%, or 5% in respect of dividends arising from participations consisting of more than 10% of the voting power of the US company.

UK resident companies satisfying certain conditions under the limitation of benefits article and with a holding exceeding 80% of the voting power in the US company, which they have held for a minimum of twelve months, are entitled to receive dividends subject to zero withholding (Article 10(3)(a)). A UK investment trust with such a holding would qualify for zero withholding under these provisions. A unit trust, whether authorised or unauthorised, would not be eligible to benefit under this provision.

UK approved pension schemes qualifying for full treaty benefits are also entitled to receive dividends without deduction of withholding tax provided that such dividends are not derived from the carrying on of a business, directly or indirectly, by the pension scheme (Article 10(3)(b)). Under the 19 July 2002 Protocol, schemes investing via US-regulated investment companies or US real estate investment trusts will also preserve their entitlement to the zero rate. As noted above, a response is awaited from the IRS on the question of whether unauthorised unit trusts whose unitholders are all UK approved pension schemes can themselves be treated as pension schemes for this purpose and benefit accordingly.

Interest (Article 11)

11.82   The standard rate of withholding tax on interest under US domestic law is 30%.

Interest payments between residents qualifying under the limitation of benefits article remain free from withholding tax under the treaty.

Capital gains (Article 13)

11.83   The old treaty afforded no protection from double taxation on capital gains as it allowed each country to tax gains in accordance with its domestic laws. The new treaty article follows the OECD model, subject to some additional provisions dealing with gains arising to temporary non-residents and gains arising on shares deriving the greater part of their value from real property. In general, relief is now afforded by awarding exclusive taxing rights to the residence country, or where the source country taxes the gain, by the residence country giving credit relief.

Japanese government bonds – status of investment fund holders

11.84   Certain non-Japanese resident holders of Japanese government bonds are eligible to receive interest payments on such bonds without deduction of withholding tax. This exemption from withholding tax applies to interest payments made to a qualifying non-resident if:

* the bonds are deposited by a financial intermediary participating in the Bank of Japan Book-Entry system, also known as the *Furiketsu* system, or

* the bonds are deposited with a global custodian authorised by the Bank of Japan as a Foreign Indirect Participant ('FIP') and by the tax authorities as a Qualified Foreign Intermediary ('QFI').

Participants in the *Furiketsu* system may be direct or indirect. A direct participant is a Japanese designated financial institution who holds a *Furiketsu* account directly in the Bank of Japan and who is a member of the BOJ-Net system (the online computer settlement system for transactions between the Bank of Japan and financial institutions). An indirect participant is a Japanese designated financial institution approved by the Bank of Japan as an indirect participant, who has appointed direct participants as its custodians.

QFI status was introduced in 2001. In order to obtain QFI status, the foreign entity must be a financial institution resident in a country with whom Japan has concluded a double tax treaty incorporating exchange of information provisions and must be approved by the Bank of Japan as a foreign indirect participant in the *Furiketsu* system. A QFI is responsible for confirming the identity of the beneficial owners of Japanese government bonds held by it, and must submit documentation concerning the holders via their sub-custodian. Details of transactions must also be notified to the sub-custodian.

Eligibility of investment funds

11.85   The exemption in respect of Japanese government bonds deposited with QFIs originally applied to non-resident individuals and corporate bodies, which included investment trusts and OEICs. The scope of the exemption was widened with effect from 1 April 2002 to include payments of interest to unincorporated investment funds provided the following conditions are met:

* The fund's main purpose must be to invest in securities or money market instruments.

* The fund should not be marketed to Japanese residents.

* The fund should be publicly marketed to investors resident outside Japan.

* The QFI should confirm the eligibility of the fund and submit an application on its behalf to the tax authorities.

* The holdings of each individual fund should be accounted for separately in the *Furiketsu* system.

These conditions may be satisfied by an authorised unit trust. As unauthorised unit trusts are not marketed to the public, they are only permitted to qualify if they disclose the names of their beneficial owners.

In addition, approved occupational pension funds are also treated as eligible. A copy of an Inland Revenue letter confirming approved status will be required to confirm their eligibility.

Taxation of foreign scrip dividends in the UK

11.86   Collective investment schemes investing overseas may sometimes be offered a choice between receiving a cash dividend or additional shares. Where the cash option is taken, the dividend received will be taxable as usual under Schedule D Case V. If the option of additional shares is taken, this is known as a 'scrip' or stock dividend. Such a dividend does not constitute income falling within Schedule D Case V, whether or not the shareholder was given the option of receiving cash instead of shares, nor does it fall within the scope of the *ICTA 1988, s 249* stock dividend provisions. This treatment has been established in a number of cases, notably the House of Lords decision in *CIR v Blott* 8 TC 101 and the Court of Appeal decision in *CIR v Wright* 11 TC 181.

For capital gains tax purposes, the additional shares acquired via a foreign scrip dividend are treated as acquired at no additional cost.

Part II
Taxation of Investors

12 Authorised Unit Trusts and OEICs

Lucy Shirley

Deloitte

Introduction

12.1 The overriding principle behind the taxation both of authorised investment funds and their investors is that investors should be in the same position, neither better nor worse off, through investing in a collective investment scheme than they would have been if they had held the underlying investments directly. Whilst this is largely achieved, there remain are certain exceptions, largely to avoid the complexity that would otherwise arise.

Taxation of UK residents

Taxation of individuals

Income

12.2 The amount shown as available for distribution by an AUT or an OEIC will be taxable as investment income in the hands of the investor, either as Schedule D Case III or Schedule F depending on whether the distribution is shown as a dividend distribution or an interest distribution. In accordance with general principles, the income is taxed under self-assessment on a fiscal year basis and the usual rates and allowances apply.

Although an investor may hold accumulation units, such that he does not actually receive a cash distribution but an accretion to the capital value of his holding, *ICTA 1988, s 468H* requires that he is taxed on his share of the distribution as if he had received it. Similarly, if an investor has instructed the manager to use his income distributions to purchase additional units ('income reinvestment'), he is still taxed on the distributions as they arise.

As mentioned in CHAPTER 1, both equity and bond funds are permitted to pay their distributions as dividends but only bond funds may pay them as annual interest.

Dividend distributions

12.3 A dividend distribution from an authorised fund bears a notional tax credit of 10% that may be used to pay or partly pay the investor's liability to tax on the income.

For higher rate taxpayers, Schedule F income is currently taxable at a rate of 32.5% of which 10% is covered by the tax credit. A recipient of a dividend worth £90 declares it as £100 in his tax return and his tax liability thereon is £32.50. £10 is deemed to have been discharged by the tax credit, so additional tax of £22.50 is payable and the net dividend is worth £67.50.

For lower and basic rate taxpayers, dividends are currently taxable at a rate of 10% which means that their tax liability is fully covered by the notional credit. A dividend of £90 received is, therefore, worth £90 after tax.

For non-taxpayers, the fact that the credit is only notional means that they may not claim a repayment of the credit and they are in exactly the same position as a lower or basic rate taxpayer.

12.4   It should be noted that except for pure UK equity funds, the taxation of the investor may not exactly mirror his treatment if he held the investments directly. A fund that does not qualify as a bond fund (so is treated as an equity fund in the legislation) but which holds overseas equities, interest-bearing investments or rental properties, for example, will only be able to pay a dividend. If the underlying investments were held directly the investor would have received Schedule D Case V income (possibly subject to withholding tax and eligible for double tax relief), Schedule D Case III income (possibly subject to deduction of tax at source) or Schedule A income, not dividends. The lack of streaming of the underlying income can in some cases lead to differences in the treatment of direct and indirect holdings. However, against this the investor has effectively received tax relief for the expenses of management, which would not be the case had they invested directly.

Interest distributions

12.5   Bond funds are able to pay interest distributions, which are treated as annual interest in the hands of the investor. For a UK resident individual, income tax at the rate of 20% must be deducted at source and this tax may be used to pay or partly pay the investor's tax liability on his income.

For higher rate taxpayers, interest income is currently taxable at a rate of 40% of which 20% is covered by the tax credit. A recipient of interest of £80 declares it as £100 in his tax return and his tax liability thereon is £40. £20 is deemed to have been discharged by the tax credit, so additional tax of £20 is payable and the net receipt is worth £60.

For basic rate taxpayers, interest is currently taxable at the savings rate of 20%, which means that their tax liability is fully covered by the tax credit. Interest received of £80 is, therefore, worth £80 after tax.

For lower rate taxpayers, the applicable rate is 10% so their liability is exceeded by the amount of the tax credit and they may obtain a repayment of the difference so that the net receipt is worth £90 after tax.

Non-taxpayers may claim a repayment of the whole of the credit so the distribution received equals £100. In contrast to bank or building society interest, distributions paid by authorised funds must have tax withheld even if the recipient is a non-taxpayer.

Equalisation

12.6   In CHAPTER 1 it was explained that equalisation received on creations is returned to Group II unitholders as part of their first distribution after purchasing units. Of the total distribution received, part is income and is taxable as such, and part is equalisation, treated as a return of capital so not subject to income tax. The amounts of income and equalisation are disclosed to investors in the tax vouchers received. Equalisation does have consequences for capital gains tax purposes, discussed below.

Capital gains

12.7   Units of AUTs and shares in OEICs are regarded for tax purposes as being shares or securities and thus subject to the usual capital gains tax rules on pooling, taper relief, indexation allowance, etc.

It should be noted that another instance where treatment of an indirect holding differs from that of a direct holding relates to gilts or qualifying corporate bonds (QCBs) held in an authorised fund. Disposal of the units in the fund triggers a capital gains tax charge, whereas a direct investment in gilts or QCBs would be exempt on disposal under *TCGA 1992, s 115*.

Basic calculation

12.8   The chargeable gain on disposal of units is the sale proceeds received, less base cost and any allowable expenditure, less the annual exempt amount, taper relief and, if applicable, indexation allowance. In most senses, this is exactly as it would be for disposal of any kind of share.

Taper relief

12.9   Non-business taper relief is available to an investor who has held his units for more than three years. The amount of taper given is increased for each complete year in which the units have been held up from 5% after three years up to 40% after ten years.

See *Tolley's Capital Gains Tax*, Chapter 61 for further information about the rules governing taper relief.

Indexation

12.10   Where units have been held since before April 1998, indexation allowance will be available in addition to taper relief. Indexation allowance is available only in respect of expenditure incurred up to 31 March 1998 and computed up to April 1998 only.

An example of taper relief and indexation is as follows:

EXAMPLE 12.10

> Bernard purchased units in the ABC OEIC on 1 March 1997, and his wife Clara bought units on 1 April 2000. Both disposed of their units on 1 September 2003.
>
> Bernard is entitled to indexation allowance in respect of the period from 1 March 1997 to 5 April 1998, and thereafter may take taper relief in respect of the period from 6 April 1998 to 1 September 2003 (five complete years, plus a bonus year for holding the units on 17 March 1998).
>
> Clara is not entitled to indexation allowance as her units were purchased after April 1998 and is only able to take taper relief, which runs from 1 April 2000 to 1 September 2003. She benefits from three complete years' holding.

Equalisation

12.11   Equalisation paid as part of a distribution is a return of capital and is not taxable upon receipt. Instead it is effectively taxed on disposal of the units to which it relates, as it is deductible from the base cost of the units.

Notional distributions (accumulation units)

12.12   Where accumulation units are held, the distribution is not paid to the investor but added to the value of his units. Nonetheless, as described in **12.2** above, the investor is still deemed to have been paid taxable income at the time the accumulation is made.

To prevent double taxation of the same amount, the notional distribution is treated as allowable expenditure for CGT purposes.

If indexation allowance is available, it is given on each separate notional distribution from the date the unitholder became entitled to it. Taper relief, however, is calculated with reference to when the units were acquired and is unaffected by the notional distributions.

Reinvested distributions (income units)

12.13   Where an investor's income is neither accumulated nor paid out as cash, but used to purchase additional units (income reinvestment), the investor will, as described earlier, be taxed on the income at the time the distribution was paid.

These additional units are treated as new holdings with acquisition date and base cost relevant to the date and value of the distribution reinvested. Where applicable, indexation allowance and taper relief are given on each new holding.

Switches within/between subfunds

12.14 Umbrella funds are required by the FSA regulations to permit switching between subfunds upon demand. Each subfund is regarded for tax purposes as a separate pool of assets and, indeed, a separate company.

TCGA 1992, s 100 provides that *section 127* shall not prevent switches from one subfund to another from being regarded as a disposal and acquisition for capital gains tax purposes. In other words, unless it is part of a reorganisation or reconstruction of share capital, a switch from one subfund to another will be a CGT event, the rationale being that the unitholder has ceased to have an interest in one pool of assets and has acquired an interest in another pool.

On the other hand, should an investor switch from one type of units to another in the same subfund to another (for example, switching from income to accumulation units) there will not be a disposal for capital gains purposes and the new units are treated as standing in the shoes of the old in terms of acquisition date and base cost, as per *Revenue Interpretation 169*.

Monthly savings schemes

12.15 Many managers offer the option for investors to make small monthly investments in AUTs or OEICs as part of a savings scheme. Where numerous small holdings are acquired over a period of time, the calculation of indexation and taper relief can very quickly become disproportionately complicated and cumbersome, especially where distributions have been accumulated.

For holdings acquired before April 1999 the Inland Revenue concessionally allow an individual in a monthly savings scheme to opt to perform averaging calculations for each tax year for all investments in the same unit trust in order to simplify their calculations (*Statement of Practice 2/99*). Taking this option requires a written request to the tax office on or before the first anniversary of 31 January following the first tax year in which the individual disposes of such units, supposing that either his *total* gains for the year exceed the annual exemption, or his total proceeds exceed twice the exemption, or his disposals of other assets result in a net loss.

The simplified arrangements allow the individual to calculate gains as if he had made a single annual investment in the seventh month of the trust's accounting year.

The capital gains tax calculations where monthly sums were invested after 6 April 1999 must, however, be calculated on the normal statutory basis and the difficulty of performing numerous fiddly computations remains.

Inheritance tax

12.16   Holdings of units in UK authorised unit trusts and OEICs are UK situs assets and are therefore within the scope of UK inheritance tax (IHT) for both UK domiciled and non-UK domiciled but UK resident individuals. The usual rules apply to chargeable transfers of holdings as they would for other assets.

Taxation of corporates

Income

12.17   The taxation of distributions (or accumulations) by an AUT or an OEIC to a UK corporate investor will depend on whether the distribution is in dividend or interest form in accordance with general principles.

Dividend distributions

12.18   It was mentioned in **CHAPTER 1** that dividend-paying funds stream their distributions into franked (dividend) and unfranked elements and inform corporate investors of the relative proportion of their income falling into each category.

To the extent that the distribution relates to underlying franked investment income ('FII'), the investor treats it as FII in its computation and is not subject to tax on the receipt. To the extent that it relates to underlying unfranked income, such as UK interest or overseas income, it is treated as Schedule D Case III income and tax is payable on it. The unfranked element is treated as having been received under deduction of 20% income tax, and this deemed credit may be used to offset against the recipient's corporation tax liability. Some or all of the credit may be repaid if the recipient does not have a tax liability. See **CHAPTER 1** for further details on the calculation of tax that may be reclaimed.

Interest distributions

12.19   No streaming calculations are required for interest distributions paid by bond funds, and the whole amount is taxable under Schedule D Case III. Where the recipient is a company or a UK branch of an overseas company within the charge to corporation tax on the income, no tax should be withheld on the payment by the unit trust in accordance with *ICTA 1988, ss 349A–D*.

Capital gains

12.20   The taxation of gains or losses on the disposal of holdings in an AUT depends on the type of fund, namely whether the funds are equity or bond funds. The definition of a bond fund for these purposes is contained in *FA 1996, Sch 10 para 8*, although this is to all intents and purposes identical to the *ICTA 1988, s 468L* definition covered in **CHAPTER 1**.

Equity funds are capital gains assets, and their units are treated as normal shares or securities, so are subject to the usual corporation tax rules on pooling, indexation allowance, etc.

Unlike the CGT treatment for individuals, indexation allowance still remains available for corporation tax payers and there is no taper relief.

Mark to market on bond funds

12.21   Bond funds are not capital gains assets where they are held by corporate investors but are deemed to be creditor loan relationships under *FA 1996, Sch 10 para 4*. Accordingly, the corporate investor is required to mark to market its holding on an annual basis, with any uplift being taxable as a non-trade loan relationship credit, and any loss of value being relievable as a non-trade loan relationship debit, in accordance with the usual rules.

Upon disposal, the difference between sale proceeds and the previous year's valuation is taxed as a non-trade loan relationship debit or credit, as appropriate, so that over the life of the holding, all returns – whether income or gains and whether realised or unrealised – are taxed as income, not capital. The treatment is identical to that the investor would have if it held the underlying investments directly.

Annual deemed disposal by insurance companies

12.22   Under *TCGA 1992, s 212*, life insurance companies holding units in a unit trust (and also relevant interests in offshore funds) in their long-term insurance fund are deemed to dispose of their holdings annually at market value and to reacquire them immediately afterwards. The provisions were introduced to counter the use by life companies of in-house authorised unit trusts to hold equities and therefore shelter corporation tax on capital gains. The effect of the provisions is to tax gains and allow losses on unit trusts over the term of the holding.

The legislation only applies in relation to the corporation tax charge on capital gains. Accordingly, the deemed disposal provisions only apply to unit trusts held to support basic life and general annuity business (BLAGAB). The provisions do not apply to unit trusts held to support other categories of long-term business as they are specifically exempted from corporation tax on capital gains.

Specific provisions require gains and losses arising on deemed disposals to be spread over a period of seven years. There are also provisions allowing deemed losses to be carried back and set against deemed gains in previous years.

This annual taxation of capital gains applies only to holdings in equity funds. Where the company's holding is in a bond fund, the annual mark-to-market rules described at 12.21 above apply as they would for an ordinary corporate.

Dealer in securities

12.23   Under *ICTA 1988, s 95*, a dealer in securities is taxable on UK dividends received as part of his trading profits under Schedule D Case I or II, as opposed to being exempt as an ordinary UK corporate would be or taxable under Schedule F as an individual would be.

A person is subject to these rules for income from securities if he would also be taxable on the profits of sale of the same securities as part of his trade. A unit trust manager or ACD is subject to these rules.

Taxation of Non-Residents

Taxation of individuals

Income and gains

12.24   Investors resident outside the UK are, of course, subject to tax on income and gains made on their investments in authorised funds in accordance with the rules in their home countries.

The UK does not impose withholding taxes on payments of dividends to non-residents. Double tax treaties in theory allow residents of other countries to reclaim a proportion of the notional 10% tax credit attached to dividends, after deduction of any applicable withholding tax, but in practice the value of these is likely to be negligible. Dividend distributions paid to UK and non-UK residents are, therefore, handled in exactly the same way by the fund manager.

Payments of interest must generally be made under deduction of income tax in accordance with *ICTA 1988, s 349*, and non-residents are generally entitled to reclaim tax suffered if there is a treaty between their home country and the UK. However an interest distribution may be paid without withholding income tax where an investor provides the trustee of the fund with a valid NOR (not ordinarily resident) declaration. The investor is required to confirm his residential address outside the UK, state that he is not ordinarily resident in the UK and undertake to inform the trustee if he does become ordinarily resident.

12.25   For distributions made on or after 16 October 2002, *FA 2003* has amended *ICTA 1988, ss 468M–P* and introduced a new *section 468PA*. The legislation now allows that interest distributions may not only be paid gross where a valid NOR declaration is held, but also where the 'reputable intermediary condition' is satisfied and where the unitholder is a company or trustee of a unit trust scheme.

The reputable intermediary condition allows an overseas investor who buys units through an adviser to avoid the need to file a NOR form.

12.26   Before *FA 2003*, the proportion of an interest distribution that could be paid gross to non-residents depended on the levels of 'eligible income' within the fund. Eligible income was broadly any type of income that was derived from shares and securities and was not itself subject to deduction of tax at source. As such, rental income, franked investment income etc were excluded from the definition. Now the eligible income test has disappeared and fully gross interest distributions may be made by all funds irrespective of the composition of their income.

The rules regarding deduction of tax at source on interest distributions are discussed in greater detail in CHAPTER 1.

Inheritance tax

12.27   As mentioned at **12.16** above, holdings of units in UK authorised unit trusts and OEICs are within the scope of UK inheritance tax (IHT) for non-UK domiciled but UK resident individuals.

However, following *Finance Act 2003*, any holding in a UK authorised fund by individuals domiciled outside the UK is treated as excluded property for IHT. This applies to transfers of value occurring on or after 16 October 2002.

If the individual becomes domiciled in the UK for inheritance tax purposes, the holding will cease to be excluded property. However, if the individual settles the holding on trust before becoming domiciled, it will continue to be treated as excluded property.

In the case of individuals (as opposed to offshore trustees), there may be a potential trap with the new rules, in that the holding in question appears still to be a UK situs asset for income tax and CGT purposes. If a non-UK domiciled individual brings funds into the UK in order to purchase such a holding, he may trigger a charge under the remittance legislation. Furthermore, if the individual decides to dispose of the holding, this will be a disposal for UK CGT purposes.

Taxation of corporates

Income and gains

12.28   A non-UK corporate investor may also receive the distribution gross, like a non-resident individual, upon completing a declaration of non-residence in the UK. The declaration is required to include the address of its registered or principal office, confirmation that the company is not resident for tax purposes in the UK and an undertaking to inform the trustee should that change.

Stamp duty

12.29   Units in authorised funds are chargeable securities for the purposes of *Stamp Duty Reserve Tax* legislation. Transfers of holdings are subject to imposition of an *ad valorem* charge of 0.5% which is normally borne by the fund rather than the individual. CHAPTER 3 explains the basis for the charge.

Saving for children

12.30   Children are not permitted to hold investments in their own name until they reach the age of 18 and can enter into a legal contract. If a relative or friend wishes to make an investment in a unit trust in a child's name, they will generally do so using a designated account. The individual making the gift is registered as the legal owner of the units but will designate the account for the benefit of the child.

Where an individual holds an investment with the intention of it being for the benefit of another, an informal and very simple trust arrangement known as a bare trust is accepted to exist, under which the child is the beneficiary and the parent (for example) is the trustee and settlor. All income and gains generated by the investment should, therefore, be taxable on the child, subject to three provisos.

12.31   First, if the gift has been made by a parent, and produces income of £100 or more in a tax year, anti-avoidance legislation provides that this income will be taxable as the parent's, not the child's. This does not apply to gifts from other relatives or friends.

Secondly, having made the gift, the investment becomes a potentially exempt transfer for IHT purposes. Provided, however, that the donor survives for seven years after making the gift, no IHT will be payable upon it. Smaller gifts may also be covered by an annual exemption (currently worth £3,000 per fiscal year) or a small gifts exemption.

Thirdly, the income of the investments must be accumulated and not spent, unless it is for the maintenance, benefit or education of the child.

If the income and capital gains are taxable on the child, he is entitled to the usual annual allowances for income tax and CGT. In many cases these will be sufficient to ensure the child is a non-taxpayer and if this is so, tax withheld on any interest distributions may be reclaimed in full.

To ensure that a designated account is treated as a bare trust for legal and tax purposes, so that there is no doubt that the parent is not the beneficial owner of the units, it is generally advisable to draw up a proper trust deed setting out the rights and obligations of the arrangement.

Savings Tax Directive

12.32 In an attempt to combat tax evasion achieved by individuals placing money offshore and failing to declare the income or gains arising, the member states of the EU have negotiated the Savings Tax Directive, which is likely to be implemented on 1 January 2005. Certain aspects of the Directive have an impact from 1 January 2004, which was until recently to have been the date for full implementation.

The key impact of the Directive can be summarised as follows:

- There will be an automatic exchange of information between most EU member states of cross-border payments of interest to EU resident individuals.

- The method of reporting these cross-border payments of interest will be that all such payments will be reported by EU paying agents to their home tax authority. The home tax authority will then automatically exchange this information with the recipient jurisdiction's tax authorities.

- Three EU member states (Austria, Belgium and Luxembourg) will operate a withholding tax on cross-border interest payments to EU tax resident individuals rather than automatically exchanging information relating to such payments. This rate of withholding tax will increase over a transitional period starting at 15% from 1 January 2005, rising progressively to 35% after six years. Tax withheld is to be shared by the two jurisdictions' tax authorities, with 25% retained by the paying jurisdiction and 75% paid over to the recipient jurisdiction.

12.33 Implementation from 1 January 2005 is subject to dependent territories of EU members applying the same measures as those of the Directive and certain non-EU countries (known as 'third countries') applying equivalent measures to those of the Directive. This is considered necessary to ensure that EU member states remain competitive in international financial services provided to individuals.

The third countries included in the negotiations have in most cases been selected on the basis that they operate strict banking secrecy rules which might otherwise enable EU residents to shelter their money out of sight of their tax authorities. Negotiations to date with these third countries, which include Switzerland, Monaco and Liechtenstein, suggest that acceptable equivalent measures will be introduced in the form of a withholding tax on the same terms as for Luxembourg, Austria and Belgium. Dependent territories such as the Channel Islands also appear to be moving towards a withholding tax system.

What is reportable?

12.34   Any cross-border payment of interest made by a paying agent to an EU resident will be reportable. Included in the meaning of interest are payments by UK paying agents in respect of UCITS funds and other collective investment funds based outside the UK, which includes non-EU funds.

Payments by a fund must be reported if the fund is significantly invested in debt-claims. The types of payment caught are both distributions made and proceeds paid on sale or redemption.

For distributions, reporting will not be required if no more than 15% of a fund's investments are in debt-claims. 15% is a considerably lower threshold for a fund to be regarded as significantly invested in debt-claims than is the case in UK legislation, where it is 60%. Funds marketed as equity funds will need to consider whether their investment strategy should be changed so they fall beneath the threshold and avoid the need to report.

Sale proceeds paid by a UCITS fund to an exiting investor are reportable if the fund exceeds a 40% threshold for investment in debt-claims.

12.35   In both cases, the member states have the option of requiring the total amount of the payment to be reported, or just the proportion that is derived from debt-claims. At the time of writing, the UK has published draft legislation that will implement the Directive into national law. The draft legislation offers paying agents the choice of reporting the whole amount of a payment or just the element that relates to debt-claims. It has also opted to base the test for whether a fund exceeds the thresholds on the stated investment policy in the fund rules or instrument of incorporation, rather than the precise asset composition of the fund. Where a paying agent has no information as to whether the threshold has been breached, reporting is the default option.

The paying agent is any person who is directly responsible for making the payment to the beneficial owner. Where the bank, UCITS fund etc making the payment has a direct relationship with the customer, it will report the payment itself. If it uses a third party to process the payment or if the customer has used an intermediary, it is the last person in the chain who must report.

Who is reportable?

12.36   Payments are only reportable where the beneficial owner of the income is an individual resident in one of the EU member states, so payments made to companies are excluded.

Paying agents must comply with fairly detailed rules to establish the identity and place of residence of beneficial owners, and the rules differ according to whether a relationship was established before or after the date when the Directive took effect.

What impact does it have on the investor?

12.37   Obviously the intention is that the impact of the Directive will be most strongly felt by anyone attempting to evade tax in not being able to get away without declaring all taxable income. The impact on law-abiding investors is twofold.

First, individuals may be questioned about their tax affairs on the basis of information received about them from overseas. There is a good chance that in some cases the tax authority will have received information about a person's income that is not quite correct, as a result of the fact that the Directive is a blunt instrument and cannot perfectly distinguish between different types of income.

Secondly, where the money is held in a country which has elected to apply a withholding tax as the default option, the investor will receive his income net of this withholding tax unless he specifically requests that information be exchanged instead. The withholding tax suffered will be capable of being used to offset a UK tax liability or will be repaid.

13 Offshore Funds

Martin Smith and Simon Davies

PricewaterhouseCoopers LLP

Offshore fund rules

Introduction

13.1 [**Note**: As mentioned in CHAPTER 4, the Inland Revenue are currently consulting on the future of the offshore fund rules. The taxation of UK investors in offshore funds may therefore change, either in Finance Act 2004 or subsequently.]

The main offshore fund legislation can be found in *ICTA 1988* within *sections 757–764* and *Schedules 27* and *28*. The legislation was introduced in *FA 1984* in response to what the Inland Revenue perceived to be the widespread avoidance of UK tax liabilities by individuals through the use of offshore investment vehicles (primarily money market funds) to roll up investment income.

In such 'roll-up' funds, income arising on the underlying investments accumulates tax free and adds to the capital value of the shares in the fund. Prior to *FA 1984*, the profits arising on disposal or redemption of interests in roll-up funds were subject to capital gains treatment. At the time this had very significant tax advantages, as the taxation of capital gains was considerably more favourable than that of income. For UK individual investors:

- income tax was levied at a higher marginal rate than capital gains tax;

- an annual exemption for capital gains applied; and

- generous indexation allowances were available to reduce capital gains (reflecting high inflation in the early 1980s).

Today these benefits are less marked, as the marginal rates of tax for both income and capital gains are broadly the same, although individual investors still retain the benefits of an annual exemption and taper relief for capital gains. What is still important is that the roll-up of fund income gives the investor the ability to defer the point at which tax becomes payable until the date on which the investor's holding is disposed of. In certain cases, UK taxation is avoided altogether if the individual has emigrated (eg on retirement) and ceases to be UK resident and ordinarily resident.

13.2 Since existing UK anti-avoidance legislation was proving ineffective as a means of combating the conversion of income into capital gain (see **13.42** on *ICTA 1988, ss 739* and *740*), the offshore fund legislation was introduced to differentiate between those funds that distributed the bulk of their investment income ('distributing funds') and those funds that rolled up their investment income ('non-qualifying funds').

The process by which an offshore fund may obtain certification as a distributing fund for any particular account period is described in CHAPTER 4. A UK investor in a distributing fund is taxed periodically on distributions of income to him; and his residual gain (subject to special rules on equalisation) on the eventual disposal of his holding in the fund remains subject to taxation as a capital gain. A UK investor in a non-qualifying fund avoids the periodic taxation of income (unless such income happens to be distributed by the fund), but is taxed on the whole of his gain (which will reflect capital appreciation as well as any rolled-up income) as though this were income, at the date of disposal of his holding.

Definition of an offshore fund

13.3 As has been seen in CHAPTER 4, the general term 'offshore fund' covers many types of investment vehicle established outside the UK. However, not all such vehicles fall within the definition of an 'offshore fund' for the purposes of the UK tax legislation.

In order for a UK person's holding in an offshore vehicle to fall within the offshore fund regime, that person's holding must constitute a 'material interest in an offshore fund' as defined in *ICTA 1988, s 759*. The definitions of 'material interest' and 'offshore fund' are discussed below.

Offshore fund

13.4 An offshore vehicle falls within the definition of an offshore fund if it meets both of the following requirements:

(1) it is a 'collective investment scheme' as defined by *Financial Services and Markets Act 2000 (FSMA 2000), s 235*; and

(2) it is structured as:

    (a) a company resident outside the UK; or

    (b) a unit trust scheme, the trustees of which are not resident in the UK; or

    (c) any arrangements under foreign law which create rights in the nature of co-ownership.

Most offshore investment vehicles will fall within one of the categories at (2) above. However, some investment vehicles (particularly those which are companies) will not be 'collective investment schemes' as defined by *FSMA 2000, s 235*.

Under *section 235*, a collective investment scheme means:

> 'any arrangements with respect to property of any description, including money, the purpose or effect of which is to enable persons taking part in the arrangements (whether by becoming owners of the property or any part of it or otherwise) to participate in or receive profits or income arising from the acquisition, holding, management or disposal of the property or sums paid out of such profits or income' (*s 235(1)*).

13.5   The arrangements must be such that the persons who are to participate do not have day-to-day control over the management of the property, whether or not they have the right to be consulted or to give directions. In addition, one or both of the following criteria must be met:

(a)   the contributions of the participants and the profits or income out of which payments are to be made to them must be pooled; and/or

(b)   the property must be managed as a whole by or on behalf of the operator of the scheme.

The nature of most bodies corporate established as investment vehicles means that they will satisfy the above requirements. However, there are a number of exclusions that prevent certain arrangements from being a collective investment scheme. These can be found in the *Collective Investment Schemes Order 2001 (SI 2001/1062)*. The Schedule of that order excludes from the definition of a collective investment scheme certain bodies corporate as well as any other body corporate except a limited liability partnership or an open-ended investment company. Therefore if a body corporate is an open-ended investment company it will not be excluded from the definition.

Open-ended investment companies

13.6   For a body corporate to be an open-ended investment company, as defined in *FSMA 2000, s 236(1)*:

•   it must be a collective investment scheme;

•   it must satisfy the property condition in *section 236(2)*; and

•   it must satisfy the investment condition in *section 236(3)*.

These definitions are not straightforward and a detailed commentary is outside the scope of this section. However, an open-ended investment company can be described in general terms as a body corporate, the aim of which is the spreading of investment risk by giving its members access to the benefits of the management of funds by or on behalf of that body corporate, most or all of the shares or securities of which can be realised within a reasonable period. 'Realisation' will typically involve the redemption or repurchase of shares in, or securities of, the body corporate. The value of the participant's investment must be based on the value of the property that the body corporate holds, ie the net asset value.

13.7 The Financial Services Authority (FSA) has produced guidance in the FSA Handbook as to the meaning of an open-ended investment company. In this the FSA confirms that, in determining whether a body corporate is an open-ended investment company, it will look at the vehicle as a whole. Therefore, if, for example, the body corporate were to issue a mixture of redeemable and non-redeemable shares or securities, the existence of the non-redeemable shares or securities would not, of itself, rule out the possibility of the body corporate falling within the definition of an open-ended investment company, but a number of circumstances would have to be considered.

The FSA has also set out its response to a number of frequently asked questions in relation to the application of the definition of an open-ended investment company. One such response deals with the situation of a body corporate holding out redemption or repurchase of its securities every six months. The FSA's view of such a situation is that a period of six months would generally be too long to be a 'reasonable period' within which a reasonable investor can realise their investment in a liquid securities fund. As such the body corporate would not satisfy the definition of an open-ended investment company.

What is clear is that the tests set out in *FSMA 2000* result in a degree of uncertainty as to whether an offshore vehicle would be a collective investment scheme. It is possible to structure vehicles so that they would fall either inside or outside the collective investment scheme definition.

Material interest

13.8 Once it has been identified that the offshore vehicle would fall within the definition of an 'offshore fund', it must be considered whether a particular person's holding in the fund would constitute a 'material interest' such that the holding would fall to be dealt with for UK tax purposes under the offshore fund regime. Shares in a non-UK resident company and units in a foreign unit trust would certainly be 'interests', although less clear is the status of certain derivative instruments that have interests in or rights over such shares or units.

An interest is defined as 'material' if, at the time a person acquired the interest, it could reasonably have been expected that, within seven years of the date of acquisition, he would be able to realise the value of the interest for an amount which was reasonably approximate to that portion which the interest represented of the market value (at that time) of the assets of the fund. This definition was originally the sole determinant as to whether the holding in the non-UK company, unit trust or co-ownership arrangements comprised a relevant interest for the purposes of the offshore fund rules. It potentially caught a wide range of situations, including the one where a closed-ended investment company specified a date within seven years when it would either be liquidated or convert to an open-ended form. There was an issue as to whether such shares would constitute a material interest in an offshore fund. Indeed, it was possible to have situations where, depending on the date on which an investor acquired his interest in the company, he might or might not hold a material interest. Differential tax regimes thus resulted for different investors in the same company.

13.9 The above anomalies were largely eradicated in *FA 1995*, when the general definition of an 'offshore fund' was restricted to those non-UK vehicles or arrangements that also constituted 'collective investment schemes' under what was then the *Financial Services Act 1986*. Interestingly, the changes to the definition of an open-ended investment company that were introduced in *FSMA 2000* echo, to a degree, the concept of 'material interest' that was originally introduced in the 1984 tax legislation, perhaps demonstrating the increasingly closer interaction between UK tax and regulatory authorities.

Occasion of charge

Taxation of income

Corporate offshore funds

13.10 Subject to their specific circumstances, investors resident in the UK for taxation purposes will be liable to UK income tax or corporation tax in respect of distributions of income received from a corporate offshore fund, whether or not such distributions are reinvested on their behalf (see **CHAPTER 4**, which deals with dividend reinvestment schemes). This is the case irrespective of whether the fund is a distributing or a non-qualifying fund.

UK individuals

13.11 UK resident individuals are liable to UK income tax under Schedule D Case IV/V on any dividend distributions that they receive from their shares in a corporate offshore fund. Currently, UK higher rate taxpayers are taxed at 32.5% on the amount received/reinvested, with basic rate taxpayers taxed at 10%. Unlike distributions by comparable onshore vehicles, there is currently no distinction between an 'interest distribution' and a 'dividend distribution' to a UK individual (although the future implementation of the EU Savings Directive (see **13.71** below) will cause the 'interest' element of distributions by certain non-UK funds, eg Luxembourg SICAVs, to suffer local withholding tax that will be creditable against the UK tax liability on the distribution).

It would therefore seem advantageous, with respect to the taxation of income distributions, for individuals to invest in an offshore bond or money market fund as opposed to an onshore equivalent, because distributions from the offshore fund are subject to a maximum rate of tax of 32.5%, while distributions from the onshore equivalent are treated as an interest payment and are taxed under Schedule D Case III at a maximum rate of 40%. There is also a tax cash flow advantage (subject to the aforementioned Savings Directive effects) in that UK withholding tax is suffered on an interest distribution to an individual by a UK authorised fund (see examples at **13.41** below).

UK corporate investors

13.12   For UK corporate investors, including investment trust companies, distributions of income by a corporate offshore fund are generally taxable under Schedule D Case IV/V at the normal rate of corporation tax. In the financial year to 31 March 2004, this is 19% (if a 'small' company for the purposes of the legislation), or 30% (if total profits are greater than £1.5m), with marginal rates in-between. No corporation tax is payable if profits chargeable to corporation tax are under £10,000.

Unlike individual investors, it is not tax advantageous for corporate investors to invest in debt instruments via an offshore fund. Special loan relationship rules apply, and are explained at **13.61** et seq below.

Authorised unit trusts/open-ended investment companies (OEICs)

13.13   Distributions received are taxable at the special corporation tax rate of 20%, subject to the application of the loan relationship rules in appropriate cases.

Unauthorised unit trusts

13.14   Distributions received are taxable at the basic rate of income tax. For the fiscal year to 5 April 2004, the basic rate is 22%.

Pension funds and charities

13.15   UK exempt approved pension schemes and qualifying UK charities are generally exempt from UK income tax if the investment is held for the purposes of the scheme, or for charitable purposes.

Transparent offshore funds

13.16   A fuller discussion of the taxation of UK investors in 'transparent' offshore funds is included at **13.29** ET SEQ. In summary, UK investors in a foreign limited partnership that is viewed as fiscally transparent are subject to UK taxation on their proportionate shares of the underlying partnership income as this arises, irrespective of when the income is distributed to them. Technically, the same is true of investment in many contractual funds (such as a Luxembourg Fonds Commun de Placement (FCP)), although, as indicated in CHAPTER 4, it is not uncommon in practice for taxation to proceed by default as if the fund were corporate in nature. In the case of a foreign unit trust, a hybrid form of taxation as regards the fund's income will generally result.

Taxation of capital gains

13.17 The treatment of a gain on the disposal of an investment in a corporate offshore fund will broadly depend on whether the fund is a distributing fund or a non-qualifying fund. The disposal of an interest in a non-qualifying offshore fund gives rise to an 'offshore income gain', taxable as income under Schedule D Case VI; whereas the gain arising on the disposal of an interest in a distributing fund retains, for the most part, its character as a capital gain. This assumes that the interest in the offshore fund was not held for the purposes of a trade or profession (in which case any gain on disposal would be taxed as income under Schedule D Case I/II). There are special rules (see **13.61** below) for UK companies investing in offshore bond or money market funds.

Disposal of interests in non-qualifying offshore funds

Offshore income gains

13.18 Under *ICTA 1988, s 757* an offshore income gain arises on a disposal if:

(a) at the time of the disposal, the asset constitutes a material interest in an offshore fund which is or has at any material time been a non-qualifying fund; or

(b) at the time of the disposal, the asset constitutes an interest in a company resident in the United Kingdom or in a unit trust scheme, the trustees of which are at the time resident in the United Kingdom; and at a material time after 31 December 1984 the company or unit trust scheme was a non-qualifying offshore fund and the asset constituted a material interest in that fund.

A disposal will include the sale, redemption or other disposal of the material interest.

An offshore fund is a non-qualifying fund except during an account period of the fund in respect of which the fund is certified by the Inland Revenue as a distributing fund (*ICTA 1988, s 760*).

CERTIFICATION PROCEDURE

13.19 CHAPTER 4 provides details of the certification procedure.

If an offshore fund has not applied for certification as a distributing fund, there is provision (*ICTA 1988, Sch 27 para 18*) for a UK investor to request that the Inland Revenue invite such an application by the fund. If the fund does not then make an application, the Revenue are required to determine the question of certification on the basis of whatever fund accounts and associated information are supplied by the UK applicant(s).

13.20   *Offshore Funds*

MATERIAL TIME

13.20   *Section 757* defines a 'material time', for the purposes of (a) at **13.18** above, as any time on or after the earliest date on which any relevant consideration was given for the acquisition of the asset; or, if that is earlier than 1 January 1984, any time on or after 1 January 1984. The fund will be a non-qualifying fund in relation to that investor's disposal if it has failed to obtain certification for any of its account periods which are comprised in whole or in part within the UK investor's period of holding since 1 January 1984.

EXAMPLE 13.20

B acquires shares in an offshore fund on 8 July 1990 and his shareholding constitutes a material interest in an offshore fund. The offshore fund has a 31 December year end and has been certified as a distributing fund since its first account period ended 31 December 1988. In March 2003 the offshore fund receives certification for the year ended 31 December 2002 and B decides to sell his shares for a substantial gain at the end of March 2003. B has until 31 January 2004 to submit his income tax return for the 2002/03 fiscal year, and in his return B records his gain on disposal as a capital gain. However, in March 2004 the offshore fund fails to obtain certification for the year ended 31 December 2003 because it has breached one of the investment restrictions. Therefore, between January and March 2003, B held an interest in a non-qualifying fund, and B's entire gain should have been taxed as an offshore income gain under the income tax rules.

13.21   Condition (b) at **13.18** above was intended to cover those instances where a non-qualifying fund migrates to the UK prior to the disposal of an interest in it. Without this provision, it would have been possible to roll up income offshore in a non-qualifying fund and then bring the vehicle onshore, for example via a change in the location of central management and control of the vehicle, at which point the disposal of the holding of shares or units in that vehicle would have been outside the offshore funds regime.

An offshore income gain can also arise on the disposal of an interest in an offshore fund that has been certified as a distributing fund throughout the period of ownership but which at the time of disposal is operating 'equalisation' (see 'Equalisation gains' at **13.34** below).

CALCULATION OF THE OFFSHORE INCOME GAIN

13.22   The calculation of an offshore income gain follows capital gains tax principles, but without the benefit of indexation allowance (for corporate investors and, where applicable, individuals) or taper relief (for individuals). Because the gain is subject to tax as income under Schedule D Case VI, the annual capital gains tax exemption for individuals is unavailable.

There is no such thing as an offshore income loss. If the calculation of the offshore income gain results in a loss, the Schedule D Case VI liability is treated as nil. Where an offshore income gain arises, there is in principle also an occasion of charge to capital gains tax; but the capital gain arising is fully offset by the offshore income gain. However, in the case of a loss on disposal, a capital loss will arise under the normal computational principles. As with other capital losses, a capital loss arising on the disposal of a holding in an offshore fund cannot be offset against offshore income gains.

CHARGE TO TAX OF THE OFFSHORE INCOME GAIN

UK individuals

13.23   UK resident individuals are liable to income tax under Schedule D Case VI at the basic (currently 22%) or higher (currently 40%) rates of tax, as appropriate. Individuals who are not domiciled in the UK are not liable to income tax unless the offshore income gain is remitted to the UK.

UK trustees (generally)

13.24   Under *ICTA 1988, s 764*, offshore income gains arising to UK trustees are generally charged to income tax at the rate applicable to trusts (currently 34%).

UK corporate investors

13.25   Offshore income gains arising to UK companies are subject to the normal rates of corporation tax (see 'Taxation of income' above). Special rules apply to the taxation of holdings in bond and money market funds (see **13.61** below).

Authorised unit trusts/OEICs

13.26   Offshore income gains are taxable at the special corporation tax rate of 20%, subject to the application of the loan relationship rules in appropriate cases (see **13.61** below).

Unauthorised unit trusts

13.27   The rate at which the trustee of an unauthorised unit trust is charged to tax in respect of an offshore income gain will, in the authors' view, depend in the first instance upon whether the gain is accounted for as capital, or recognised as income available for payment to unitholders (or for reinvestment). In the former case, the general rule in *ICTA 1988, s 764* (see **13.24** above) will apply to charge the gain to income tax at the rate applicable to trusts. Where, however, the offshore income gain is recognised as distributable income which, under *ICTA 1988, s 469(3)* and *(4)* is deemed to be received by unitholders in the form of an annual payment, it is considered that the provisions of *ICTA 1988, s 3* will operate so as to restrict the tax charge on the trustees to the basic rate of income tax, to the extent that the offshore income gain is franked by deemed annual payments in the relevant year of assessment. This approach would appear to be confirmed by the guidance notes to the income tax return for trustees.

Pension funds and charities

13.28   UK exempt approved pension schemes and qualifying UK charities are generally exempt from income tax on offshore income gains if the investment is held for the purposes of the scheme, or the gain is applied for charitable purposes.

Transparent offshore funds

13.29   An offshore income gain can only arise if there is a disposal of an asset for capital gains tax purposes. In the case of an investment in an offshore fund that is constituted as a fiscally transparent partnership (and also, it is considered, in the case of an investment in a contractual fund such as a Luxembourg FCP), the chargeable 'asset' in the hands of the UK investor is not the interest in the fund itself, but rather the investor's proportionate interest in each of the underlying assets of the fund. Thus, an occasion of potential charge to taxation of capital gains occurs each time an underlying fund asset is disposed of. The ultimate disposal by the investor of the interest in the fund itself does not trigger a charge to tax, regardless of whether the fund is a distributing or a non-qualifying fund.

Offshore unit trusts are generally regarded as fiscally transparent to a degree as regards their income (see **13.38** below). For capital gains tax purposes, however, units in most unit trust schemes are treated as though they were shares in a company (*TCGA 1992, s 99*), and offshore income gains (or capital gains) will arise for UK tax purposes on their disposal.

Disposal of interests in distributing funds

13.30   Although not defined as such in the tax legislation, a distributing fund is any offshore fund that is not a non-qualifying fund.

For interests in distributing funds, which comprise assets for capital gains purposes (see **13.29** above as regards transparent funds), any gains arising to investors resident or ordinarily resident in the UK on a sale, redemption or other disposal of their holdings are taxed not as offshore income gains, but as capital gains under the normal capital gains tax rules at the point of disposal. However, as explained at **13.34** below, if the distributing fund operates 'equalisation arrangements', such part of the proceeds on a disposal of the holding as represents income of the fund accrued since the previous distribution date is ring-fenced and taxed as income under Schedule D Case VI as an 'equalisation gain'.

UK individuals

13.31 For UK individual investors, capital gains are taxed at the relevant marginal rates, which are currently 10% (starting rate), 20% (basic rate) and 40% (higher rate).

The advantage of capital gains treatment is that any realised gains may be relieved by a number of allowances under the capital gains tax rules. First, the unindexed gain can be reduced by the indexation allowance according to the length of the holding period pre-April 1998. Capital losses in the current year and those brought forward from previous years can be used to further reduce any capital gain arising. Individual UK investors have the additional ability to relieve gains through taper relief according to the length of the holding period post-5 April 1998, as well as an annual exemption in relation to capital gains arising in a tax year.

In the case of investors who are not domiciled in the UK, capital gains are only subject to UK tax on their remittance to the UK.

UK corporate investors

13.32 For UK corporate investors, and subject to the application of special rules in the case of holdings in bond and money market funds (see **13.61** below), capital gains realised on the disposal of holdings in distributing funds are taxable at the corporation tax rate applicable to the company at the time of disposal. Capital losses and indexation allowances can be used to reduce the taxable gain.

Other investors

13.33 UK exempt approved pension funds, UK qualifying charities, UK investment trust companies, UK OEICs and UK authorised and exempt unauthorised unit trusts are all generally exempt from tax on capital gains realised on the disposal of an interest in a distributing offshore fund.

Equalisation gains

13.34 Where a fund operates equalisation arrangements, payments made to an investor in respect of disposals of shares or units during an account period of the fund will include an income component (to reflect the investor's share of the fund's accrued income since the last distribution date), with the balance representing the capital value of the shares or units. (See fuller discussion in CHAPTER 4.)

On the disposal by a UK investor of an interest in a distributing fund which operates such arrangements, that portion of the disposal proceeds which comprises accrued income is subject to UK tax as income under Schedule D

Case VI, in the form of an 'equalisation gain' (*ICTA 1988, s 758(3)*). The balance of disposal proceeds is dealt with under capital gains tax principles. As in the case of a mainstream offshore income gain, an equalisation gain carries no entitlement to indexation allowances, taper relief or annual capital gains tax allowances for individuals.

Equivalent equalisation gains on disposals of interests in non-qualifying offshore funds are excluded from separate taxation, as the disposal gives rise to an offshore income gain calculated by reference to the entire disposal proceeds.

13.35   The equalisation gain is the amount which would be credited to the fund's equalisation account in respect of accrued income if, at the time of disposal, there had been an acquisition of the interest by another investor by way of initial purchase.

The equalisation gain is reduced, where appropriate, by the amount of any accrued income credited to the equalisation account in relation to that holding which relates to a period before the acquisition of the holding concerned or to a period of ownership before 1 January 1984. If the amount credited to the equalisation account includes profits from dealing in commodities, half of such profits are left out of account.

However, in no circumstances may the equalisation gain exceed the offshore income gain that would have arisen on the disposal of the holding, had the fund not been certified as a distributing fund throughout the period of ownership.

Merger and reconstruction of offshore funds

13.36   The tax implications of share etc reorganisations and mergers in relation to offshore funds are heavily dependent on whether the fund or funds in question are distributing or non-qualifying offshore funds. In some cases, the distinction can result in a particular transaction being subject to tax or wholly exempt. See CHAPTER 9 for a full commentary.

Transparent funds

13.37   So-called 'transparent funds' have been touched on in CHAPTER 4, to the extent that fiscal transparency may affect the taxation at the level of the local jurisdiction or impact on the distribution requirement when applying for UK distributor status. However, the tax impact of holding interests in such funds is most important to the investors themselves.

Limited partnerships are a common form of transparent entity and the tax implications of investing in a limited partnership are covered fully in CHAPTER 5.

As mentioned in CHAPTER 4, there are two other main types of non-UK investment vehicle that have 'transparent' characteristics. The first is an FCP

(Luxembourg/France), which is deemed to be transparent for UK tax purposes as regards its underlying income (and probably its gains also). However, such a vehicle is seldom offered to UK investors, partly because of the level of information that a UK taxable investor would need in order to complete their tax return.

13.38   The other investment vehicle that can be considered to be transparent to a certain degree is the foreign unit trust scheme (as found in Ireland, the Channel Islands, the Isle of Man etc). The UK Inland Revenue generally classify foreign trusts by reference to two established tax cases, *Baker v Archer-Shee* and *Archer-Shee v Garland*. The Inland Revenue's interpretation of these two cases can be broadly summarised as follows:

- The beneficiary of a 'Baker'-type trust is entitled to his appropriate share of each item of income as and when it arises to the trust, subject only to a charge for trustee's expenses and remuneration. The beneficiary is taxable on his share of the trust income, less the relevant portion of the trust expenses.

- The beneficiary of a 'Garland'-type trust is entitled only to his appropriate share of the net trust income remaining after the trustees have ascertained the balance available. A beneficiary taxable on an arising basis is liable to UK tax by reference to the actual income receivable from the trust, whether remitted to the UK or not, and without regard to the nature of the income as it arose to the trustees.

13.39   Where a foreign trust is constituted as a unit trust and is governed by trust law which broadly follows that of the UK, the Inland Revenue's approach in practice has generally been to regard a UK unitholder as entitled to (and thus taxable on) his share of the net income of the trust at the time that is indefeasibly allocated to him – at which time it will either be paid to him or accumulated on his behalf, depending on the types of units held. However, in taxing that share of income, the Inland Revenue generally give credit for foreign (or, indeed, any UK) tax suffered in relation to each income source. This suggests that the Inland Revenue are inclined to view such a unit trust as having certain 'Baker'-type features (ie the underlying income of the trust retains its source characteristics), but are content to defer the taxation of income arising to UK investors until the time of its periodic distribution or accumulation.

In practice it is not uncommon for sponsors of offshore unit trust funds which are to be marketed to UK investors to submit the trust deed to the Inland Revenue, in order to obtain confirmation of the tax position of UK unitholders and to agree a suitable form of tax voucher for issue to UK unitholders in respect of each periodic distribution or accumulation of income. These vouchers would typically identify foreign tax (and UK tax credits, where applicable) attached to the various sources of income, thus enabling UK unitholders to maximise the tax reliefs available.

Death of an investor – inheritance tax

13.40   An individual investor domiciled, or deemed for UK tax purposes to be domiciled in the UK may be liable to UK inheritance tax on his offshore fund holding in the event of death or on making certain categories of lifetime transfer.

Under the normal capital gains rules, death is not an occasion of charge. However, under *ICTA 1988, s 757(3)–(4)* and *TCGA 1992, s 62*, on the death of an investor who was competent to dispose of their holding in a non-qualifying fund, there is deemed to be a disposal of that holding and the triggering of an offshore income gain, where relevant. The deemed disposal proceeds must be taken as an amount equal to the market value of the holding at the date of death. This modification of the capital gains tax rules is designed to prevent income gains from falling out of charge on a person's death. There is no such deemed disposal of an interest in a distributing fund, even if the fund operates equalisation arrangements (see **13.34** above).

Taxation of onshore versus offshore investment

13.41   The following two worked examples illustrate the effect of taxation on the comparative returns to different types of UK investor from a distributing offshore fund, a non-qualifying offshore fund and a UK OEIC.

Example 1 illustrates in particular the beneficial effect to a UK higher rate taxpayer of the favourable rate of UK taxation on foreign dividends versus interest.

Example 2 further illustrates the effect of foreign withholding taxes and double tax treaty access on the comparative post-tax returns from a UK and an offshore equity fund.

The examples are broad in nature, and a detailed comparison would need to factor in, inter alia, the generally positive effect of tax deferral in the case of investment in a non-qualifying fund, assuming that the fund accumulates all its income.

EXAMPLE 13.41A – EUROBOND FUND

		UK OEIC	Distributing offshore fund	Non-qualifying offshore fund
		(Income shares)		
Taxation of the fund				
Gross interest income (no withholding tax)		1,000	1,000	1,000
Expenses		(100)	(100)	(100)
Roll-up to capital		–	–	(900)
Gross distribution		900	900	–
Withholding tax thereon (where applicable)		–/(180)	–	–
Cash distribution		900/720	900	–
Capital gains		1,000	1,000	1,000
Roll-up from income		–	–	900
Total capital appreciation		1,000	1,000	1,900
Taxation of pension fund				
Cash distribution (gross)		900	900	–
Capital gain		1,000	1,000	1,900
Total post-tax yield		1,900	1,900	1,900
Taxation of ISA investor				
Cash distribution (gross)		900	900	–
Capital gain		1,000	1,000	1,900
Total post-tax yield		1,900	1,900	1,900
Taxation of higher rate tax payer				
Cash distribution (net/gross)		720	900	–
Taxable income/offshore income gain	900		900	1,900
Tax thereon at 32.5%/40%[1]	360		292	760
Income tax credit	(180)		–	–
Income tax payable	180	(180)	292 (292)	760 (760)
Capital gain	1,000		1,000	1,900
Tax thereon at 40%[2]		(400)	(400)	–
Total post tax-yield		1,140	1,208	1,140[3]

[1] Cash distributions from the OEIC are taxed as interest income at a marginal rate of 40%. Cash distributions from the distributing offshore fund are taxed as overseas dividends at a marginal rate of 32.5%. Offshore income gains from the non-qualifying offshore fund are taxed as income at a marginal rate of 40%.

[2] Capital gains are taxed at a marginal rate of 40%. In practice the effective rate may be lower by virtue of taper relief, an individual's annual exemption and capital losses.

[3] No account has been taken of the time value of money as a result of the deferral of the entire tax charge until realisation of the holding.

EXAMPLE 13.41B – US EQUITY FUND

	UK OEIC	Distributing offshore fund	Non-qualifying offshore fund
	(Income shares)		
Taxation of the fund			
Gross US dividends	800	800	800
Expenses	(300)	(300)	(300)
Withholding tax on US dividends (15%/30%)[1]	(120)	(240)	(240)
Taxable income	500	–	–
UK tax due (20%)	100	–	–
Less credit relief for WHT suffered	(100)	–	–
	–	–	
Roll-up to capital	–	–	(260)
Gross distribution	380	260	–
Withholding tax thereon	–	–	–
Cash distribution	380	260	–
Capital gains	1,000	1,000	1,000
Roll-up from income	–	–	260
Total capital appreciation	1,000	1,000	1,260
Taxation of pension fund			
Cash distribution	380	260	–
Capital gain	1,000	1,000	1,260
Total post-tax yield	1,380	1,260	1,260
Taxation of ISA investor			
Cash distribution	380	260	–
Reclaim of dividend tax credits[2]	42	–	–
Capital gain	1,000	1,000	1,260
Total post-tax yield	1,422	1,260	1,260
Taxation of higher rate tax payer			
Cash distribution	380	260	–
Taxable income/offshore income gain	422	260	1,260
Tax thereon at 32.5%/40%[3]	137	84	504
Income tax credit	(42)	–	–
Income tax payable	95 (95)	84 (84)	504 (504)
Capital gain	1,000	1,000	1,260
Tax thereon at 40%[4]	(400)	(400)	–
Total post tax-yield	885	776	756[5]

[1]   A withholding tax rate of 15% has been assumed for US dividends received by the UK OEIC and 30% for the offshore funds.

[2]   ISA investors can only reclaim UK dividend tax credits until 5 April 2004. The tax credit is equivalent to one-ninth of the net distribution.

[3]   Cash distributions from the OEIC and distributing offshore fund are taxed as dividend income at a marginal rate of 32.5%. Offshore income gains from the non-qualifying offshore fund are taxed as income at a marginal rate of 40%.

⁴ Capital gains are taxed at a marginal rate of 40%. In practice the effective rate may be lower by virtue of taper relief, an individual's annual exemption and capital losses.

⁵ No account has been taken of the time value of money as a result of the deferral of the entire tax charge until realisation of the holding.

Offshore Funds – Technical Areas

Transfer of assets abroad – ICTA 1988, ss 739–740

13.42   Income arising abroad to a person who is not resident in the UK is, in general, not subject to UK tax. Where a person is resident but not domiciled in the UK, the income is only assessable to the extent that it is remitted to the UK.

If a person ordinarily resident in the UK could arrange for income to be received by a non-resident person, while somehow retaining the right to benefit from the income, they might thus avoid a charge to UK tax.

To counter such tax planning by individuals ordinarily resident in the UK, *ICTA 1988, ss 739* and *740* contain complex anti-avoidance provisions which impose a charge to UK income tax on such individuals who, in consequence of a transfer of assets, have the power to enjoy income arising to a person resident or domiciled outside the UK or may otherwise benefit from the transfer. If an individual ordinarily resident in the UK receives a capital sum, the payment of which is in any way connected with such a transfer of assets, a similar charge to UK income tax is imposed.

13.43   The broad effect of the provisions is to treat income that has become payable to the non-UK resident or domiciliary by virtue of the transfer as though it were the income of the UK individual.

The provisions only apply to the UK taxation of individuals. The Controlled Foreign Company (CFC) legislation in *ICTA 1988, Part XVII Chapter IV* (described at **13.56** below) contains somewhat equivalent measures for UK companies.

An important escape clause exists in order that arrangements which are not made with a view to avoiding tax, and bona fide commercial transactions which are not for the purposes of avoiding tax, are not caught by the legislation.

The provisions of *sections 739* and *740* are widely drawn, in terms of what constitutes a relevant transfer of assets, what 'power to enjoy' means, and what may constitute a benefit provided out of assets. The legislation has been the subject of a number of significant cases in the courts.

13.44   While the legislation has, over the years, been closely associated with the establishment of foreign 'family trusts' and private companies, it has been of potential application also to investment by UK ordinarily resident individuals in offshore funds, in that the subscription for shares or units in an offshore fund would undoubtedly constitute a transfer of assets for the purposes of *section 739*. Equally, the UK individual investor would have the 'power to enjoy' his share of the income arising within the fund within the wide definition of that phrase.

However, it was one thing for the UK Inland Revenue to pursue *section 739* challenges in selected and material cases involving offshore trusts and private companies; and another thing entirely to attempt to use *section 739* as a means of combating the large scale flight of UK 'retail' money into offshore funds during the early 1980s, following the abolition of UK exchange controls in 1979. Not only were the administrative difficulties daunting, but also the motive test associated with *section 739* would have had to be addressed in the case of each individual UK investor. The latter would have been problematic, given the nature of any fund investment. Thus, the offshore fund legislation was introduced in 1984 as a more straightforward means of countering the problem as the Revenue saw it.

Nevertheless, *sections 739* and *740* remain on the statute books, and continue to be of potential application to investment in non-qualifying funds by UK individual investors.

Allocation of underlying capital gains – TCGA 1992, s 13

13.45   Generally, UK investors in an offshore fund that is not treated as tax transparent are taxed only when they dispose of their holding in the fund or when they receive a distribution from it. However, under the provisions of *TCGA 1992, s 13*, the investor may in certain circumstances also be charged to tax when a fund constituted as a company itself realises chargeable gains, eg on the disposal of its underlying investments. This charge on the investor is made regardless of whether the fund itself is taxed on such gains (which in most cases will not be the case).

The rationale for this legislation (which is of general application) is that, without it, a UK resident individual, company or trust could defer or avoid a liability to tax on chargeable gains by holding assets through an offshore company.

13.46   The provisions of *section 13* will only apply to a UK investor in a corporate offshore fund if, at the time when a chargeable gain accrues to the fund, the following conditions hold:

- the investor is a 'participator' in the fund; and

- the investor is resident or ordinarily resident in the UK (and, in the case of an individual, is domiciled in the UK); and

- the investor (including connected parties) would be entitled on an apportionment to more than 10% of the chargeable gain; and

- the fund is controlled in such a manner as to render it a 'close company' for UK taxation purposes, were it to be resident in the UK.

These provisions, if applied, would result in the investor being treated as if a part of the gain accruing to the fund had accrued to the investor directly, for the purposes of UK capital gains tax or corporation tax on chargeable gains. Offshore income gains arising to the fund on the disposal of any interests in non-qualifying offshore funds would be similarly attributed to the UK investor.

The 'part' referred to above will be equal to the proportion of the gain that corresponds to the extent of the investor's interest as a participator in the fund.

In the event that a UK investor invests in a 'close' offshore feeder fund or fund of funds that itself invests in a 'close' fund, the gains of the underlying fund can be indirectly apportioned to the UK investor.

Close company legislation

13.47   Generally, a close company is one that satisfies one or more of the following tests:

- it is under the control of five or fewer 'participators' (see below); or

- it is under the control of participators who are directors of the company (with no limit on the number); or

- on a winding-up (on a specified basis) five or fewer participators or participators who are directors (with no limit on the number) would be entitled to receive more than half of the amount of the company's assets available for distribution to participators.

The basic definition of a 'participator' is a person having a share or interest in the capital or income of the company, and therefore includes shareholders and any loan creditor of the company. Typically, an investor in a corporate offshore fund would be a participator.

However, the scope of the definition is extended by the attribution to a person of the rights and powers of his 'associates' (see below), nominees and certain other companies which he and his associates control. Thus, an individual who does not meet the basic definition may still be a participator, eg if his father is a shareholder or if some of the company's shares are held by another company which he controls.

The definition of 'associate' is complex, but it includes business partners and certain relatives of a participator.

There are some important exceptions to the definition of a close company (including companies controlled by non-close companies, and quoted companies, 35% of whose voting power is held by the public).

Can a unit trust scheme come within the provisions of section 13?

13.48   The application of *section 13* to unit trust schemes with non-resident trustees is unclear. *Section 13* applies in respect of chargeable gains arising to:

- a company which is not resident in the UK; and

- which would be a close company if it were resident in the UK.

In respect of the first test, *TCGA 1992, s 99* states that the *1992 Act* shall apply in relation to a unit trust scheme as if it were a company. This test would therefore be satisfied.

However, the situation is less clear with respect to the second test, which must also hold in order for *section 13* to apply. It is generally thought by commentators that, in the context of *section 13*, a close company must be a company as defined under *ICTA 1988, s 832*. That definition states that a company must be either a body corporate or an unincorporated association. While a UK authorised unit trust is deemed to be a company for these purposes, an offshore unit trust would not appear to fall within either category. It is also the case that a foreign unit trust, even assuming that it were resident in the UK, could not be 'authorised' unless it had received such authorisation on application to the Financial Services Authority. There appears, therefore, to be a technical case that *section 13* cannot apply to a foreign unit trust scheme; although, given the underlying principles of *TCGA 1992, s 99*, a purposive interpretation of the legislation would perhaps suggest the contrary.

Calculating the offshore fund's chargeable gains

13.49   In the relevant cases, the offshore fund's chargeable gains (including offshore income gains) are calculated as if it had been resident in the UK. The normal computational rules apply, including those on indexation and rebasing in the case of capital gains.

Gains on certain assets used for the purposes of a non-UK trade are exempt from the charge.

Apportioning the gain to the investor

13.50   As stated above, the gain is attributed to each investor according to the extent of his interest in the fund. This interest is measured in proportion to the interests of all participators in the fund, not just those who are UK resident, and is calculated using a just and reasonable apportionment. Methods of apportionment could include, for example, entitlement to income or capital. Inland Revenue manuals provide guidance here.

When calculating whether the investor's proportion of the gain exceeds 10% of the total (and is therefore taxable), it is necessary to include gains apportioned to persons connected with the investor.

If the disposal by the non-resident fund gives rise to a loss, that loss cannot generally be apportioned to UK investors for them to offset against their other capital gains. However, the loss can be offset against gains apportioned to the investor under *section 13* in relation to gains made by the same fund or other non-resident companies, where the gains arise in the same year of assessment as the loss arises. Surplus losses cannot be carried back or forward to a different year of assessment.

Calculating the tax charge on the attributed gain

13.51   A capital gain (but not an offshore income gain) attributed to a UK investor may be offset by capital losses and, for an individual, the net capital gain may be reduced by the investor's annual exemption. The usual rates of capital gains tax or corporation tax on chargeable gains (or income tax or corporation tax in the case of an offshore income gain) apply.

When the capital gain has been subject to foreign tax outside the UK, the UK investor is allowed credit for an appropriate proportion of that foreign tax suffered.

The impact on subsequent disposals of, or distributions arising from, the shares in the fund

13.52   *Section 13* charges tax on a relevant investor when the fund realises capital gains and offshore income gains. At that stage, the investor has not necessarily made any actual disposal of an asset. Consequently, the investor retains his shares in the fund and may incur an additional tax charge on the disposal of those shares or on a distribution from the fund.

The legislation provides that, if the fund makes a distribution in respect of the gain to the investor within a certain time after the date on which the original *section 13* gain accrued, the investor will get credit for the original tax paid against tax due on the subsequent distribution.

If the investor who has been charged to tax on the apportioned gain subsequently disposes of his shares in the company otherwise than on the receipt of a distribution, they will get an element of relief for the tax originally paid. In calculating the capital or offshore income gain chargeable to tax on the subsequent disposal, a deduction is allowable for any capital gains tax or income tax suffered under *section 13*. However, full tax credit is not granted in this situation and therefore a *section 13* charge can lead to an element of double taxation.

Application of section 13 to an offshore fund structured as an umbrella fund

13.53   Sub-funds of a UK umbrella authorised unit trust or OEIC are deemed in UK tax legislation to be individual unit trusts or OEICs in their own right. By contrast, *section 13* does not address whether sub-funds of offshore fund entities should be regarded as separate entities or not, and therefore the application of *section 13* to an offshore umbrella fund is determined by the legal nature of the entity. A corporate 'umbrella' should be treated as a single legal entity for the purposes of *section 13;* however, in relation to other forms of 'umbrella' fund, the answer will depend upon (a) whether the fund constitutes a 'company' at all for these purposes; and (b), if so, whether there is a single company or multiple companies represented by different sub-funds.

Application of section 13 to temporary non-residence

13.54   As a basic principle, individuals can only be subject to capital gains tax in respect of chargeable gains accruing to them in a year of assessment during any part of which they are either resident or ordinarily resident in the UK. It was therefore a tax planning strategy for individuals to emigrate offshore for a period so that they were no longer either resident or ordinarily resident in the UK, realise their chargeable gains offshore thus avoiding a UK capital gains tax liability and then subsequently return to the UK.

13.55   To kerb this activity, anti-avoidance legislation was introduced in *FA 1998* in the form of *TCGA 1992, s 10A*. This temporary non-residence provision applies to an individual where:

(i)   having been UK resident for at least four out of the seven years of assessment immediately preceding his year of departure from the UK, the individual becomes not resident and not ordinarily resident; and

(ii)   the period in which he is not resident and ordinarily resident lasts for less than five years of assessment.

Where the relevant conditions are satisfied, gains arising while the individual has been temporarily non-resident, and that would have been chargeable gains had the individual remained resident in the UK, will be subject to capital gains tax in the year of his return to the UK. Such gains would include any gains apportioned under *TCGA 1992, s 13*. There are, however, exceptions to this rule, the main one being that a charge generally does not arise on an asset that was acquired by the individual at a time in the year of departure or any intervening year when he was neither resident nor ordinarily resident in the UK.

Controlled Foreign Companies (CFCs) – ICTA 1988, Part XVII, Chapter IV

13.56   As in the case of the loan relationship rules (see **13.61** below), the CFC legislation (contained within *ICTA 1988, Part XVII Chapter IV*) applies only to UK corporate investors.

The objective of the legislation is to prevent tax avoidance by companies resident for tax purposes in the UK which hold an interest in companies in low tax jurisdictions, in order to benefit from the fiscal advantages offered by those jurisdictions. Unless the offshore company paid regular dividends to its UK shareholder(s), UK taxation of the company's underlying income would be deferred, possibly indefinitely.

As an anti-avoidance measure, the income profits of an offshore company, should it fall to be treated as a CFC, are therefore notionally apportioned amongst its shareholders, and profits allocated to UK resident company shareholders are charged to UK corporation tax should they exceed a certain level.

As in the case of *TCGA 1992, s 13*, the CFC rules are of general application but can encompass investment in corporate offshore funds. The legislation is complex, and the paragraphs that follow contain a broad summary only.

What is a CFC?

13.57   A CFC is a company that satisfies all of the following conditions:

- the company is tax resident outside the UK; and

- the company is controlled by persons resident in the UK; and

- the company in its country of residence is subject to a 'lower level of taxation'; broadly, a tax charge which is less than three-quarters of the 'corresponding' tax charge in the UK.

Consequences of a company being a CFC

13.58   Subject to certain defences (see below), the 'chargeable profits' of the CFC are apportioned as appropriate to the UK resident corporate shareholders and are taxed on those shareholders. The chargeable profits consist of the total profits of the CFC as defined for corporation tax purposes, but, importantly, exclude chargeable (capital) gains.

The chargeable profits are apportioned among the persons who have an interest in the company at any time in the accounting period, the split being made on the basis of such interests. No charge arises unless more than 25% of the CFC's chargeable profits for the period in question is apportioned either to the UK resident company or to persons 'connected' or 'associated' with it.

The amount of the tax liability in respect of the chargeable profits apportioned is reduced by the CFC's 'creditable tax'. The creditable tax of a CFC includes:

- any foreign tax paid on its income – provided the company could have had double tax relief for this tax had it been UK resident; and

- any income tax or corporation tax paid by deduction at source or on an assessment (for example on the profits of a UK branch).

Defences against being deemed to be a CFC

13.59 There are a number of defences against an offshore company (including a corporate offshore fund) being treated as a CFC. It is sufficient to satisfy one of the following conditions:

(1) The company pursues an 'acceptable distribution policy'.

The CFC distributes more than 90% of the relevant portion of its chargeable profits (less creditable tax) to UK residents, either during or within 18 months of the end of the accounting period in question. There are detailed rules for calculating the profits from which the company pays the dividends.

(2) Exempt activities test.

The CFC is engaged in certain exempt activities. The activities of an offshore investment fund will not generally satisfy this test.

(3) Public quotation test.

This exclusion is for quoted CFCs that have shares owned by the public. The public must hold shares carrying at least 35% of the voting rights, and there must be dealings in those shares on a recognised stock exchange situated in the territory in which the company is resident. Whereas many offshore funds do have a stock exchange listing (if only to satisfy the conditions under which certain institutional investors may invest), these are frequently 'cross-border' listings (eg a Cayman Islands fund listed on the Dublin or Luxembourg stock exchange), and as such would not satisfy the quotation test.

(4) Motive test.

It must be demonstrated that diverting profits from the UK is not the main or one of the main reasons for the existence of the company in the accounting period.

(5) Excluded countries.

The Inland Revenue have published in regulations a list of 'excluded' countries. Where a company meets certain conditions with regard to residence and income and gains in relation to a listed country, no apportionment falls to be made. An offshore fund would rarely meet these conditions.

(6) De minimis profits.

No apportionment will be made where the chargeable profits of a company for the accounting period in question do not exceed £50,000 (proportionately reduced for periods of less than twelve months).

Impact of CFC rules in relation to offshore funds

13.60 Offshore funds that obtain distributor status will have distributed at least 85% of their net income on an annual basis, and many of these might also be expected to have satisfied the acceptable distribution policy test for CFC purposes.

In addition, the Inland Revenue's guidance notes have indicated that the motive test is satisfied in the case where an offshore open-ended investment company is controlled by a UK resident company and the facts show that the main reason for the existence of the offshore company is to invest in cash and bonds, and as a result the offshore company fails the non-qualifying investment test in *FA 1996, Sch 10 para 8* (see **13.61** below). The Revenue have confirmed that whilst the existence of the offshore company achieves a reduction in tax, the UK tax charge on the parent demonstrates that one of the main reasons for the offshore company's existence was not to achieve a reduction in UK tax by a diversion of profits from the UK. As a result the CFC rules would not be applicable.

The application of the CFC rules is therefore most likely to be in point in the case of non-qualifying offshore funds that invest otherwise than in cash and bonds. Even then, there is a problematic interplay between the CFC rules (which aim to combat tax deferral, but are subject to a motive test) and the specific anti-avoidance legislation on offshore funds (which permits tax deferral, but is mandatory in its application). A UK company that invests in a non-qualifying offshore fund in the knowledge that its capital gains (as well as any rolled-up income) will eventually be taxed as income might well argue that its investment is not primarily tax-motivated. Moreover, a double charge to UK tax would often result if a CFC apportionment were made in relation to the profits of a non-qualifying offshore fund.

Given the above considerations, and the relatively high level of participation in an offshore fund that would be required for a UK corporate investor to fall within the CFC rules, CFC issues have in practice tended to be restricted to 'captive' offshore funds of large UK financial institutions.

Impact of the loan relationship rules – FA 1996, Schedule 10

13.61   Where a UK resident company holds government or corporate debt indirectly, through an equity interest in an offshore investment fund, *FA 1996, Sch 10* deems such an interest to constitute a creditor relationship under the loan relationship rules if:

- it constitutes a material interest in an offshore fund (or, in the case of non-corporate funds, would do so if the fund constituted a collective investment scheme); and

- the offshore fund's 'qualifying investments' have exceeded 60% (by market value) of the fund's total investment at any time in the accounting period of the UK corporate investor concerned.

'Qualifying investments' are broadly those which yield a return directly or indirectly in the form of interest, and include deposits, securities (other than shares), shares in a building society and units in a unit trust scheme or shares in an OEIC or other offshore fund where the underlying fund itself satisfies the 60% test as regards its qualifying investments.

13.62   If a UK corporate investor's interest in an offshore fund is recharacterised as a loan relationship, the offshore fund rules are of no consequence. Instead, the UK company is taxed annually on the increase in value of its holding in the fund on a mark-to-market basis, or will obtain annual tax relief for any equivalent decrease in value. Distributions of income by the fund are taxed as interest receipts.

For accounting periods beginning on or after 1 October 2002, UK authorised unit trusts and OEICs which invest in offshore funds whose qualifying investments meet the 60% standard described above are subject to a modified version of these loan relationship rules. Broadly, profits, gains and losses on the deemed creditor relationship will only be taxed (or tax relieved) if they are recognised as income items within the statement of total return. To the extent that they are accounted for as capital items in accordance with the prevailing Statement of Recommended Practice (SORP), they are ignored for all tax purposes.

Taxation of Life Companies

Background

13.63   There are two main bases on which investment income and gains are taxed within a UK life company, namely:

- Schedule D Case VI (but computed under Case I principles); and

- Income + Gains – Expenses (I–E).

Where a policy falls into one of the categories of pension business, life reinsurance business, overseas life assurance business or individual savings account business, the income and gains on assets backing such policies are not subject to tax in the hands of the life insurer. Instead, a profits calculation is performed and the profits the life insurer makes from writing such policies are taxed. The charge to tax is under Schedule D Case VI with the computations being carried out on Case I principles. Depending upon the tax position of the policyholder and the type of policy, the policyholder may pay tax on the proceeds arising from the maturity of the policy.

Where an insurance policy is a basic life or general annuity policy, the income and gains arising on assets backing that policy are subject to tax on the life insurance company as if it were an investment company (under the I–E regime). The policyholder receives a tax credit on the maturity of such a policy to take account of the tax suffered by the life company.

13.64   Some assets are solely linked to either life business or a class of Case VI business and, where this is the case, all income and gains on those assets are allocated to that class of business. Where assets are not so linked, it is necessary to apportion the income and gains arising on such assets between the classes of business. The proportion of income and gains on non-linked assets which is brought into either the Case VI computation or the I–E computation will depend on the tax profile of the life insurance fund writing the business.

Treatment of offshore fund holdings attributable to Case VI pension business

13.65   As discussed above, pension business is taxed on the profits arising from the business, not on the income and gains arising from assets used to back that business.

ICTA 88, s 438 provides that:

> 'exemption from corporation tax shall be allowed in respect of income from, and chargeable gains in respect of, investments and deposits of so much of an insurance company's long-term insurance fund as is referable to pension business'.

Any chargeable gains arising under *TCGA 1992* and referable to pension business will not come into the charge to tax.

If there is a disposal of a material interest in a non-qualifying offshore fund under *ICTA 1988, s 757, section 761* applies to treat the amount of the gain as income arising at the time of the disposal. Such income is exempt from tax by virtue of *section 438*.

Treatment of offshore fund holdings attributable to life insurance business

13.66   The comments that follow are relevant wherever income or gains are attributable to life insurance business.

Bond funds

13.67   Bond funds (>60% invested in interest-bearing securities) are taxed under the loan relationship rules. Income and market movements in the year are brought into the charge to tax in accordance with *FA 1996, Sch 10 para 4*.

'Transparent' funds

13.68   If the investment is in a unit trust established in a common law territory (eg the Isle of Man or Bermuda) or a country which recognises trusts (eg Jersey), and the trust is a 'quasi-Baker'-type trust (see **13.39** above), the income (but not the gains) of the trust is taxable on the life company as it is indefeasibly allocated.

Other offshore investment vehicles (eg certain limited partnerships) are fully transparent, such that the underlying income and gains are attributed to UK participators (including life insurers) as they arise.

TCGA 1992, s 212 charge

13.69 At the end of each accounting period, there is a deemed disposal of relevant interests in offshore funds. For the purposes of *section 212*, an 'offshore fund' also includes entities which are not collective investment schemes, and therefore the deemed disposal rules extend more widely than the definition at *ICTA 1988, s 759*.

Where the fund is a distributing fund within *section 760*, a capital gain or loss will arise on the deemed disposal, subject to any element of equalisation gain. One-seventh of the capital gain is brought into tax for the current year and each of the following six years. If a loss arises, that loss can be utilised against current year capital gains, carried forward or carried back to prior years on a LIFO basis, reducing the capital gains brought into tax in those periods. The maximum carry-back is currently two years. Any equalisation gain is charged to tax as Case VI income for the year in which the deemed disposal occurs.

Where the fund is a non-qualifying offshore fund within the strict definition of the offshore fund legislation, a Case VI offshore income gain charge or a capital loss will arise. If a Case VI income charge arises, the entire amount is brought into the charge to tax in that year. As noted at **13.22** above, it is not possible to offset capital losses against the Case VI income charge. Capital losses arising can, however, be offset against other capital gains within the life company.

Where the investment does not fall within the *section 759* meaning of a 'material interest' in an offshore fund but does fall within the *section 212* definition (ie the investment is not in a collective investment scheme), a capital gain will arise and be spread under *section 212*.

Interaction between the offshore funds legislation and the CFC legislation

13.70 An investment may constitute a material interest in an offshore fund as described above and may also, in certain circumstances, be a CFC for UK tax purposes (see **13.56** above). In such situations, it is necessary to look very closely at the structure in order to determine whether double taxation is suffered.

The Future

Information reporting and the Savings Directive

13.71 The EU Savings Directive is a step towards closer cooperation between member states in the field of direct taxation. It will unquestionably have a major impact on the financial services industry throughout the EU, and in particular the investment management industry.

Under the Directive, member states, with the exception of Austria, Luxembourg and Belgium (which will initially operate a withholding tax regime) will automatically exchange information about interest payments originating in their territories which are paid on or after 1 January 2005 to individual beneficial owners in other member states (although new customer documentation procedures will need to be in place from 1 January 2004).

Who will be caught by the Directive?

13.72 The Directive will apply to any paying agent in an EU member state which makes an interest payment to an individual beneficial owner resident in another member state. The definitions of 'paying agent' and 'interest payment' are wide enough to include payments by a wide variety of institutions, including investment funds, private equity funds, hedge funds, transfer agents, custodians, trustees etc.

Paying agents will be required either to report information about relevant cross-border interest payments to their domestic tax authorities, or, for a transitional period applicable to paying agents in Austria, Belgium and Luxembourg, to levy a minimum level of withholding tax on such payments.

When will the Directive be implemented?

13.73 The Directive applies to interest payments made on or after 1 January 2005. However, the Directive will apply from this date only if a number of other European countries (including Switzerland) agree to apply equivalent measures and if member states' dependent and associated territories (including the Channel Islands, the Isle of Man, and Caribbean dependent territories) apply either automatic exchange of information or a withholding tax.

Individual investors

13.74 The Directive employs the term 'beneficial owner', which broadly means any individual resident in a member state who receives interest payments. An offshore fund which has individual investors may need to comply with new procedures set out in the Directive for establishing the identity and residence of its investors.

Interest payments

13.75 Interest is defined very widely and all payments of interest relating to 'debt claims' are subject to the Directive. It is worth noting that the definition of debt claims is likely to be interpreted differently by different member states (eg local interpretations may vary as to whether or not derivative contracts give rise to interest payments).

The Directive also applies to distributions by, and redemptions or sales of shares or units in investment funds, depending on the extent to which the assets of such funds are invested in debt claims. Member states have the option of excluding distributions made by funds established in their territory where no more than 15% of these assets are invested in debt claims. This exclusion is, however, not available where the fund is located outside the EU (eg a Cayman Islands domiciled fund). In addition, all redemptions or sales of shares or units in investment funds will be ignored where the fund, irrespective of where it is established, invests less than 40% of its assets in debt claims.

Paying agents

13.76 The key to the operation of the entire Directive is the identification of the 'paying agent', as it is the paying agent that is ultimately responsible for complying with the rules. The paying agent is the entity which, under the Directive, is deemed to have made or secured the payment of interest to the investor. The Directive focuses on the last 'paying agent' in a chain of interest payments which are ultimately paid to the beneficial owner – thus for each payment there should only be one 'paying agent'. However, it remains to be seen whether this seemingly simple proposition will be as clear following its implementation into national law by the member states, as local interpretations of the Directive may differ.

14 Investment Trust Shareholders

Ian Sayers

AITC

Introduction

14.1 In recent years, the investment trust industry has made a concerted effort to attract more retail investors. Indeed, the investment trust sector is probably the only sector of the UK stock market to have seen a significant rise in the proportion of its shares owned by private shareholders. Many generalist trusts, for example, are well over 50% owned by retail shareholders. The increased level of share ownership by retail investors has been boosted by the creation (normally by the management groups which manage the investment portfolio of the investment trust) of 'wrapper' products which make it possible for investors with smaller sums (eg £50 on a regular monthly basis, or £250 lump sum) to invest in the shares of investment trusts in a cheaper and administratively more convenient manner. The most common forms of wrapper products used to hold the shares of investment trusts are Investment Trust Savings and Investment Schemes, Investment Trust Personal Pensions and Individual Savings Accounts.

Where the taxation of private investors is concerned, shareholders in investment trusts are, by and large, treated in exactly the same way as shareholders in any other listed company. However, there are certain tax issues which arise which can be seen as largely unique to investment trusts owing to the types of investment opportunity they offer (eg warrants, split capital structures etc) or by the way in which such investments are bought (eg regular monthly contributions to an Investment Trust Savings and Investment Schemes).

Split capital investment trusts

14.2 As mentioned in the earlier discussion on the tax position of investment trusts (see CHAPTER 7) the shares of split capital investment trusts have been popular with private investors and offer some tax planning opportunities. The main types of share available, and their tax treatment, are as follows:

- zero dividend preference shares ('zeros') – shares which offer a predetermined capital return payable out of the assets of the trust on liquidation. Any gain on such shares is normally subject to capital gains tax.

- income shares – shares which offer a high level of income during the life of the trust, payable out of the income generated by the trust's investments, and sometimes a predetermined return of capital (eg a return of the initial

355

invested capital) on liquidation. Any dividends on such shares are treated as Schedule F income and any gain or loss on the sale of the shares is subject to capital gains tax (however see analysis at **14.4** below in respect of annuity income shares).

- capital shares – shares which receive the balance of any sum remaining on liquidation after the payment to other classes of shareholder. Any gains on such shares are subject to capital gains tax.

From a personal tax perspective, it is easy to see why split capital shares have been popular, as they enable different types of return to be 'matched' to an individual's particular tax position. For example, it is quite common for UK higher rate income taxpayers not to fully utilise their annual capital gains tax exemption. Such investors can therefore be attracted to invest an amount in zeros so that, on redemption, a capital gain roughly equal to the annual exemption would arise. Non, lower and basic rate taxpayers (perhaps also in retirement) might be more attracted to income shares, where the tax credit would settle any UK income tax liability.

14.3   The tax position of zeros is worthy of further comment. Prior to the late 1990s, these shares were perceived as being extremely low risk and, before the beginning of the new millennium, no zero had failed to pay its predetermined redemption amount. They were therefore often considered to have characteristics similar to gilts and certainly it was true that their values were often more heavily influenced by movements in interest rates than by consideration of, say, the composition of the underlying portfolio.

There was, therefore, consideration given by the UK Government, at the time of the introduction of what became the loan relationship legislation in *FA 1996*, as to whether the returns on zeros should be taxed as income. Eventually it was decided that the loan relationship legislation should not extend to equities and the recent problems experienced by some highly-geared split capital trusts (where some zeros have failed to pay back anything to investors) have demonstrated that zeros are equities and that the predetermined redemption value is not guaranteed.

The commentary below assumes that the shareholder (or warrant holder) is a UK resident individual.

Annuity income shares

14.4   The term 'annuity income share' is a colloquial term used to refer to a specific form of income share issued by split capital investment trusts. The shares are normally entitled to substantially all the income from the investment trust's assets and their issue price is significantly greater than their future redemption value, which is fixed and normally of a nominal amount. As such, on redemption a loss arises to the individual, being the difference between the issue price and the redemption price. The question arises as to whether this loss is also a capital loss which could be used by the investor to offset against other capital gains.

The main reason why relief may be denied for the loss arising is due to the affect of the wasting asset provisions of *TCGA 1992, s 46*. *Section 46* states that in computing the capital gain on disposal of a wasting asset, the base cost of the asset allowable as a deduction is calculated by the following formula:

$$C - \frac{T \times (C-R)}{L}$$

where:

L is the predictable life of the asset,

T is the length of time between the acquisition and disposal of the asset,

R is the predictable residual value of the asset at the end of its predictable life, and

C is the acquisition cost of the asset

Therefore for the normal annuity income share held to redemption the above formula would reduce the allowable cost to a minimal amount or to nil.

EXAMPLE 14.4

A shareholder subscribes for 10,000 annuity income shares with a nominal value of £1 each, for which the shareholder pays £10,000. The shares will be redeemed in 10 years time at 1 penny per share and the shareholder holds the shares until redemption.

If the wasting asset provisions apply then the shareholder's capital gains position would be:

	£
Redemption proceeds (10,000 x 1p)	100
Base cost:	
$£1 - \dfrac{10 \times (£1 - 1p)}{10} \times 10,000 =$	(100)
Capital gain/loss	NIL

If the wasting asset provisions did not apply then the shareholder would have a capital loss equal to redemption proceeds less original cost (ie £100 – £10,000 = £9,900).

14.5 A wasting asset is defined as 'an asset with a predictable life not exceeding 50 years' (*TCGA 1992, s 44(1)*). There is no provision in the legislation precluding shares from falling within the definition, although most shares do not have a predictable life.

The legislation also states (*TCGA 1992, s 44(3)*) that:

357

'The question what is the predictable life of an asset, and the question what is its predictable residual or scrap value at the end of that life, if any, shall, so far as those questions are not immediately answered by the nature of the asset, be taken, in relation to any disposal of the asset, as they were known or ascertainable at the time when the asset was acquired or provided by the person making the disposal.'

In guidance to its members, the AITC concluded that, whilst the wasting asset legislation was clearly never originally intended to apply to shares, there is nothing in the tax legislation which prevents it applying to shares. The Inland Revenue indicated, and the AITC agreed, that the question of whether or not an annuity income share is a wasting asset can only be determined on the individual facts of each case.

14.6   The difficulty in deciding whether an annuity income share has a predictable life of less than 50 years stems from the fact that, whilst the investment trust issuing them may have a planned life of, say, 10 years (after which the company will normally be wound up) the shareholders may have the right, at least in theory, to extend the life of the investment trust and hence the life of the annuity income shares. In other words, this ability to extend the life of the company means that one cannot say with certainty that the predictable life of the annuity income share is less than 50 years. The Revenue's point of view, however, is that 'certain' and 'predictable' are not the same thing.

In addition, where a company is liquidated but shareholders are provided with replacement shares or units in another investment vehicle, such that the capital gains roll-over provisions apply, then those shares or securities are treated as the same asset as the original shares (*TCGA 1992, s 127*). Therefore, the fact that the investment trust itself only has a predictable life of 10 years does not necessarily mean that, for the purposes of capital gains tax, the shares in that company also have a predictable life of less than 50 years, as they could continue to exist as shares in a different company for many years to come.

Warrants

14.7   A warrant is a form of option which confers a right, but not the obligation, to the warrant holder to subscribe for new shares in an investment trust at a fixed price at some time within a limited future period. Warrants are normally issued 'free' as a 'sweetener' to the original subscribers for the shares of the investment trust in proportion to the amount of shares that are subscribed for (eg on a one warrant for five shares basis). After the initial allotment of the shares and warrants, they are separately traded on the London Stock Exchange.

As warrants themselves do not give rise to income during the period of ownership, investors in warrants will only potentially be subject to tax when a disposal arises for UK tax purposes. Essentially there are four different ways in which warrant holders can become divested of their warrants. The warrants can be:

(a) sold in the open market;

(b) exercised;

(c) abandoned; or

(d) bought back by the company.

Sale

14.8   The sale of a warrant in the open market is a normal disposal for capital gains tax purposes. However, as the warrant is issued 'free' with the shares, the first question that arises is what the base cost of the warrant is for capital gains tax purposes. The Inland Revenue take the view that *TCGA 1992, s 43* applies and that a warrant is an example of an asset where the value of the asset (the warrant) is derived from an asset in the same ownership (the other shares issued). In such cases it is necessary to split the total cost of acquiring the shares and warrants in a 'just and reasonable' way. Under current Inland Revenue practice, the total subscription proceeds are normally apportioned between the shares and warrants by reference to the relative market values of the shares and warrants when they are first traded separately.

EXAMPLE 14.8

An investment trust issues shares for £1 and warrants on a one warrant for five share basis. The market value of the shares and warrants on the first day that they are traded separately are 95p and 15p. The total amount subscribed for each batch of five shares and one warrant is £5. However, for capital gains tax purposes this will have to be apportioned between the shares and warrants as follows:

Market value of shares 5×95p=	475
Market value of warrant=	15
Total	490p
Base cost of shares=(475/490×500)/5=	97p
Base cost of warrant= (15/490×500)=	15p

When calculating the capital gain on the disposal of a warrant, the full base cost as calculated above is taken into account regardless of how far into the 'life' of the warrant the sale takes place. This is because a warrant is excluded from the wasting assets provisions (*TCGA 1992, 146(1)*).

Exercise

14.9   On the exercise of a warrant the warrant holder will have to subscribe an additional amount for the issue of the share. The exercise of a warrant is not a disposal for capital gains tax purposes (*TCGA 1992, s 144(3)*). On disposal of the share issued as a result of exercising the warrant, the base cost of the share for capital gains tax purposes will be the total of the amount treated as the warrant's base cost on the original subscription (ie 15p in the above example) plus the additional amount subscribed for the share.

Abandonment

14.10   Usually warrants can only be exercised for a fixed period of time. If during that period the quoted share price of the investment trust does not rise above the amount the warrant holder has to subscribe on exercise of the warrant, it would not be logical for the investor to exercise his warrant. When a warrant is abandoned the investor will realise a capital loss equal to the base cost attributed to it on the original subscription for shares (*TCGA 1992, s 144(4)*).

Buy-back

14.11   As the section below on the tax treatment of share buy-backs sets out (see **14.20**), the tax treatment of a buy-back of a financial instrument can change depending on whether the transaction is carried out 'on market' or 'off market'.

Essentially there are two possibilities:

(a)   that the buy-back is a distribution (at least in part) by the company and assessable as Schedule F income; or

(b)   that the buy-back is simply another type of disposal for capital gains tax purposes and therefore is subject to the usual rules for disposals.

If the share buy-back is conducted 'on market' then, as with share buy-backs, the investor will be subject to capital gains treatment. If, however, the company makes a direct offer for the warrants, then the question arises, as is the case with shares, whether Schedule F income may arise.

14.12   The rules governing whether a buy back of warrants amounts to a qualifying distribution for Schedule F purposes are covered by *ICTA 1988, s 209*. The AITC had call to consider this question from the company's perspective when the question was raised as to whether a buy-back of warrants gave rise to a distribution on which advance corporation tax (ACT) was potentially payable. Although ACT has been abolished, the issues raised in determining whether a buy back of warrants is a distribution on which ACT is payable are the same as for whether a buy back of warrants could give rise to Schedule F income.

In order to be a qualifying distribution, a buy-back of warrants would have to be either:

(a)   a distribution in respect of shares, except so much as is equal to any new consideration received by the company (*ICTA 1988, s 209(2)(b)*); or

(b) a transfer of assets by a company to its members where the value of the benefit received by the member exceeds the amount of any new consideration given by the member (*ICTA 1988, s 209(4)*).

14.13 Following a consultation with tax counsel, the AITC advised its members that it considered that:

(a) a buy-back of warrants by an investment trust is not a distribution under general law;

(b) even if a buy-back of warrants is a distribution, it is not a distribution in respect of shares;

(c) even if a buy-back of warrants is a distribution in respect of shares, new consideration (ie the warrant holder giving up the right to acquire new shares in the investment trust) is received by the investment trust; and

(d) to the extent that a buy-back of warrants is a transfer of assets (ie cash) by an investment trust to its members, new consideration (again, the giving up of the right to acquire new shares in the investment trust) is given by the members.

As a result, it is considered that the buy-back of warrants should be treated as a capital gains tax event.

Taper relief and investment trust savings schemes

14.14 Although investment trust savings schemes offer investors a convenient mechanism to purchase small regular (normally monthly) amounts of investment trust shares, the mechanics of the UK tax system has not been particular accommodating to investors faced with calculating their UK capital gains position on disposal of shares acquired through such schemes. Under the previous system of indexation, although some attempts have been made to simplify the process (eg SP 2/99), for most private investors such calculations remain a daunting task.

The change from a system of indexation allowance to a system of taper relief has, if anything, further complicated the position and therefore the AITC issued a guide to explain the problems that arise and to show how the calculations can be simplified to some extent. This guide is reproduced in full below. However, it is known that some investors choose to hold their investment trust shares in, for example, Individual Savings Accounts, even though it is extremely unlikely that they would ever have to pay capital gains tax, simply to avoid the potential problems of performing the calculations if required to do so.

A Basic Guide to the Calculation of Capital Gains on an Investment Trust Savings Scheme

14.15 This Guide shows you the basic way to work out capital gains arising on a sale of investment trust shares if you acquired them by saving regular amounts through an Investment Trust Savings Scheme ('Savings Scheme').

Introduction

14.16   The principles set out below should only be taken to apply to disposals of shares of investment trusts acquired through Savings Schemes started after 6 April 1999. Before this date, shares may be subject to the previous indexation rules. If you acquired shares before this date, the Inland Revenue's *Statement of Practice SP2/99 Monthly savings in investment funds* has more details on how you should calculate capital gains on these shares. This Statement of Practice is contained in the Inland Revenue's document *IR 131 Statements of Practice* which is available on the Inland Revenue's website at www.inlandrevenue. gov.uk/leaflets/c13.htm.

More general information on how to calculate capital gains and your capital gains tax liability is also available in the Inland Revenue's booklet *CGT1: Capital Gains Tax*. This is available on the Inland Revenue's Website at www.inlandrevenue.gov.uk/leaflets/c4.htm or can be obtained from Inland Revenue Tax Enquiry Centres and Tax Offices.

Basic principles

14.17   In the days of indexation, there was a special concessionary basis for calculating capital gains on shares acquired through Savings Schemes (see SP 2/99 for more details). With the introduction of taper relief and the cessation of indexation, these special rules are no longer required and the calculation of taper relief follows the same rules as for shares acquired in lump sums.

In order to work out your capital gains on shares, and any taper relief that is available, the first two things you need to know are:

- Which shares you are selling out of the 'pool' of shares that you have built up over time.

- How long you have held those particular shares.

Identifying shares

14.18   The basic rule for identifying which shares you have sold is what is sometimes referred to as 'LIFO', which stands for 'Last In First Out'. In other words, you are treated as having sold first the shares you acquired most recently.

Holding period

14.19   Once you have identified which shares you have sold, you then have to work out how long you have held them. This is because taper relief rewards long-term ownership of assets by reducing the amount of the gain you make on the shares.

Number of whole years in holding period	Percentage of gain chargeable
Less than 1 year	100
1	100
2	100
3	95
4	90
5	85
6	80
7	75
8	70
9	65
10 or more	60

It is worth noting that, unless you hold the shares for a full three years, you will not be entitled to any taper relief at all. Therefore, unless you wait at least three full years from the last purchase of shares in your Savings Scheme before you sell, you will not receive any taper relief on some or all of the shares (remember the LIFO rules).

In addition, 'part years' do not count, so if you are thinking of selling shares 4 years and 11 months after acquiring them, it may be worth waiting a few extra weeks to reduce your capital gain by a further 5%. However, you are taking a chance on what will happen in the stock market while you wait.

EXAMPLE 14.19

Jane starts up a Savings Scheme in January 2001 and invests £200 per month into the shares of a capital growth investment trust that pays no dividends. Contributions are invested on the 25th of each month. Jane stops contributing to the scheme after three years. On 31 March 2006 she decides that she needs to raise £10,000 so she sells 4,724 shares at a share price of £2.12.

[Note: the example ignores stamp duty and other costs that may be payable on the purchase or sale of shares.]

Jane – Purchases through Savings Scheme

Month	Price	Shares	Cost
	(£)		(£)
Jan 01	1.00	200	200.00
Feb 01	1.02	196	199.92
Mar 01	1.03	194	199.82
Apr 01	1.03	194	199.82
May 01	1.05	190	199.50
Jun 01	1.07	187	200.09
Jul 01	1.06	189	200.34
Aug 01	1.06	189	200.34
Sep 01	1.09	183	199.47
Oct 01	1.10	182	200.20
Nov 01	1.13	177	200.01
Dec 01	1.12	179	200.48
Jan 02	1.12	178	199.36
Feb 02	1.10	182	200.20
Mar 02	1.09	183	199.47
Apr 02	1.11	181	200.91
May 02	1.13	177	200.01
Jun 02	1.15	173	198.95
Jul 02	1.16	173	200.68
Aug 02	1.14	175	199.50
Sep 02	1.13	177	200.01
Oct 02	1.16	173	200.68
Nov 02	1.19	168	199.92
Dec 02	1.21	165	199.65
Jan 03	1.25	160	200.00
Feb 03	1.20	167	200.40
Mar 03	1.19	168	199.92
Apr 03	1.18	169	199.42
May 03	1.20	167	200.40
Jun 03	1.24	161	199.64
Jul 03	1.27	158	200.66
Aug 03	1.26	158	199.08
Sep 03	1.28	157	200.96
Oct 03	1.30	153	198.90
Nov 03	1.34	150	201.00
Dec 03	1.35	148	199.80
Total		6,281	£7,199.51

The first step is to identify the shares that have been sold. As mentioned above, we have to use a LIFO basis for this, so we count up shares back from December 2003 until we reach 4,724 shares. Conveniently, these are all the shares acquired from September 2001 onwards.

Having done this, we now need to sort these 4,274 shares into batches by reference to whole years leading up to the date of sale (ie the years from 1 April to 31 March leading up to 31 March 2006). We divide up the 4,724 shares according to which of these periods they were acquired in to give the following:

Period	Number of Shares Acquired	Total Cost
1 Apr 05 to 31 Mar 06	NIL	NIL
1 Apr 04 to 31 Mar 05	NIL	NIL
1 Apr 03 to 31 Mar 04	1,421	£1,799.86
1 Apr 02 to 31 Mar 03	2,057	£2,400.63
1 Apr 01 to 31 Mar 02	1,264	£1,399.19
Total	4,742	£5,599.68

We can now start to work out the capital gains on each of these batches of shares.

1 April 2003 to 31 March 2004

These 1,421 shares have all been held for a period of less than three years when Jane comes to sell them. They therefore receive no taper relief.

The capital gain is therefore:

Proceeds	
(1,421 shares at £2.12 per share)	£3,012.52
Less cost	(£1,799.86)
Capital gain	**£1,212.66**

1 April 2002 to 31 March 2003

These 2,057 shares have all been held for a period of more than three years but less than four years when Jane comes to sell them. Therefore only 95% of the gain made on the shares will be chargeable.

The capital gain is therefore:

Proceeds	
(2,057 shares at £2.12 per share)	£4,360.84
Less cost	(£2,400.63)
Gain	£1,960.21
Capital gain (£1,960.21×95%)	**£1,862.20**

1 April 2001 to 31 March 2002

These 1,264 shares have all been held for a period of more than four years but less than five years when Jane comes to sell them. Therefore only 90% of the gain will be chargeable.

The capital gain is therefore:

Proceeds	
(1,264 shares at £2.12 per share)	£2,679.68
Less cost	(1,399.19)
Gain	£1,280.49
Capital gain (£1,280.49×90%)	**£1,152.44**

Finally, all you have to do is add up all the gains to arrive at the total capital gain on the sale of the shares:

$$
\begin{array}{rr}
& £1,212.66 \\
& £1,862.20 \\
& £1,152.44 \\
\hline
\textbf{Total capital gain} & \textbf{£4,227.30} \\
\hline
\end{array}
$$

Whether there will be any capital gains tax to pay, of course, will depend on Jane's personal tax position (eg whether she has made other capital gains or losses in the year).

Share buy-backs

14.20   Share buy-backs have become increasingly common since the abolition of advance corporation tax in 1999 removed any tax cost to the company (other than stamp duty). Share buy-backs are viewed as a means of helping, by reducing the supply of shares on the market, to reduce the discount at which the price of an investment trust share normally trades below its net asset value per share.

From the private investor's perspective there are two possible tax treatments that could apply to a private shareholder on a share buy-back:

- the shareholder will be treated as having made a normal capital gains tax disposal; or

- a 'distribution treatment' will arise, under which part of the proceeds received by the shareholder will be treated as Schedule F income.

Where the distribution treatment applies, the shareholder is treated as effectively receiving net UK dividend income equal to the difference between the price paid for the share on the buy-back and the original subscription price (not the price paid for the shares).

As the example below shows, the question of which treatment applies can make a significant difference depending on the tax position of the shareholder.

EXAMPLE 14.20

ABC Investment Trust plc, whose shares were issued at £1 per share, decides to buy back some of its shares. The buy-back price is set at £10. Mr Smith bought his shares in ABC Investment Trust plc one year ago for £9.

If a capital gains treatment applies (ignoring indexation, taper and other potential reliefs) Mr Smith will be subject to capital gains tax on his gain of £1 per share. If the distribution treatment applies, Mr Smith will be treated as receiving dividend income of £9 per share (ie £10 less the original issue price of £1). This dividend income will carry with it a tax credit of £1.

If Mr Smith is a higher rate taxpayer (and the shares are not held in a PEP/ISA), he is faced with either a potential capital gains tax liability of up to 40p per share (40% x £1), or an income tax liability of up to £2.25 per share (£9 dividend income plus £1 tax credit = £10 taxable income x 32.5% = £3.25 less £1 tax credit = £2.25).

In other words, Mr Smith could end up making a profit of £1 on the sale of his shares and end up paying £2.25 in income tax. In such circumstances, however, Mr Smith would be entitled to a capital loss of £8 per share (£1 return of capital less cost of £9).

The Inland Revenue's Manual gives guidance on this issue as follows (CT1756):

'Shares which are...in the official list of the Stock Exchange...will normally pass through the hands of a market maker in those shares.

The market maker acts as principal. Where such a company purchases its own shares there are two stages in the sale:

- the shareholder sells to the market maker then

- the market maker sells to the company...

Exceptionally, the shareholder and the company may not pass the shares through the hands of a market maker. Instead, they may use a broker to execute the transaction ... In these circumstances the shareholder has sold the shares direct to the company. As a result, the distribution provisions will apply...However, usually the company will use a market maker. The shareholder will sell the shares to the market maker, rather than the company. Hence, the shareholder does not receive a distribution.'

Therefore, if the investment trust conducts an 'on market' share buy-back, investors selling their shares back to the company (who will not know, of course, that they are doing so) will be subject to capital gains tax. On the other hand, a tender offer, under which the investment trust makes a direct offer to shareholders to buy back a proportion of their shares, may give rise to Schedule F income.

15   Venture Capital Trusts

Philip Hare

PricewaterhouseCoopers LLP

Investors' tax reliefs

15.1   To encourage investment in VCTs there are four important tax breaks available to personal investors who are aged 18 or over.

'Front-end' tax reliefs

15.2

- income tax relief of up to 20% of the investment (see **15.5** below); and
- deferral of capital gains (see **15.10** below).

These reliefs are only available to investors who subscribe for new ordinary shares in a VCT and can have a significant impact on the return of an investment.

Other reliefs

15.3

- dividend exemption, where dividends received in respect of ordinary shares in a VCT are exempt from income tax (see **15.18** below); and
- exemption from capital gains tax on disposal of ordinary shares in a VCT ('disposal relief') (see **15.19** below).

These reliefs are available to both purchasers and subscribers alike.

All the tax reliefs mentioned above are available on the first £100,000 invested by an investor in a tax year in one or more VCTs. There is a general requirement that the shares are acquired for bona fide commercial purposes and not as part of an arrangement for the avoidance of tax.

15.4   Where shares are acquired in excess of the permitted maximum of £100,000 per tax year:

- shares acquired on a later date are allocated to the excess before those acquired earlier;
- if shares in different VCTs are acquired on the same day, the excess is apportioned to each holding based on their respective values.

Those shares acquired in excess of the permitted maximum do not attract tax reliefs.

'Front-end' income tax relief

Description of relief

15.5 When an individual subscribes for eligible shares in a VCT, he is entitled to income tax relief for the year in which the shares are issued to him. The maximum subscription in one or more VCTs available for relief in any one tax year is £100,000.

To be 'eligible' shares, the shares have to be new ordinary shares, which throughout the three-year period beginning on the date of issue, have no preferential rights to dividends or assets on a winding up, nor any rights of redemption. For shares issued before 6 April 2000, the period is five years.

15.6 Income tax relief is available at the lower rate of tax, which for 2003/04 is 20% (and has been for a number of years). The relief is restricted to an amount which reduces the individual's income tax liability for the year to nil. The individual's income tax liability is the amount calculated before:

- Enterprise Investment Scheme income tax relief;

- personal allowances;

- relief for certain types of interest paid;

- double tax relief; and

- tax deducted at source on charges on income.

EXAMPLE 15.6

George, whose only income is salary of £15,000 in the 2003/04 tax year, subscribes for 12,000 eligible £1 shares in an approved VCT. His tax computation is:

Salary	15,000
Less: personal allowance	4,615
Taxable income	10,385
Tax payable:	
1,960 @ 10%	196
8,425 @ 22%	1,853.50
	2,049.50
Less: income tax relief in respect of VCT subscription	
20% of £12,000 (restricted)	2,049.50
Net tax payable	–

Eligibility

15.7   The initial relief is only available to individuals who are at least 18 years of age and subscribe for shares on their own behalf. Therefore, relief is not available to institutional investors, trustees or where subscriptions are made in a nominee arrangement. However shares can subsequently be transferred to a nominee, provided that the individual retains beneficial ownership of the shares.

The shares must be subscribed for and issued for bona fide commercial reasons, and not as part of a scheme to avoid tax.

There is no requirement for the individual to be UK resident. However since this tax relief is dependent on income tax being payable, it is necessary that the individual has some UK income tax liability against which to set the relief.

15.8   In order to retain the relief, the individual must meet certain conditions during the 'relevant period'; this is the period beginning two years before the share issue (or if later, beginning on the date of incorporation of the VCT) and ending three years after the share issue. For shares issued before 6 April 2000, the period ends five years after the share issue.

A VCT must issue the subscriber with a certificate of investment. With this certificate, the investor can make a claim in his tax return for the year of subscription. If the claim is not made on the tax return, the claim must be made in writing within five years of 31 January following the end of the tax year in which the subscription was made. If the subscription is made early in the tax year, an investor in employment can ask his Inspector of Taxes to adjust his notice of PAYE coding so that relief is obtained during the current tax year.

Pitfalls

15.9   Relief will not be available if the individual subscribing for the shares has no UK income tax liability, perhaps due to his being non-resident, or his having losses.

Income tax relief is only available for VCT shares acquired within the £100,000 limit, and acquisitions (whether by subscription or purchase) count towards the limit in order of acquisition – the investor cannot choose. Therefore, if an individual has purchased existing shares in a VCT, or subscribed for VCT shares under a nominee arrangement, they will count towards his £100,000 annual limit, even though no income tax relief is available in respect of those shares. His ability to claim income tax relief and deferral relief in respect of later subscriptions may therefore be affected.

Relief will be withdrawn if within the relevant period:

● the individual disposes of the shares; or

371

- the individual subscriber or his associate is advanced a loan which would not have been advanced to him had he not subscribed (or planned to subscribe) for the VCT shares.

Capital gains deferral relief

Description of relief

15.10   Investors who subscribe for shares in a VCT can defer capital gains of the amount of their subscription up to the permitted maximum of £100,000 per tax year.

Eligibility

Gains and time limit

15.11   Gains which can be deferred are those arising from actual disposals, or crystallised gains which were previously deferred under the VCT or Enterprise Investment Scheme. The gain must arise within twelve months of (before or after) the date of subscription of the new VCT shares.

Upon obtaining a certificate from the VCT the investor can make a deferral relief claim. The claim is made in the tax return for the year in which the gain arises. If that return has already been filed, a claim can be made in writing. In any event, the claim must be made within five years of the 31 January following the tax year in which the subscription is made.

Individuals

15.12   In order for deferral relief to be available, investors must have obtained income tax relief on their investment. Therefore investors must:

- be at least 18 years of age; and
- have a UK income tax liability in the year of subscription.

In addition, they must also be resident in the UK for tax purposes both at the time of the disposal which gave rise to the gain to be deferred, and also at the time of subscription for the VCT shares.

It is important to note that it is the gain *before the application of taper relief* which is deferred. Any entitlement to taper relief on the original gain is applied when the gain eventually crystallises.

Investments

15.13 The investment in a VCT must be a subscription for new eligible shares (see **15.5** above). The investor must subscribe for the shares on their own behalf, and not through a nominee.

Commentary on gains coming back into charge

15.14 The deferred gain will crystallise on a 'chargeable event', which includes:

- Disposal of the VCT shares (other than to the investor's spouse). A disposal also includes the instance where the shares are exchanged for other shares or securities (except where the shares are exchanged for shares in another VCT in certain circumstances (see below));

- The investor ceasing to be resident in the UK during the relevant period (unless under a contract of full-time employment abroad, and the investor becomes resident in the UK again within three years having held the VCT shares throughout that time);

- The VCT ceasing to be approved as a VCT; or

- The income tax relief is withdrawn for a reason other than those stated above.

The crystallised gain will be chargeable to capital gains tax at the prevailing rate at the date of crystallisation, not at the date at which it originally arose. This may mean that the gain is covered by losses or the annual exemption which may not have been available at the time of the original gain. Any entitlement to taper relief for the original gain is given at the time the gain crystallises, and at the rate applicable at the time of the original gain.

The crystallised deferred gain (before taper relief) can be reinvested by subscribing for shares in a VCT or under the Enterprise Investment Scheme within the time limits applicable to each scheme based on the date of crystallisation.

15.15 Where only some of the VCT shares are disposed of, the capital gain which crystallises is that which has been deferred against the shares disposed of.

Where VCT shares have been acquired on different days, those acquired earlier are deemed to be disposed of first. Where shares have been acquired on the same day, and some of those shares have gains deferred against them, then on a disposal, the shares which do not have gains deferred against them are deemed to have been disposed of first.

Where shares in a VCT are exchanged for shares in another VCT such that the merger provisions of *FA 2002, Sch 33* are satisfied, the exchange will not be treated as a disposal, and so the capital gains deferral will be preserved.

Interaction with disposal relief

15.16   Although a disposal of VCT shares acquired within the annual £100,000 limit is exempt from capital gains tax, investors should note that the previously deferred capital gain will crystallise. Therefore a deferred gain can crystallise where there is a sale or an exchange of shares (except for a qualifying exchange for shares in another VCT).

Problem areas

15.17   Where investors subscribe for in excess of £100,000 for shares in one or more VCTs in a tax year, the ability to defer gains may be restricted. Investors have no choice as to which shares represent the excess; shares acquired later in the tax year are treated as being the excess, and so do not attract relief. In such situations, the only gains which can be deferred are those which arise within twelve months of the earlier subscriptions which fall within the £100,000 limit. It may not be possible to defer later capital gains using VCT investments unless there is a further subscription in the next tax year.

EXAMPLE 15.17

Eleanor subscribed for shares in an approved VCT as follows: £40,000 on 10 April 2003 and £75,000 on 10 August 2003. On 15 May 2004 she incurs a capital gain of £80,000 (before taper relief) on the disposal of property. The subscription on 10 April 2003 cannot be used to defer the capital gain. Only £60,000 of the subscription on 10 August 2003 qualifies for deferral relief and the remaining £20,000 gain cannot be deferred unless Eleanor makes a further subscription in an approved VCT of at least £20,000 by 14 May 2005.

Dividend exemption

15.18   Dividends received by individual investors in a VCT are exempt from income tax provided that:

- the dividend is paid out of capital or revenue in respect of an accounting period at the end of which the company was a VCT;

- the shares on which the dividend is paid are ordinary shares which the individual acquired when the company was a VCT and when the individual was at least 18 years old; and

- The shares were acquired (whether by subscription or purchase) within the annual £100,000 permitted limit.

Investors are not required to include the dividends received on their annual tax return.

This tax relief is not available to institutional investors.

Disposal relief

Description of relief

15.19   Capital gains arising on the disposal by individuals of ordinary shares in a VCT are exempt from capital gains tax. Losses are not allowable.

Eligibility

15.20   Disposal relief is available to individual investors who have acquired their shares when aged 18 or above and within the annual £100,000 limit, whether by subscription or purchase.

The VCT must be a VCT both at the time of acquisition and disposal of the shares.

Share identification rules regarding disposals

15.21   Where there is a disposal of VCT shares, and either:

● shares have been acquired on different days; or

● shares have been acquired in excess of the annual permitted maximum,

it is necessary to identify which of the shares are disposed of first. The identification rules help preserve income tax relief and capital gains deferral relief where this has been claimed. The general rule is that shares acquired on an earlier date are disposed of first.

15.22   For shares acquired on the same day, those acquired in excess of the permitted maximum are treated as disposed of before other shares acquired on that day. If any shares were acquired before the company was approved as a VCT, they are treated as disposed of before any other shares in the company.

Gains which are exempt need not be reported on the individual's annual tax return.

EXAMPLE 15.22

Jonathan makes the following acquisitions of VCT shares during 2003/04:

15 April 2003	North VCT plc	Subscription 30,000 shares for £30,000
15 June 2003	North VCT plc	Purchase 50,000 shares for £60,000
15 June 2003	South VCT plc	Subscription 40,000 shares for £40,000

The purchase on 15 April is wholly within the £100,000 limit. Of the acquisitions made on 15 June, £30,000 is in excess of the limit. This is apportioned as follows: £18,000 (6/10ths×£30,000), ie 15,000 shares to the North VCT plc shares, and £12,000 (4/10ths×£30,000), ie 12,000 shares to the South VCT plc shares.

If Jonathan sells 55,000 shares in North VCT plc on 7 November 2004 for £88,000, he is deemed to sell 30,000 shares acquired on 15 April 2003 and 25,000 shares acquired on 15 June 2003. Of these 25,000 shares, 15,000 are deemed to be those acquired in excess of the £100,000 limit and are treated as disposed of first.

Jonathan's taxable capital gain (before annual exemption) is as follows:

Proceeds (15/55ths×£88,000)	24,000
Base cost	18,000
Capital gain	6,000

Where shares in a VCT are exchanged for shares in another VCT such that the merger provisions of *FA 2002, Sch 33* are satisfied, the exchange will not be treated as a disposal, and so the capital gains exemption will be preserved.

Effect on investors of loss of approval by the VCT

15.23   If a VCT loses its approval, having first obtained full approval, the investors' tax reliefs are withdrawn as follows:

- Upfront income tax relief – if approval is lost within the investor's relevant period, the income tax relief is withdrawn from the date of loss of approval.

- Dividend exemption – dividends paid in respect of periods where the VCT is not approved will be subject to income tax.

- Disposal relief – investors will be deemed to have disposed of their VCT shares at the date of loss of approval. Any gain will be exempt from capital gains tax and any loss is not allowable. Gains or losses from that date are subject to capital gains tax in the usual way.

- Capital gains deferral relief – the deferred gain will crystallise at the date of loss of approval.

15.24   If a VCT obtains provisional approval, and does not obtain full approval, the investors' tax reliefs are withdrawn as follows:

- Upfront income tax relief – the income tax relief is withdrawn in full, and treated as if it were never due. There will be a charge to interest on overdue tax.

- Dividend exemption – all dividends received will be subject to income tax.

- Disposal relief – disposal relief is not due and any gains or losses are subject to capital gains tax in the usual way.

- Capital gains deferral relief – the gain deferred is treated as if it had not been deferred. Interest on overdue tax may arise.

Death of investor

15.25 The death of an investor does not trigger withdrawal of any of the tax reliefs, even if death occurs before the end of the relevant period. The income tax relief is not clawed back, and any deferred gain does not crystallise.

Since VCT shares are quoted, they do not qualify for Business Property Relief for inheritance tax purposes.

The beneficiary inheriting the VCT shares is treated as though he purchased them at the market value at the date of death of the previous investor. Therefore, provided that he is aged at least 18 years of age and has acquired them within the annual permitted £100,000 limit, he is entitled to dividend exemption and disposal relief as detailed above. Any gain that was previously deferred by the original investor effectively disappears.

16 Taxation of Holders of Life Policies

Chris Marshall

Legal & General

Onshore life policies

16.1   This section deals with the taxation of holders of onshore life policies – that is those where the insurer is a UK company. The tax treatment largely depends on whether the policy is qualifying or not, the qualifying rules being set out in the *ICTA 1988, Sch 15*.

Broadly speaking for a qualifying policy there will be no tax liability on a payout unless it is surrendered in the first ten years. Most regular premium policies are qualifying. For non-qualifying policies (virtually all single premium ones) most payments are potentially subject to income tax at the higher rate less basic rate. The following sections expound the details.

Qualifying policies

16.2   To be a qualifying policy the policy must meet all the following tests which differ according to the type of policy.

Endowment policies

16.3

(a)   The policy must secure a capital sum payable on survival to the end of the term, or earlier death (or disability). Other benefits may be included, except those of a capital nature payable before death, disability, or survival. Surrenders and bonus encashments are ignored for this purpose.

(b)   Premiums must be payable at annual, or shorter, intervals for at least ten years, or until earlier death (or disability). The term of the policy must be at least ten years.

(c)   The total premiums payable in any one year must not exceed twice the total premiums payable in any other year.

(d)   The total premiums payable in any year must not exceed one-eighth of the total premiums payable over the whole term.

(e)   The sum assured on death must be at least 75% of the total premiums payable if the policy ran for its full term. Where the sum assured is payable by instalments, the total of the instalments is used for this purpose, rather than any cash alternative which might be offered by the office on maturity. However if a cash option is quoted in the policy then this is taken instead. For policies effected on or after 1 April 1976, the 75% is reduced by 2% for each year by which the age of the life assured at outset exceeds 55.

Whole life policies

16.4

(a)   The policy must secure a capital sum on death (or on death or earlier disability) and no other benefits. Participation in profits, surrender values, annuity options, increasability options, waiver of premiums on disability, and disability benefits of a capital nature do not count as other benefits.

(b)   Premiums must be payable at annual, or shorter, intervals for at least ten years, or until earlier death (or disability).

(c)   The total premiums payable in any one year must not exceed twice the total premiums payable in any other year.

(d)   The total premiums payable in any one year must not exceed one-eighth of the total premiums payable over the whole term (or over the first ten years where premiums are payable throughout life).

(e)   For policies effected on or after 1 April 1976 the capital sum on death must not be less than 75% of the premiums which would be payable if death were to occur on the life assured's 75th birthday. Where the sum assured can be paid as a lump sum or as a series of sums, the rule will operate on the smallest total payable.

Term assurance policies – over ten years

16.5

(a)   The policy must secure a capital sum on death (or on death or earlier disability) and no other benefits. Participation in profits, surrender values, annuity options, increasability options, waiver of premiums on disability, and disability benefits of a capital nature do not count as other benefits.

(b)   Premiums must be payable at annual or shorter intervals for at least ten years, or three-quarters of the term, whichever is the shorter.

(c)   The total premiums payable in any one year must not exceed twice the total premiums payable in any other year.

(d)   The total premiums payable in any one year must not exceed one-eighth of the total premiums payable over the whole term.

(e)   For policies effected on or after 1 April 1976, the capital sum on death must be not less than 75% of the premiums which would be payable if death were to occur on the life assured's 75th birthday. Where the sum assured can be paid as a lump sum or as a series of sums, the rule will operate on the smallest total payable. However, a term assurance which has no surrender value, and which does not run beyond age 75, is exempted from this rule

Term assurance policies – ten years or less

16.6

(a) The policy must secure a capital sum on death (or on death or earlier disability) and no other benefits. Participation in profits, surrender values, annuity options, increasability options, waiver of premiums on disability and disability benefits of a capital nature do not count as other benefits.

(b) The policy must provide that any surrender value must not exceed the premiums paid.

(c) The term must not be less than one year.

Joint life policies

16.7 When applying the 75% rule for whole life and term assurances to joint life policies, the 75th birthday to be used is as follows:

(a) Joint life first death policy, the older life;

(b) Joint life second death, the younger life.

Friendly society policies

16.8 The qualifying rules are modified for friendly society tax-exempt policies issued (or varied) on or after 19 March 1985. The policy must be for a term of at least ten years and premiums must be level and payable at annual or shorter intervals for at least ten years. However, the term can be reduced to five years for an assured under 18 if it is one of a series of payments falling due at intervals of not less than five years, and the amount of any payment, other than the final payment, does not exceed four-fifths of premiums paid in the interval before its payment. Any term or whole life sum assured must be at least 75% of total premiums payable, subject to the normal age 55 rule.

Industrial assurance policies

16.9 There are special rules for industrial assurance policies. An industrial policy that fails the normal rules will still qualify if it complies with the following condition:

(a) The total sum assured under the policy, together with all the individual's other non-qualifying industrial policies, does not exceed £1,000.

(b) Premiums meet the normal ten-year, 'twice times' and 'one-eighth' rules.

(c) No capital sum, other than on death or surrender or one allowable under (d) below, can be payable in the first ten years.

(d) If the policy provides a series of payments:

- the first payment must not be due in the first five years and the others must be at intervals of at least five years;

- the amount of any payment, other than the final payment, must not exceed four-fifths of the premiums paid in the interval before payment. This condition does not apply to policies issued before 6 April 1976 or to policies issued after 6 April 1979 in substantially the same form as policies so issued before 6 April 1976.

Extra premiums and debts

16.10   When applying the qualifying rules, any extra premiums charged for any exceptional risk of death or disability (whether medical or otherwise) can be disregarded. The Inland Revenue have confirmed that this applies to the removal as well as the imposition of a loading. The same applies to any debt on the sum assured, imposed for any such exceptional risk. This treatment only applies if there is evidence of an exceptional risk of death or disability. It does not apply merely because the proposer declines to provide medical evidence or the insurer decides not to ask for any. When applying the 75% rule, any loading for paying premiums more frequently than annually can also be ignored.

From 1 December 2001 if a policy provides for payment other than annually, without providing an annual amount, 10% of those premiums can be disregarded for the 75% test.

Backdating

16.11   If a policy is backdated by up to three months, it will be regarded as having been made on the date to which it is backdated. However, if the policy is backdated more than three months, it will be regarded as having been made on the date the contract was actually completed. This may result in an otherwise qualifying policy being non-qualifying – often because the 'one-eighth' rule will be broken, due to well over one year's premiums being payable in the first actual year of its existence.

For example, if a 15-year endowment, completed on 1 January 2003 with an annual premuim of £1,000, were backdated five months, the amount due in the first actual year of risk would be £2,000 (ie £1,000 due 1 January 2003 plus £1,000 due 1 August 2003). The policy would thus fail the one-eighth rule as 2000/15,000 is greater than one-eighth.

Reinstatement

16.12   If a qualifying policy lapses due to non-payment of premiums, this can affect its qualifying status. If it is reinstated within 13 months this is ignored and the policy can continue to qualify but only if the policyholder gets exactly the same policy as he had before. Thus, if the premium is increased because of a health problem revealed on a declaration of health, it is treated as a new policy. If reinstatement occurs after 13 months then it is also treated as a new policy which may prevent it qualifying – eg if there is less than ten years still to run.

Substitutions and variations

16.13   A policy effected on or before 19 March 1968 is not subject to the qualifying rules on a variation, except if the variation is to increase the benefits or to extend the term of the policy. Where the term of an endowment is reduced and the premiums consequently increased, this is regarded as an increase in the benefits. The same applies to the addition of profits to a non-profit policy, unless the sum assured is correspondingly reduced.

If a post-19 March 1968 policy (or a pre-1968 policy in the cases mentioned above) is substituted or varied then it has to be re-tested under the rules contained in *ICTA 1988, Sch 15 para 17*. In these rules 'the old policy' means the policy prior to the substitution or variation and 'the new policy' means the policy after the substitution or variation.

The rules are as follows:

(a) If the new policy would, apart from this provision, be a qualifying policy, but the old policy was not, the new policy is not a qualifying policy unless the person making the insurance was an infant when the old policy was issued, and the old policy was one securing a capital sum payable either on a specified date falling not later than one month after attaining 25 or on the anniversary of the policy immediately following attainment of that age.

(b) If the new policy would, apart from this provision, be a qualifying policy and the old policy was qualifying, the new policy is a qualifying policy unless:

- it takes effect before the expiry of ten years from the effecting of the old policy, and

- the highest total of premiums payable for any period of twelve months expiring before that time is less than one-half of the highest total paid for any period of twelve months under the old policy, or under any related policy issued less than ten years before the issue of the new policy ('related policy' meaning any policy in relation to which the old policy was a new policy, any policy in relation to which that policy was such a policy and so on).

(c) If the new policy would not, apart from this provision, be a qualifying policy, and would fail to be so by reason only of the ten-year premium term, 'one-eighth', or 'twice times' rules, it is nevertheless a qualifying policy if the old policy was a qualifying policy and:

- the old policy was issued more than ten years before the taking effect of the new policy, and the premiums payable for any period of twelve months under the new policy do not exceed the smallest total paid for any such period under the old policy, or

- the old policy was issued outside the UK, the circumstances being as follows:

    – the person in respect of whom the new insurance is made became resident in the UK during the twelve months ending with the date of its issue;

    – the issuing company certify that the new policy is in substitution for the old, and that the old was issued either by a branch or agency of theirs outside the UK or by a company outside the UK with whom they have arrangements for the issue of policies in substitution for those held by persons coming to the UK, and that the new policy confers on the holder benefits which are substantially equivalent to those which he would have enjoyed if the old policy had continued in force.

Where the new policy referred to in the above rules is one issued on or after 1 April 1976, then in determining its qualification that part of the first premium payable which derives from the value of the old policy is left out of account.

These rules apply to both contractual and non-contractual substitutions and variations.

Certification

16.14   No policy effected on or after 1 April 1976 can qualify, even if it meets the rules, unless it is certified as qualifying by the Inland Revenue or confirms to a standard form of policy which has already been so certified. Furthermore, no additional policy wordings are allowed unless they have been certified by the Inland Revenue as compatible with a qualifying policy.

Thus, all policy forms and wordings for qualifying policies have to be submitted to the Inland Revenue for certification by the life office, before selling that type of policy.

Non-qualifying policies

16.15   All life policies that do not meet the qualifying rules are non-qualifying policies. Non qualifying policies are almost always single premium investment bonds, although a few will be policies that were originally qualifying but became non-qualifying by some type of alteration, or lapsing followed by reinstatement.

Taxation of life policyholders

16.16   The main tax applicable to life policyholders is income tax under the provisions of *ICTA 1988, ss 539–552*. The aim of the legislation is to tax gains (called chargeable gains) usually at the higher rate only.

Qualifying policies are treated much more beneficially as in general terms only gains in the first ten years are taxable, whereas for non-qualifying policies all gains are taxable.

Exempt policies

16.17   The following four types of life policy are exempt from these rules and therefore free from income tax.

1   Policies effected on or before 19 March 1968, unless varied after that date so as to increase the benefits or extend the term.

2   Policies which have as their sole object the provision on death or disability of a sum substantially the same as that outstanding under a mortgage of the policyholder's residence or business premise. This means decreasing term policies only.

3   Policies issued in connection with an approved pension scheme, retirement annuity or personal pension.

4   Certain group life policies where benefits are payable to an individual or a charity, either direct or via a trust.

The tax charge

16.18   Tax is only payable if:

(a)   a chargeable event occurs; and

(b)   a chargeable gain arises therefrom; and

(c)   when the gain is added to the taxpayer's total income for that year it falls partly or totally within the higher rate tax bracket (subject to exceptions for policies owned by Lloyd's members, and tax-exempt friendly society policies).

These factors will now be dealt with in turn.

Chargeable events

16.19   The chargeable events for a non-qualifying policy are:

(a)   death (if it gives rise to a benefit);

(b)   maturity;

(c) surrender;

(d) certain part surrenders and part assignments (see below);

(e) policy loan if the policy was effected after 26 March 1974;

(f) assignment for money or money's worth.

16.20   The chargeable events for a qualifying life policy are:

(a) death (if it gives rise to a benefit);

(b) maturity;

These are chargeable events only if the policy is made paid-up within ten years, or 3/4 of the term if sooner.

(c) surrender;

(d) certain part surrenders and part assignments (see below);

(e) policy loan at non-commercial rate of interest, if the policy was effected after 26 March 1974;

(f) assignment for money or money's worth.

These are chargeable events only if they occur during the first ten years, or 3/4 of the term if sooner or the policy has been made paid-up within that time.

The time limits run from the commencement of the policy, or from any variation by which premiums are increased, unless the increase is solely due to a variation in the life or lives assured or the exercise of an option under a policy entered into on or after 1 April 1976.

16.21   Assignments by way of mortgages are ignored, as are assignments between spouses living together. If a policy issued prior to 26 June 1982 was assigned for money or money's worth before that date, no subsequent event can be a chargeable event. However, this does not apply if – after 23 August 1982 – the policy is reacquired by the original beneficial owner, a further premium is paid, or a policy loan is given.

A policy loan at a non-commercial rate of interest on a qualifying policy is not a chargeable event if it was made before 6 April 2000 by the issuing office to a full-time employee for house purchase or improvement. A loan to buy a life annuity where the interest is eligible for tax relief is not a chargeable event.

If a loan is a chargeable event it is treated as a part surrender and the gain is calculated as set out in the rules for part surrenders.

Payment of a critical illness benefit or a terminal illness benefit is not a chargeable event and so cannot give rise to a tax charge.

Chargeable gains

16.22 When a chargeable event occurs a calculation must be made to see if a gain has arisen. A chargeable gain arises in the following cases:

(a) on maturity or surrender – if the amount paid out, plus any relevant capital payments, exceeds the premiums paid plus the total gains on previous surrenders or part assignments. Where the sum assured is payable by instalments the amount taken for the calculation is the capital value of the instalments;

(b) on death, if the surrender value immediately before death, plus any relevant capital payments, exceeds the premiums paid plus the total gains on previous part surrenders or part assignments;

(c) on assignment, if the price received, plus any relevant capital payments, exceeds the premiums paid plus the total gains on previous part surrenders or part assignments.

Where the chargeable event is an assignment between persons connected with each other, the gain is based on the market value, not the price received. This would affect assignments to a spouse, brother, sister, parent, child or grandchild. An assignment in connection with a divorce or pre-nuptial settlement is an assignment for monies' worth. However, if it is a result of a divorce court order it is not for monies' worth, even if the court is only ratifying an agreement reached by the divorcing parties.

Relevant capital payments are any benefits of a capital nature (other than those attributable to a person's disability) paid under the policy prior to the chargeable event.

Gains can also occur on part surrenders and part assignments and the special rules for these are explained in the next section.

Part surrenders

16.23 A part surrender (which would include a bonus encashment or a loan) can be a chargeable event if it exceeds a certain limit. The law looks at the total part surrenders in any policy year and not to individual part surrenders. A chargeable event only occurs if at the end of a policy year the 'reckonable aggregate value' exceeds the 'allowable aggregate amount'. The 'reckonable aggregate value' is the total amount withdrawn from the policy and the 'allowable aggregate amount' is the total of 'appropriate portions' – the annual 5% allowances, described below.

Each policy year there is an allowance of 5% of any premium paid in that year plus 5% of any premium paid in previous policy years, subject to a maximum allowance of 100% for any premium. However, no allowance is given for any policy year prior to the first policy year falling wholly after 13 March 1975. Any allowance not used can be carried forward to future years. So an investor with a single premium policy can withdraw 5% of the single premium each year for 20 years without a chargeable event occurring.

Under this system, at the end of each policy year the total of part surrenders is compared with the accumulated allowances. If the surrenders exceed the allowances a chargeable event has occurred and the amount of the excess is the chargeable gain. When this happens the allowances which have accumulated so far are deemed to have been used up and the process of cumulative allowances will start again. A gain can thus only occur on the last day of a policy year.

16.24   When a policy is terminated by death, maturity or full surrender, then the period from the previous policy anniversary to the termination (which may not always be a full year) is treated as the final year. If that final year begins and ends in the same tax year, then the final year and the year preceding it are treated as one year.

On the final termination of the policy there is a 'sweep-up' calculation to tax the total profit under the policy. If the termination is a chargeable event, a chargeable gain will arise if the total of the final proceeds plus any previous partial surrenders exceeds the total of premiums paid plus any chargeable gains arising on any previous part surrenders. Withdrawals under the 5% limit are thus tax-deferred rather than fully tax-free.

If a policy is owned jointly, the chargeable gain produced by a withdrawal in excess of the 5% limit is shared between the joint owners even if it is actually paid to just one of the owners.

If a policy is assigned during the policy year the calculations are first done with regard to withdrawals made before the assignment (for which the assignor is liable) and then for withdrawals made after the assignment (for which the assignee is liable).

Part assignments

16.25   The part surrender rules also apply to assignments of part of the rights of a policy, but only if it is for money or monies worth. However this does not apply to assignments between spouses living together. A part assignment is any assignment where one of the assignors is also one of the assignees – eg A and B to A, or A to A and B. Frequently on a divorce one of the owners of a joint life policy will assign his or her rights to the other ex-spouse, and as this is for consideration it could create a chargeable gain. The value to be used is the surrender value of the rights being assigned – eg half the surrender value in the usual case of one joint owner assigning his half share in the policy to the other. In this case half the surrender value would have to be compared with any available 5% allowances to decide whether a gain had arisen.

If a policy is part assigned for consideration, any gain caused by the part assignment is taxable on the part assignor, although the date of the chargeable event for income tax purposes is still the end of the policy year.

Examples of chargeable gains

16.26   These examples use single premium bonds for simplicity and also because the vast majority of chargeable gains occur on them, as opposed to regular premium qualifying policies.

EXAMPLE 16.26A – A SIMPLE SURRENDER

Single premium bond effected 1 January 1995 for a premium of £10,000 and surrendered on 1 July 2003 for £16,000.

	£
Surrender Value	16,000
Less premium	10,000
Chargeable gain	6,000

The date of the chargeable event is 1 July 2003.

EXAMPLE 16.26B – A DEATH CLAIM

Single premium bond effected 1 January 1994 for a premium of £10,000. Life assured died on 5 April 2003 when the surrender value was £15,000 but the claim value of £15,500 was paid 1 July 2003.

	£
Surrender value immediately prior to death	15,000
Less premium	10,000
Chargeable gain	5,000

The date of the chargeable event is the date of death, 5 April 2003 (tax year 2002/03), not the date the claim was paid, 1 July 2003 (tax year 2003/04).

EXAMPLE 16.26C – PART SURRENDERS

Single premium bond effected 1 January 1993 for a premium of £10,000.

1 July 1993	Part surrender £500 – not a chargeable event as it did not exceed 5%.
1 August 1995	Part surrender £1,000 – not a chargeable event as it did not exceed the two 5% allowances for policy years 1994 and 1995.
1 May 1996	Part surrender £1,000 – a chargeable event as it exceeds the 5% allowance for 1996 – chargeable gain £500.
1 June 1998	Part surrender £1,500 – a chargeable event as it exceeds the 5% allowances for policy years 1997 and 1998 – chargeable gain £500.
1 September 2001	Part surrender £1,500 – not a chargeable event as it does not exceed the three 5% allowances for 1999, 2000 and 2001.
1 July 2003	Full surrender for £16,000 – a chargeable event.

The calculation on full surrender is:

	£
Surrender value	16,000
+ 1993 Part surrender	500
+ 1995 Part surrender	1,000
+ 1996 Part surrender	1,000
+1998 Part surrender	1,500
+ 2001 Part surrender	1,500
Total paid out	21,500
– Premium	10,000
– 1996 Chargeable gain	500
– 1998 Chargeable gain	500
Final chargeable gain	10,500

The date of the 1996 chargeable gain was 31 December 1996. The date of the 1998 chargeable gain was 31 December 1998. The date of the final chargeable gain was 1 July 2003.

Taxation of the gain

16.27   Once a chargeable event has occurred and a chargeable gain has arisen, then the tax can be calculated. Normally the gain will only be subject to the higher rate of income tax. The person chargeable to tax is the beneficial owner of the policy. However, if it is mortgaged, the mortgagor is chargeable and if it is under trust, the creator of the trust or the trustees, or in certain circumstances the beneficiaries of the trust, are chargeable as explained at **16.33** below.

16.28   For an individual policyholder, the tax is calculated as follows:

(a) Top-slice the gain by dividing it by the number of full years between the date the policy was effected and the date of the chargeable event. If the gain is on a part surrender (or assignment), the period is the number of full years back to the start of the policy from the first part surrender (or part assignment) or back to the previous part surrender (or part assignment) giving rise to a chargeable event for a second or subsequent part surrender (or part assignment).

(b) Add the top-sliced gain to the individual's total income for that tax year.

(c) Calculate the tax liability on the total income including the top-sliced gain.

(d) Calculate the tax liability on the income without the top-sliced gain.

(e) Deduct the figure in (d) from the figure in (c) and this difference is the theoretical tax liability on the top-sliced gain.

(f) Deduct tax at the basic rate on the amount of the top sliced gain from the figure in (e) so that the balance represents higher rate tax only.

(g) Multiply the figure in (f) by the number of years used in the top-slicing procedure to give the actual tax liability on the whole gain.

Top-slicing is only of any benefit to policyholders who are not already higher rate taxpayers on the basis of other income. Personal pension contributions do not reduce total income for this purpose, but the basic rate band is extended by the gross contribution.

Examples of tax calculations

16.29

EXAMPLE 16.29A

Bill Jones is a basic rate taxpayer and makes a chargeable gain of £10,000 on the surrender of a single premium bond he has held for five and a half years. His other income is £28,000.

(a) Top-slicing – number of full years is 5

$$Top-sliced\ gain = \frac{10,000}{5} =$$ £2,000

Individual's other income that tax year	£28,000	
(b) Total income		£30,000
(c) Income tax with gain £1,960×10%=	£196	
+£28,040×22%=	£6,168.80	
	£6,364.80	
(d) Income tax without gain £1,960×10%=	£196	
+£26,040×22%=	£5,728.80	
	£5,924.80	
(e) Difference between (c) and (d)		£440
(f) Less basic rate tax on top-sliced gain		
£2,000×22%=	£440	
	0	

There is therefore no tax liability in this case because even with the addition of the top-sliced gain, Bill's income for that tax year was below the higher rate tax threshold of £30,500. Without the benefit of top-slicing he would have been pushed into the higher rate tax bracket by the chargeable gain.

EXAMPLE 16.29B – A HIGHER RATE TAXPAYER

Fred Smith is a higher rate taxpayer and also makes a chargeable gain of £10,000 on the surrender of a single premium bond he has held for five and a half years. His other income is £48,000.

16.30   *Taxation of Holders of Life Policies*

(a) Top-sliced gain is £2,000 as in Example 16.29A
     Fred's other taxable income is £48,000

(b)	Thus total income is	
	£48,000+£2,000=	£50,000
	£1,960×10%	£196.00
(c)	Income tax with gain £28,540×22%=	£6,278.80
	£19,500×40%=	£7,800.00
		£14,274.80
(d)	Income tax without gain £1,960×10%=	£196.00
	£28,540×22%=	£6,278.80
	£17,500×40%=	£7,000.00
		£13,474.80
(e)	Difference between (c) and (d)	£800
(f)	Less basic rate tax on top-sliced gain	
	£2,000×22%=	£440
	Tax on top-sliced gain	£360
(g)	Therefore tax liability on whole gain	
	£360×5=	£1,800

It will be seen that the effective rate of tax on the gain is thus:

	%
Top rate of tax	40
Less basic rate tax	22
Effective rate on gain	18

ie tax is £1,800 which is 18% of the gain of £10,000

EXAMPLE 16.29C – GAIN STRADDLING THE HIGHER RATE THRESHOLD

Bill Bloggs makes a chargeable gain of £5,000, on a bond that has been in force for five years. His other income is £500 less than the higher rate threshold. The top-sliced gain is £5,000÷5=£1,000.

So half the top sliced gain is in the basic rate band and half the top sliced gain is in the higher rate band. Thus on half the full gain there is no further tax and on the other half of the full gain there is tax at the higher minus basic rate.
Thus the tax bill= £2,500×(40−22)%
              =   £2,500×18%
              =   £450

Without top-slicing relief, £4,500 of the gain would have been taxable at 18%, ie tax of £810.

Some further tax points to note

16.30   The basic rate credit will reduce to 20% for chargeable events on or after 6 April 2004 and thus the effective top rate for higher rate taxpayers will be 20% (assuming the higher rate stays at 40%).

If a gain is made on a tax-exempt friendly society policy there is no basic rate credit and thus the full rate of tax is payable.

Any tax payable would be due on 31 January following the tax year in which the chargeable event occurred.

If a policy is owned jointly, *ICTA 1988, s 547(1)(a)* splits the gain in the same proportion as the ownership regardless of the person to whom the money was actually paid. Each owner would thus be taxed (or not) on his or her share of the gain. If the joint owners are married to each other, the Revenue consider that *section 282A* overrides *section 547A* so that each spouse would be taxed on half the gain. However, if the spouses hold the policy in unequal shares they can make a declaration under *section 282B* to enable them to be taxed on their actual shares. *Section 547A* was amended by *FA 2001* to deem ownership to be in equal shares where part assignments are involved.

It may be advantageous for a higher rate tax-paying spouse to assign a policy before the chargeable event so that the gain forms part of a basic rate tax-paying spouse's income. This would avoid any tax bill even if the higher rate tax-paying spouse has been taking 5% withdrawals for years. The assignment to the other spouse would not itself be a chargeable event or a chargeable transfer for inheritance tax.

16.31   It is possible that part surrenders in excess of the 5% allowances can produce 'artificial' gains. For example, consider a unit-linked bond taken out for £20,000 which grows after one year to £22,000 and where a part surrender of £10,000 is made at the end of the first year. The chargeable gain is £10,000 less 5% of £20,000, ie £9,000. However, the bond has really only grown by £2,000. Nevertheless, these artificial gains are taxed if the policyholder is a higher rate taxpayer. Thus, very large partial surrenders should be avoided if possible.

The situation would be even worse if the bond had dropped in value to £18,000 and a part surrender of £10,000 was taken. The chargeable gain would still be £9,000, even though in reality there has been a loss of £2,000. Tax can thus actually be paid on losses, for example, £1,620 in this case (£9,000 @ 18%).

Some relief is allowed by *ICTA 1988, s 549* for this type of situation. This provides that, if on the eventual final termination a loss arises, then the policyholder is entitled to a corresponding deduction from his other income for that tax year as long as it does not exceed the previous chargeable gains. The deduction operates for higher rate tax only and would have the effect of reducing the tax otherwise payable on his other income for that year. This is called 'corresponding deficiency relief', and only applies where individuals (not trustees) are liable.

16.32   The chargeable gain is included in a taxpayer's income (without top-slicing) in order to calculate entitlement to age allowance, Child Tax Credit and Working Tax Credit. It may thus reduce, or even eliminate, a taxpayer's eligibility for these allowances.

Under Inland Revenue Extra-Statutory Concession B53, any individual who is not resident in the UK in the tax year in which the gain is chargeable will not have to pay tax on it.

If a life policy is held by a member of Lloyd's as part of his Lloyd's trust fund, the gain is chargeable under Schedule D, not *section 547*. Thus the full gain is chargeable as income, with no top-slicing relief or notional basic rate tax credit.

Trust policies

16.33   Originally the rule was that if a policy was subject to a trust, the person chargeable was the individual who created the trust, although he could recover the tax from the trustees. If the creator of the trust was dead and had died in a tax year prior to the year of the gain, there was no-one on whom the Revenue could tax the gain – the so-called 'dead settlor trick'.

The rule was changed in the *FA 1998*. The situation is now as follows:

(a) If the individual who created the trust was both alive and UK resident immediately before the chargeable event, the gain is treated as part of this individual's income. He or she can recover any tax paid from the trustees.

(b) If the individual who created the trust was dead, or resident outside the UK, immediately before the chargeable event and one or more of the trustees are resident in the UK, the trustees are chargeable on the gain. The charge is at the rate applicable to trusts, which is 34% resulting in a 12% liability for a UK policy, after allowance for the basic rate credit. This tax cannot be reclaimed by the trust beneficiaries, even if they would not be liable in their own right because they were well below the higher rate threshold.

(c) If the trustees are not resident in the UK, any UK beneficiary receiving a benefit under the trust from the gain will be taxable on that amount at his or her tax rates, but without top-slicing relief.

16.34   The new rules apply to chargeable events which occur on or after 6 April 1998. They do not apply to policies effected prior to 17 March 1998, where the trust was also created prior to this date and the creator of the trust died before then. For these cases, the dead settlor trick will still apply, as long as the policy was not varied on or after 17 March 1998 so as to increase the benefit or extend the term.

The 12% tax charge referred to in (b) above can be avoided if the beneficiaries are non-taxpayers or they are starting or basic rate taxpayers. This can be done by arranging for the UK trustees to retire and be replaced by foreign trustees (eg in the Channel Islands or Isle of Man) before the chargeable event. Then (c) above would apply and the beneficiaries would be liable at their rates. There would be no tax if their incomes were low enough to avoid the chargeable gain (without top-slicing) putting them in the higher rate tax band.

The process could be reversed for cases in (c) above where the beneficiaries are higher rate taxpayers who would thus suffer tax at 18%. If the foreign trustees are replaced by UK trustees, then (b) will apply and the tax charge will be 12%.

16.35   For chargeable events on or after 9 April 2003, where the trust is a charitable trust the charge is on the trust (not the settlor) and at the basic rate, leaving no tax to pay on a UK policy.

Administration of the tax

16.36   The taxation of chargeable gains is not the responsibility of the life office and all policy payments would be made without deduction of tax. It is the responsibility of the policyholder to declare the gain on the tax return for the tax year in which the chargeable event occurred.

The life office has to issue a chargeable event certificate to the policyholder, unless it is satisfied that no gain has occurred. The certificate has to be issued before the end of three months after the latest of:

● The date of the chargeable event.

● The end of the policy year for a part surrender or part assignment.

● The written notification of a death or assignment.

16.37   The certificate must show the following details:

● The policy number.

● The nature of the chargeable event.

● The end of the policy year for a part assignment.

● The amount of the chargeable gain.

● The amount of any basic rate credit.

● The number of years for top-slicing.

● If the event is a full assignment, the amount of any relevant capital payments, the total premiums paid, the value of any previous part assignments and the total previous chargeable gains caused by part surrenders or assignments.

The information on the certificate enables the policyholder to complete the details on the tax return. A certificate must be sent to each policyholder for a jointly owned policy, although only one certificate is required where the policyholders live at the same address, or are trustees.

A certificate must also be sent to the Inland Revenue within three months of the end of the tax year in which the event occurred if the chargeable event is a full assignment, or the gain (plus connected gains) exceeds half the basic rate limit for the tax year concerned – ie currently £15,250. The Inland Revenue may also request a certificate in any other case. A certificate sent to the Inland Revenue must be in the form specified by them. The certificate will enable the Inland Revenue to tax a policyholder who omits to declare the chargeable gain on the tax return.

The Inland Revenue has the power to audit a life office's system used to produce these certificates, and regulations specify what records a life office must keep for this.

When a life office receives notification of an assignment it is entitled to assume it is not for consideration unless it is told otherwise.

Second-hand endowments

16.38   Capital gains tax is not normally charged on life policies because *TCGA 1992, s 210* provides that a disposal is not subject to CGT unless the policy has at any time been acquired by any person for actual consideration. For this purpose premiums do not count as actual consideration, and neither does a post-marriage disposal. A post-marriage disposal is one made in the course of the dissolution or annulment of a marriage, by one party to the other, made with the approval, agreement or authority of a court. On most life policies the pay-out is either to the original beneficial owner or to someone who has acquired it otherwise than for actual consideration – eg a donee or trustees.

There is however a flourishing market in second-hand endowments whereby the original owner sells the policy to a new owner, although the cover still continues on the original life assured. This section deals with the relevant tax considerations of this subject.

Income tax on the seller

16.39   If a qualifying policy is sold after at least ten years (or three-quarters of the term, if sooner), the sale is not a chargeable event and there can be no income tax liability.

If a qualifying policy is sold within the ten-year period (or three-quarters of the term), the sale will be a chargeable event. If a non-qualifying policy is sold, the sale will always be a chargeable event.

If the sale is a chargeable event, the seller will make a chargeable gain if the sale price exceeds the total premiums paid. The gain will then be subject to higher rate income tax minus basic rate tax resulting in a maximum rate of 18% on current rates (subject to top-slicing relief), as explained in the previous sections.

CGT on the seller

16.40   There will be no CGT on the seller if he is the original beneficial owner of the policy, as it was not acquired for actual consideration.

Income tax on the buyer

16.41   If the buyer holds a qualifying policy to maturity (or death claim), there is no chargeable event and thus no income tax liability. If the buyer holds a non-qualifying policy to maturity (or death claim), this is a chargeable event. There will be a chargeable gain if the maturity value (or surrender value immediately prior to death on a death claim) exceeds the total premiums paid by the buyer and the seller. The purchase price paid by the buyer does not enter into the calculation. If a gain arises the buyer will pay income tax at the higher rate minus the basic rate subject to top-slicing relief, as explained earlier.

If the buyer sells the policy rather than holding it until a claim arises, the second sale would only be a chargeable event on a qualifying policy if it occurred in the first ten years (or three quarters of the term if sooner). On a non-qualifying policy the second sale will always be a chargeable event. The normal chargeable gains consequences will then ensue.

CGT on the buyer

16.42   When the buyer disposes of the policy there is the possibility of a CGT charge. The following count as disposals:

(a) payment of sum assured (on death or maturity);

(b) payment of surrender value;

(c) a further assignment for value, or as a gift.

Where a policy is subject to CGT the gain is calculated by deducting from the proceeds of disposal the market value on 31 March 1982 if the policy was held on that date, or the acquisition cost if acquired since then. Also allowed as a deduction is an indexation allowance representing the effects of inflation from March 1982 or acquisition, whichever is later, to April 1998. In addition, any incidental costs of acquisition or disposal (such as legal fees) are allowed, as are premiums paid by the assignee from March 1982 or acquisition, whichever is later. All these items (except disposal costs) can benefit from indexation. Taper relief might also apply depending on how long the policy has been held by the buyer. The acquisition cost is the purchase price paid for the policy (with indexation allowance). The disposal proceeds of a life policy would be the sum assured, surrender value or market value as the case maybe. If the gain exceeds the annual CGT allowance of £7,900 (taking into account any other gains or losses that year), the excess will be subject to CGT at 10%, 20% or 40%, depending on which band the gain takes the buyer's income into.

16.43   The CGT calculation takes no account of whether the policy is qualifying or not, although the taxable capital gain is reduced by any amount which is subject to income tax (ie a chargeable gain). Thus, it is unlikely that the same policy will be subject to income tax and CGT.

A life office does not have to inform the policyholder or the Inland Revenue when a disposal subject to CGT occurs.

In the past it has been possible for the CGT charge to be avoided by the buyer gifting the second-hand policy straight away to a trust or a member of his family who would thus have been exempt from the CGT charge as they had not acquired it for money or money's worth. This loophole was closed for disposals on or after 9 April 2003 by *FA 2003*, and thus the CGT charge will still apply in these circumstances.

Example

16.44

EXAMPLE 16.44

Rob bought a house in 1987 with the aid of a 25-year endowment mortgage for £30,000 – premium £100 per month. As a result of receiving an unexpected legacy from a grandparent, he repaid his mortgage in 1992. The endowment policy was then surplus to requirements. The life office quoted him a surrender value of £4,500 but Rob managed to sell the policy on the second-hand market for £5,500.

Selling the policy in the first ten years was a chargeable event, but there was no gain, because the sale price was less than the total premiums paid.

The maturity of the policy in 2012 will not be a chargeable event, so the buyer will not be liable for income tax. The buyer will, however, make a CGT disposal by claiming the maturity value. He will have a CGT liability on the gain, which will be the maturity value less the sale price paid and premiums paid by the buyer from 1992 to 2012.

Indexation allowance will also be given on the sale price and these premiums (up to April 1998), and taper relief for the period since then plus the added year, because the buyer owned the policy before 17 March 1998.

Inheritance tax

16.45   Inheritance tax is relevant whenever the beneficial owner of a policy dies. It is also relevant each time a person pays premiums on a policy which is for someone else's benefit.

IHT on premiums

16.46   If an individual pays premiums on a policy which is for the benefit of another person, that is a transfer of value because it reduces the payer's estate. The value of the transfer is the amount of the premium.

Thus, if a life assured pays premiums on a policy where the assured is someone else or where it is under trust for someone else, that will be a transfer of value.

The transfer will usually be covered by one of the exemptions. The most common exemptions utilised for this are as follows:

398

Annual exemption

16.47 If the premium is less than the annual exemption of £3,000 (and this exemption is not already being used, it will be exempt (*IHTA 1984, s 19*).

Spouse exemption

16.48 If the policy is for the benefit of the payer's spouse, the premium will be completely exempt whatever the amount (*IHTA 1984, s 18*). The spouse has to be legally married and domiciled in the UK.

Small gifts exemption

16.49 If the policy is for the absolute benefit of someone else (that is, not under a trust other than a bare trust) then the premium will be exempt if it is not more than £250 per annum (*IHTA 1984, s 20*).

Normal expenditure exemption

16.50 The premium will be exempt if all the following conditions are met:

● it was part of the normal expenditure of the payer;

● it came from income (not capital);

● after allowing for all gifts from normal expenditure the payer was left with sufficient income to maintain his usual standard of living (*IHTA 1984, s 21*).

This exemption can be used in conjunction with the annual exemption to allow quite a high premium to be paid free of tax for those with high incomes. However, it must be added that withdrawals from another life policy, such as a single premium bond, are not income for this purpose (even if they exceed the 5% limit for higher rate income tax).

Potentially Exempt Transfers (PETs)

16.51 If premiums paid into a trust policy exceed the available exemptions it is often thought that the excess will be a PET, assuming the trust has as interest in possession. However, because of the wording of *IHTA 1984, s 3a(2)(b)*, the transfer will only be a PET to the extent that the donee's estate is increased. The Inland Revenue have stated that where premiums are paid by the settlor direct to the life office, the full premium will not always be a PET. This is because the value of the policy owned by the donee is not always increased by the full amount of the premium. Examples of such cases would be:

(a) term assurance where because the policy has no surrender value, in a way its value is not increased at all;

399

(b) with-profits policies where the surrender value does not increase by the amount of the premium; and

(c) unit-linked policies during the initial allocation period where no, or a reduced, percentage of units is being purchased.

In these cases, the transfer would be (a) exempt up to the limit of the available exemptions, (b) a PET for the excess, but only to the extent of the increase in value (if any) of the policy, and (c) chargeable as to any balance. The problem only arises in the case of second or subsequent premiums and will only apply where all the exemptions are being exceeded or have been used for other transfers.

In all these cases, the problem can be avoided if the settlor pays premiums directly to the trustees (thereby increasing the trust's value by the amount of the premium) and the trustees then paying the premium on to the life office. In that way the excess over the exemptions would definitely be a PET.

Chargeable lifetime transfers

16.52   If the premium is neither exempt nor a PET (for instance if a discretionary trust was being used), then it will be a chargeable transfer. Tax will thus be payable at the life rates, if it takes the payer's seven-year cumulative total over the IHT threshold of £255,000. If the payer died within seven years of paying the premium, then the donees would be liable for extra tax on the difference between the life rates actually used and the death rates in force at the date of death.

IHT on policies gifted during life

16.53   Inheritance tax can also be chargeable if a policy is gifted, or put into trust, during its lifetime rather than at outset. In this case, there will be a transfer of value of the value of the policy at the date of the gift, and all future premiums paid by the transferor will also be gifts and treated as above.

The value of the policy when gifted will normally be its open market value: its surrender value. However, there is a special valuation rule for life policies and this must be used if it produces a higher value. This is the 'premium valuation' set out in *IHTA 1984, s 167*.

Under this rule, the value is not less than the total premiums paid under the policy minus any sums previously paid out. This special valuation rule does not apply to term assurances for three years or less or where, if the term exceeds three years, premiums are payable for at least two-thirds of the term and premiums payable in any one year do not exceed twice those in any other year.

There is also a variation of the rule for unit-linked policies in that any drop in the value of units since they were allocated is allowed as a deduction from the total premiums.

16.54 The transfer may be exempt under one of the exemptions, and if not exempt will be a PET, provided it is an outright gift to an individual, or the trust used is an interest in possession trust, accumulation and maintenance trust or a disabled trust.

If it is exempt, no tax will be payable at all. It if is a PET, there will be no tax if the donor lives for seven years but there could be a tax liability if the donor dies during this period. If so, the transferee has to pay tax based on the following:

● the value of the policy at the time of the transfer;

● the transferor's seven-year cumulation at the time of the transfer; and

● the death rates in force at the date of death

If the transfer is neither exempt nor a PET (for instance, if a discretionary trust is used), then it will be a chargeable transfer and tax will be payable at the life rates if it takes the transferor's seven-year cumulation over the IHT threshold. Extra tax will then be payable by the transferee, based on the death rates, if the transferor dies in the seven years after the transfer.

IHT on death

16.55 The proceeds of an own life policy which is not under trust or assigned will be part of the deceased's estate on a death claim. Tax may thus be payable if the value of the total estate plus the previous seven years' chargeable transfers exceeds the IHT threshold.

If the policy is life of another, on trust or assigned, the death of the life assured will not result in the proceeds being taxed because no transfer has taken place on death, and it was not part of the deceased's estate.

Inheritance tax planning

16.56 Whole life policies are frequently used for IHT funding. The way this works is for the potential IHT bill on death to be calculated and then a policy written under trust for this amount. The trust should be for the benefit of the major beneficiaries of the estate who will effectively bear the burden of the tax. The sum assured will be tax free and can be used to pay the IHT bill and enable the grant of representation to be obtained and the estate distributed.

For married couples, where the major IHT liability tends to occur on second death, the policy would be a joint life second death policy.

There are also many IHT plans based on single premium bonds but they are beyond the scope of this work.

However the following table gives brief details of the most common plans.

Gift And Loan Plans	These involve a gift of (usually) a de minimis amount to a trust, followed by a loan of a much larger amount. The trustees invest the loan in a single premium bond, using the 5% withdrawals to repay the loan.
Split Trust Bonds	These involve a client effecting a single premium bond under a split trust as to x% for himself and the balance for his beneficiaries. This is a gift of part of the investment at outset and the client can withdraw capital from his portion of the trust.
Back To Back Plans	A combination of a whole life policy and an annuity. The whole life policy is under trust and pays out IHT free on death, whilst the annuity provides a tax efficient income for life.
Discounted Gift Plans	These involve a combination of a pure endowment policy and a term assurance. The pure endowment is retained by the investor and the term assurance is put into trust at outset. The value of the gift is a discounted value reflecting the donor's age, sex and state of health.

Offshore life policies

16.57   Offshore life policies are policies issued by non-UK life offices – usually in low tax countries such as the Channel Islands, the Isle of Man or Luxembourg. Often these are subsidiaries of well-known UK companies.

In theory an offshore policy effected prior to 17 November 1983 could be qualifying, but in practice this is very rare.

From 17 November 1983, a policy issued by a non-UK life office cannot be certified and thus will not qualify until either:

- the life office becomes UK authorised and premiums are payable to a UK branch, or

- the policyholder becomes resident in the UK and the life fund income is chargeable to UK corporation tax.

These policies are known as 'new non-resident policies' and a pre-17 November 1983 policy will become a new non-resident policy if it is varied after that date so as to increase the benefits or extend the term.

Chargeable gains

16.58   When a new non-resident policy pays out, there is a chargeable event for income tax purposes as it is a non-qualifying policy. However, the chargeable gain is reduced by multiplying it by the following fraction:

$$\frac{\textit{Number of days policyholder was resident in the UK}}{\textit{total number of days policy has run}}$$

Thus, the whole gain is chargeable if the policyholder was resident in the UK for the whole term of the policy. However, if he or she was resident for, say, six out of the ten years the policy was held, only 60% of the gain is chargeable. If the policyholder was resident outside the UK the whole time, the chargeable gain is nil. However, there is no time apportionment if the policy has ever been held by a non-resident trustee – in such cases the whole gain is chargeable.

Where a gain arises it is chargeable to starting and basic as well as higher rate tax. The number of years used for top-slicing is reduced by the number of complete years for which the policyholder was not resident in the UK. The number of years to be counted goes back to the policy date for all chargeable events – including all part surrenders and part assignments (unlike an onshore policy). Top-slicing only applies to higher rate tax – it cannot be used to reduce the tax from basic to starting or nil rates.

16.59 The effect of this is to make UK policyholders with offshore policies liable to income tax at their highest rate(s) on the whole of their gain, with some relief for any periods spent outside the UK during the term of the policy. This reflects the fact that no UK tax is paid on the underlying life fund.

However, the charge is reduced to higher rate minus basic rate if:

(a) the insurer is based in a country which is a member of the EU or the EEA; and

(b) in its home state the insurer is taxed on the investment income and gains accruing for its UK policyholders at a rate of not less than 20%; and

(c) the insurer has not reinsured the investment content of the policy.

The remittance basis for non-UK domiciled taxpayers does not apply to these gains. Thus gains made on offshore policies by non-UK domiciled UK residents are taxable, whether or not they are remitted to the UK.

Tax planning

16.60 The main advantage of an offshore bond is that the income rolls up gross. Over the long term (probably ten years or more), the compounding effect of this can make a substantial difference to the eventual overall return, despite the higher tax on final encashment. If a UK expatriate has an offshore life policy and is planning to return to the UK, it may be preferable to cash the policy while the investor is still non-resident and pay no UK tax. This may be better than cashing the policy some time after returning to the UK and paying tax at basic and higher rates on some portion of the gain. A substantial part surrender could be taken while the investor is non-resident, leaving a policy with a minimal value to be taken back to the UK. Later, it could be topped up in the

UK and the gain produced by the subsequent premium paid in the UK would still benefit from the full-time apportionment calculation.

Inheritance tax

16.61   The inheritance tax aspects of offshore life policies are exactly the same as onshore policies as far as UK domiciled policyholders are concerned. This is because for UK-domiciled taxpayers their worldwide assets are subject to IHT.

However for a non-UK domiciled policyholder, even one resident in the UK, there will be no IHT on an offshore policy as this is not a UK asset.

Personal portfolio bonds

16.62   Personal portfolio bonds are non-qualifying single premium life policies where an investor effectively wraps a life office bond around his own portfolio of investments, instead of investing in the life office's publicly available funds. The bond is linked to the investor's own fund to which no other investors have access. The fund might be managed by the investor or his own investment managers, although it will be administered by the life office.

Definition

16.63   The exact definition of a personal portfolio bond is in *ICTA 1988, s 553C* and the *Personal Portfolio Bonds (Tax) Regulations 1999 (SI 1999/1029)*.

It is a life policy where:

(a) some or all of the benefits are determined by reference to the value of, or the income from, property of any description (whether or not specified in the policy or contract) or fluctuations in, or in an index of, the value of property of any description (whether or not so specified); and

(b) some or all of the property, or such an index, may be selected by, or by a person acting on behalf of the holder of the policy or a person connected with him.

However a bond is not a personal portfolio bond if the fund is available to policyholders in general or invested in cash, authorised unit trusts, investment trusts or OEICs.

The Willoughby Case

16.64   The Inland Revenue never liked personal portfolio bonds, particularly offshore ones, and claimed that they could apply the anti-avoidance legislation in *ICTA 1988, s 739* against them. *Section 739* states that where:

- because of a transfer of assets, income becomes payable to persons resident or domiciled outside the UK; and

- as a result, an individual who is ordinarily resident in the UK has the power to enjoy that income, either at that time or in the future,

the Inland Revenue can then treat that income as if it was paid to the individual ordinarily resident in the UK and tax him or her on it.

The Revenue's view was tested in the *Willoughby* case which went all the way to the House of Lords in 1997 and where the Revenue were soundly defeated, partly because the taxpayer was resident outside the UK when the bond was effected. The Revenue's response was to change the law so that *section 739* applies to income arising on or after 26 November 1976, whatever the residence status of the individual when the transfer was made, where a purpose of the transfer is to avoid any form of direct taxation.

Taxation of personal portfolio bonds

16.65   The Inland Revenue also enacted specific legislation against these bonds in *FA 1998* by imposing a penal tax on a deemed gain. The deemed gain is 15% of the total premiums paid at the end of a policy year plus the total deemed gains from previous years less any chargeable withdrawals. The effect of this is to tax the policyholder as if the investment was yielding 15% compound, regardless of any actual growth. However, it is worse that this, as the deemed gain is on top of the normal tax charge which would arise on a part surrender. The deemed gain can be deducted from a final termination gain. For an onshore policy, there is a credit for the basic rate tax paid by the life fund. The normal rules for chargeable gains apply to the deemed gain, except that there is no top-slicing relief.

The intent seems to have been to extinguish these bonds, which is what has happened, at least as far as UK-resident investors are concerned.

17   Taxation of Pension Fund Investors

Chris Marshall

Legal & General

Introduction

17.1   The taxation of pension fund investors divides neatly into two – the tax treatment of the contributions and the tax treatment of the benefits.

Tax treatment of contributions

17.2   This varies according to the type of pension arrangement.

Occupational Schemes

17.3   An occupational pension scheme that is approved as exempt by the Inland Revenue enables the employee to receive income tax relief on the contributions. The employee can contribute up to 15% of gross remuneration into the pension scheme. Remuneration includes the taxable value of benefits in kind as well as salary, bonuses and commission from the employer.

Employee contributions are virtually always deducted from pay by the employer and paid directly into the pension scheme along with the employer's contribution. Tax relief is given by incorporating an allowance for the pension contribution into the PAYE code. The effect is therefore to give income tax relief at the employee's highest rate on the contribution at source.

The employer's contribution is not taxable on the employee as a benefit in kind, making a pension scheme a very tax efficient investment. The employer can claim tax relief on the contribution as a business expense, whether this is for income tax as a sole trader or partnership, or corporation tax as a company.

However an employee's contribution is not deductible from earnings for National Insurance purposes.

Additional voluntary contributions

17.4   As stated, an employee can pay up to 15% of remuneration into an occupational pension scheme. All schemes must allow members to pay

407

additional voluntary contributions (AVCs) into the scheme. The AVC could be an add-on extra to the employer's scheme, or a personal AVC – known as a free-standing or FSAVC. This is a plan owned by the member separate from the employer's scheme, with a pension provider of the member's choice.

Thus, if the scheme is non-contributory the full 15% can be paid into an AVC. If the scheme is contributory, only the balance can be paid into an AVC. So if the scheme requires, for example, a 6% contribution, a maximum of 9% can be paid into an AVC.

For an employer-sponsored AVC, contributions can be deducted by the employer directly from pay effectively giving full tax relief immediately via the PAYE system. For an FSAVC, contributions can be paid net of basic rate tax with the pension provider reclaiming the tax relief from the Revenue. Higher rate taxpayers are able to claim the balance of this relief direct from the Revenue on their annual tax return. A contribution certificate is issued by the pension provider but need only be supplied to the Revenue on request.

17.5   The 15% limit is based on taxable remuneration which may be much more than the figure used to work out pension entitlement under the main scheme. Often the employer's definition of final salary will exclude such items as overtime, bonuses and the taxable value of a company car. All these can be included in the definition of remuneration for AVCs. An FSAVC provider would need evidence of these benefits, for example a coding notice or employer's confirmation. In any event an FSAVC provider will need to obtain evidence of earnings, for example a payslip.

For schemes set up on or after 14 March 1989 and new entrants on or after 1 June 1989, an earnings cap (currently £99,000) applies to the 15% limit. Thus the maximum contribution is now £14,850. In this connection the relevant date is when the main scheme started, not when the AVC started.

Personal Pensions

17.6   Personal pension contributions attract full income tax relief, but there are complications involving limits on contributions, basis years, cessation of earnings and how the relief is allocated and administered.

Limit on contributions

17.7   Anyone who is eligible for a personal pension can contribute up to a certain threshold, currently £3,600, regardless of their level of earnings. They can even contribute if they have no earnings – for example, a houseperson or carer.

Contributions over £3,600 can be made if they are within the following limits which relate to net relevant earnings. Earnings over the earnings cap, currently

£99,000, do not count for this purpose, thus limiting the maximum contribution to the figure in the third column.

2003/04

Age on 6 April	Net relevant earnings, %	Maximum, £
35 or under	17.5	£17,325
36 to 45	20.0	£19,800
46 to 50	25.0	£24,750
51 to 55	30.0	£29,700
56 to 60	35.0	£34,650
61 to 74	40.0	£39,600

The limits for the previous year, which are relevant for the carry-back provisions (see **17.15** below), were as follows:

2002/03 – Earnings cap £97,200

Age on 6 April	Net relevant earnings, %	Maximum, £
35 or under	17.5	£17,010
36 to 45	20.0	£19,440
46 to 50	25.0	£24,300
51 to 55	30.0	£29,160
56 to 60	35.0	£34,020
61 to 74	40.0	£38,880

The basis year rule

17.8   The basis year rule can be used to make contributions which are higher than those normally allowable under the above limits. An individual's net relevant earnings in any tax year can be used as the basis for contributions in the next five tax years, even if the subsequent net relevant earnings are much lower, or there are no net relevant earnings at all. However, the applicable percentage will depend on the person's age at the beginning of the tax year in which the contribution is made, not the person's age in the basis year.

EXAMPLE 17.8

Michael was born in August 1967 and has the following pattern of earnings and pension contributions.

17.9 *Taxation of Pension Fund Investors*

Tax Year	Years since Basis Year	Applicable %	Net Relevant Earnings £	Normal Contribution £	Basis Year Rule Allows £
2001/02*	Basis Year	17.5	40,000	7,000	7,000
2002/03	1	17.5	35,000	6,125	7,000
2003/04	2	17.5	25,000	4,375	7,000
2004/05	3	20	20,000	4,000	8,000
2005/06	4	20	15,000	3,600x	8,000
2006/07	5	20	10,000	3,600x	8,000
2007/08	6	20	10,000	3,600x	7,000

* Net relevant earnings before 2001 are assumed to be less than £40,000.
x Threshold figure applies.

The high basis year earnings of £40,000 in 2001/02 can be used to justify contributions of £7,000 in the next two years, and £8,000 in the following three years because the applicable percentage has increased as Michael is 36 at the start of the tax year. In 2007/08, the basis year can no longer be 2001/02 and the new basis year can be taken as 2002/03, allowing a pension contribution of £7,000, ie £35,000 x 20%.

Cessation of earnings

17.9 If an individual ceases to have net relevant earnings, they can contribute up to £3,600 as long as they are eligible. Higher contributions are possible for the tax year in which earnings cease and the following five tax years if there are relevant earnings in the cessation year and higher contributions were possible under the basis year rule in one or more of the cessation year and the five previous years. These six years are called the reference years. This effectively allows higher contributions to be paid for up to ten years after the basis year, because the contribution can be based on any of those reference years. The net relevant earnings can be used as the basis for contributions in any of the next five tax years following earnings cessation.

EXAMPLE 17.9

Adam Ball has the following earnings, assuming a 17.5% applicable percentage throughout.

Tax Year		Net Relevant Earnings £	Normal Contribution Allowable £	Maximum Contributions Allowable £
2001/02	Basis Year	40,000	7,000	7,000
2002/03	BY + 1	35,000	6,125	7,000
2003/04	BY + 2	25,000	4,375	7,000
2004/05	BY + 3	20,000	3,600x	7,000
2005/06	BY + 4	15,000	3,600x	7,000
2006/07	Cessation Year	8,000	3,600x	7,000
2007/08	CY + 1	0	3,600x	7,000
2008/09	CY + 2	0	3,600x	7,000
2009/10	CY + 3	0	3,600x	7,000
2010/11	CY + 4	0	3,600x	7,000
2011/12	CY + 5	0	3,600x	7,000
2012/13	CY + 6	0	3,600x	3,600

x Threshold figure applies.

In 2012/13, the maximum contribution falls to £3,600 because it is more than five years after the cessation year. The right to pay higher contributions in relation to earlier earnings stops if earnings start again or if the person becomes a member of an occupational pension scheme for the whole of a tax year within the five-year period.

Employer's contributions

17.10   Where an employer contributes to a personal pension the employee's maximum contribution is reduced by the amount the employer pays, but any NICO contracting-out rebate is ignored for this purpose. Any existing retirement annuity premiums also count towards the maximum, so it effectively applies to the total premiums for both contracts from all sources except the NICO. The employer can obtain tax relief on the contribution as a business expense, but it is not taxable on the employee as a benefit in kind.

Relevant earnings

17.11   Relevant earnings are:

(a)   earnings from a non-pensionable office or employment;

(b)   income from property attached to or part of the earnings of a non-pensionable office or employment;

(c)   income chargeable under Schedule D immediately derived from a trade, profession or vocation;

(d)   patent rights income treated as earned income.

The income of an external Lloyd's name from his syndicate is included in (c).

17.12   Relevant earnings do not include:

(a)   income from the acquisition or disposal of shares under share option and share incentive schemes;

(b)   golden handshake payments;

(c)   a controlling director's fees if the company's income is mainly investment income.

It is not possible for a controlling director to take early retirement benefits from his occupational pension scheme on the basis introduced by *FA 1989* and then pension further earnings from the same employer (or an associated employer) by a personal pension. For this purpose the Act removed these earnings from the definition of net relevant earnings. However, the retired individual would nevertheless be able to contribute up to £3,600 per year, ie the threshold, until age 75.

17.13   A married woman's relevant earnings are not treated as her husband's. Each spouse can therefore have his or her own contract based on his or her own earnings, regardless of what the other spouse does. Net relevant earnings are relevant earnings after deduction of annuities payable out of profits, patent or mining royalties, necessary expenses, losses and capital allowances, but before deduction of loan interest, personal reliefs and other allowances.

17.14   Where an individual has two associated employments, one of which is pensionable and one of which is not, and the pensionable remuneration exceeds £99,000, the earnings from the non-pensionable employment do not count as relevant earnings. Employers are associated if directly or indirectly one is controlled by the other or both are controlled by a third person. The object of this rule is to prevent the earnings cap being avoided by ie the creation of associated non-pensionable employments (fragmentation).

Allocation of relief

17.15   The tax relief on premiums is normally given in the tax year the premium is paid. However, there can be exceptions to this and the rules are as follows:

(a)   Current year.

Tax relief is obtained against the taxable earnings in the tax year in which the contribution is made.

Examples:

- A director or employee who makes contributions in 2003/04 can obtain tax relief against income for that year. In practice only higher rate relief is obtained in this way, as basic tax relief is given at source.

- A self-employed person carrying on a trade or profession is normally assessed in each year on the basis of earnings in the accounting period ending in that tax year.

Thus, if a self-employed person has an accounting period ending on 1 June in each year, contributions to a personal pension scheme made between 6 April 2003 and 5 April 2004 are relieved against the assessment for 2003/04 which is based on the earnings in the accounts for the year ending 1 June 2003.

(b)   Carrying back.

An individual can pay a premium and elect to have the tax relief applied against the income for the previous tax year under certain circumstances.

The contribution must be made by 31 January in a tax year, and the election must be made at or before the date the contribution is paid. Contributions made between 31 January and 6 April cannot be carried back, so the last date for a carry-back contribution in 2003/04 is 31 January 2004.

The carry-back can only be made to the tax year immediately prior to the year in which the contribution is made, ie 2002/03 for a contribution made in 2003/04. So a contribution made by 31 January 2004 (ie in the tax year 2003/04) can only be carried back to before 6 April 2003 (ie the tax year

2002/03). Payment would be made net of the basic rate for the year to which the contribution is carried back, even if this is different to the rate for the year of actual payment.

Claims for carry-back relief at the higher rate can be made on a stand-alone basis or as part of the tax return.

Administration of tax relief

17.16 All contributions by an individual are payable net of basic rate income tax relief under a system of tax relief by deduction, often called PTRAS, Pension Tax Relief At Source. The deduction normally has to be made at the basic rate in force at the date of payment. However, if the contribution is carried back to the previous year, the deduction is at the rate for the previous year. The pension provider will then reclaim the relief deducted from the Inland Revenue each month in a block reclaim for all its relevant policyholders. Thus if a gross contribution is £1,000, the individual will pay £780 to the pension provider who will reclaim £220 from the Inland Revenue. Higher rate taxpayers can get higher rate relief from the Inland Revenue either by adjustment of their PAYE code or on their assessment. The pension provider can provide a Contribution Payment Certificate for this purpose but the Inland Revenue do not normally require to see this. A non-taxpayer or starting rate taxpayer does not have the tax relief reclaimed.

The £3,600 threshold referred to earlier is a gross limit, so will net down to £2,808 at 22% basic rate tax.

Higher rate relief is actually given by extending the basic rate band by the amount of the gross pension contribution. However the gross pension contribution can be used to reduce total income for those claiming age allowances. The extension of the basic rate band also applies to deciding whether the basic rate band has been exceeded for CGT purposes, and for chargeable gains on life policies (see **CHAPTER 16**). Evidence of earnings is required only where gross contributions exceed £3,600 in a tax year. The evidence has to be produced to the pension provider for the basis year being used. Evidence required is as follows.

Employed individual

17.17

(a) P60 or week 52 payslip, or

(b) declaration from employer showing amount paid or to be paid, or

(c) tax return or assessment, or

(d) P45 from a previous employer, showing cumulative pay from the previous 6 April to the date that employment ended.

Self-employed individual

17.18

(a) Copy accounts, or

(b) copy of tax return or assessment, or

(c) a written statement from the individual's accountant, solicitor or auditor showing net relevant earnings.

Normally, the evidence must be provided within 30 days of payment of a contribution over £3,600 gross, or if higher, the amount justified by evidence already produced.

Stakeholder pensions

17.19   Stakeholder pensions are treated in exactly the same way as personal pensions for taxation purposes and thus all the rules in **17.6** et seq above apply. Thus in effect a stakeholder pension is really a personal pension with a charge cap which must be made available by most employers who do not have an existing pension scheme.

Retirement annuities

17.20   These contracts were the forerunners of personal pensions and were replaced by them on 1 July 1988. From that date no new retirement annuities could be sold but existing ones could be continued and contributions can still be paid in. Some details must be given of these contracts as they affect any subsequent personal or stakeholder pensions effected by the same individual. They were often called self-employed retirement annuities, although they were also available to individuals in non-pensionable employment.

17.21   In many ways retirement annuities are similar to personal pensions, though there are vital differences.

Contributions attract full income tax relief, but they are not within the **PTRAS** scheme. Thus payment must be made in full with tax relief being claimed via the tax return.

Employers are not permitted to contribute to retirement annuities. The maximum contribution levels are different from personal pensions and are as follows:

Age on 6 April	Percentage of net relevant earnings
Up to 50	17.5
51 to 55	20.0
56 to 60	22.5
60 to 74	27.5

The £3,600 threshold, basis year rules and cessation of earnings rules do not apply. The earnings cap also does not apply to retirement annuities. However if an individual contributes to both a retirement annuity and a personal (or stakeholder) pension the earnings cap does apply to the total contributions. Thus it can still limit contributions, and for a very high earner paying substantial retirement annuity contributions this rule might prevent any contribution to a personal pension.

Net relevant earnings

17.22   Another difference from personal pensions is that the definition of net relevant earnings is wider. It includes earned income from share schemes and the taxable element of golden handshake payments. It also includes the earnings of a controlling director who continues to work for the company after taking retirement benefits from an occupational pension scheme.

Carry back and forward

17.23   These rules also differ from personal pensions. A contribution paid in any tax year can be carried back to the previous year or, if there were no net relevant earnings in that year, to the year before that. A carry-back election must be made by 31 January in the tax year following that of payment.

If an individual has paid less than the maximum possible contribution for any of the previous six years the unused relief can be carried forward and a contribution paid in the current year to mop that up. This can only be done if the maximum contribution for the current year has been paid already. The carried-forward relief is then given on the current year's assessment.

The carry-back rule can be used in conjunction with the carry-forward rule to effectively go back seven years. However this is subject to an overall limit that total contributions in a tax year cannot exceed the net relevant earnings for that year.

Pension life cover

17.24   All forms of pension can include life cover (often called death in service cover) although none have to.

Occupational pension scheme death in service cover

17.25   Most occupational pension schemes provide death in service cover which will inevitably be paid for by the employer's contribution, and which ranks for tax relief in the normal way.

Personal and stakeholder pension life cover

17.26   A personal pension effected before 6 April 2001 can include life cover up to age 75. The maximum premium for the life cover element is limited to 5% of net relevant earnings, and this still applies for contracts continued after that date. The maximum life cover contribution must be based on actual net relevant earnings, not on a basis year figure. However the life cover premium counts towards the overall contribution limit and thus reduces the amount that can be contributed to the pension element.

For personal pensions effected on or after 6 April 2001 and for stakeholder pensions the maximum premium for the life cover element is 10% of the total contributions (including any employer's contribution but not National Insurance rebates). The total of life cover premium and pension contribution cannot exceed the relevant maximum contribution. Thus again, a life cover premium reduces the maximum pension contribution.

The effect of the post-2001 rules is that if pension contributions stop, the life cover premiums must also stop, and the cover will cease. This is not the case for pre-2001 contracts.

Income tax relief on the premium is available in the same way as for the personal pension contribution.

Retirement annuity life cover

17.27   Retirement annuities can provide life cover by a contract often called a *section 226A* policy, after the original section of the *ICTA 1970* which introduced it. No new contracts could be sold after 30 June 1988, but existing ones could be continued.

The maximum premium is 5% of net relevant earnings, which counts towards the overall maximum retirement annuity contribution limit. Tax relief is available in the normal way for retirement annuities.

Taxation of benefits

17.28   The taxation of the benefits depends on the form it takes.

Death benefit

17.29   Any death benefit payable from an occupational pension scheme is not subject to income tax and, because it is almost always payable under a discretionary trust, it is free of inheritance tax as well.

Any rights under an approved occupational scheme are excluded from the estate for IHT purposes under *IHTA 1984, s 151*.

Any death benefit from a personal or stakeholder pension or retirement annuity is also free of income tax and usually inheritance tax because it will normally be payable under trust. The Inland Revenue has confirmed that the reservation of benefit rules do not apply to pension contracts. If this were not so then putting the death benefit in trust would be a reservation, as the right to the pension must be retained by the individual.

Inheritance tax aspects of personal pensions

17.30   When the death benefits of a personal (or stakeholder) pension or retirement annuity are put under trust this is a transfer of value for IHT purposes. The value of the transfer is the reduction in value of the transferor's estate. This is the difference between the premium paid and the open market value of the rights retained by the transferor where the trust is created at outset. Where the trust is created after the start of the contract it is the open market value of the whole contract less the open market value of the rights retained by the transferor.

This value is regarded by the Inland Revenue as nominal if the transferor is in reasonably good health at the time of the transfer. As a general rule, in practice the Inland Revenue do not raise the point in any case where the transferor survives for two years. However they could query a case where the transferor was known to be in poor health at the time of the transfer.

17.31   A further problem is that *IHTA 1984, s 3(3)* provides that an omission to exercise a right is a transfer if it reduces one individual's estate and increases that of another, unless it can be shown that the omission was not intentional. The Inland Revenue have stated that if an individual does not exercise an option when first entitled to do so, this can be a transfer unless it was not intentional. A tax charge could thus arise at the latest time at which the right could have been exercised – the moment before death. Any tax charge would be on the reduction in the estate caused by the omission, ie the retirement lump sum plus the open market value of the pension that could have been taken.

This situation rarely applies because usually an individual takes the pension during his or her lifetime, or dies before retirement. The Inland Revenue have confirmed to the Association of British Insurers that it will not raise the point in cases of genuine pension arrangements, but might if there was evidence that the intention of not taking the pension was to increase the estate of the beneficiaries of the death benefit, ie 'death bed' cases.

Even then the Inland Revenue have said that they would not pursue the matter if the death benefit was paid to the individual's spouse and/or dependants. However, the Inland Revenue do reserve the right to look at each case individually.

Lump sum on retirement

17.32   The lump sum payable on retirement from any type of approved pension is not subject to income tax. This is so even if it is then used to buy a purchased life annuity.

The pension annuity

17.33   Annuities from any occupational, personal or stakeholder pension or retirement annuity are subject to income tax in full as earned income. The annuity payer operates a PAYE system which effectively deducts the correct amount of income tax via a system of code numbers, incorporating the taxpayer's allowances and reliefs.

However this does not apply to retirement annuities which are paid after deduction of basic rate tax. A higher rate taxpayer will have to pay the extra tax (18%) via the annual assessment. A non-taxpayer or starting rate taxpayer can reclaim all, or some, of the tax from the Inland Revenue, using the tax deduction certificate supplied by the pension payer.

Income drawdown

17.34   For personal and stakeholder pensions a policyholder can elect to have an income drawdown facility instead of buying an annuity. This enables withdrawals to be taken from the pension fund, which are treated as income, and purchase of the annuity to be deferred until age 75.

If the policyholder elects for income withdrawals, the lump sum can be taken and income withdrawals can be made at an amount of the policyholder's choice between limits. The maximum withdrawal is the level single life annuity calculated by reference to the Government Actuary's Tables and the pension fund available for the age and sex of the policyholder. The minimum is 35% of the maximum. The actual amount withdrawn must be between these limits, but can be varied each year. The pension provider is responsible for ensuring that the amount is within the limits.

A similar system operates for money purchase occupational pension schemes.

When income withdrawals are being taken they are treated as pension annuities and taxable under PAYE. Income withdrawals are not allowed for retirement annuities.

Trivial pensions

17.35   Very small pensions can be commuted into a lump sum to save all concerned the trouble of paying trivial amounts.

For an occupational pension commutation is allowed if the pension is less than £260 pa. The pension scheme has to deduct income tax at 20% from the lump sum. This tax cannot be reclaimed if the pensioner is a non-taxpayer or starting rate taxpayer. There is no further liability for basic or higher rate taxpayers.

An AVC can only be commuted if the total of the main scheme and AVC pensions is below the limit, and both pensions are being commuted.

For a personal or stakeholder pension commutation is possible if the annuitant is at least 60, if there are any protected rights benefits, or 50 if not, or is retiring early due to incapacity or as a consequence of an Inland Revenue approved occupation. The annuitant must have no other benefits under any other personal pensions. The fund must be £2,500 or less, or insufficient to provide an annuity of at least £260 pa. The lump sum is chargeable to income tax under PAYE. Commutation is not possible where income withdrawals are being taken. Retirement annuities cannot be commuted.

AVC surpluses

17.36   It is possible that the total funds from the main scheme and an AVC at retirement exceed what is needed to provide the maximum approvable benefits. In this case benefits are still restricted to the maximum but the excess funds have to be refunded to the member. The excess is regarded as arising from the AVC and the refund is subject to income tax at 32%. This is deducted by the AVC administrator and paid to the Inland Revenue. The member is deemed to have received income equal to the net refund grossed up at the basic rate of tax. If the member is not liable to tax or is a starting rate taxpayer, there can be no repayment of the tax. If a member is a basic rate taxpayer there is no further liability.

However, if the member is a higher rate taxpayer, the excess rate will be charged on the grossed-up refund. For example, if the excess refund is £2,500 the administrator will deduct £800 and the member will receive £1,700. This is then grossed up at 22% to give £2,179.49 on which tax of 18% (ie 40%–22%) is charged, resulting in a further tax bill of £392.31. The total tax is thus £1,192.31 or 47.7%. There is no higher rate liability if the repayment arises on death.

Unapproved pension schemes

17.37   Prior to 1989 it was an Inland Revenue condition of approval of a pension scheme that an employer could not have any other scheme that would take total retirement benefits over the various limits. This effectively prevented an employer running a 'top-up' scheme to pay benefits over the limits.

However since 1989 employers have been able to operate unapproved top-up schemes without jeopardising approval of the main scheme. Such schemes are taxed differently from approved schemes. They can be Funded Unapproved Retirement Benefit Schemes (FURBS) or Unfunded Unapproved Retirement Benefit Schemes (UURBS).

Funded Unapproved Retirement Benefit Schemes

17.38   When an employer pays into a FURBS, the employee is subject to income tax and NICs on those payments as if they were salary. The employer can claim tax relief as a business expense. If an employee pays into a FURBS, there is no tax relief.

If a FURBS pays out a pension it is subject to income tax in the normal way for occupational pension schemes. A lump sum is, however, tax free. Thus because there are no limits on the lump sum, in practice all FURBS benefits are paid out as lump sums.

Unfunded Unapproved Retirement Benefit Schemes

17.39   With an UURBS there are no contributions into the scheme to fund benefits. Thus all retirement and death benefits are taxable on the member as income when paid out, whether as an annuity or a lump sum. Where an employer buys an annuity for an employee on retirement, there is an income tax charge on the employee on the purchase price of the annuity as well as on the annuity payments as and when made.

The employer's payments gain corporation tax relief as a business expense at the point when the employee is taxed.

Inheritance tax on unapproved pension schemes

17.40   Lump sum death benefits from UURBS are not subject to IHT unless the lump sum is payable as of right to the deceased's estate (which would be very unusual). There will be no IHT if the benefit is under trust and the trustees have a discretion as to whom to pay, even if in the event they decide to pay the estate.

For a FURBS the normal IHT exemption may not apply as it is only given where some part of the cost is met by the employer. As the member is charged to tax on the employer's contribution, the Inland Revenue consider that the member is bearing the whole cost and so the exemption does not apply. Lump sum death benefits could thus possibly give rise to IHT under the settled property rules.

However, the Inland Revenue have stated that when separate and identifiable payments are made by the employer to meet expenses incurred in setting up or administering the scheme, and these are not passed on to the employee, then it will benefit from the exemption. Thus employers generally take this course to secure the IHT exemption.

Foreign pensions

Contributions to foreign pensions

17.41   A foreign pension arrangement will virtually never be approved by the UK Inland Revenue for tax purposes. Nevertheless if the benefits provided by a foreign pension arrangement are broadly similar to those that can be provided by a UK approved retirement benefit scheme the Inland Revenue may be prepared to treat the employer's contributions as not being pay for Schedule E income tax. It may also allow employee contributions to be deductible if they are made out of foreign earnings. Often the Inland Revenue will only allow this where the taxpayer agrees to restrict the rights under the foreign scheme. An example of this would be made where the foreign scheme allowed a greater lump sum than a UK scheme.

17.42   The above was the situation up to October 2002 when it was modified by the European Court of Justice in the case of *Rolf Dieter Danner* (C-136/00). Danner was a Finnish resident who claimed tax relief in Finland on contributions to a German pension scheme. The Finnish tax authorities refused relief and the case ended up in the European Court of Justice.

The court decided that voluntary pension contributions paid to pension providers in other EU states should be allowed as tax deductible in the country of residence of the taxpayer (provided that country gives relief on its own pensions). The court added that a country of residence could disallow tax relief on contributions to foreign pensions only if its law precluded taxation of the resultant pension. Thus, in theory, the UK Inland Revenue will have to allow UK income tax relief on contributions by a UK resident to a pension in another EU state.

The UK Inland Revenue do not seem to have officially responded publicly to this decision so it remains to be seen exactly how it will work in practice.

Foreign pension benefits

17.43   A UK resident receiving a foreign pension is only subject to UK income tax on 90% of that pension. This includes pensions paid by a former employer or state pensions. Any lump sum paid from a foreign pension arrangement is not subject to UK tax if it relates solely to work performed outside the UK.

However if the UK resident is not domiciled in the UK the foreign pension is only taxed to the extent that it is remitted to the UK.

Double taxation

17.44   The foreign pension might also have been taxed in the country of origin as well as in the UK. If so, the double taxation may be mitigated if the UK has a double taxation agreement with the country concerned. Details of double taxation agreements vary but often any foreign tax paid is allowed as a credit against UK tax. In addition many double taxation agreements provide that pensions paid for government service are taxed only in the country which is paying the pension.

Even if there is no double taxation agreement with the country concerned, the UK Inland Revenue may be prepared to allow unilateral relief by setting off the foreign tax against the UK tax.

Pensions for Nazi persecution

17.45   Any pension payable under any special provision for victims of National Socialist persecution made by the laws of Germany or Austria is exempt from income tax.

Pensions and divorce

17.46   Pensions are often neglected in divorce settlements, which is strange as they can often involve considerable sums of money. There are basically three methods of dealing with pensions on divorce:

● Offset

● Earmarking

● Pension sharing

Offset

17.47   This is the commonest way of dealing with pensions. It involves treating pension rights as part of the total assets of the divorcing parties. The divorce settlement can then divide up the matrimonial assets as agreed, leaving the pension untouched. Thus the main earner might retain their pension but transfer other assets to compensate for this.

This is simple and easy to understand but can leave one ex-spouse with assets but no pension, and the other with a pension but few assets. It is obviously not a sensible method to use if there are not enough other assets with which an offset can be done, or where both parties want to have an interest in the pension rights.

Earmarking

17.48 The *Pensions Act 1995* introduced earmarking, although it has not been very popular. The way it works is that the court issues an order to the trustees of a pension scheme or the pension provider specifying that a proportion of the member's benefits is paid directly to the ex-spouse, but only when the member retires. The order is thus deferred in effect until retirement. The court may also override the pension scheme trustees' normal discretion over lump sum death benefits by ordering a percentage to be paid to the ex-spouse.

The disadvantage of earmarking is that there is no clean break between the parties. The ex-spouse has to wait until the member's retirement before getting any payment. The member could defer retirement to age 75 in an extreme case. Pension benefits will also cease on the member's death so it could be that an ex-spouse received very little benefit from earmarking if the member died shortly after retirement. In addition, if the ex-spouse dies or remarries the earmarked benefits revert to the member. There is also a huge tax disadvantage for the member because any earmarked pension is fully taxable on the member even though he (or she) does not receive it. Many members might regard this as adding insult to injury!

Pension sharing

17.49 The problems of earmarking led to pension sharing being introduced by the *Welfare Reform and Pensions Act 1999*. It only applies to divorce petitions filed on or after 1 December 2000. Pension sharing works by the court dividing pension benefits between the parties. Thus each party has their own share of the pension rights, not dependent on the other, and so a clean break is achieved.

The pension split is based on the Cash Equivalent Transfer Value (CETV) and can be any percentage ordered by the court. These rules apply to all types of pension (including SERPS and S2P) except the basic state pension. The rules apply to pensions in payment as well as rights to a pension in the future. In order to enable the legislation to work, trustees of occupational schemes have to quote CETVs within certain time limits, as do providers of other types of pension.

17.50 A funded pension scheme can either give a transfer value or separate membership to the ex-spouse. Many such schemes just offer a transfer value for administrative ease. With a personal pension the ex-spouse effectively gets a lump sum to establish their own personal pension, either with the existing provider or, via a transfer, with another pension provider. The same applies to stakeholder pensions.

The situation is different for retirement annuities. There has to be a transfer to a personal or stakeholder pension because the law does not allow a new retirement annuity to be effected now.

For unfunded pension schemes (eg many public sector schemes) the rules require the scheme to make an internal transfer which gives the ex-spouse their own independent membership. A transfer to another scheme does not have to be offered.

17.51   The pension share given to an ex-spouse is called a pension credit. For the maximum benefit rules this is treated as still belonging to the original member. From the original member's viewpoint this is a pension debit. A pension debit does not count for maximum benefit purposes unless the member is a controlling director and had earnings of more than 25% of the earnings cap in the tax year before divorce, ie currently £24,750.

For these members the pension debit will reduce their maximum benefit. The pension debit is revalued under Government Actuaries Department guidance to arrive at a notional value at the original member's retirement date and then deducted from the normal maximum benefit to arrive at the member's actual maximum benefit.

The effect of these rules is that divorce may reduce a member's pension and lump sum, and also deny them the opportunity to replace the lost pension. The ex-spouse who receives a pension credit is still entitled to their own normal maximum benefit as well as the pension credit. An ex-spouse could in theory have a pension greater than their earnings – for example, a two-thirds earnings pension from their own scheme plus a pension credit from a high-earning ex-spouse.

There is no limit to the pension produced by a pension credit. The credit can be used to provide a lump sum of up to 2.25 times the pension from the credit. The pension which is bought by the credit is taxable as the income of the payee, not the original member.

Very few pension sharing orders have been made to date, possibly due to the unfamiliarity of divorce lawyers with the new legislation.

Tax planning and pensions

17.52   Inland Revenue-approved pension arrangements are very efficient vehicles for tax planning – possibly the most tax-efficient investments currently available in the UK. The reasons can be summarised as follows:

1   Full tax relief is available on contributions, whether from an individual or an employer.

2   Contributions by an employer are not benefits in kind and thus not subject to income tax or NICs.

3   The investment fund is not subject to income tax, corporation tax or capital gains tax. Investments can thus grow faster than they would in a fund which is taxed. However, since 1997, pension funds have not been able to reclaim the tax credit on UK share and unit trust dividends.

4   Lump sums payable on retirement are tax free.

For these reasons pensions are a very tax-efficient way for the owner of a business to extract profits – whether that business is a sole trader, partnership or company.

Personal pensions

17.53   The rules introduced in 2001 along with stakeholder pensions have opened up a number of tax planning areas, including the following:

1   Contributions of up to £3,600 (£2,808 net of basic rate tax relief) can be made regardless of earnings. In an extreme case someone might have no earnings, no other income and thus no income tax liability and still effectively get tax relief of up to £792, ie 22% of £3,600.

2   The basis year rules (see **17.8** above) can be used to enable large contributions to be made, and thus a large amount of tax relief to be claimed, even where earnings are very low or nil.

3   The cessation rules (see **17.9** above) can be used to enable large contributions to be made, and large amounts of tax relief claimed, for the year in which earnings cease and the following five years.

4   The basis year rules can be used in conjunction with the cessation rules.

5   The carry-back rules (see **17.15** above) can be used to claim tax relief in the tax year prior to that in which the contribution was made. This might be very beneficial if tax rates generally, or an individual's own rates, were higher in the previous year.

What type of individual pension?

17.54   For someone who has a pre-1988 existing flexible premium retirement annuity there is the option of putting extra contributions into that contract, or into a personal or stakeholder pension. The following factors should be borne in mind.

1   The earnings cap does not apply to retirement annuities, thus for someone with higher earnings than the cap, a retirement annuity might be better. However as the net relevant earnings percentages are not the same, the lack of a cap must be balanced against the lower percentage. The following table shows the earnings levels above which the retirement annuity limits give a higher contribution than the personal pension limits.

Age on 6 April	£
Up to 35	99,000
36 to 45	113,142
46 to 50	141,428
51 to 55	148,500
56 to 60	154,000
61 to 74	144,000

2   If the individual wants the maximum lump sum, retirement annuity contributions might be preferable because the lump sum is potentially higher on these contracts.

3   The different retirement ages may be relevant. Retirement annuity pensions cannot be taken before age 60, whereas the limit is 50 for personal and stakeholder pensions. If retirement before 60 was required a personal or stakeholder pension would be preferable.

4   A new personal pension might well have a lower charging structure than a retirement annuity, and a stakeholder pension almost certainly will.

5   There is a cash flow advantage to personal and stakeholder pensions as basic rate tax relief is given by deduction at source rather than via the annual tax return.

6   The six-year carry forward facility (see **17.23** above) is available for retirement annuities, although this may not be as beneficial as the basis year and cessation rules for personal and stakeholder pensions.

Salary Sacrifice

17.55   Salary sacrifice is a tax-planning device used by employees. The employee voluntarily gives up part of their salary and in return the employer pays an equivalent sum into the employee's pension plan. Although this looks like a personal contribution from the employee's viewpoint, it is actually an employer's contribution and the employer can obtain tax relief on it as a business expense, subject to the normal limits.

17.56   For an employee it is beneficial because:

- It reduces income tax by reducing income.

- It saves on NICs, particularly now that there is no ceiling for the extra 1% imposed in 2003.

- It enables an employee to top up benefits even if the employer is not willing to meet extra costs.

- It can be an efficient means of avoiding tax and NICs on an annual basis.

17.57   For an employer it is beneficial because:

- There is no extra cost – it matters not to the employer whether the amount is paid as salary or a pension contribution, the amount is the same.

- The pension contribution is eligible for tax relief, as would have been the salary.

- It saves on NICs.

- It can be done by directors as well as employees.

17.58   A salary sacrifice agreement can be done by a simple exchange of letters between employer and employee. However the exchange must take place before the salary sacrifice and must not refer to any pension contribution. If the salary sacrifice exceeds £5,000 the employer's Inspector of Taxes must be notified.

The only potential disadvantages are that the reduced level of salary is taken into account for:

- state second pension entitlement;

- maximum death benefits under the pension scheme;

- maximum pension benefits.

The Pensions Green Paper

17.59   The Government published The Pensions Green Paper in December 2002. This proposes a major overhaul of the pensions system, including the tax rules. The proposals are not yet final and could well change before implementation. The most important proposals are as follows:

- All the existing tax regimes will be abolished and replaced by a single tax regime for all types of pension.

- Pension rights built up prior to implementation will be respected, but all pension rights accruing after implementation will be subject to a single set of rules.

- The current annual contribution limits will be replaced by a single lifetime limit of saving that will benefit from tax relief. This will be £1.4 million at implementation and indexed thereafter.

- When benefits are taken any excess over the lifetime limit would be subject to a 'recovery charge' (or tax) of one-third before being applied to purchase a taxable pension.

- An annual contribution limit of 100% of earnings for earners and £3,600 for non-earners. This would be subject to an overall ceiling on inflows of value into an individual's pension fund of £200,000 at implementation, indexed thereafter.

- Individuals to be able to draw pension benefits whilst still working.

- The minimum age at which pension benefits can be taken will increase from 50 to 55 by 2010.

- A single set of rules for all pensions in payment.

- A tax-free lump sum on retirement of 25% of the pension fund.

- The death before retirement benefit will be limited to the lifetime limit of £1.4 million (indexed).

- Commutation of trivial funds will be allowed for funds of up to £10,000 for anyone over 65, although 75% of this will be subject to income tax.

- In the case of serious ill health before age 75, full tax-free commutation of pension rights.

- No earnings cap.

- No restrictions on transfers between different types of pension.

- No restrictions on concurrent membership of different pension schemes.

- No normal retirement dates.

The Government has announced that the changes will not be implemented until April 2005. Consultation will continue with draft legislation due some time in 2004.

18 Individual Savings Accounts and Personal Equity Plans

Peter Shipp

PIMA

Background/history

Origins in PEPs and TESSAs

18.1   Launched on 1 January 1987, Personal Equity Plans (PEPs) in their original form (*SI 1986/1948*) were designed to encourage new investors to invest directly in the shares of UK companies. The annual subscription limit was £2,400 of which no more than £600 could be used to buy unit trusts or investment trusts, the balance had to be held in the shares of individual UK companies. The scheme was re-launched three years later (*SI 1989/469*) with what remain the principal Regulations to this day, now amended by some sixteen amending Regulations over the ensuing years (*SIs 1990/678, 1991/733, 1991/2774, 1992/623, 1993/756, 1995/1539, 1995/3287, 1996/846, 1996/1355, 1997/511, 1997/1716, 1998/1869, 2000/3109, 2001/923, 2001/3629, 2001/3777, 2003/2748*). These saw the investment restrictions widened progressively to the point where today they are identical with those of the stocks and shares ISA and the subscription limit eventually increased to £6,000 (fully available for collective investments from 1992) until the scheme was closed to subscriptions on 5 April 1999 (*SI 1998/1869*). Holders of PEPs existing at that date can continue to enjoy the tax-free status of the investments held within the PEP wrapper for as long as they keep the plan open.

The Tax Exempt Special Savings Accounts (TESSAs) were introduced in 1990 (*SI 1990/2361*), allowing savers to enjoy untaxed gross income on their savings in return for a commitment to lock them into the TESSA scheme (although not necessarily to remain with the same provider) for five years. The subscriptions to TESSAs were limited to £9,000 overall but there was an option to retain the savings in a follow-on TESSA for a further five years. Similarly, no new accounts could be opened after 5 April 1999 although all accounts open at that date can continue to operate under the TESSA Regulations until their maturity at five years so that savers with such accounts may continue to subscribe under the TESSA Regulations.

Initial ISA proposals

18.2   In 1997 the Chancellor of the Exchequer, Gordon Brown, introduced the new Individual Savings Account (ISA) proposals, which were intended to 'encourage people, through tax relief, to raise the level of their long-term savings building on the experience of TESSAs and PEPs'. In practice, the proposals did not look particularly new, being closely based on the Regulations for TESSAs (without five-year limit) and PEPs. The initial proposals, published in a consultation document, were that each investor would use one single manager to operate cash, insurance and stocks and shares components and that there would be a £5,000 annual subscription limit raised to £7,000 for the 1999/2000 year only. It was proposed that there should be an overall lifetime contribution limit to ISAs of £50,000 per individual and that any PEP they might hold would be rolled into a stocks and shares ISA and would itself contribute towards the £50,000 ceiling. There was also a proposal that there might be a regular prize draw to encourage people to use the scheme.

Original 1999 ISA Regulations

18.3   As a result of detailed industry consultation, a number of features of the original proposals were changed before the principal Regulations (*SI 1998/1870*) were laid in July 1998. By this time, the requirement for a single manager had been replaced with the option of using separate managers for cash, insurance and stocks and shares. Both the £50,000 lifetime limit and the rolling of PEPs into ISAs had been removed, as had the prize draw.

When comparing the stocks and shares section of the new ISA Regulations with the PEP Regulations, the ISA was allowed a much wider choice of investments than was permitted under the, then current, PEP Regulations. Whilst the PEP investor was still restricted to shares in European companies, the ISA investor could buy shares in companies worldwide. The ISA investor could choose gilts which were not allowed in PEPs but in other respects most of the investment rules were very similar, if not identical, to those of PEPs at that time.

The original Regulations were further amended (*SI 1998/3174*) before the scheme launched in April 1999, which altered the definition of 'relevant UCITS' (Undertaking for collective investment in transferable securities within the meaning of Article 1 of *Council Directive 85/611/EEC* – OJ No L375, 31.12.1985, pp 3–18, amended by *Council Directive 88/220/EEC* (OJ No L100, 19.04.1988, pp 31–32)) and extended Government securities beyond UK gilts to include certain equivalent foreign governments' securities.

Subsequent developments

18.4   Further changes have extended the £7,000 subscription, initially to the year 2000/01 (*SI 2000/809*) and subsequently until April 2006 (*SI 2001/908*). Shares deriving from an approved share-ownership plan were brought within the special subscription Regulation (*ISA Reg 7(2)(h)*) with effect from 21 August 2000 (*SI 2000/2079*), allowing them to be transferred into an ISA in the same way as shares from other approved all-employee schemes. A technical problem with eligible foreign shares, dealt through CREST Depository

Interests (CDIs) was addressed with effect from 13 December 2000, making Depository Interests eligible if the investments they represented were themselves eligible (*SI 2000/3112*).

From April 2001 (*SI 2001/908*), cash ISAs became available to 16-year-olds and from the same date the spouses of Crown employees working abroad became eligible to subscribe to an ISA. The *Financial Services and Markets Act 2000 (FSMA 2000)* required some consequential amendments to the ISA Regulations (*SI 2001/3629*), which took effect on 1 December 2001. The Inland Revenue amended their interpretation of the term 'listed on a recognised stock exchange' (*SI 2001/3778*) in December 2001 and further amendments (*SI 2002/453*) were introduced, with effect from 6 April 2002, principally to ensure the same treatment for charitable event gains arising on insurance policies held within an ISA as for those held outside.

18.5   Alterations were made to the Regulations regarding transfer of ISAs between managers (*SI 2002/1974*) with effect from 1 October 2002, giving the investor the right to specify within limits how quickly the transfer should be executed. Various new ISA Regulations (*SI 2002/3158*) were introduced with effect from 8 January 2003 to allow the repair of inadvertent investor errors which breach the subscription rules and previously would have resulted in the investors second and subsequent ISAs being made void.

Following the recent UK implementation of the UCITS Amending Directive (*2001/108/EEC*), amendments have been made to the ISA Regulations (*SI 2003/2747*) to enable Chapter 5 UCITS to be held in an ISA from 17 November 2003. Most Chapter 5 UCITS may be held in a PEP from the same date.

Separate regulations for insurance

18.6   Alongside the principal ISA Regulations, separate Regulations of concern only to insurance companies conducting ISA business were also laid in July 1998 (*SIs 1998/1871* and *1998/1872*) enabling them to continue to reclaim tax credits on distributions in respect of their investments that relate to their ISA business until April 2004 and making modifications to various other Acts to include relevant references to ISA business.

Minor changes have since been made to the ISA Insurance Companies Regulations in amendments laid in December 1998 (*SI 1998/3174*), August 2000 (*SI 2000/2075*) and November 2001 (*SI 2001/3629*). Further amendments were also laid in December 2001 (S*I 2001/3974*).

Regulation and guidance

18.7   The operation of both the PEP and ISA schemes is regulated by secondary legislation to which reference has already been made, in the form of Statutory Instruments issued from time to time by HM Treasury. However the day-to-day operation of the scheme is the responsibility of a special Inland Revenue department ('SPS': Inland Revenue, Savings and Pensions Schemes (SPS) Services Team 2, St John's House, Merton Road, Bootle, Merseyside L69 9BB) to which managers can refer on operational matters. In order to facilitate this process, SPS issues the Guidance Notes for PEP and ISA Managers (Inland Revenue Guidance Notes for PEP and ISA Managers issued by SPS and available at www.inlandrevenue.gov.uk/isa/isagn.htm updated by PEP and ISA Bulletins at www.inlandrevenue.gov.uk/isa/bullmenu.htm) which are updated from time to time through regular bulletins and, where necessary, revised pages are issued. Whilst this guidance has no binding force in law, managers would obviously be ill advised to ignore it.

Tax benefits of PEPs and ISAs

18.8 Both the PEP and the ISA are wrappers, they are not themselves investments although with some types of ISA product in particular the distinction is not immediately apparent. The advantage of using PEPs/ISAs is that any gains made on the investments held within them are free from Capital Gains Tax (CGT) and income is free from income tax on interest and dividend tax credits may be recovered until April 2004.

Current ISA subscription limits and structure

Subscription limits for 2003/4 and beyond

18.9 Any individual aged 18 or over who is resident and ordinarily resident in the UK may subscribe to an ISA subject to an overall annual subscription limit, currently £7,000 per tax year. This limit was originally set for 1999/2000 only but has subsequently been extended until 5 April 2006, after which it will drop to £5,000 unless further amendments to the Regulations are made in the meantime. The ISA may contain any or all of the three components, cash, insurance and stocks and shares, each of which have their own annual limit within the overall £7,000 figure. The limit for cash ISAs is £3,000 (currently until 5 April 2006) and for insurance £1,000. If the investor has chosen to use separate managers for each component (see mini subscription rules below) he will be limited to £3,000 also in stocks and shares. However, if the investor chooses to use one manager for all his ISA requirements in that particular tax year then anything up to the whole £7,000 may be directed into the stocks and shares component of that maxi ISA.

Mini/maxi/TESSA-only subscription rules

18.10 The terms mini and maxi ISA have caused some confusion, particularly as the Regulations refer to them as mini accounts and maxi accounts. A close examination of the Regulations shows that, in fact, they are subscription rules which apply in any particular tax year and which, under certain circumstances, may be varied from one tax year to another.

Distinction between types and components

18.11   Using the maxi subscription route, the investor will place all their ISA subscriptions for that year with one manager. In order to offer the maxi the manager must at least offer the stocks and shares component and may offer a cash and/or insurance component alongside it. Even where the manager offers all three components, the investor is not obliged to use them and could, for example, subscribe £500 to the cash component and £6,500 to the stocks and shares component or indeed the full £7,000 subscription into the stocks and shares component.

The mini subscription route allows the investor to use separate managers for each component to which he subscribes. In this case he could use one manager for cash, another for insurance, and maybe a third for stocks and shares. However, the maximum that can be subscribed to a mini stocks and shares ISA is £3,000.

18.12   The rules do not allow the investor to subscribe to both mini and maxi ISAs in the same year (*ISA Reg 10(2)(b) & (c)*), either with the same manager or different managers. Therefore, any investor who wishes to invest more than £3,000 in stocks and shares will have to use the maxi subscription route.

Under the TESSA Regulations (*TESSA Reg 7B inserted by SI 1995/1929*) savers were permitted to roll their savings into a follow-up TESSA to be held for a further five years. An equivalent facility is provided as part of the ISA Regulations (*ISA Reg 5*) to allow matured TESSA capital to be 'transferred' into the cash component of an ISA within six months of the TESSA maturing. Although this procedure is a subscription to the ISA (the investor has to be eligible to subscribe etc), the amount of capital does not count against the annual subscription limit (currently £3,000) for the cash component or the overall annual limit (currently £7,000).

The capital may be put into an existing mini cash ISA or into the cash component of an existing maxi ISA. However, because investors would be disadvantaged if they had a maxi ISA with no cash component, the ISA Regulations additionally provide the third subscription route – the TESSA-only ISA. This consists of a cash component (only) to which the investor subscribes the matured TESSA capital (and nothing else). Unlike the prohibited maxi/mini combination, an investor may subscribe to a TESSA-only ISA alongside a maxi ISA or mini cash ISA in the same tax year.

How the mini/maxi/TESSA-only labels can fall away

18.13   Most ISA investors will have made a 'continuous' application where the wording makes it clear that the application will apply not only to the year of initial subscription but also to all subsequent tax years until such time as the arrangement is terminated – either at the request of the investor or because a complete tax year has passed without any subscription being made. Where continuous applications are in use, a further subscription in a subsequent tax year will automatically retain the same subscription type (maxi/mini) so that, normally, an account will continue year on year to be the same type.

It is, however, possible for an investor to change, eg from mini to maxi. An investor may have subscribed to a mini stocks and shares ISA in the first year because he had already subscribed to a mini cash ISA with another manager. When he comes to consider his options in the second year, he may decide to put his whole annual allowance (£7,000) into stocks and shares in which case he should make a new maxi application to his stocks and shares manager before making any cash subscription in that second year.

Similarly with a TESSA-only ISA the label will fall away after the end of the tax year in which the matured TESSA capital was subscribed, leaving simply a cash component in subsequent years. This may be relevant in transfer cases as we shall see later. Theoretically, the manager could (in these subsequent tax years only) allow the investor to make maxi/mini subscriptions to this component but, in practice, most managers keep TESSA-only accounts separate for ease of administration. (For similar reasons, some banks' terms and conditions will only allow them to accept matured TESSA capital into a TESSA-only account.)

ISA application process

Written applications

18.14   Under the ISA Regulations, an investor has to apply to subscribe to an ISA and applications fall into two categories, written and non-written. A written application must be made on an application form provided by the ISA manager. There is no proscribed Inland Revenue form but the appropriate wording must be included on the manager's documentation. Investors are required to give personal information including their name, permanent residential address, national insurance number (NINo), if they have one, and date of birth. They are also required to make a declaration that they are 16 or over (18 or over where the ISA is not just a cash component), that they have not subscribed and will not subscribe to another ISA of the same type in that tax year and any subsequent tax years to which they subscribe to this ISA and furthermore that they are resident and ordinarily resident in the UK for tax purposes or treated as such by virtue of being a Crown employee or that they are a spouse of such a Crown employee. The application also authorises the manager to hold their subscription, investments etc on their behalf and to make claims to the Inland Revenue on their behalf for the tax relief available through the ISA scheme.

Applicants with physical or mental incapacity

18.15   Where applicants are physically or mentally incapable of signing a written application or communicating their wishes, special arrangements exist for applications to be accepted from a person appointed to look after their affairs (this may be a guardian, curator bonis, attorney or continuing attorney or the person may have been appointed by a sheriff under an intervention order, authorised under an enduring power of attorney or appointed by the Court of Protection as a receiver). Whilst all ISA applications should be made by the investor personally in order to satisfy the requirements of tax law concerning applications for tax relief, the Inland Revenue's position on this point has relaxed over time, most recently in a bulletin to ISA managers (www.inlandrevenue.gov.uk/isa/bullmenu.htm – Bulletin No 9) issued on 8 January 2003 which allows the ISA manager to accept an application by someone legally appointed or authorised to act on behalf of the incapacitated investor. Furthermore, managers may also accept applications made by certain relatives (parent, guardian, spouse, son or daughter) of an investor suffering from a mental disorder. In all these cases, managers are required to record the fact that they have seen evidence of the appointment or relationship as appropriate.

Powers of Attorney (PoA)

18.16   Whilst an application may be made under a PoA on behalf of an incapacitated person as explained above, applications cannot be accepted under a PoA in any other circumstances, notwithstanding the fact that the PoA is perfectly valid. This is because of the requirement for applications for tax relief to be made in person. This does not prevent a manager accepting other instructions (eg to switch investments, make a withdrawal or even close the account) under a valid PoA.

Non-written applications

18.17   The ISA Regulations also allow for investors to apply in non-written form. Signed application forms, faxes of signed application forms and e-mail applications with an electronic signature (as defined in the *Electronic Communications Act 2000*) are treated as written applications. Applications in any other form are treated as non-written. In this case the investor is still required to give the same information that they would otherwise have given on a printed application form. Because the application has been made in non-written form (eg by telephone), the manager is required to send a written declaration to the investor confirming all the details that have been provided, thereby giving the investor the opportunity to check the accuracy of the information captured by the manager in his ISA system. The investor has 30 calendar days to notify any corrections to the manager who must then issue a revised declaration if necessary. There is no requirement for the investor to sign this declaration.

ISA cash component – eligible investments

Deposits

18.18   The majority of cash ISAs take the form of a deposit account or similar earning gross interest (ie without deduction of tax). These may take the form of a deposit or share account with a building society, a deposit account with a licensed deposit taker or with a relevant European institution, which has been designated as an ISA account.

Unit trusts and OEICs (money market schemes)

18.19   The ISA Regulations also allow the ISA cash component to hold units or shares in money market schemes (see **18.26** below) or units in fund of fund schemes, which qualify for the cash component (by investing in money market schemes) (see **18.26** below).

National Savings

18.20   The cash component may also hold securities issued under the National Loans Act 1968 or the National Savings Bank Act 1971, on terms that allow them to be held in an ISA. National Savings and Investments (previously known as National Savings) offer cash ISAs in this format.

The Tax Deduction Scheme for interest does not apply to income arising on investments held in the Cash component.

ISA insurance component – eligible investments

Policies of life insurance

18.21   The ISA insurance component can hold certain polices of life insurance. The policy must be on the life of the ISA investor alone and the terms and conditions of the policy must require that it may only be owned as a qualifying ISA investment, terminates automatically if it ceases to be so owned, cannot be transferred to the investor and cannot be assigned. It must not form a contract to pay an annuity, be a personal portfolio bond or a contract, which constitutes pension business within the meaning of *ICTA 1988*. After the first payment of premium there must be no contractual obligation to make any further such payments.

Insurance ISAs are offered by relatively few providers – mainly life companies and friendly societies. Take-up of insurance components has been disappointingly low. Subscriptions to insurance components represented less than three-quarters of 1% of total ISA subscriptions in 2002/3 (www.inlandrevenue.gov.uk/stats/isa/isa_t01_1.htm).

ISA stocks and shares component and PEP – eligible investments

Previous PEP Regulations

18.22   Prior to 6 April 2001, PEPs continued to operate under existing PEP Regulations which drew a distinction between general PEPs and single company PEPs (SCPs). This distinction was abolished from that date (*SI 2001/923*) following which any PEP (including those that previously were SCPs) could be invested in any number of qualifying investments. At the same time, the Regulations defining PEP qualifying investments were also aligned with the corresponding Regulations for Stocks and Shares ISAs.

Qualifying shares

18.23   The first category of qualifying investments defined in the Regulations (*PEP Reg 6(2)(a); ISA Reg 7(2)(a)*) covers shares (other than those of a UK Investment Trust) issued by a company from anywhere in the world so long as the shares are officially listed on a recognised stock exchange (the term 'recognised stock exchange' refers to a stock exchange recognised by the Board of Inland Revenue under *ICTA 1988, s 841*). The Inland Revenue interpretation of 'listed on a recognised stock exchange' was revised with effect from 28 November 2001 (*PEP: SI 2001/3777; ISA: SI 2001/3778*) in such a way that several European secondary markets – NASDAQ Europe (formerly EASDAQ); Nouveau Marché and Neuer Markt Frankfurt – were excluded from qualification after that date. There were, however, special arrangements put in place to permit the continued holding of shares dealt on those secondary markets, which were held within a PEP or ISA on that date.

Within the PEP/ISA Regulations (*PEP Reg 2(1)(a); ISA Reg 2(1)(a)*), the definition of 'company' excludes an open-ended investment company (within the meaning given by *FSMA 2000, s 236*). The definition does allow a close-ended investment company based outside the UK to qualify for PEP/ISA holdings, so long as the company's shares are officially listed. This has been used by some investment houses to construct PEP/ISA qualifying funds that do not have to meet the restrictions imposed on UK investment trusts, authorised funds and European UCITS.

Corporate bonds etc

18.24   A corporate bond may be held within an ISA (*PEP Reg 6(2)(b); ISA Reg 7(2)(b)*) if it meets certain listing requirements and has more than five years to maturity at the date on which it is purchased for the PEP/ISA. The corporate bond meets the listing requirement if it is officially listed on a recognised exchange or the shares of the issuing company are officially listed or the issuing company is a 75% subsidiary of a listed company.

A corporate bond issued by an investment trust will be a qualifying investment so long as it meets the above requirements.

Gilts etc

18.25   This category (not available in PEPs prior to 2001) includes Government gilt edged securities (*TCGA 1992, Sch 9 paras 1, 1A*), gilt strips and equivalent securities and strips issued by Governments of any EEA state; ie a state, other than the UK, which is a contracting party to the Agreement on the European Economic Area signed at Oporto on 2 May 1992, as adjusted by the Protocol signed at Brussels on 17 March 1993. These must also have at least five years to maturity when purchased for the PEP/ISA.

UK funds – unit trusts and OEICS

18.26   To be held in a PEP/ISA, an authorised fund has to meet both the 50% rule and also the definitions of 'security scheme' or 'warrant scheme', or be a qualifying 'fund of funds scheme' (see Table below).

Authorised fund	covers both a unit trust scheme authorised by the FSA under *FSMA 2000, s 243* and a UK incorporated OEIC authorised by the FSA under *Reg 14* of the *OEIC Regulations 2001*)
The 50% rule	not more than 50% in value of the investments of the trust, scheme or UCITS, or investments subject to the trusts of the scheme, as the case may be, are either corporate bonds or gilts which had less than five years to maturity at the date when they first became investments of the trust, scheme or UCITS or, as the case may be, investments subject to the trusts of the scheme – *PEP Reg 6(8); ISA Reg 7(8)*
Security scheme	an authorised fund which, according to the terms of the scheme, belongs to the category of securities scheme as established by the FSA, and a part of an umbrella scheme which would belong to that category if the part were itself an authorised fund
Warrant scheme	an authorised fund which, according to the terms of the scheme, belongs to the category of warrants scheme as established by the FSA, and a part of an umbrella scheme which would belong to that category if the part were itself an authorised fund
Fund of funds scheme	an authorised fund which, according to the terms of the scheme, belongs to the category of fund of funds scheme as established by the FSA, and a part of an

	umbrella scheme which would belong to that category if the part were itself an authorised fund and where the terms do not allow the scheme to invest in any funds other than securities schemes or warrant schemes

These terms are defined within the Regulations (*PEP Reg 2(1)(b); ISA Reg 2(1)(b)*) by reference to the categories established by the FSA, which have since been overtaken by the new UCITS directive (*2001/108/EEC*) that will be fully adopted in the UK by 2007. To be qualifying PEP/ISA investments, such funds will continue to be subject to the 50% test until 5 April 2004 or they adopt Chapter 5 status (see **18.28**). From 6 April 2004, the 50% test no longer applies to funds (although it will still apply to investment trusts – see **18.29**) and will be replaced by the new 95% test (see **18.28**). Any 'old style' funds validly held within a PEP or stocks and shares ISA at 5 April 2004 which fail the 95% test, may continue to be held but they will not qualify for further investment.

Relevant UCITS

18.27   The PEP/ISA Regulations allow for UCITS situated in other European Union States (other than the UK) to be included within a PEP/ISA so long as they have been authorised by the competent authorities in their home state, are a 'recognised scheme' (within the meaning of *FSMA 2000, s 264*) and again meet the 50% requirement (*PEP Reg 6(8); ISA Reg 7(8)*). The 50% test will be replaced by the new 95% test from 6 April 2004 (see **18.26**). (The requirement that a relevant UCITS would fall within the definitions of security scheme or warrant scheme if it were subject to regulation by the FSA was removed with effect from 17 November 2003.)

Chapter 5 UCITS

18.28   Currently launched funds now need to comply with Chapter 5 of the Collective Investment Schemes Sourcebook and existing funds must convert by 2007. The previous fund categories used in the PEP/ISA Regulations have been replaced by one mixed fund category. Because the Government does not wish to see any further ingress of cash-like investments into the stocks and shares component (or a PEP), they have introduced a test to distinguish between cash-like and other UCITS schemes based on the proportion of capital which an investor could be certain, or near certain, of receiving from their investment. If the investor is exposed to risk of loss of at least 5% throughout the first five years that the fund is held in the PEP or stocks and shares ISA, it will qualify. (Funds that fail this test would be eligible to be held in the cash component of an ISA.)

Investment trusts

18.29   We have noted earlier that a close-ended investment company based outside the UK may qualify under the category of qualifying shares. However, UK investment trusts (*ICTA 1988, s 842*) have their own PEP/ISA Regulations (*PEP Reg 6(2)(f); ISA Reg 7(2)(d)*) which require that they must have no eligible rental income (*ICTA 1988, s 508A*) and must again meet the 50% requirement (*PEP Reg 6(8); ISA Reg 7(8)*).

The net effect of this Regulation and the corporate bond Regulation is that both shares and corporate bonds issued by a qualifying investment trust may qualify to be held within a PEP/ISA but no other instruments (eg warrants) qualify. There is, however, an exception in cases where a new investment trust is launched in the form of units comprising shares with warrants attached. In such a case, if application is made by a PEP/ISA manager with funds from within the wrapper, any units applied for and allocated may be retained in the PEP/ISA. Once the shares and warrants are unstapled (traded separately, usually about a month after the launch), both shares and warrants may continue to be held within the PEP/ISA.

Shares from approved share schemes

18.30   Shares which employees acquire by virtue of their participation in an approved all-employee share scheme (*ISA Reg 7(2)(h)*), may be transferred directly into the stocks and shares component of an ISA as a subscription, valued at market value on the date of transfer against the current year's subscription limit. In other words, the maximum value of shares that could be transferred into a newly opened maxi ISA would be £7,000 worth. Note that, via this route, investors may legitimately hold shares, which would not otherwise be qualifying investments (eg shares in unlisted companies that operate one of the qualifying schemes).

Depository interests

18.31   This mechanism is used by most dematerialised systems, such as CREST, particularly in cases where investors hold and trade in non-UK shares. The Government were advised that the PEP/ISA Regulations did not permit the holding of depository interests which created an anomaly given that, on the one hand, investors were being encouraged to dematerialise their holdings for the greater efficiency of share dealing and, on the other, the PEP/ISA Regulations allowed share holdings in foreign companies to a larger extent than before. This was addressed by a change in the Regulations (*PEP: SI 2000/3109; ISA: SI 2000/3112*) to allow depository interests to be held where they represent what would otherwise be qualifying investments.

Historical anomalies (PEP and ISA)

Amended listing interpretation

18.32 In November 2001 the Inland Revenue adopted a revised interpretation of the phrase 'listed on a recognised stock exchange' (see **18.23**). There is, however, a special rule (*PEP: Reg 6(2)(o) inserted by SI 2000/3109; ISA: Reg 7(2)(k) inserted by SI 2000/3112*) for shares and securities validly held at 28 November 2001 in a PEP or stocks and shares ISA by virtue of their listing on NASDAQ Europe, Nouveau Marché and Neuer Markt Frankfurt. Although no longer qualifying shares for new purchases, such shares will remain as qualifying investments for as long as they remain held within the PEP/ISA.

If these investments should change in any way, PEP/ISA managers will be required to apply two tests:

1   If they would now qualify for a PEP/ISA without the special rule, from that point the investments lose their protection under this special rule. Should they later change again, they must then satisfy the same rules as any other investments held in a PEP/ISA.

2   If the investments would still not otherwise qualify for a PEP/ISA, they still retain the protection of the special rule and may remain in the PEP/ISA provided they would have satisfied the PEP/ISA Regulations applying prior to 28 November 2001.

Historical anomalies (PEP only)

Alignment with ISA investment rules

18.33   The PEP investment rules were aligned with those for ISAs with effect from 6 April 2001. Broadly speaking, this represented a widening of the scope of qualifying investments for PEPs, almost without exception. However provision is made, with another special rule (*PEP: Reg 6(2)(m) inserted by SI 2001/923*), that any investments validly held in a PEP on that date, that would not qualify under the Regulations after that date, can continue to be held in the PEP. However, if the investments change in any way then the manager should apply the two tests as set out in the previous paragraph.

The one area that this rule would seem to cover is that of Housing Investment Trusts which would have been eligible under the pre-April 2001 PEP Regulations and, if already held at that date, may therefore continue to be held to the present day.

Restriction of collectives allowed in PEPs after 5 April 1990

18.34   The principal PEP Regulations (*SI 1989/469*) (within certain subscription limits) allowed investors to invest during 1989/90 in any authorised unit trust or investment trust. This was tightened up in April 1990 (*SI 1990/678*) when a requirement was introduced that qualifying unit trusts and investment trusts must have at least 50% in value of their investments held in shares of UK companies. As a result, some previously qualifying holdings became non-qualifying.

However, a special rule (*PEP Reg 6A* (later removed by *SI 2001/923* with effect from 6 April 2001)) was also introduced to allow such non-qualifying investments validly held on 5 April 1990 to be continue to be held. This rule was eventually swept away on 6 April 2001 when the qualifying investment rules for PEPs were aligned with those for stocks and shares ISAs. Nevertheless, in the unlikely (but possible) event of an investor continuing to hold such non-qualifying investments since before 5 April 1990, the combined effect of this special rule and the previously mentioned rule concerning qualifying investments held on 5 April 2001 is to allow them to continue to be held.

Other investments that cease to qualify

18.35   The special rules discussed in the preceding paragraphs are designed to retain within existing PEPs/ISAs any investments that no longer otherwise qualify because the Regulations have been changed.

The opposite situation occurs when a qualifying investment ceases to qualify because something about the investment changes. A common example is where shares that previously were officially listed on the Stock Exchange are delisted and trading in the shares moves to the Alternative Investment Market (AIM). Another example would be where an authorised fund or an investment trust alters the balance of its portfolio and ceases to meet the 50% rule.

The Inland Revenue guidance gives the investor two alternatives in these circumstances. The first choice is to sell the investment within 30 days of it ceasing to qualify, in which case the proceeds remain within the PEP/ISA and may be used to buy replacement qualifying investments, thereby maintaining value within the PEP/ISA wrapper. Alternatively, if an investor believes that the investment is worth retaining, notwithstanding the fact that it cannot be held in the PEP/ISA, they may use the second option which is to transfer the investment in specie (an off-market transfer of legal title from the PEP/ISA manager's nominee to the investor; see **18.49**) to be held in their own name outside the PEP/ISA.

Cash

18.36   In the past, there has been some friction between the Inland Revenue and a minority of investors and their managers where large sums of money, having been subscribed to a PEP or stocks and shares ISA, have been left in cash for prolonged periods of time without being invested. The Inland Revenue view is that the stocks and shares ISA/PEP is a vehicle for investment in stock market based instruments and not one for holding cash (which should be held in the ISA cash component or, previously, in a TESSA).

Purpose for which cash is held

18.37   Neither the PEP nor ISA Regulations are specific about how long cash may be held pending a suitable investment opportunity nor about how much cash may reasonably be held. They simply state that cash may be held for the purpose of buying qualifying investments (in due course) (*PEP Reg 6(2)(n); ISA Regs 7(2)(j)* and *9(2)(b)*). The PEP/ISA Regulations allow investors to hold cash in this way for the very good reason that the Government does not want them to force an investor to make an investment at a time when all advice might be to wait. This could easily lead to bad press and lurid headlines about the way in which some deserving case has lost most of the value of their life savings, not through bad investment advice, but as a direct result of a time or monetary limit in the regulations.

The delay in investing the cash may be because the investor is waiting for the market to move in their favour before investing an ISA subscription (or the proceeds of selling a previous investment within the PEP/ISA) or perhaps because the cash concerned represents miscellaneous income which has not yet built up sufficiently to justify a cost effective purchase of further investments.

18.38   This is not an issue for the traditionally marketed unit trust where the PEP/ISA wrapper is placed around the units but every penny of the subscription is immediately invested and income is either paid out or re-invested so that there is no separate cash balance at any time. Some managers operating this type of PEP/ISA are not authorised to hold client money in the PEP/ISA. The issue is very much more of concern to managers operating PEPs/ISAs where direct investment in shares and other securities is allowed (whether on a self-select or discretionary basis) and to a certain extent it may apply to some types of self-select/supermarket type fund products that have been developed in more recent years.

One of the remaining differences between the PEP and ISA Regulations is the way in which any interest on such cash on deposit is treated.

PEP treatment of interest on cash on deposit

18.39   In the case of PEPs, interest on cash on deposit is credited to the account without deduction of tax (*PEP Reg 17A* and Guidance 10.24–10.28). If any such interest is withdrawn from the PEP without first having been invested the amount of interest withdrawn is subject to tax in the investor's hands outside the PEP. There is however a de minimis disregard limit of £180 per plan per tax year. If the amount of interest withdrawn is less than £180 no tax is deducted by the manager and no liability incurred by the investor.

In order to administer this, managers of these types of PEP need to keep a running total (per individual per plan) of interest credited to the account and also any amounts of that interest that have been paid out to the investor during the year. If the amounts paid out exceed £180, then the whole amount paid out must have tax deducted at the lower rate by the manager and is then subject to the his marginal tax rate in the investor's hands (so that he needs to record the interest on his tax return).

In determining whether a cash withdrawal from a PEP contains any interest, the uninvested interest is treated as the last cash to be withdrawn. Similarly, it is treated as the first cash to be used when a legitimate debit is applied to the PEP (whether in settlement of a purchase of qualifying investments or in respect of fees due to the manager for the administration of the PEP wrapper).

ISA treatment of interest on cash on deposit

18.40 By the time the ISA Regulations were drafted in 1999, the Inland Revenue felt it could take a simpler approach to the issue of dealing with uninvested interest in the stocks and shares (and insurance) components of an ISA. As a result the ISA Regulations allow interest to be credited gross but require the manager to deduct a 20% flat-rate charge (technically not income tax) which he then passes to the Inland Revenue usually by adjusting his next interim claim. This applies equally to stocks and shares and insurance components of an ISA, although it would be very unusual for an insurance ISA to hold cash on deposit in the first place (*ISA Reg 23* and Guidance 10.29–10.31).

Clearly, the ISA rule is easier for the manager to administer, albeit the investor suffers a 20% deduction which the PEP investor does not (so long as he orders his affairs accordingly). However, the Inland Revenue decided that the existing PEP rule described in the previous paragraphs should remain unchanged in order to avoid unnecessary alterations to managers' systems (and the expense incurred thereby). Each rule, in its own way, is designed to achieve the same end, namely to discourage people from holding cash long term in the PEP/stocks and shares ISA.

Investment income

Dividends and dividend distributions – reclaim of tax credits until 6 April 2004

18.41 Managers can claim UK tax credits arising on dividends and dividend distributions, payable prior to 6 April 2004 in respect of investments held in the PEP/stocks and shares ISA by making claims to the Inland Revenue (SPS).

Note that, if an investor chooses to accept scrip dividends (further stock in place of the cash dividend), there is no tax credit that may be reclaimed even where a 'notional tax voucher' may be incorporated in the documentation.

Interest on corporate bonds and gilts – reclaim of income tax

18.42 Managers may also claim UK income tax deducted at source from income in respect of PEP/ISA investments in corporate bonds etc. The reclaim of income tax on interest in this way is not affected by the 6 April 2004 cut off for the reclaiming of tax credits mentioned in the previous paragraph. In most cases, gilts will pay interest gross so there will be no income tax for the manager to recover.

Insurance ISAs – reclaims of tax credits and income tax

18.43 ISA managers who are insurer managers can claim UK tax credits on dividends payable prior to 6 April 2004, UK tax deducted at source from interest on bonds, and foreign withholding tax (all in respect of income referable to ISA business) from their own tax office (guidance for insurers is included on the claim form R19 and in the note sent out with the CT61 return form).

Reclaim procedures

18.44 All managers are required to make an annual claim (*PEP Reg 20; ISA Reg 26*) to the Inland Revenue (SPS) in respect of all the tax credits and income tax that they are claiming in respect of the tax year to which the claim refers.

PEP10/ISA10 interim claims

18.45 In addition to the mandatory annual claims, managers may also make interim claims (*PEP Reg 19; ISA Reg 25*) on PEP10/ISA10 forms on a tax month basis. Whilst managers are not compelled to make interim claims, most do since not to do so would deprive their investors of the tax credits/income tax to which they are entitled for a longer period of time than is necessary. These same claim forms are used to reclaim both tax credits on dividends and dividend distributions and also income tax deducted at source from interest paid by corporate bonds and from interest distributions. The interim claim forms must be submitted to the Inland Revenue by the end of the calendar month during which the tax month ends and repayment is made electronically directly into the manager's ISA client money account on the 17th, or into his PEP client money account on the 21st, of the following month.

It is a requirement that managers only reclaim tax credits/income tax for income where they hold the distribution voucher. Interim claims can be made to cover a period up to a maximum of six months (all within one single tax year) if necessary in order to make supplementary claims for tax credits from earlier periods where tax vouchers had been delayed etc.

ISA14/PEP14 annual return and claims

18.46   These mandatory returns have to be submitted within six months of the end of the tax year (ie by 5 October each year) and until recently required the signature of an external auditor. This usually meant that the manager had to arrange a special audit of his PEP/ISA function before such a sign off could be given. The Inland Revenue have more recently relaxed their requirements (www.inlandrevenue.gov.uk/isa/bullmenu.htm – Bulletin No 5) so that, as an alternative, a manager may now submit a copy of his audited Report and Accounts for the accounting year ending during the tax year to which the annual claim refers. This has made the process of completing the annual return on time much simpler and has also reduced the cost to managers because, in most cases, an external audit visit is no longer necessary.

Withdrawals and transfers

18.47   The PEP and ISA Regulations do not impose any restrictions on withdrawals either in cash or in specie from these accounts. However, in designing some PEP/ISA products, managers may impose their own restrictions within their business Terms and Conditions. Withdrawals from PEPs and ISAs are entirely tax free (provided the plan or account is not in breach of the Regulations).

Cash withdrawals

18.48   It is common for managers to allow one-off lump-sum withdrawals and there are also many products on the market allowing regular income withdrawals, usually paid electronically directly into the investor's own bank account.

Where an investor wishes to withdraw a cash lump sum from his PEP/stocks and shares ISA, this may well involve the manager in selling shares or cashing units to raise the sum required for the withdrawal. There is no tax liability on the investor because any gain that may occur is protected within the PEP/ISA wrapper and is therefore free of any CGT liability. Likewise any loss incurred within the PEP/ISA cannot be offset against gains elsewhere.

In specie withdrawals

18.49   A manager may be required to make an in specie withdrawal from a PEP/ISA either because the investor has requested it or perhaps because the investment concerned has become non-qualifying (as discussed earlier).

Regardless of the reason for the in specie withdrawal, the manager will have to arrange the re-registration into the new name, which need not be the PEP/ISA investor's own name so long as it is the investor who gives the instruction. The manager is also obliged to provide the market value at the date of withdrawal.

For CGT purposes, the investor is deemed to have acquired the investment on the date of transfer. The market value on that date is the investor's acquisition cost for CGT purposes for the new holding outside the PEP/ISA. If the transfer involves qualifying shares or securities which are officially listed, the value is calculated by reference to a well-established formula (*TCGA 1992, s 272*). If units or OEIC shares are being transferred, the managers bid price should be used This is not reduced by any exit, redemption or withdrawal fees that the manager may charge

Transfers to/from another manager

Transfer of whole plan/account

18.50   Under the PEP/ISA Regulations, the investor has, at all times, the fundamental right to transfer the whole of his PEP/ISA from his existing manager to another manager. All managers must provide the facility to transfer the whole PEP/ISA (*PEP Reg 4(6)(f)(i); ISA Reg 4(6)(f)(i)*).

Partial transfers

18.51   With the introduction of ISAs in 1999 (*ISA Reg 4(6)(f)(ii)*) and subsequently in PEPs (*PEP Reg 4(6)(f)(ii)* as amended by *SI 2001/923*), investors have also been able to transfer a part of their PEP/ISA to another manager. Managers are not obliged to offer this facility, known as a 'partial transfer', although many do. With a partial transfer, the investor can choose to define that part of the PEP/ISA that is to be transferred in any manner acceptable to the manager (under his terms and conditions) subject to the one constraint that the current subscription year (if any) cannot be split. The current year must either be transferred complete within the part of the ISA being transferred to the new manager or retained completely within the part remaining with the existing manager.

Correct procedures

Documentation

18.52   There is no obligatory transfer documentation and managers can, if they wish, simply include all the required information within a letter to the other manager. However, many managers will use their own transfer forms based on the model forms provided by the Inland Revenue (paras 11.34/5 of the Guidance Notes). Neither is there a standard procedure for the transfer between managers other than the fact that the Inland Revenue require that the two managers concerned agree the terms of the transfer and the date when it is going to happen. The Regulations require the old manager not only to provide the new manager with sufficient information (*PEP Reg 16(3); ISA Reg 21(6)*) for him to continue to manage the PEP/ISA but also to make a declaration

(PEP Reg 16(4); ISA Reg 21(7)) that he has done so and fulfilled his obligations under the PEP/ISA Regulations.

Transfers in cash or in specie

18.53 The PEP/ISA Regulations concerning the transfer of plans/accounts to another manager (*PEP Reg 16; ISA Reg 21*) provide that the transfer between managers may be in cash (by liquidating existing holdings with the old manager prior to transfer) or in specie (by transferring actual assets) or in a combination of the two.

Transfers in cash are common where the existing PEP/ISA is held in a traditionally marketed unit trust because a transfer in specie to another fund manager would not be appropriate. Commonly such PEP/ISA products will include in their terms and conditions a requirement that all transfers will be in cash.

For managers operating PEPs/ISAs where direct investment in shares and other securities is allowed and also with some of the self-select/supermarket type fund products that have been developed in more recent years, the managers will commonly allow transfers of assets in specie. Depending on the type of PEP/ISA, there will often be an uninvested cash balance to be transferred alongside.

ISA subscription and component information must be given

18.54 Where the transfer of an ISA is (wholly or partially) in cash, the old manager must indicate what proportion of the cash belongs in each of the three ISA components. He should also indicate the amount of any subscriptions made in the current tax year together with an indication of whether they have been made under a mini, maxi or TESSA-only agreement.

This information is essential in order to enable the new manager firstly to allocate assets and cash to the correct components and secondly to record whether he is now managing the current year subscription for the investor and, if so, what subscription type (maxi/mini) it is. If the ISA being transferred is shown to include subscriptions made in the current tax year through the old manager prior to the date of transfer, the new manager must take these subscriptions into account in determining what further subscriptions (if any) the investor may make. He should also maintain the same subscription type as previously.

The principle is that in regulatory terms, whilst the new manager will see this as a 'new' ISA business and will require customer agreement etc, this is the same ISA that was previously managed by the old manager and is now managed by the new manager. For this reason, the Regulations do not require the investor to complete an application form to the new manager purely to transfer the ISA. The investor will, however, need to make an application if he wishes to make any subscriptions.

PEP uninvested interest must be accounted for

18.55 We have seen earlier in this chapter (see **18.39**) that interest on cash that the investor holds on deposit in a PEP, pending a suitable investment opportunity, is entitled to receive interest without deduction of tax but that such interest is taxable, subject to a £180 disregard limit, if paid out of the PEP. This must be accounted for when transferring a PEP to another manager.

If the whole PEP is being transferred, the old manager must provide details of both the total amount of interest on cash on deposit credited to the PEP which has not been invested in qualifying investments (or used to meet legitimate fee debits on the account) prior to the date of transfer and also the amount of such interest that has been paid out from 6 April up to the date of transfer. This enables the new manager to incorporate that information into his own PEP system and continue to monitor such interest and any withdrawals during the rest of the tax year.

Where there is a transfer of part of a PEP (a 'partial transfer'), this information is not required by the new manager who, for these purposes, is effectively deemed to have a 'new' PEP and starts with both totals at zero. The old manager continues to monitor, as before, the part of the PEP remaining with him.

Implications of incorrect procedures

18.56 Whilst transfers commonly involve passing a cash lump sum between the managers, as discussed earlier in this section, it is essential that the old manager sends these cash amounts directly to the new manager and that they are not inadvertently sent to the investor.

If the investor were to receive a cheque representing the cash element of a transfer and to bank the cheque, the Inland Revenue would regard this as a withdrawal from the PEP/ISA. Even if that were not what the investor had intended, the Inland Revenue will not allow that withdrawal to be unwound. The effect therefore would be that the investor had lost the PEP/ISA tax benefit for all time.

In the event that such an error has been made, the manager responsible should seek guidance from the Inland Revenue (SPS) who may allow the situation to be corrected if the cash is deemed not to have left the PEP/ISA environment. If the investor returns the cheque unbanked (and in certain circumstances where cash has been transferred to another account with the same institution but has not been used) then SPS may allow correction but managers cannot rely on this and it is obviously incumbent on them to ensure that correct procedures are followed in the first place.

Closure of PEPs/ISAs

Investor chooses to close his PEP/ISA

18.57   An investor may close his plan/account at any time without any loss of tax benefits, assuming it is valid and not in breach of the PEP/ISA Regulations. The Regulations do not require this instruction to be given in writing although many firms will include this as a requirement in their terms and conditions. Neither do the Regulations prevent the manager from accepting instructions given by another person, whether under a Power of Attorney or otherwise, if he wishes to accept them.

In many cases, the PEP/ISA will be due to receive further tax credits or income tax after the date of the instruction to close the plan/account. In such cases, there is no requirement to withhold processing the closure and/or distribution of the cash/assets to the investor. Typically this process will take place promptly on receipt of the investor's instructions and, following receipt of the proceeds of any sale of assets, payment will be made to the investor – this date is normally recorded as the closure date for the account. This leaves the PEP/ISA with a nil balance ready to receive outstanding tax credits and reclaimed income tax in the course of the monthly reclaim cycle.

18.58   When these outstanding amounts have been received by the manager and processed onto the account, they will also be paid away to the investor as a supplementary payment. In cases where the investor, as part of their instruction to close the account, has requested that some of the assets be transferred in specie to themselves, the re-registration process may take some further time after the recorded date of closure.

Where an ISA has been closed and, in the same tax year, the investor subsequently wishes to make further subscriptions (assuming they had not already fully subscribed), the manager may re-open the account (Guidance 12.5) and accept further subscriptions up to the limits for that year. In such cases, the account will be recorded as if it had never been closed but had been open throughout the year, albeit with a nil balance and no assets for part of that time.

Other reasons for closure of the PEP/ISA

18.59   Some managers may require that plans/accounts will be closed automatically if the balance falls below a particular level. This is acceptable so long as it is clearly stated in their terms and conditions.

When an investor ceases to meet the residency requirements, whilst they are no longer eligible to subscribe to an ISA, there is no requirement for the PEP/ISA to be closed. In cases where an investor has emigrated, for example, their PEP/ISA may remain open and will continue to be eligible for the tax reliefs, assuming that the manager does not require closure in his terms and conditions. The investor may, however, be liable for tax in his new country of residence.

Death of an investor

18.60   The death of an investor also forces the closure of the PEP/ISA, although this may take time whilst the normal procedures for dealing with a deceased account are followed. The PEP/ISA status is lost after the date of death.

Tax credits etc

18.61   The manager is not entitled to claim tax credits on dividends or to reclaim income tax on corporate bond interest where the pay date is later than the date of death. For earlier pay dates, the manager will reclaim in the usual way and credit the amounts recovered from the Inland Revenue to the deceased account, which is technically no longer a PEP/ISA although for administrative convenience it may continue to be held within the manager's PEP/ISA system.

Interest on cash on deposit

18.62   Interest on cash on deposit within the PEP/ISA which is paid or credited after the date of death is subject to tax in the hands of the estate and managers should deduct tax at the lower rate. However, the Inland Revenue will allow managers to apportion such interest up to the date of death and treat that portion as arising in the PEP/ISA.

In the case of a cash ISA, this means that it will not be subject to deduction of tax.

18.63   In a stocks and shares (or insurance) ISA, it will be subject to the flat rate deduction (*ISA Reg 23*). Frequently, where notification of death is less than prompt, the manager will have applied this flat rate deduction to interest relating to the period after the date of death. Technically this should be recovered and repaid to SPS and lower rate tax then deducted. However, because the flat rate charge equates to the lower rate tax due (both are 20%) the manager simply treats as lower rate tax that part of the deduction that relates to interest covering the period after the date of death (Guidance 12.12–12.14).

In a PEP, any interest paid to the personal representatives which was credited up to the date of death but had not been invested will be subject to tax if, together with withdrawals of such interest earlier in the tax year, it exceeds the £180 de minimis limit discussed earlier (see **18.39**).

Information to be provided to personal representatives

18.64   The manager will have to report the market value of the PEP/ISA, including any cash balance, as at the date of death. If, as a result of late notification of death, further transactions such as sales and purchases of investments have taken place after the date of death, full details (date and proceeds/costs) must be provided to the estate together with supporting tax certificates (R189K, R185 or Section 352 as appropriate).

The manager should make it clear to the representatives that, subject to any contrary provisions in his terms and conditions, the assets held within the PEP or stocks and shares ISA do not necessarily have to be sold and may be transferred to the estate or to a beneficiary. In the case of an insurance ISA, the rights conferred by the policy vest in the personal representatives who are obliged to make a prompt claim under the policy which must pay out on the death of the investor (by definition the insured).

Voiding PEPs/ISAs

Reasons to be void

18.65   A PEP/ISA may be found to be invalid as a result of which, depending on the cause, either the whole or a particular part has to be made void. The possible causes are many but all will either be as a result of manager errors or of investor errors.

Some errors can be put right ('repaired') whilst those that cannot require the complete PEP/ISA status be removed retrospectively, unwinding the situation and then rolling forward again as if the PEP/ISA had never existed. The latter cases may be quite complex to calculate in some cases but all tax benefits of the scheme have to be recovered and repaid to the Inland Revenue.

'Simplified voiding' to correct manager errors

18.66   All registered managers are subject to regular examination (now at roughly 3-year intervals, although this will vary depending on the size and nature of the manager's PEP/ISA business) by Inland Revenue auditors who operate to a published set of objectives (Guidance Appendix H). Where the manager is found to have made inadvertent errors that can be put right, SPS has introduced the concept of simplified voiding as an option within the Guidance Notes. It is not compulsory and both the manager and the Inland Revenue can insist on dealing with the errors found strictly in accordance with the PEP/ISA Regulations. The manager can elect, as an alternative and subject to Inland Revenue approval, to adopt simplified voiding in respect of a particular audit visit but he cannot 'pick and mix' between the two. In practice, most audited managers elect to use simplified voiding and the Inland Revenue almost always allow it.

Errors that cannot be repaired

18.67   A typical error that cannot be repaired would be the discovery that a PEP/ISA investor had not met the necessary requirements (residency/age etc) at the time of subscription. The PEP/ISA must be totally unwound. Another example would be a PEP/ISA that had been opened before the end of one tax year where the subscription was actually made after the next tax year had started.

Repairable errors

18.68   Many inadvertent manager errors can be repaired using simplified voiding, a procedure that is available through the Inland Revenue Guidance Notes.

If, for example, the manager has lost the ISA application form and cannot produce it for the auditors inspection, the ISA is invalid and, under a strict application of the rules, will have to be made void, no doubt considerably annoying the investor. Using simplified voiding, the manager can ask the investor to complete a duplicate application form and place that on file. The manager will then settle with the Inland Revenue on the basis of the period of time that this ISA was in breach – in this example from the date the subscription was credited until the date of repair.

Another example would be where the audit discovers that a PEP or stocks and shares ISA is found to be holding an investment that is not a qualifying investment. If this is accepted as an inadvertent error (as opposed to a lack of adequate procedures to check the eligibility of investments being made by the manager) the manager can now sell the investment and replace it with a qualifying investment. The settlement will be based on the length of time that the non-qualifying investment has been held. The same would apply if an investment which qualified at the time of purchase, subsequently became non-qualifying and was not noticed at the time.

18.69   These are just two examples. In most cases where simplified voiding is used, the manager will be required to make a settlement payment to the Inland Revenue based on a formula that is intended to recover (across all cases) broadly the same amount of incorrect tax relief as if the rules had been strictly applied and tax recovery calculated accordingly. The advantage to managers is that precise and detailed calculations, often resulting at the end in relatively small amounts of tax to be repaid, are not required and, perhaps most importantly from the managers point of view, the investor gets to retain the PEP/ISA status rather than losing it as a result of an administrative error by the manager.

The settlement formula (Guidance 17.54) is currently £5 per year per £1, 000 subscribed to a PEP (£10 for periods prior to 6 April 1999 to reflect the 20% tax credit recovery then applicable to PEPs), an insurance or stocks and shares ISA and £10 per year per £1,000 subscribed to a cash ISA (SPS PEP & ISA Bulletin No 10 (£15 for periods prior to 6 April 2002 to reflect higher interest rates then offered on cash deposits)).

Investor errors can now be repaired

18.70 Whilst manager errors can be repaired under Guidance, that has not previously been possible for investor errors. Having looked at the experience from the first two ISA subscription years, the Inland Revenue set about introducing Regulations that would allow repair of many of the most common investor errors. These were eventually laid and took effect from 8 January 2003 (*SI 2002/3158*), at which point the Inland Revenue promptly started their compliance review of the 2001/02 subscription year using the new Regulations. It appears that this approach has benefited somewhat more than half the investors who had managed to breach the rules and, in previous years, would have had their ISAs made void. Measured by the reduction in the Inland Revenue's complaints postbag, this appears to have been very successful. There are three common ways in which investors get the ISA subscription rules wrong, all of which can now be repaired.

'Self-transfer'– 2001/02 and 2002/03

18.71 It is quite common to find that an investor with a cash mini ISA who wished to transfer it to another manager (often to get a better rate of interest) actually closed it and took the proceeds to the new manager with whom he opened what is actually the second mini cash ISA for that year and thereby breaches the rules. Under the previous rules the second would be void as a result and, as the investor had closed the first, he would be left with nothing. The new rules (*ISA Reg 4A* inserted by *SI 2002/3158* and Guidance 12.30–12.33) allow this to be repaired so long as the first was completely closed before the second was opened and the second is of the same type. The second loses all tax benefits (in the case of a mini cash ISA this will involve taxing all interest at the lower rate and in the case of a mini stocks and shares ISA of recovering all tax benefits) up to the date of repair, after which the second ISA continues as a fully valid ISA going forward. However, it is very important to note that this only applies to the first self-transfer in a tax year. If the investor makes more than one self-transfer in a tax year, all the ISAs involved are void and none can be repaired.

The self-transfer repair can be used for two mini cash ISAs, two mini stocks and shares ISAs and two TESSA-only ISAs but not for mini insurance ISAs or maxi ISAs.

'Self-transfer'– 2003/04 onwards

18.72 From subscription year 2003/04 onwards, the first self-transfer is valid and no repair is necessary. However it is still the case that this only applies to the first self-transfer in a tax year (*ISA Reg 4B* inserted by *SI 2002/3158*).

Disallowed combination (mixing minis and maxis etc)

18.73 The great fear in 1999 was that investors would be confused about their mini and maxi options, would mix them in a single tax year and thereby make the second void. Whilst many thousands of investors did just that, the number of cases was encouragingly less than either the Inland Revenue or the industry had expected. Nevertheless, the effect for those that did get it wrong was no less painful.

The new rules (Guidance 12.34–12.35) allow repair of the *second* ISA within the overall subscription limits for the year so that total subscriptions to all valid and repairable ISAs do not exceed £7,000, total subscriptions to insurance ISAs do not exceed £1,000 and total subscriptions to cash ISAs do not exceed £3,000. The *first* ISA subscribed to in any year is, by definition, valid so that the repair will always be applicable to the second (and possibly subsequent) ISAs. Subscriptions of matured TESSA capital and subscriptions to closed self-transferred ISAs are ignored. Excesses (if any) above these limits have to be removed and lose all tax benefits (this may involve representing the subscriptions to be removed by an agreed mix of current assets and/or cash). The remaining (second) ISA loses all tax benefits up to the date of repair but proceeds thereafter as a fully valid ISA. Detailed procedures are set out in the Guidance Notes (Guidance 12.37 onwards).

Matured TESSA capital

18.74   Where TESSA capital has been transferred into a cash mini ISA or (less typically) into the cash component of a maxi ISA and subsequently the cash component, for whatever reason, has been declared void, the previous rules would have made the whole cash component void including the (potentially £9,000) TESSA capital. This scenario probably accounted for the highest proportion of complaints to the Inland Revenue, particularly where a husband and wife each lost their entitlement to gross interest on their TESSA allowance for all time.

The repair procedure (Guidance 12.36) quite simply ring fences the TESSA capital and excludes it from the voiding of the remainder of the cash ISA. The interest (if any) already credited to the account in respect of the TESSA capital has to be taxed but, going forward, it earns gross interest as a fully valid cash ISA.

Information reporting by the PEP/ISA manager

18.75   Managers are required to make certain returns to the Inland Revenue on a regular basis.

Subscription and other investor information

Quarterly ISA statistical returns – ISA25

18.76   For each tax year, managers make cumulative quarterly returns to the Inland Revenue (*ISA Reg 31(2) and (7)* and Guidance Chapter 16) with details of the number of ISAs to which subscriptions have been made and the amounts subscribed, analysed by subscription type and component. Where current year accounts are received transferred from other managers, the manager should receive a full subscription history for the year and include subscriptions made to the previous manager prior to transfer in his subsequent returns. Equally, where current year accounts are transferred out, the manager should pass a full subscription history to the new manager and should exclude that investor from subsequent quarterly returns.

The data collected from the industry is published by the Inland Revenue central statistical service as Tables 9.4 (www.inlandrevenue.gov.uk/stats/isa/isa_t01_1.htm) and, for TESSA-only subscriptions, Table 9.5 (www.inlandrevenue.gov.uk/stats/isa/isa_t03_1.htm). Table 9.4 is updated roughly four months after the period to which the returns relate and Table 9.5 annually.

Returns of information

18.77   ISA Managers are required to make a return of investor information (Guidance Chapter 14) to the Inland Revenue within 60 days (*ISA Reg 31(1) and (3)*) and PEP managers within 3 months (*PEP Reg 24A(1) and (2)*) of the end of the tax year. These returns are usually made on magnetic media although managers with very small databases may use paper forms (PEPCOM100(Z) at Guidance 14.23 and ISACOM100(Z) updated by SPS PEP & ISA Bulletin No 11) which are also used to notify the Revenue of any omissions from the manager's magnetic return.

The PEP version lists all investors whose PEPs were open at the reporting date (5 April) recording their account number, name, address, date of birth, NINo (if any) and the market value of the PEP on that date.

The ISA version lists all investors whose ISAs were open at the reporting date, including any transferred in during the year, plus any that were open for any part of the reporting year but have since been closed. The manager should not include ISAs transferred out in full, made void or cancelled within 30 days of opening under cooling-off/cancellation arrangements. The return records the investor's account number, name, address, date of birth, NINo (if any), amounts subscribed by component, the date of the first subscription and the date of closure (if any), any amount subscribed by share transfer (from approved schemes) and the market value of each component on the reporting date.

Annual statistical returns of market value

18.78   Both PEP and ISA managers are required to make annual statistical returns (*ISA Reg 31(1), (4) and (5); PEP Reg 24A(1) and (3)*) by completing PEP14(Stats) (Guidance 15.13) and ISA14(Stats) (Guidance 15.14) respectively. These record the overall market value of the PEPs/ISAs managed by them at 5 April each year, broken down by asset type and, in the case of ISAs, by components.

The data is published annually as:

- Table 9.2 (www.inlandrevenue.gov.uk/stats/peps/pep_t02_1.htm) for PEPs; and

- Table 9.6 (www.inlandrevenue.gov.uk/stats/isa/isa_t02_1.htm) for ISAs.

19   The Sandler Review

Nathan Hall

Investment Management Association / KPMG

> 'The Review therefore recommends that, in future, governments should avoid introducing new tax-based savings incentives if their aim is to increase aggregate savings levels. The core objective of policy in this area should be simplification' (*Medium and Long Term Savings in the UK*, paragraph 10.166).

Introduction

19.1   Against a backdrop of falling equity markets and press focus on the 'savings gap' and mis-selling, the Treasury commissioned Ron Sandler to investigate the competitive forces at play in the retail savings industry. The project had been prompted by Paul Myners in his March 2001 report on 'Institutional Investment in the UK'. The result, entitled 'Medium and Long Term Retail Savings in the UK' (hereafter referred to as 'the Review'), was published in July 2002.

The remit of the Review was broad and Sandler put forward a number of recommendations to increase competition in the retail savings industry and to strengthen the position of the consumer. Taxation features prominently and this chapter discusses those recommendations that could have a significant impact on the way authorised funds, investment trusts, insurance based savings products and pensions are taxed.

19.2   It is not possible to assess the Review in isolation. In the past year a raft of consultation papers have emanated from the Treasury, Inland Revenue, Customs and Excise, Department for Work and Pensions (DWP) and the Financial Services Authority (FSA). Some arose directly as a result of Sandler's recommendations, others independently, but even in the case of the latter the influence of the Review is noticeable. This chapter takes stock of its impact as at October 2003. It is important to state this as a reference point because the landscape is fast changing.

The Review in summary

19.3   The overall message conveyed is that the UK retail savings industry is sufficiently complex and opaque to cause concern. Complexity and opacity are undesirable because in such an environment providers are unlikely to operate as efficiently as possible and individuals, particularly the Government's target middle to lower income group, are less likely to save. The taxation recommendations should not be taken out of context as tax is just one of several contributing factors.

19.4   First, because of the complex nature of the industry consumers are in a weak position. The choice of products can be overwhelming, relative costs and performance are difficult to gauge and the benefits of investing are long term and, therefore, not immediately obvious.

19.5   Second, advice is needed and this necessitates layers of intermediary between investor and product provider. The evolution of efficient and innovative distribution networks such as the fund supermarket shows that the consumer can benefit from added layers, but the Review concludes that the current system of remuneration by way of commission could be improved upon. Currently, it claims, providers compete to impress the distributor rather than the end consumer, to whom it is far from clear how much is being paid for advice.

19.6   Third, regulation imposes costs on providers and ultimately investors (although Sandler shirks from measuring the cost effectiveness of the current regulatory regime). The Review focuses on the sales process and product regulation. In respect of the latter, Sandler sees the merits of 'voluntary benchmarking', whereby minimum standards are set for achieving some form of endorsement, but admits that improvements could be made to the CAT mark and stakeholder models.

19.7   Fourth, with-profits policies attract criticism for their 'general opacity', the conflict of interest between policyholders and shareholders, and the distorting effects of inherited estates. In short, it is claimed, competition amongst with-profits providers is not solely concerned with generating value for money and investment returns.

19.8   The fifth area of concern stoked most controversy immediately after publication of the Review. Sandler suggests that investment decisions are not entirely made with the retail investor's interests in mind. Too much emphasis is placed on past performance and inappropriate timescales are used to assess returns, insufficient attention is paid to asset allocation, and the preference for active management is hard to justify. Throughout the past year the industry and regulators have traded blows on these subjects.

19.9   Taxation then follows. The taxation of investment products is complex for three main reasons: different categories of product are taxed in very different ways (compare an authorised unit trust and a unitised life product); products that compete in the same market are taxed differently (compare an authorised unit trust and an investment trust); and certain treatments are inherently complicated (for example that of life policies). Tax too often drives investment decision-making and contributes to the aura of confusion that deters many potential investors. Consequently, Government policy should be directed towards levelling the playing field on which similar products compete. The current rules mean that investors fail to focus on the cost and quality of a product and often decide on an investment solely because it gives a favourable tax outcome. In addition, many are put off from investing altogether; advice is required to wade through the quagmire and this can be prohibitively expensive.

Stakeholder products

19.10   The Review proposes a number of recommendations to counter the concerns outlined above. The suite of stakeholder products is at the heart of these. It is worth outlining Sandler's thinking in this area because an understanding of what type of product he envisages as suitable for lower income groups could indicate what the future holds for established savings vehicles.

In a stakeholder world, the emphasis is on regulation of the product rather than the provider. Products that adhere to consumer friendly criteria would be able to enjoy special branding. To reach out to the lower to middle income group such products should be cheap, perhaps subject to a 1% price cap, and easy to understand. The sense of security conveyed by the stakeholder brand would mean that, controversially, such products could be sold without regulated advice.

19.11   Three types of product are catered for: a mutual fund or unit-linked life fund; a pension (essentially the current stakeholder pension); and a with profits product. Sandler goes into some detail as to how the with profits product should be structured, recommending for example a 100/0 charging structure (whereby 100% of bonus distributions are made to policyholders) and that management charges be made by a separate management company from within the same group as the life company.

19.12   In February 2003, the Treasury and DWP launched a consultative paper on the proposed product specifications for Sandler stakeholder products and it is clear that the Government sees promise in the proposals. The consultation developed Sandler's suggestions and set out the risk profile such products should adhere to, placing a 60% cap on equity exposure but no minimum. Moreover, the FSA is consulting separately on changes to the sales process that would be needed to complement the stakeholder range. In July, the results of the Treasury consultation were announced but, as yet, there has been no decision on the price cap. Debate over the wisdom of focusing on product regulation to this extent and the imposition of a 1% price cap is ongoing. The response did state that the new range will keep the stakeholder label and will include CAT-standard ISAs. The product range will consist of a short term product (CAT-standard cash ISAs), medium term products (in unitised or smoothed form) and a long term product (the current stakeholder pension). The range is expected to be available from April 2005.

19.13   Intriguingly, given the Review's concerns that different tax treatments distort behaviour, the February consultative paper shrank from designing a 'one size fits all' regime for unitised and with profits products:

'It has been argued that [tax] differences provide a complicating factor. But it is not clear to what extent any lack of understanding is likely to have a material impact on the appropriateness of product choices' (Paragraph 54, 'Proposed product specifications for Sandler "stakeholder products"').

As will be explained below, this does not mean that an alignment of taxation regimes has been ruled out in a wider context.

The taxation recommendations in summary

19.14   A plethora of tax anomalies and distortions stand in the way of Sandler's vision of cheap, easy to understand and directly comparable savings products. The Review places much of the blame at the feet of successive Governments that have sought to incentivise saving by complicating product features with tax breaks of one form or another. The most thought-provoking conclusion is that quoted at the head of this chapter, viz that tax relief is not an effective tool for increasing the propensity to save amongst low-income groups. In addition, a number of specific recommendations are made to level the playing field between different types of product and provider.

This chapter discusses where the 'tax as incentive to save' debate leaves the Individual Savings Account (ISA) and what other forms of inducement have caught the imagination of the Government. It then moves on to assessing the potential impact of Sandler's specific recommendations for both medium and long-term savings vehicles. Such an assessment cannot be made without mentioning recent regulatory change (CP185: The CIS Sourcebook – a new approach) and a number of concurrent consultations (on the offshore funds regime, pensions tax simplification and corporation tax reform).

Tax as an incentive to save

19.15   Prior to publication of the Review, the Government was already of the view that tax incentives are ineffective at increasing the propensity to save amongst lower and middle income groups (the Saving Gateway and Child Trust Fund were already being developed). Intuitively, the promise of tax-free income means more to those taxed at the higher rate than to those taxed at the lower or basic rates. Sandler concurs, a central tenet of his Review is that tax incentives are unlikely significantly to increase the overall level of saving, but they can affect asset allocation.

Perhaps the introduction of ISAs encouraged more people to save who otherwise would not have, but, Sandler argues, the evidence is not clear and chances are that the majority of ISA investors would have been minded to save anyway. Moreover, tax incentives are a form of Government meddling, increase complexity and, paradoxically, may even discourage saving. The Review cites research that indicates that some consumers are put off by the word tax even in the context of tax breaks. A key recommendation of the Review is that future policy should be driven by simplification. A corollary of this view is that matching schemes rather than traditional methods of tax relief should be used to encourage saving amongst lower income groups.

Matching schemes

19.16 The Government appears to agree with Sandler as the Child Trust Fund and Saving Gateway are proposals that it is taking very seriously. This is clear from the Treasury report of November 2001, 'Delivering Saving and Assets: The modernisation of Britain's tax and benefit system', that summarised the results of an earlier consultation phase. The theory is that the concept of a matching scheme is easier to understand because a gift of cash that matches amounts saved by the investor is more concrete and direct than tax relief. After a brief summary of the latest position, it is worthwhile asking what the future holds for the ISA given this preference for matching.

The Child Trust Fund

19.17 The Government's commitment to the Child Trust Fund was reiterated in the 2002 Pre-Budget Report and a brief outline of the proposals was revealed in the subsequent Budget. Each child born from September 2002 will be granted £250 (or £500 if from low income families entitled to the full Child Tax Credit) that will be held on trust until the child reaches 18 years of age when it is hoped (and it appears that no restrictions will be imposed) that the accumulated fund will be invested wisely. Crucially, to foster the interest of product providers, parents, other family members and friends will be able to contribute to the fund.

Detailed proposals were published on 28 October 2003. The maximum level of contribution from family and friends will be £1,200 per annum. Contributions will not attract tax relief but within the fund the income and gains will be tax free and there will be no charge on maturity. In addition, where parents contribute, the settlements legislation will not apply and income from the CTF will not count towards the annual limit of £100. However, contributions will attract no relief from inheritance tax beyond existing reliefs for lifetime giving.

Child Trust Fund accounts are expected to be available from April 2005 as part of the stakeholder regime outlined above.

The Saving Gateway

19.18 The Child Trust Fund is intended to encourage the young to get into the savings habit from an early age. With the Saving Gateway, the Government hopes to provide any individual on a low income with a means of accumulating savings perhaps for the first time. First, money saved will be matched by a Government contribution; second, basic information will be made available to increase understanding of the savings industry. Once again, full details have not been finalised but a number of pilot schemes are running across the country. These are scheduled to end in February 2005.

All contributions to date have been paid into bank accounts but to the extent that the concept is designed to introduce many to saving for the first time, the outcome of the pilots is of interest to the wider savings industry. Certainly the Government regards the scheme as a potential bridge to other forms of saving.

Individual Savings Accounts

19.19   The ISA regime is due to be reviewed in 2009. With the current preference for matching over tax relief, and the Government's continued commitment to end the repayment of the dividend tax credit to ISA and PEP managers from April 2004, is the future of ISAs guaranteed beyond this date?

It is important to keep in mind that the matching schemes are not universal solutions. They are specifically targeted at those on lower incomes who probably would not have contributed to an ISA anyway. Importantly, the Government and industry agree that the regime has been a success with 14 million individuals now holding an account. In a Commons debate on 1 July 2003 over the expiry of the repayable tax credit, the Economic Secretary to the Treasury proudly declared that ISAs are starting to reach those groups that were underrepresented in terms of saving through PEPs and TESSAs.

19.20   The ISA is a widely recognised, well-understood concept and many argue that the regime has been successful at reaching out to those who had not saved previously. At present the ISA is set to remain, as stated in the 2003 Budget Report, 'the Government's primary vehicle for tax advantaged saving outside pensions'.

Sandler acknowledges that 'dismantling the regime would not be desirable' and has few recommendations on how to improve the regime. His sole concern is the distinction between mini and maxi ISAs, which in the wake of depolarisation might well be otiose. The Review anticipates that freeing up of distribution channels will enable more providers to offer a range of cash, equity and insurance products. It will be interesting to see what impact the loss of the repayable tax credit has, to put to the test the Review's conclusion that tax relief does little to boost aggregate savings levels. Following abolition, the basic rate taxpayer investing in equities will essentially be no better off within an ISA wrapper than outside, although some marginal benefits will remain such as the exemption from capital gains tax and the removal of the need to calculate gains annually (for a reminder of what a chore this could be, see Statement of Practice 2/99 on the subject of monthly share schemes).

19.21   The challenge facing those responsible for devising the stakeholder regime and the above matching schemes is how to co-ordinate the many different strands of savings policy to form an ordered whole. A solution that gives rise to some stakeholder or Child Trust Fund products sitting outside the ISA regime and some within would not be simple and clear.

Compulsion

19.22   Finally, in this discussion of incentives, it is worth mentioning that the Review touches upon the thorny issue of compulsion, which would be the most radical way of filling the perceived savings gap. As a parting shot, it recognises that forcing individuals to save is a difficult issue but one that has been tried elsewhere and that could at least be usefully debated. However, no more is said and the impression is given that this remains too contentious an issue for the short term.

Specific recommendations – medium-term retail savings

19.23   The Review places great emphasis on unnecessary differences of tax treatment between similar products. However, rather than attempt to devise a single framework for authorised funds, life products and investment trusts, Sandler recommends a small number of targeted improvements. First, he asserts that life products have historically enjoyed favourable tax treatment and questions the need for the 5% withdrawal rule and distinction between qualifying and non-qualifying policies. Second, he argues that investment trusts should be afforded the same Stamp Duty Reserve Tax (SDRT) and Value Added Tax (VAT) exemptions as authorised funds.

Life insurance taxation

19.24   The current regime is criticised because it draws a distinction between policies that involve a 'nominal' life insurance element and other forms of saving. The Review argues that any differences in substance between qualifying and non-qualifying policies do not justify the significant tax advantages available to holders of the former. Moreover, because the entire liability of holders of qualifying policies is deemed to be met by the life company, higher rate payers pay the same as non-taxpayers. Although he acknowledges the special status of pure protection policies, Sandler asserts that the qualifying regime 'ties in with no apparent policy objective' and should therefore be abolished for new business.

The 5% withdrawal rule attracts similar criticism. In times of low inflation this rule has real benefits to higher rate taxpayers, which give life policies an advantage over other savings products. Sandler particularly objects to the emphasis distributors place on this tax feature. He therefore recommends that the previous partial disposal rules be reinstated.

19.25   It is easy to see why Sandler objects to these two characteristics of the regime: they run counter to the spirit of the Review by introducing complexity and favouring higher rate taxpayers. However, whether or not the Government should press ahead with Sandler's recommendations is another matter. If the tax treatment of life and non-life products is to be aligned, more radical reform is necessary, not a couple of tweaks around the edges. Sandler suggested as much at paragraph 10.176:

> 'Even after these changes, life taxation would still be a source of complexity. In particular, the treatment of unit linked life policies would remain very different from the tax treatment of mutual funds, even though these are virtually identical products in other respects.'

19.26   The industry's response to the specific recommendations was that the Government should wait and consider the wider context. It appears that the message has got through; having announced in the 2002 Pre-Budget Report that it was keen to press ahead with the life insurance recommendations, the Government has since paused for thought:

> '...industry representatives have argued that the Government should look at Sandler's tax proposals in the wider context of other tax issues affecting the market for life insurance and other pooled investment products such as unit trusts. The Government agrees, and will consider these recommendations further within a wider framework that takes account of ongoing regulatory change and other developments such as corporation tax reform' (The Budget Report 2003, paragraph 5.63).

The Review coincided with a number of related consultations that could give rise to major changes in the way onshore and offshore funds and life companies are taxed. This is a rare opportunity to devise a competitive and robust tax regime for UK-based savings products.

Offshore funds review

19.27   First, in April 2002 the Inland Revenue released a consultative paper on the offshore funds regime that has been in place since 1984. Four options were presented: maintaining the status quo; modifying the current regime; replacing the regime with another; and abolition of the existing regime. It soon became apparent that the tax treatment of offshore funds could not be viewed in isolation. Some, including the IMA, considered change to the taxation of UK funds coupled with abolition of the regime. This would enable savings to roll up free of tax until disposal, which would give rise to a capital gain, and provide UK investors with a level of tax efficiency that many Continental investors expect.

19.28   Of course, serious thought should be given to the impact such a measure could have on the nation's tax receipts, but the differentiation between capital gains tax and income tax rates that spawned the growth of 'money box accounts', and in response the offshore funds regime, no longer exists. Admittedly, taper relief and the annual exemption tip the scales in favour of a capital treatment but, for equity funds, compare a 25% income tax charge today with a 28% tapered capital gains tax charge eight years down the line (IMA research indicates that investors typically hold on to their holdings in UK funds for 8.1 years – see Unit Trust Information Service: Market Research Survey and Report, April 2002). The only other long-term answer is some form of information reporting regime; however, the more one considers the detail of such a solution the greater the number of concerns that spring up.

Reform of corporation tax

19.29   Secondly, August 2002 saw the publication of a consultative paper on the reform of corporation tax. This questioned the need for certain anachronisms at the heart of the UK's corporate tax regime, for example the schedular system, the investment versus trading distinction and the capital revenue divide. A further consultation paper was issued in August 2003 with the same issues discussed. To allay fears that reform would be used as an excuse to tax capital gains within collective investment schemes, both papers recognise that authorised funds and investment trusts are special and that new rules will be required to reflect this. However, much of the mainstream debate is still relevant particularly if the trading versus investment divide is revisited. Imminent regulatory reform could pave the way for hedge funds to be established onshore, albeit for the non-retail market, and it is widely held that it is only uncertainty surrounding whether or not investment strategies will fall foul of the traditional badges of trade tests that would keep them offshore.

Thus, two significant consultations point in the direction of significant change. In addition, the following external factors are expediting the process.

CP185 The CIS Sourcebook – a New Approach

19.30   The regulatory status of a fund currently dictates how it is taxed. Because the FSA's CP185 proposes to stretch the regulatory boundary, such that a number of unauthorised funds under the current regime could well become authorised, it could necessitate radical changes to the current system of funds taxation. There will be three categories of authorised fund: those that comply with the Amended UCITS Directive, non-UCITS retail funds and authorised non-retail funds. The Revenue are closely involved in the consultation process and are aware that current tax rules and attitudes could render the regulatory developments ineffective.

First, many of the regulatory obstacles that prevent property funds establishing themselves as authorised vehicles in the UK will be removed. Limited redemption will be allowed and gearing perhaps up to 100% of the value of the fund. However, as things stand, the authorised fund is not an efficient vehicle because rental income is taxed at fund level.

Secondly, the new vehicle for non-retail funds could be suitable for certain hedge funds, for example, long/short funds. It is clear though, as mentioned above, that such funds will not be managed onshore unless there is a shift in attitude as to what constitutes trading. The test is subjective and depends inter alia on the manager's intent. However, as far as the investor is concerned, they have made an investment and how actively the fund is managed should not affect their tax treatment.

19.31   The regulatory changes are due to take effect from February 2004, so *FA 2004* is the first opportunity to bring into line the tax legislation. This timetable could well be too tight.

International Financial Reporting Standards (IFRS)

19.32   A theme of the corporation tax review is the ever closer relationship between taxable profits and accounting profits. For example, *FA 2002* brought authorised funds within a quasi-loan relationships regime that, referring specifically to the Statements of Recommended Practice for authorised funds, relies very much on the accounting method of apportioning returns between income and capital.

Following an EU Regulation, from 1 January 2005 listed companies will have to prepare group accounts in accordance with IFRS. It is unclear to what extent unlisted entities will have to follow suit as member states have the option of extending the scope of the Regulation. The Department of Trade and Industry consulted on the subject and it was announced on 17 July 2003 that unlisted entities or listed entities not preparing group accounts would be granted the option of complying fully.

19.33   There is still some uncertainty, therefore, for all authorised funds and many investment trusts. Nevertheless, the Revenue should not expect the accounts of funds or investment trusts to remain the same. First, the accounting framework will change even for those entities that do not opt for full compliance with IFRS. Second, many entities not caught automatically may choose the full compliance route. For example, for an effective cross-border market in authorised funds, consistency in reporting is a must.

The most obvious risk is that the current boundary between income and capital will shift. If there is to be no change in tax take or the tax base, tax legislation will need to keep track of any change in accounts presentation. By way of illustration, International Accounting Standard 32 shows just how important it is closely to follow developments. Paragraph 22B states that the unit or shareholder's interest in a fund is akin to a putable instrument and therefore is technically a liability. Dividend distributions could therefore take the form of interest, which would have significant tax implications unless the change is anticipated.

Authorised funds and investment trusts

19.34   Sandler highlights two differences in tax treatment between investment trusts and authorised funds that he considers unnecessary. First, to enable authorised funds to compete with life companies in the personal pensions arena, holdings in an authorised fund are exempt from SDRT if held within an Individual Pension Account (IPA); however holdings in an investment trust are not. Secondly, Customs regard authorised funds, but not investment trusts, as 'special investment funds', the management of which is an exempt supply.

Stamp Duty and SDRT

19.35   In the context of the pensions Green paper and simplification of the pensions tax regime, the SDRT 'discrepancy' is a minor point; the priority for the industry is to devise a workable IPA (see below). Sandler should have discussed SDRT in a wider context. Because of their open-ended nature, authorised funds are subject to a different regime to investment trusts. In effect, *FA 1999, Sch 19* deems the manager to be a normal third party intermediary transferring units from outgoing to incoming unit holders. The accuracy of this charging mechanism depends on the incidence of creations and cancellations and the extent the fund is invested in exempt assets.

Because it is complicated and in many ways unique, it is difficult to assess the fairness of the *Schedule 19* charge and to gauge how level the playing field is. Indeed, the foremost challenge is to ensure that authorised unit trusts (AUTs) and open-ended investment companies (OEICs) receive the same treatment. Because of their different structures the same transaction can give rise to different stamp duty or SDRT results, notwithstanding that it is generally the Government's intention to treat the vehicles as equivalent. Thus, there are rough edges to the regime, and the distinction highlighted by Sandler is but one example, but, as abolition of SDRT is the only way to guarantee a level playing field, real simplification is a long way off.

VAT

19.36   Unlike the Review's SDRT proposals, the scope of the special investment funds VAT exemption has generated significant excitement over the past year, partly because of Sandler, partly because of Customs' recent defeats at Tribunal (*Prudential Assurance Co Ltd*, EDN/00/37 and *Abbey National plc*, LON/00/928).

Article 13B(d)6 of the Sixth VAT Directive provides an exemption for the 'management of special investment funds as defined by Member States'. It is open to each member state to define special investment funds how it sees fit. In the UK the exemption has been restricted to AUTs and OEICs because such vehicles are widely marketed to the public and are subject to regulation.

19.37   The investment trust community has long argued that, based on these criteria, it is illogical to exclude investment trusts. In addition, many would like to see charitable common investment funds included. Because investment trusts compete in the same market as AUTs and OEICs, Sandler believes that they should be treated the same for VAT purposes and asked that Customs review the scope of the exemption in the UK. Consequently, in November 2002, interested parties were asked their opinion as part of the consultation on 'The VAT treatment of pension fund management'.

19.38   The decision whether or not to extend the number of funds eligible for exemption has not yet been taken. On 16 June 2003 regulations were laid to effect the decisions of the *Prudential* and *Abbey National* Tribunals from 1 August 2003 but the legislation is unlikely to remain static for long. First, consistency in application of the Directive across Europe is a long way off. Second, the thorny question of what constitutes 'management' still has to be settled. A Business Brief was issued in July confirming Customs' view that management must contain the core portfolio management function to fall within the exemption and, importantly for UK-based managers of overseas funds, that the exemption is restricted to AUTs and OEICs that are incorporated in the UK.

Specific recommendations – long-term retail savings

19.39   Pensions and the market for long-term savings have been in the spotlight for some time. Falling stock markets, the abolition of the repayable dividend tax credit and FRS 17 have all focused minds on the savings gap and the need for some sort of regulatory or tax reform to encourage us to save more.

The Review fell within the bounds of a wider debate: Myners had explored whether pension funds were being served well by institutional fund managers and trustees; the Inland Revenue had been reviewing the taxation of pensions since March 2001; and Alan Pickering had been commissioned to examine the wider challenges facing the industry (his 'A Simpler Way to Better Pensions: an independent report' was published in the same month as the Review). Sandler, whose interest is individual pensions sold either directly or via employers, focuses on two areas: the complexity of pensions taxation and the level of competition amongst providers.

Pensions taxation

19.40   The Review questions the need for the continuation of eight sets of rules (four separate codes for occupational schemes, retirement annuity contracts superseded by personal pensions, funded unapproved schemes, and unfunded unapproved schemes). Complexity is undesirable because it increases the cost of advice, discouraging the less well off from saving, increases administration costs, shifts emphasis away from product suitability to tax features and acts as a barrier to entry. In addition the current rules are rigid and are not suited to modern work patterns. Sandler therefore asks the Revenue to be radical and recommends that the eight regimes be whittled down to the minimum necessary, ideally one.

To the surprise of many, the Revenue duly complied. In December 2002, alongside the Pensions Green Paper, the Inland Revenue and Treasury issued a joint consultation paper entitled 'Simplifying the taxation of pensions: increasing choice and flexibility for all'.

19.41   If its proposals get the go-ahead, the existing eight regimes will be replaced by one set of rules. There will be no grandfathering of old regimes and a much needed clean break with the past. Contributions or the value of growth will be restricted to £200,000 a year with any excess accounted for as a benefit in kind. An indexed lifetime limit of £1.4m will be imposed and any benefits drawn in excess will be subject to a recovery charge of 33% and then taxed on the individual at the marginal rate. Other proposals include a standard 25% tax-free lump sum, a rise in the minimum age at which benefits can be drawn to 55 by 2010 and a more flexible, albeit still annuity based, post-vesting phase. The consultative paper aimed for an implementation date of April 2004 but, in response to requests for deferral, the revised target is April 2005.

Initial reaction concentrated on the need to limit both annual contributions and the total value of entitlements. Because the limits are linked to inflation rather than wages growth they could become a significant restraint in years to come. However, at this stage it appears that the Revenue have risen to Sandler's challenge to simplify pensions taxation. In addition, the consultative paper presents an opportunity to address his second concern.

Competition in the pensions industry

19.42   The IPA was introduced in April 2001 to enable providers to manage personal pension accounts outside of a life company and to help deliver the stakeholder pension. However, the product has not been a success, with only one provider marketing their stakeholder as an IPA since its introduction. In the UK, long-term saving has traditionally been regarded as a form of insurance and the scale of operations required to administer contributions and the complexity of the tax rules act as real obstacles to new entrants. Given that the 401k retirement plan in the United States is widely regarded as a success, the Review was justified in investigating this aspect of the UK market. Sandler duly concluded that the playing field is not level and asked the Government to revisit the IPA rules and, rather unhelpfully, to investigate the VAT exemption for management fees charged by insurance groups.

The IPA

19.43   The objectives for the IPA were laudable; with a name redolent of the ISA and features borrowed from the 401k, the intention was to create a portable, transparent and flexible account. Originally called the 'pooled pensions investment', the IPA was intended to be a means of providing investors with a sense of ownership of their pension and a degree of control. The Self Invested Personal Pension (SIPP), introduced in 1989, already achieved this but not for the mass market. It was hoped, therefore, that the IPA would be a more accessible version of the SIPP and the asset management industry duly awaited the outcome of the Government's proposals with some enthusiasm.

The structure was outlined in a Treasury paper published in July 2000 and the detail can be found in *SI 2001/117*. An IPA is an account within which assets can be held. The funds are held by the trustees, managers or administrators of the scheme on behalf of the investor, the beneficial owner. Although the investment criteria are not as relaxed as for SIPPs, the IPA can be invested in a range of authorised funds, investment trusts or UK and EEA Government debt securities. The account can be moved from one pension scheme to another and becomes subject to the rules of the prevailing scheme.

19.44 To ensure parity with the unit linked business of a life company (but note Sandler's comments on investment trusts above), *Finance Act 2001, sections 93* and *94* granted an exemption from any *FA 1999, Sch 19* charge for surrenders of units or shares held within an IPA account. A Stamp Office Customer Newsletter of 15 May 2001 described the three ways this exemption can be achieved. First, no monthly return is required if all units in a unit trust are held in an IPA. Secondly, surrenders of shares in an OEIC are left out of the monthly calculation if they form part of a separate IPA share class. Finally, surrenders of units in a unit trust that has both IPA and non-IPA unitholders are left out of the calculation if the return certifies that the trustees or managers are able to distinguish between those units held outside of or within an IPA and that no amount of tax has been recovered from the IPA unitholders.

19.45 Despite the good intentions and assurances that the IPA would be like an ISA, it has not been as successful as hoped. Reasons often cited include that the concept is too complicated and cannot be explained to would-be investors. The IPA was introduced at the same time as the stakeholder regime and it was difficult to understand where the IPA belonged amidst the morass of pensions tax regimes and terminology. The IPA must still sit within an approved pensions arrangement that means costs have to be borne establishing an irrevocable trust and expensive administrative machinery is required to keep track of contribution limits. Such barriers to entry and the 1% price cap mean that there is little incentive for providers to break the mould.

However, it has been explained how the Revenue's consultation promises to reduce compliance costs by replacing the various age-related contribution limits with universal contribution and life time limits. Prompted by Sandler, the paper also recognises that increasing competition could drive down prices and improve choice. This is an opportunity for the industry to design a workable IPA.

19.46 The IPA should be a stand-alone wrapper that attracts tax relief like an ISA. Currently, it must 'sit within' an approved pension scheme that meets the Inland Revenue's criteria and it is not fully portable. Reform along these lines would open up the prospect of new providers, both fund managers and fund supermarkets, coming into the market for personal pensions during their accumulation phase and greatly improve the scope for product innovation.

VAT – 'Insurer' versus 'non-insurer' investment managers

19.47   It has already been mentioned that in November 2002 the industry was presented with a consultative paper on 'The VAT treatment of pension fund management'. The scope of the paper was unexpected because it is primarily concerned with an anomaly in the legislation that had lain unnoticed by many; it is certainly of low importance when compared with the disputes arising over the UK's interpretation of the Article 13B(d)6 exemption.

Investment management is a taxable supply, but exemptions are available in certain restricted cases. One such case is when the investment manager is also a 'permitted insurer'. In practice, this means that the management of personal pension schemes is exempt (the vast majority of such business is carried out by a life insurer) and management of the majority of occupational schemes is taxable.

19.48   Sandler affords the matter two sentences at the foot of his analysis of the taxation of pensions and recommends 'that the Government considers making the playing field level wherever possible by, for example, extending the VAT exemption for pension fund management fees to include those levied by life insurance companies'. The context of this recommendation is the personal pensions arena and the uneven treatment of IPAs and insured pension arrangements.

The scope of Customs' consultation was therefore surprising in that it offered the prospect of radical changes across the board and considered a 'one size fits all' approach for both personal and occupational schemes. Note that Sandler specifically excluded occupational pension schemes (other than insured schemes) from his remit (see paragraph 2.2 of the Review). Interested parties were asked to consider three options: extending the exemption to cover management of all pension funds (perhaps by including pension funds within the definition of 'special investment funds'; treating management of all pension funds as taxable; and 'redrawing the borderline', the most enigmatic option.

19.49   The second option was effectively ruled out by Customs themselves in the consultative paper. It is unlikely that such a move would be popular in the current climate and stakeholder providers would be unable to pass the cost on because of the 1% stakeholder cap.

19.50   The deadline for consultation was 31 January 2003 and the industry anticipated Customs' conclusions to be announced as part of the 2003 Budget report. Silence reigned but it is understood that the Government is carefully considering responses that broadly fell into two camps, those favouring exemption and those supporting the status quo. The decision will not be an easy one to make, not least because it is unclear who the winners and losers might be.

In the context of Sandler, limited redrawing of the borderline would be the most appropriate outcome so that management of all personal schemes would be afforded an exemption, but the current, generally taxable, treatment of management of occupational schemes would be preserved. This would level the playing field as far as personal pensions are concerned. By contrast, wholesale exemption, covering personal and occupational schemes, could do more harm than good as many managers would be unable to pass on the cost of irrecoverable input tax to the funds and some might even consider transferring the management function overseas.

The impact of the report

19.51   One year on, it is not yet possible to gauge the impact the Review has had on the medium or long-term savings industry. However, the extent to which the Government has acted on a number of the proposals suggests that it has struck the right note as far as the policymakers are concerned. In particular, the central recommendation, the suite of stakeholder products, is likely to take effect in the near future. It remains to be seen how successful this emphasis on product regulation will be at encouraging the target audience to participate more in the savings industry.

Leaving aside the debate of how best to encourage those on lower incomes to save more, the tax recommendations are a mixed bag.

19.52   The observations on the long-term savings industry are valid and, to the extent that they have informed the Inland Revenue's consultation on the simplification of pension taxation, could well have a long-term impact. Fundamental reform is promised and hopefully the Revenue will not lose its appetite for seeing the changes through.

However, the recommendations for the medium-term industry are less welcome. It is a pity that the question of more fundamental alignment is left hanging. The areas concentrated on, for example the differences between authorised funds and investment trusts vis-à-vis SDRT and VAT, are not earth shattering. Perhaps it is a good thing that the Government is revisiting the areas of legislation that are singled out for criticism, for example the VAT exemption for special investment funds, but there is a danger that Sandler's comments could be taken out of context and do more harm than good. Customs' consultation on pension fund management is a case in point.

19.53   The specific recommendations should not be viewed in isolation. The Review is useful in that it brings together a number of strands and helps focus various influences, the offshore funds consultation, corporation tax reform and CP185. The opportunity is there for the industry in tandem with the Government to design a competitive and long-term regime for savings products. The Budget Report suggests that the Review has encouraged the Government to consider the wider context; it could therefore be the catalyst for important change. However, as with the review of pensions taxation, the Government must rise to the challenge and the lead up to this year's Pre-Budget Report will be a critical period.

Index

J

Clarke: Offshore Tax Planning Tenth Edition

Giles Clarke, MA, PhD, FTII, Barrister

Offshore Tax Planning is the essential guide to successful planning through offshore trusts and companies. It also focuses on the tax treatment of foreign domiciliaries. For all taxation advisers, accountants and lawyers with international clients this is the indispensable guide to understanding the legislation, opportunities and pitfalls associated with offshore tax planning.

The tenth edition of **Offshore Tax Planning** has been revised to take account of recent developments. It will ensure that you are fully abreast of all the relevant issues.

The book is divided into seven parts each dealing with a different aspect of offshore tax planning and takes you straight to the area you need guidance on immediately:

- Fiscal Connection
- UK Domiciliaries
- Non-domiciliaries
- Practical Issues
- Anti-Avoidance Legislation
- Sheltering Business Profits
- Migration

Offshore Tax Planning is a must have for you in your day-to-day offshore tax planning work.

Published: October 2003   **Format:** Soft Cover   **Price:** £93.50   **ISBN:** 0 406 96804 7   **Product code:** COT10

Tax Direct is the ultimate online service that provides you with instant access to the most authoritative information ... all via the internet.
For more information on all of our products, please visit our website at www.lexis.nexis.co.uk

Prices may be subject to change

LexisNexis™ UK

Gibraltar – International Financial Centre *Fourth edition*

By Hassans, Gibraltar and Caplan Montagu, London with a foreword by The Hon. Peter R Caruana QC, Chief Minister of Gibraltar

"A precise update concerning tax legislation and commercial aspects in Gibraltar"

The rapid development of International Financial Centres in recent years makes it vital for a new edition of the highly regarded book **Gibraltar - International Financial Centre**. This text develops and updates the previous edition and is a detailed and comprehensive guide to the tax legislation and commercial aspects of Gibraltar aimed at tax consultants, accountants, lawyers and all involved in offshore taxation. The fourth edition will include:

- All changes since the 1999 edition
- Developments as a result of the Gibraltar Budget 2003
- A new section on E-Commerce
- The implementation of the pass porting of banking services
- An examination of the Edwards Report and OECD
- reports on Tax Havens
- Further consideration on money laundering
- legislation and reports about harmful tax competition
- New trading directives
- Implementation of company law
- An update of case law/precedents

Containing commentary on almost every aspect of finance in Gibraltar and the only book available on this subject, **Gibraltar –International Financial Centre Fourth edition** is an essential point of reference for all involved in business and trading in Gibraltar.

Price:	£55.00
Product Code:	TIG02
ISBN:	0 7545 1340 8
Published:	December 2003

Tolley's Taxation of Stakeholder Pensions

By **Alec Ure**, Bacon & Woodrow,
Douglas Sleziak, Nabarro Nathanson,
John Frith, Consultant, Bacon & Woodrow

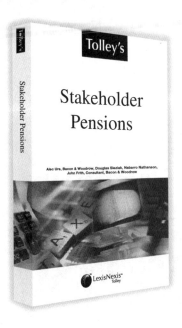

Tolley's Taxation of Stakeholder Pensions deals with the legislation relating to stakeholder pensions as introduced in the Welfare Reform and Pensions Act and the taxation aspects introduced in the following year's Finance Act.

This unique publication guides the professional through the legislation centring around the rule that employers who do not offer their employees access to occupational pension schemes will have to permit them access to a stakeholder scheme via the payroll.

Tolley's Taxation of Stakeholder Pensions provides a thorough, unambiguous explanation of this new pensions scheme which is intended to provide a low cost, privately funded supplement to the basic state pension. The book also defines the tests that employers need to apply to establish whether they are exempt from the stakeholder legislation.

The title outlines the measures employers should take to ensure that they comply with the legislation which could help them avoid a heavy fine from the Occupational Pensions Regulatory Authority.

Tolley's Taxation of Stakeholder Pensions is ideally suited to employers, pension providers (including insurance companies), general tax practitioners, accountants and all those working in pensions who should be aware of the changes directly affecting them.

Product Code: TSP   **ISBN:** 0 7545 1460 9   **Price:** £41.95   **Publication Date:** December 2001

How To Order

To order, please contact LexisNexis UK Customer Service Dept: LexisNexis UK, FREEPOST SEA 4177, Croydon, Surrey CR9 5WZ
Telephone: 020 8662 2000   Fax: 020 8662 2012

35 Chancery Lane, London WC2A 1EL
A division of Reed Elsevier (UK) Ltd
Registered office 25 Victoria Street London SW1H 0EX
Registered in England number 2746621
VAT Registered No. GB 730 8595 2

Tax Direct is the ultimate online service that provides you with instant access to the most authoritative information ... all via the internet.
For more information on all of our products, please visit our website at www.lexis.nexis.co.uk

Prices may be subject to change

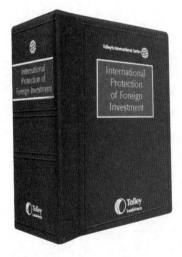